THE BIBLE THROUGH THE SEASONS

11/28/07

Dear Evelyn,
 Thank you for your kindness and support of this special ministry. I will be with you each day through God's Word.

Lovingly,
Rick

THE BIBLE THROUGH THE SEASONS

A THREE-YEAR JOURNEY WITH THE BIBLE

Nicholas J. Connolly

iUniverse, Inc.
New York Lincoln Shanghai

The Bible Through the Seasons
A Three-Year Journey with the Bible

Copyright © 2007 by Nicholas J. Connolly

iUniverse books may be ordered through booksellers or by contacting:

iUniverse
2021 Pine Lake Road, Suite 100
Lincoln, NE 68512
www.iuniverse.com
1-800-Authors (1-800-288-4677)

ISBN-13: 978-0-595-41503-8 (pbk)
ISBN-13: 978-0-595-85852-1 (ebk)
ISBN-10: 0-595-41503-2 (pbk)
ISBN-10: 0-595-85852-X (ebk)

Printed in the United States of America

Season	Year A	Year B	Year C
Advent to Epiphany	NIV	NRSV	NKJV
Lent and Easter	NKJV	NLT	NRSV
Pentecost	NRSV	NRSV	NRSV
Kingdomtide	NLT	NKJV	NIV
Torah Portions	NRSV		

To Georgina

You came into my life
At its mid-course
And filled it with faithful love
As spouse and companion in ministry.
Thank you for
Your encouragement, your wisdom
And for making this journey through the Bible
such a part of our life together.

CONTENTS

Acknowledgements xiii

Introduction xv

How to Use This Book xvii

The Bible Through the Seasons at a Glance xxi

The Bible Through the Seasons

Solar Seasons are reversed in the Southern Hemisphere.

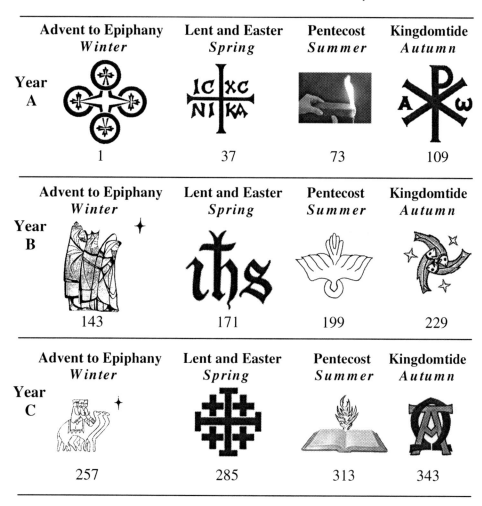

	Advent to Epiphany *Winter*	Lent and Easter *Spring*	Pentecost *Summer*	Kingdomtide *Autumn*
Year A	1	37	73	109
Year B	143	171	199	229
Year C	257	285	313	343

Alphabytes

Weekly object lessons following the Alphabet
See the beginning pages of the four seasons of Year A.

Advent to Epiphany: *A to M* 3

Lent and Easter: *N to Z* 39

Pentecost: *A to M* 77

Kingdomtide: *N to Z* 110

The Sabbath Torah Readings

Page 371

Articles:

Weaving the Word 431

Timescaping 433

Bible Study Through the Seasons 434

Solar and Sacred Seasons...435

A Heavenly City Comes to Earth 439

Additional Tables:

Perpetual Calendar of the Church Year 440

The Books of the Bible by the Seasons 442

Names of Sundays Corresponding to Lectionary-Based Church Years 444

Dates of Easter and Cycle Letters for the 21st Century 446

Resources **447**

About the Author **449**

Abbreviations for the Names of the Seasons

The first two letters of the seasons. These are found in the tabs at the edge of the pages for each week. These provide easy navigation across the four seasons and the three years.

Ad-Advent; Ep-Epiphany; Le-Lent; Ea-Easter;
Pe-Pentecost; Ki-Kingdomtide

Solar seasons are reversed in the southern hemisphere.

ACKNOWLEDGEMENTS

I give thanks to my parents, Wilhelmina and John, who immersed me in the love of Jesus Christ from my earliest years, and to my brothers in the Society of Jesus for their holiness and inspiration. From seminary days, my dear friend, the late Cantor Sidney Venetianer, opened me to the joy of the Sabbath and the Holidays. I am especially grateful to the United Methodist Church and the support I find in my colleagues in ministry in the Greater New Jersey Conference.

Mario and Camelia Pando, my wife's parents, shared their enthusiasm by sending helpful resources wrapped with their love. Along with my parents, they now bless me from heaven.

Appreciation is extended to Tom and Pam McGovern for printing the first edition, to Ethel Durka for her unique support and for the many in the congregations of the First United Methodist Churches of Keansburg and Vineland, N.J., who walked together on the three-year journey through the Bible. My thanks to Laurence Vogel who introduced me to the ancient arrangement of the Sabbath Torah Readings.

I am indebted to Ted Nelson for his help with biblethroughseasons.com, to those who proofread or offered other support: Ralph, Betty and Patricia Barrett, Dona Dute, Alfredo and Carmina Feigelmüller, Dale Keepfer, Yvonne Luengo, June McCullough, David and Donna Pickett, Dick and Joyce Prochaska, Bill and Diane Rafferty, Barbara Robidoux, Roger and Judy Scull, Beverly Slimmer, Robert Steelman, Robin Van Cleef and Wellington Woods. I am grateful to *Wesley Without Walls (WWW),* an internet community for those following the plan; their messages have been an inspiration.

I appreciate the love and support of my dear friends, Rafael Pimentel, Denise and Tony Ragone, Jorge and Elia Sánchez, Carl Bowser, Judy Kurtz, Roscol Pearce, and Heather Sneath.

I give thanks to my brothers, John and Frank, for their abiding love and to my sisters-in-law, Martha, Margarita and Laura who found strength in this devotional. I am grateful to my sister-in-law, Cindy, who continues to find peace in what has become for her a meaningful, daily ritual of reading God's Word in this plan.

Bearers of many gifts are my children. I am grateful to Manny, for his valuable feedback—one of the first to complete the three-year cycle; to Teresa for sharing her exciting ideas about the project and for her belief in me through the years; to Laura Elena, for allowing herself to be moved by the text as she proofread and to Jorge, for his life-commitment to protect our country. My appreciation to their spouses, Richard Nelson, Yara La Fossé-Prendes and Andrew Walls. My grandchildren, Richard, Ashley, Amber, Dylan, Madeleine, and Jorgito color all my seasons with laughter and joy.

Finally, my gratitude to John and Charles Wesley for their inspiration "To spread Scriptural holiness across the land."

I offer this work for the greater glory of God.

INTRODUCTION

The Vision

How can it be that the Bible is one of the best selling books of all time, yet one of the most under read? Favorite passages are often prayed, perhaps daily. Yet what about the whole Bible, read not as a once-in-a-lifetime project, but rather as a habit for everyday living?

These are the issues that awakened me on a cold winter's night in January 1996. In the course of the hours until dawn, a flow of ideas leapt as sparks from the heart.

- A way to read the entire Bible in a relaxed manner, one passage a day, over the course of three years
- Books of the Bible chosen with sensitive reference to seasons instead of a fixed sequence from Genesis to Revelation
- Parts of the Bible dedicated to each day of the week
- A daily, inspirational message for every reading
- Connection with many reading the same passage on the same day.

The Lord unfolded the plan that night. The four solar seasons in the northern hemisphere correspond to sacred ones:

Winter: Advent to Epiphany
Spring: Lent and Easter
Summer: Pentecost
Autumn: Kingdomtide

Sunday is dedicated to the Gospel from *The Revised Common Lectionary,* identical texts for worship across many denominations. Monday-to-Friday resembles a worship service with readings moving from the Hebrew Scriptures to the New Testament.

Monday	—	**The Prophets**
Tuesday	—	**Hebrew History and the Writings**
Wednesday	—	**The Psalms**
Thursday	—	**The New Testament**
Friday	—	**The Gospels**

Saturdays offer something unique and unprecedented. Christians join with Jewish people in synagogues around the world as together we ponder common passages from the *Torah* (Genesis to Deuteronomy). Fifty-four portions of the Torah form a sacred sequence of readings dating from the time of Ezra and the Second Temple, rebuilt in 515 B.C. For Jesus in the synagogue of Nazareth in Luke 4, to Paul in the synagogues the Book of Acts, a similar arrangement of readings was followed.

For two years after that January night, I rose very early everyday with the excitement of a child on Christmas morning. "It's time to write "Firestarters"! These are one-minute meditations designed to ignite the imagination and heart of the reader as the daily passage is prayerfully read. They are like the blocks of compressed, combustible material used to start the flames in a fireplace. They burn for a time and then are gone, leaving the logs to burn on for hours. A *Firestarter* is an "advertisement" for the daily reading. One minute is the usual time for a TV commercial; that's how long I gave myself to write these brief messages for the some eleven hundred readings of the Bible in the three-year plan. Each *Firestarter* carries with it this prayer: may what I offer burn out as the Holy Spirit burns on in your heart for the rest of the day through the Scripture passage.

The vision in summary:

- Live each day in a biblical context.
- The Word becomes flesh in our lives.
- Not only *read* the Bible in three years, but also *live it* every three years.

I welcome your exploration of various articles and tables in the book. The entire reading cycle at a glance is on page xx. As a map for a journey, return to this chart at the beginning of each season to feel where you are on the journey, finding what authors of the various books of the Bible will be your "experts" in helping you find God everyday. The article "Solar and Sacred Seasons," p. 435, further explains the ordering of the year for the purposes of this Bible plan. It also simplifies the church year, offering a solution toward reconciling current methods of naming the Sundays of the year for worship. The article, "The Books of the Bible by the Seasons," p. 442 directs you to the *Firestarters* for all the books of the Bible in order. It is hoped that these brief messages will help enkindle the imaginations of pastors, for example, as they prepare to preach.

A Personal Note

The spiritual energy of this book comes from God and from the author's desire to be a faithful disciple of Jesus Christ. While intended for those wanting to grow in this faith, it is my hope that any person from whatever spiritual affiliation or from no affiliation at all, will find this approach to the Bible to be a source of inspiration and support.

Nicholas J. Connolly
Vineland, New Jersey   October 17, 2006

HOW TO USE THIS BOOK

"OK," you say. "It seems like a good idea. Sounds doable, different, attractive—maybe even intriguing. But how do I go about it?" It's as easy as A B C!

A. *Find the current year in the three-year cycle.*

Divide the present year by three. A remainder of one is Year A, a remainder of two is Year B and a year divisible by three is Year C. It is as though the first year in the Christian era were Year A. A point to remember: Advent begins a new sacred year, taking its cycle letter from the year beginning the following January. For example, the First Sunday of Advent that begins Year A, 2008, occurs on Nov. 30, 2007.

B. *Find the current week in the year, from the tables on the following pages.*

Find the Sunday nearest a given date that is last Sunday, or today, if it is a Sunday. This is the current sacred week in the year. The only exception to this is the combined season of *Lent and Easter*, which varies due to the changing date of Easter Sunday. This has the effect of having *Lent and Easter* "float" back and forth across the final weeks of *Epiphany* and the beginning weeks of *Pentecost*. The six Sundays before Easter are *Lent*; the seven Sundays after are the season of *Easter*. You will find simple instructions in the concluding weeks of *Epiphany* informing you when to begin *Lent and Easter;* at the beginning of *Pentecost*, you will be guided as to how to begin that season.

Winter *Advent to* *Epiphany*	Spring ← *Lent* *and Easter →*	Summer *Pentecost*	Autumn *Kingdomtide*

C. *The Sabbath Torah Readings*

After Fridays of every week you will find a list of dates when a particular Sabbath Torah reading occurs on Saturday of that week. Go to the Sabbath Torah section beginning on page 371 and read the portion number indicated.

An "Alphabyte," an object meditation following the alphabet, moving two times through the year, heads each of the fifty-two weeks of the year. They are offered as themes for the weeks or as spiritual disciplines on which to focus. Sometimes the *Firestarters* draw from the image of the week. The *Alphabytes* are found at the beginning of the four seasons in year A.

Begin! Three years later you will arrive at the place where you started, having prayed through the entire Bible. An ever-widening community will be joining you on the journey; it will be an honor for me to be a guide.

Finding the Current Week in the Season of the Year

Advent to Epiphany
Winter in the Northern Hemisphere

	Week	Begins on the Sunday nearest ...	Year A Page	Year B Page	Year C Page	Alphabytes Page
	First	Nov. 30	10	144	258	Advent Wreath—3
	Second	Dec. 7	12	146	260	Bible—4
	Third	Dec. 14	14	148	262	Chimes—4
	Fourth	Dec. 21	16	150	264	Darkroom—5
Christmas Week		Dec. 28	18	152	266	Evergreen—5
	First	1st Sun. in Jan.	20	154	268	Frankincense—6
	Second	2st Sun. in Jan.	22	156	270	Gold—6
	Third	3rd Sun. in Jan.	24	158	272	Homing Pigeon—7
	Fourth	4th Sun. in Jan.	26	160	274	Ice Dancing—7
	Fifth	Feb. 1	28	162	276	Journal—8
	Sixth[1]	Feb. 8	30	164	287	Kiln—8
	Seventh[1]	Feb. 15	32	166	280	Laser—9
	Eighth[1]	Feb. 22	34	168	282	Myrrh—9

[1] Depending upon how early Lent begins due to the changing date of Easter, a week or two (rarely three) at the end of Epiphany leap ahead and become a preliminary week(s) at the beginning of the season of Pentecost. Depending upon how late Easter is, a week (rarely two) leap back from the season of Pentecost and is added to the end of Epiphany.

Lent and Easter
Spring in the Northern Hemisphere

	Week	Relation to Easter	Year A Pg.	Year B Pg.	Year C Pg.	Alphabytes Page
	First	6 Wks before	46	172	286	Nadir—39
	Second	5 Wks before	48	174	288	Olive Tree—40
	Third	4 Wks before	50	176	290	Plumb Line—40
	Fourth	3 Wks before	52	178	292	Quarters—41
	Fifth	2 Wks before	54	180	294	Rooster—41
	Holy Week	1 Wks before	56	182	296	Supper—42
	Easter Week	**Easter Sunday**	58	184	298	Temple—42
	Second	1 Wk after	60	186	300	Universe—43
	Third	2 Wks after	62	188	302	Vine—43
	Fourth	3 Wks after	64	190	304	Wax—44
	Fifth	4 Wks after	66	192	306	Xylophone—44
	Sixth	5 Wks after	68	194	308	Yoke—45
	Seventh	6 Wks after	70	196	310	Zenith—45

Pentecost

Summer in the Northern Hemisphere

Week	Begins on the Sunday nearest ...	Year A Pg.	Year B Pg.	Year C Pg.	Alphabytes Page
First[2]	June 1	82	202	316	Arc—77
Second[2]	June 8	84	204	318	Beach Ball—77
Third	Jun 15	86	206	320	Clock—78
Fourth	Jun 22	88	208	322	Drink—78
Fifth	June 29	90	210	324	Eyes—78
Sixth	July 6	92	212	326	Firestarter—79
Seventh	July 13	94	214	328	Gears—79
Eighth	July 20	96	216	330	Hurricane—79
Ninth	July 27	98	218	332	Ink—80
Tenth	August 3	100	220	334	Juggling—80
Eleventh	August 10	102	222	336	Knots—80
Twelfth	August 17	104	224	338	Loops—81
Thirteenth	August 24	106	226	340	Metal Detector—81

2   See footnote 1 at the end of Epiphany to understand changes to Epiphany and Pentecost due to the changing date of Easter. The first two Sundays in this season are *Pentecost and Trinity Sundays* respectively. At the end of the Easter Season, for every year, there will be instructions for how to begin the readings for the season of Pentecost.

Kingdomtide

Autumn in the Northern Hemisphere

Week	Begins on the Sunday nearest ...	Year A Pg.	Year B Pg.	Year C Pg.	Alphabytes Page
First	August 31	116	230	344	Nose—110
Second	September 7	118	232	346	Oak—110
Third	September 14	120	234	348	Pencil—111
Fourth	September 21	122	236	350	Quilt—111
Fifth	September 28	124	238	352	Rainbow—112
Sixth	October 5	126	240	354	Streams—112
Seventh	October 12	128	242	356	Trapeze—112
Eighth	October 19	130	244	358	Usher—113
Ninth	October 26	132	246	360	Violin—113
Tenth	November 2	134	248	362	Well—114
Eleventh	November 9	136	250	364	Xerography—114
Twelfth	November 16	138	252	366	Year—115
Thirteenth	November 23	140	254	368	Zoom Lens—115

The Bible Through the Seasons at a Glance

Solar seasons are reversed in the Southern Hemisphere.

Winter / Advent to Epiphany

	Year A: 2008, 2011, etc.	Year B: 2006, 2009, etc.	Year C: 2007, 2010, etc.
Sunday – Lectionary	Matthew 2—6	Mark 1—2	Luke 3—6
Monday – Prophets	Isaiah 1—12	Isaiah 40—55	Isaiah 56—66
Tuesday – Hebrew Writings	Joshua, Proverbs 1—3	Judges, Proverbs 4—6	Ruth, Esther, Proverbs 7—9
Wednesday – Psalms	Psalms 1 to 13	Psalms 48 to 60	Psalms 95 to 107
Thursday – New Testament	Titus, Philemon, Gal, Phil	Letters of John and Jude	Letters of Peter
Friday – Gospels	Luke 1—2; Matthew 1—7	Luke 1—2; Mark 1—3	Luke 1—8
Saturday – Torah	Gen 32—48: Exodus 1—28	Gen 32 to 48: Exodus 1—28	Gen 32 to 48: Exodus 1—28

Spring / Lent and Easter

	Year A: 2008, 2011, etc.	Year B: 2006, 2009, etc.	Year C: 2007, 2010, etc.
Sunday / Lectionary	Various passages from Matthew and John	Various passages from Matthew, Mark and John	Various passages from Matthew, Luke and John
Monday / Prophets	Lent: Jeremiah 1—17 / Easter: Ezekiel 1—16	Lent: Jeremiah 18—35 / Easter: Ezekiel 17—32	Lent: Jeremiah 36—52 / Easter: Ezekiel 33—48
Tuesday / Hebrew Writings	Lent: Job 1—14; 38; / Easter: Prov 10—2; Song of Sgs	Lent: Job 15—21; 39—40 / Easter: Prov 17—19; Ezra	Lent: Job 22—37; 41—42 / Easter: Prov 24—26; Nehemiah
Wednesday / Psalms	Lent: Psalms 120—124 / Holy Wk & East; Pss 14 to 21	Lent: Psalms 125—129 / Holy Wk & Easter: Pss 61 to 68	Lent: Psalms 130—134 / Holy Wk Ps 108; Easter Ps 119
Thursday / New Testament	Lent: Eph, 1 Cor 11—12 / Easter: Acts 1—9	Lent: Col, 1 Cor 11:23—13:13 / Easter: Acts 10:1—18:22	Lent: James: 1 Cor 14—15 / Easter: Acts 18:23—28:31
Friday / Gospels	John: 1st third of Gospel	John: 2nd third of Gospel	John: 3rd third of Gospel
Saturday / Torah	End of Exodus, Leviticus, Beginning of Numbers	End of Exodus, Leviticus, Beginning of Numbers	End of Exodus, Leviticus, Beginning of Numbers

Summer / Pentecost

	Year A: 2008, 2011, etc.	Year B: 2006, 2009, etc.	Year C: 2007, 2010, etc.
Sunday Lectionary	Matthew 7—16	Mark 2—6; John 6	Luke 7—13
Monday Prophets	Isaiah 13 to 27 Lamentations 1—2 at 9th Week	Hosea Lamentations 3 at 9th Week	Joel to Nahum Lamentations 4—5 at 9th Week
Tuesday Hebrew Writings	Proverbs 13—14; 1Samuel	Proverbs 20—21; 1 Kings	Proverbs 27—29; 1 Chronicles
Wednesday Psalms	Psalms 22—34	Psalms 69—81	Psalms 109—137
Thursday New Testament	Romans	2 Corinthians	1 Timothy; Hebrews
Friday Gospels	Matthew 8—18	Mark 4—9	Luke 9—19:27
Saturday Torah	Remainder of Numbers, Half of Deuteronomy	Remainder of Numbers, Half of Deuteronomy	Remainder of Numbers, Half of Deuteronomy

Autumn / Kingdomtide

	Year A: 2008, 2011, etc.	Year B: 2006, 2009, etc.	Year C: 2007, 2010, etc.
Sunday Lectionary	Matthew 16—25	Mark 7—13	Luke 14—23
Monday Prophets	Isaiah 28—39	Daniel	Habakkuk to Malachi
Tuesday Hebrew Writings	Proverbs 15—16; 2 Samuel Ecclesiastes 1—4	Proverbs 22—23; 2 Kings Ecclesiastes 5—8	Proverbs 30—32; 2 Chronicles Ecclesiastes 9—12
Wednesday Psalms	Psalms 35—47	Psalms 82—94	Psalms 138—150
Thursday New Testament	1 Corinthians	1 & 2 Thess; Rev. 4—10:18	2 Timothy; Revelation 12—22
Friday Gospels	Matthew 19—28	Mark 10—16	Luke 19:28—24:53
Saturday Torah	Remainder of Deuteronomy to Genesis 32	Remainder of Deuteronomy to Genesis 32	Remainder of Deuteronomy to Genesis 32

The Star Cross on the facing page is baked in tiles in a nineteenth century Anglican monastery in York, England. A meditative gaze upon it reveals the inner flow of the season of *Advent to Epiphany*, winter in the northern hemisphere. The tips of the cross suggest the four candles of the Advent Wreath. The cross becomes the Star of the Magi, sign of the Savior from heaven, coming to earth in the wood of the manger of Bethlehem and the cross of Calvary, shining forever in the brilliance of resurrection. Thus not only does the symbol embrace winter, but it does the same for *Lent and Easter* in the spring. Indeed, the wholeness of the image is maintained alive by the fire of the Holy Spirit in summer and *Pentecost*, as well as being the ongoing, triumphant sign of the cross as we live in autumn and *Kingdomtide*, the season of fullness. The ends of the cross also suggest the four Gospels preached to the four corners of the world.

ADVENT
TO
EPIPHANY

WINTER

Northern Hemisphere

Year A
2008, 2011, 2014 …

Advent begins every year
on the Sunday nearest November 30, St. Andrew's Day.
See the entire cycle of readings at a glance on page xx.

1

Alphabytes

Poems and object lessons following the Alphabet twice through the year.
They are inserted at the beginning of the four seasons in year A;
they are the same for all three years in the cycle.

Advent to Epiphany: *A–M*

The First Week in Advent

*A*dvent Wreath

We were all running around in circles,
   since the fall of Adam and Eve had us spinning out of control.
Waiting, we were, for thousands of sun-cycles,
   hoping that the downward spiral might be reversed to an upward one
   that leads to a heavenly somewhere.
That heavenly somewhere, thought to be nowhere, is now here.
A new circling spiral begins with Advent and its wreath.
The wreath is a circle seared with four lights,
   one for each of the four thousand years
   since the Biblically conceived time from Adam's fall to Jesus' birth.
They are ages—great spans of time past looked from above, hope increasing with
each week's light.

CANDLE ONE: **Noah**—Rainbow-light: the first of new covenants after the loss of
   Adam's.
CANDLE TWO: **Abraham**—Countless star-flung lights promised in another
   covenant: God's own people.
CANDLE THREE: **Moses**—Fire-light draws this freedom warrior who leads
   God's beloved to their own land.
CANDLE FOUR: **David**—Star-Shepherd and King: head of the house whence
   Jesus would come.
Feel the flow of the ages. Sense the beginning of a new one for yourself, as spinning
   wheels taking you nowhere, now engage at this year's beginning with an
   inward spiraling flight to heaven.

The Second Week in Advent

*B*ible

A Meditation for the Five Senses

Take your Bible into your hands.
    Feel the texture of the text—the cover, the binding,
    the wholeness of it, the oneness of its many books.
Gaze upon its completeness. The whole of life is before you.
Smell its fragrance. Inhale the breath of life.
Listen to the silence as the book is closed—
    as the curtain down before the play begins.
Now open it … pause …
Descend to the place of the day's reading.
Look to the right and left, front and back at the countless others
    beyond your room, yet within your heart, who read and pray with you.
Hear the reading—don't just read it. Hear it together. Go further …
"Taste and see the Lord is good."
This is communion—a sacramental taste of God inside of you.

The Third Week in Advent

*C*himes

Winter is here.
Gone are the birds, the sounds of leaves, the laughter of children
    playing in the light-long day.
Windows are closed … Silence pervades.
Thus, it is that bells and chimes have special power to awaken the soul
    delighting the ear in the silence, even as candles bring joy
    to the eye in the darkness.

Be careful of enemy noises seeking to turn the attention to the outer,
    the frenetic, the hastenings for things and plans.
We're not meant to despise the gifts and even the shopping.
Just be attentive to those bells and gentle chimes that call to inwardness,
    to quiet, to a space that is hedged about by the Angel of the Lord
    so that there can be announced to your heart as to Mary's:
             "You will conceive in your womb
        and bear a son, and you will name him Jesus."
                Luke 1:31

The Fourth Week in Advent
*D**arkroom*

A closed space it is—free from the intrusion of unwanted light
    from altering what happened when once a fleeting beam was admitted,
    snatched up by the hungry film, etching an image upon it.
The image is bathed in developer, till slowly, the then conceived,
    yet unseen form, can withstand the flood of light all about.

Ponder this darkroom time of the year.
Enter its quiet, protected space, where that image of your very self
    etched by your Creator from the beginning,
    can emerge unaltered into the fullness of the sun.
Bathe yourself in darkness. Trust it, in faith.
Take time to hold the larger lights at bay
    so that the Spirit can baptize you in the holy developer
    of that quiet inner touch of love and water and fire.
Hold the self in stillness so that the Word of Life
    can continue to make its image upon your face … your heart …
    the way you walk and live and love.
Spend time each day in God's darkroom—
    even if only to close the eyes for some minutes,
    holding in check the pressing claims of others
    wanting to make you into their image.
Protect the image of you: it is the only one God ever made.
He waits to see it develop to the full, till your face and the face of Jesus
    look longingly at each other forever.

Christmas Week
*E**vergreens*

There are a few trees that defiantly resist the choke-hold of the cold,
    squeezing away the green of summer.
They are curved into wreathes twisted into garlands,
    clustered as centers for the table.
We invite one to visit us, wrenching it from what would have been
    its never changing place, asking it to spend its final days
    as a member of our family, reminding us of the Life
    that has come to the world in Jesus.
When it is all decorated with lights and ornaments of memory
    spend time alone with this Christmas guest.
Recall the places and trees of the past. Welcome feelings that well up.
They are—like the branches—something ever-green inside you,
    memories ever-alive, seeking to be expressed for deeper healings.
And when the season is past, thank the tree—no longer evergreen—
    as it takes its place with all its sister trees
    whose leaves have long turned brown upon the ground,
    making next summer even more green than ever.

*F*rankincense

Gift of the Magi in worship of their King:
> trees from Arabia offer resin resembling stone—
> rigid, resistant to change … apparently.

One would think that by pouring these pieces of earth onto hot coals,
> the fire would go out.

But no. The rocks melt into fire, into air,
> sending sizzling sweet-smelling smoke heavenward,
> those present ascending to spaces beyond the pull of earth.

> Temperaments, moods, dispositions emanate from us either as incense
> inviting to worship lifting others up, or
> as black smoke from which others must flee.

Sit. Drop onto the hot coals of the Lord's love for you.
Let go of what is rigid and rock-resistant within.
Blend your incense with the Word of life both swirling heavenward.
Rise. The day is fragrant because fire has transformed you.

The Second Week in Epiphany

*G*old

Kings and gold go together.
And so the Three Kings bring their gifts of gold to the little King who has none.
Yet the three do not know that this is the One
> in whom all the earth and gold is found.

Gold: the ultimate possession. Earth holds it … Heaven gives it away.
What do you claim and cling to as ultimate in life?
Let go. Nothing can be possessed as yours.
Even your body is not yours, but rather a gift given
> by the One in whom we live and move and have our being.

Two things are truly ours: thoughts and feelings.
So go to that place deep within where lie these buried treasures and
> give them to the Infant King.
They become gold in the offering.

The Third Week in Epiphany
*H*oming Pigeon

From thousands of miles away, these pigeons will know how to come home, flying constantly until they arrive. Rest comes only then. How do they do it? The mystery remains, yet we know it has something to do with the angle of the sun and its polarized, ultra-violent rays. In a similar way, the sun is the source for how honeybees make their configured dances, each design a special message for the other bees to know where the flowers are with their nectar. Yet homing pigeons seem to have something else—a memory system creating an internal map for them to follow when clouds get in the way of familiar landmarks below.

Home: there's no place like it, as the carol sings. *Welcome Home*—next to *I love you*, are our favorite words to hear. We have been created to rest in God alone. St. Augustine wrote: "You have made us for Yourself, O God, and our hearts are restless until they rest in You."

The outpoured Spirit of Jesus has given you an innate sense of what will bring you home with the Lord—even now, while heaven may seem far away. The map and manual are the Scriptures. When read with faith, they will imprint the directions homeward, and give the energy to keep flying without stopping until the Sabbath rest is complete in Jesus.

Be at home with the Lord in the Word for some precious time each day. Then, when you go about your day, others will find in you a landmark that will invite them also to come home to Jesus.

The Fourth Week in Epiphany
*I*ce Dancing

Each of the two perfected dancers across the smooth arena
    could well be doing it alone. Less dependent ... less risky ...
    much simpler, it would seem.
But there is a call upon the two to blend themselves
    into one ever-changing figure and form,
    folding themselves into patterns of silent sailing
    across the slippery, open plane.
They spin in cycles only possible by the pulse of now pulling against,
    now yielding to the energies in each.

The Trinity could have chosen that they alone do the divine dance.
However, they decided to create dancers in their image,
    so that all could join together and move through life with shapes and designs
    decided by the Creator-Father, completed by Jesus, the Son,
    in the power of the Spirit.

Ice dance with the Word each day.
Resist going it alone—decisions, plans, relationships
    without the clinging to the Spirit who clings as fire to the soul.
Let the choreography of the day be set by the creative interplay
    between you and the Word for the day.
Let all the events and people that move into each hour's rounded space
    take their shape from the dance
    you've well rehearsed in prayer with your God.
Do not fear that some intrusion need have you fall from the hold
    that the Lord has upon you.
Bond and blend with your God today as you pray and dance with the Word.

The Fifth Week in Epiphany

*J*ournal

What would have happened if the sacred writers had not completed the inspirations of the Holy Spirit and moved beyond inward hearing to outward writing? There would have been no Bible—only traditions handed down by word of mouth, along with all the impressions of words to ear alone, instead of words to eye. The Bible needed to be written.

However, in addition to preserving the sacred words, the Lord uses the process of writing as a way to access the soul of the sacred writer. The open space of papyrus or page becomes the arena within which the Word and the writer through alphabets and languages release the creative Word. A journal is a way for this to continue.

A journal originally meant a book of worship for the day hours. It comes from the Latin *diurnalis,* the word "day" being related to the first syllable. Later, the word came to mean the daily happenings that one records.

From the pages of a journal, the personal Word of God can well up from their point of origin—the deepest recesses of the spirit. The process determines the outcome. There are some things that will not be understand without the struggle—as ice dancers—with the tugging, pulling and yielding that takes place in writing.

As you move through the hours of the day and interplay with events that sometimes seek to intrude upon your peace, take time—even mere minutes—to stop, pause, and write some phrases that will unleash the Spirit. The Lord is actively using what is happening to you along with the Word for the day as a sacred counterpoint to show you God's will, to unfold God's love. God needs your attentive listening, as well as your obedient fingers in writing to give you a more complete expression of God's purposes in your life. Writing lifts thoughts, feelings, and images that would otherwise be lost in the darkness of the sea inside us.

The Sixth Week in Epiphany

Depending on how early Easter is this week, the Seventh and Eighth Weeks in Epiphany
may "leap ahead' to the beginning weeks of the season of Pentecost

*K*iln

What a darkroom is to a picture, a kiln is to clay cup.
In the one, light is frozen, in the other shape.
Though we need to be pliable for further ongoing shaping by the Lord,
   a time comes when shape needs to be fixed … final,
   for only a vessel harden by fire can hold the sacred blood of Jesus,
   can become a cup of grace outpoured in love upon the other.

Prayer-time is the kiln. Motion ceases.
The fire of the Word increases until the formless in us
   takes on the shape of the Creator, until it is set,
   able to withstand being reshaped by the preferences of others.
Stay in the kiln until your shape is set.

The Seventh Week in Epiphany

*L*aser

Light means more than floods of waves of the right length for the eye to see. Rays can now be gathered into a single length and sent in one selected direction, making three additional results of light possible: sounding, printing, and fusing. So too does the Scripture share in these qualities.

First, there is a **FLOODING** of your being with the passage, bathing all of you in the love-light of the Word. Prepare the next day's passage the night before, so that you can sleep and dream with it, as God's Word blends with the restoration that so beautifully happens in sleep.

> **"I think of you on my bed, and meditate on you in the watches of the night"**
> (Psalm 63:6)

The Word **SOUNDS** within the soul. Listen inwardly to the movement of the passage.

> **"Faith comes from what is heard, and what is heard**
> **comes through the word of Christ."**
> (Rom 10:17).

Then there is the **PRINTING** of the Word, as the laser-like quality of the Word is etched, inscribed, and written upon the heart. Here a close, meditative reading takes place. What are you going to remember and memorize about the passage for the day?

> **"Do not let loyalty and faithfulness forsake you; bind them**
> **around your neck, write them on the tablet of your heart."**
> (Pro. 3:3).

Finally the Word **FUSES** broken, disconnected parts of the mind, as faulty thinking continues to hurt the heart from sins of the past—yours or others. Allow a laser ray to touch attitudes and ways of thinking that need to be soldered and fused by the Spirit. Where in the body does the ray need to penetrate, bringing healing to your body as well?

> **"The Spirit of the Lord has sent me to bind up the brokenhearted"**
> (Isaiah 61:1; Luke 4:18).

Everyday, let the Word of God do *all* that it can
to have you transformed into Jesus.

The Eighth Week in Epiphany

*M*yrrh

This is the last gift of the Magi to Jesus. Just as frankincense, myrrh is a gum resin from trees in the Middle East. The name in Arabic means "bitter." It was a gift at the beginning of Jesus' life, to become one at the end; a Roman soldier attempted to soothe Jesus' pain on the cross. While Jesus accepted the gift at the beginning of his life, he refused it at the end. No anesthesia would diminish the pain that transformed death into the beginning of resurrected life for Jesus and for us.

Myrrh is a symbol of suffering. Pain has within it, the power to transform. We often seek to mask suffering through activity. Resist this anesthesia—or any other addiction that seeks to bury the pain. Receive and accept suffering; do not recoil from it. May suffering be a creative force to purify and transfigure our lives.

The First Sunday in Advent

Begins on the Sunday nearest St. Andrew's Day, Nov. 30. Alphabyte: Advent Wreath, p. 3

Sunday   *The Ark of Sacred Time*   **Matthew 24:36–44**

**You also must be ready, because the Son of Man will come
at an hour when you do not expect him. v. 44**

Noah began to build the ark, not when it looked like rain, but when the Lord commanded. Imagine how Noah must have been mocked—building a great ship far away from the sea! Still, day after day, he built the ark, ready for the waters to become chaotic again, just as in the beginning.

Most of the world will not take notice that a new sacred "ark" of time begins with this First Sunday in Advent. Just as Noah, The Holy Spirit invites you to build each day's spiritual portion of the year as you ready yourself for the coming of the Lord, whenever, and however that will occur. Be safe and secure in the ark of Christ's body. Be safe and secure in this ark as worldly waters with chaotic energies pound against you from without, seeking to put a leak into the sacred seal of your sacred ark.

Monday   *New Life in Your Inner House*   **Isaiah 1**

**Though your sins are like scarlet, they shall be as white as snow;
though they are red as crimson, they shall be like wool. 1:18**

"The Holy One of Israel" is Isaiah's favorite name for God. The Lord states his case against his children. Judgment and tenderness intermingle. Allow Isaiah's poetic images to so move you that you sense in your spirit all the variations on the theme of rebellion that Isaiah lays before you. Listen inwardly as you read. Be one with all humanity that has been in open rebellion against the Lord, yet still the object of the Lord's tender love when hearts turn to God once again.

This is a new beginning of the cycles of grace. Present yourself before the Lord. Perhaps you feel as that abandoned shack in the field after the farm workers have moved on. May you know by faith that the Spirit of the Lord Jesus is waiting to breathe new life into your inner house. May you receive the Lord and be one with God.

Tuesday   *The Red Streamer*   **Joshua 1—2**

**Have I not commanded you? Be strong and courageous.
Do not be terrified; do not be discouraged,
for the LORD your God will be with you wherever you go. 1:9**

Advent, Joshua, Jesus, you: all are involved in thresholds to new life. Read with an Advent longing, with yearning and expectation. Listen carefully to the commands of the Lord upon Joshua, hearing them directly addressed to you. You are the most important person to hear this. God's Word is alive now for you through a personal, intimate encounter with God, as though you were the only one to hear it. This personal revelation comes to you through the Spirit of Christ risen.

Joshua is the Hebrew name for Jesus, the latter coming to us through the Greek New Testament. God called both Joshuas to take God's people into a new Promised Land. For the first Joshua, this was the actual land promised by God to Moses; for Jesus, it is the inner, spiritual Promised Land called the Kingdom of God.

Find a piece of red ribbon and use it as a marker in your Bible, or hang it somewhere where you can often see it. It will remind you of the scarlet rope in chapter 2 as well as the streaming blood of Jesus from the cross, sign of salvation.

| Wednesday | *Water for Everyday* | Psalm 1 |

His delight is in the law of the LORD,
and on his law he meditates day and night. v. 2

The three-year journey through the sacred land of the Bible has begun. Weaving through the center of each of the one hundred and fifty-six weeks of these years is a psalm. Take the admonition of Psalm 1 as you stand before the open space of time before you.

When Moses was about to "pass the torch" to Joshua, Moses put life and death before the people, encouraging them to "Choose life." As you enter the Promised Land of God's presence each day, there will be a word from God to guide you. The Living Waters of the Word will soak the roots of your life.

The trees of winter hardly look as though life will spring from them in the next season. Yet snow is needed now to warm the plants and when melted, to be the first waters for new life.

Fill let each day of your life with Living Water.

| Thursday | *A Leader in Your Own Way* | Titus 1 |

To the pure, all things are pure, but to those who are corrupted
and do not believe, nothing is pure. v. 15

Just as Moses prepared Joshua for leading God's people into the Promised Land, so does Paul instruct Titus as a leader of the Church on the Island of Crete. As in the First Letter to Timothy, here are the qualities needed for a leader in the church. Similar to the contrasts in Psalm 1 are the contrasts between good and evil leaders.

God calls you to take a special place of leadership for God's People. Beyond administrative leadership associated with the office of bishop, gifts and graces are given to you to be a leader in your own way. Meditate on the list of virtues required for spiritual leaders. What are the areas where you need to grow?

Be a steward of God and the things of God. May your daily contact with the Word steadily purify you and clarify the sacred call God has placed upon your life.

| Friday | *The Unexpected* | Luke 1:1–25 |

He [John] will be great in the sight of the Lord …
and he will be filled with the Holy Spirit even from birth. v. 15

Noah's Ark and the Holy of Holies: both are sacred spaces where God acts. Here in the center of the holiest place in the Temple, an aged man lifts his hands to the Lord—longing, waiting, interceding, and pleading. All the emotions of a desperate people converge upon him.

St. Luke is presenting *Yom Kippur*, the holiest of holy days. Perhaps because he is so overwhelmed with this once-in-a-lifetime stand before God, Zechariah is not prepared to hear astounding, unexpected news. While he prays for deliverance, he does not expect it to come so clearly, so closely, so personally through his own wife Elizabeth and him.

Are you ready for the unexpected to happen to you? Remember the words of Jesus: "The Son of Man will come at an hour when you do not expect him." (Luke 12:40).

Saturday | The Sabbath Torah Reading

Dec 08, 2007 #10A	Dec 03, 2016 #6A	Dec 06, 2025 #8A	Dec 09, 2034 #10A
Dec 04, 2010 #10A	Dec 07, 2019 #7A	Dec 09, 2028 #9A	Dec 05, 2037 #10A
Dec 07, 2013 #11A	Dec 03, 2022 #7A	Dec 06, 2031 #9A	Dec 08, 2040 #10A

The Second Week in Advent
*Begins on the Sunday nearest December 7. Alphabyte: **Bible**, p. 4*

Sunday　　　　　　　*The Voice from Wild Emptiness*　　　　　**Matthew 3:1–12**
**A Voice of one calling in the desert, "Prepare the way for the Lord,
make straight paths for him." v. 3. Cf. Isa. 40:3**

Last week's voice of Gabriel from the tightly bounded Holy of Holies contrasts with this week's call from the limitless wild of the desert. The barren void of Elizabeth's womb has received the conception of John the Baptist. Today we hear the silence of the barren wilderness broken with the voice of John completing the prophecy of Isaiah centuries before.

The beginning of newness occurs with a fresh voice of God welling up from the inner, open expanse of the soul. Be there in silence. Feel the wild emptiness of your own spirit—that place of virgin openness beneath the more constructed space contaminated by routine, boredom, low expectation of life—just plain sin. The voice from within calls you to a completely new depth in your relation with God. This begins with repentance. Fall in with the crowds about John allowing their intense desire for spiritual change to do the same for you. John's purifying water prepares the way for the fire of the Holy Spirit of God to ignite your soul.

Monday　　　　　　　　　*Loosened from Self*　　　　　　　　**Isaiah 2**
**The Lord Almighty has a day in store for all the proud and lofty,
for all that is exalted and they will be humbled. 2.12**

Nothing but a radical re-focus will dispose the people for God's salvation. Words of promise mingle with those of judgment. The "mountain of the Lord's house" is a physical image of the new center that must fill the hearts of the people.

The tender power of the Lord works its way into the mountain of resistance that may be inside you. Is your *self* consuming you? Is there pride pounding at you? The images of Isaiah can do their work to tear down pride until all that is left is a heart humbled and ready to surrender to the Lord. Accept all that is challenging you, paining you—even your temptations—as ingredients that God wants to use to loosen you from self-sufficiency, to a total surrender and trust in the Lord.

Tuesday　　　　　　　　*Waking to New Wonders*　　　　　　**Joshua 3—5**
**Consecrate yourselves, for tomorrow
the Lord will do amazing things among you. 3:5**

The Jordan River, familiar to us from the Baptism of John, is encountered and crossed for the first time by God's people. It is about 1200 B.C. Join those making the miracle passage to new life, just as you were one with the crowd baptized by John in the Jordan—those on the brink of knowing Jesus.

The verse for today can become part of your every night's prayer. Prepare yourself as you are about to fall asleep, with the expectation of the wonders God is going to do in you as the waters of the "Jordans" in your life spread wide to receive your entry into the Promise.

In keeping with Joshua's instruction in chapter 4, you might find a few stones and place them where you pray, as memorial stones for what God has done for you, and for what God is going to do. You are a living stone—a testimony, a witness, a reminder to others of what God can do in our lives.

Wednesday   *Nice Try, Evil!*   **Psalm 2**
The One enthroned in heaven laughs
the Lord scoffs at them. v. 4

In a flash of awareness, we scan from the birth of Jesus to the Ascension, celebrated six months from now. Jesus first allowed himself to experience the chaos of sin in all its fury on the cross; he becomes the risen and ascended One who reigns in love above all kingdoms, nations and any other system that sets itself against God.

The victory has been won against any godless kingdom that comes against you such as past generational sin in your family that tends to continue to have its effect upon you and yours. The victory of Jesus confronts all that attacks you. May the Holy Spirit give you that sense of free, joyous laughter, as though you say with the power of God: "Nice try, Evil!"

Christ's love for you is far greater than any hatred mounted against you. Remember Paul's words from Romans 8:31: "If God is for us, who can be against us?"

Thursday   *The Glorious Appearance of God*   **Titus 2**
Jesus Christ gave himself for us to redeem us from all wickedness
and to purify for himself a people that are his very own,
eager to do what is good. v. 14

Pause before each of the virtues listed by Paul to Titus. They will wash you as the Baptism of John, cleansing you to receive ever-deeper penetrations of these gifts from the fire of the Holy Spirit.

The text from v. 11 is often the reading for Christmas Eve. These words of profound hope will launch you into a loving embrace of Jesus who wants to appear before you right now and come to you. May your heart long to possess the One with you in every successive minute of your life.

Repeat today's reading often, such as at the hours that mark the quarter parts of the day. In this way, this holy Word of life, which encourages you and makes you eager to do the good, will transform the entire day.

Friday   *Flesh of His Flesh*   **Luke 1:26–56**
For the Mighty One has done great things for me—
holy is his name. v. 49

Morning, afternoon and evening can beautifully receive these three parts of today's Gospel—the annunciation to Mary in the morning, the afternoon visit of Mary to Elizabeth and the evening song of Mary's praise, the *Magnificat*. Each of these three segments take their movement from the stirrings of the Holy Spirit within the two women.

You will come to appreciate why for centuries the *Magnificat* has been the church's evening prayer in the Catholic and Anglican traditions. Your heart will be one with the heart of Mary in her explosive prayer, if the prior hours of your day are filled with the awareness of what God wants to do for you as God did for Mary. Witness God's compassion as Mary did to Elizabeth. May Jesus grow within you as he did within Mary. For you too, Jesus will be bone of your bone, and flesh of your flesh.

Saturday   **The Sabbath Torah Reading**

Dec 15, 2007 #11A	Dec 10, 2016 #7A	Dec 13, 2025 #9A	Dec 16, 2034 #11A
Dec 11, 2010 #11A	Dec 14, 2019 #8A	Dec 16, 2028 #10A	Dec 12, 2037 #11A
Dec 14, 2013 #12A	Dec 10, 2022 #8A	Dec 13, 2031 #10A	Dec 15, 2040 #11A

The Third Week in Advent
Begins on the Sunday nearest December 14. Alphabyte: Chimes, p. 4

Sunday   *The Sweep of Saving Grace*   Matthew 11:2–11
**The blind receive sight, the lame walk,
those who have leprosy are cured, the deaf hear,
the dead are raised, and the good news is preached to the poor. v. 5**

Winter's cold holds trees captive, wrenching away all evidence of life. Trees that once swayed with summer songs are now touched and come to a silent, stark stillness.

John the Baptist, captive in prison, is also cut off from the evidences of the life-giving presence in Jesus. John begins to doubt, longing for a release from the torturing question, which throws him this way and that: "Are you the one who was to come, or should we expect someone else?"

Does doubt dangle questions before you as well? The words that reassured John will do the same for you with the clarity of bells making these dark nights of the year echo with a summoning call to worship and to joy. Listen in the silence to the sounds of saving grace that sweep across your silent, emptied soul.

Monday   *A Cry in the Winter Night*   Isaiah 3
**Woe to you who add house to house and join field to field
till no space is left and you live alone in the land. v. 8**

Disobedience and betrayal of God's people, just as the betrayal of Joseph's brother in Genesis, result in stark emptiness and life weakened by evil. God's people ignore those powerless in their world—women and children.

How similar is the worldly noise these weeks before Christmas! So many merchants and enterprises not interested in the coming of Jesus to the poor, only want great riches to be accounted when this season of buying and selling is over.

Isaiah's prediction of the loss of finery is as a great blackout that reduces the colorful, flickering lights of stores and houses to an awesome darkness. It is from the darkness and emptiness of all distraction that the soul cries out more clearly to the Lord in the winter night.

Tuesday   *The Spirit Breaks In*   Joshua 6—8
**Do not say a word until the day I tell you to shout.
Then shout. 6:10**

Jericho is taken, not by worldly strategies, but in the Lord's unique way. It is time for what is "Jericho" in you to fall. Do some walking today in silence. Do not talk. It is Advent. Wait upon the Lord. Allow God to tell you when to make a move with your mouth. The decisive moment will come when God prompts you to speak or shout, breaking in upon any lying spirit that may lurk within your heart behind walls that need to fall. Like the shout when a karate chop breaks wood, let the Spirit break open the stuck and stubborn stuff in your spirit.

The Israelites hoarded enemy treasures intended only for the Lord. They were powerless before their enemies until they repented and released these treasures. Is there anything that you are clinging to or hoarding that belongs to the Lord?

I lie down and sleep;
I wake again, because the LORD sustains me. v. 5

In the middle of this week that is itself the middle of Advent, there comes a cry in the midst of enemy territory. John the Baptist could have groaned this psalm from his prison cell. Christians, Jews, and Muslims persecuted today around the world can do the same. Strengthen their prayer by binding yourself to them with these words of salvation.

May your inner conviction of this psalm ring out with the same deep resounding toll of a great bell. The emptier and darker the night, the more the clarion-call of God's salvation can silence those taunting, tempting voices that may be keeping you fretfully, frightfully awake. Be assured of God's salvation upon your life as you sleep in peace and rise in confidence.

Thursday *The Wash of Regeneration* Titus 3

He saved us through the washing of rebirth and renewal
by the Holy Spirit, whom he poured out on us generously
through Jesus Christ our Savior ... v. 5

Prepare an inner manger of the heart for Jesus. Paul's concluding chapter in this letter uplifts humility and gentleness which must precede the soul about to be immersed in the miracle of God's presence in Christ. Thus, your spirit will be ready to receive the regenerating wash of the Holy Spirit expressed in verses 4 to 6. These are verses, which place the wonders of our redemption into tiny space; I suggest you memorize them. The verses are in preparation for the bath of grace; the following verses unfold the ways we are to live our transformed life.

Do not argue about theology; it only makes for division. Receive the measure of faith that God gives you and come into God's presence. Jesus said, "Where two or three are gathered in my name, I am there among them" (Matt 18:20).

Friday *At Work in Your Inmost* Luke 1:57–80

Praise be to the Lord, the God of Israel,
because he has come and has redeemed his people. v. 67

Zechariah must have benefited from the months of his muted mouth, consequence of doubt and distrust of Gabriel's message. Unable to communicate, he enters into that inmost sacred space where God does a precious work, just as God was doing in the dark, silent wombs of Elizabeth and Mary.

Thus, Zechariah was ready to let prayer be the first expression of his loosened tongue. What flows forth would be repeated daily for centuries as the Church's Morning Prayer after the silence of the night.

Hold your tongue often during these darkening days of Advent. Believe that God is at work in your inmost, just as God was molding the major personalities of the first Advent. The more you wait and relish the silence, the greater will be the fire of prayer that starts within, expressing itself without through your loosened tongue.

Saturday **The Sabbath Torah Reading**

Dec 22, 2007 #12A	Dec 17, 2016 #8A	Dec 20, 2025 #10A	Dec 23, 2034 #12A
Dec 18, 2010 #12A	Dec 21, 2019 #9A	Dec 23, 2028 #11A	Dec 19, 2037 #12A
Dec 21, 2013 #13A	Dec 17, 2022 #9A	Dec 20, 2031 #11A	Dec 22, 2040 #12A

The Fourth Week in Advent

Begins on the Sunday nearest December 21. Alphabyte: Darkroom, p. 5

Sunday   *Waking to the Lord's Plan*   **Matthew 1:18–23**

**When Joseph woke up, he did what the angel of the Lord
had commanded him and took Mary home as his wife. v. 24**

Two Josephs are with us this season—the patriarch and the husband of Mary. The Saturday readings about Joseph in Genesis blend with those in the Gospels relating with Joseph, foster father of Jesus. Both receive directions from God through dreams; both go to Egypt; both are "just men" of the Lord.

Enter into the scene of the Annunciation to Joseph. Imagine his pain before the intervention of the angel. Mary is pregnant by someone else. Just as for the patriarch, Joseph, Mary's husband moves beyond being a victim of circumstances. He is more concerned for Mary's well-being than for his own condition. God can work wonders with those who die to self.

Meditate upon Joseph as he falls asleep in anguish; be with him in the wonder of his waking.

Monday   *The Embrace of the Branch*   **Isaiah 4**

**In that day the Branch of the LORD will be beautiful and glorious,
and the fruit of the land will be the pride and glory of the survivors in Israel. v. 2**

The Messianic image of "The Branch of the Lord" opens this chapter of just six verses. As occurred in the Exodus, the cloud of smoke by day and the pillar of fire by night will once again lead the people to places of purification, joy, and peace.

The days are the shortest in the northern hemisphere. However, with winter, the days begin to be longer. Thus, we remember the birth of Jesus at this time. The light of God in Christ has come. Whatever is the darkness of your circumstances or the filthiness of your sin, Jesus offers himself to lead you into paths of light. Jesus loves you. Only embrace and stay clinging to "The Branch of the Lord" and allow the Branch to embrace you in total love and forgiveness.

Tuesday   *Victory Over Inner Enemies*   **Joshua 9—10**

**All these kings and their land Joshua took at one time,
because the LORD God of Israel fought for Israel. 10:42**

War is being waged, not for land, but for a spiritual space in your heart where you can live with God alone. Advent is a time to take possession of this space. However, there are spiritual enemies that have "dug in" to that same territory—perhaps old family strongholds passed on to you through negative, prideful, sinful tendencies that seek to sap the peace that God wants to share with you. Name those "enemies." Recall in the letter to the Ephesians: "We do not wrestle against flesh and blood ... but against spiritual hosts of wickedness in the heavenly places" (6:12).

God gives you the heart of Joshua and especially the heart of Jesus, born in the silence of the night in the stable of your heart.

Wednesday	*God's Protective Presence*	Psalm 4

**In your anger, do not sin; when you are on your beds,
search your hearts and be silent. v. 4**

Κing David's anointing for intimacy with the Lord comes through deeply and sweetly in this psalm. Pray it often throughout the day and especially as your night prayer. Commit all or part of it to memory.

The verse for the day deserves special reflection. If you fulfill the second part of the verse first, then you will be less likely to sin. When we yield in a reactive manner to anger, sin occurs. Place a silent buffer zone between the feeling of anger and your response to it.

Whatever might have made David angry, his meditative space has enlarged his awareness. The overwhelming sense of God's protective presence to him makes the source of his anger a mere speck against the shining light of the Lord's countenance before him.

Thursday	*Forgiving Love*	Philemon

**If he has done you any wrong or owes you anything,
charge it to me. v. 18**

Βriefest of Paul's letters, here is an invitation to forgiveness. Instead of what could have been harsh treatment and even death for Onesimus, the runaway slave, Paul pleads for reconciliation between him and his master, Philemon.

Meditate before the manger. See Mary, slave and handmaid of the Lord. Joseph is wrapped in the swaddling cloths of silence. Here is the place of forgiving love. Jesus has come, writing with his birth and later with his blood, a letter of intercession for us to the Father. All our wrongs have been charged to Jesus' "account." Jesus became a slave so that we might be set free and live with the Father as God's child.

Is there someone who needs a letter like Paul's coming from you—something more than a hasty "Seasons Greeting" card?

Friday	*Movement and Stillness*	Luke 2:1–20

**Mary treasured up all these things
and pondered them in her heart. v. 19**

Μovement and stillness are carefully contrasted in the Christmas Story. First, there is the tedious moving of Mary and Joseph from Nazareth to Bethlehem, a journey by donkey of some seventy miles. Accompany them. Take the reigns of the donkey so that Joseph can tend to Mary without distraction. Kneel with them in the stillness and awesomeness of the birth. Drink in all the power of that silent night.

Energy shifts to the angels announcing and singing before the shepherds. By faith your spirit mounts with theirs. From the stillness of a winter's night-watch over their sheep, they run in haste to the manger. Their out-of-breath-ness slows to an immense peace, and then energy again as they become the first missionaries of the new presence.

Where does all this leave you? Take your cue from Mary who "treasured up all these things and pondered them in her heart."

Saturday   The Sabbath Torah Reading

Dec 29, 2007 #13A	Dec 24, 2016 #9A	Dec 21, 2025 #11A	Dec 30, 2034 #13A
Dec 25, 2010 #13A	Dec 28, 2019 #10A	Dec 30, 2028 #12A	Dec 26, 2037 #13A
Dec 28, 2013 #14A	Dec 24, 2022 #10A	Dec 27, 2031 #12A	Dec 29, 2040 #13A

Christmas Week

Sunday   *Ministry Unfolds*   **Matthew 2:13–23**

So was fulfilled what was said through the prophets:
"He will be called a Nazarene." v. 23

Joseph, a dream, and Jesus—again we find meaning in relating this story to the saga of the patriarch, Joseph, read on Saturdays.

Today's reading is the sequel to the account of the Magi and Herod proclaimed next week on Epiphany Sunday. We read of the aftermath of Herod's rage in the terrible massacre of the Holy Innocents and the safe refuge of Jesus, Mary, and Joseph in Egypt. From the very beginning, Jesus is one with his people, at first protected in Egypt, then delivered from the slavery that would develop.

Follow the journey of the Holy Family to and from Egypt; join them as they settle in Nazareth for the long, quiet years of the presence of God in Jesus. He becomes ready for the saving ministry that will unfold.

As you quietly live each day, God continues to prepare you for your unique ministry that is unfolding.

Monday   *Fruit or Ornaments?*   **Isaiah 5**

Yet for all this, his anger is not turned away,
his hand is still upraised. v. 25

Hebrew poetry is at its best here, as Isaiah unfolds an image familiar to his listeners. There is tenderness in the poetry, especially in those verses where God's hurt, pain and frustration about his withered vineyard are most expressed.

What kind of fruit has your life been giving? Wait … Ask God to tell you. Perhaps you do not discover much fruit, but only ornaments as on your Christmas tree. No matter; God can transform all in the coming year.

When we are hurt and frustrated, our moods and feelings change rapidly. So too with God, in whose image we are made. Feel the shifts and changes in the movement of God's heart. Worship. Take hold of God's hand stretched out to heal.

Tuesday   *Manger Outward—Cross Upward*   **Joshua 11—12**

Joshua left nothing undone
of all that the LORD commanded Moses. 11:15

The summary list in chapter 12 bears witness to one clear truth: God longs for a people wholly dedicated to God. The Lord does not want us to make deals with the Enemy, as the Israelites did with Canaanite neighbors with whom they mingled.

Christmas contrasts with the conquests of Joshua. The wood of the manger is at the center of the space of *God-with-us,* won for us, not with the edge of the sword, but with the laser-beam of Jesus' love. From the manger outward, to the cross upward, Jesus' love is the weapon that has given us a "holy land" where we can live right now and forever.

Feel the contrasts in the silence—lists of conquered kings in Joshua … your list of spiritual enemies overcome … Joshua's sword … Jesus' manger … Come to the stable!

Wednesday	*Go Straight to God*	Psalm 5

**In the morning I lay my requests before you
and wait in expectation. v. 3**

If last week's psalm can become your night prayer, this Psalm is perfect for mornings. The first attention of David upon awakening is God. Learn from David. Direct your words and your eyes straight into the Lord's presence as soon as you awaken.

We are creatures who need the rhythms of daily cycles. Just as children love the security of routine, so we need that sense of comfort that comes through the repetition and return of regular practices of prayer. These can deepen our entry into God's presence.

What are the habits of daily devotion that the Lord urges upon your heart? Though my own life has been through so many changes, I find continuity and peace to gently whisper into the morning what we used to pray as novices in religious life: *"Laudetur Jesus Christus:"* Praised be Jesus Christ.

Go straight into the presence of your God and from there only, live out your day.

Thursday	*Jolted into Inwardness*	Galatians 1

God set me apart from birth and called me by his grace. v. 15

Paul in Galatians will help you ponder in your heart as Mary did. The credentials he offers come from the decisive move of God upon his life on the road to Damascus. Paul first goes to the Arabian Desert, then on to a three-year period in Damascus. God gave the Gospel to Paul, unmediated by anyone else. Damascus was the jolt to Paul; later came the deep, inner preparation of the wondrous Apostle to come. Paul too, has his desert, just as John the Baptist, Jesus, and God's people in the wilderness.

God's unique intervention in history through Jesus breaks all the assumptions about how we think God is going to act. God wants to do great things in you by grace. Let God shake you. However, you receive your "wake-up call," get busy with the daily, inner work of responding to God's Word … for three years, like Paul!

Friday	*Because of You*	Matthew 1

**Jacob was the father of Joseph, the husband of Mary,
of whom was born Jesus, who is called Christ. v. 16**

Three great divisions of generations place Jesus into the immense tapestry of God's activity in history. Each of these has fourteen generations—two times the perfect number—seven. They are described by Matthew in the conclusion of the genealogy in v. 17.

The New Testament begins with a grand sweep of the First Covenant. The list is taken from the paternal line. However, the symmetry is interrupted by the mention of foreign women: Tamar, Rahab, Ruth, and Bathesheba. The ways that God worked through these women outside the strictly male, Jewish line, set the stage for the miraculous intervention through Mary. This also anticipates the way in which God's saving grace would include Gentiles.

The Lord has placed you in the generational list of those who will bear Christ. How will the next generation be brought to worship God because of you?

Saturday   The Sabbath Torah Reading

Jan 05, 2008 #14A	Dec 31, 2016 #10A	Jan 03, 2026 #12A	Jan 06, 2035 #14A
Jan 01, 2011 #14A	Jan 04, 2020 #11A	Jan 06, 2029 #13A	Jan 02, 2038 #14A
Jan 04, 2014 #15A	Dec 31, 2022 #11A	Jan 03, 2032 #13A	Jan 05, 2041 #14A

The First Week in Epiphany

*Begins on the first Sunday in January. Alphabyte: **F**rankincense, p. 6*

Sunday   *Innovation in the Skies*   **Matthew 2:1–12**

We saw his star in the east and have come to worship him. 2:2

Energy enters into a search for God. Pagan foreigners peer into the skies, seeking meaning to the new star they discover in the heavens. They leave everything to discover where it is leading. They follow the star shining in their hearts, as well as the one in the skies.

At polar opposites are Herod and the Jewish leaders. Nestled in complacency and inner blindness, they are not interested in God's new King, but rather are anxious that he might overthrow the tables of their own power. Fear and hostility enter and possess them.

How are you when it comes to some new entry of God into your life? Are you open to search the inner skies of your own possibility for some innovation and direction there, or are you tempted to be your own "king," resisting God's reign in your life?

Monday   *Here I Am*   **Isaiah 6**

**Then I heard the voice of the Lord saying, "Whom shall I send?
And who will go for us?" And I said, "Here am I. Send me!" v. 8**

The fire of God's Holy Spirit falls upon the quivering mouth of Isaiah, releasing the incense of prophesy. The first news is not good. The Lord reveals to Isaiah a people whose hearts have become as heavy and hardened as Herod's.

Notice how quickly the move of the fire of God upon the prophet loosens him from the guilt and shame of his own sinfulness. Though made the more noticeable because of the contrast between human sinfulness and God's immense holiness, Isaiah still allows God to do a new and wondrous work in him. He is ready to be sent. Shame is burned away; only the sweet smelling fragrance of being alive to God's personal mission upon his life remains.

Pray until you are as ready as Isaiah to respond to the "whatever" of God's will, with your very own "Here I am."

Tuesday   *The Life-Pledge*   **Joshua 13—14**

**To the tribe of Levi, Moses had given no inheritance;
the LORD, the God of Israel is their inheritance, as he promised them. 13:33**

Deeds of land of the Twelve Tribes are described. However, the lands are unlike those that are bought with a bank's money as a mortgage—a "death-pledge" upon it. These are inherited lands given by God alone to God's chosen people through Moses.

We live in a society where we earn, buy and sell possessions and properties; only then do we will them as inheritance. But the Psalmist declares in 89:11 "The heavens are Yours, the earth also is Yours; the world and all its fullness." Today be aware of all that you have as *given* to you by the Lord. You have something greater, given by the death of Jesus on the cross. He is the inheritance of God—a "life-pledge." Christ shares this with you in the inner Kingdom where he calls us to live by this outpouring of God's love.

Approach with the Magi and adore.

Wednesday   *A Heavy Heart's Answered Prayer*   **Psalm 6**
Away from me, all you who do evil,
for the LORD has heard my weeping. v. 8

God's grace in the shining star penetrates the earth, revealing the fragile goodness and hardened arrogance that lurk there. Here in the middle of Epiphany Week, David's bed of suffering evidences the struggle between good and evil. Verse after verse come as waves of feeling expressing the extent of David's pain. However, the heart of this man extends even more, stretching his prayer to the utmost until he knows that God is answering him.

The coming of Christ brings turmoil to resistant ones. The more you turn your life over to God, the more persecution you will receive. Expect it! However, expect all the more that God will bring you beyond your pain to the triumphant experience by faith of God's love and power in your life. Nothing nor anyone can take this away from you.

Thursday   *Christ Lives in Me*   **Galatians 2**
I have been crucified with Christ and I no longer live,
but Christ lives in me. v. 20

In the Magi, Gentiles have free access to the living God in Christ. Here the great apostle to the Gentiles, Paul, depicts the essence of his call: Gentiles have total access to the grace of God without having to fulfill the prescriptions of the law. We catch a glimpse of the conflict in personal terms, imagining what must have been the sparks that flew between Peter and Paul.

Along with the first chapter, this one completes the first of three parts of the letter—the call and credential of Paul himself. The end of the chapter presents the point of doctrine, which will Paul develops in chapters 3 and 4: the human person is justified by faith, and not by works.

Memorize verse 20 and let it fall upon your heart as the coals of fire upon the lips of Isaiah—as the burning embers of frankincense, gift of the Magi.

Friday   *Abuse of the Innocent*   **Matthew 2**
The angel of the Lord appeared to Joseph in a dream.
"Get up," he said, "take the child and his mother and escape to Egypt." v. 13

The readings for this week mingle marvelously with each other in Epiphany themes. Today, return to the Magi story, this time linking it with the tragedy in the reaction of Herod. Evil resists God outlandishly, always harming the innocent. Consider the children who are victims of abuse, murder, and genocide.

As we begin reading Exodus as the Sabbath readings about this time, Matthew sees Jesus as a New Moses who will lead us out of the bondage in the "Egypts" of our lives. God's eternal plan is that we be free from all "Pharaohs" or "Herods" who scramble to protect their power by destroying ours.

Saturday   **The Sabbath Torah Reading**

Jan 12, 2008 #15A	Jan 07, 2017 #11A	Jan 10, 2026 #13A	Jan 13, 2035 #15A
Jan 08, 2011 #15A	Jan 11, 2020 #12A	Jan 13, 2029 #14A	Jan 09, 2038 #15A
Jan 11, 2014 #16A	Jan 07, 2023 #12A	Jan 10, 2032 #14A	Jan 12, 2041 #15A

The Second Week in Epiphany
Begins on the second Sunday in January. Alphabyte: Gold, p. 6

Sunday   *Embrace of Saving History*   **Matthew 3:13–17**
**Heaven was opened, and Jesus saw the Spirit of God
descending like a dove and lighting upon him. v. 16**

Jesus launches his public ministry as he emerges from the waters of the Jordan. Biblical themes about water are touched upon and blended in this account. Recall the Spirit hovering over the chaotic waters in Genesis, Noah, the ark, the dove, the crossing of the Jordan in Joshua 3, and the Exodus readings these Saturdays. All are gathered into one event that unites heaven and earth, the divine and the human. Jesus embraces all of God's saving history to himself. The saving energy of God is fused into one laser beam of Christ's light as we celebrate this second Epiphany of Jesus—his baptism.

It is a moment in history with cosmic dimensions. Immerse all your senses in the scene. Renew your baptism. Rise with Jesus and be free.

Monday   *Into the Center of the Future*   **Isaiah 7**
**The virgin will be with child and will give birth to a son,
and will call him Immanuel. 7:14**

If you yield to the Lord, God will do more with you than what you embrace with your conscious mind alone. When Isaiah made this famous prophecy about the virgin to Ahaz, king of Judah, he wanted to assure the king, frightened about the power of enemies all about, that a little child to come would be the source of victory. However Isaiah's prophecy reaches deep into the very center of the future; it is the Messiah of whom he speaks. Though the rest of the chapter speaks of devastation, Ahaz, you and I need to remember the name given to the child of promise to come: **Immanuel: "God-with-us."** The child of the Virgin Mary is the spark igniting the new fire of God's powerful intercession against every enemy in all history. Jesus has come. Trust in his power, even though for you, as for Ahaz, times of loss and trial may be coming against you.

Tuesday   *A Place to Settle Down*   **Joshua 15—17**
**Though the Canaanites have iron chariots and though they are strong,
you can drive them out. 17:18**

Genealogies in the Bible are tedious to read; so also the lists of the boundaries of the tribes and their cities. Don't lose the forest for the trees! While a map will help you visualize these territories, there is something obvious: a wandering people finally have a place to settle down. Identify with this in your own life.

Lands and relationships both need boundaries. The arms of the crucified, risen Lord gather others into a primary community—a spiritual land of faith, hope, and love called God's Kingdom.

Take care that you do not cross the borders of your faith by simply not believing.

Wednesday *A Song of Victory* **Psalm 7**
My shield is God Most High,
who saves the upright in heart. v. 10

David finds a time and a place of respite in his flight from King Saul and his retinue that are pursuing David. Once again, he discovers by faith that the God of his heart will prevail. All that frightens David flees from him. He stops, gathers strength in this psalm given to him and to us by the Holy Spirit.

Take time apart today to pray this psalm over and over until its cumulative effect has all fears leave, bringing you to full awareness of the deep truths of the psalm. The power of God will lead you to safety.

Jesus emerges from the chaotic waters and is ready to bring victory. He is God's beloved Son; listen to him. The Holy Spirit of God is praying this song of victory deep within you.

Thursday *Freedom by Faith* **Galatians 3**
The law was put in charge to lead us to Christ
that we might be justified by faith. v. 24

Paul plunges into the midst of his argument about faith vs. works. Catch the passion beneath these words of doctrine—the burning of his heart feeding the enlightenment of his mind.

He shakes the Galatians and us by a series of six questions. These reverberate within so that the joyous answers given by Paul may find a home in you.

Here lie the essentials of Christian teaching: we are made right with God not by what *we* do, but by what we allow *Christ* to do in us. As a great magnet, Jesus draws the curse of sin and the law to himself. The cross crushes the curse.

Read slowly Paul's understanding of the Law. Commentaries will help. May you fly by faith far beyond the law, into the freedom and love of Jesus.

Friday *Points of Combustion* **Matthew 3**
He will baptize you with the Holy Spirit and with fire. v. 11

Imagine the internal movement of your car's engine in slow motion. As each piston meets the spark plug, there is a flash explosion in the cylinder, driving the piston down, moving the pin in the crankcase in a circular motion. Then the piston returns to be fired once again. All this happens some twenty-five to seventy-five times a second.

Over the past six weeks since the beginning of Advent, there have been points of ignition when the Holy Spirit's fire has exploded in your heart, seeking to set your life into more complete movement toward the Lord. There was a point of fiery contact in the Second Sunday in Advent when we heard the first part of chapter 3, to be completed this past Sunday in the Baptism of Jesus.

Sense the new and creative cycles that these daily readings are setting in motion in your life. I pray that these *Firestarters* may be such sparks to ignite your heart.

Saturday **The Sabbath Torah Reading**

Jan 19, 2008 #16A	Jan 14, 2017 #12A	Jan 17, 2026 #14A	Jan 20, 2035 #16A
Jan 15, 2011 #16A	Jan 18, 2020 #13A	Jan 20, 2029 #15A	Jan 16, 2038 #16A
Jan 18, 2014 #17A	Jan 14, 2023 #13A	Jan 17, 2032 #15A	Jan 19, 2041 #16A

The Third Week in Epiphany

Begins on the third Sunday in January. Alphabyte: Homing Pigeon, p. 7

Sunday   *A Stable, New Future*   John 1:29–42

**The next day, John was there again with two of his disciples.
When he saw Jesus passing by, he said, "Look, the Lamb of God!" v. 35**

One time while camping with my family, I created an outdoor shower. I lashed a hula-hoop to the branches of a tree in three places, a shower curtain hanging onto it. A plastic bag of water previously heated by the sun, hung from above. It had a hose and showerhead attached—all the comforts of a shower at home … almost!

There were three points to keep the hula-hoop stable. Three gives stability. Is this another reason why sacredness and completeness are associated with this number?

In John's gospel, the episode of Jesus' first encounter with his disciples takes place on the middle day of three days. The first day is the meeting and baptism with John the Baptist; the third day is the Marriage Feast at Cana. Feel this second day: transition from old water to the stability of new life, symbolized by the new wine.

Spend time with Jesus and the first disciples. He prepares a stable, new future for you.

Monday   *Sanctuary in the Lord*   Isaiah 8

**Here am I, and the children the LORD has given me.
We are signs and symbols in Israel from the LORD Almighty
who dwells on Mount Zion. 8:18**

A child is promised who will be victorious over the enemies of the southern kingdom of Judah. The child's name, Maher-Shalal-Hash-Baz, means "The spoil speeds, the prey hastens," prophesying that Syria and the northern Kingdom of Israel would soon be destroyed by Assyria.

The Lord will give you all the resources you need to withstand any enemy. There will be "children" for you in one way or another, who will continue to bear the name Immanuel: "God-with-us."

Immerse yourself in the presence of God until what is awesome in your life is not what is coming against you, but rather the One in whose sanctuary you find refuge and in whose presence you are at home.

Tuesday   *Home of the Ark*   Joshua 18—19

**The whole assembly of the Israelites gathered at Shiloh
and set up the Tent of Meeting there. 18:1**

Before these chapters conclude with the rest of the lands apportioned to the remaining tribes, there is a simple notice given in the verse for today: the Ark of the Covenant has come to a place of rest; it has found a home. Just as the capital of a state or country is centrally located, so this city is chosen because it is near the center of the lands the Lord gave to the people. It is about 35 miles north of Jerusalem. The Ark will remain there for over 100 years until the Philistines capture it, as we read in 1 Samuel 4.

The tabernacle is the primary sacrament of the presence of God to God's people. What do you have in your home and your life that reminds you of God's enduring presence to you in Christ? During this Epiphany season, as the light of Jesus' presence grows, do something to increase awareness—perhaps a star above your front door or an ornament that stays behind, after all the others have been gathered and stored in the attic.

**You have made man a little lower than the heavenly beings
and crowned him with glory and honor. v. 5**

The wider and deeper is David's contemplation, the greater the sense of comfort and security he finds in God. David's eyes sweep over the wonders of creation. He takes countless "snapshots" that bear the name of the Creator.

Then suddenly David becomes self-conscious. How tiny is the being whose eye is embracing all this! The insignificance he feels is not negative; rather he is lifted to awareness that the human being is the greatest expression of God's creative love.

Lift your eyes to an expanse wider than the scope of your limited world and all its problems. May faith in God's creative, preferential love for you have you believe how very much at home you are in the universe, no matter how tempted you might be to feel how far away and lost you are.

Thursday   *Adopted into God's Family*   Galatians 4

**Because you are sons, God sent the Spirit of his Son into our hearts,
the Spirit who calls out, "Abba, Father." v. 6**

As though we are in the middle of a lovely garden, we find ourselves in the center of Paul's teaching about our salvation through Jesus. Simply put, God has brought us into God's house and family. You and I can do nothing to qualify us for such adoption. Only Jesus is Son, but in Jesus, we have all the rights and privileges of the first-born son.

Catch the intensity of Paul's words of love for the churches in Galatia that he urgently wants to be convinced of the truths he expresses. Meditate carefully upon the analogy he makes between Ishmael and Isaac—the former, the child of a slave, the latter, of a free woman. Receive the full impact of being a free child of God in God's own house.

Friday   *Immersion in Ministry*   Matthew 4

**The People living in darkness have seen a great light;
on those living in the land of the shadow of death a light has dawned.
v. 16; Isaiah 9:1–2**

Jesus, the sinless one, is nonetheless tempted. Three major temptations come against Jesus in the desert, occurring between the baptism and the beginning of Jesus' ministry. He takes upon himself the history of God's people in the desert. Jesus is faithful where the Israelites were not. Last Sunday's reference in John's Gospel to Jesus as "The Lamb of God" is John's way of seeing Jesus taking the place of the Paschal Lamb sacrificed in remembrance of the Exodus.

After the temptation, Capernaum becomes Jesus' home-base. Miracles abound; immense crowds follow him. Immerse yourself in Jesus' ministry. Give Jesus your history and let him transform its meaning, just as he did for our ancestors in the desert.

Saturday   **The Sabbath Torah Reading**

Jan 26, 2008 #17A	Jan 21, 2017 #13A	Jan 24, 2026 #15A	Jan 28, 2035 #17A
Jan 22, 2011 #17A	Jan 25, 2020 #14A	Jan 27, 2029 #16A	Jan 23, 2038 #17A
Jan 25, 2014 #18A	Jan 21, 2023 #14A	Jan 24, 2032 #16A	Jan 26, 2041 #17A

The Fourth Week in Epiphany

Begins on the fourth Sunday in January. Alphabyte: Ice Dancing, p. 7

Sunday   *The Dance with Jesus*   **Matthew 4:12–23**
At once they left their nets and followed Jesus. v. 20

Countless numbers of communities across the earth encounter this passage today in worship. As soon as Jesus begins his ministry, he calls others to be with him. Just as the *Alphabyte* "Ice Dancing," Jesus chooses not to "skate" alone, but rather to dance with others.

Take a place alongside these simple fishermen as Jesus calls them to be his disciples. Three of them would become his closest friends—Peter, James, and John. Perfect they were not. One would deny Jesus; two would become obsessed by positions of privilege in the new kingdom; all three would sleep during Jesus' greatest moment of anguish in the garden.

God places a call upon you. Do not deny the call, be self-centered or sleep during it. Jesus will teach you how to dance with him.

Monday   *Christmas Echoes Again*   **Isaiah 9**
For to us a child is born, to us a son is given, and the government will be on his shoulders.
And he will be called Wonderful Counselor,
Mighty God, Everlasting Father, Prince of Peace. 9:6

Every year at Christmastime, this verse is proclaimed. Perhaps you will hear the familiar ecstatic music of Handel's "Messiah" echoing within you. Sway with the joy of this verse, which forever imbeds itself against every dark and malicious enemy. Meditate upon the five names given to the Messiah. Say and sing them repeatedly during the course of this day, which the Lord has made.

Verse 8 begins to describe the judgment against Israel, referred to at the beginning of this section as "Jacob." Israel, the northern kingdom with its ten tribes, has sinfully conspired against Judah in the south. Samaria, the capital of the key tribe of Ephraim, would be destroyed.

It is said that Handel wrote the entire Messiah in three weeks, with times of ecstasy lifting him throughout. The Holy Spirit will do something wonderful for you as well, as the "Wonderful Counselor," Christ, is born in you.

Tuesday   *An Altar of Witness*   **Joshua 20—22**
The Reubenites and the Gadites gave the altar this name:
A Witness Between Us that the LORD is God. 22:34

The final allotment of lands is decided with special provisions for the priestly house of Levi. Ponder the issue of the separate altar, which those tribes and half-tribes who settled on the eastern side of the Jordan had constructed. Find out why the rest of God's people were so concerned about this and how the issue was resolved.

Once again, it is the dilemma of "The One and the Many." The one sacrifice of Christ upon the cross irradiates across the globe, blending with the ongoing suffering of others.

Do you have a special place of prayer in your house that is a sanctuary for you? If not, create one. May it be for you what the eastern altar was—place of the rising sun. As each new day dawns, may God come more fully into your life.

Wednesday   *Engravings Every Hour*   **Psalm 9**

Those who know your name will trust in you,
for you, Lord, have never forsaken those who seek you. v. 10

This psalm, together with next week is Psalm 10, forms an acrostic: the first word of each stanza begins with successive letters of the Hebrew alphabet. This literary style provides a thread of unity in the absence of a more developed sequence of thought. Some early Bibles counted these two psalms as one.

When taken individually, each letter of an alphabet stands on its own. Do the same with each group of verses that make a stanza or strophe. Imagine each one printed or engraved upon your soul. The psalms are prayers of strong expression.

From the deep, inward experience of David and other psalmists, let each stanza make a powerful impression. You might engrave and shape every hour of your day by each one.

Thursday   *Your Nine-to-Five Job*   **Galatians 5**

The fruit of the Spirit is love, joy, peace, patience, kindness,
goodness, faithfulness, gentleness and self-control. vv. 22–23

"Practical Applications for Life:" such is this third and final division of Paul's letter to the churches in the province of Galatia. Freedom and bondage; life and death: these are the two polarities. Ask the Lord to show you whether you are clinging to the freedom the Lord Jesus gives, or are losing the grip, swept away and bound up in external legalism. The opening inspiration is meant to startle you.

In freedom, you do the clinging; in bondage, an outside force does the clinging to you. God welcomes us to cling to the cross of Jesus to protect us from the vicious tide of evil that seeks to sweep us away.

Here is your "nine-to-five job:" take one of the nine fruits of the Spirit for each hour. The Spirit will birth them in you, one hour at a time.

Friday   *Inaugural Address*   **Matthew 5:1–20**

Blessed are the meek, for they will inherit the earth. v. 5

If Jesus were to give an inaugural address for his ministry, the Sermon on the Mount would be it. The message is for the disciples alone; the multitude far below is not ready for these words.

Matthew sees Jesus as the New Moses. He wants us to be aware of the lines of connection between the Mount of the Beatitudes and Mount Sinai. On Sinai God spoke face to face with Moses when God gave Moses the Ten Commandments; here God in Christ speaks face to face with the disciples. He invites you to be there and listen to the wondrous new ways of walking in the freedom of God's kingdom in the intimate, face-to-face union with Jesus.

Jesus invites you to be his closest disciple. Will you let the Sermon on the Mount lift you to new heights of your awareness of self, so very close to God?

Saturday   **The Sabbath Torah Reading**

Feb 02, 2008 #18A	Jan 28, 2017 #14A	Jan 31, 2026 #16A	Feb 03, 2035 #18A
Jan 29, 2011 #18A	Feb 01, 2020 #15A	Feb 03, 2029 #17A	Jan 30, 2038 #18A
Feb 01, 2014 #19A	Jan 28, 2023 #15A	Jan 31, 2032 #17A	Feb 02, 2041 #18A

27

The Fifth Week in Epiphany

Begins on the Sunday nearest February 1. Alphabyte: Journal, p. 8

For 2008 and 2035, this is the last week in Epiphany, beginning with Transfiguration Sunday. Easter in 2008 is March 23, the earliest date for Easter in the 21st century. (March 22 is the earliest date possible; this occurred in 1818 and will not happen again until 2285!) See p. 36 for the Transfiguration Sunday reading, continuing below for the Monday-to-Saturday passages. Ash Wednesday occurs this week. Next week turn to The First Week in Lent, Year A, p. 46.

Sunday   *The Need of God*   **Matthew 5:1–12**

Blessed are they who know their need of God. v. 1, New English Bible

As though with a magnifying glass, look more closely at the Eight Beatitudes. The first one from the New English Bible exposes the essence of what it means to be "poor in spirit." "Blessed are those who know their need of God." Poor indeed! The only source of our coming into existence is God.

Have you ever wondered why *you* came forth from your mother's womb on the day of your birth, and why it was not someone else? It is a fact of God's loving favor toward you that God decided some time ago to allow the idea of you take flesh at your conception. You need God alone for that fact. You need God alone for every breath, from the first gasp of air at birth, to the final sigh surrendering you in death.

If you truly live by the First Beatitude, the Kingdom of Heaven will be yours, not only after your final breath, but also in all the breaths, from the first to the last.

Monday   *Fires that Consume*   **Isaiah 10:1–19**

The Light of Israel will become a fire,
their Holy One a flame. 10.17

Though the Lord had used pagan Assyria to bring judgment upon Israel, the arrogance of Assyria brings its own punishment. Listen to that nation's haughty words, boasting that its cities are like the great ones that were destroyed. They blaspheme by blurting out that Judah's God is just like the pagan ones of Syria that Assyria destroyed. The poetry that Isaiah paints serves to make the arrogance and blasphemy of Assyria even bolder. The fire started here will consume.

Reflect upon the energies of the world that press about. Can you not hear similar words muttered beneath commercials conspiring that we consume more and more of the riches of the earth? Work and pray against the injustices that pervade current society, just as they did in Isaiah's day. The fire of God's love: may it burn away all pride.

Tuesday   *Tough Love and Tenderness*   **Joshua 23—24**

As for me and my household, we will serve the LORD. 24:15

We are at the end of Joshua's life. The warrior years of the young liberator are long gone. His words have the ring of "tough love." He reminds God's people of their need to be faithful to the covenant. At the same time, there are tenderness and expansive peace that well up in words of comfort, his long life seasoned by the inner joy of God's constant fidelity.

Though the enemies in your life may not be the countries bordering your house, still there are inner forces of darkness and evil that push against your "front door." Peace can be dissipated. Do not become discouraged from fidelity to those daily disciplines needed so that God's grace can grow within you.

Be with the great multitude that first heard Joshua's words, and those gathered in the silence this day, awed by the final chapters of this great book.

| Wednesday | *Driven By Deep Prayer* | Psalm 10 |

Arise, LORD! Lift up your hand, O God.
Do not forget the helpless. v. 12

The tragic irony of the prosperity of the wicked and the persecution of the innocent haunt the psalmist. The first verse begins with an outright complaint to God about God's distance in times of trouble. Ten of the next seventeen verses of the psalm cite example after example of injustices that cry to heaven for vengeance.

However negative and complaining is the psalm, at a deeper level, it is driven by intercession. Profound intimacy binds the psalmist to God, no matter what. In fact, in the verse for today, the inventory of evil results in an immense shout of intercession with confidence in God's response. Feel the flow of assurance that completes the psalm. May your prayer today be driven by the inner energy and depth of this psalm.

| Thursday | *Sowing in the Spirit* | Galatians 6 |

May I never boast except in the cross of our Lord Jesus Christ,
through which the world has been crucified to me, and I to the world. v. 14

If outrage at evil drives the verses of yesterday's psalm, today's chapter has the sweet movement of gentleness, love, and peace—three of the nine fruits of the Spirit we considered last Thursday. We learn today how real situations evidence these fruits. We are encouraged to be compassionate instead of judgmental when sin besets someone. As for any fruit, the fruits of the Spirit appear and ripen on the tree of your life by what you do. Verse 8 clearly uplifts this principle.

This glorious letter has so many verses you will want to write down and commit to memory. With these words sown as seed, how can your life not bear the fruits of the Spirit in your soul?

| Friday | *But I Tell You …* | Matthew 5:21–48 |

I tell you, Do not resist an evil person. If someone strikes you
on the right cheek, turn to him the other also. v. 39

Jesus' words from the Mount of the Beatitudes join with those given to Moses on Sinai. Jesus embraces them, but goes deeper than mere external fulfillment of the Torah, the Law. Six times, while referring to the Torah, Jesus says "But I tell you …"

Consider the power of this transference. Jesus is embodies the Torah. He is alive in the Holy Spirit, seeking to go ever deeper into your own heart, there to refine and make perfect, the inner subtleties of Jesus' law of love. The Spirit prompts you to live love from its point of depth-sowing until full fruit-bearing, as we considered in yesterday's reading from Galatians.

May you find special joy in knowing that the Spirit within you will be constantly suggesting, inclining, inspiring you this very day at every moment, to act, not as the world teaches, but as Jesus does.

Saturday   The Sabbath Torah Reading

Feb 09, 2008 #19A	Feb 04, 2017 #15A	Feb 07, 2026 #17A	Feb 10, 2035 #19A
Feb 05, 2011 #19A	Feb 08, 2020 #16A	Feb 10, 2029 #18A	Feb 06, 2038 #19A
Feb 08, 2014 #20A	Feb 04, 2023 #16A	Feb 07, 2032 #18A	Feb 09, 2041 #19A

The Sixth Week in Epiphany

Begins on the Sunday nearest February 8. Alphabyte: Kiln, p. 8

For 2029, 2032, *this is the last week in Epiphany, beginning with Transfiguration Sunday. See p. 36 for the Transfiguration Sunday reading, continuing below for the Monday-to-Saturday passages. Ash Wednesday occurs this week. Next week turn to The First Week in Lent, Year A, p. 46.*

Sunday	*"Both-And"*	**Matthew 5:13–20**

You are the salt of the earth … You are the light of the world. vv.13–14

Mount Sinai and the Mount of the Beatitudes stand beside each other in our imagination. From the former comes the foundation of how to live a godly life. Moving beyond the "Thou shalt nots," the Beatitudes begin with positive expressions of blessing: How blessed and fortunate you will be, that now having the foundation, you understand how to live in the Kingdom.

Imagine that you *are* salt and light—one at a time. Salt offers zest to others' lives; light illumines the way of Jesus.

In the second half of our reading, Jesus uplifts "both-and" of his teaching, referring to the Law and to his words. It is not "either-or" for Jesus, but rather "both-and."

Monday	*Faith-Tools*	**Isaiah 10:20–34**

Though your people, O Israel, be like the sand by the sea,
only a remnant will return. 10:22

There is joy in Isaiah's announcement of a remnant that will survive the devastation of Assyria. The glory of God rises as God uses the very instruments of war as symbols of victory. The list of vulnerable cities that lay in the path of Assyria serves to give the people strength in the face of the indignation of God against the adversary. God will avenge all enemies.

All enemies—especially those from the spiritual world of darkness and the forces set against you. They are nothing when it comes to the power of God. You will find verses of Isaiah as faith-tools to tear down the strongholds of the Enemy that may yet lurk within you. Go to that place in your heart where the remnant lives— the part of you that is faithful to the Lord because of the anointing of the Holy Spirit upon your life.

Tuesday	*The Salt of Wisdom*	**Proverbs 1**

If you had responded to my rebuke, I would have poured out my heart to you
and made my thoughts known to you. v. 23

A sacred thread is held out as we begin to read from the Book of Proverbs. Every season of grace in the three-year cycle is woven together for a few Tuesdays that become blessed by these golden words.

All of God's Word needs a space that you create within and around you—a kind of open, empty womb, as Mary's, to receive the overshadowing and in-flooding of the Holy Spirit. Therefore, be in a holy, receptive disposition of heart and mind as you listen to these words.

Remain in the kiln of prayer. Then you will be ready to respond outwardly, as you share the salt of your wisdom and the light of your life in God with a tasteless, hungry, darkened world.

Wednesday	*Faith-Flight to the Mountain*	Psalm 11

The Lord is righteous, he loves justice; upright men will see his face. v. 7

Surrounded by enemies, David finds a refuge of prayer to compose this lovely, brief psalm. He finds strength in knowing that God, who sees all, will pour out saving power on those who live uprightly.

"The Lord is in his holy temple" (v. 4). Are you in yours? While David longs to fly as a bird to a mountain to flee from his enemies, his wish can become yours. Enter that inward center of your own soul, which is the Holy of Holies of your body, temple of the Holy Spirit. By faith, flee to the Mount of the Beatitudes, as the Gospels of these weeks come from there, portions of "The Sermon on the Mount." Jesus lives this psalm, giving you strength in every circumstance.

The psalm will center you and comfort you, as you know by faith the One who is seeing you, loving you, and protecting you.

Thursday	*Pain Washed Away by Love*	Philippians 1

For me to live is Christ and to die is gain. v. 21

Profound feelings of love and affection for a community of Christians far away warms the heart of Paul as he writes from a damp, dark Roman prison. With every stroke of his pen, sentiments of joy and encouragement expand and flow outward from him. His letter rescues him from being consumed by pain.

As the season of Epiphany ends, the cross on Calvary's hill is on the horizon. Take courage. The joy of Christ manifest and with us will not diminish. The power of Christ shining from his face on the Mount of Transfiguration will continue, though blood from the crown of thorns will transfigure this face.

Is there someone who needs your love and encouragement in a letter that would send a stream of love into your heart as well as theirs, washing pain away?

Friday	*From the Secret Place*	Matthew 6:1–15

**If you do not forgive men their sins,
your Father will not forgive your sins. v. 15**

Clear, straightforward instructions come from Jesus about the dispositions of the heart when we do good deeds, and how the heart itself is to be transformed by prayer. Jesus' instruction about prayer is a blend of two inseparable aspects. Each person is encouraged to go alone to the inner, secret place of one's spirit. There is an inward privacy to prayer. However, as The Lord's Prayer reminds us, there is always a communal dimension. The prayer is **"Our Father,"** not **"My Father."**

Lent is coming soon. What does the Lord suggest to you about growth in prayer as the dark, secret place of winter yields to the open, expansive light of the coming spring?

Ponder the parting warning of Jesus in the verse for today.

Saturday   The Sabbath Torah Reading

May 17, 2008 #32A	Feb 11, 2017 #16A	Feb 14, 2026 #18A	May 19, 2035 #32A
Feb 12, 2011 #20A	Feb 15, 2020 #17A	Feb 17, 2029 #19A	Feb 13, 2038 #20A
Feb 15, 2014 #21A	Feb 11, 2023 #17A	Feb 14, 2032 #19A	Feb 16, 2041 #20A

The Seventh Week in Epiphany

Begins on the Sunday nearest February 15. Alphabyte: Laser, p. 9

For 2026, this is the last week in Epiphany, beginning with Transfiguration Sunday. See p. 36 for the Transfiguration Sunday reading, continuing below for the Monday-to-Saturday passages. Ash Wednesday occurs this week. Next week turn to The First Week in Lent, Year A, p. 46.

Sunday   *The Demands of Discipleship*   **Matthew 5:21–37**

**If you are offering your gift at the altar and there remember
that your brother has something against you, leave your gift there in front of the altar.
First go and be reconciled to your brother; then come and offer your gift. vv. 23–24**

Jesus cuts no corners on the absolute demands of integrity. The law, however strictly maintained in outer details, will not make one just or worthy of the Kingdom. Jesus "raises the bar" on life—beyond works, to actions fed by grace.

Only by grace can we steer away from the demands of the flesh in anger or lust. Anger, unless released in prayer and energy for appropriate actions on the behalf of the poor, is destructive of relationships. As for lustful feelings, even the wish to be flirtatious or inappropriate in ones behavior toward another in a sacred relationship, damages holy expressions of love.

Take Jesus literally here: why not? Why must we wiggle around and find exceptions to these exalted ideals of living? Let us examine ourselves carefully, repent, and be open to all the joys Jesus is teaching you.

Monday   *Images of Reconciliation*   **Isaiah 11**

A little child will lead them. 11:6

Intended as Hezekiah, the rod from the stem of Jesse reaches forward in time and touches Jesus. The Lord uses Isaiah for more than the immediate circumstance into which he prophesies. The Holy Spirit, referred as such by Isaiah more times than any other prophet, uses this great man of God for announcing the Messiah. With the addition of "piety," not mentioned in verse 2, the seven gifts of the Holy Spirit are listed.

This chapter and the next conclude the first of five parts in Isaiah. As a symphony raising its themes in sweeping final movements, so do these chapters lift up the ultimate triumph of God in images of reconciliation.

Let the Word of the Lord fill all your days "… as the waters cover the sea."

Tuesday   *Four Gifts of the Spirit*   **Proverbs 2**

**Wisdom will enter your heart, and knowledge will be pleasant to your soul.
Discretion will protect you, and understanding will guard you. vv. 10–11**

The Mounts of Sinai, the Beatitudes, and the Transfiguration invite us to linger in their atmosphere of contact with the divine as we listen to these words. While they are abstract, taste them nonetheless. Consider how *wisdom, knowledge, discretion,* and *understanding* are present, or absent, in your life. Let today be a special day of reflection on your life, taking the mountain images as ones of retreat, reflection and reordering of your life's priorities in keeping with the daily inspirations of God's holy Word.

Though these four gifts are abstract, they engage all the practical aspects of your life. How are you to live in the light of these gifts? This is the constant question of Proverbs. Reflect … ponder … write.

| Wednesday | *Refined Silver* | Psalm 12 |

**The words of the LORD are flawless,
like silver refined in a furnace of clay, purified seven times. v. 6**

As the shoot from Jesse's stem, as the wisdom of the Spirit coursing through Proverbs, so is this Psalm itself is as purified silver set against the rough darkness of the sins of which the psalm speaks.

Once again the number seven occurs—symbol of completion. What would it take you to encounter the Word of the Lord at each of the seven sacred quarter parts of the day? As corks holding up a net, the purifying power of God's Word cleanses your heart seven times.

Though fire hurts, it burns away the dross, the darkness, the dirt that blemishes the heart before God. As long as your heart is beating and your lungs have breath, your suffering can prepare your heart for purity and joy. Better the fire on this side of the grave than the one on the other!

| Thursday | *The Mystery in One Place* | Philippians 2 |

**… and every tongue confess that Jesus Christ is Lord,
to the glory of God the Father. v. 11**

As shining silver rising from its setting, so does this chapter contain a precious gem in an ancient hymn in verses 5 to 11. Meditate upon its circular movement. Just as the minute hand of a clock moves in a circle from top to bottom, rising to the top again, so is the movement of the Second Person of the Blessed Trinity from heaven to earth's depths in the embedded cross, and back to heaven again. It is as a dancer raising his/her hand and eye. The hand drops in a graceful swing, suspended on high again. This is the movement of saving grace in Christ leaving heaven, swinging down to earth, rising again to heaven. Though the earthly descent plummets Jesus into a horrific death, the cross carries the glory and the energy of the resurrection because of Christ's great love.

| Friday | *The Means of Grace* | Matthew 6:16–34 |

**Seek first his kingdom and his righteousness,
and all these things will be given to you as well. v. 33**

Jesus uses the image of the secret place in his teaching about fasting. This is one of the six "means of grace," taught by John Wesley and uplifted in other spiritual traditions. By setting a limit to our response to the appetite for food, the soul is purified, the focus shifting to God alone as nourishment, as is found in found in Deut. 8:3 and Matt 4:4: "One does not live by bread alone, but by every word that comes from the mouth of God." (NRSV). The other four means of grace are prayer, searching the Scriptures, Holy Communion, and holy conversation.

Listen to these words from the Sermon on the Mount as special inspirations from the Lord to live this season in the grace that flows from that mountain.

Saturday   The Sabbath Torah Reading

May 24, 2008 #33A	Feb 18, 2017 #17A	Feb 21, 2026 #19A	May 26, 2035 #33A
Feb 19, 2011 #21A	Feb 22, 2020 #18A	May 26, 2029 #35A	Feb 20, 2038 #21A
Feb 22, 2014 #22A	Feb 18, 2023 #18A	May 22, 2032 #35A	Feb 23, 2041 #21A

The Eighth Week in Epiphany

Begins on the Sunday nearest February 22, unless Lent has begun. Alphabyte: Myrrh, p. 9
For 2020, 2023, *this is the last week in Epiphany, beginning with Transfiguration Sunday. See p. 36 for the Transfiguration Sunday reading, continuing below for the Monday-to-Saturday passages. Ash Wednesday occurs this week. Next week turn to The First Week in Lent, Year A, p. 46.*

Sunday	*The Violence of Love*	Matthew 5:38–48

If you love those who love you, what reward do you have? v. 46

There are familiar sayings of Jesus here that have been misunderstood. In no way does Jesus want you to be someone else's doormat. The refusal to co-operate with violence brings forth a "violence" of love. Let us see this in the familiar "turning the other cheek."

The first blow comes to the right check. In the ancient world, this could not be a blow of attack, since this would only be done by the person's right hand; the left hand was used only for cleaning oneself. The punch with the right hand would hit the person's left cheek, not the right one. The scenario here is of one receiving a blow of insult with the back of the right hand onto the right cheek of the other. Turning the other cheek means this: "Your first attempt to degrade me by this blow has failed; would you like to try it again?" The unrighteous anger of another is turned back upon that other.

Reinterpret your life's experience according to fresh ways of understanding Jesus' teaching about transforming non-violence into the shaking violence of love.

Monday	*Welling Upward and Outward*	Isaiah 12

With joy you will drink deeply from the fountain of salvation! v. 3

The crowds were singing this verse during the water ritual at the end of the Feast of Tabernacles. It was then that Jesus shouted about the living waters flowing from him (John 7:37).

This brief chapter is a celebrative conclusion to the first part of Isaiah. It is soaked in messianic imagery. The word for "praise" in verse 4 means, "to lift up the hands." Here is a way for your body to pray this psalm-like prayer of Isaiah. Begin with your head down, your hands clenched together in a fist, pressed against your chest. Then in response to the promise of Jesus, let your palms become open, as the living water of Christ's Spirit breaks out from your inmost being, flowing upward and outward in joy to the world—so thirsty for the life-giving Spirit that can flow from you.

Tuesday	*The Aroma of God*	Proverbs 3

**Trust in the Lord with all your heart;
do not depend on your own understanding.
Seek his will in all you do, and he will direct your paths. vv. 5–6**

Whole sections of aisles in supermarkets are devoted to products designed to have your house smell fragrant. A sophisticated name, "aroma therapy," is given to further the marketing of these sprays, oils, and candles. A device will periodically spray fragrance into your room every few minutes.

The sense of smell leads us into spiritual feelings associated with our world. God's Word can do the same, especially chapters such as the one for today. An aroma of wisdom and spiritual understanding will fill your day if you let God's presence through the Word pervade it. Periodically let each verse "spray" its sweet fragrance into the agenda of your day. The aroma of God's presence will not only transform all that you do, but your life itself will smell sweet to others and lead them to God.

Wednesday	*Shifts in the Soul*	Psalm 13	8 Ep A

Turn and answer me, O Lord my God!
Restore the light to my eyes, or I will die. v.3

A brief psalm of only six verses is yours today. Three couplets of two verses each bear dramatic shifts in David's spirit as he prays. First come four repeated cries of "How long, O Lord?" However far away God seems, David believes that God is listening. What intimacy David has with his God! A couplet comes next with three imperatives for God. Two of them are commands for God to listen, the third, a plea that God put the sparkle back into David's eyes. Finally, there is the dramatic shift in the two final verses that express David's singing for joy.

It does not take long for shifts to take place in your soul, if you model your prayer-life after David's. Whether or not you identify with the eclipse of God's presence, pray this psalm in profound intercession for those at the edge of despair—or deep into it, as in some black hole. Grab hold of them with this psalm and be lifted up to peace.

Thursday	*The Upward Call*	Philippians 3—4

My God shall supply all your need
according to His riches in glory by Christ Jesus. 4:19 NKJV

These are among the most beloved chapters in the Bible. Verse upon verse needs to be present before your eyes throughout this day; you will find it hard to select your favorite one.

Yesterday you learned from David how to let the Lord lift you from the pit of darkness and despair. Today Paul is your leader. Remember, Paul penned these words from the pits of a Roman prison. Everything goes out from the dark, downward space as he responds to the "upward call" of Christ upon his life.

Though Paul likely received mere morsels of stale bread, Paul offers you a banquet of God's Word, upon which he also feasts. Nothing can restrain his joy.

A banquet of delicious food from the Lord is spread before you today. Take, eat, and pass the nourishment on to others.

Friday	*Hearing and Doing*	Matthew 7

"Anyone who listens to my teaching and obeys me is wise,
like a person who builds a house on solid rock." v. 24

Hang upon the words of Jesus in this concluding chapter of "The Sermon on the Mount." Various brief instructions are arranged one after another. Receive each of them as precious gems of Jesus' wisdom which he lovingly shares with you, his disciple. Each comes from the inmost center of Jesus; will you receive them at that same point within yourself?

The concluding six verses present an image developed in the letter of James, reminding us not only to be hearers of the word, but doers as well. As you look upon the movement of your life and learn from Jesus' words, what action is called for? You might miss this, if your reading is hasty—a hearing only.

Amid the declarations that Jesus makes, three questions are interposed. Feel the questions first, then respond from the depths of your spirit.

Saturday   The Sabbath Torah Reading

May 31, 2008 #34A	Feb 25, 2017 #18A	May 30, 2026 #35A	Jun 02, 2035 #34A
Feb 25, 2011 #22A	Feb 29, 2020 #19A	Jun 02, 2029 #36A	Feb 27, 2038 #22A
May 03, 2014 #23A	Feb 25, 2023 #19A	May 29, 2032 #36A	Mar 02, 2041 #22A

The Ninth Week in Epiphany

Begins on the Sunday nearest March 1, or February 29 in leap years, unless Lent has begun.
*Due to a very late Easter in **2011** and **2038**, (April 24 and 25th respectively), in these years turn to the First and Second Weeks in Pentecost, Year A for the readings for the entire week, from Sunday to Saturday. **For 2014, 2017 and 2041,** this is the last week in Epiphany, beginning with Transfiguration Sunday below. For the Monday-to-Saturday readings, turn to the First Week in Pentecost, Year A, p. 82. An exception to this is in **2017** when this is an extra week in the year which has no Monday-to-Friday readings. The Torah reading for Saturday, March 4, 2017 is #19. Ash Wednesday occurs this week. For next week turn to the First Week in Lent, Year A, p. 46.*

The Tenth Week in Epiphany

*For **2011** and **2038**, this is the last week in Epiphany, beginning with Transfiguration Sunday below. For the Monday-to-Saturday readings, turn to the Second Week in Pentecost, Year A, p. 84. Ash Wednesday occurs this week. For next week turn to the season of Lent and Easter, Year A, p. 46.*

Transfiguration Sundays, Year A

(The Last Sunday in Epiphany)

Feb 03, 2008	Feb 26, 2017	Feb 15, 2026	Feb 04, 2035
Mar 06, 2011	Feb 23, 2020	Feb 11, 2029	Mar 07, 2038
Mar 02, 2014	Feb 19, 2023	Feb 08, 2032	Mar 03, 2041

Transfiguration Sunday   *Suspension*   **Matthew 17:1–8**

When they looked up, they saw no one except Jesus. v. 8

There are moments of suspension and stillness in the movements of ice dancers. The male skater lifts his partner high with outstretched arms. As two statues intertwined, they glide effortlessly across the ice—a time of pause in spinning and dancing.

In the dance of Jesus' saving grace, the Transfiguration is a moment of suspension and stillness on the heights. All the glory of the dance of salvation is gathered into one moment, a suspension in time that Peter wishes to hold onto forever. The glimpse of eternal glory serves to strengthen the faith of the three disciples, awestruck before three great figures in the history of God's gracious intervention in human life. Relish the pause, the suspension of time, drinking in the power of Jesus as soon we will descend the mountain into Lent. There the dance goes on, drawing us closer and closer to our Lord who alone lifts us high from the cross and from the grave.

The Cross on the Facing Page

In the upper left, **IC** are the first and last letters of **IHCUC**, the Greek for "Jesus." The upper right bears the first and last letters of **XPICTOC**, "Christ." The lower left and right spell the word **NIKA**, "victory" in Greek. The name "Nicholas" means "Victorious People."

LENT
AND
EASTER

SPRING

Northern Hemisphere

Year A
2008, 2011, 2014 …

Lent begins six weeks before Easter Sunday.
See the entire cycle of readings at a glance on page xx.

The First Sundays in Lent, Year A

Feb 10, 2008	Mar 05 2017	Feb 22, 2026	Feb 11, 2035
Mar 13, 2011	Mar 01, 2020	Feb 18, 2029	Mar 14, 2038
Mar 09, 2014	Feb 26, 2023	Feb 15, 2032	Mar 10, 2041

Alphabytes

Lent and Easter: *N–Z*

The First Week in Lent

N*adir*

I recall as a boy, peering into a pure puddle—the surface unruffled by the wind,
  perfectly mirroring the clouds suspended somewhere between
  the surface of the water and an endless bottom of a blue, inverted heaven.
The gaze down revealed up.
Searching inward unfolded the outward and far away.
In the nadir of the puddle was the zenith of the sky.

The ashes of our sin mix with the desert sands beneath the feet of Jesus.
The salty sweat of the Savior dries crusty upon his face,
  eyebrows knitted as the ancestral journey from the bottom of the Sea
  through the wilderness of temptation and fall is traversed again by Jesus.
The nadir of desert temptation and his faithfulness release the promise of
  the zenith of Ascension: both together at once. In the bottom is the top.

The hardest bottom gives a ball its highest bounce.
There is no death, no ashes, no loss, no sin but that they become
  the surface to allow the fall to become the rise—
  the death to become the resurrection.
Surrender to your Jesus at the bottom of the cross and be lifted to highest heaven
  with him throughout these precious days.

The Second Week in Lent
*O*live Tree

Yearning to embrace resistant Jerusalem with peace,
    hundreds of evergreen olive trees cluster and clutter
    the mountain to the east, dancing in the breeze,
    waving their branches over the city of tumult
    seeking to distract those with fists tight and raised in anger against Jesus.
Other tree branches will lie on the road, dead from grief
    when **"Hosanna"** becomes **"Crucify."**
Faithful over their many years, the olives stretch their twisted,
    gnarled branches offering fruits to the press,
    dying to oval loveliness, till their blood is squeezed out,
    becoming the oil of gladness.

Their oil delights the senses:
    Sight: light at night, making a way;
    Smell: sweet fragrances added to their substance, lifting mind and heart to wider
space.
    Taste: foods given tenderness in the mouth.
    Touch: dried skin becomes soft and moist, anointed for healing and mission,
    divine, heavenly life penetrating to earthy, inward depths.
    Hearing: silence only, as its awesome, sacramental power plummets us into the
depths of prayer.

The Third Week in Lent
*P*lumb Line

The Lord was standing beside a wall
built with a plumb line, with a plumb line in his hand. Amos 7:7

The once plumb people of God had become tilted, warped, crooked, off balance
    by rebellion, idol worship, and idleness inclining them to the brink of death.

Take the image to the self.
How is it with you and balance, symmetry, steadiness, straightness and stillness?
Sit and do nothing, until you are plumb.
Let the downward pull of your own weight be as a sign of
    the inner weight of God's presence,
    pulling you inward until you become nothing but a creature centered
    and steadied in adoration of the Creator.
Be kind to yourself, as gentle as the hand that steadies the weight from swinging.
Wait till the weight becomes still and you are just there, before your God.
Then go to the Word for the day that will steady you
    through the winds of the world that would have you whirl and be dizzy again.

The Fourth Week in Lent

*Q*uarters

Ponder the ways life is divided into quarters: four sides of house and room,
   private quarters for rest, quadrants of a clock's circle, quarter hours,
   days and nights, quarter time to march or dance,   quarts for liquid,
   quarters of dollars and games, four directions, four seasons, four Gospels.

Sit in silence, protected and embraced by the fours about you,
   whether walls or winds.
In front and back, to right and left is your God and three more"
   Above, beneath and within is your God.
The sum of the sacred numbers, three and four, makes the most complete
   and perfect number—seven.
In these sevenfold sacred spaces does your Triune God dwell
   within the walls of your person, now made sacred by divine presence:
   the Trinity embraced by you—you embraced by the Trinity.

The Fifth Week in Lent

*R*ooster

Peter: surrounded by wrong walls, warmed by wrong fire,
   lingers near, but all too far away from his Lord.
That night of accusation, trial and coming murder
   freezes the heart of Peter for a time, wearing out the warning of Jesus
   just a few hours earlier: Peter would deny he even knew him.

I wonder which rooster it was whose routine, daily early morning call
   shook Peter to wakefulness?
All the quaking mind and limbs of Peter
   were shattered by that distant cry in the night.
   It scratched his soul into recalling what Jesus said.
And then the rush of goodness in the man as weeping washes fear away,
   sadness plummeting him to a sober space of waiting
   till Jesus looks at him again with love, another morning not far away.

Calls to awakening: what are yours?
Chime of clocks … beeps of watches:
   they are all it takes to topple those muscle-bound temptations
   that throttle and throw you to the ground
   in your brand of denial of your Lord.
Let the rooster noises of your days be sounds for summoning the soul to sobriety,
   fresh awakening, new awareness, lifting the self into new and sacred space
   with all the joy that the forgiving look of Jesus can bring upon the heart.

Holy Week
*S*upper

The Holy Week: the blood of Jesus writes a sacred script
    across the movement of each day and hour,
    the intensity of anguish squeezes blood to the surface of his skin.
The last supper this side of the grave becomes
    the first supper in a new way of being with Jesus:
    bread and wine bear his body and blood—
    a promise, a pledge, a peace of being with him, even as he is soon to be taken
    away in arrest, trail, death, returning again in resurrection,
    leaving again in Ascension, returning still again in a total,
    complete way in the Holy Spirit who lives and breathes
    the life of Jesus in Eucharist.

No greater closeness could God give than being food.
Outer receiving joins inner hearing, sealing the sacred promise of
    supper with the Master—first, last and always.

"Listen! I am standing at the door, knocking;
if you hear my voice and open the door,
I will come in to you and eat with you, and you with me." Revelation. 3:20

Easter Week
*T*emple

Well before he broke ground for the First Temple,
    Solomon yielded to an inner listening,
    A mounting energy from the vision of what was to come …
Then came the day when a long string stretched to its limit,
    marked the place where this great edifice would come to rise.
The root of "temple," as its sister word "tense," is "to stretch, to pull,"
    making listless string meet the demands of perfect alignment,
    perfect centering, from whence buildings spiral upward and outward.

Jesus breaks ground, stretching to limitless rising,
    offering his body as the place within for life, for work, for worship.
Every human created rising from the ground
    is to find it breathing Jesus' risen breath.
No place can confine the presence of such a risen Lord.
No time but that which is stretched about, encircled and defined by
    the sacred plummeting of Jesus back into our lives,
    resurrecting endless cycles of tedium to a rising spiral of divine energy
    welling up from the ground of our being, breaking the soil of the soul,
    loosening the death grip of all the "whatevers" in our lives to
    the "Who" who lives in our midst.

The Holy Week has birthed a Holy Temple.
Jesus is the sacred space whence to breathe resurrection life,
    bursting forth into sacred fire.

The Second Week in Easter

*U*niverse

Stillness and silence do not at first unfold slowly spinning spirals
  beyond imagining.
We are blended into a uni-verse: one thing that turns.
Earth daily turns on its axis, revolving in the yearly circle about the sun;
  sun rolling about its place in the galaxy, turning and dancing
  with clusters of sun systems.
Somewhere there is a center to it all, a still point around which everything turns,
  making one pulsing, waving entity adoring the Creator at the living center.

In a single verse of God's Word, a uni-verse exists.
Whether telling of good or ill, lists or wisdom, each verse finds its place
  in the whole that turns.
Be part of this wider, spiraling converging mass of text
  leading deeper and deeper beneath the surface spinning of life,
  to that living center of the whole where all is still, joyous, silent, present,
  laughing, loving, tender, holding all together.
God knows your dance, its turnings, whether smooth or jagged.
Stop the spin. Yield to the wider dance until,
  lost in understanding, you rest in the One who knows all, loves all,
  and keeps you in the rocking, turning embrace.

The Third Week in Easter

*V*ine

"I am the vine, you are the branches."
John 15:5

Vast stretches of rolling earth blanketed with lines upon lines of vines,
  grapes heavy in their moist fruit, held aloft, so their faces can see the sun,
  gently bounce in the soft breeze.
Each branch, each twig, each fruit finds who it is as long as the inner wine
  of the centering Spirit reaches each one—dead ones cut away and burned.
When one looks at the whole, the vine is seen, not the branches—
  as thread is lost in the larger whole, disappearing
  so the image in the tapestry can leap forth.

Sit in silence.
Descend till you rest by faith in the Vine, touching the point where who you are,
  is lost in the look of the whole.
Be no longer alone, apart, but joined as one to the Vine—
  one life coursing through yours, connecting you to all who in like manner
  choose to define their being as nothing but the bouncing, buoyant, joyful fruit
  in the Vine that lives forever.

The Fourth Week in Easter

*W*ax

A single tongue of fresh fire burns high above from the noble Easter candle—
   faithful, sturdy, proud, fruit of countless bees sealing a people into oneness.
Lost in the stately column, the wax of faithfulness melts into larger love.

How else could a length of string burn on so long!
Without wax, a flash of flame it would be—quick heat and light,
   and then a tiny clump of Ash Wednesday again.
The nectar presence of the Spirit is within,
   turning what is offered into sacred wax, embracing, surrounding,
   covering the wick so that it can hide the sacred fuel for the sacred fire.

You are wax—and whole candle too.
Surround yourself with believing bees, hiding in a hive of Kingdom life.
Be comforted, for you can burn long, when burning in Jesus.
Be joyful. There is no fire like yours when leaping from such a candle.

The Fifth Week in Easter

*X*ylophone

Bars of wood, *xylon,* ascending in sound, *phone.*
Hear the sounds of cross-wood making a scale until
   the octave, Easter to Pentecost, resonates in sweet harmony.
No more the sound of banging, howling, wailing, crying, shouting
   of twisted body made straight, hammers pounding hands,
   feet and ears with death-dealing sounds.
Silence alone echoes from the cross as Good Friday evening finds
   all bodies gone—dead and living.
Only wind's whistle passes through bare beams braced against the sky.

Now the cross is buried into paper-wood.
Word of God sounds forth as the Spirit knocks and skillfully strikes
   the soundboard of the heart, echoing sounds of heaven
   from selves once dead, now brought to life
   as Jesus' touch of love awakens new music in the soul.

Yoke

Yokes bind, burden, but also bless.
A young ox learns to pull the plow, blended with a brother beast
    who knows the pace and patient plodding of the path
    for the new seeds' growth,
Never alone—always together as the life-work moves.

Jesus invites you to take his yoke heavy with the world's weight,
    yet light now because the crossbeam yoke has broken the harsh
    resistance to love, to goodness, flowing now the lighter,
    since always yoked with Christ in the pull-power of the Spirit.
So learn from this meek and humble Lord ever at your side, always teaching,
    always pulling, until the whole field of your life is sown with the Word.

The fields are planted.
Yokes and oxen rest while gently day by day, sun and rain draw food and flowers
    from the moist earth, soon to send their leaves dancing in the breeze.

The Seventh Week in Easter

Zenith

A half-year has passed since its nadir when winter's cold
    felt the warmth of Advent's first candle.
A tiny light won over the enveloping black.
Each day the Sun pushed aside the dark on either end of winter's day and night,
    passing through springtime's midway point, on to the summer-zenith
    soon to come.

Nadir of Lent becomes zenith of Ascension.
Disciples dizzy from the upward look strain to catch a final glimpse of
    their Master disappearing behind the clouds.
From the contemplative, downward gaze upon God's nadir descent
    as the Christ in the manger,
to the upward stretch of the eyes to see him
    in the zenith of the skies,
    God's grace in Christ moves wider and fuller into the year, into life.

What is completed is beginning again.
Wait with Mary and the apostles in novena days.
The Spirit is coming into the nadir-bottom of your soul,
    lifting you now to the zenith-height of heaven's life.

The First Week in Lent

Six weeks before Easter. Alphabyte: Nadir, p. 39

Sunday   *Into the Promise*   **Matthew 4:1–11**
**You shall worship the Lord your God
and Him only you shall serve. Matt 4:10/Deut 6:13**

The Israelites wandered in the wilderness for forty years because they were so often lost in sin. Complaining, lack of faith, idolatry, and pride: all these held them back from a free-flowing movement into the Promised Land.

The Blessed Trinity says with great love, "We will intervene once again. This time, the Son will take upon himself the sin of the past, gathering new followers for a new Promised Land."

The days of Lent are as the years of wandering. Beset with the same temptations of God's people in the desert, Jesus reduces each one to ashes by the power of God's Word from Deuteronomy. These are the same verses that the Israelites could have applied to their temptations, but did not. Cling to Jesus and let him move you into the Promise.

Monday   *Face to Face*   **Jeremiah 1—3**
**"Return, O backsliding children,"
says the LORD, "for I am married to you." 3:14**

Of all the feats that skiers do in the Olympics, no one has ever attempted to ski backwards. Yet this catches the essence of the Biblical concept of *meshubah* "backsliding." Of the twelve times that the noun is used in the Bible, nine of them are found in Jeremiah.

When we turn our eyes away from the Lord, it is impossible not to fall—literally sliding down on one's back, feet sprawled in mid-air. To repent means to turn back again, with eyes and life totally focused upon God.

The Lord will pound away at your heart through Jeremiah these Mondays of Lent, until you stop, pick yourself up, and turn back again, face to face with the Lord, the spouse of your soul. Listen with the same energy as Jeremiah speaking.

Tuesday   *Put to the Test*   **Job—3**
**Naked I came from my mother's womb, and naked shall I return there.
The LORD gave, and the LORD has taken away;
Blessed be the name of the LORD. 1:21**

We know something Job does not: God and Satan have decided to test him. How far can Satan push Job by the powers of evil in his life, and Job still not curse God? God, sets the boundaries of the test—not Satan; Satan is not permitted to touch the life-core of Job.

So begins this book of the Bible, dealing with the ancient problem posed in the Garden of Eden—how to understand good and evil. God forbade us to eat of that tree.

The test for Job and for us: how much do we trust God, no matter what?

| **Wednesday** | *Ashes* | **Psalm 120** |

In my distress I cried to the Lord and He heard me. v. 1

Quick to ignite into a blazing fire with long-lasting coals: such is the broom tree. This image occurs to the psalmist to describe the deceitful mouths that surround him, an image that James would use in his letter about the tongue.

The psalmist walks with those making their way to Jerusalem for the pilgrimages three times a year for *Passover, Pentecost and Tabernacles*. We interrupt the numerical flow of Psalms on Wednesdays, to catch this sense of movement to Jerusalem each Lent. This year, one third of the fifteen "Songs of Ascent" (Psalms 120 to 134) will be our weekly Wednesday meditation-points to Holy Week and Easter.

Burn away your old self, so that a new self can live. If you are as dead to self as the ashes of last Wednesday, the fires of life can harm you no longer. On the contrary, you will burn on and on in the Spirit!

| **Thursday** | *The Prizes* | **Ephesians 1** |

Blessed be the God and Father of our Lord Jesus Christ,
who has blessed us with every spiritual blessing
in the heavenly places in Christ. v. 3

1
Le
A

Picture the gaping mouths and wide eyes of winners of a T.V. quiz show. The curtain is pulled back; they gasp at all the prizes they have won.

In Ephesians, the curtain of the heavens is drawn back so that we can see all the spiritual prizes poured out from the heights of heaven to the depths of our hearts. Read this chapter slowly while savoring each gift. Rejoice that you have been selected to receive all the prizes that Jesus won, and more: you are adopted into the very family of the One who gives the prizes! The loving, generous Father of Jesus is yours. The Holy Spirit guarantees on earth that these prizes will last into heaven. Their value never diminishes, but rather grows with you into everlasting life

| **Friday** | *Tent of Flesh* | **John 1:1–28** |

The law was given through Moses,
but grace and truth came through Jesus Christ. v. 17

As a masterpiece painted with broad strokes of bold colors, so is the prologue of John's Gospel. The themes of the Gospel are drawn: *life, light, glory, truth*. John begins his painting of the New Creation with the same words as Genesis: "In the beginning."

Another beginning took place for God's people with Moses in the wilderness. There the glory of God as a cloud clung to the tabernacle, center of divine presence. Now the Eternal Word pitches divine presence in the tent-tabernacle flesh of Jesus.

The Gospel of John will be our guide through the wilderness of Lent into the glory of Easter. The Lord Jesus is with us and in us all the way.

Saturday

The Sabbath Torah Reading

Feb 16, 2008 #20A	Mar 11, 2017 #20A	Feb 28, 2026 #20A	Feb 17, 2035 #20A
Mar 19, 2011 #25A	Mar 07, 2020 #20A	Feb 24, 2029 #20A	Mar 20, 2038 #25A
Mar 15, 2014 #25A	Mar 04, 2023 #20A	Feb 21, 2032 #20A	Mar 16, 2041 #24A

The Second Week in Lent
Five weeks before Easter. Alphabyte: Olive Tree, p. 40

Sunday   *Gospel at a Glance*   **John 3:1–17**
For God so loved the world that He gave His only begotten Son,
that whoever believes in Him should not perish
but have everlasting life. 3:16

Feel the searching, the silence, and the secrecy that fills the night air as Nicodemus meets alone with Jesus. Take your place of quiet and listen to the dialogue of the two. This Pharisee probes at the mystery of Jesus; the Lord responds with new, divine turns of meaning. We are to be born from what flows from above; the saving blood of the Savior will seep into the soul of the searcher, giving life-beyond-death.

 The bronze serpent of Moses lifted on high was the sight from above that prevented those bitten by the serpents from being killed. Lift your head high to the cross and there find new life saving you from all the deadly bites of the evil one. Find eternal comfort in verse 16, which expresses all of salvation and the entire Gospel at one glance.

Monday   *God Hurts*   **Jeremiah 4—6**
Break up your fallow ground,
and do not sow among thorns. 4:3

The Lord calls Jeremiah to be the emotional expression of a God outraged, grieved, and simply hurt at the infidelity of the people.

 God feels. How could it be otherwise, since we are made in God's image? The Lord expresses all these emotions through Jeremiah, longing that the people be shaken from their evil, adulterous, idolatrous practices, and turn to the Lord once again.

 Get ready with a heart open to receive the pain of your divine spouse. Do not stop short with guilt and shame; these block your spirit. Go deeper. Let the hard, numb soil of your soul be loosened to receive the pure seed of God's Word. Drop down to that place within where there is deepest sorrow for your sins, all of which are variations on the theme of infidelity to the Lord. Pour out your heart in repentance. The Lord wants you back.

Tuesday   *Improving the Silence?*   **Job 4—5**
But as for me, I would seek God
and to God I would commit my cause. 5:8

A Chinese proverb says, "Never speak unless you are improving on the silence." Job's so-called "friends" would have been much better at being quiet those seven days, than in speaking their hurtful words. Presence in silent love with one in grief releases more power than words.

 However, silence is not enough for Eliphaz, Bildad and Zophar. As you read their speeches, do so with the discerning heart that the Spirit will give. Their words are tempting fruit from the Tree of the Knowledge of Good and Evil. Many of the verses are true and beautifully expressed in the dance of poetry that abounds in this book. However, it is not the whole truth, and nothing but the whole truth will do; anything less is a lie.

 The friends become part of Job's problem, instead of part of his solution. Be aware of the power of your silent presence.

Wednesday   *A Hedge Around*   **Psalm 121**
My help comes from the Lord
Who made heaven and earth. v. 1

Picture Jesus in the crowds making their way to Jerusalem. Since he was twelve years old, three times a year he walked to the great city surrounded by pilgrims chanting this psalm and all the psalms that fill our Wednesdays in Lent. There would be a final journey to Jerusalem and the lament over the city heard only by the olive trees on the mount, and then the final walk up Calvary's hill with the cross.

Six times in the psalm, the word *shamar* sings itself, naming the Lord as "keeper" and "preserver." Meditate on this word, sighing its sweet sound over and over as you mull over its inner meaning of God as a *hedge* around you. No matter what lies before you in your journey—challenge or temptation—the grace, power, and presence of God press on before you and hedge you all around.

Thursday   *Pure Gold*   **Ephesians 2**
We are God's work of art,
created in Christ Jesus for good works. v. 10

One of the deepest desires in the Middle Ages was the search for a secret formula that would turn base metals into gold. It was called alchemy.

In the verse for the day, Paul uses a Greek word *poiema*, from which comes our word, "poem." It means a "work of art." By grace, your Creator can make the base and tarnished "metal" of your being into a golden masterpiece.

Read this chapter joyfully and tenderly receiving all the gifts of oneness with God that Christ has gained for you. Believe that everything else in your life can be blended into the pure gold of this awesome grace. Verse after verse of this chapter unfolds the vision of what God wants to do with you, God's irreplaceable work of art. The work is God's, not yours.

Friday   *Crescendo*   **John 1:29–51**
Behold! The Lamb of God
who takes away the sin of the world! v. 29

If the Prologue of John's Gospel were likened to a work of art, the second half of this chapter would be the movement of a symphony. There is a sweep from the single tone of John's cry in the desert, to the climactic expression of Nathaniel: "Rabbi, you are the Son of God! You are the King of Israel!" Each new disciple crescendos into the next, as they come to Jesus. John points out the Lamb of God and unfolds who Jesus is. Place yourself in line as one of those first disciples of Jesus. Spend the whole day with him.

The transition from John to Jesus is complete. In these weeks of Lent, we open ourselves to Jesus teaching us as he did his dearest disciples.

Saturday   **The Sabbath Torah Reading**

Feb 23, 2008 #21A	Mar 18, 2017 #21A	Mar 07, 2026 #21A	Feb 24, 2035 #21A
Mar 25, 2011 #26A	Mar 14, 2020 #21A	Mar 03, 2029 #21A	Mar 27, 2038 #26A
Mar 22, 2014 #26A	Mar 11, 2023 #21A	Feb 28, 2032 #21A	Mar 23, 2041 #25A

The Third Week in Lent
Four weeks before Easter. Alphabyte: Plumb Line, p. 40

Sunday   *To New Depths*   John 4:5–42
The water I shall give him will become in him
a fountain of water springing up into everlasting life. v. 14

Once again, a dialogue takes place between Jesus and another with whom you can identify. This time it is a woman, a public sinner, who encounters Jesus at noontime, contrasting with the midnight visit of righteous Nicodemus.

Jesus dares to do what no Jewish man would ever do—talk to a woman, a Samaritan as well. As is typical in John's Gospel, the conversation is on two dimensions—a literal, earthly one on the part of the woman, a sacred, heavenly one on the part of Jesus.

Listen carefully as the Lord loosens you from sin in your spirit. Do you also feel isolated and rejected as this woman? Jesus addresses you face-to-face and heart-to-heart in her. Yield to the Lord. Let the plumb line image help you to descend straight down into the depths of your inner well. Receive the living waters that spring forth.

Monday   *Gift of Tears*   Jeremiah 7—9
Oh, that my head were waters, and my eyes a fountain of tears,
that I might weep day and night for the slain of the daughter of my people. 9:1

Verse one gave Jeremiah the name: "The Weeping Prophet." He grieves over the people's lost condition, so much of which has to do with leaders lying to the people.

What is your experience of crying? Do you weep easily, or is it hard for you to pour out the sin and sadness in your life through tears? Shame often enters to gridlock the emotion of pain that needs the loosening release of sobs. The tears of others often help to free this "liquid prayer."

Read slowly, carefully, reflectively. You might take a chapter for each of the three hours in the quarter parts of the day. Let your heart be touched; your head may flow with tears. Listen for the tears of Jeremiah until you hear your own. Pray for what spiritual writers call "The Gift of Tears," a gift from God for intercessory prayer.

Tuesday   *When Love is Absent*   Job 6—8
God will yet fill your mouth with laughing,
and your lips with rejoicing. 8:21

Though Job is filled with immense pain, anguish, and anger, there is beauty in the poetry that flows from his mouth.

Paul's words from 1 Corinthians 8:1 apply to the attitude of Job's friends: "Knowledge puffs up, but love edifies." Love, not knowledge, is greater than evil. All the truth in the world, without love, amounts to nothing—amounts to evil. The absence of love allows evil to rush into the vacuum created. In all of Bildad's judgmental words about Job and his wrongs, Bildad fails to see the arrogance of evil imbedded in his own loveless heart.

If you were to write or cry out the current "chapter" in your life just as Job does in his, how would the words flow? Will you trust the Lord and pour out your heart in prayer, sharing with the Lord how you feel about all aspects of your life?

Wednesday	*Pilgrim-Joy*	Psalm 122

I was glad when they said to me,
let us go into the house of the LORD. v. 1

Excitement irrupts from the back seat of the car: *Are we there yet?* The child simply cannot wait any longer to arrive at the longed-for destination. A similar holy anxiety fills the mass of marchers on their way to Jerusalem. They see the beloved city part of the crowd is already there.

A focus on Jerusalem—this is what sustains the joy of the pilgrim. While we are moving toward Jerusalem and Holy Week, the spiritual realities celebrated there are already present within you and within the church, the New Jerusalem. The One that you are seeking as the goal in your life is already walking with you on your journey. Recall the chorus of the 1913 hymn by C. Austin Miles, "In the Garden." "And He walks with me, and He talks with me, and He tells me I am His own."

Thursday	*Waves of Glory*	Ephesians 3

Now to Him who is able to do exceedingly abundantly above all that we ask or think,
according to the power that works in us,
to Him be glory in the church by Christ Jesus to all generations. vv. 20–21

Picture the prison walls where Paul writes this letter. Go there. Enter the heart of this great apostle. The personal joy he shares overflows beyond the walls of his cell. Nothing on an external level can take away this joy.

Let it be the same for you. Whatever may be pressing about you, holding you hostage, inner freedom is being offered you at this very moment. To experience this, take each phrase of glory in this chapter and let it turn your "prison cell" into a prayer cell—a space of energy that launches you into total freedom, beyond all that would hold you captive.

Nothing needs change in your circumstances. Only your heart needs to be open to free, transforming grace.

Friday	*The New Wine*	John 2

Whatever He says to you, do it. v. 5

Six heavy, earthen urns sit awkwardly; ashamedly empty in the midst of the energy of a wedding feast. Six—number of incompleteness. The wine of the old law has been consumed. Place yourself there. Stand next to the mother of Jesus and listen to her instruction: "Whatever He says to you, do it."

Does your life sometimes feel as one of those empty urns—empty, heavy, waiting to be filled? The bridegroom is with you right now as you enter into this sacred passage. Open yourself to be filled. Let all that is old in you yield to the New Wine that the Spirit of Jesus is ready and longing to pour into your heart.

The glory moves from the wedding to the Temple. Jesus overturns the tables of that place where the glory used to be, but is no longer. Is there anything in your life that needs to be to overturn?

Saturday			The Sabbath Torah Reading
Mar 01, 2008 #22A	Mar 25, 2017 #22–23A	Mar 14, 2026 #22–23A	Mar 03, 2035 #22A
Apr 02, 2011 #27A	Mar 21, 2020 #22–23A	Mar 10, 2029 #22–23A	Apr 03, 2038 #27A
Mar 29, 2014 #27A	Mar 18, 2023 #22–23A	Mar 06, 2032 #22–23A	Mar 30, 2041 #26A

The Fourth Week in Lent
Three weeks before Easter. Alphabyte: Quarters, p. 41

Sunday   *Seeing Jesus*   **John 9:1–41**

Jesus heard that they had cast him out; and when He had found him,
He said to him, "Do you believe in the Son of God?" v. 35

In the time of the early church, anyone who confessed Jesus as Lord was expelled from the Temple and the local synagogues. Those beloved walls would no longer embrace the ones who had embraced Jesus. There would be no more pilgrimages to Jerusalem for them!

Herein lies the significance of the account of "The Man Born Blind." Here too is that irony that threads its way through John's Gospel. The miracle of being able to see for the first time since birth contrasts with the blindness of those who arrogantly claim to see, but who are in fact, blind.

May you be enriched by the confession of the blind man given the gift of sight by faith. No longer are the Pharisees there, "expelled" from Jesus' presence by their disbelief. Remain with the blind man and Jesus. What is happening to you as you share this silent, loving space together?

Monday   *Honesty*   **Jeremiah 10—12**

O LORD, correct me, but with justice;
not in your anger, lest You bring me to nothing. 10:24

The people of Jeremiah's time had lost a sense of the power of God, placing more confidence in idolatry. Pray that words of the prophet will break you free from any brands of idolatry in your life.

Have a page of your journal open. Make a list of what the Spirit brings to your awareness as manifestations in your own life of what Jeremiah is preaching. What are your fears and worries that may be symptoms that your faith in the power of God is weakening in the face of temptation? Be honest … courageously honest. Feel the links that connect you with these people seven centuries before Christ.

Chapters 11 and 12 contain two of six personal laments of the prophet. They have Job-like power and beauty. How would you express laments about your own personal losses?

Tuesday   *Snapped into Pain*   **Job 9—11**

God is wise in heart and mighty in strength.
Who has hardened himself against Him and prospered? 9:4

As a child of Adam, Job cries out with the pain that flows into him and into us from Adam's fall. The poetry of chapter 9 is Job's attempt to stretch himself beyond the circle of his suffering into the larger sphere of God's world. However, as a great bungee cord stretched to its limit, it snaps Job back into his pain that is the center of everything. Zophar makes all this worse when he, third of Job's so-called friends, intervenes with his theology of sin. Instead of living with questions that evade easy answers, Zophar sets his speech to be the last word on the subject.

Give the Jobs in your life the compassion they need, but which they do not receive. Return this compassion to yourself at those points where your spirit quivers with Job's.

| **Wednesday** | *Eyes Upon You* | **Psalm 123** |

As the eyes of a maid to the hand of her mistress,
so our eyes look to the Lord our God, until He has mercy on us. v. 2

In the archives of our home movies, there is a clip of me as a child playing in the surf while my mother looks on lovingly and caringly. At that moment of play, I was only aware of the delight of the waves at low tide washing over me. While viewing the film as an adult, the love of my mother moved me, as did my love for her.

In the verse for today, the psalmist uses an image similar to mine to stir devotion to the Lord. Recalling also "The Man Born Blind" from last Sunday's Gospel, let these images stir about within until you find your own image offered. How do you sense the presence of your tender and caring Lord who never removes God's eyes from you?

| **Thursday** | *Jottings and Joltings* | **Ephesians 4** |

4
Le
A

I, therefore, the prisoner of the Lord, beseech you to walk
worthy of the calling with which you were called. v. 1

From the boundaries of Paul's prison come these words that leap in freedom beyond those walls. A careful, meditative reading of this chapter will penetrate walls of resistance that may yet lurk within the prison of your own heart. Here are words that bear potential for personal transformation. Read and reread them slowly, until the power of God in Paul moves within you as well.

Pause with Paul at those places where you find your spirit shaken positively or negatively. These are the areas where you need to grow so that you can meet the challenge of Paul to respond to grace. Make jottings in your journal where joltings occur. A spontaneous list of areas to grow may emerge. The very process of writing will help to unfold the list; you will have a "blueprint" for the work that yet needs to be done in your life.

| **Friday** | *Banquet of God's Will* | **John 4** |

My food is to do the will of Him who sent Me,
and to finish His work. v. 34

The story of "The Woman at the Well" from the Third Sunday in Lent is filled with so many dimensions that it is well for us to consider it once again. You might focus today upon the scene with Jesus and the disciples, while the woman leaves and witnesses to her people about her encounter with Jesus.

Jesus moved the woman and she moved him. The greatness of his hunger is revealed—hunger for her salvation and the salvation of all of us.

Meditate upon the image of food and doing the will of God. Jesus teaches in the Sermon on the Mount: "Blessed are those who hunger and thirst for righteousness, for they shall be filled" (Matthew 5:6). Discovering and doing the will of God give a joy and satisfaction to the soul far surpassing any other banquet table.

Saturday   **The Sabbath Torah Reading**

Mar 08, 2008 #23A	Apr 01, 2017 #24A	Mar 21, 2026 #24A	Mar 10, 2035 #23A
Apr 09, 2011 #28A	Mar 28, 2020 #24A	Mar 17, 2029 #24A	Apr 10, 2038 #28A
Ap5 05, 2014 #28A	Mar 25, 2023 #24A	Mar 13, 2032 #24A	Apr 06, 2041 #27A

The Fifth Week in Lent

Two weeks before Easter. Alphabyte: Rooster, p. 41

Sunday   *Loose Him*   **John 11:1–45**

I am the resurrection and the life.
He who believes in Me, though he may die, he shall live. v. 25

The miracle of Lazarus brought back to life is a prelude to the death and resurrection of Jesus. If Jesus has power over this death, what must this say about Jesus' power over his own life? The Jewish leaders ironically miss the whole point. Lazarus alive becomes the precipitating event that enrages the scribes and Pharisees to seek Jesus' death. Ultimately their spiritual death occurs.

John dramatically tells the story. Human and divine elements fill the scenes. Verse 35 is the shortest verse in the Bible: "Jesus wept." Meditate upon the movements and levels of meaning in this wondrous chapter of the Bible. Take to your own heart the words of verse 44 spoken by Jesus on Lazarus' behalf: "Loose him and let him go."

Monday   *Power of Confession*   **Jeremiah 13—15**

Your words were found and I ate them, and
Your word was to me the joy and rejoicing of my heart. 15:16

The Lord orders Jeremiah to express the sin of the people through various symbolic acts—wearing a rotting, linen sash, and later, wine bottles that the Lord would have smashed. Feel the impact of these images in your own spirit. Jeremiah will do for you what God had him do for the people of those times. God's Word is eternal; it is alive for you today.

Come to appreciate the value of confessing specific sins. Each confession unfolds disorders in your spirit, gradually uncovering some basic, sinful tendency that needs the touch of the Lord to bring healing to your heart.

Pray with Jeremiah in his third lament in 15:10–21. Just as he does, take personal time to be with the Lord so that intimacy of expression will develop.

Tuesday   *Intimacy with God*   **Job 12—14**

"Only two things do not do to me … withdraw Your hand far from me
and let not the dread of You make me afraid." 13:20–21

In waves of poetry, Job expresses praise as well as pain. Notice the verbs in chapter 12 assigned to God. The very act of Job's expression loosens the constant pounding of the pain in his heart, freeing him to come to the poignant prayer in the verses for the day. Dwell on them until they engrave prayer upon your heart.

Competition instead of compassion: this is what Job's friends contribute. Their responses are blocks in the path to where the Lord is leading him. Job's words reveal the intimacy that he really has with the Lord. It is trust in God that ultimately brings Job to the place of resolution from all that is torturing him. God is even using the heartless responses of Job's friends in the process.

Will you be open to how God's hand is upon you, though you may not see it?

Wednesday	*Images of the Enemy*	Psalm 124

Our help is in the name of the LORD
Who made heaven and earth. v. 8

The final "Song of Ascents" for this year brings us near the entry of Jesus into Jerusalem on Palm Sunday. Jesus, Job, and the psalmist experience the onslaught of enemy power coming against them. Do you identify with them? Three images are uplifted that describe these enemies. Feel them. In what way do they serve to have you sense enemy power coming against you?

The verse for the day, the final one in the psalm, has been used from earliest times in worship as a prelude to the final blessing. Meditate upon the blessings that will come to you when you know with your entire being that the one who is your defense is the One who made heaven and earth. Is there any power greater than this? Is there anyone more disposed to come to your aid than the Lord?

Thursday	*Practical Ways*	Ephesians 5—6

Speak to one another in psalms and hymns and spiritual songs,
singing and making melody in your heart to the Lord … 5:19

Virtues move from being mere abstractions when placed against the vices that Paul lists. Note the specific ways of behaving that Paul enjoins. Decide to practice them.

How could you make the verse for the day come alive for you as you literally speak to others in words of Scripture? Look at the agenda of your day. Ask the Lord to give you verses applied to the persons with whom you interact each day.

These are vital chapters for families. When reading about the submission of wives, remember that this applies only to those marriages where the husband loves his wife as Christ loves the church.

You would be well to memorize the elements of the whole armor of God in 6:14–17. Put them on as you would the clothes you wear.

Friday	*Peering into the Mystery*	John 5

Most assuredly, I say to you, he who hears My word and believes in Him who sent
Me has everlasting life, and shall not come into judgment,
but has passed from death to life. v. 24

Feel the frustration of the lame man beside the pool. Thirty-eight years of trying to get to the waters, someone else always beating him to it … thirty-eight years for bystanders to know him, have compassion for him, and hence joy at his healing. Nevertheless, not for the Jewish leaders … Legalism blocks and blinds them from the Good News of the healing Jesus.

Exalted words of Jesus well up as sparks and then flames from the friction between the leaders and him. We are peering directly into the mystery of Jesus' divinity and oneness with God the Father. Contemplate the mystery and live it, for Jesus shares with you the very life he has with the Father. Rest in this life, this love, this healing touch of God upon you. Rise and walk!

Saturday			The Sabbath Torah Reading
Mar 15, 2008 #24A	Apr 08, 2017 #25A	Mar 28, 2026 #25A	Mar 17, 2035 #24A
Apr 16, 2011 #29A	Apr 04, 2020 #25A	Mar 24, 2029 #25A	Apr 17, 2038 #29A
Apr 12, 2014 #29A	Apr 01, 2023 #25A	Mar 20, 2032 #25A	Apr 13, 2041 #28A

Holy Week

The week before Easter. Alphabyte: Supper, p. 42

Alphabyte: Supper, p. 42

Palm Sunday   ***The Passion***   **Matthew 26:14—27–66**

**So when the centurion and those with him, who were guarding Jesus, saw
the earthquake and the things that had happened, they feared greatly saying,
"Truly this was the Son of God!" 27:54**

We enact through ritual, the triumphal entry of Jesus into Jerusalem. The mood shifts, however, with the reading of the Passion account later in worship. Matthew unfolds twenty-one scenes in telling the story. Hold your palm branches while prayerfully reading Matthew's Passion throughout the day, a few scenes at a time.

Matthew wants us to feel the connection of this Passion with the Infancy Narrative. Now the chief priests, scribes, and elders are in the place of Herod. As Jesus partakes of the Passover meal with his apostles, he relives the Exodus theme, just as he did in the flight to Egypt. Matthew alone tells the story of the death of Judas, the dead rising at the moment of Jesus' death, and the guards to be placed at the tomb. The New Testament's only references to God's appearance through dreams are in the divine messages to Joseph and to Pilate's wife.

What does the Holy Spirit tell you personally, as you pray?

**HW
A**

Monday   ***The Prophet's Pen***   **Jeremiah 16—17**

**Heal me, O Lord, and I shall be healed;
Save me, and I shall be saved, for You are my praise. 17:14**

The Lord forbad Jeremiah to marry, intended to shock the people into awareness of the coming disaster of exile that would come upon them, if they failed to repent. God did not want children to be brought into such a world.

Sometimes we hear that from parents about today's world. The way you live points others to the reality of God's presence to them. When the Lord calls persons to celibacy it is to witness to the absolute sufficiency of Christ in one's life.

Chapter 17 is a blending of verses that will remind you of the Psalms and the Book of Proverbs. Read Jeremiah slowly here, as the prophet etches the power of his pen upon your heart. Embrace these words, which will be food for you this day that the Lord has made. Does the Lord invite you to write?

Tuesday   ***God at Last***   **Job 38**

**Have you commanded the morning since your days began,
and caused the dawn to know its place? v. 12**

At last Job listens to the Lord. The strategy of God is not to answer the questions that have been the debate of the previous chapters, but rather, to pose more questions! The Lord simply repositions Job into his place in the universe. The result is silence. Job's arguing and complaining ceases as he yields to pure wonder at the beauty of the world. It is beyond his capacity to understand. Contemplation wins out over competition and complaining.

The secret of your own peace lies in totally listening to the Lord speaking to you and asking these same questions. God speaks to you through the pen of Job. Pick up your own pen and let the Lord do the same through you. What does the Lord have to say to you after the debate in your head is over?

Wednesday   *Against Unbelief*   **Psalm 14**

The fool has said in his heart, "There is no God." v. 1

[Note: This psalm and psalm 53 are the same, except for this one's use of the name *Yahweh* for God.]

Though there are many who say with their mouth that they believe in God, by the way in which they live, their heart betrays that they do not. This psalm does not seek to breed a "holier than thou" attitude, but rather to be a sobering reminder that the world does not live with the Lord in charge, and despises those do.

The last verse gathers all this into a cry for the world, to free it from captivity. In the name of Jesus, stand against the spirit of unbelief that chokes the world. Pray for you and your loved ones. Is there anything that is holding you captive? By the power in the Holy Name, command that all that stands between you and the Lord be removed.

Holy Thursday   *Communion and Community*   **1 Corinth. 11—12**

For as the body is one and has many members,
but all the members of that one body, being many, are one body,
so also is Christ. 12:12

Picture the Upper Room where Jesus is sharing the Passover with his apostles. This Last Supper becomes the First Supper of a New Creation. Something only from heaven is about to take place; divine communion and community is incarnated in our human flesh through the Sacrament of Bread and Wine.

Keep your awareness of communion and community central as you read these two chapters of Paul. They treat of both. Though we peer into the particular problems of the church in Corinth long ago, the essence of the issues of strife and competition rear their ugly faces in every time and place religious institution. May the power of Christ transform you by the radiant light of his love. Pray for the oneness of the world.

Good Friday   *Close to Jesus*   **John 18:1—19:42**

"Woman, behold your son!"
Then He said to the disciple, "Behold your mother!" 19:26–27

As you pray through the Passion Narrative, recall your experience of doing this last Sunday with Matthew. Both evangelists find themes of Exodus and Jesus as King. What variations and nuances can you find?

Let your whole day be soaked with the saving Blood of Jesus by reading scenes in the narrative. Here is a suggested outline:

1) **6 am** (or on rising)	*Arrest, Trial, Denial of Peter*	**18:1–27**
2) **9 am**	*Jesus and Pilate*	**18:28–40**
3) **12 pm**	*Scourging, Crown of Thorns, Crucifixion*	**19:1–30**
4) **3 pm**	*Piercing the Side; Burial*	**19:31–42**

Be close to your Lord throughout this day, just as did the beloved disciple and Mary, mother of Jesus.

Saturday   **The Sabbath Torah Reading**

Mar 22, 2008 Passover	Apr 15, 2017 Passover	Apr 04, 2026 Passover	Mar 24, 2035 #25A
Apr 23, 2011 Passover	Apr 11, 2020 Passover	Mar 31, 2029 Passover	Apr 24, 2038 Passover
Apr 19, 2014 Passover	Apr 08, 2023 Passover	Mar 27, 2032 Passover	Apr 20, 2041 Passover

Easter Week
Alphabyte: Temple, p. 42

Easter Sunday *Mourning to Joy* John 20:1–18
Woman, why are your weeping? Whom are you seeking? v. 15

New Adam, new Eve, new Eden, new creation: this is Easter morning. Mary Magdalene, figure of Eve and all humanity, weeps at the tomb of her beloved. St. John has the beginning of chapter 3 of The Song of Songs in mind, as we will see in the final four Tuesdays in Easter this year. Be in touch with your own inner weeping for deeper union with the Lord.

Unrecognized, because utterly unexpected, Jesus appears. Come close. The spiritual fragrance of this morning penetrates your soul until there is a resurrection-shift from tears of mourning to tears of joy. The source of the joy is what has happened to Jesus. The spouse of your soul is before you. Leap beyond the prison of your own self-consciousness of sin, to the presence of your Jesus who receives you and loves you completely.

Monday *Eating the Word* Ezekiel 1—3
He said to me, "Son of man, feed your belly,
and fill your stomach with this scroll that I give you."
So I ate, and it was in my mouth like honey in sweetness. 3:3

A desperate, broken, exiled people are about to have the power of God revealed to them through Ezekiel. First, however, a dazzling vision envelopes the prophet.

As you read, believe that this same God of might wants to reveal the divine presence to you. The Lord embraces you with the Word, coming to you from four directions, as imaged in the prophet's vision. Receive in faith. Be prepared to respond.

Is there anything of a rebellious spirit in you as described of Israel? Unbelief in the Lord's sovereignty in your life is rebellion. Repent. Allow the Lord to intervene in your life. Resist the mental wrestling that may be going on within, as though you alone have the power to make the changes that need to take place in yours and others' lives. Eat. Commune with God.

Tuesday *Seasoned with Wisdom* Proverbs 10
He who winks with the eye causes trouble,
but a prating fool will fall. v. 10

The first three Tuesdays in Easter find us penetrating truth through the Book of Proverbs. The Holy Spirit as always is our teacher. Each one of the four seasons over the three-year cycle has a few chapters from this book to "season" our lives with the wisdom of the Spirit.

"On the one hand … on the other hand …" this expression uses the physical weighing of two open palms to consider contrasting points. This book of peace expresses proverbs in a similar manner. Receive each side of these wise sayings, as though you weigh each half of the truths in your hands, until the wisdom that feeds the proverbs centers you. Pause at special proverbs such as the one for today. The one that winks and looks the other way at evil is the one who causes trouble!

Wednesday	*What Not to Do*	Psalm 15

Lord, who may abide in Your tabernacle?
Who may dwell in Your holy hill? v. 1

There is no other joy in life than to sense that you are in the presence of God. This presence for God's people in David's time was the resting place of the Ark of the Covenant. Your soul is intended to be the resting place for God when you surrender to the Lord Jesus. "If anyone loves Me, he will keep My word; and My Father will love him, and We will come to him and make Our home with him" (John 14:23).

The psalm makes a list of what not to do, so that you may dwell with God. Pray the list item by item, opening yourself to the immense inner freedom that comes to those whose lives flow in agreement with the list. If anything jolts your spirit, it means that the Lord is convicting you by awakening you to sin. Turn to the Lord in immediate repentance and receive the peace that only God can give.

Thursday	*The Holy Spirit in You*	Acts 1

You shall receive power
when the Holy Spirit has come upon you. v. 8

The Book of Acts *is* the risen Lord living in his new community through the Holy Spirit. Though we focus on the coming of the Spirit fifty days after Easter on Pentecost, recall that the night of the Resurrection, Jesus appeared to the disciples and said, "Receive the Holy Spirit!"

Rejoice this Easter season that this same Holy Spirit wants to act in you and through you as you are engrafted onto the Lord's risen life through a community of faith. As you enter the picture of the first days of the Church, can you find these spiritual energies alive with you? You will, if you "Seek first the Kingdom of God and His righteousness, and all these things shall be added to you." (Matthew 6:33).

Friday	*From the Ashes*	John 3:1–21

Most assuredly, I say to you, unless one is born again,
he cannot see the kingdom of God." v. 3

Adam was the firstborn; Jesus is the New Adam born again. Adam was born of the barrenness of the earth. The Spirit of God hovered over it and breathed into the clay of the earth so that Adam might live with the breath of God. Jesus was born in the barrenness of Mary's womb. The Holy Spirit hovered over that abyss until she conceived the flesh of the New Adam. From her womb and from the tomb, Jesus lives.

Are you ready for the funeral of the old self so that from its ashes, the new you can be born? Die to the old Adam-self and live the very life of God through the Holy Spirit.

Saturday   The Sabbath Torah Reading

Mar 29, 2008 #26A	Apr 22, 2017 #26A	Apr 11, 2026 #26A	Mar 31, 2035 #26A
Apr 30, 2011 #30A	Apr 18, 2020 #26A	Apr 07, 2029 Passover	May 01, 2038 #30A
Apr 26, 2014 #30A	Apr 15, 2023 #26A	Apr 03, 2032 Passover	Apr 27, 2041 #29A

The Second Week in Easter
Alphabyte: Universe, p. 43

Sunday   *Presence by Faith*   **John 20:19–31**
Jesus breathed on them and said to them,
"Receive the Holy Spirit." v. 22

The evening of the first day of the new creation finds Jesus breathing peace into the chaotic clay of the disciples and making them new creatures. John recalls the time when God created Adam by forming a nose and breathing God's life into it. Some have found liturgical traces in this reading—the kiss of peace offered to one another from ancient services of worship. Thomas missed the kiss of peace and joy, left only to his own devices and prerequisites for him to know if Jesus was alive. He too needs a touch—however, one more radical than the one he demands. When Jesus does come, I do not imagine that Thomas needed to feel the wounds of Jesus; the presence of the Lord was enough for him.

Is the presence of Jesus by faith enough for you? Jesus said such ones are more blessed than the Thomases who have seen.

Monday   *Divine Outrage*   **Ezekiel 4—5**
You shall set your face toward the siege of Jerusalem
and with your arm bared you shall prophesy against it. 4:7 (NRSV)

Symbols can raise awareness to acute levels. This is evident in these chapters. Ezekiel is deeply conscious of the sins of the people for whom he intercedes.

You will read about the power of God and the divine outrage at the people and their high places in the mountains where they worship idols. That any person, place, or thing be more important than the Lord is to commit idolatry. God has made us to adore and worship the Lord alone.

Great pain occurs when life is lived without God as center. Is there anything of this kind of pain in your life? What images come to you in prayer? Jesus took all your pain and anguish so that you would not have to bear them any longer. Give all to God; adore and worship God alone.

Tuesday   *The Suffering of Servants*   **Proverbs 11**
He who is surety for a stranger will suffer,
But one who hates being surety is secure. v. 15

Be especially aware of the key words on each side of the contrasts in these proverbs. You might jot them down on the left and right side of your journal. The cumulative effect of these wise sayings will deepen their common truth. Just as raking the soil back and forth prepares the ground for seed, so does the back and forth praying of these proverbs sift your soul as soil for the seed of God's holy Word.

Ponder the truth of the verse for today. It reminds me of the ironic saying someone once said about a school: "This would be a wonderful place if it weren't for the students!" The security of those who do not take risks serving is the stale air of those bored in life.

Write down those proverbs that especially ignite your soul. Return to them often today and be warmed by their fires.

| Wednesday | *Profound Comfort* | Psalm 16 |

You are my Lord,
My goodness is nothing apart from You. v. 2

Once there was a person tormented night after night, waking from terrible nightmares of a pack of vicious dogs attacking the person. One night, the person prayed before going to sleep that this nightmare would cease. The dream occurred again, but this time the self in the dream faced the dogs; they immediately turned to flowers.

In this psalm, David leads you into a prayer of absolute awareness of the power and presence of God to turn all repugnant or frightening aspects of your life, into goodness and peace. David knows that with God's hand on his life, everything takes on the fragrance and beauty of God's presence. Even a nightmare like Goliath became a blessing for David. By faith in God's power, David became "taller" than the height of this great giant. So may you pray in the same manner.

| Thursday | *Soaked with Spirit-Power* | Acts 2 |

Therefore let all the house of Israel know assuredly
that God has made this Jesus, whom you crucified, both Lord and Christ. v. 36

Again, God acts in the fullness of time. The waiting and expectancy are over; now God is moving in the final outpouring of divine life and love in the Holy Spirit.

There is a shift from the waiting for, to the outpouring of the Spirit in the words of Peter. The once impulsive, frightened, and reactive man now becomes a pure vessel for God's strong, yet sweet activity through the Spirit.

The same changes can happen in you. Watch and wait with the disciples. The same Holy Spirit desires to infill you right now with power and love, transforming your unredeemed character into a personality totally soaked with Spirit-power and ready to move.

| Friday | *The Weight of Glory* | John 3:22–36 |

He must increase, but I must decrease. v. 30

Imagine a scale and the contents of your awareness—your world, with all its problems and challenges on one side, God and God's power and glory on the other. Which side is heavier?

The verse for the day is the center verse in this passage. As you read, let each verse increase the weight of the Lord in your spirit, filling your mind and heart with a deepening consciousness of God's presence to you.

The Hebrew concept of God's glory, *kabod* means "weightiness." Welcome the glory of God sinking into your soul as a weight that centers you. Feel the shift in the scale as your problems become lighter in the balance, the Lord filling you more and more with God's glory.

Saturday   The Sabbath Torah Reading

Apr 05, 2008 #27A	Apr 29, 2017 #27–28A	Apr 18, 2026 #27–28A	Apr 07, 2035 #27A
May 07, 2011 #31A	Apr 25, 2020 #27–28A	Apr 14, 2029 #26A	May 08, 2038 #31A
May 03, 2014 #31A	Apr 22, 2023 #27–28A	Apr 10, 2032 #26A	May 04, 2041 #30A

The Third Week in Easter
Alphabyte: Vine, p. 43

Sunday   *Awakened to Joy*   **Luke 24:13–35**
Beginning with Moses and all the Prophets,
He expounded to them in all the Scriptures the things concerning Himself. v. 27

Each Resurrection appearance of Jesus involves a process of coming to know that it is truly Jesus. So also with these two disciples on the road to Emmaus; tradition believes one of them to be St. Luke. The stranger to them is no stranger to the meaning and movement of God's word. They are broken in sadness, returning home very disappointed to return to "business as usual." However, in the course of the day, they awaken to the truth of God's bringing life through suffering.

Full recognition for them only comes at the breaking of the bread, the Sacrament of encounter that draws them into the presence of Christ by faith. Their hearts, ignited along the way, are now aflame; Jesus is with them.

Imagine Jesus walking with you from morning to evening as your heart awakens to joy.

Monday   *Shocked into Repentance*   **Ezekiel 6—7**
No one will strengthen himself
Who lives in iniquity. 7:13

If you find yourself shocked by the anger and violence of God, know how God is appalled even more by the evil of idolatry, which enrages God's heart. No, you might not adore an idol of plaster of Paris, yet it is easy to be tempted to place the center of preference in some project, some plan, and some *thing* as empty as a cheap idol, in place of God.

The day of trouble *has come*: Good Friday. The Easter season is one continuous day of salvation. For those who resist God's plan in their lives, there are not enough physical or emotional anesthesias to ward off the pain.

Be sobered by the verse for the day. Remember "the bottom line." God is forgiving. Yet God wants your heart now, not postponed until later. God's anger is short; God's love is everlasting—but this life is not! Repent now and live.

Tuesday   *Extenders to Proverbs*   **Proverbs 12**
A fool's wrath is known at once,
But a prudent man covers shame. v. 16

The same Spirit of the living God that gave wisdom to the writer of Proverbs is ready and available now to pour wisdom into your heart. Just as these proverbs come to us in writing, so can the Spirit use your own hand in writing what could be called "extenders" to the proverbs. These are your own personal expressions of truths as they especially touch your own life. Perhaps people and circumstances will come to your awareness; lift them in prayer as the Spirit prompts. Images, further wisdom sayings of your own, and the Spirit's creation will flow forth.

Once again, make use of the pauses that the Spirit urges you to make. Lift your eyes in silent pondering until the words of wisdom take flesh in your own life.

| Wednesday | *Apple in God's Eye* | Psalm 17 |

Keep me as the apple of your eye;
Hide me under the shadow of Your wings. v. 8

Clear a space at the center of your self. It is the middle of the week where the work-struggle is strong for so many. The first words of this psalm lead you into the presence of the Lord. The Holy Spirit prays through you as a defense attorney for yourself and the rest of humankind.

Even more than David's surrender in trust, you, adopted son or daughter of the living God, have the right to come into the presence of God.

Examine yourself and your tongue, not with the knitted eyebrows of tight judgment, but with the open-handed, openhearted honesty that draws you closer to the Lord.

Here is your prayer for the day. Pray it often. Linger a long time with the last verse.

| Thursday | *Power in the Name* | Acts 3—4 |

Silver and gold I do not have, but what I do have I give you:
In the name of Jesus Christ of Nazareth, rise up and walk. 3:6

Perhaps Jesus often saw this lame man sitting by the door as Jesus went in and out of the Temple. He might have said to himself, "This one will be healed soon through my Spirit in Peter and John." The Acts of the Apostles are the continuation into the Church of the ministry of Jesus' healing, loving, teaching.

The evidence of the resurrection is immediate in the lives of the Apostles. Jesus lives in them. Not only has he died and risen, but so have the first Christians died and risen in him. Nothing can keep them from being with Jesus, for his Spirit dwells in them. They draw forth riches for healing, calling on the Name of Jesus that brings the power of this presence.

Easter power is yours.

| Friday | *Miracle Bread* | John 6:1–21 |

Jesus took the loaves and when He had given thanks
He distributed them to the disciples … v. 11

Jesus could have turned the stones around him into bread to feed the crowd; this was the temptation of the devil when Jesus was hungry at the end of his forty-day fast at the beginning of his ministry. Instead, Jesus takes what food is there. The lunch of a young boy becomes the seed for the miracle.

Bring what you have to the Lord. God has made you good and can multiply that goodness to feed many. Feed your spirit with the Word of the Lord who hands you miracle bread of his body right now. Walk with him on top of the turbulent waters of your life. He wishes to bring you in the Easter season through a new Exodus to life on the other side of anguish and pain.

Saturday — The Sabbath Torah Reading

Apr 12, 2008 #28A	May 06, 2017 #29–30A	Apr 25, 2026 #29–30A	Apr 14, 2035 #28A
May 14, 2011 #32A	May 02, 2020 #29–30A	Apr 21, 2029 #27–28A	May 15, 2038 #32A
May 10, 2014 #32A	Apr 29, 2023 #29–30A	Apr 17, 2032 #27–28A	May 11, 2041 #31A

The Fourth Week in Easter
Alphabyte: Wax, p. 44

Sunday *Resting with the Shepherd* John 10:1–10
I am the door. If anyone enters by Me, he will be saved,
and will go in and out and find pasture. v. 9

Christians of ancient Rome buried their dead and worshipped in underground chambers called catacombs. The earliest images of art found on those dark walls are drawings of Jesus as the Good Shepherd. The entrances to the catacombs were reminders that Jesus is the door to the Sheepfold. There Christians were safe from the emperor-thief intent upon destroying God's beloved ones.

Today is "Good Shepherd Sunday." There is an ancient tradition of reading from John 10 on this center Sunday of the Easter Season. We read three sections of this chapter in the three-year cycle.

On Tuesday we will begin to read from the Song of Songs where the beloved of the Shulamite woman is a shepherd. Rest in the love of the Good Shepherd who came to life again.

Monday *The Hole in the Wall* Ezekiel 8—9
"Son of man, dig into the wall;"
and when I dug into the wall, there was a door. 8:8

Go with Ezekiel lifted on high between heaven and earth. Behold the visions the Lord unfolds for him. Abominations of idolatry are committed. Feel the jealousy of God as worship of idols is described, with all the horrible practices that accompany this. The purity of God cannot tolerate such contamination. Those that continue to practice idolatry must be eliminated.

Look into the hole in your own heart, as into the eye-piece of a microscope. What do you see going on there? The pace of life, the demands of others can lure us into living out priorities that are not God's—idols that God abhors. What do you see that fills your inner space? Release your hold on any idol. "Sigh and cry over all the abominations that are done within" (9:4).

Tuesday *Your Beloved* Song of Songs 1—2
Tell me, O you whom I love, where you feed your flock,
Where you make it rest at noon. 1:7

There are love expressions in this book as clear and beautiful as are its origins obscure. We find examples of similar poetry in cultures surrounding the ancient Hebrews. How did this book, which never mentions God, find its way into the Bible? This answer is simple, enunciated centuries later by St. John in his first letter: "God is love" (4:7–8). All of God's people, Jewish and Christian, have found this book filled with the intimacy with which God wishes to relate to us.

Jewish people read the Song of Songs in synagogues on the Sabbath during the intermediate days of Passover. It is spring. The earth turns to love. This book will refresh you; it is unique from others in the Bible. There are fifty words in it not found anywhere else in Scripture!

May you be as passionate in your love for Jesus as Jesus' love is for you.

Wednesday *God's Strength* **Psalm 18**
For You will light my lamp;
The Lord my God will enlighten my darkness. v. 28
[This Psalm is also found in 2 Samuel 22]

Why is it so easy to talk about the weather? It is because we find a common experience for conversation. So often, we define a day as good or bad by how the weather is. For David, the variety of weather changes only serves to lead him into deeper awareness of the power and strength of the Lord who has protected him from all his enemies—Saul and his army.

Images of safety in the midst of turmoil abound. Picture these same physical settings for yourself, along with David. Security in the Lord's protection will comfort you. Call upon the Lord and his angels to protect those you love.

Someone once said: "Criticism of the weather is a mild form of blasphemy!" Penetrate to the sun present behind the clouds.

4
Ea
A

Thursday *Joy and Suffering* **Acts 5—6**
They departed from the presence of the council,
rejoicing that they were counted worthy to suffer shame for His name. 5:41

Though the death of Ananias and Sapphira did not come as violently as did the idolaters in Monday's reading from Ezekiel, it came as swiftly. Do not lie to God!

Water and oil do not mix; but joy and suffering can. Be aware of this blending in today's reading.

How do you suffer? Is it with anger and complaints as a victim asking, "Why is this happening to me?" Give a name to the suffering and let this name turn into the name of Jesus. Offer your pain and suffering for others who do not have the faith that gives meaning to their pain. The joy of the Lord is your strength, making sense out of your suffering, which brings power in intercession for others.

Friday *Clinging Fire* **John 6:22–40**
This is the will of Him who sent Me,
that everyone who sees the Son and believes in Him may have everlasting life;
and I will raise him up at the last day." v. 40

Long for the Bread of Heaven to fill your entire being. You will become hungry again with other breads; Jesus' gift of himself in the Sacrament of his love will satisfy the hunger in your spirit.

There is a quiet, unrelenting joy in this season, which proclaims the abiding presence of Jesus as the nourisher of your soul. Jesus has already raised you up on the "last day," which for St. John has reference to Good Friday. Jesus draws you to himself on the cross and embraces you as he rises. Adhere to Jesus; this is the meaning of belief in John. If you cling to the cross, you will cling to Jesus in the resurrection. Just as fire clings to the wood it burns, the Spirit will cling to you.

Saturday **The Sabbath Torah Reading**

Apr 19, 2008 #29A	May 13, 2017 #31A	May 02, 2026 #31A	Apr 21, 2035 #29A
May 21, 2011 #33A	May 09, 2020 #31A	Apr 28, 2029 #29–30A	May 22, 2038 #33A
May 17, 2014 #33A	May 06, 2023 #31A	Apr 24, 2032 #29–30A	May 18, 2041 #32A

The Fifth Week in Easter
Alpbabyte: Xylophone, p. 44

Sunday   *Dwelling with God*   **John 14:1–14**

**In My Father's house are many mansions; if it were not so,
I would have told you. I go to prepare a place for you. v. 2**

The setting of the Last Supper before Jesus is lifted up on the cross is offered here before Jesus is lifted to heaven in the Ascension. Jesus has just heard the protestations of Peter that he would never deny Jesus. Jesus must have descended in an instant to an inner garden of agony. Nonetheless, from these depths of Jesus' heart we begin to hear the most exalted words ever addressed to humans: we are called to live with God.

The essence of this living-with is found in the Greek word *meno* meaning "to dwell, remain, abide," etc. The noun form, "mansions," or "dwelling places," occurs only two times in the Bible, in the verse for today and in verse 23. The way in which the Father and Son mutually indwell becomes the model for how we are meant to live with God.

Take this Greek word, *meno* and repeat it repeatedly today until it burrows its way into you.

Monday   *Four Faces*   **Ezekiel 10—11**

**I will give them one heart, and I will put a new spirit within them, and take the
stony heart out of their flesh, and give them a heart of flesh ... 11:19**

Forty-seven times the number four appears in Ezekiel, seven times in just six verses in chapter 10. As the *Alphabyte* "Quarters" suggests, four is basic to life, symbol of fullness and completion.

Slow down your reading so that the images in Ezekiel can come alive in you. Go with him to the places where he leads. The four faces have led to various later interpretations of finding the faces of the Evangelists. St. John is the Eagle as he soars in heights of sublime understanding of Jesus.

Be ready for the heights of communion with God where the Lord wants to take you. The Lord is doing a miracle of re-creation in you as anything stony in your heart is transformed into a heart of flesh.

If you were to be one of those faces, which one would it be and why?

Tuesday   *Love's Expression*   **Song of Songs 3—4**

**"I will rise now," I said, "and go about the city,
in the streets and in the squares I will seek the one I love." 3:2**

See today's reading in the light of the resurrection account in John 20:1–18. You will find the search for Jesus' body by Mary Magdalene expressed in ways similar to those found in the beginning of the passage for today. The clinging of Mary to Jesus finds echo in 3:4.

Lush images flow throughout the dialogue between the Shulamite woman and the Beloved. This is the way God loves you in Jesus. Fall in love with God again.

You might write a prayer-letter to God using images here as elements of your expression. May your search for love and for God be as strong and adamant as the search for the Beloved.

Wednesday *Cosmic Meditation* **Psalm 19**

Let the words of my mouth and the meditation of my heart
Be acceptable in Your sight,
O LORD, my strength and my Redeemer. v. 14

Have you ever noticed when you are worried or afraid that your eyes are downcast? As you begin to pray this psalm, lift up your gaze and see the whole expanse of the sky. Gently study the detail that you see. Cosmic space covers you. Be open to the presence of God in this massive meditation, allowing the movement of the verses of the psalm to take you high in awareness of God that is greater than your worries. With David, picture the sun as a bridegroom rejoicing to come up and out to meet his bride—a theme from the Song of Songs

There's a shift in the meditation that comes in verse 7. Rest in the closing verse enshrined in Jewish and Christian liturgies for centuries untold.

Thursday *Stephen the Martyr* **Acts 7**

Stephen knelt down and cried out with a loud voice,
"Lord, do not charge them with this sin." v. 60

Stephen gathers the entire history of rebellion of the people of Israel into one place. This same history stares at him in the faces of his accusers. However, even more intently present to him are the glory of God and the sight of Jesus sitting at God's right hand as he is being stoned to death. In words and disposition of heart the same as Jesus, Stephen commits his spirit to the Lord in today's verse.

Jesus lives in his disciples and in you. The Holy Spirit fills you as you immerse yourself in the scene of Stephen's martyrdom. Empty your hands of stones to throw, for you are not without sin. No more accusing others, or yourself.... Open yourself to awesome love.

Friday *Bread and Breath* **John 6:41–71**

He who eats my flesh and drinks My blood
abides in Me, and I in him. v. 56

Along with our Hebrew ancestors in the wilderness, the spirit of complaint blinds the Jewish leaders from receiving the gift in front of them of Jesus as the Bread of Life. Similar to Thomas the apostle who doubted, the leaders come to Jesus with their own concepts and norms for how God would touch and communicate with God's people.

Complaining is poison. Do not do it. Receive the Bread of Life. Commit to the Lord that problem, that situation as you exhale each breath. With each inhale, take in the Bread of Life who is also the "breath" of life in the Holy Spirit. Receive the covenant blood of Jesus that brings salvation, joy and the immense love of Jesus.

Saturday **The Sabbath Torah Reading**

Apr 26, 2008 Passover	May 20, 2017 #32–33A	May 09, 2026 #32–33A	Apr 28, 2035 Passover
May 28, 2011 Passover	May 16, 2020 #32–33A	May 05, 2029 #31A	May 29, 2038 #34A
May 24, 2014 #34A	May 13, 2023 #32–33A	May 01, 2032 #31A	May 25, 2041 #33A

The Sixth Week in Easter
Alphabyte: Yoke, p. 45

Sunday   *Behind the Veil*   **John 14:15–21**

**I will pray the Father, and He will give you another Helper,
that He may abide with you forever. v. 16**

6
Ea
A

On Good Friday, the veil in the Temple was torn in two; the separation between the divine and human was removed. In the final weeks of Easter, we peer into the mystery of God behind the place where the veil used to be.

The key to understanding is once again, *meno*, "to abide." Repeatedly this word appears, weaving Jesus' profound expression in this and the following chapter.

The word for the Holy Spirit that John uses is the Greek *parakletos*, sometimes simply transferred into English as "paraclete." The word literally means "one who is called to be at your side" as a lawyer, advocate, counselor, "helper," or in the King James version, "Comforter."

Meditate upon these and other words that may be given to you, all variations of the intimate living-with that the Spirit brings.

Monday   *Prophetic Symbols*   **Ezekiel 12—14**

**"None of My words will be postponed any more,
but the word which I speak will be done," says the Lord GOD. 12:28**

The word "prophesy" literally means, "to speak on behalf" of God. However, in addition to the voice, God often speaks through symbolic gestures of the prophets such as Jeremiah commanded not to marry and Hosea ordered to marry a prostitute. These gestures express the infidelity that wounds the heart of God who loves so much. In today's reading, Ezekiel is to gather up his belongings as though going into exile—sign of what is going to happen to God's rebellious people.

Beyond the anger of God, read God's hurt as that of a beloved treated with indifference and infidelity on the part of the spouse. The denial of bread, a consequence to immanent siege, is similar to the refusal of the Bread of Life in last Friday's reading.

What symbolic gestures does God suggest to you, to express how you are relating to the Lord these days?

Tuesday   *Disconnected Love*   **Song of Songs 5—6**

**I sought him, but I could not find him;
I called him, but he gave me no answer. 5:6**

The readings from The Song of Songs come in sharp contrast with Monday's stark passages from Ezekiel. The tender, sensual love poetry of the Song is set against the violence, famine, death, and exile spoken by Ezekiel. However, God's intense love for his people and their absence from this love still emerge in both readings as a common theme. Surely, the verse for the day was in St. John's mind when he developed the scene of Mary Magdalene searching for Jesus in this year's Easter Gospel.

Though faithful, yet without her proper clothing, the security guards of the city believe the Shulamite is a prostitute. Even when love is faithful, there are disconnections, misunderstandings and confusions that can have the timing of love be out of sync.

Receive the description of the Shulamite of her Beloved as expressions of the beauty of the Body of Christ.

Wednesday	*All You Need*	**Psalm 20**

Some trust in chariots, and some in horses;
But we will remember the name of the Lord our God. v. 7

A series of loving blessings flow from the heart of the psalmist. He is an intercessor for you. The Holy Spirit groans inwardly to set you free and brings the gift of God's helping presence to you. What are the circumstances in your life that come to mind that concretely unfold for you just how and where you need help from the Lord?

The same power that raised Jesus from the dead is available to you. Take the verse for today and treasure it. The power of Jesus' name has been given to you. He stands before you now as the risen Lord. See the smile and feel the arms of Christ who embraces and protects you.

Thursday	*A Path Through the Word*	**Acts 8**

"Do you understand what you are reading?"
And he said, "How can I, unless someone guides me?" vv. 30–31

The church grows as an explosion in the Book of Acts. The rage of persecutions only fans the flames of fervor. Joy expands.

There is saying of Tertullian from the second century: "The blood of martyrs is the seed of Christians." Saul was present at the blood bath of Stephen. It quickened his personal resolve to persecute. However, this is the last chapter about Saul; in the next one, he is Paul with energies transformed for Christ.

Simon is a wheeler and dealer, reminding us to beware of turning the power of the Spirit to selfish ends. Give God all the glory for the wonderful things God wants to do in you and through you. May the Spirit guide you through these daily readings, as Philip guides the eunuch on his path through the Word of God.

Friday	*Near Death—Near Life*	**John 10:1–21**

I have come that they may have life,
and that they may have it more abundantly. v. 10

Those who have had a near-death experience speak about passing through a tunnel having a great light at the end. Actually, these are "near-life" experiences.

Jesus is the door. As you approach Jesus in faith, you are having such a near-life experience. Pass through the door, which is Jesus, and rest with the Good Shepherd.

Do not be satisfied with merely a near-death experience of self, but rather a whole-death one. Lift your heart into the open doorway of the side of Jesus. His heart waits to receive you as the bridegroom of your soul. Return often during the day to the image of Jesus as your Good Shepherd

Saturday			**The Sabbath Torah Reading**
May 03, 2008 #30A	May 27, 2017 #34A	May 16, 2026 #34A	May 05, 2035 #30A
Jun 04, 2011 #35A	May 23, 2020 #34A	May 12, 2029 #32–33A	Jun 05, 2038 #35A
May 31, 2014 #35A	May 20, 2023 #34A	May 08, 2032 #32–33A	Jun 01, 2041 #34A

The Seventh Week in Easter
Alphabyte: Zenith, p. 45

Next week is Pentecost Sunday, the beginning of the season of Pentecost. The reading for Pentecost and Trinity Sunday are found at the beginning of the next season, *Pentecost*. You will also find further directions for finding the Monday-to-Saturday readings for the beginning weeks of the season of Pentecost which has slight yearly variations due to the changing date of Easter.

Sunday　　　　　　　　*Temple Without Limit*　　　　　　　　**Luke 24:44–53**
He opened their understanding,
that they might comprehend the Scriptures. v.45

The final scene in Luke's Gospel is described again in the opening chapter of the Book of Acts. It is the Ascension of Jesus. Before Jesus departs, he does for the disciples what he did for the two on the road to Emmaus—he opens minds to understanding.

Luke's Gospel begins and ends in the Temple. The closed, empty, inner Holy of Holies of waiting, longing, and finally God's intervention in Gabriel, contrasts with the whole Temple. The veil of separation is torn; the new community expands the sacred space of God's presence as they wait for the Holy Spirit. This Spirit will take them beyond the boundaries of the old Temple to endless limits of the new temple of Christ's body.

Spend these days of waiting, in watching, longing, and hoping for what is yet to come.

Monday　　　　　　　　*The Outcast Wife*　　　　　　　　**Ezekiel 15—16**
"When I passed by you and saw you struggling in your own blood, I said to you in
your blood, 'Live!' Yes, I said to you in your blood, 'Live!'" 16:6

Vine-wood has only one purpose—to give grapes. Jesus shares the same image in John 15: "I am the vine, you are the branches."

Sense in your spirit the pain of the Lord as that of a husband of a wife who has become the most debased of whores that ever existed. The pain of God yields not "grapes of wrath," but grapes of love—wine for Eucharist. Our blood lives because Jesus' was poured out for us. Greater is the redemptive blood of Jesus than all our infidelity. The tenderness of God is described with all the exuberance of the Song of Songs.

However unfaithful you have been to the call of the Lord upon your life, be less in awe about this, than in awe about the constancy of God's love for you. Greater is God's love than your sin. Engraft yourself on the vine again—the only way your life will bear fruit.

Tuesday　　　　　　　　*Your Spouse*　　　　　　　　**Song of Songs 7—8**
Set me as a seal upon you heart, as a seal upon you arm;
For love is as strong as death ... 8:6

Love is so great that it can only be described by what it is like. So does the Beloved stretch his imagination to the wide expanses of nature itself to describe the beauty of the Shulamite woman.

The best of wine—think of this image in recalling the reading from Ezekiel yesterday. The only exception is that here it is a source of joy in love, in place of the pain of unfaithfulness. Jesus at the marriage feast at Cana kept the best wine until now.

Connect the verse for the day with the rest of the phrase that completes it. God is a jealous God, commanding that you find no other taking the place of God. If you are married, may you find your spouse in the *Spouse*.

| Wednesday | *Prayer with Power* | Psalm 21 |

Be exalted, O LORD, in Your own strength!
We will sing and praise Your power. v. 13

Listen to a confident cry in the power of God to save. Pray it riding on the faith and joy of the psalmist and on the joy of the first disciples waiting in praise in the Temple. Christ the Lord has finally entered into the New Jerusalem. Breathe the stability and the security of God's saving grace.

Pray with ever deepening confidence. Be sensitive to those transition points of the day. Pause to pray verses that will re-energize your activity. God's power and grace come against melancholy, depression, resentment, or any other de-energized state of soul. As so many whacks in karate, your very being is loosened and made receptive to the power of God lifting you on high.

| Thursday | *Prostrate in Prayer* | Acts 9 |

He is a chosen vessel of Mine to bear My name
before Gentiles, kings and the children of Israel. v. 15

Our reading from the Acts of the Apostles this year ends with the conversion of St. Paul. Then he was Saul, with one driving compulsion—to persecute those who follow Jesus. Jesus shakes his very being. Enter the scene. Experience the profound shift in Paul to a fire that burns for love and joy, no longer for death.

Are you also ready to be shocked and astonished by the call of God on your life? As you pray, you are bathed in the same light that threw Paul to the ground, rising as a new creature. You might physically prostrate yourself in prayer. Welcome the gifts for ministry that the Spirit pours into you.

| Friday | *Secure in Jesus' Hands* | John 10:22–42 |

I give them eternal life and they shall never perish;
neither shall anyone snatch them out of My hand. v. 28

Jesus meets persistent resistance in the Jewish leaders. They choose to argue Jesus out of their lives. Arguments have no place with faith. Mental battles keep energy in the head, blocking that faith which comes from the heart. We are called to pass from death to life in Jesus.

Belief is a vigorous, total surrender to the Lord. Surrender in faith and rest secure in the hands of Jesus. The Lord Jesus is with you; no one can snatch you away from his hands.

Tell whatever or whomever else pushes for prominence to back off. All that matters is the presence of the Lord in whom you live, move, and have your being.

Saturday

May 10, 2008 #31A	Jun 03, 2017 #35A	May 23, 2026 Pentecost	May 12, 2035 #31A
Jun 11, 2011 #36A	May 30, 2020 Pentecost	May 19, 2029 #34A	Jun 12, 2038 #36A
Jun 07, 2014 #36A	May 27, 2023 Pentecost	May 15, 2032 #34A	Jun 08, 2041 #35A

The Sabbath Torah Reading

PENTECOST

SUMMER

Northern Hemisphere

Year A
2008, 2011, 2014 …

Pentecost begins the Sunday after the Seventh Sunday in Easter.
See the entire cycle of readings at a glance on page xxi.

The Beginning of the Season of Pentecost

Due to the changing date of Easter, the beginning of the season of Pentecost varies a few weeks from year to year. The first two Sundays of the season are always Pentecost and Trinity Sundays. When Easter is early, up to two weeks (rarely three) at the end of the season of Epiphany "leap ahead" to become the Monday-to-Saturday readings for the corresponding number of weeks needed to fill in the beginning of the season of Pentecost. When Easter is late, one week (rarely two) "leaps backs" to become the Monday-to-Saturday readings for the corresponding number of week(s) needed to fill in the end of the season of Epiphany. For the changes in Year A, simply follow the table below. When Easter occurs in its mid-range of dates (April 10 to 16), omit the Sunday readings for the first and second weeks, substituting them for Pentecost and Trinity Sundays. After these initial weeks, continue in the usual way of finding the Sunday nearest a given date. For more detailed information on suggested revisions of the Christian year, see the article "Solar and Sacred Seasons" in the Appendix.

The First Week in Pentecost, Year A, is on p. 94, after the *Alphabytes*.

Year A	Pentecost Sunday *See facing page*	Monday-to-Saturday Readings	Trinity Sunday *See facing page*	Monday-to-Saturday Readings
2008	May 11	1st of 3 Extra Weeks See Sixth Wk in Epiphany	May 18	2nd of 3 Extra Weeks See Seventh Wk in Epiphany
			Sun after Trinity, May 25	3rd of 3 Extra Weeks See Eighth Wk in Epiphany
2011	June 12	Third Week in Pentecost	June 19	Fourth Week in Pentecost
2014	June 8	Second Week in Pentecost	June 15	Third Week in Pentecost
2017*	June 4	First Week in Pentecost	June 11	Second Week in Pentecost
2020	May 31	First Week in Pentecost	June 7	Second Week in Pentecost
2023*	May 28	1 Extra Week No Mon-Fri Readings Torah Reading for Jun 03: #35C	June 4	First Week in Pentecost
2026	May 24	1 Extra Week See Eighth Wk in Epiphany	May 31	First Week in Pentecost
2029	May 20	1st of 2 Extra Weeks See Seventh Wk in Epiphany	May 27	2nd of 2 Extra Weeks See Eighth Wk in Epiphany
2032	June 9	1st of 2 Extra Weeks See Seventh Wk in Epiphany	June 16	2nd of 2 Extra Weeks See Eighth Wk in Epiphany
2035	May 13	1st of 3 Extra Weeks See Sixth Wk in Epiphany	May 20	2nd of 3 Extra Weeks See Seventh Wk in Epiphany
			Sun after Trinity, May 27	3rd of 3 Extra Weeks See Eighth Wk in Epiphany
2038	June 13	Third Week in Pentecost	June 20	Fourth Week in Pentecost
2041	June 9	Second Week in Pentecost	June 16	Third Week in Pentecost

*Years that have fifty-three weeks in the Christian Year.

Pentecost Sunday   *Spirit-Water*   **John 7:37–39**

**Let the one who believes in me drink. As the scripture has said,
"Out of the believer's heart shall flow rivers of living water." v. 38**

In seasons of drought, there are strict limits on the use of water. Even then, extreme scarcity of water in affluent countries is non-existent. This is not the case for the Middle East in ancient times. For the Hebrew people, water was a blessing from God, especially manifest during the years of wandering in the desert when miracle-water from the rock flowed.

The great autumn festival of Tabernacles celebrates all these years of wandering. On the last day of this feast, the priest would walk about the altar with water freshly drawn. Today rabbis pray for rain at the close of this festival.

Picture the Temple with Jesus standing amid the crowd as the ritual of water takes place. He has overturned the money tables in chapter 2 at the Passover Festival. Now he breaks in upon the singing crowd with the ear-piercing cry of today's verse. Let it break open the rock of your heart, letting Spirit-water flow.

Trinity Sunday   *Three as One*   **Matthew 28:16–20**

**Go therefore and make disciples of all nations, baptizing them in the name
of the Father and of the Son and of the Holy Spirit. v. 19**

Though the persons of the Trinity never act alone, their separateness does suggest modes in the life of grace that honor each person of the Trinity in a special manner. *Advent to Epiphany* stirs within us a longing for God as Creator and Father to intervene in an unjust and sinful world. God does this: Jesus, Messiah and Son of God is born. The season of *Lent and Easter* focuses upon the saving acts of Jesus in his life, death, and resurrection. This third season is dedicated to the Holy Spirit, taking its name from the festival linked to the Spirit—*Pentecost*.

The church in the west has been celebrating Trinity Sunday on the Sunday after Pentecost since 1334. We gather the movement of God over the previous seasons, into a single contemplation of the wholeness of God. You do the same today.

Alphabytes

Pentecost: *A–M*

The First Week in Pentecost

Depending on how late Easter is, this week and the next
may "leap back" to the end of the season of Epiphany.

*A*rc

Two points inseparably distant embrace in the union of a fire leap.
Standing rigidly apart, creative kinship bonds the two,
    eternally made to face each other.
There is the Father, there is the Son and the leaping love between them:
    the Holy Spirit.
There is God, there is you, and the Spirit-arc of fire across the gap.
There is the Bible soaked in sacred speaking;
    there is your ear soaked in sacred silence,
And the Word becomes flesh in yours through the leaping joy of the Holy Spirit.

Pause to poise before you listen.
Ready yourself to hear the ageless Word become the now-Word for you—
    just for you—as though yours is the only face
    that stands before the face of God.

The Second Week in Pentecost

*B*each Ball

Airless, flat, dusty, hidden, the plastic wrinkled mass made it through
    the cold of winter and the hope of spring.
Now breath makes it rise to global fullness, barely touching the earth and water,
    dancing freely in the kindred air that puffs about it.
Down it plunges as children play and push it beneath the surf,
    pressing upward as though gasping for the very air of which it's made,
    joyous in its upward surge as at last the children yield the hold and let it go.

Energies from within the soul seek to make their way above,
    pushed relentlessly to drowning depths.
Call these energies by basic, beach ball names:
    ANGER, FEAR, SADNESS, JOY, LOVE.
Get out of their way till they rise and dance about
    on the sacred waters of your soul.

The Third Week in Pentecost
*C*lock

As old as my memory, the face of a family clock turns toward mine.
In steady, relentless rhythm, the hands weave and wave the minutes
    in the space of each hour.

The clock rests beside the person of the hour with whom I seek to pastor,
    to listen and share the Word of life.
The face of the other one changes often—brows bent in resentment,
    arched in fear, bowed in weeping, uplifted in joy.
So many changes beside that other changeless face that simply and silently points
    to the moment in the hour's space of feeling's shift.

Wisdom comes again:
A moment's intensity is never greater
than the flow of time. "This too shall pass."

The Fourth Week in Pentecost
*D*rink

It's summer and everything is drinking in liquid life all about.
Rounded glasses filled with pleasure or poison, punctuate patios of restful ease.

Your soul too—from what does it drink to quench its endless thirst?
Wells of living water lie silently beneath Bible pages.
Pick up and drink.
Sip slowly and sigh your YES to all that wants to flow into your soul,
    until it—as the water-well itself—is nothing but the Lord's liquid life.

The Fifth Week in Pentecost
*E*yes

Signs that say, "DO NOT TOUCH" adorn the shops of delicate figures.
So let it be for the thoughts and things of the soul.
Look at, but do not touch—or much less handle or wrestle—
    those thoughts from darkness and death that thrash about from within,
    seeking to have you grasp at them till they topple you and hold you
    to the ground, refusing to let go.
Give them—without touching them—to the Lord of all thoughts.

What about those thoughts that lead toward light and life?
Receive them, treasure them, and hold them gently in open hands.
Watch the Spirit weave them into creations of delight before your very eyes.
Then, you will not have to touch them, for they will be one with your hands
    that touch others till they quiver with life.

The Sixth Week in Pentecost
*F*irestarter

A block of burnable bits, pressed tight, lodged among logs,
    willing to burn and disappear, as long as logs linger with fire …

Clear the space of the hearth of the heart.
Allow your breathing to become quiet, deep, regular, rhythmic—
    each exhale as a sacred sigh that sweeps the self
    of all the ashes of yesterday's pain, of any concern other than
    the one that is about to happen: you becoming the Word.

The minute's meditation presenting the Word
    furthers the mellowing of the heart, moving it to readiness
    to receive the fire of the Spirit to burn on,
    just as the bush that lit and warmed the heart of father Moses forever.

The Seventh Week in Pentecost
*G*ears

He was a brave man who took me on in my later years to learn the guitar.
The music in my spirit grabbed all at once at the fingers, making them spasm
    in tightenings and loosenings.
With an accent from Italy, tinged with impatience he blurted:
    "You've got to practice slowly. The movements of the hand
    are as many tiny gears that must meet and mesh perfectly
    so the music's whole can happen."

Magnify the gaze at the many movements of your heart's hands
    that freeze in fear, or ring with rage.
Look at your frenzied heart through the glass of God's Word
    till you can see in large space, just how to move.
Then, with joyful ease, your soul will sing the music that magnifies the Lord.

The Eighth Week in Pentecost
*H*urricane

Islands where hurricanes abound are so often those of the poor.
Theirs are not storm-proof homes.
When the great winds come, the door in the front and the door in the back
    must be open to welcome the unfriendly guest, and show him the way out.
The alternative? A sure explosion from within.

So too with the humble house of the soul.
When the winds of arrogance, judgment, hatred, guilt and shame
    threaten to blow the self away, be sure that the door in the front
    and the door in the back are open wide, letting all the angry winds
    pass straight through, till the gentle winds of the Spirit return
    and breathe softly across your soul.

The Ninth Week in Pentecost
*I*nk

Wood-pounded, mashed, soaked, dried, is what you hold right now—
    paper made white to bear pen's piercing mark.
Body—pounded, mashed, soaked, open, is Jesus on that wooden death—
    heart pierced to open the sacred flow.

Ink—it means to burn.
Old burnt offerings are no longer needed; only the heart aflame will do for God.
Take the open, white space that waits to serve you.
Pause, pen poised for the promptings of God, calling you to be poet and prophet
    faithful to the peace the Spirit gives.
Let the Spirit shape the fingers as you watch and see the Word become flesh,
    burning the paper—burning the heart.

The Tenth Week in Pentecost
*J*uggling

I never was very good at baseball.
That is why I loved that day on the beach many years ago,
    when my body arched above in motion slow,
    to catch the friendly Frisbee saucer.
I thought that this must be a game for heaven.
I once saw someone juggle ten of these, flinging them into the upper air
    of the circus tent, easily, quietly receiving and dispatching each
    as they playfully returned to the hand that made sure
    they would be borne on air again.
What patience, what falls, what discouragement must have been
    in the life of that artist till he could fling those airy discs
    as easily as breathing in and out!

So much comes your way to juggle; you know the list.
Practice slowly, a few at a time, till many plots and peoples
    and places can revolve about your life, while you watch it all,
    just as the folks in the bleachers do … and the Lord of heaven and earth.

The Eleventh Week in Pentecost
*K*nots

None was better than Dad at casting a four-ounce weight into the sea,
    sinking and searching for a catch.
Before I got the knack, the knot came—huge … endless …
    making the smoothly spinning reel an inert mass of mess,
    slowly to be unwound, unpuzzled so that the flow could happen again.
Like a faithful pet, Dad's pole would patiently wait beside him,
    as he turned his eyes from the preferred outward, seaward,
    longing look, to the close search for the answer, so I could cast again.

Backlashes, they're called—life spinning too fast
   for gentle control and directing movement.
Look at the spool of life with its minutes and hours that unroll for you.
How does it feel—this reel?
Wait … watch … letting your Father take your life into his lap, teaching you
   how to unravel the knots, so you can cast out into the deep again.

The Twelfth Week in Pentecost

*L*oops

Look long at the looping of life.
Far and wide it swings out, seeking a point of return to stop,
   to gather, to nourish, to let go, to forgive, and with love's energy,
   to move out wider yet.

Where are the points of return, of pause for your spirit?
Daily let the Word connection be one of those places
   that makes crosses on the face of life.
Let Jesus set fire to that place of intersection, igniting your heart again
   launching it into the wide expanse, going freely and joyfully.
That still point will return when rest for the soul will be offered,
   only to gather yet wider loops into the harvest of love that is your life.

The Thirteenth Week in Pentecost
*M*etal Detector

As though itself coming to the end of a long day in the sun,
   summer is almost past.
Sands have been pounded, dug, thrown and mixed with many a treasure.
Now is the time for the gentle detective dancers,
   armed with Geiger's divining rod, to sweep across the gridded expanse,
   eager to catch the beeps of beach buried treasures longing to be lifted,
   though hopeless to be returned to the ones who grieve their loss.

Silently buried beneath Bible print lie the treasures of the Word of life,
   waiting, hoping that you will make the sweeping dance across its lines,
   resurrecting their life in the flesh of the heart.
Sounds of recognition, delight, hope, and strength leap from page to heart.
Note the place.
Catch the treasure lying there, just for you, waiting since the first writing
   to have you receive it, so that its revelation power can live in you—
   and through you, can touch the heart of the next person longing to believe.

The First Week in Pentecost

Begins on the Sunday nearest June 1, unless the Easter Season is still in effect. Alphabyte: Arc, p. 77

Sunday   *The House on Hard Rock*   **Matthew 7:21–39**

**Everyone who hears these words of mine and does not act on them will be
like a foolish man who built his house on sand. v. 26**

An admonition and an image conclude "The Sermon on the Mount." Jesus warns about commitment to God with one's mouth only, and not with a life of obedience to God's word. Such response does not place us in God's "radar." "I never knew you" (v. 23). The image of two houses is then held before us—one built on sand, the other on rock. Similar to the admonition of speaking and not doing, the image is a warning about hearing and not doing the teachings of Jesus.

The shifting sands of our own will cause our houses to fall. The regular focus of the daily Word of life put into action will assure a steady, sturdy house that will not collapse. Obedience is the cement that turns sand into a hard rock foundation for your inner house.

What is the verse or phrase from today's and every day's reading that summons your life to one of obedient discipleship?

Monday   *Resistance to Grace*   **Isaiah 13**

**I will punish the world for its evil, and the wicked for their iniquity;
I will put an end to the pride of the arrogant, and lay low the insolence of tyrants. v. 11**

The Holy Spirit intervenes on behalf of the earth in an immense fullness. Still, individuals, cities, and even nations are free to resist this move of God upon them, but not without eventual consequences.

Just as Sodom and Gomorrah were symbols of absolute evil in the Second Millennium B.C. in the age of the Patriarchs, so is Babylon an image of evil in the beginning of the Seventh Century, B.C. In the Book of Revelation, John uses Babylon as a type of Rome and all the evils that ensued when the emperor made himself into a god.

Continued resistance to God demands justice. Mondays of summer this year will be sobering reminders of this. Do not be frightened. Now is the moment to receive the rush of God's love into your heart. Say a more complete YES.

Tuesday   *Counterpoint*   **Proverbs 13**

**The appetite of the lazy craves, and gets nothing,
while the appetite of the diligent is richly supplied. v. 4**

Each day of your life in God flows into the next, in counterpoint—the name given in music to independent melodies moving together in harmony.

Today's litany of proverbs develops inward, personal reflections in counterpoint to yesterday's sobering passage from Isaiah. The Sunday-to-Friday readings in the one hundred and fifty-six weeks in the three-year cycle are stitched together into themes set against each other in counterpoint. Though the Sabbath *Torah* readings thread their way through the year according to lunar and not solar cycles, still basic areas of the *Torah* are wedded to the rest of the week, making a rich variety of God's Word against which your life itself is in counterpoint.

Each proverb is set in twofold counterpoint movements. Feel this music of the Spirit, either challenging you to change, or soothing your soul, according to your need.

Wednesday   *No More Suffering Alone*   **Psalm 22**
My God, my God, why have you forsaken me?
Why are you so far from helping me, from the words of my groaning? v. 1

Return to the cross and hear the anguished cry of Jesus as he begins to pray this psalm. The price of the outpoured Spirit was the blood and water from Jesus' side.

Your most desperate cry of suffering is nevermore a cry alone. The Spirit of God weeps within you, groaning your prayer even before it enters your mind. Verse after verse pours out the anguish of a God who experiences your pain, giving images and names to it. The psalm recalls the pain of Job from Lent—this time prayed by the Son of God who draws your prayer to saving completion in the Holy Spirit.

In verse 21, there is a profound shift in awareness. God has in fact not forsaken David, Jesus, and you, but has answered. Waves of confidence and joy rush into the soul as immense hope returns.

Some themes in music must be exhausted, before others come.

Thursday   *Soaked in the Spirit*   **Romans 1**
For I am not ashamed of the gospel; it is the power of God for salvation
to everyone who has faith, to the Jew first and also to the Greek. v. 16

Summer Thursdays this year are immersed in the waters of the Spirit found in this letter of Paul to the church at Rome. The time of the year of fullness finds us pondering the thought of Paul in all its maturity. The letter is acclaimed to be the greatest exposition of Christian doctrine ever written.

The Roman Christians are waiting to meet Paul in person; you meet him as well. Yet deeper than seeing his face, is knowing his heart. The letter is filled with teachings about the Holy Spirit. Before reading, pray that the same Spirit who inspired Paul will be with you now.

The mercy of God lasts longer than God's justice, as expressed in Monday's passage from Isaiah. The New Testament soaks the First Covenant in waters of the Spirit, transforming judgment into mercy.

You will encounter verses that speak of the morality of homosexuality. Bear in mind that Paul does not understand this apart from the context of his letter—total godlessness, with a litany of vices that flow from those who disdain God.

1
Pe
A

Friday   *The Fire of Healing Love*   **Matthew 8**
To the centurion Jesus said, "Go; let it be done for you according to your faith."
And the servant was healed in that hour. v. 13

Action follows thought, as we come down the mountain after pondering "The Sermon on the Mount." There at the foot of the mountain is one of the rejects from Jewish society—a leper. Rather than keeping his distance, Jesus approaches and does the unthinkable: he touches him. As sparks leap from one pole to another, so do the hands of Jesus ignite the fire of healing love in those desperately bound by sickness in one form or another.

Wonder at the healings in this chapter. Reflect upon the demands of discipleship. Jesus has authority over the winds and the seas, yet the power over your own heart the Lord reserves until you surrender all to him. Therefore, do it now and live every hour of this and every day in God.

Saturday   **The Sabbath Torah Reading**

Jun 07, 2008 #35A	Jun 10, 2017 #36A	Jun 06, 2026 #36A	Jun 09, 2035 #35A
Mar 05, 2011 #23A	Jun 06, 2020 #35A	Jun 09, 2029 #37A	Mar 06. 2038 #23A
Mar 08, 2014 #24A	Jun 10, 2023 #36A	Jun 05, 2032 #37A	Mar 09, 2041 #23A

The Second Week in Pentecost
Begins on the Sunday nearest June 8. Alphabyte: Beach Ball, p. 77

Sunday   *The Breeze of Eternal Life*   **Matt. 9:9–13; 18–26**
Those who are well have no need of a physician, but those who are sick. v. 12

Three persons find themselves in Jesus' presence—a tax collector, a bleeding woman and a dead girl. The Lord invites the first one to follow him. Like the abandoned nets of the three disciples, Peter, James, and John, Matthew drops the nets binding him to the unholy task of exacting taxes for Rome. The woman pursues Jesus, bound by a severe hemorrhage threatening her life. If only she can touch the hem of Jesus' cloak, she will be healed. Finally, there is the young girl bound by death.

Relate with all three. Are you in a work that binds you? Are you bleeding emotionally? Is there a little child within you that has died? As a beach ball pressed beneath the surface of the water, so are each of the three until the touch of Jesus releases them to rise to the surface of the saving waters, dancing with joy and freedom in the breeze of eternal life that blows across their faces.

Monday   *My Will or God's?*   **Isaiah 14**
For the Lord of hosts has planned, and who will annul it?
His hand is stretched out, and who will turn it back? v. 27

The three examples of salvation in yesterday's reading are contrasted with three doomed to destruction. Babylon, Assyria, and Philistia are singled out for their unique arrogance toward God that results in their downfall.

The outcome of these three countries is the result of what Mary sings in the Magnificat: "He has put down the mighty from their thrones, and exalted the lowly" (Luke 1:52). Again with the image of the beach ball pressed down for later release, the pride that seeks to puff itself up before others, actually results in their being pressed down to death.

In this context, the fall of Lucifer is described. Tradition has linked him to Satan. Ponder the five arrogant assertions in verses 13 and 14 that begin with the words "I will." The one whose name means "light-bearer" is plummeted into darkness.

Which is it for you—your will or God's?

Tuesday   *Refreshing Pauses*   **Proverbs 14**
The perverse get what their ways deserve, and the good,
what their deeds deserve. v. 14

Each proverb contrasts the positive and negative examples of the first two days of this week. The opening verse is a rare proverb about the feminine. As you pray through each of the thirty-five proverbs, weigh each of their sides in the hands of your heart, as though tossing a beach ball back and forth from one hand to another. Read the proverbs slowly, pausing where you find yourself released upward by the wisdom that sets you free.

Can you put your own names to the classes and categories listed in the proverbs? Do not judge, but rather discern the people, places, and things in your life that are concrete examples of the types in the proverbs.

Write out your favorites. Place them nearby where you bump into them throughout the day for refreshing pauses. What can you do to be creative with these wise sayings that have come down to us from almost three millennia?

Wednesday   *A Beloved Psalm*   **Psalm 23**

He restores my soul. He leads me in right paths for his name's sake. v. 3

This favorite psalm of countless persons over the ages is yours today. Millions know it from memory. If you need to refresh your memory, the task will be as sweet as the psalm itself if you link the images together. Be as the sheep in the first four verses. Sense the sequence of resting and movement. The word for comfort in verse 4 is *nacham*, making a sound, just as it does—the deep sighs of those receiving comfort, as well as those giving it.

Verse 5 shifts to the image of an army arrayed for battle. Victory is so assured by the Lord that the troops sit down to a banquet as the enemy looks on. The anointing for spiritual warfare takes place. The sixth and last verse combines the image of movement with rest again. Notice how right living causes goodness and mercy to pursue David.

Move through this prayer and you will be dwelling in the house of the Lord today, looking forward to forever.

Thursday   *Admonition*   **Romans 2:1—3:20**

Do you despise the riches of his kindness and forbearance and patience?
Do you not realize that God's kindness is meant to lead you to repentance? v. 4

As though admonishing his readers down through the ages to resist the temptation to point fingers after reading chapter 1, Paul begins chapter 2 with a sharp rebuke about judgment. You will need to read slowly to catch the argumentation of his thought about the law and its relation to Jew and Gentile. However, the basic thought is clear: we are to mind our own business and examine our own selves. God gives a conscience to each person, whether Jew or Gentile, as the means to come to a basic understanding and reception of God and God's ways.

Paul wants to loosen the Jewish Christians from any arrogance in their unique call through the ages. The heart needs to be circumcised—to respect and respond to God's presence that is offered to every person.

Where in your life do you feel admonished in this reading?

Friday   *Seven Appointments with Jesus*   **Matthew 9**

Ask the Lord of the harvest to send out laborers into his harvest. v. 38

The wider context for last Sunday's Gospel is before you. Jesus has returned to his home base, Capernaum. Beginning with the freeing of a paralytic, there are seven brief accounts, each no longer than eight verses. Four of these are healing stories, with remaining units reporting the call of Matthew, a comment by Jesus about fasting and the new wine, and a concluding statement about the profound compassion of Jesus.

You might divide the day and evening into seven parts, each one beginning with a meditation from this chapter. Among your appointments for the day, make seven brief ones with the Word of God. Surely even the busiest of days offers moments to read eight verses; it would only take a minute. If the Lord were to come up to you and ask, "May I have a minute of your time?" Would you deny him?

Saturday   **The Sabbath Torah Reading**

Jun 14, 2008 #36A	Jun 17, 2017 #37A	Jun 13, 2026 #37A	Jun 16, 2035 #36A
Mar 12, 2011 #24A	Jun 13, 2020 #36A	Jun 16, 2029 #38A	Mar 13, 2038 #24A
Jun 14, 2014 #37A	Jun 17, 2023 #37A	Jun 12, 2032 #38A	Jun 15, 2041 #36A

The Third Week in Pentecost
Begins on the Sunday nearest June 15. Alphabyte: Clock, p. 78

Sunday   *Radiating Outward*   **Matthew 9:35—10:8**

**When he saw the crowds, he had compassion for them,
because they were harassed and helpless, like sheep without a shepherd. 9:36**

The word in Greek for the pity and compassion of Jesus refers to a profound inner emotion. The root of the word is *splanchna*, the Greek for "bowels." From the tenderest feeling of love to the strongest outrage, the physical center of our bodies is the place from where deep feelings come.

Chapter 10 begins "The Missionary Discourse" of Jesus, the second of five major addresses in Matthew's Gospel. The twelve apostles are named and sent forth, even as the hands of a clock point to the twelve hours that radiate outward to mark the movement of the day and night.

Today when you look at a clock or watch with a face, be reminded that you are going forth to a day of loving compassion and healing with the same energy of Jesus.

Monday   *The Sounds of Suffering*   **Isaiah 15—16**

**Therefore my heart throbs like a harp for Moab,
and my very soul for Kir-heres. 16:11**

Moab was a son of Lot by his eldest daughter. As though continuing the perversity from which he was born, the Moabites were characterized by idolatry with all the sacrilegious behaviors that accompany false worship. Isaiah describes the outcome of their behavior in a manner in keeping with the very rebellion of this people against God. Listen for the sounds of suffering in the wailing and weeping that weave themselves throughout this reading.

From 16:8, summer is emptied of its fullness as invaders ravage the land of Moab. Unrepented sin has its consequences. However, even for Moab, there is a remnant that will become seed for a new summer, even as from the seed of Ruth, the Moabitess of old, came Jesus. Jesus is relentless in compassion for those bound by sin. Stay close to the Lord today.

Tuesday   *The Spirit Moves Again*   **1 Samuel 1—2**

**Hannah prayed and said, "My heart exults in the Lord; my strength is exalted in my God.
My mouth derides my enemies, because I rejoice in my victory. 2:1**

If there were faces on clocks three millennia ago, countless would have been the turnings of their hands from one day to the next, from one year to the next without a clear word from the Lord God. Listen to the sounds of sadness of Hannah. Eli the priest thought she was drunk. Her grief contrasts with the joy of the outpoured Spirit at Pentecost. The disciples were also thought to have been drunk!

The Holy Spirit of God is about to move again. We begin with God's unique intervention through Samuel. The story of the birth and dedication of this pure and gentle boy will be a joy for you. Watch for similarities with Jesus. Mary's *Magnificat* that we sang six months ago in Advent, is the echo of one of its sources in the song of Hannah, mother of Samuel.

The purity and wickedness that are to come are set against each other in the opening chapters of this great book. Where do you find yourself in these contrasts?

| Wednesday | *Empty Hands and Heart* | Psalm 24 |

**Lift up your heads, O gates! and be lifted up,
O ancient doors! that the King of glory may come in. vv. 7 & 9**

The gates of heaven—picture them in your faith-filled imagination. The heaven you hope to enter after death has its gate here on earth.

Heaven can be now! Enter into that heavenly space at this moment. The Psalm does give you some prerequisites—"clean hands and a pure heart." Come empty-handed and empty-hearted into the presence of the Lord who will fill your hands with spirit-riches, and your heart with spirit-love. Keep the focus upon the majesty of the Lord this Pentecost season.

Jesus' hands and heart were opened for you on the cross and are open now as your resurrection-refuge in the Spirit. Be aware of the majesty of God today as you open the door of your heart to God.

| Thursday | *Gratuity of God's Grace* | Romans 3:21—4:25 |

**Do you despise the riches of his kindness and forbearance and patience?
Do you not realize that God's kindness is meant to lead you to repentance? 3:22**

Law and grace, faith and works, human righteousness and Jesus' justification: Paul holds these polar opposites before the face of the Roman recipients of this letter. He goes beneath the level of debate, linking the apparent newness of his teaching about the law of faith with the prototype of all faith—Abraham. Citing Genesis 15:6, Paul grounds his case upon the righteousness of Abraham in his faith.

May the energy of Paul's teaching bring you beyond and beneath mental understanding of his thought, to a spiritual grasp of this teaching. It is not what you do that brings salvation, but rather your surrender by faith to the One who saved us through the blood of the cross.

Here is the essence of our joy—the gratuity of God's grace.

| Friday | *Ready for Transformation?* | Matthew 10 |

**As you enter the house, greet it. If the house is worthy, let your peace
come upon it; but if it is not worthy, let your peace return to you. v. 12–13**

Gather with the Twelve and listen to Jesus tell them and you about how to go about spreading God's Good News.

The reception of God's peace, which each household must have, begins with you. Wait before you begin to read. Silence descends, giving a wide setting for whatever distracting thoughts may be buzzing in your head. Give them attention for a moment, but only long enough for you to collect them and turn them over to the Lord. Do not suppress distractions; give them a way out and a direction into God.

The thought of Jesus is not complicated here; however, be ready to be transformed by grace.

Saturday   **The Sabbath Torah Reading**

Jun 21, 2008 #37A	Jun 24, 2017 #38A	Jun 20, 2026 #38A	Jun 23, 2035 #37A
Jun 18, 2011 #37A	Jun 20, 2020 #37A	Jun 23, 2029 #39A	Jun 19, 2038 #37A
Jun 21, 2014 #38A	Jun 24, 2023 #38A	Jun 19, 2032 #39A	Jun 22, 2041 #37A

3
Pe
A

The Fourth Week in Pentecost

Begins on the Sunday nearest June 22. Alphabyte: Drink, p. 78

Sunday   *All Fear Is Gone*   **Matthew 10:24–39**
Do not fear those who kill the body but cannot kill the soul;
rather fear him who can destroy both soul and body in hell. v. 28

I hope you are finding vacation space from the year's work. The Spirit will speak to your heart before you return to the challenges to come, as you spend quiet time with the Lord.

The message of grace today intends to take fear away. Widen you faith-awareness of being one with Jesus; this will help flush out fear. The One within you is stronger than the negative forces without that may be pressing against you. St. John and St. Paul express it this way: "The Spirit who lives in you is greater than the spirit who lives in the world" (1 John 4:4). "I am convinced that nothing can ever separate us from his love" (Rom. 8:38). How would you express this conviction in your own words?

Monday   *Focus Upon God*   **Isaiah 17—18**
The nations roar like the roaring of many waters, but he will rebuke them,
and they will flee far away, chased like chaff on the mountains before
the wind and whirling dust before the storm. 17:13

Nations that have risen against Judea and Jerusalem are marked for destruction. Those bent on defying God are doomed. They will not harvest the rich fruits resting in ripeness in the field, but rather the beasts of the field and the birds of the air will do the gathering. So says the master of the harvest who rests in the heat of the summer sun.

I wonder if John the Baptist had 17:13 in mind when he preached the way clear for Jesus in Matthew 3:12—the chaff blown to oblivion by the wind. Efforts in your life will be similarly scattered if there lacks a clear, fundamental purpose and call in your life.

Ask the Lord to gather your energies according to God's plan. What does the final verse mean for you as you place your life and will into God hands?

Tuesday   *Someone Who Listens*   **1 Samuel 3—4**
Now the Lord came and stood there, calling as before, "Samuel! Samuel!"
And Samuel said, "Speak, for your servant is listening." 3:10

At last, God found someone who will listen! The story of Samuel's call and first prophecy is one mixed with as much charm and purity as it is with expressions of dire consequences to Eli and his family. Eli was a priest set aside to listen, but he refused. He was deaf to the warning about his sons who likely started out simply as spoiled children, but wound up in brazen wickedness.

So careful was Samuel to listen to God that no word of God fell worthless to the ground. In their own way, Samuel's words were as the sparrow of last Sunday's Gospel that does not fall to the ground apart from God's will.

Let your words flow carefully from your mouth, so that none of them will be worthless—or those you wish you had recalled!

Wednesday	*Your Closest Friend*	Psalm 25

The friendship of the Lord is for those who fear him,
and he makes his covenant known to them. v. 14

Imagine you are at a great reunion. Almost everyone has arrived, including some you would rather not see. However, there is only one person that you *really* want to embrace. All your attention is on the loved one for whom you are waiting. Then the arrival—full joy, total attention, everything and everybody else recedes into the background.

That is how the psalmist is today. Waiting for the Lord and union with God are all that matters. The psalm breathes the air of expectancy and hope as the writer waits for God to intervene against all that is pressing upon him. Each verse blends with the next one, expressing growing intimacy with God.

Pray this psalm often in the course of your day as you take breaks to be with your closest friend who is also your God.

Thursday	*Saving Grace*	Romans 5

God proves his love for us in that
while we still were sinners Christ died for us. v. 8

Chapter 5 is like the fifth gear in a standard shift car. The previous four chapters have gathered the momentum of the past, so that Paul can have us cruise into the present. The verses flow easily, each one with a potential to open your spirit more and more to the power of God to drive your life.

Rejoice to rediscover what God has done to restore us to friendship with God. Just as in the case of the Psalm yesterday, spend today being deeply aware that friendship in all its depths is what God is offering to you in Christ.

From verse 12, Paul develops a comparison to continue his thought, this time setting Adam and Christ before you. Pray these verses slowly until you experience by faith the power of God's grace to move you on the road of your life to its heavenly destination, empowered by the saving grace of God.

Friday	*Kingdom Boundary*	Matthew 11

Truly I tell you, among those born of women no one has arisen greater than John the Baptist;
yet the least in the kingdom of heaven is greater than he. v. 11

The dungeon of John the Baptist stinks with the stench of doubt. John is cut off from the evidence of Jesus' saving grace. Perhaps prisoners with him taunt him: "No big changes happening outside your cell." Now his voice cries in the wilderness of prison, "Are you really the Messiah we've been waiting for, or should we keep looking for someone else?" How the message from Jesus must have comforted him as a glass of cool, clear water to his parched spirit!

As great as is John, the least in the Kingdom is greater than he is. No matter what your circumstances, whether bound by the prison of doubt, or simply resting in the confines of your patio or summer garden—go deeper. There is within you an inner boundary of the Kingdom into which the Lord invites you to enter as his most intimate friend.

Saturday / The Sabbath Torah Reading

Jun 28, 2008 #38A	Jul 01, 2017 #39A	Jun 27, 2026 #39–40A	Jun 30, 2035 #38A
Jun 25, 2011 #38A	Jun 27, 2020 #38A	Jun 30, 2029 #40A	Jun 26, 2038 #38A
Jun 28, 2014 #39A	Jul 01, 2023 #39–40A	Jun 26, 2032 #40A	Jun 29, 2041 #38A

The Fifth Week in Pentecost
Begins on the Sunday nearest June 29. Alphabyte: Eyes, p. 78

Sunday   *Intense Identity*   **Matthew 10:40–42**
Whoever welcomes you welcomes me,
and whoever welcomes me welcomes the one who sent me. v. 40

Three verses ring out from countless churches across the globe concluding the "Missionary Discourse" of Jesus. The disciples rejoice to find the presence of Jesus filling them to such an extent that when people receive them, they receive Jesus. Dwell on the immensity and the intensity of the identity!

The Dutch priest Henri Nouwen said: "You find the God you want to give, in the person to whom you want to give him." This is the joy of ministry.

Look about your world. Observe without grabbing, as the *alphabyte* "Eyes" suggests. Be aware today of God's presence in your interactions with others. Even the simplest and the most mundane of these can be filled with divinity, if filled with faith and love.

Monday   *Hitting Bottom*   **Isaiah 19—20**
The Lord will strike Egypt, striking and healing; they will return to the Lord,
and he will listen to their supplications and heal them. 19: 22

The great stock market crash of 1929 provoked a variety of responses from people. Some jumped out of windows when financial disaster hit home; others found the Lord in a totally new way.

So it will be for Egypt. Isaiah foretells the total collapse of its economy. The Nile River will no longer bring life. There will literally be no more "stock" in its waters. Isaiah describes the devastation to come in detail. Suddenly in 19:18, there is a shift. Often when Isaiah uses the phrase "in that day," he is prophesying Messianic times. Egyptians will begin to speak Hebrew, the sacred language of Canaan. They will come to know the Lord and God's Word. Greater than the waters of the Nile will be the waters of the Torah that shall bring them life.

Do you bounce when you "hit bottom"? Living waters are ready to bubble up within you from the Spirit.

Tuesday   *God at Home in You*   **1 Samuel 5—7**
The cows went straight in the direction of Beth-shemesh along one highway,
lowing as they went; they turned neither to the right nor to the left,
and the lords of the Philistines went after them as far as the border of Beth-shemesh. 6:12

The Philistines have captured the Ark of the Covenant. It is as though they took God as a prisoner of war! Read what happens to their god, Dagon. Lesson: when we try to manipulate God into our own space, instead of surrendering into God's space, false treasures and "idols" will fall.

In the center of the reading, there is a tender and charming shift in tone and feeling you will not want to miss. Picture the cows drawing the wooden cart as they lead the Ark back to God's people. There is no human driver. Listen in the silence to the hobbling of the wheels and the mooing of the cows as slowly the Ark makes its way back home again to God's people.

What is God doing to bring the divine presence into your center? Are there any animals that come to mind that God is using for this?

| Wednesday | *The Gyroscope* | Psalm 26 |

My foot stands on level ground;
in the great congregation I will bless the Lord. v. 12

Here is the assurance of a person aware of his integrity. An examination of his conscience results in seeing himself apart from outright evildoers. Yet he is not boasting as the Pharisee in Luke 28:9; he hates hypocrites.

In keeping with the reading of yesterday, our psalmist goes to where God is, instead of taking God to where he is. He exults in being about the altar, expressing his love for worship.

The verse for the day is a way of life. Remain steadfast in faith as you walk in God's presence. Though evil press about you and seek to throw you off balance, pray this psalm and find God as your gyroscope. You can be at rest in the midst of the storm.

| Thursday | *Delivered from Death* | Romans 6—7 |

For I know that nothing good dwells within me, that is, in my flesh.
I can will what is right, but I cannot do it. 7:18

Paul returns to a thoughtful development of the doctrine of freedom by grace. More than understanding in the mind, there needs to be a sense in the heart of his thought. The key lies in acknowledging whether your life is bound by slavery to some sinfulness, or free because you are a slave to God. The quality of life is determined by the one to whom one is slave. Whom do you obey in your life?

Take comfort in identifying with Paul about the great challenge to live this doctrine. How candidly Paul confesses his weakness in the second half of chapter 7! Make a similar, fearless inventory of your life, praying over the passage. The cumulative effect of your reflection will bring you to the place where it brought Paul, as your spirit is released along with his in the final two verses.

| Friday | *The Will of the Father* | Matthew 12 |

For whoever does the will of my Father in heaven
is my brother and sister and mother. v. 50

The essences of all the readings of the week are found in today's Gospel. Jesus' image of the divided house recalls Isaiah's focus on the downfall of Egypt. The Ark of the Covenant of Tuesday's passage is recalled when Jesus tells the Pharisees that there is "one greater than the Temple" in their midst. Wednesday's psalm about worship balances Jesus' teaching about the divine preference for "mercy and not sacrifice." Paul's teaching about sin and grace forms a backdrop to the sin of blasphemy against the Spirit. This is to grieve the Holy Spirit so deeply by claiming that it is the devil at work in Jesus.

Think of it this way: when the cows led the Ark back among God's people, how would the Holy Spirit have felt if the people turned the cows around, to walk back down the road again?

Saturday   The Sabbath Torah Reading

Jul 05, 2008 #39A	Jul 08, 2017 #40A	Jul 04, 2026 #41A	Jul 07, 2035 #39A
Jul 02, 2011 #39A	Jul 04, 2020 #39–40A	Jul 07, 2029 #41A	Jul 03, 2038 #39A
Jul 05, 2014 #40A	Jul 08, 2023 #41A	Jul 03, 2032 #41A	Jul 06, 2041 #39A

5
Pe
A

The Sixth Week in Pentecost

Begins on the Sunday nearest July 6. Alphabyte: Firestarter, p. 79

Sunday   *Power in the Present*   **Matthew 11:16–19; 25–30**

Come to me, all you that are weary and are carrying heavy burdens,
and I will give you rest. v. 28

At times, I hear a person say something like this: "I wonder what it would have been like to have actually been with Jesus when he walked this earth?" Today's Gospel is a sobering reminder of what happened to many who had this blessing. Moses was able to bring water from the rock at God's command; but even God cannot make the rock-hard soul of a person flow with living water, unless the person is willing.

You needn't prefer any other time or place than your *here* and your *now*. The fullness of God's power in the Holy Spirit is available to you at this very moment. Repent of hardness of heart toward any person, place, or thing. Be open to God's invitation to rest in him.

Take the final three verses and memorize them so that they will be the *Firestarter* in the center of the logs of your life, falling into place to light your fire.

Monday   *The Release of Fear*   **Isaiah 21**

Therefore my loins are filled with anguish; pangs have seized me,
like the pangs of a woman in labor; I am bowed down so that I cannot hear,
I am dismayed so that I cannot see. v. 3

Isaiah envisions the fall of Babylon, the city called "The Wilderness of the Sea." In 703 B.C., Sennacherib of Assyria takes the city. Isaiah experiences within, the terror of Jerusalem as the thought, "You're next" brings pain to God's people as of a woman in labor.

Is there anyone or any circumstance coming against you that is frightening you? Isaiah describes the crippling power of fear. Just as he identifies with the fear of Jerusalem, so can this chapter serve to have the fears in your life come to the surface so that you can face them, releasing them to the Lord who has ultimate power against all the "bullies" in your life.

Are there persons in your life who are being frightened? Perhaps the Lord will have you intercede for them by experiencing their fear, just as Isaiah stands in for Jerusalem and its terror, until God's saving power enters in.

Tuesday   *The New King*   **1 Samuel 8—10**

Then the spirit of the Lord will possess you, and you will be in a prophetic frenzy
along with them and be turned into a different person. 10:6

The kingship has very shaking beginnings. Due to the corruption of the sons of Samuel appointed by their father to be judges over Israel, God moves to "Plan B." The original plan had God alone as king. However, in the face of the desire of the Israelites to be like all the other nations, God complies with the people's wishes.

Chapter 10 cites the first use of oil to anoint a king, previously used only for the sanctuary and for priests. Saul receives the inrush of the Spirit and begins to prophesy. He is indeed transformed, but not enough; watch for a stronghold of sin that remains which becomes tragedy as the rest of the book unfolds.

The final verse of the reading touches on the evil of jealousy. The question of the rebels. It is like how like the question Satan must have asked when he looked ahead to Jesus. Is there prideful questioning going on in your life?

Wednesday *Light and Salvation* **Psalm 27**
The Lord is my light and my salvation; whom shall I fear?
The Lord is the stronghold of my life; of whom shall I be afraid? v. 1

The psalmist stitches together a variety of pleas flowing from a heart intimate with God. The opening twofold question loosens you to respond in abandoned prayer.

The psalm is one of my favorites; may it bring you comfort. There is joy in every verse moving from the images of security and protection from the Lord. The psalm will remind you of Psalm 23 as David experiences confidence in the presence of enemies, and the joy of dwelling in the house of the Lord.

In *The Bible Through the Seasons* Wednesdays are usually days when the readings are shorter. Spend time reading and re-reading the psalms. Review previous days' readings, or catch up, if you want.

Just as Wednesday is the link between the first and second parts of the week, so do the psalms bond Jewish, Christian as well as Muslim Scriptures.

Thursday *Fire in Four-Quarter Time* **Romans 8**
If the Spirit of him who raised Jesus from the dead dwells in you,
he who raised Christ from the dead will give life to your mortal bodies also
through his Spirit that dwells in you. v. 11

One of the most powerful chapters in the whole Bible is before you. We peer into the depths of Paul's heart and mind as we consider the essence of what it means to live a life in the Spirit.

This chapter forms a centerpiece to the whole letter to the Romans, coming in the middle of this season dedicated to the Holy Spirit. It is the *Firestarter* that has Paul burn on and on with his passion for the Spirit. Pray that the same Spirit that burned in Paul will burn in you. You will encounter very profound thought. Ask the Lord to give you a spirit of deep understanding as you embrace the truths that are laid forth here.

You may find it helpful to take the four quarter parts of the day, devoting these four parts of the chapter to each one: verses 1–8, 9–17, 18–30, 31–39. It will be "Fire in Four-quarter Time"!

Friday *Throwing Your Way* **Matthew 13**
Truly I tell you, many prophets and righteous people longed to see what you see,
but did not see it, and to hear what you hear, but did not hear it. v. 17

Parable: here is a word associated with Jesus, almost as much as the word *Gospel*. Today begins "The Sermon of Parables," the third of five major discourses in the Gospel of Matthew. Envisioning Jesus as the new Moses, Matthew parallels the first five books of the Bible, the Torah.

Parallel and *parable*: the words are related through the common Greek prefix *para* meaning "alongside." Parallel lines are those that move alongside each other at the same distance, uniting only in infinity. The third syllable in the word parable means, "to throw." A parable is an image that is "thrown alongside" some aspect of the Good News, so that we can see grace reflected in the image.

Remember the list of seven parables in this chapter. Be alert today for other parables that the Spirit will throw your way, as the Spirit within your heart teaches you about the mysteries of the Kingdom of God.

Saturday **The Sabbath Torah Reading**

Jul 12, 2008 #40A	Jul 15, 2017 #41A	Jul 11, 2026 #42–43A	Jul 14, 2035 #40A
Jul 09, 2011 #40A	Jul 11, 2020 #41A	Jul 14, 2029 #42–43A	Jul 10, 2038 #40A
Jul 12, 2014 #41A	Jul 15, 2023 #42–43A	Jul 10, 2032 #42–43A	Jul 13, 2041 #40A

The Seventh Week in Pentecost

Begins on the Sunday nearest July 13. Alphabyte: Gears, p. 79

Sunday   *Silence and the Seed*   **Matthew 13:1–9; 18–23**
Let anyone with ears listen! v. 9

Silence: the word comes from the ancestral root *si*, meaning "to rest," "to let the hand fall." Our word *seed* is sister to *silence*. The falling seed from the hand of the sower becomes an image that Jesus uses in "The Sermon of Parables."

For the next three Sundays, the seven images that Jesus uses to describe the Kingdom are set forth in meditative detail. The *alphabyte* "Gears" for this week suggests a slowing down of life to magnify the movements of God in you. Receive these parables and other images God will be sending your way into the silence of your being.

Silence embraces every word of Jesus. May this minute meditation with you here, be as a seed dropping into the some one thousand minutes of your waking day, so that your day may bear fruit.

Monday   *Groaning and Grieving*   **Isaiah 22**
**I will place on his shoulder the key of the house of David; he shall open,
and no one shall shut; he shall shut, and no one shall open. v. 22**

Reckless abandon to one's own methods and disdain for God's help guarantee a headlong descent to destruction. Hezekiah's tunnel is a parable of the ways in which our own plans, apart from God, push us to where we alone want to go. We can be like Balaam who refused to listen to his donkey block his path to evil in Numbers 22. The world adopts v. 13 as its "Verse for the day."

The siege of Jerusalem in 701 B.C. anticipates the future destruction of Jerusalem and the Temple over a hundred years later in 589. The Book of Lamentations echoes the sounds of grief.

The messianic figure of Eliakim comes as a ray of divine energy. John uses the verse for the day as the power of the risen Christ in the Book of Revelation 3:17.

Groan and grieve freely as the Spirit moves.

Tuesday   *Like Samuel or Saul*   **1 Samuel 11—13**
**Moreover as for me, far be it from me that I should sin against the Lord by ceasing to pray for you;
and I will instruct you in the good and the right way. 12:23**

As gears out of sync in a machine, so are Saul and the Israelites. Decisions are made apart from prayer; rather they are impetuous reactions, prompted by fear, power and pride.

Alone among them completely doing the Lord's will, is Samuel. Listen to him once again say to the people as he said to God as a boy, "Here I am" (12:3). His transparency to God makes him able to be used by God. Nothing is between him and his Lord. He lives uncontaminated by the evils that enter and gradually push their way deeper and deeper into Saul, disconnecting his heart from the Lord. Samuel, on the other hand, always holds God's people in prayer.

Discern those inner movements that make for oneness with the Lord and those that disrupt and break away from God. As you listen to the promptings of the Spirit, are you like Samuel or Saul?

Wednesday　　　　　　　　　*Mounting Confidence*　　　　　　　　　**Psalm 28**

The Lord is my strength and my shield; in him my heart trusts; so I am helped,
and my heart exults, and with my song I give thanks to him. v. 7

Contrasted with Saul and yesterday's reading, here is David and his psalm—the prayer of one whose heart is one with God. The very outpouring of his heart in anguished prayer lubricates the "gears" of his inner being. His spirit loosens; deeper and wider expanse of joyous expression flows from verse 6 to the end. David knows it is God, not he, who will avenge enemies and shepherd his people. Breathe with relief and confidence as the prayer rises to the concluding verse.

Return to this psalm often today, especially when temptations press you to regain control of things, disqualifying you from making this prayer as sincere and open as David. Watch how you are vulnerable to temptations of this kind; thus, you will know to what precise inner places you need to ask the Spirit to direct laser-beams of healing love.

Thursday　　　　　　　　　*Living with Questions*　　　　　　　　　**Romans 9**

But who indeed are you, a human being, to argue with God?
Will what is molded say to the one who molds it, "Why have you made me like this?" v. 20

The self-effacement of Paul is starkly described in the opening verses. Imagine willing to be cursed and separated from Christ, if it meant the salvation of Paul's beloved Jewish people! Samuel, David and Paul, and of course Jesus, stand before you this week as those willing to live and die that others might have life.

The questions posed in verses 20 and 21 are designed to have the image of the potter and the clay shift us away from Job-like questions that nag at us. There is yet another question that the clay could ask the pot with equal silence in response: "Why did you make me at all?"

Why were *you* conceived and the born on the day of your birth, and not someone else? No answer to that question … Neither are there answers to many others. Live with these questions and adore the Lord who made you.

7
Pe
A

Friday　　　　　　　　　*Miracles Birthed in Silence*　　　　　　　　　**Matthew 14**

After he had dismissed the crowds, he went up the mountain by himself to pray.
When evening came, he was there alone. v. 23

How would you feel if your cousin was beheaded and the head placed on a platter for public ridicule? The death of John the Baptist must have affected Jesus in a similar way. He seeks solitude in a silent place … no such thing. The crowds are so excited about Jesus and the miracles that they track him down by the thousands.

The chapter is marked with strong changes. The multiplication of the five loaves and the two fish deeply moves the crowd, not to mention the disciples. I remember a retreat director during my seminary years suggesting that while the disciples were gathering the leftovers into the twelve baskets, they instigated the crowd, starting the chant: "Make him king! Make him king!" Jesus would have none of it. He dismisses the crowd and sends the disciples into a boat. Jesus seeks quiet, this time on a mountain. Then see what happens!

Expect silence to birth your miracle as you seek solitude and surrender to Jesus.

Saturday　　　　　　　　　　　　　　　　　**The Sabbath Torah Reading**

Jul 19, 2008 #41A	Jul 22, 2017 #42–43A	Jul 18, 2026 #44A	Jul 21, 2035 #41A
Jul 16, 2011 #41A	Jul 18, 2020 #42–43A	Jul 21, 2029 #44A	Jul 17, 2038 #41A
Jul 19, 2014 #421A	Jul 22, 2023 #44A	Jul 17, 2032 #44A	Jul 20, 2041 #41A

The Eighth Week in Pentecost

Begins on the Sunday nearest July 20. Alphabyte: Hurricane, p. 79

Sunday   *Wheat for the Bread*   **Matthew 13:24–30; 36–43**

Let both of them grow together until the harvest; and at harvest time I will tell the reapers,
"Collect the weeds first and bind them in bundles to be burned,
but gather the wheat into my barn." v. 30

There is a basic point in "The Parable of the Wheat and the Tares." It is difficult to distinguish between weeds and wheat. Lest there be any wheat killed by "friendly fire," Jesus invites us to hold back. Discernment about good and evil is a gift we need from the Spirit; yet Jesus admonishes us not to judge. There is a time and place for judgment and for the eternal separation of the good from the bad, but it is not now, and it is not for us to judge; this is reserved for God at the end of time.

There is still time for you and me! This suggests another interpretation: "tare-like" qualities in a person can be transformed into wheat! Yet another point of the parable: it discourages living in someone else's head, instead of in your own. Self-examination, rather than the examination of others, is what will have what is "tare-ible" in you, become wheat for Christ's bread.

Monday   *Swept Away by Pride*   **Isaiah 23**

The Lord of hosts has planned it—to defile the pride of all glory,
to shame all the honored of the earth. v. 9

Isaiah's list of cities proclaimed for downfall concludes with the cities of Tyre and Sidon, merchant centers for ancient Phoenicia. This country, to which we owe the alphabet, becomes bound in persistent pride and arrogance in their worship of false gods. It will mean their destruction.

Pride is at the head of all sin—a deadly hurricane that sweeps destruction in its path. Continue the self-examination suggested in yesterday's approach to "The Parable of the Wheat and the Tares." Allow the power of the Holy Spirit to sweep through you and make your house clean with the strong winds of the Spirit.

Is worship and dedication to God and God's will absolutely at the center of your inner house? If it is not, your house is one built on the fickle, shifting sands of the world; the winds will blow it away.

Tuesday   *A Shift in God's Plan*   **1 Samuel 14—16**

So Saul said to his servants, "Provide for me someone who can play well,
and bring him to me." 16:7

Samuel recedes to the background while the exploits of Saul and Jonathan against the enemies of God's people come to the fore. The rash oath that Saul inflicts upon his people and his hoarding of the spoils of war instead of dedicating them to the Lord, prompts God to intervene again in the night to Samuel. Contrasted with the first nightly visit of the Lord to Samuel as a boy, this encounter brings anguish to the heart of Samuel and to God; God repents of having chosen Saul to be King. Listen in on the words of Samuel to Saul in 15:22–23; they are addressed to you and to me.

As the peace that comes out after a hurricane, so is chapter 16 with the beginning of the story of David. Samuel must have found some of that early joy as a boy return, as he sees God doing something similar to David as was done to him many years before. Return in prayer to the times when God spoke to your heart when you were a child.

Wednesday   *Split by Flames of Fire*   **Psalm 29**
The voice of the Lord flashes forth flames of fire. v. 7

The awesome presence and power of God in strong weather moves David in this psalm. You might ask yourself, "If God already possesses glory and strength, what does it mean for us to *give* God these attributes?"

The answer lies in the intimacy between God and creature. God receives expressions of glory and strength through God's people. The creature participates not only in receiving the Creator's life and its power, but also in returning it to God through worship and offering of self.

Jewish people pray this psalm on the festival of Pentecost. Likely, St. Luke had this psalm in mind and this Jewish celebration when he describes the coming of the Holy Spirit in the image of today's verse.

An earthquake can split great cedars down the middle. The images of the psalm will split your heart apart by flames of inner fire.

Thursday   *Winds of the Spirit*   **Romans 10**
So faith comes from what is heard,
and what is heard comes through the word of Christ. v. 17

As a mighty wind, the Spirit rushes into the house of the First Testament giving new and exciting meaning to familiar passages. Paul weaves quotations from the Hebrew Scriptures into twelve of the twenty-one verses of this chapter. The newness and freshness of Paul's thought is launched from the foundation in the First Testament. The Holy Spirit quickens these words with fresh, profound meaning.

The weeks of the three-year cycle consist of a stitching of passages from both Covenants. These readings are wedded together for the regular return of the week every three years. Look for common threads that bind these readings together. Look back over previous days as you move through the week to discover their unity. Link the readings with each week's *Alphabyte* as well—the *Hurricane* being the mighty wind of the Spirit that rushes into your inner house!

Friday   *Blows of Truth*   **Matthew 15**
It is not what goes into the mouth that defiles a person,
but it is what comes out of the mouth that defiles. v. 11

Two kinds of persons are before us today. The first are blind nit-pickers who see only what they want to see—Jesus violating some laws. The second is a foreign woman who also sees only what she wants to see—a daughter healed. Listen to Jesus respond to each of them. The first group is the Pharisees and scribes; Jesus angrily confronts them with truths that go far deeper than external regulations. Jesus does a kind of spiritual karate, seeking to chop through the resistance with blows of truth. He praises her for pursuing what she wants, after passing a test in humility as Jesus pretends to put her off.

Find yourself in these two episodes. Is there anything that Jesus is telling you about what you are seeing, and what you refuse to see? Take to the heart the teaching of Jesus about what makes for a defiled life.

Saturday   The Sabbath Torah Reading

Jul 26, 2008 #42A	Jul 29, 2017 #44A	Jul 25, 2026 #45A	Jul 28, 2035 #42A
Jul 23, 2011 #42A	Jul 25, 2020 #44A	Jul 28, 2029 #45A	Jul 24, 2038 #42A
Jul 26, 2014 #43A	Jul 29, 2023 #45A	Jul 24, 2032 #45A	Jul 27, 2041 #42–43A

The Ninth Week in Pentecost

Begins on the Sunday nearest July 27. Alphabyte: Ink, p. 80

Sunday   *Fire-Seeds*   Matt. 13:31–33; 44–52

**The kingdom of heaven is like treasure hidden in a field, which someone found and hid;
then in his joy he goes and sells all that he has and buys that field. v. 44**

Jesus presents five images as ways to understand the Kingdom of Heaven. All of them, especially the first four, have something in common. What is it? A hint: *Firestarters* might be included in the list.

The first two illustrations are similar: something small becomes big over time. The flowers that are delighting your summer were once seeds in the ground. Each day they were stitched from within until their leaves and petals played in the sun. The persistence of planted seeds has something to do with the Kingdom of Heaven: it grows inside of you.

The time you spend with the Word each day is as a fire-seed for what can grow within you during the day, then day after day, until your whole life is bathed in the awareness that God is reigning, protecting, covering, and directing your life. What other words and images can you discover to express what the Kingdom means to you?

Monday   *Creative Burning*   Lamentations 1—2

**Is it nothing to you, all you who pass by?
Look and see if there is any sorrow like my sorrow, which was brought upon me,
which the Lord inflicted on the day of his fierce anger. 1:12**

On or about this time, Jewish people grieve over the destruction of two Temples. The first is the one Solomon dedicated in 959 B.C., destroyed on the 9th day of the month of *Ab*, July 18, 587 B.C. The other Temple is the one rebuilt after the Exile, which the Romans destroyed in 70 A.D. The synagogue readings are from the Book of Lamentations, attributed to Jeremiah.

The verses of the first four chapters of the book are an acrostic, similar to some psalms. Each verse begins with the next letter of the Hebrew alphabet—every three verses, for chapter 3.

Ink: the word means "to burn." The Spirit transforms the burning fires of overwhelming grief into a precious book of the Bible. Will you allow the Spirit to burn creatively inside of you as you face great losses in your life?

Apply the verse for the day to the sufferings of Jesus—then and now.

Tuesday   *Two Giants*   1 Samuel 17—19

**The Lord does not save by sword and spear;
for the battle is the Lord's and he will give you into our hand." 17:47**

Fear shakes the hands and hearts of the Israelites as they learn about Goliath, the great giant of their Philistine enemy. He eclipses God's presence to the people, but not for David. Confidently aware of the presence of his God, far greater than the power of any giant, David stalks closer to his enemy. A tiny stone hurled with focus is enough to make the giant drop—how like the mustard seed of last Sunday's parable!

If fear overwhelms God's people, another destructive emotion, once small, now a "giant," burns away in the heart of King Saul—jealousy. The Philistines are a relatively easy match for David; however, now he spends much of his time hiding from Saul as this wicked king pursues God's anointed, instead of God's enemies.

"Religious" people often chew each other up by jealousy and still another giant—gossip! Reflect upon the many lessons that these chapters can stir within you.

Wednesday	*Dancing in the Morning*	Psalm 30

For his anger is but for a moment; his favor is for a lifetime.
Weeping may linger for the night, but joy comes with the morning. v. 5

Place the grief over the loss of the Temple in the Book of Lamentations against this song attributed to David at the dedication of the Temple. Sadness and joy are set against each other in this psalm, with its message of ultimate joy for those who trust in the Lord. Surely, this prayer comes from David's recollection of the triumph over Goliath, and the sadness of Saul's destructive jealousy.

Whatever emotions you are experiencing as you come to this psalm, they are all present as a collage of verses. Link up with the ones that are taking place as you begin to read, allowing the Spirit to transform all your feelings into an immense joy in God's presence.

The Hebrew word for "joy" in verse 11 is *rinnah*, meaning a joy that is so strong that it sends the person into a whirling dance. The Lord wants to give you joy—intense, explosive, dance-like, and expanding. Get ready: this kind of joy can come for you, even when you get up in the morning!

Thursday	*Pro-Semitism*	Romans 11

The gifts and the calling of God are irrevocable. v. 29

Imagine a child disinterested in the gift of a toy. The parent says, "Well, if you don't want it, I'll give it to the child down the street who will *love* to have it." Sometimes this causes a fresh interest in the toy. Verse 11 is Paul's way of saying something similar with respect to the Jews; he hopes that a holy jealousy might quicken desires in them to embrace the Good News.

If only this chapter were carefully meditated upon, the ages-long, "anti" in semitism might have been changed to "pro." Instead, the child down the street who receives the unwanted gift comes back to bully and taunt the child who originally received it.

Do not boast about the gifts God has given you. Rather humbly and fully receive them. Allow your expressions of wonder and praise for God to increase until your whole being is living the final verse of the reading.

Friday	*The Leaven of Pride*	Matthew 16

Jesus told his disciples, "If any want to become my followers,
let them deny themselves and take up their cross and follow me. v. 24

Leaven is an image Jesus uses with both positive and negative meanings. Last Sunday we listened to leaven as an image of the Kingdom growing within a person. Here, the leaven is that of the Pharisees and Sadducees—pride and ambition. Repent if you find these vices in you.

Peter receives the gift of knowing who Jesus is. From yesterday's reading, God is to receive the glory for the gift. Yet Peter seems to take the gift in a prideful manner, presuming to question Jesus in the first prediction that Jesus was going to suffer and die. Similar to the challenge to Peter about having his feet washed at the Last Supper, the name that Peter has just been given, "Rock," is quickly changed to "Satan" in the hopes that Peter will be shaken into belief and obedience.

Are you impetuous as Peter, quick to take in the leaven of pride?

Saturday · The Sabbath Torah Reading

Aug 02, 2008 #43A	Aug 05, 2017 #45A	Aug 01, 2026 #46A	Aug 04, 2035 #43A
Jul 30, 2011 #43A	Aug 01, 2020 #45A	Aug 04, 2029 #46A	Jul 31, 2038 #43A
Aug 02, 2014 #44A	Aug 05, 2023 #46A	Jul 31, 2032 #46A	Aug 03, 2041 #44A

The Tenth Week in Pentecost
Begins on the Sunday nearest August 3. Alphabyte: Juggling, p. 80

Sunday   *Juggling God's Gifts*   **Matthew 14:13–21**
Jesus said to them, "They need not go away;
you give them something to eat." v. 16

The gruesome death of John the Baptist urges Jesus to seek solitude. However, crowds track Jesus down, interrupting the gift of spending time alone. Compassion for the crowd shifts Jesus' awareness from grief over the death of his beloved cousin. The multiplied loaves and fish prefigure another miracle related to his own death—Holy Communion.

The miracle of the loaves and fish does not occur without the cooperation of the disciples: "You feed them," commands Jesus.

Do the needs of others—and sometimes their unreasonable claims upon you—seem so hard to juggle? Slow things up, through prayer and contemplation. Spend time alone with your Lord; God will teach you how to have your few gifts pass through the Lord's hands into yours for multiplied cycles of flight to heaven.

Monday   *Loosened by Repentance*   **Isaiah 24**
Then the moon will be abashed, and the sun ashamed;
for the Lord of hosts will reign on Mount Zion and in Jerusalem,
and before his elders he will manifest his glory. v. 23

There need be no fear as you read these chapters, referred to as "Isaiah's Apocalypse." It is not "Apocalypse Now," but "Apocalypse When." In figurative, rather than literal language, Isaiah prophesies that God will come against unrepented evil.

But for now, God's mercy is in full measure. God wants you to put an end to unrepented sin in your life, lest such sin put an end to you!

Isaiah wants the power of the images to make deep impressions upon you. There can be much denial in how sin gets to us. Isaiah's poetry can loosen the hold that any sin has upon you. Do not get stuck in guilt; guilt is a gridlock that freezes movement into the eternal life that can be yours now.

The chapter sounds like the reversal of the power of God in the creation account in Genesis. The truth is that unrelenting, unrepented sin destroys the beauty of God's creation. However, there is still time! Be loosened by the sweet joy of repentance.

Tuesday   *Always in God's Presence*   **1 Samuel 20—22**
Jonathan made David swear again by his love for him;
for he loved him as he loved his own life. 20:17

Saul's jealousy mounts to blind fury as he recklessly seeks to kill David. How similar it would in for the blind pride and jealousy of the Pharisees seeking to kill Jesus, son of David, a thousand years later!

In David's desperate need for food, he partakes of the Bread of the Presence. The three synoptic evangelists tell of Jesus' reference to this incident as an example of how sacred regulations yield to human need (Mt 12:3,4; Mk 2:25,26; Lk 6:3,4). Though David flees from Saul, David is ever in the Lord's presence.

Amid the tide of Saul's hatred, which mounts to a massacre of priests, there flows the sweetness of profound friendship between Jonathan and David. Cherish such gifts of friendship in your life. Covenant with such a friend to share the daily scriptures—a spiritual accountability that will give energy for you to walk always in God's presence.

Wednesday   *Rock of Safety*   **Psalm 31**
Into your hand I commit my spirit;
you have redeemed me, O Lord, faithful God. v. 5

Ingredients of David's pain flow out from him with abandon, mingling with verses that celebrate the comfort he finds in the Lord's protection. Be aware of the intimacy that David has with God—the tenderness in his pleas that need to sweeten your own petitions in prayer.

The verse for the day was on the lips of Jesus and Stephen at the moment of their deaths (Luke 23:46; Acts 7:59). From verse 9, there comes a series of statements that can be applied to the most abject of society through your intercessory prayer.

The Lord as a rock of safety is the first of the images of protection David uses. Find others with which your soul especially relates, writing them down on post-it notes to stick in places where you can see them in the course of the day. These will be places to rest on the rock of safety, which is the Lord.

Thursday   *Exhortations*   **Romans 12—13**
Owe no one anything, except to love one another;
for the one who loves another has fulfilled the law. 13:8

The final chapters of Paul's letter shift from teaching to exhortation. Make a list of the imperatives that he uses to encourage his beloved Roman Christians to grow in their commitment to Christ.

The essence of Jewish worship was animal sacrifice. Paul takes this concept and urges his listeners to have their bodies become a "living sacrifice."

Similar to his thought in 1 Corinthians 12, Paul reminds his people that their oneness in the body of Christ means that they belong to one another. It is Paul's way of stating a truth found in the very beginning of the Bible about Cain and Abel: you are your brother's keeper. Spiritual gifts unique to each person are described just as Paul did in that same chapter of 1 Corinthians.

When you conclude the reading, rest … wait … write what further exhortations the Spirit may be expressing from deep within.

10 Pe A

Friday   *Tabernacles Unmade*   **Matthew 17:1–13**
Peter said to Jesus, "Lord, it is good for us to be here; if you wish,
I will make three dwellings here, one for you, one for Moses, and one for Elijah." v. 4

Jesus invites Peter, James, and John to pray with him in the Agony in the Garden. That moment brought drowsiness upon them as great as was the suffering of Jesus. Likely it was Jesus' intent to take these special three apostles and prepare them for his approaching death, by giving them an anticipation of the glory to come. The Transfiguration prefigures the resurrection. Here on the last Sunday in Epiphany we glimpse at glory before the season of Lent begins. Take your place beside the apostles as they look at the other three—Jesus, Moses, and Elijah.

A thought to ponder: two of the three great Jewish festivals find Christian fulfillment in the Trinity. Passover is fulfilled in the resurrection of the Son; Pentecost is completed in the coming of the Spirit; Tabernacles … no Christian counterpart for the Father's plan. Given the divisions that exist among religions, we are a long way from one tabernacle of peace, tolerance, and worship of the one God in whom we claim to believe.

Saturday		**The Sabbath Torah Reading**	
Aug 09, 2008 #44A	Aug 12, 2017 #46A	Aug 08, 2026 #47A	Aug 11, 2035 #44A
Aug 06, 2011 #44A	Aug 08, 2020 #46A	Aug 11, 2029 #47A	Aug 07, 2038 #44A
Aug 09, 2014 #45A	Aug 12, 2023 #47A	Aug 07, 2032 #47A	Aug 10, 2041 #45A

The Eleventh Week in Pentecost

Begins on the Sunday nearest August 10. Alphabyte: Knots, p. 80

Sunday   *The Sea of Faith*   **Matthew 14:22–33**

**Jesus immediately reached out his hand and caught him, saying to him,
"You of little faith, why did you doubt?" v. 31**

The chaos of water is subject to the command of God. It must obey the limits assigned to it by its Creator. Thus, it was in the beginning when God rolled back the seas and the dry land appeared (Gen. 1:9–10). Again, water bowed to the rainbow covenant of God when the ark finally rested on the mountaintop. The Chosen People later walked through the Red Sea on dry ground. Jesus shares power over water with the first of his friends: Peter walks upon the impossible—water … but only for a while.

What is missing is *consistent* and not merely *impulsive* faith. A block of fear comes between the eyes of Peter and those of Jesus, when Peter looks down and sees water below his feet. Peter's dread is similar to that which will take hold of him when the servant girl in the courtyard outside of Jesus' trial will shake Peter's heart into denying that he ever knew Jesus.

What has you turn your eyes away from Jesus and sink? Cast your cares and your self into the sea of faith. Jesus takes hold of your hand.

Monday   *Praise and Promise*   **Isaiah 25**

**He will swallow up death forever. Then the Lord God will wipe away the tears
from all faces, and the disgrace of his people he will take away from all the earth,
for the Lord has spoken. v. 8**

Ten weeks of readings predicting destruction for godless, nasty nations, yield to three weeks of exuberant release of praise and promise. Get in touch with the aftermath of the downfall of cities that have made themselves into gods. Now God's reign covers the face of the earth. Find your joy in the expressions of God's protection of the poor and needy. Recall the calming of the storm of yesterday's reading as images of God's protection fill verses 4 and 5.

Isaiah joins John and Paul as two verses are lifted into the New Testament. Revelation 19:9 finds inspiration in verse 6; Revelation 21: 4 and 1 Corinthians 1:59 are inspired by verse 8.

Pray for nations that continue to rule apart from an awareness of God's presence, lest destruction happen for them, just as for those ruthless, ancient nations.

Are there any inner storms or knotted emotions in you that need quiet space for unraveling?

Tuesday   *React or Enact?*   **1 Samuel 23—25**

**"The Lord forbid that I should do this thing to my lord, the Lord's anointed,
to raise my hand against him; for he is the Lord's anointed." 24:6**

Monstrous jealousy drives Saul, while quiet, inner direction from God guides David. Even when he is enraged by the wicked Nabal and wants revenge, there is a space inside David that listens to the touching intervention of Nabal's wife, Abigail that frees David to be open to God's plan.

Here and again in next week's reading is the principle David invokes for resisting the urge to kill Saul before David himself is killed. David invites us to look beyond the personal character of religious leaders, and respect those whom God has anointed for spiritual leadership, even when they are hardly acting in accord with the anointing. They need more prayer so that they remain faithful.

There are divine principles shining through these chapters as expressed by David and Abigail. How would you put them in your own words as the Spirit prompts?

**11
Pe
A**

Wednesday   *A Hiding Place in God*   **Psalm 32**

You are a hiding place for me; you preserve me from trouble;
you surround me with glad cries of deliverance. v. 7

Today's psalm comes as a joyful release for David, a prayerful commentary after the episodes in yesterday's reading.

Verse 3 expresses the freeing power of confessed sin. Is there some sin that you are allowing guilt or shame to prevent you from confessing? Find out what it is, and confess it to God and to a person that you trust. In so doing, the place within ceases to be a dungeon where you are held hostage by guilt or shame; instead you are transported into God's secret hiding place within God's own heart. Confession will shift you from the self-absorption of guilt and shame, into a divine awareness of God's enduring and unconditional love.

Ask God to enable you to discern the moods that have been affecting you at this time in your life—even right now as you begin to pray. Be careful of getting stuck and stubborn by sulking. This psalm will inspire you to let go of all that garbage!

Thursday   *Live and Let Live*   **Romans 14**

If we live, we live to the Lord, and if we die, we die to the Lord; so then,
whether we live or whether we die, we are the Lord's. v. 8

John Wesley summarized the opening verses by stating: "In essentials, unity; in non-essentials, liberty; in all things, charity."

The idea of one day being holier than another comes from a deeply subjective, yet real feeling. Each day has a sense about it. I hope that you will grow in a unique and holy feeling about each day of the week, due to the associations that all seven days of the week have with parts of the Bible.

As Paul develops his line of thought, be aware of those verses that especially summarize him. You will discover basic principles of human freedom and edification of your neighbor as guides for you, not only in living your own life, but also in allowing others to live theirs.

Examine yourself: do you do anything that stops the free flow of your brother or your sister's life from flying freely into the depths of God?

Friday   *Three Responses*   **Matthew 17:14–27**

For truly I tell you, if you have faith the size of a mustard seed,
you will say to this mountain, "Move from here to there," and it will move;
and nothing will be impossible for you. v. 20

The night of the Last Supper, Jesus says through the Gospel of John, "Anyone who believes in me will do the same works I have done, and even greater works, because I am going to be with the Father." Apparently, the resurrection community around St. Matthew needed to hear the rebuke of Jesus about their lack of faith, the same condition placed at the beginning of the verse from St. John. Some manuscripts add verse 21 with Jesus saying, "But this kind of demon won't leave unless you have prayed and fasted."

Faith, prayer, fasting: the first is a gift; the next two are disciplines that loosen the way for the healing power of Christ. While there is mystery in how some people are healed and some are not, be sure there are positive check marks on the list of these three spiritual responses in your life.

Yesterday's teaching of Paul about one's behavior not being a stumbling block for another is exactly held by Jesus in verse 27.

Saturday   **The Sabbath Torah Reading**

Aug 16, 2008 #45A	Aug 19, 2017 #47A	Aug 15, 2026 #48A	Aug 18, 2035 #45A
Aug 13, 2011 #45A	Aug 15, 2020 #47A	Aug 18, 2029 #48A	Aug 14, 2038 #45A
Aug 16, 2014 #46A	Aug 19, 2023 #48A	Aug 14, 2032 #48A	Aug 17, 2041 #46A

The Twelfth Week in Pentecost

Begins on the Sunday nearest August 17. Alphabyte: Loops, p. 81

Sunday *Pressing for the Miracle* **Matthew 15:21–28**

Jesus answered her, "Woman, great is your faith! Let it be done for you as you wish."
And her daughter was healed instantly. v. 28

Perhaps Jesus has been looking for that time apart which he never was able to find, due to the pressure of the crowds to hear him, and the scribes and Pharisees to reject him. Jesus goes to the northern seacoast around Tyre and Sidon as a place of retreat by the sea. His reputation has gone before him. A pagan woman approaches Jesus and beseeches him to heal her daughter. Was the reason for his harsh response to the woman because Jesus did not want to give up on God's chosen people? She refuses to take his remark personally, but rather presses on. She keeps to her purpose in coming to Jesus—to have her daughter healed. Jesus' response to her faith brings joy to his heart, and healing to her daughter.

Is there anyone or anything distracting you from a relentless pursuit of your heart's deepest desires in life? Does fear, pride, or lack of faith prevent you from pressing on for your miracle?

Monday *Pause for Personal Pouring* **Isaiah 26**

Those of steadfast mind you keep in peace—
in peace because they trust in you. v. 3

Isaiah rests from the intensity of previous prophecies. With the freshness and intimate approach of David, Isaiah pours at this chapter of personal expression. Just as the points of energy described in the week's *Alphabyte*, "Loops," so does Isaiah pause in the forward movement of speaking to the people on behalf of God, now speaking to God on behalf of the people, and simply, on behalf of himself.

Take your cue from Isaiah and allow him to be a "firestarter" for your own moment of prayer—a resting in the forward movement of your life to catch the upward surge of expression that the Spirit is stirring within you. As you find yourself awakened spiritually by special verses, go further in your expression and tell the Lord just how it is with you. Note the particular verse or verses that have started your fire. May the intimacy that Isaiah has with God be yours today.

Tuesday *Saul and Judas—David and Peter* **1 Samuel 26—28**

As your life was precious today in my sight, so may my life be precious in the sight of the Lord,
and may he rescue me from all tribulation. 26:24

Once again, David restrains himself from killing Saul. Today's verse is a foretaste of the Lord's Prayer: "Forgive us our trespasses as we forgive those who trespass against us."

Saul has lost all contact with his Lord, focusing obsessively on David, instead of a passionate centering upon God. In his desperate attempt to establish contact with the spiritual world, he sinks into the forbidden practice of seeking help from a medium. Samuel indeed comes forward by the power of God, much to the fright of the medium.

David too seeks allies in the enemy, instead of in the Lord. In his impetuosity, he is like Peter, as Saul is like Judas. Sense the difference between the two—the *hope* in David, the *despair* in Saul.

When God is silent, go deeper within, not searching outside of God for cheap answers. Accept no substitutes!

Wednesday   *Return to Basics*   **Psalm 33**

Let your steadfast love, O Lord, be upon us, even as we hope in you. v. 22

Everyday reading of God's Word offers you rest from outer activity and commitment, so that you can gather energy from your commitment to what is inward. A psalm in the middle of the work-week provides this moment of rest in a special way. Pause to look around you at a world that hastens to fulfill its own will, instead of God's will. The world needs intercession; the Psalms are perfect for that.

Notice what the psalmist does today for his "coffee break." Quickly and easily, he gets in touch with a contemplation of the whole world, catching the awesome power of Godly awareness, as did the writer of the opening chapters of Genesis. This pause for refreshment has the psalmist return to what is most basic in his life. May the psalm lift you to the same perspective and call forth new songs from your heart.

Thursday   *Encouraging Words*   **Romans 15**

**For whatever was written in former days was written for our instruction,
so that by steadfastness and by the encouragement of the scriptures
we might have hope. v. 4**

As happened in last Monday's reading from Isaiah when we caught the spirit of the prophet, so also today, the essence of Paul shines forth. Extravagant in his travels to begin churches where no one else has ever been, he yet finds time to pause, to write, to share with the Romans a letter that would come to be in your hands across the millennia.

Let yourself be encouraged along with his first readers. He quotes verses from the Torah, the Psalms, and Isaiah that express the point he makes in the verse for the day. Do with Paul's letter what he does with the Hebrew Scriptures; find verses in this chapter that quicken you to all the joy of being called to intimacy with Christ in the Spirit.

Paul asks for prayers. We might forget that he, just as Jesus in his agony, needed the prayer of his disciples. Be open for the Spirit to bring to your mind those spiritual leaders who need your prayers.

**12
Pe
A**

Friday   *Only Children May Enter*   **Matthew 18:1–20**

**Truly I tell you, unless you change and become like children,
you will never enter the kingdom of heaven. v. 3**

Over the gates of the Kingdom is this sign: "Only Children May Enter." Read this familiar passage expanding its meaning in your imagination.

First, remove some negative associations with children. They can be cruel. There are many times when peers pick on, ridicule, and shun innocent children. However, this generally happens as a reaction to some grave dysfunction in family and society. There are many adults who are candidates for that millstone to be hung around their necks and cast into the sea, because of scandal to children.

On the positive side, children are needy and dependent. When they are safe and loved, they naturally tend to radiate love in return, as well as spontaneity, trust, hope, and wonder.

Be as a child whose joy in life bursts as a response to divine love welling up from the center of your heart.

Saturday   **The Sabbath Torah Reading**

Aug 23, 2008 #46A	Aug 26, 2017 #48A	Aug 22, 2026 #49A	Aug 25, 2035 #46A
Aug 20, 2011 #46A	Aug 22, 2020 #48A	Aug 25, 2029 #49A	Aug 21, 2038 #46A
Aug 23, 2014 #47A	Aug 26, 2023 #49A	Aug 21, 2032 #49A	Aug 24, 2041 #47A

The Thirteenth Week in Pentecost

Begins on the Sunday nearest August 24. Alphabyte: Metal Detector, p. 81

Sunday	*Faith Given Flesh*	Matthew 16:13–20

"Who do you say that I am?" v. 15

Jesus is in the northern part of Galilee in the ancient city of Caesarea Philippi. It lies spread out on a terrace 1,150 feet about sea level. To the northeast Mt. Hermon rises in splendor to 9,100 feet. To the south the fertile Jordan valley stretches. The city was a center of Greco-Roman Civilization, as well as a place associated with various Semitic deities. Picture the setting. Jesus stands against the background of ancient pagan gods—a fitting place for him to inquire of his disciples about who he is.

Peter answers with true, Spirit-filled spontaneity, not with his usual fleshly impulses. The Father through the Holy Spirit gives him revelation-knowledge about who Jesus is.

Be there. As you respond in faith to who Jesus is for you, know that it is the Spirit that makes faith have flesh in you.

Monday	*Restoration*	Isaiah 27

**On that day the Lord will thresh from the channel of the Euphrates
to the Wadi of Egypt, and you will be gathered one by one, O people of Israel. v. 12**

As we enter the final week of *Pentecost*, feel an inward lift in this glorious chapter of Isaiah. If you had a chance to have vacation by the sea, picture the vast expanse of ocean with all its mysterious depths as you hear about the end of ancient sea monsters—symbols of all the chaotic energies of water first subdued in the creation story in Genesis. God will triumph over all enemies. You can be part of that restored people of which Isaiah speaks. If your vacation has been to the mountains, let that place be a symbol of the spiritual mountain where the New Jerusalem rests.

With your spiritual "metal detector," scan the verses of this chapter of strength and renewal before the next section of Isaiah to come in *Kingdomtide*. There will be more challenges for you not to fall into the woes predicted for those who are obtuse to God.

Tuesday	*Victories and a Tragic End*	1 Samuel 29—31

**David was in great danger; for the people spoke of stoning him,
because all the people were bitter in spirit for their sons and daughters.
But David strengthened himself in the Lord his God. 30:6**

Again a comparison between Saul and Judas, David and Peter … David's seeking favor from the Philistines is over, similar to Peter wanting to be on the side of Jesus' adversaries in the courtyard with the servant girl. Both Saul and Judas ended their lives by committing suicide.

Peter and Judas both sinned. While Peter quickly repented, Judas sank deeper and deeper into guilt. David and Saul sinned, but David, like Peter, had a heart quick to return to God. Saul, on the other hand, went deeper into infidelity, and into that vice that ends so many relationships, and even lives—jealousy.

Here they are: the first and second kings of Israel. The stage is set for a long history of kings—most of them unfaithful as Saul, ending their lives in disgrace, just as he. Reflect upon yourself.

Wednesday *An Alphabyte of David* **Psalm 34**

The Lord is near to the brokenhearted, and saves the crushed in spirit. v. 18

Here is another Psalm among David's "alphabytes." Each of the twenty-two verses begins with successive letters of the Hebrew alphabet. What is more, we could single out every one of these verses as the verse for the day. Your spiritual "metal detector" will find gold in every one. The one selected here is the verse I often find on my lips as I seek to bring comfort to those in great suffering.

This is the psalm most often quoted in the New Testament. A familiarity with it over this center day of the last week of the season will show you why. It takes its place along with Isaiah, Paul, and Matthew, who are especially uplifting to the spirit. Linger on verse five at the end of the day, as it will link beautifully with the name Phoebe that Paul will mention in the last chapter in Romans.

Can you find words from A to Z that would summarize each verse?

Thursday *To God Be the Glory* **Romans 16**

**To the only wise God, through Jesus Christ,
to whom be the glory forever! Amen. v. 27**

This is the close to what is acclaimed as the greatest treatise on Christianity in the New Testament. You are reading what moved the "greats"—Martin Luther and John Wesley, just to name a few.

Most of the passage is Paul's commendation to those especially endeared to him. The woman's name, Phoebe, in verse 1, means "The Radiant One." By the way in which you are, you radiate or obscure the goodness and acceptance of God through yourself to others. Your radiance of God's unfailing love is what people need to find the peace for which they long. Recall verse 5 from Psalm 34 of yesterday.

The center of the chapter contains Paul's final appeal to unity. When you discuss issues, beware of self-interest, which fosters division.

As you see the setting sun on the day and the season, lift your voice in prayer and praise of God in the final verse of this great letter.

**13
Pe
A**

Friday *Fire in Forgiveness* **Matthew 18:21–35**

**Should you not have had mercy on your fellow slave,
as I had mercy on you? v. 33**

Parts of words have fire in them. The key to today's reading comes from the word "forgive." The word has the root, "give" and the prefix, "for." The prefix comes from the Latin *foris* meaning "outside." Those who speak Spanish will recognize the word *fuera*, which has the same meaning.

What does "forgive," mean? Simply this. Take the feelings of pain, resentment, frustration, sadness, fear, etc., which are associated with what someone did to you, and "give them outside yourself." This is a slightly more complicated way of saying, **"Let go."** It means that I will no longer allow the other to have power over me by the resentment that lingers all too long in my heart. In this sense, forgiveness has nothing to do with whether the other has apologized or not; that too makes my serenity depend upon the other. Forgiveness is up to you, prompted by the grace of God.

Saturday **The Sabbath Torah Reading**

Aug 30, 2008 #47A	Sep 02, 2017 #49A	Aug 29, 2026 #50A	Sep 01, 2035 #47A
Aug 27, 2011 #47A	Aug 29, 2020 #49A	Sep 01, 2029 #50A	Aug 28, 2038 #47A
Aug 30, 2014 #48A	Sep 02, 2023 #50A	Aug 28, 2032 #50A	Aug 31, 2041 #48A

The Cross at the beginning of the season of Kingdomtide for this year has been called the monogram of Christ. The first two letters of XPICTOC, form the Greek name for "Christ."

The letter *Chi* in Greek (Ch in English) has the form of a cross. On either side are the first and last letters of the Greek alphabet, Alpha and Omega. Jesus is the first and the last.

KINGDOMTIDE

AUTUMN

Northern Hemisphere

Year A
2008, 2011, 2014 …

Kingdomtide begins on the Sunday nearest August 31.
See the entire cycle of readings at a glance on page xxi.

Alphabytes

Kingdomtide: *N–Z*

The First Week in Kingdomtide

*N*ose

God looked upon a space of clay, reached forward, gathered it, caressed it,
　　shaped it into a mound of nose, then breathed into it and Adam was created.
So it was that the nose was the first part of Adam's anatomy.
Breath from inside God to inside the man came first—an air link that bonded
　　the two together ... essences blending—divine and human.
　　All of God's creation and the Creator too, are taken in and breathed forth
　　in gratitude and surrender.

Thus the first sense to be created was smell.
Smells restore to the origin of things:
　　familiar fragrances fly us back over time and space.
Past becomes present in an instant.
Autumn: season of fullness is season of remembrance.
Children leap to a new school grade. We take the cue and do the same.
Smell deeply.
Let life be restored by memories that though they hurt, can also heal.
Cycles of breath, fill and empty; cycles of life, empty and fill.

The Second Week in Kingdomtide

*O*ak

The voice of the year changes with each season:
　　SPRING: former dark and silent mornings now engraved by song of birds
　　　　from choir branches in the ever increasing light.
　　SUMMER: soothing swish of full-blown leaves in the breeze.
　　AUTUMN: rhythmic, crispy crunch of leaves as children march to school.
　　WINTER: whistle of wind as air skates between frozen branches.

All the sounds come from trees—faithful messengers of seasons' change.
Yet there is one more sound of autumn:
　　acorns from great oaks bouncing and pinging on sidewalks and streets.
Though most never wed to earth to rise again as another oak,
　　still are their gentle jolts as the Creator's knocking at soul's door,
　　that the Word not bounce off and die, but find entry
　　into moist hearts in any season,
　　there to bear fruit as Word becomes flesh in yours.

The Third Week in Kingdomtide

*P*encil

Hovering over the relentless movement of time from past to future
    is the point called NOW.
The goal: perfect at-one-ment with the now,
    as the contented feeling of being on a journey,
      enjoying the changing landscape, never preferring the scene just past,
      or impatient for the beauty to come.
Each moment of the journey is worthy to be journaled, drawn.
The secret: self suspended above the moment, like a pencil standing on its end,
    open palm pressing the eraser, balanced to support the hand.
A move away from the vertical … the hand falls.
When guilt and shame push from the present,
    when fear of future nudges from now,
    a fall takes place, a bruise on the spirit.
So take the now and sink into it:
              "The Point of Power Is the Present."

The Fourth Week in Kingdomtide

*Q*uilt

Calendar days are square
    so weeks and months and seasons can be stitched together.
Each day's portion of the quilt bears colors, feelings, revelations unique to each—
    none to be repeated.
Every minute and hour offer microscopic shafts of colors
    of their own to the great quilt.
Though shocking be the present moment's jolting news, stunning one to fear,
    time's flow stopping in the gaping of the mouth—still, the intensity
    of their colors soon find their place in the expanse of the season's larger quilt.

Live each day colored by the tapestry of God's Word weaving minutes and hours
    into a masterpiece of God's making.
No one can destroy what God intends to do. Trust God.
The quilt is in God's hands, though your fingers do the stitching.

The Fifth Week in Kingdomtide

*R*ainbow

Light and water meet, spreading the parents of all colors from earth's end to end.
God posts the promise to Noah in the sky again.
However, rainbows are rare.
We need regular mindings of God's delightful color presence.
Take the Bible and blend rainbow colors into it,
    each day's passage passing one color to the next.
Sunday: Gospel *GOLD*
Monday: Prophet *PURPLE*
Tuesday: Dark *BLUE* **of Old Testament Days**
Wednesday: Psalm's *GREEN* **Pastures**
Thursday: New Testament *ORANGE*
Friday: The *RED* **Blood of Christ's Gospel**
Saturday: Torah's Royal *BLUE*
Color your days with the feel of God's promise.

The Sixth Week in Kingdomtide

*S*treams

Down the sacred mountain peak of transfigured time,
    three streams have been flowing separately,
    now converging one upon another, meeting as they join the level earth
    in one great, sweet river of adoration:

Evangelical energy in God's total Word
Pentecostal power in the Spirit outpoured
Liturgical light in the dance of worship.

Drink from these three streams as they descend ever deeper into the earth,
    meeting the Living Water that gushes from beneath
    sending the streams mountain-high again—this time, together.

The Seventh Week in Kingdomtide

*T*rapeze

A short man walks meekly amid myriad faces.
He lifts himself above the crowd to a high trapeze where he can do
    what no one else can—three and a half times whirling from his swing
    into the arms of his brother who receives him
    till they perch on the platform on the other side.
The crowd beneath watches with breath suspended as he spins,

like a machine's gear gone wild in disconnected flight
till it stops with perfect engagement in the cog of the brother gear.
What grace, practice, trust and risk go into these gasping seconds of life!
Arms stretch out to let go and receive.
What will be, is grasped only by letting go of what was.

Be as this artist.
Stand with hands outstretched to your brother Jesus
    whose arms are cross-stretched to receive you,
    taking you into Paradise space now.

The Eighth Week in Kingdomtide

U*sher*

A modest, humble task, it would seem—pointing out a place to sit.
The root of the parent from ancient Latin gives more life to the pointing.
It means **OPENING**.
Think of the grace of taking one
    whose being is closed in fear to what is opening forth:
    the mouth of the Word—an opening in God's arms—
    an embrace that needs an open heart.

The usher is the link between what is open and closed.
So simple to do—a smile, a hand, a gesture of welcome so gentle
that what is tight in the other becomes loose.
This tiny moment of welcome at worship
    opens countless meetings with people after.
Will you let yourself be open to the Lord, so that with this same gift
    others can enter into the open side of Jesus
    where saving blood and water flow?

The Ninth Week in Kingdomtide

V*iolin*

It soars, it stretches, it strains—so does the sound of heaven sing in the strings.
How joyous must the wood feel, wedded to wire, waiting for the drawing touch!

If the wood would speak, someone once imaged it saying:

"Dum in silvis, silui—Nunc mortua, cano."
"While I was in the forest, I was silent.
Now that I'm dead, I sing."

113

The Tenth Week in Kingdomtide

Well

If you were told to be on the lookout for a thief that wants to get at you,
    you would suppose that you would need to see all the avenues of approach,
    supposing the enemy would come from without.
But the enemy lurks inside already, lodging between the old stuff
    in the cellars of our lives, past generations and experiences
    that pile up in uninventoried abandon in the forgotten corners of the soul.

No discouragement, now!
For beneath your house, far below your cellar, there is a well of water alive.
It unleashes its upward surge to refresh, whenever you open the precious Word
    expectant to find the Water of life leap forth,
    rushing with the Spirit's healing, loving, ever new power
    to wash away the debris, filling your house with the fragrant,
    sweet waters of life.
You will never thirst again, for Christ has decided never to withdraw
the flow of his blood or his water from you.
But your heart: will it be open?

The Eleventh Week in Kingdomtide

Xerography

It is as taken for granted these days, as writing with a pen:
    that ink dust could come to life at electric's command,
    lining up perfectly with the blackened image that hovers over it;
    in a second comes a copy of a masterpiece of many hours.

Ashes and toner—the same in the Spirit.
When we are spiritually dead—self burned away—
    then our ashes are ready to come to life,
    taking the shape as a perfect spirit-copy of the master—Christ.
When we have nothing left to hold,
    making no changes of shape or contour on our own,
    then we can be formed, changed, transformed into the likeness of him
    who died for us that we might live.

Open the Bible.
Let it hover over you, page by page, till you become the flesh version today
    of what once was sweat and flesh and blood and praise
    in the inspirations of past millennia.

The Twelfth Week in Kingdomtide

*Y*ear

Horos: "that which passes" parents the words "year" and "hour."
Year—a circle, a cycle path of earth about the sun.
Hour—clock's hands dropping and lifting in constant dance.
Some despaired in thinking that such cycles
    would be endless repeatings of the same—
    locked into some predetermined madness.
But spirals they are, not circles.
Returns, yes, but an ever-forward movement up,
    as "always the same" mixes with "always new," generating excitement
    for the next moment to come.
Now the Bible cycles and spirals in life, making a torque through the very center,
    changing routine works and habits into new possibilities.
The Word, ever old, ever new, blends repetitions in passages spiraling
    themselves deeper into the soul.
Civic dates become sacred days in sacred weeks.
Calendars become soaked in Spirit time, as each day's Word becomes
    the Divine presence pressing against the hours and the years,
    returning triennially, lifting the soul ever upward.
            "Heaven and earth will pass away,
        but My words will by no means pass away" (Matt. 24:35).

The Thirteenth Week in Kingdomtide

*Z*oom *Lens*

I need a zoom lens for this year that is over—an inner eye that
    widens the angle to catch the whole landscape from the first Advent Candle
    to the exalted light of Christ the King.
And then a turning of the lens zooms into an hour and minute's meaning,
    as each is cycled into days that make wholeness of the year,
    as some great search for clues or fingerprints.

A tiny drop of blood carries with it the whole of a life's unique, wide expanse.
So too, the way you live each moment
    says something about how your whole year is,
    for every moment's *yes* or *no* to life sets the flow of time's next movement,
    just as the energy of the flow is released by repentance.
Whatever you see—whether close up or far away—
    is filed away in the pages of the Book of Life, ever to be perfected
    as you pause and relish each page,
    creating change by grace in the empty pages that lie stretched out before you.

The First Week in Kingdomtide
Begins on the Sunday nearest August 31. Alphabyte: Nose, p. 110

Sunday   *The Cross in Front*   **Matthew 16:21–28**

**"If any of you wants to be my follower, you must put aside
your selfish ambition, shoulder your cross, and follow me." v. 24**

Peter has just been given revelation knowledge about who Jesus is: "You are the Messiah, the Son of the living God." Now for the first time, Jesus predicts his suffering and death at the hands of the religious authorities. Feel the contrast of Peter's former confession of faith with the rebuke that he now gives Jesus.

As Peter participates in the pride of Jesus' adversaries, the heart of the Savior begins to be in passion already. Peter must be shaken by "tough love." The Lord looks through Peter's eyes into his soul—the place where war is waged between Peter and the Enemy. "Get behind me, Satan!"

The only way for Satan to get behind you is if you let Jesus take the lead. Let the cross be in front of you today. Greater than the struggle is the victory that Jesus has won. He holds the war prize—your own soul! Do not let pride, unforgiveness and other unrepented sin wrench it from his hand.

Monday   *The Brink of Hope*   **Isaiah 28**

**"Look! I am placing a foundation stone in Jerusalem. It is firm,
a tested and precious cornerstone that is safe to build on." v. 16**

The season of hurricanes finds us seeing people on T.V. who have totally lost their homes. They stand stunned at first, then weep over so many treasures washed away—memories only. They are pushed to the limit with the question: "Why me?" As the answer eludes them, they stand at the brink of either despair or hope. What is God going to do about such loss?

Isaiah presents a similar challenge to the pride of the city of Ephraim, capital of Samaria. Here the loss comes not from without, but from within—drunkenness. Notice the many times there are references to being intoxicated: five times in verse 7 alone.

Is there a "hurricane" of spiritual or actual drunkenness that pound away at the house of your being, threatening its foundations? Be sobered by the amazing grace of the Lord who can rebuild you from the bottom up.

Tuesday   *Rocking the Soul*   **Proverbs 15**

**A gentle answer turns away wrath,
but harsh words stir up anger. v. 1**

As a sweet anointing, so the rhythmic flow of Proverbs gently rocks your soul from side to side, as you rest in the Lord. Read slowly, pausing often and long, as the wisdom of three thousands years wells up and breaks through the way the world thinks.

Clear many small spaces for yourself in the course of the day to read a few of these precious gems. The beginning of *Kingdomtide* this year has two Tuesdays dedicated to Proverbs. They are awesome ways to begin the school year and the reflective season of autumn. Notice memories that well up from within.

As your spirit sways back and forth with the reading, so do the shadows of darkness and the light of the Lord sway as each proverb is balanced off with descriptions of good and evil. Sift and weigh each proverb. Take to heart those that particularly strike you. Stop … write … pray … share inner movements with someone you love.

Wednesday   *Sparks for a New Fire*   **Psalm 35**

I will praise the LORD from the bottom of my heart. v. 10

In a dying fire, most is ash with only a few sparks left. Such an image might describe this psalm of David. The ashes of his suffering at the hands of evil enemies are described in verse upon verse. Yet sparks of a new fire kindle in his soul and in yours, if you cherish the sparks and let them light a new fire.

A fresh, new fire needs the ashes of the old to be removed. So it is that David's very expression of mounting injustices against him are as the ashes being taken out of the hearth of his heart so that from the bottom of his being he can praise the Lord in new ways.

May this psalm do for you what it does for David—new praise, new awareness of God's faithful dedication to defend and rescue the poor and the innocent. When mistreatment and even slander come your way, may this psalm bring you comfort in the company you keep—David and Jesus.

Thursday   *Mid-Course Correction*   **1 Corinthians 1**

God chose things despised by the world, things counted as nothing at all,
and used them to bring to nothing what the world considers important. v. 28

Thursdays in autumn this year find us rolling back the centuries to the birthing and growing of a first century church in a great metropolis. Paul's First Letter to the Corinthians offers a powerful example of a church struggling with the momentum of a lifestyle prior to commitment to Christ—idolatry, sexual immorality, lawsuits, worldly philosophy, etc.

Corinth is situated on a narrow isthmus between the mainland part of Greece in the north and the Peloponnesian peninsula to the south. It is perfectly placed to meet the ships sailing from the east and moving westward after a brief portage across the isthmus. It was the center of world trade, much like New York City in the cosmopolitan nature of its population.

Paul founded this church about 50 A.D. Now he writes to give them "mid-course correction" on their way to salvation. Let Paul do the same for you.

Friday   *The Impossible Made Possible*   **Matthew 19**

Many who seem to be important now will be the least important then,
and those who are considered least here will be the greatest then. v. 30

This is a challenging chapter on the supreme values of the Kingdom. Three aspects are uplifted: fidelity in marriage, living as children, and the danger of riches. Only when one is living in the Kingdom, with the Lord as center of all choices and ways of life, does Jesus' teaching on these three subjects make sense.

The world does not see things this way. Marriage is by convenience, "children are to be seen and not heard," and riches of money and fame are treasured as absolutes.

What happens to you as you listen to these words of Jesus? Take an inventory of the "things" that you treasure the most. How do they fit with Jesus' values in this chapter? If there is sin, repent now for the Lord forgives you. Remember: only God can give fidelity to marriage and indifference to riches. When you respond to graces that make the impossible possible, you will be ready for the Kingdom riches in the last two verses.

1
Ki
A

Saturday   **The Sabbath Torah Reading**

Sep 6, 2008 #48A	Sep 9, 2017 #50A	Sep 5, 2026 #51–52A	Sep 8, 2035 #48A
Sep 3, 2011 #48A	Sep 5, 2020 #50A	Sep 8, 2029 #51A	Sep 4, 2038 #48A
Sep 6, 2014 #49A	Sep 9, 2023 #51–52A	Sep 4, 2032 #51A	Sep 07, 2041 #49A

The Second Week in Kingdomtide

Begins on the Sunday nearest September 7. Alphabyte: Oak, p. 110

Sunday   *Prayer-Power*   **Matthew 18:15–20**

Where two or three gather together because they are mine,
I am there among them. v. 20

Jesus presents three powerful teachings in six verses. In the first half, he admonishes us to confront with love a brother who is doing wrong against us. In verse 18, the Lord repeats what he said to Peter about the connection between heaven and earth in binding demons and loosening them from people. The last two verses celebrate the power of "two against one," the one in question being Satan who comes against God's people in sickness, disease, and strife. Praying in agreement with another brings the power of the witness of two against the one source of evil. While speaking about two, Jesus adds the third teaching, the verse for today, also rendered as "gathered in my name."

How does your life measure itself against these standards of the Lord?

Monday   *The Mouth-Heart Connection*   **Isaiah 29**

These people say they are mine.
They honor me with their lips, but their hearts are far away. v. 13

The theme of yesterday's Gospel about *saying* versus *doing* continues in today's reading. Words of worship of the mouth are empty and vain unless connected to a heart filled with devotion. When this connection is broken, words scatter themselves about in the wind as dead crackling autumn leaves. The awesome power of worship become"s a sacrilege; the sacred becomes secular. The root of the word "secular" means, "to be scattered." The secular is that which is not rooted and defined by the holiness of God.

What will happen if your heart is not right with God? Begin there. Go to where your heart is, and make an honest confession to the Lord and repent. The sweet feelings of devotion in worship will come after your mouth honestly expresses the sinfulness that may be lurking in your heart. Then your mouth will find itself expressing the grace of the Lord that floods from within.

Tuesday   *Roll Over*   **Proverbs 16**

Commit your works to the LORD, and then your plans will succeed. v. 3

Once again, the original language helps us to picture what is abstract in English. The Hebrew word for "commit" is *galal*. It literally means to "roll over." The image comes from the action of a camel as the animal lets go of the burden it is bearing. It drops to its knees and rolls to one side, allowing the heavy load simply to drop to the ground.

Drop to your knees and roll over your plans, your works, your burdens, to the Lord. Then your planning and your thinking will be grounded in God.

Pause and kneel before the Lord when you read a proverb that especially touches you. Highlight your Bible and your heart with the soothing words of the Lord that are meant to fill your mind with God's thoughts and God's ways—letting go of yours.

Wednesday   *Whisperings*   **Psalm 36**

**Your unfailing love, O LORD, is as vast as the heavens;
your faithfulness reaches beyond the clouds. v. 51**

Soon leaves and acorns will be falling away, leaving a silence that increases with each passing day of autumn. For those inclined to evil, the silence offers an inner space where the soft voice of sin whispers into the ears of their hearts.

The psalmist's awareness of this perversion of silence is accounted in the first four verses. Then the verse for the day breaks forth as he finds his spirit awakening to holy assertions that come from one who has been listening to the voice of the Spirit within. Each succeeding verse penetrates the silent mystery of God, with many verses that gloriously manifest God's goodness, greatness, and generosity.

To whose whisperings are you listening? Pray for the gift of discerning the spirits, to enable you to sift the source of the sounds in the silence. Pray only to respond to the promptings of God.

Thursday   *In Tune with God*   **1 Corinthians 2**

**Only those who have the Spirit
can understand what the Spirit means. v. 14**

Here is a way of making a stringed instrument sound without touching the strings. Try it with a guitar. Place the body of the guitar near your mouth and sing one of the tones to which the guitar is tuned. You will hear the sound of the note echo back to you. This is because the frequency of your voice and the string are the same. With any other note you sing, the guitar will be silent.

Are you tuned to the frequency of the Lord's voice? Does your life echo the sound of the Spirit singing inside of you? Do you keep silent when others speak "notes" not tuned to love? Paul decides, "To concentrate only on Jesus Christ and his death on the cross" (v. 2). As you read and pray, become tuned to the wisdom of God, which is out of tune to the wisdom of this age. Be one with those in tune with the Lord.

Friday   *Kingdom Fame*   **Matthew 20**

**Whoever wants to be a leader among you must be your servant,
and whoever wants to be first must become your slave. vv. 26–27**

The story of the request of the mother of James and John vividly portrays what makes for greatness in the Kingdom. The world surrounds us with adulation given to those who become famous in political life, the movies, and the world of sports. What is fame from the world's point of view fades with the newest fad on the scene.

Kingdom fame is something different. Jesus is the model. He came to serve, to redeem, to set free, and to heal. Those who act in his name and do the same will receive the reward of the Father now, with the peace and joy in the secret place of the heart.

My Uncle Spence humorously requested to be buried with his checkbook—"Just in case you *can* take it with you!" The rewards of the world decay with you in the grave; the rewards of the Kingdom go with you into the world that awaits you.

**2
Ki
A**

Saturday   **The Sabbath Torah Reading**

Sep 13, 2008 #49A	Sep 16, 2017 #51–52A	Sep 12, 2026 Rosh Ha	Sep 15, 2035 #49A
Sep 10, 2011 #49A	Sep 12, 2020 #51–52A	Sep 15, 2029 #52A	Sep 11, 2038 #49A
Sep 13, 2014 #50A	Sep 16, 2023 Rosh Ha	Sep 11, 2032 #52A	Sep 14, 2041 #50A

The Third Week in Kingdomtide

Begins on the Sunday nearest September14. Alphabyte: Pencil, p. 111

Sunday   *Forgive Yourself*   **Matthew 18:21–35**

"Shouldn't you have mercy on your fellow servant,
just as I had mercy on you?" v. 33

The parables of Jesus are soul-experiences. Make this one especially personal. The amount is an immense sum, beyond the power to comprehend. The sense is of a great national debt.

Out debt to God is infinitely greater. Take the sin of the world in its "original" form in Adam and Eve. That offense to God has come down through the ages in an avalanche of sin in the human family. A debt has so accumulated that we simply cannot pay it, because *God* has been offended.

Jesus took all this sin to the cross. In that act of love, God forgave all our debt of sin. Consider this: if God has forgiven you for all that you have done, ought you not treat others, including yourself, with that same forgiveness?

Monday   *The Lord or Egypt?*   **Isaiah 30**

"Only in returning to me and waiting for me will you be saved.
In quietness and confidence is your strength." v. 15

Isaiah not only reveals the Lord's judgments about the rebelliousness of Israel, but he vividly expresses God's feelings as well. Sense the Lord's heart and catch the longing that God's people rest and wait upon God alone. Memorize the verse for the day, repeating it often until your spirit does what the verse invites.

My Dad often used to remind us: *"Man proposes, but God disposes."* As you enter into the activities of the day, do this with an inner sense that you are responding to what God is doing in you, rather than what you are doing. Then your activities will blossom into prayer as you rely upon the Lord alone—not upon the shadowy "Egypts" that come your way with but a bare pretense of power.

Tuesday   *Singing with Sadness*   **2 Samuel 1—2**

How I weep for you, my brother Jonathan! Oh, how much loved you!
And your love for me was deep, deeper than the love of women! 1:26

The Second Book of Samuel is dedicated to the reign of King David. The threads of tragedy woven in 1 Samuel continue in this book. Yet even stronger and deeper do the power of God and his redeeming love weave a fabric of sacred history, which ultimately triumphs.

The book begins with David's song of mourning over the deaths of Saul and Jonathan. David wants the earth to share in his grief as well, "fasting," as it were, from the usual splendor of creation, to share David's pain. I remember having a similar sense when my father died. It did not seem quite right that everything just went on "business as usual," without everyone feeling his death.

Right now, take your suffering and allow the Spirit to turn it into a song. Take comfort in knowing that your Lord receives and shares your pain.

Wednesday	*Be Still in the Presence*	Psalm 37

Be still in the presence of the LORD,
and wait patiently for him to act. v. 7

Solomon learned how to pray and write from his father, David. The many proverbs attributed to Solomon find a pattern similar to the flow of today's psalm of David. The outcomes of those dedicated to good and those bent on evil are contrasted. Last Wednesday's chapter 16 from Proverbs echoes today's verse 5: "Commit everything you do to the LORD …" In fulfilling the verse for today, David was open to pray this psalm that flows naturally from a heart poised and quieted in the silent center of the present moment.

You too, dear faithful follower of God's Word: take time to stop and drop into the same silence that connects you to David and all the saints on earth and heaven. Pray the psalm, being open to what the Lord is teaching you.

Thursday	*Fire-starting and Fire-testing*	1 Corinthians 3

Everyone's work will be put through the fire
to see whether or not it keeps its value. v. 13

When there is a violent forest fire, another fire is deliberately set around the perimeter of the endangered space, so that when the fire arrives at the burned-out border, there is nothing left to consume.

Divisions and party strife are as a fire gone wild. Paul speaks in terms of fire in verse 15; one's material loss through fire becomes a source of salvation.

My desire in firestarting today is that the Holy Spirit *fire-test* you. Allow the Spirit to burn away at this very moment, all that is not of the Lord's doing. As the preferred temple of the Lord, become more and more filled with the fire of the Lord's presence. Let the strong words of Paul be as breath-blows on the wood of that fire, so that all that needs to be consumed in you may be done so completely. Upon the ashes of that loss lies the saving grace of knowing that you are resting on the foundation which is Christ Jesus.

Friday	*The Leaves Speak*	Matthew 21

Most of the crowd spread their coats on the road ahead of Jesus,
and others cut branches from the trees and spread them on the road. v. 8

We have come to that place in Matthew's Gospel of Jesus' triumphal entry into Jerusalem. Though Palm Sunday comes in the spring in the northern hemisphere, there is meaning of this entrance of Jesus into his Passion and death from the perspective of autumn, the season when the southern hemisphere celebrates Lent.

The palm branches lie strewn upon the ground just as do the leaves falling from the trees. As you walk about and hear leaves crunch beneath your feet, think about Jesus' walk upon those dead palm branches and the people's disloyalty to Him: "Hosanna," one day—"Crucify Him," another.

Be thoughtful and prayerful as only the speaking of the leaves breaks the silence of your walk.

3
Ki
A

Saturday — The Sabbath Torah Reading

Sep 20, 2008 #50A	Sep 23, 2017 #53A	Sep 19, 2026 #53A	Sep 22, 2035 #50A
Sep 17, 2011 #50A	Sep 19, 2020 Rosh Ha	Sep 22, 2029 #53A	Sep 18, 2038 #50A
Sep 20, 2014 #51–52A	Sep 23, 2023 #53A	Sep 18, 2032 #53A	Sep 21, 2041 #51–52A

The Fourth Week in Kingdomtide

Begins on the Sunday nearest September 21. Alphabyte: Quilt, p. 111

Sunday *Ponder a Punch Line* **Matthew 20:1–16**

"Is it against the law for me to do what I want with my money?
Should you be angry because I am kind?" v. 15

Suppose you are working all day on a project for which you will receive a fee. Imagine someone coming in at the last hour to help, receiving the same payment as you. How would you feel? This is the issue of the famous "Parable of the Eleventh Hour Worker."

Parables, similar to jokes, have punch lines. Linger on the impact of the verse for today, until the Kingdom way of thinking rises in your heart. Let go of worldly ways of weighing in the mind—not minding one's own business … jealousy … looking for rewards. The Spirit gives the Kingdom heart; it does not come from the flesh. In the Kingdom, there is love of serving, joy in another's good fortune, and praise for the Master's love of the forgotten.

Ponder, pray and wait for the Lord to give you peace—God's choicest blessing for this, the current hour of your life. Do you have the right to demand another hour after this?

Monday *The Lord: First or Last Resort?* **Isaiah 31**

Destruction is certain for those who look to Egypt for help,
trusting their cavalry and chariots
instead of looking to the LORD, the Holy One of Israel. v. 1

God's people were regularly tempted to have recourse to an old enemy—Egypt and its "horse-power"! They continued to do what repeatedly their ancestors did in the wilderness wanderings—be impatient with Moses and with God, and look back to the fleshpots of Egypt for security.

Here is another opportunity to see where you are placing your confidence. Is it in worldly powers of one form or another, or in the power of God? Make a list of any "Egyptian horses" that you are looking to in place of God who alone can lead you through the impasses in your situation.

For you, is the Lord the first recourse in your prayer, or the last resort? Turn to the Lord with all your heart and look to God alone for the way out of what presses against you.

Tuesday *Previews of Coming Distractions* **2 Samuel 3—4**

"Your hands were not bound; your feet were not chained.
No, you were murdered—the victim of a wicked plot." 3:34

David mourns the murder of an innocent man. From the first king of Israel, Saul, there were grave difficulties when God's people came under a human king. Recall God's response to the people's demand for a king in 1 Samuel 8. God alone was to be the King of his people. Nevertheless, God gave in to their demands. There would always be a struggle between divine anointing and human sinfulness in the monarchy. Jesus said, "A Kingdom divided against itself cannot stand" (Matt. 3:24).

These chapters are "previews of coming distractions" from the Lord's ways that would result in two separate Kingdoms during the reign of King Solomon, son of David. Intrigue, power, and murder draw their lines now. However, the saving power of God is at work through David who holds no grudge. David's inner goodness is the way out for those forces that seek to wrench God's people apart. How are you when it comes to inner goodness?

Wednesday	***Silence Before Enemies***	**Psalm 38**

I am deaf to all my enemies' threats.
I am silent before them as one who cannot speak. v. 13

David seeks the help of God in the face of his enemies. Instead of listening to their threats, David chooses silence, speaking only to his God. Rather than being a victim, David focuses upon his need for confession of his sins so that he and God will be in harmony with each other.

The purpose of this psalm is that David return to that closeness with God, which will assure him of the protection for which he longs. The psalm begins and ends in the imperative mood, while all the contents are in the declarative. David pours out his suffering in all its details. How comforting it is to do this!

Place your awareness on what needs to happen in your situation, so that your relation with God is in harmony. Receive God's power to save. Just as David does in the verse for the day and the one following, choose not to hear the threats of your enemies. Listen instead to your own confession and the saving, loving response of your God.

Thursday	***Doing God's Thing***	**1 Corinthians 4**

The Kingdom of God is not just fancy talk;
it is living by God's power. v. 20

The key word in this chapter is "steward." The word in Greek is the one which gives us the word "economy." *Oikos* is the word for "house," and *nemo,* the word for "manage." A steward is the one who "manages the house."

Now the "house," here in Paul refers to God's House. Remember that *you* are to be the place where God dwells in the Holy Spirit. How you manage your life and your body is God's business, not yours. We are also called to "manage" the wonderful things of God—divine priorities and plans. Everything about our world belongs to God and is given to us for our safekeeping and furthering.

"Do your own thing"—that is the world's way. "Do God's thing"—the way of being God's steward.

Friday	***Wasting God's Good Time***	**Matthew 22**

"Your problem is that you don't know the Scriptures,
and you don't know the power of God." v. 29

Controversy heightens between Jesus and his adversaries. The Lord confronts the arrogant religious leaders who have wasted Jesus' time by trying to trip him up. Gone forever are what could have been precious moments of simply sitting at his feet, drinking in the wisdom of his teaching and the healing of his touch.

Three Sundays in October are devoted to sections of this chapter. Let today be a preview of what is coming, allowing yourself to get a sense of the whole chapter.

Do you fight what the Lord wants to do in your life? Do you find yourself arguing with God? Instead of complaining about what is happening to you, listen closely to the inner meaning of what is taking place. Seek the Lord's wise and tender voice in the midst of the chaos of your own compulsions.

4
Ki
A

Saturday
The Sabbath Torah Reading

Sep 27, 2008 #51A	Sep 30, 2017 Yom Ki	Sep 26, 2026 Tabern	Sep 29, 2035 #51–52A
Sep 24, 2011 #51–52A	Sep 26, 2020 #53A	Sep 29, 2029 #54A	Sep 25, 2038 #51–52A
Sep 27, 2014 #53A	Sep 30, 2023 Tabern	Sep 25, 2032 #54A	Sep 28, 2041 #53A

The Fifth Week in Kingdomtide

*Begins on the Sunday nearest September 28. Alphabyte: **R**ainbow, p. 112*

Sunday   *The Cross—Near or Far?*   **Matthew 21:23–32**
"I assure you, corrupt tax collectors and prostitutes
will get into the kingdom of God before you do." v. 31

One act of surrender to Jesus is worth more than a million words of promise. Think of the "Good Thief" on the cross. His act of love for Jesus and repentance of sinfulness won him full entry into paradise in the final moment of his life. All the Jewish leaders were restless with preparing other paschal lambs for Passover, blind to the power of *the* Paschal Lamb whose saving blood was already flowing from the cross.

What decisions do you make that reveal whether you are spending your life for the One who spent his life for you? It is not what you say, but what you do that defines surrender. Is what you do in life tending to have you cling to the cross—or are you sometimes far away from it, busy about other kingdoms?

Monday   *Affliction and Comfort*   **Isaiah 32**
My people will live in safety, quietly at home.
They will be at rest. v. 18

Isaiah is like a great symphony. There are majestic tones of glory and promise of messianic deliverance, as well as somber ones of judgment and call to repentance. Both of these contrast with each other in this chapter. A glorious expansion of the heart comes with the assurance of the reign of peace and justice; then there come strong admonitions to the complacent. Notice the future tense used—what God is going to do in Jesus. Isaiah speaks the words of promise; there are only two months until Advent.

These two themes in counterpoint remind me of a phrase I once heard about the prophets: "They came to comfort the afflicted and to afflict the comfortable."

Appreciate vv. 16–18. Dwellings will be secure—very close to the promise of Jesus in John's Gospel to those who keep the Word: "We [the Father and Jesus] will come to him and make Our home with him" (14:23).

Tuesday   *Dancing with God*   **2 Samuel 5—6**
I am willing to act like a fool
in order to show my joy in the Lord. v. 21

The dance of David before the Ark expresses the energy released in spontaneous worship. There is joy, for the Ark finally arrives at fixed place for worship. As the hands of a clock move freely about the center point, so does David find extravagant expression as he reels about while grounded in the joy of the presence of God centered in his life.

Michal criticizes David. She wastes her time judging him, instead of entering into the source of his joy. The same will happen to you, if you criticize and judge others. As a downward spiral, energies will go inward and bind, instead of spiraling outward in joyous expression.

Find a place in your house where you especially find the presence of God—a prayer closet, a special chair—some place where you find yourself drawn to be in God's presence, where your spirit can dance.

5
Ki
A

Wednesday   *Life Is Short*   **Psalm 39**

"My life is no longer than the width of my hand. An entire lifetime
is just a moment to you; human existence is but a breath." v. 5

Whatever are the sufferings you are undergoing in your life, this psalm will offer your sweet comfort. As you move through the verses, let the specific sufferings in your life attach themselves to these expressions. You will find yourself delivered from a focus upon the suffering, to a growing and glowing awareness of the presence of God who alone can give meaning to your pain. In addition, something else that expands your spirit: through your fervent praying of this psalm, the outpouring of David becomes a vehicle for the many kinds of sufferings of all God's people. The psalm touched Paul; he cites verse 22 in Romans 8:36–39.

You may find it helpful to note the areas of your pain, praying along with the millions today and over the centuries who have found peace through this psalm. Those verses that express the brevity of life will sober you.

Thursday   *Without Wax*   **1 Corinthians 5**

Let us celebrate the festival, not by eating the old bread of wickedness
and evil, but by eating the new bread of purity and truth. v. 8

The word "purity" in verse 8 can also be translated as "sincere." This word is from the Latin *sin-cera* meaning "without wax." The word in turn translates the Greek *eilikrineia*, meaning, "judged by sunlight." Stay with me—there is soul food here!

In ancient flea markets, unscrupulous merchants would fill wax into the cracks and broken pieces of a work of art to fool the interested into thinking the piece was whole. Careful buyers would take the piece and hold it up to the sunlight to be sure that it was "sincere"—without wax.

Take the sweet urging of Paul that your heart be without bad leaven. As you read, see where there are "cracks" in your spirit. Do not hide them by dishonesty, feigning, pretense, flattery, manipulation, etc. Take your soul and expose it to God's holy light and let the Lord burn away impurities until you shine as pure gold.

Friday   *The Greatest Sin*   **Matthew 23**

"Hyprocrites! You are like whitewashed tombs—
beautiful on the outside but filled on the inside
with dead people's bones and all sorts of impurity." v. 27

Jesus uses the word "hypocrites" to describe his adversaries. The word comes directly from Greek. The prefix *hypo* means "under" and *krites,* "to judge"—the same root as yesterday's word *eilikrineia.* A hypocrite originally meant an actor—someone who "judges under another character." Later it came to mean a "pretender" and what we would come to understand as a hypocrite.

It is the sin that Jesus denounces the most. Words speak of holiness, goodness, worship, etc., but the real thinking that flows "under" is pride, arrogance, lying and pretense. Apparently, God is first, but really, the self is number one. Two commandments are violated—idolatry and false witness.

As you read the "woes," is there any "under" areas of you that are false? As in yesterday's reading, lift yourself up to God's light.

**5
Ki
A**

Saturday   **The Sabbath Torah Reading**

Oct 04, 2008 #52A	Oct 07, 2017 Tabern	Oct 03, 2026 #54A	Oct 06, 2035 #53A
Oct 01, 2011 #53A	Oct 03, 2020 Tabern	Oct 06, 2029 #1B	Oct 02, 2038 #53A
Oct 04, 2014 Yom Ki	Oct 07, 2023 #54A	Oct 02, 2032 #1B	Oct 05, 2041 Yom Ki

The Sixth Week in Kingdomtide

Begins on the Sunday nearest October 5. Alphabyte: Streams, p. 112

Sunday   *Abusing What God Holds Precious*   **Matthew 21:33–46**
**The Kingdom of God will be taken away from you
and given to a nation that will produce the proper fruit. v. 43**

The Lord confronts the Pharisees in "The Parable of the Wicked Vinedressers." They are about to plot what the parable portrays—the murder of the Son of the Landowner.

God does not take the sin of our "No" as the final word. Ever since the original sin of abusing the sacred space of the Garden of Eden, the Lord has been seeking to create a lush vineyard in the midst of ensuing chaos. Read Isaiah 5:1–7 and the song about the tender care that the Lord has for his vineyard.

The Lord never gives up on you or me. However, is there abuse of any kind toward yourself or another? Repent. Stop abusing yourself with guilt and shame; God does not want you to treat one of his precious children that way!

Monday   *Stability in Hard Times*   **Isaiah 33**
**In that day he will be your sure foundation,
providing a rich store of salvation, wisdom, and knowledge. v. 6**

Jesus and Paul would echo the admonition at the beginning of this chapter: "Whatever measure you use in judging others, it will be used to measure how you are judged" (Matt. 7:2). "You will always reap what you sow" (Gal 6:7).

There are images of *stability* as in the verse for the day. The Hebrew word for "times," *et*, means "a particular time or season of life." The "times" of your life are set against larger, ill-defined, hostile, "hard times" from the world. Enemy eras will not be able to cross the sacred boundaries of your soul, because you are finding stability through the Spirit's gifts of wisdom and knowledge.

Jerusalem will be firm with strong stakes and cords to prevent her from being blown away by enemies from without. What do you need to do to set the stakes of your life's tent more securely?

Tuesday   *Sitting Before the Lord*   **2 Samuel 7—8**
**When you die, I will raise up one of your descendants,
and I will make his kingdom strong. 7:12**

David does what yesterday's reading from Isaiah implored. David's plan to build a house for God is reversed: God is going to build *him* a house! Feel the burst of promise in the coming Messiah in today's verse. Sit with David as he prays a glorious prayer of thanksgiving from verse 18. He reviews what God has done in his life. You do the same. Make this prayer your very own. Reflect upon the movement of your life and see in it the hand of the Lord redeeming and remaking what your mistakes and sins have damaged.

All the successes of chapter 8 come because David sits before the Lord in chapter 7. Is there a new chapter in your life that is about to begin, but which needs you to sit in prayer where you are now?

6
Ki
A

Wednesday   *Intercessory Pain*   **Psalm 40**

He lifted me out of the pit of despair, out of the mud and the mire.
He set my feet on solid ground and steadied me as I walked along. v. 2

A young woman dying of AIDS found comfort in this psalm. The intensity of her suffering found a place to express itself in this prayer. The psalms will comfort you in times of anguish. Let David be your "coach." Allow his suffering to become one with yours, giving you words and phrases that are expressions of your own pain.

Most of all, Jesus, the Son of David, has already taken the essence of your suffering to the cross. Join your suffering to Jesus' who leads you on the path toward the redemption of your pain and your own salvation. Pray to the Lord that you learn to suffer well—not in self-pity or anger; not in guilt and shame; not as a victim. Just as David and Jesus, let your pain become intercessory for others. It is then given so much meaning and a special kind of joy that lifts the suffering itself. Then you will see your suffering placed into the galaxy of the Lord's blessings.

Thursday   *With Whom Are You Joined?*   **1 Corinthians 6**

Don't you know that your body is the temple of the Holy Spirit,
who lives in you and was given to you by God? v. 19

Paul uses the image of sexual union to address the Corinthian Christians who had once surrendered their lives to Jesus, later committing fornication, along with other vices. From verse 15 Paul uses this principle: your identity is found from the one with whom you are joined. If joined to a prostitute, you are a prostitute; if joined to Christ, you are "one spirit with him."

Clear boundaries must be set between those who live in Christ's body, and those who do not. It is a sacrilege for those who profess oneness in Christ to settle disputes by recourse to those outside this sacred boundary.

Paul's admonition is strong—as strong as his love for these children begotten of him. Write down the loving and perhaps confronting words the Lord speaks to your heart.

Friday   *Adhere Closely to Him*   **Matthew 24**

Heaven and earth will disappear,
but my words will remain forever. v. 35

The Good News is not reserved to every other chapter of the Gospels but this one! Greater than the disasters predicted, is the presence of the Lord to those who remain faithful to him. What comfort in this fact! Paul would later exult in Romans 8: 35: "Who shall separate us from the love of Christ?" When you experience a resounding "NO ONE" in the depths of your being, then the peace of the Lord will well up from within.

Do not fail to catch the significance of the first verse of the reading. "Jesus departed from the Temple." Never again would Jesus enter the physical temple. When he left it, so did the Holy Spirit. Evil rushes into the vacuum left when Jesus is not there. Adhere ever more closely to him. Remember: you are a living stone—part of the new temple.

6
Ki
A

Saturday   **The Sabbath Torah Reading**

Oct 11, 2008 #53A	Oct 14, 2017 #1B	Oct 10, 2026 #1B	Oct 13, 2035 Yom Ki
Oct 08, 2011 Yom Ki	Oct 10, 2020 #54A	Oct 13, 2029 #2B	Oct 09, 2038 Yom Ki
Oct 11, 2014 #54A	Oct 14, 2023 #1B	Oct 09, 2032 #2B	Oct 12, 2041 Tabern

The Seventh Week in Kingdomtide

Begins on the Sunday nearest October 12. Alphabyte: Trapeze, p. 112

Sunday   *Wedding-wear*   **Matthew 22: 1–14**

"Friend how is it that you are here without wedding clothes?" v. 12

In every culture, in every age, one celebration that stands out as unique in its joy is a marriage. The Lord uses this image to have his chosen people catch the essence of the intimacy the Lord wants to have with his people. God wants to marry us!

Jesus furthers this image in the famous "Parable of the Wedding Feast." Once again, Jesus pounds the Pharisees with another parable, spotlighting their rejection of that which God longs to share with us.

The invitation to the wedding is universal. However, a "yes" means more than just showing up. You must be wearing clothes to fit the occasion. Paul in his letter to the Colossians 3:12 ff. lists the proper garments. Meditate upon them. Some clothes *do* make the person!

Monday   *God's Protection Voided*   **Isaiah 34**

Come here and listen, O nations of the earth.
Let the world and everything in it hear my words. v. 1

Isaiah envisions the judgment of those nations set against the Lord. An example is made of Edom, the land that originated from Esau, as typical of those nations that have made themselves enemies to God and his people. The chief city, Bozrah, meaning "Impenetrable," will have its boundaries invaded by animals that usually inhabit the wild. With a nature-lover's detail, Isaiah pictures how these various animals will be making their home within the walls of that worldly city that prided its protection by its own power.

In effect, Isaiah says that these wild animals do God's will more than many humans! That is why God protects them and provides them with progeny by being sure that each animal has its mate.

Jesus said, "You are more valuable than a whole flock of sparrows." (Matt. 10:31). Is there arrogance in you, which voids the protection, and care the Lord longs to give you?

Tuesday   *An Adopted Son of David*   **2 Samuel 9—10**

"Don't be afraid! I've asked you to come so that I can be kind to you
because of my vow to your father, Jonathan." 9:7

David has a sense of reverence for the gifts from the Lord he had received in his life. Of these, one of the most precious was his deepest friend, Jonathan. Out of respect for his memory, David welcomes Jonathan's son Mephibosheth into his household and in effect, adopts him as a son.

Notice what happens to those who do not receive David's kind approach. In the refusal of the Ammonites and the Syrians to receive reconciliation with David, they sow the seeds of their own destruction.

The Lord reaches out to you and takes you as one of his children, not only to eat at his table, but to partake of his body and blood. Be as Mephibosheth and find yourself welcome in intimate communion with the Lord.

Who needs your special acts of kindness?

7
Ki
A

128

| Wednesday | *Betrayal* | Psalm 41 |

**Even my best friend, the one I trusted completely,
the one who shared my food, has turned against me. v. 9**

Pray this psalm aware of David and Jesus. The "friend" in verse 9 was perhaps Ahithopel, a close associate of David's (2 Sam. 17:23). For Jesus, this friend was, of course, Judas.

If you have ever experienced betrayal in some form or other, turn this special suffering over to the Lord Jesus who has been with you in the most painful of betrayals. You are not alone in *anything* that you suffer. There is simply no pain that you or I can ever experience that was not first lived by Jesus.

Consider this in some detail. What are those sufferings that tend to consume your spirit's energies? Look in the Gospels, and you will find some connection with the essence of that suffering with Jesus' own. This will be prayer. Be bonded to the Lord in deeper communion with him. What awaited Jesus at the end of his suffering, awaits you—the resurrection and the life.

| Thursday | *Standards for Marriage* | 1 Corinthians 7—8 |

**The Christian wife brings holiness to her marriage,
and the Christian husband brings holiness to his marriage. v. 14**

Paul seeks to reorient the Corinthians according to moral principles, especially about sexuality. His understanding rests on the power of the Christian life to make holy a marriage with an unbeliever. Greater is the power of holiness than the power of unbelief. This holy fidelity can result in the conversion of the unbeliever. Both faith and love can move mountains.

There is strength, yet gentleness in the teaching of Paul. Perhaps you have come to a place in your life and are sharing it with someone, without having previously adhered to these standards. Live the standard now, by the grace of the Lord. Renew your repentance for past sin, asking the Lord to let holiness of life flow through you to all those who depend upon the commitment of your love.

| Friday | *Responsive* | Matthew 25 |

**"I assure you, when you did it to one of the least
of these my brothers and sisters, you were doing it to me!" v. 25**

This is the last chapter in Matthew's Gospel before the Passion of Jesus. It consists of two parables and the description of the final judgment. They are as three murals that fill the wall of a great hall. Your imagination will creatively continue the stories and the images before you.

If there is one word that gives unity to the three scenes, it is *responsibility*. Take the word in the sense of "being responsive." The wise virgins, the persons with five and three talents, and those at the final judgment who were compassionate to the needy—each of these were responsive to the demands and the details of the presence of Jesus as Bridegroom, Master, and Son of Man.

Meditate on where you find yourself in each of these stories, noting the changes needed in your responsiveness—before it is too late.

**7
Ki
A**

Saturday			**The Sabbath Torah Reading**
Oct 18, 2008 #54A	Oct 21, 2017 #2B	Oct 17, 2026 #2B	Oct 20, 2035 #54
Oct 15, 2011 #54A	Oct 17, 2020 #1B	Oct 20, 2029 #3B	Oct 16, 2038 #54
Oct 18, 2014 #1B	Oct 21, 2023 #2B	Oct 16, 2032 #3B	Oct 19, 2041 #54A–1B

The Eighth Week in Kingdomtide

Begins on the Sunday nearest October 19. Alphabyte: Usher, p. 113

Sunday   *Outlaw or Outrage*   **Matthew 22:15–22**
"You hypocrites! Whom are you trying to fool
with your trick questions?" v. 18

If you were to select the "Top Ten Sayings" of Jesus, which ones would they be? Likely, you will include, "Give to Caesar what belongs to him; everything that belongs to God must be given to God" (v. 21). Many have fixed on that saying of Jesus as the morality for paying taxes.

True enough. However, if you were to ask Jesus about *his* "Top Ten," I doubt he would pick that one. Why? Because Jesus was only fending off the vicious word game of "one-up-manship" the Pharisees were inviting him to play. They had a dilemma. If Jesus said, "Don't pay taxes," he would be an outlaw to Rome; if he said, "Pay taxes," he would be an out-*rage* to the Jewish people.

What a tragedy! The Pharisees had the Word of Life in front of them, and they played games. What about you as you sit before the Lord? He does not come to play games when abundant, eternal life is at stake.

Monday   *Highway of Holiness*   **Isaiah 35**
A main road will go through that once deserted land.
It will be named the highway of Holiness. v. 8

This chapter concludes the first part of Isaiah, making a joyous ending to the judgments against those nations who refuse to follow the Lord's way. Many verses will draw you into the feeling of Advent. The ending of God's year of grace has strong similarity with its beginning; the theme "What Is Coming?" pervades them both.

Read these verses with faith knowing that God will protect you and give you prosperity, as long as he finds you responding to grace by being on the Highway of Holiness.

If you were to imagine the movement of your life as a journey down a road, how would you describe the road? What do you sense spiritually about what is coming? Are you cruising along the road or have you broken down on its shoulder, needing help?

Tuesday   *Repentance*   **2 Samuel 11—12**
David confessed to Nathan
"I have sinned against the LORD." 12:13

Instead of being the leader with his men in battle, David is idle at home being a voyeur—gaping at Bathsheba bathing. David's sin of lust and murder ushers in a future laden with the same and similar sins in his descendants.

David repented and became purer and greater. Greater too than your sin is Jesus risen. Repent of your sinfulness. The sins of you family's past need no longer cripple the future. Jesus ended this on the cross. The power of the Lord's resurrection is to have you break with areas of sin in your lives that bring grave consequences such as death.

David … you … Jesus … reflect upon your life in the light of this episode. Go deeper into repentance, total forgiveness, and joy.

8
Ki
A

130

Wednesday   *Thirsting for God*   **Psalm 42**
As the deer pants for streams of water,
so I long for you, O God. v. 1

Take time for your inner person to become quiet. Be as the deer thirsting for water brooks until you sense the deep longing for God that lies at the base of your being. Every person thirsts for God with great intensity. However, if the pangs of thirst are anesthetized, then life goes on searching for the dry riverbeds of the world—wealth, fame, pride, human respect. It is easy to thirst for these, missing the deeper brook that flows within—the Living Waters of the Spirit in Christ Jesus.

Read the opening verse of this psalm slowly, repeatedly, until your soul awakens to its thirst for God. Then let the rest of the psalm carry you along the "stream" of images that will lead you more and more to the source of your life in God who alone can quench your thirst.

Thursday   *A Way Out*   **1 Corinthians 9—10**
When you are tempted, God will show you a way out
so that you will not give in to it. v. 13

The passion of Paul to preach the gospel is especially present in chapter 9. He finds the example of running a race as an image to describe this intense focus of his life.

The verse for today will bring comfort to you in times of trial. There is nothing too great for you to endure. The Lord God will give you a way out by the light and power of grace.

From verse 14, there is a sacred principle at work: do everything that would have the conscience of another aided in coming to the gospel; do nothing that would hinder this approach. You will find other verses as you read that I suggest you write down in your best handwriting and place near you to engrave in your mind for continual recall in your heart.

Friday   *Absolute Evil—Absolute Good*   **Matthew 26:1–35**
"I assure you, wherever the Good News is preached throughout the world,
this woman's deed will be talked about in her memory." v. 13

There are strong contrasts of good and evil in this half chapter. It is the beginning of Jesus' Passion. Until now, Jesus has been in *action* against the domains of evil in disease, hypocrisy, and unbelief. Now he allows himself to be acted upon, to be in *passion*.

There are contrasts in the plot to kill Jesus and the extravagant gesture of the woman who pours costly oil upon Jesus expressing her great love.

In the face of coming death, Jesus gives us the promise of his body's resurrection in the gift of Communion—even as he faces the evil of Judas' betrayal and the imminence of Peter's denial.

The shifts between absolute good and absolute evil will move you. Be shaken, humbled and awed by all the grace this is quietly triumphing.

**8
Ki
A**

Saturday   **The Sabbath Torah Reading**

Oct 25, 2008 #1B	Oct 28, 2017 #3B	Oct 24, 2026 #3B	Oct 27, 2035 #1B
Oct 22, 2011 #1B	Oct 24, 2020 #2B	Oct 27, 2029 #4B	Oct 23, 2038 #1B
Oct 25, 2014 #2B	Oct 28, 2023 #3B	Oct 23, 2032 #4B	Oct 26, 2041 #2B

The Ninth Week in Kingdomtide

Begins on the Sunday nearest October 26. Alphabyte: Violin, p. 113

Sunday   *Jesus Is the Answer*   **Matthew 22:34–46**
**"You must love the Lord your God with all your heart, all your soul,
and all your mind ... Love your neighbor as yourself." vv. 37 and 39**

Jesus quotes from the first half of the Jewish *Shema* which pious Jews repeat twice daily (Deut. 6:4–5). After many questions on the part of the scribes, Sadducees and Pharisees, Jesus now takes the offensive. He presents a dilemma, forcing his listeners to face the question of how the Messiah would come to be. They are finally rendered speechless.

Life poses many questions about how, when or even whether God is intervening or not. There needs to come a moment when questions are silenced by the very presence of the Lord, perhaps by further questions, such as those posed to Job. God's questions reduce Job to silence. They remind him about how incapable he is to dominate questions for which the Lord alone has answers.

Ponder these words of the song of Scott Wesley Brown: "When answers aren't enough—there is Jesus."

Monday   *God Said So!*   **Isaiah 36**
**"So what makes you think
that the Lord can rescue Jerusalem?" v. 20**

One of God's favorite actions is to defend his people against arrogant, bully enemies. Outlandish, blasphemous assertions come from the mouth of the representative of King Sennacherib of Assyria. In fact, they appear twice in the Bible, as Chapters 36 to 39 are almost identical to 2 Kings 18:17–20:19. The confidence, which godless Assyria has in their military power, prompts the representative to summarize his arrogance in the verse for today.

This verse was a challenge to the first listeners—and is one for you as you listen to the taunting question, and boldly live out its answer in your life. It might be similar to an unbeliever who might question your belief in the presence of Jesus by faith in Holy Communion. The answer to that question and to the one in the verse for the day is the same: "He said so: I believe him!"

Tuesday   *Hot Coals of Unforgiveness*   **2 Samuel 13—15**
**Our lives are like water spilled out on the ground,
which cannot be gathered up again. That is why God tries to bring us back
when we have been separated from him. 14:14**

David sows the sin of lust in his family. He makes an opening for evil to fester. Incest becomes hatred, further blowing up into conspiracy and murder.

As you read this story, know in your heart that the Lord is at work to bring reconciliation and peace to your family. No one alone can make it happen, but know that Jesus has risen to bring wholeness to brokenness in your life and in the lives of those you love.

Are there any dark emotions of resentment and vengeance that vibrate inside you as you read? Be honest with yourself. Forgive. Don't let the tail wag the dog anymore! Let go and forgive. Thus, you will find that there will no longer be that inner pushing and shoving going on that takes its energy from negative emotions that burn within. When you forgive, you release the hot coals of unforgiveness that would otherwise burn you up.

Wednesday   *The Altar and the Day*   **Psalm 43**

There I will go to the altar of God,
to God—the source of all my joy. v. 4

For many centuries, the Catholic Mass began with the priest standing at the foot of the altar praying this psalm. It was a personal prayer as he entered worship.

As you stand at the foot of the altar, which is the day that lies before you, this psalm becomes a powerful prayer invoking the presence of the Holy Spirit. The Spirit is your own personal lawyer to plead your case against those personal forces in dark places that are set against you. Greater is God's power to overcome them, than their power to overcome you.

Go forth to your day, walking upon the ground as upon an altar on which you are worshipping the Lord in all you say and do.

Thursday   *Members of One Body*   **1 Corinthians 11—12**

Now all of you together are Christ's body,
and each one of you is a separate and necessary part of it. 12:27

Ask the Holy Spirit to teach you the truths expressed here, discerning what is proper to the Corinthian church alone, and what touches our own day. Chapter 11 treats about the mutuality of men and women, and the roles that each share—even as the Father, Son, and Spirit are equal, while still relating distinctly to each other.

The theme of diversity and identity continues in chapter 12, which begins the teaching about spiritual gifts. Each person is unique; so are the gifts given. However, we become one with each other, because the origin of the gifts is from the one Holy Spirit.

You are one with your brothers and sisters as members of the Body of the risen Jesus. What changes do you need to make in the way you live because of this awesome fact?

Friday   *Jesus Needs Prayer*   **Matthew 26:36–75**

"Keep alert and pray. Otherwise temptation will overpower you.
For though the spirit is willing enough, the body is weak!" v. 41

Agony, arrest, trial, and denial are four movements that bring Jesus closer to Calvary. As you pray the Passion Narrative, go slowly, allowing the scenes of this tragic, yet salvific drama draw you into their mystery.

In the Agony in the Garden, Jesus' suffering was the more intense because his closest friends slept while he was in such great emotional pain. Sleep was the anesthesia to avoid being with Jesus at his hour of agony. Is sleep sometimes a pain-deadener for you also?

Think of it: Jesus needs you to pray with him. We are ordinarily aware of ourselves doing the praying, God doing the answering. However, the Lord needs your prayer for his Body that still suffers. Pray so that the agony of others may be the less because you are vigilant in prayer beside them.

Saturday   **The Sabbath Torah Reading**

Nov 01, 2008 #2B	Nov 04, 2017 #4B	Oct 31, 2026 #4B	Nov 03, 2035 #2B
Oct 29, 2011 #2B	Oct 31, 2020 #3B	Nov 03, 2029 #5B	Oct 30, 2038 #2B
Nov 01, 2014 #3B	Nov 04 2023 #4B	Oct 30, 2032 #5B	Nov 02, 2041 #3B

The Tenth Week in Kingdomtide
Begins on the Sunday nearest November 2. Alphabyte: Well, p. 114

Sunday   *Jesus Denounces His Enemies*   **Matthew 23:1–12**
"The greatest among you must be a servant." v. 11

In the trial scene of the play and movie by Richard Bolt, "Man for All Seasons," Thomas More breaks the silence he had previously kept while striving to be both faithful to God and loyal to the King, Henry VIII of England. When he is finally convicted and sentenced to death, he declaims the evil of putting temporal before eternal law.

In a similar way, Jesus denounces the scribes and Pharisees in his last words to them. He pours out his anger upon those who had relentlessly opposed the grace of the Good News.

Be moved by the grief of Jesus as he laments over Jerusalem in the last three verses. He then departs forever from the Temple. Jesus doesn't want to depart from your spirit, his temple. Is there anything you are doing that is driving Jesus away?

Monday   *Time to Recover*   **Isaiah 37:1–20**
You alone are God of all the kingdoms of the earth.
You alone created the heavens and the earth. v. 16

Ignatius Loyola, the founder of the Jesuits, was once asked how long it would take him to recover if the Pope were to suddenly dissolve the new religious order Ignatius had founded. His answer: "About fifteen minutes." He was speaking from experience. He had heard one time that a cardinal, who had opposed the Jesuits, had himself become Pope. Ignatius said that his knees shook. He went into the chapel to pray. Fifteen minutes later he emerged—his face radiant.

Hezekiah's hands must have shaken when he read the threatening letter of King Sennacherib. Then he placed this letter before the Lord in the Temple. The small piece of material which contained all those threats must have seen small in comparison to the vastness of the Temple and of God who was especially present there; Hezekiah must have felt peace.

We do not know how long it took Hezekiah to recover, but I like the fifteen minutes it took Ignatius. Today's verse will help you rebound from your fears.

Tuesday   *Grief of David and Jesus*   **2 Samuel 16—18**
"O my son Absalom! My son, my son Absalom!
If only I could have died instead of you!" 18:23

The treason against David reminds me of the same against Jesus on the part of Judas. Absalom, part of David's family, betrays his father, and wants the power of the kingdom to fall to him. Judas, one of Jesus' apostles, betrays his Lord. Just as Absalom, Judas does not like the way the lines of power in Jesus' Kingdom are being drawn. The fates of Absalom and Judas are similar—hanging from a tree. The grief of David over the fate of his son is similar to the grief that Jesus must have felt for Judas' betrayal and the way he ended. The prayer of David, "If only I had died in your place," is fulfilled in Jesus who died in your place and mine, so that our sin would not do to us what Absalom's and Judas' did to them. The tree, upon which Jesus hung in agony, became a new tree of life.

Spend time praising the Lord for the extent of his love for you. How much more can you yet respond?

Wednesday   *Vehicle for Pain*   **Psalm 44**
O God, we give glory to you all day long
and constantly praise your name. v. 8

The outpourings in this psalm become vehicles for all the ways in which God's people suffer. Paul cites verse 22 in Romans 8:36–39 as he finds the words of this psalm expressing the suffering he experienced in his reborn life in Christ. Allow this psalm to carry you through your pain. Moving slowly through the psalm, painful memories, and other sorrows will attach themselves to this prayer and move outward into God's presence. Your awareness will shift from pain to the presence of God who alone gives healing and meaning to the suffering.

You may find it helpful to note down specific concerns that come to mind. You blend in with millions of people today and over the centuries who found peace and the soothing comfort of God's abiding presence through this and all the psalms.

Thursday   *From Mind to Spirit*   **1 Corinthians 13—14**
I will pray in the spirit, and I will pray in words I understand.
I will sing in the spirit, and I will sing in words I understand. 14:15
(The *Firestarter* and the reading are repeated on Thursday, Holy Week B.)

However familiar you may be with chapter 13, read it today as though for the first time. Though this chapter does not mention God, the traces of God who is love penetrate every verse, challenging the listener to go beyond the world's mind about love, deep into divine understanding. Reflect upon the spiritual gifts outlined in chapter 14. Paul describes the gift of tongues, a spiritual language that many discover the Holy Spirit continuing to give. Ordinary language tends to keep one in the mind alone; a language of the Spirit allows the recipients to yield the heart to those communications from the Lord that transcend the limitations of the mind; they are one-on-one contacts with the Spirit.

Pray that the Lord give you understanding about these gifts—surely offered today as well as to the community of Corinth.

Friday   *The Deliverer Is Delivered*   **Matthew 27:1–31**
Pilate ordered Jesus flogged with a lead-tipped whip,
then turned him over to the Roman soldiers to crucify him. v. 26

Two grave sins were committed in Jesus' Passion—betrayal and denial. Peter wept bitterly over the sin he committed; profound sorrow and the Lord's forgiveness cleansed his soul and prepared the way for the greatness of the Peter to come. Judas' sin of betrayal results in a tragic consequence. The killing emotion of guilt overwhelms Judas and he hangs himself. If only he had allowed himself to catch the pained, yet loving glance of Jesus, he might have clung to that glance, rather the rope that hung him!

There is sin all over this narrative. Consider the aimless gesture of Pilate washing his hands, as though that would free him from responsibility.

Keep yourself very close to Jesus as you pray the Passion. Distance from him makes you vulnerable to the Enemy. The Deliverer is delivered to be crucified.

10
Ki
A

Saturday   **The Sabbath Torah Reading**

Nov 08, 2008 #3B	Nov 11, 2017 #5B	Nov 07, 2026 #5B	Nov 10, 2035 #3B
Nov 05, 2011 #3B	Nov 07, 2020 #4B	Nov 10, 2029 #6B	Nov 06, 2038 #3B
Nov 08, 2014 #4B	Nov 11 2023 #5B	Nov 06, 2032 #6B	Nov 09, 2041 #4B

The Eleventh Week in Kingdomtide

Begins on the Sunday nearest November 9. Alphabyte: Xerography, p. 114

Sunday　　　　　　　　*Here I Come!*　　　　　　　　**Matthew 25:1–13**

"So stay awake and be prepared,
because you do not know the day or hour of my return." v. 13

If there is any outdoor game we all played as children, it is *"Hide 'n Seek,"* with its ringing cry: "Ready or not: here I come!" Think of this shout coming from Jesus as we start the fire on the lamps of our hearts with "The Parable of the Wise and Foolish Virgins." Ten are asked to meet the bridegroom; five are ready, five were not.

There is a difference between those playing *Hide 'n Seek* and those lost and not yet found. For the latter, the bridegroom becomes the Good Shepherd who goes in search of the lost sheep. Those already found need to stop playing *Hide 'n Seek* with Jesus, and simply get ready, for he is coming!

About your heart: is it soaked in the oil of the Holy Spirit so that when he touches your heart with a tongue of fire, you will shine as a light to the world?

Monday　　　　　　　　*God's Plans*　　　　　　　　**Isaiah 37:21–38**

"I know you well—
your comings and goings and all you do." v. 28

The Lord speaks through the mouth of Isaiah, responding as only God can do. The former blasphemies of the Assyrians, as well as the pride of God's people and their lack of reliance upon God, are unmasked with strong assertions of what God is going to do.

There are verses that need to take deep root in your heart, saved from the scorched grass of verse 27. Meditate upon the following in verse 26: "Long ago I planned what I am now causing to happen …" You may think that your present situation is the result of what you have done. On another level, God is working with even your mistakes and sins to bring forth God's plan in your life. Will you let God do this?

The three-year reference to eating the fruits of the land in verse 30, draws attention to the three-year cycle of praying through the Bible. Can you sense the growth in your spiritual life by defining each day by God's Word?

Tuesday　　　　　　　*Healing Divisions*　　　　　　**2 Samuel 19—21**

"I am content just to have you back again, my lord!" 19:30

Power, division, and disloyalty continue, eventually resulting in the two separate kingdoms of Israel and Judah after the death of Solomon. The verse for today comes from the lips of Mephibosheth, Saul's grandson whom David had taken as his own. The return of King David is all that Mephibosheth wants; everything else can go. The presence of the Lord Christ in your heart—what else do you need?

The side of Jesus was opened and divided, so that there could be healing and reconciliation among those torn by division. Even the inner divisions that may be breaking your heart are healed, because Jesus had his heart broken for you.

Greater is the power of Jesus' love than the powers that would split you apart.

Wednesday   *An Overflowing Heart*   **Psalm 45**

My heart overflows with a beautiful thought!
I will recite a lovely poem to the king,
for my tongue is like the pen of a skillful poet. v. 1

The messianic joy of yesterday continues. Hebrews 1:8–9 applies these verses to Christ. From this understanding, the bride is the church, as the writer of Ephesians describes in 5:32.

If there is any event of great joy in human life, it is a marriage. Married love begins with a burst of energy and direction in life. The two look to the future together with anticipation and fresh joy.

For mystic writers, the soul is feminine before God. As the bridegroom, Christ seeks to carry you as his beloved into the house of his risen body. What plans he has for you as you move into the future together!

Picture the "oil of gladness" of verse 7 flowing over you, completely transforming you.

Thursday   *Your New Resume*   **1 Corinthians 15—16**

Christ has been raised from the dead.
He has become the first of a great harvest of those
who will be raised to life again. 15:20

Chapter 15 teaches the intimate connection that exists between Christ's resurrection and ours. One gets its meaning from the other. We are not to believe in the resurrection of Jesus as a reality for Jesus alone, apart from its impact upon the very nature of our own lives.

This chapter is a glorious new resume about who you are in Christ Jesus. It expresses the very essence of your faith. The reading stands in contrast to any less worthy way that you see your life—worthiness not of your own doing, but rather of what Christ Jesus has recreated you to be in his own body.

As you prayerfully read this and the final chapter, the very familiar verses will take on a greater, inner illumination for your own nourishment. Give thanks to the Lord for this great letter … and for your new resume!

Friday   *Die with Jesus*   **Matthew 27:32–66**

"Truly this was the Son of God!" v. 54

Ask Simon of Cyrene to let you carry the cross with Jesus for a while. Allow your senses to come alive in the scene, letting the Lord use your imagination to take you beyond the imaginable—God's Son dying for you. Live the darkness of the sixth to the ninth hour (Noon to three PM). Hear Jesus' cries against the harsh background of blasphemy. Die with Jesus as he dies for you. The presence of God becomes accessible as the curtain between the Holy Place and the Holy of Holies is torn in two. Dead saints break loose from the grave. At the very moment of death, signs of Jesus coming to life are present!

May your contemplation of the death of Jesus have you ready to die with him. Let go of all that needs to die in you, so that you can rise with Jesus.

11
Ki
A

Saturday   **The Sabbath Torah Reading**

Nov 15, 2008 #4B	Nov 18, 2017 #6B	Nov 14, 2026 #6B	Nov 17, 2035 #4B
Nov 12, 2011 #4B	Nov 14, 2020 #5B	Nov 17, 2029 #7B	Nov 13, 2038 #4B
Nov 15, 2014 #5B	Nov 18 2023 #6B	Nov 13, 2032 #7B	Nov 16, 2041 #5B

The Twelfth Week in Kingdomtide

Begins on the Sunday nearest November 16. Alphabyte: Year, p. 115

Sunday   ***What Talent!***   **Matthew 25:14–30**

**To those who use well what they are given,
even more will be given ... v. 29**

Reflect carefully upon "The Parable of the Talents." Was the man with five talents five times more valuable than the man with one? Could it be that he had a high sense of his worth, more open to taking risks, since his self-worth was greater than the man with one talent? Here is the problem. We have transferred not only the name "talent" from money to innate gifts, but we have a society that compares and judges one another by the amount of talent that one has.

How are you when it comes to taking spiritual risks about who you are and how you see yourself? Do you bury your talents with judgments about yourself and comparisons with others that crush the hidden dreams the Lord offers you? The resurrection of Jesus pulls your out from being buried alive! What a talent you have and are, when the Spirit lives within!

Monday   ***The Evening of Life***   **Isaiah 38**

**Yes, it was good for me to suffer this anguish,
for you have rescued me from death and have forgiven all my sins. v. 17**

Autumn is the evening time of the year, as the earth "dies" in winter. The colder days and diminishing light continue to draw us into that inwardness which is the gift of autumn. Separate time this evening to review again the psalm-like prayer of King Hezekiah. It is the "evening" of his life, soon to end. His words flow with the wisdom of the Holy Spirit as a model for your prayer.

Hezekiah discovers images in the movement of his prayer. If you were to place yourself on your death-bed, what images of your own life would the Spirit give you? Even though you may only be imagining this hour as your last, are you sure of yet another whole hour when the clock chimes?

Tuesday   ***Praise Focus***   **2 Samuel 22—24**

**I will call on the Lord, who is worthy of praise,
for he saves me from my enemies. v. 4**

The Lord acts to bring justice and victory to those who trust in him. (Chapter 22 and Psalm 18 are identical.) Pray this song of David over his whole life and receive the same joy in God's protection for yourself. This can only happen when you humble yourself and look only to the Lord as your protector. Jesus saves you from all your enemies of whatever kind. Praise him. Focus on him. The Lord brings triumph and victory over all that besets you.

This song is a prayer-lift in the presence of chapters of tragic history. David's prayer will uplift you. Mull over the images; make them yours.

No one can take away your peace unless you let him or her do it. Do you let this happen at times because there is something wanting in your focus of praise?

Wednesday	*God Is Our Refuge*	Psalm 46

"Be silent, and know that I am God!" v. 10

Someone once said: "The only thing you need is the ground beneath your feet." In a world, which creates so many needs, we are tempted to find absolute what is only relative.

However, today's psalm goes even further. "We will not fear even if earthquakes come and the mountains crumble into the sea" (v. 2). Here is a psalmist whose only trust is in the Lord as his refuge. Though the ground is removed beneath his feet, his confidence in God is unshaken. The twentieth century theologian, Paul Tillich, referred to God as "The Ground of our being."

Feel the contrast in v. 4 as the image of the peaceful stream brings joy. The verse for the day, sometimes translated as "Be still and know …," means simply this: "Stop *your* doing and let God act."

Thursday	*Sharing the Vision*	Revelation 1

"I am the Alpha and the Omega—the beginning and the end," says the Lord God." v. 8

A year of grace is ending with the beginning of the last book of the Bible, Revelation. John reveals the visions he received from the Lord about the events between the first and second coming of Jesus. The contents of the book consist of seven groups, seven being the symbolic number of perfection and fullness.

Not only picture the images, but also receive them by faith just as they are revealed to John. Find comfort in the assurance of Christ's final victory over evil. He is already reigning. The only power that Satan has is to deceive us into thinking that the victory has not taken place. There is glorious hope here. Read in triumph.

Friday	*Two Empty Places*	Matthew 28:1–15

"Don't be afraid! Go tell my brothers to leave for Galilee, and they will see me there." v. 10

Catch the shift of emotions as Mary Magdalene and "the other Mary" move from grief, to surprise, wonder, and absolute joy as they meet Jesus on the road. Contemplate the scene as Jesus alive takes action again, now that the passion is over.

Look at the two empty places that bear witness to Jesus alive—the cross and the tomb, both without Jesus filling them.

In the emptiness, allow the faith in the resurrection to well up deep within your spirit. Jesus is alive for you just as he was alive to the women on the road and the disciples in Galilee. As this sacred season comes to a close with the end of Matthew's Gospel, what do you notice about your commitment to the Lord who lives inside you?

Saturday

The Sabbath Torah Reading

12
Ki
A

Nov 22, 2008 #5B	Nov 25, 2017 #7B	Nov 21, 2026 #7B	Nov 24, 2035 #5B
Nov 19, 2011 #5B	Nov 21, 2020 #6B	Nov 24, 2029 #8B	Nov 20, 2038 #5B
Nov 22, 2014 #6B	Nov 25 2023 #7B	Nov 20, 2032 #8B	Nov 23, 2041 #6B

The Thirteenth Week in Kingdomtide
Begins on the Sunday nearest November 22. Alphabyte: Zoom Lens, p. 115

Sunday   *The Open Book of Life*   **Matthew 25:31–46**
"I assure you, when you did it to one of the least
of these my brothers and sisters, you were doing it to me!" v. 40

There comes a time of judgment for you and I—the moment at our deaths when we will stand before King Jesus with the Book of Life open. While salvation depends upon accepting Jesus as Lord and not upon our works, there is a connection to accepting Jesus that must be seen in action. There are consequences in our surrender to the Lord that need to be evidenced in our sensitivity to the needs of others and to meeting these needs. No one ever presuming to give his or her life to the Lord ought to be blind to the needs summary that Jesus offers in this chapter.

Jesus said, "The decisive issue is whether they obey my Father in heaven" (Matt. 7:21). Are you doing the will of the Lord now as was outlined in the criteria for eternity in the reading for today? Spend time in the quiet, until any defensiveness within yields to surrender in action to the Lord.

Monday   *Two Sides of a King*   **Isaiah 39**
"They saw everything," Hezekiah replied.
"I showed them everything I own—all my treasures. v. 4

Hezekiah is better at praying than at being a diplomat. Recalling the prayer of King Hezekiah in last week's reading and contrasting it with today's chapter, we discover a king who is a mixture of fervor in prayer on the one hand, weakness and co-dependency on the other.

Our last taste of Hezekiah is in his weakness. Look at the final verse of the reading. He displays the treasures of the kingdom to foreigners. He has no boundaries. He reveals precious articles intended only for the worship of the Lord, to a people with no respect for God. Jesus would say that he is "Giving pearls to swine" (Matt. 7:6).

Have respect for what the Lord says to you in the privacy of your own prayer, revealing and witnessing to others according to God's invitation. Beware of sharing emotions and personal graces with those who at best could care less or who worse, despise the things of the Lord.

Tuesday   *The Lasting and the Passing*   **Ecclesiastes 1—4**
"Everything is meaningless," says the Teacher,
"utterly meaningless!" 1:3

Jewish people have a tradition of reading this book in the fall. They recognize that the author, attributed to be Solomon, was writing these words of wisdom in the autumn of his life. We retain this tradition in closing the final Tuesday of the three-year cycle with this book.

The theme of the work is in the verse for the day. The word "meaningless" (sometimes translated as "vanity") occurs throughout the whole book, translating the Hebrew word *yitron*, meaning "breath"—all that is empty and without substance.

Read these chapters with the wisdom that the Spirit gives you in Jesus—the Way, the Truth and the Life. Everything in life is ultimately empty and meaningless without the grounding and centering that life in God brings.

Wednesday   *Applause for Creation*   **Psalm 47**
Come, everyone, and clap your hands for joy!
Shout to God with joyful praise! v. 1

I remember a delightful evening many years ago, walking with some dear brothers on the lovely grounds of the former novitiate of *St. Andrew-on-Hudson* in Hyde Park, New York. We asked ourselves, "Why do we only applaud when someone performs? Why don't we clap for God's beautiful creation … like that tree over there?" We began to applaud the tree, turning to other ones whose beauty was revealed to us the more we clapped. There was a simple, clear joy in our abandon.

For our Jewish ancestors, clapping the hands for the Lord's victory over enemies was as spontaneous as our society's standing ovation after a great performance, or during a ticker-tape parade of heroes on Broadway in New York City.

Do not allow secular settings to be the only ones for applause—especially since clapping first began with the sacred. Applaud God in all manifestations of the divine in creation.

Thursday   *Letters to Seven Churches*   **Revelation 2—3**
"Look! Here I stand at the door and knock. If you hear me calling and open the door,
I will come in, and we will share a meal as friends. 3:20

As you read these letters to the seven churches, catch the essence of the point of John's writing to each of them. Evils that attack the church from within beset them.

Does your heart nod, acknowledging any of these points as applying to you? If so, repent. Also, hear these letters as though you yourself were one of the churches to whom John is writing. Thus your repentance will not only be personal, but communal, as you ask the Lord's forgiveness for how the Church today has fallen into the same areas of sin as these early communities. Intercede for the Body of Christ as you read and pray.

An evening supper with the Lord in the Book of Revelation marks this last Thursday of *Kingdomtide*.

Friday   *The Great Commission*   **Matthew 28:16–20**
"Teach these new disciples to obey all the commands I have given you.
And be sure of this: I am with you always, even to the end of the age." v. 20

Recall the mountains in this Gospel—the setting for the Beatitudes in "The Sermon on the Mount," Mount Tabor where the Transfiguration of Jesus took place, Mount Calvary, and finally this mountain where your King bids farewell and gives "The Great Commission."

On this last week of another year of grace, place yourself among those first disciples who heard the commission. Feel yourself a part of the Church, bonded together in such a way that Christ lives in you and works through you because of the connections you have with the members of Christ's body.

Take the Great Commission personally. How are you living it? What changes in your life need to take place? Advent begins in two days: will you be disposed to live in the Kingdom? A new year of grace is about to rush in for you!

13
Ki
A

Saturday   **The Sabbath Torah Reading**

Nov 29, 2008 #5B	Dec 02, 2017 #7B	Nov 28, 2026 #7B	Dec 01, 2035 #5B
Nov 26, 2011 #5B	Nov 28, 2020 #6B	Dec 01, 2029 #8B	Nov 27, 2038 #5B
Nov 29, 2014 #6B	Dec 02 2023 #7B	Nov 27, 2032 #8B	Nov. 30, 2041 #7B

ADVENT
TO
EPIPHANY

WINTER

Northern Hemisphere

Year B
2009, 2012, 2015 …

Advent begins every year
on the Sunday nearest November 30, St. Andrew's Day.
See the entire cycle of readings at a glance on page xx.

The First Week in Advent

Begins on the Sunday nearest St. Andrew's Day, Nov. 30. Alphabyte: Advent Wreath, p. 3
Alphabyte: Advent Wreath

Sunday   *With Faith Awakened*   **Mark 13:24–37**

Therefore keep watch because you do not know when the owner of the house
will come back—whether in the evening, or at midnight,
or when the rooster crows, or at dawn. v. 35

Jesus' words that you will read sound more like something ending, rather than the beginning of a new church year. It appears to be the reversal of the first verses of Genesis when God created light, the sun, and the moon. Darkness comes again, as though chaos, first bound by God at the beginning of the Bible, is swallowing up God's creation again. These are signs of the beginning of something gloriously new—the total reign of Jesus in creation. However, as often happens in our own personal lives, "Things have to get worse before they get better." Present with you right now, the Lord seeks to turn the chaos of your life into one of order and light, even when you do not see it.

Walk awakened in faith and not in fear.

Monday   *Comfort Ye*   **Isaiah 40**

Comfort, comfort my people, says your God. v. 1

Beginning on a lofty note and dropping down four tones as on a doorbell or a clock in slow motion, the tenor in Handel's *Messiah* rings out the cry: **"COMFORT YE!"** He lingers long on the **"YE."** The first one to ring out this cry was the Lord through the prophet, Isaiah. Three times in two verses, "Comfort" is repeated.

Do you have a need to be comforted this Advent and Christmas? Expose the pain in your life without hiding it. You will do this only if you know it is safe to do so, in the presence of someone who will accept the pain.

Believe by faith that you are in the presence right now of The Comforter, the Holy Spirit, who longs to dwell deep within you and release healing rays of comfort and peace.

Tuesday   *Longing To Be Led*   **Judges 1—2**

Whenever the LORD raised up a judge for them, he was with the judge
and saved them out of the hands of their enemies as long as the judge lived;
for the LORD had compassion on them as they groaned under those who oppressed
and afflicted them. 2:18

We begin to consider a period in Jewish history from 1380 to 1050 B.C. Joshua, the Lord's special warrior, has entered into the Promised Land. Once there, possession of all the land begins to take place. Each person begins "to do their own thing." Leadership is needed; the Lord gives gifts of direction to special persons to govern the people, make decisions, and win military victories over the enemies of God's People. The Bible calls them "Judges." Actually, they are a combination of what we would come to divide into three areas in our democratic nation—legislative, executive, and judicial. In addition, they combine military and civil, which we keep separate.

Advent is the time to ask: "Do I long to be led to inner freedom? Reach inward in faith to the Holy Spirit given to you as your personal lawyer and spiritual director.

Wednesday   *The Temple of Time*   **Psalm 48**

Within your temple, O God, we meditate on your unfailing love. v. 9

The only remains of the Temple of Jerusalem are what is now called the "Wailing Wall." This psalm must increase the feelings of grief for Jews as they pray beside this relic of the greatness of the former Temple.

However, more than a building in space, the new temple is the Body of Christ in time. We have entered this holy temple of sacred time through the gateway of Advent. There is a new and heavenly Jerusalem that is to come down from heaven, as we read in Revelation 21:1–4; still, ahead of you lies the daily opportunity to be aware of the intimacy you share with those bonded by the spiritual bones and sinews of the Body of Christ. Time is soaked with eternity.

Let go of all those "former things" in your life that need to pass away that blind and block you from this union with Christ, such as resentments, fears, sins. Let the Holy City descend into your heart.

Thursday   *Old Year—New Year*   **1 John 1**

That which was from the beginning, which we have heard,
which we have seen with our eyes, which we have looked at and our hands have touched—
this we proclaim concerning the Word of life. v. 1

An aged St. John writes this letter in exile on the island of Patmos, near Greece. Just as a pious Jew faces toward the holy city of Jerusalem when he prays three times a day, so does John "turn his eyes upon Jesus" present in the communities of faith which were alive because of Jesus' resurrection. There is a tradition that says that in his nineties, John used to keep repeating: "Little children, little children: love one another."

John's ending years are your beginning ones, as daily Bible reading becomes part of a way of life for you. Get ready! This is a splendid letter. Feel John's enthusiasm as he tells you in the first verses, about how tangible and lovely Jesus was in his earthly flesh.

Your relation with the Lord: how tangible is it?

Friday   *Astounding News*   **Luke 1:1–25**

"The Lord has done this for me," she said."
In these days he has shown his favor and taken away my disgrace among the people." v. 25

Once a year on *Yom Kippur*, the Day of Atonement, a Jewish priest would be privileged to offer incense in the Holy of Holies, the innermost sanctuary of the Temple. Lots were drawn to see who it would be. In today's passage, they fell to Zechariah. The moment of a lifetime had come.

He is there to atone for his people, and to pray longingly for the Messiah. There was an additional heartache for him; he and his elderly wife Elizabeth were yearning for their own child. However, it seemed too late; she was just too old.

Enter Gabriel with astounding news—a son for Zechariah and Elizabeth, intimately connecting the child with the coming of the Messiah! Zechariah was not prepared to listen to this, and so he was unprepared to shout out its news. He is struck dumb.

How open are you to the wonderful things the Lord wants to do with you?

Saturday   **The Sabbath Torah Reading**

Dec 3, 2005 #6B	Dec 6, 2014 #8B	Dec 9, 2023 #9B	Dec 4, 2032 #10B
Dec 6, 2008 #7B	Dec 9, 2017 #9B	Dec 5, 2026 #9B	Dec 8, 2035 #7B
Dec 3, 2011 #7B	Dec 5, 2020 #8B	Dec 8, 2029 #10B	Dec 4, 2038 #7B

The Second Week in Advent
Begins on the Sunday nearest December 7. Alphabyte: Bible, p. 4

Sunday   *God Is Up to Something*   **Mark 1: 1–8**
**This was John's message: "After me will come one more powerful than I,
the thongs of whose sandals I am not worthy to stoop down and untie." v. 7**

If you find yourself caught in the humdrum of your own expectations of how things are going to be, then Advent is the time to be shaken to new awareness. The Lord wants to leap into your world and offer you the power to change it.

This shaking is not an outer violence, but an inner one. If you are alone, lost and thirsty in a desert, then the faint voice of another promising to lead you out will be very refreshing. This is the voice and water of John.

Listen to the beginnings of this Gospel, which shall be with us this year. Your heart quivers as you hear these words with millions of believers throughout the earth. God is up to something great for you in fire and in the Holy Spirit.

Monday   *Back Home from Exile*   **Isaiah 41**
**So do not fear, for I am with you; do not be dismayed, for I am your God.
I will strengthen you and help you; I will uphold you with my righteous right hand. v. 10**

Look for quiet times of the day, perhaps in the morning. If it is evening, let the first two candles of an Advent Wreath push back the darkness that moves in more and more to take light from the day as winter comes. Make an Advent Bible Journal for yourself so that you can note spiritual movements in your soul.

Prepare such a prayerful setting as you read Isaiah, the blessed Advent prophet. This chapter begins with all of the cities by the Mediterranean shore as witnesses to the goodness of God in raising the pagan Persian King Cyrus to lead the Chosen People back to their land.

Do you sometimes think that things are just not working out for you in the deep, quiet, places in your heart? Do you relate to being in a kind of exile at times? Pour out your feelings to the Lord and let God lead you "home."

Tuesday   *Going It Alone?*   **Judges 3—4**
**Then Deborah said to Barak, "Go! This is the day the LORD has given Sisera into your hands.
Has not the LORD gone ahead of you?" 4:14**

Various judges introduce themselves in this book—heroes who single-handedly take charge and win over enemies. They are fearless, bold, and risk-taking. There is one exception to this, however; they are very aware of the power and the presence of God who gives them wisdom, discernment, courage, and whatever else needed at each moment.

They are constant examples of one basic principle in the spiritual life: fidelity means victory; faithlessness and idolatry mean defeat. The judges do not go it alone. They have a deep sense of the presence of God who is always with them. Learn from Deborah, the first woman "General" in the Bible, and Supreme Court Justice to boot!

Today, think about how you face the challenges in your life. You are not alone.

Wednesday   *Drawn into Serenity*   **Psalm 49**

But God will redeem my life from the grave;
he will surely take me to himself. v. 15

This psalm breathes the wisdom of proverbs. Originally, a sweet musical accompaniment softened the hearts of the first listeners to receive these truths. For you as well: let the Holy Spirit fill the silence that weaves itself between the verses, serenading you with a holy inner music that eases the pure teaching of this psalm into your own spirit.

Today's verse is one of those special places that uplift Jewish belief in the resurrection. Give thanks to the Lord for the gift of faith that you have, to affirm as true, that which escapes the five senses. Ask the Lord to let you see the essentials in your life beyond the senses, into the perspective of eternity.

What are the areas of your life that you still resist giving over to the Lord? Are there temporal, passing conditions that you have allowed to take away your peace? This psalm will draw you more and more into the serenity of a quiet, winter night in Advent.

Thursday   *Strings of Light*   **1 John 2:1–11**

Anyone who claims to be in the light
but hates his brother is still in the darkness. v. 9

Points of light spring up all over the land as the darkness of night invades late afternoon. Are there brands of darkness that seek to move in upon the light-center of your life?

As you look at areas in your life where light needs to shine, listen to John remind you that obedience to the Lord is essential for light to fill you. Otherwise, arrogance, error, and hatred—as so much darkness, will try to overtake you.

Hatred is darkness; love is light. Are there pockets of dark resentments in your life? The verses of John's letter will be as a string of lights to adorn the house of your heart. Write. The lines in your journal will continue the points of lights that the Spirit is offering to you.

Friday   *Christ Made Greater*   **Luke 1:26–56**

God has been mindful of the humble state of his servant.
From now on all generations will call me blessed. v. 48

Just as darkness and light are set against each other in this season, so the high and glorious words of Angel Gabriel contrast with the humble, receptive, gentle words of Mary. She makes her decision: "Behold the maidservant of the Lord!" God takes flesh in her womb because of her "Yes."

Mary and Elizabeth meet, as well as the children in their wombs. Mary combines humility with exaltation in her song, the *Magnificat:* "My soul magnifies the Lord."

A magnifying glass makes bigger what you see through it. Mary makes God larger to Elizabeth and us. How can you ready yourself so that when others look at you, they see Christ within and beyond you, made larger, greater, and clearer?

Saturday   **The Sabbath Torah Reading**

Dec 10, 2005 #7B	Dec 13, 2014 #9B	Dec 16, 2023 #10B	Dec 11, 2032 #11B
Dec 13, 2008 #8B	Dec 16, 2017 #10B	Dec 12, 2026 #10B	Dec 15, 2035 #8B
Dec 10, 2011 #8B	Dec 12, 2020 #9B	Dec 15, 2029 #11B	Dec 11, 2038 #8B

The Third Week in Advent

Begins on the Sunday nearest December 14. Alphabyte: Chimes, p. 4

Sunday   *Receive and Believe*   John 1:6–8,12–28
**Yet to all who received him, to those who believed in his name,
he gave the right to become children of God. v. 12**

Karl Walenda, father of the famous family of tightrope walkers, once crossed over Niagara Falls. As he was about to go, he struck up a conversation with someone standing by to watch the feat. Karl turned to the person and asked: "Do you think that I can do it?" "Of course you can," came the reply. "You're Karl Walenda!" Karl responded, "Then if you *really* believe me, jump on my shoulders and go with me!"

The heart of today's reading is the two words, "receive" and "believe." Receive Jesus and believe in him. "Believe" in John's Gospel means an active, total surrender to the Lord. The key words become two dynamic aspects of one reality. When you surrender to Jesus, he enters your heart to dwell there.

Monday   *Something New Is Coming*   Isaiah 42
**He will not shout or cry out, or raise his voice in the streets.
A bruised reed he will not break, and a smoldering wick he will not snuff out.
In faithfulness he will bring forth justice. vv. 2–3**

Does this gnawing sense make your life dull: that the future is only going to be a continuation of a boring past? If this is the case, then Isaiah is just for you. In verse 9 he cries out: "Look: the things of the past are over: new things I declare."

Something that is very new is the absence of violence as the Lord announces the future. The warriors in Judges contrast with the gentle movement and images of this chapter. As you read, prepare for a day that will be different from any day you ever experienced. Look to the Lord who is ever old and ever new to bring life to you today.

The problem with God's people of the past was those carved images. Now if there is anything that is predictable and unchangeable, it is a carved image! Our God is surprising. Wait with expectancy and see what God is up to with you today.

Tuesday   *Instruments for God*   Judges 5—6
**So may all your enemies perish, O LORD! But may they who love you be like
the sun when it rises in its strength. 5:31**

Singing and celebrating the wonders of the Lord lift energies from within and link them with the very power of God. Deborah's source of success was her total confidence that God would always be with her. She knew that victory was not *her* doing, but the Lord's.

Note the contrast after Deborah's song. You might think that such a celebration would have the sense of the divine presence flow from her to all the people. Not so … They return to evil ways of idolatry in chapter 6. Then the Lord raises up Gideon to be the next judge. Success comes because he is an instrument fitted for God's hand.

Do you want the Lord to use you? Sing in your heart to God and trust in God alone. Get ready for the special call placed upon you. You are a special instrument in God's hand.

Call upon me in the day of trouble;
I will deliver you, and you will honor me. v. 15

As intense as is the brightness of the sun from its rising to its setting, so is the brilliance and the fullness of God's presence in this psalm. Each verse is a ray of light to shine on you and shake you from routine acts of worship that fail to honor the God of light due to the dullness of the soul.

More than the sacrifices of animals, the Lord longs for us to express thanks and trust in God. Outer offerings are meaningless without expressions of inner surrender.

The strong admonitions from verse 16 confront you in those areas of sinfulness, which may yet lurk in the dark corners of the soul. May the light of God be as a search light into those areas, revealing any vestige of dishonesty and hypocrisy that the Lord abhors. The divine fire seeks to burn away everything in you, until there is nothing but radiant expressions of thanksgiving, trust, and praise.

Thursday   *The Passing and the Lasting*   **1 John 2: 12–17**

The world and its desires pass away,
but the man who does the will of God lives forever. v. 17

If you were to describe your spiritual states before God as a member of a family, what would you call yourself? Are you a "father," a "spoiled child"? How might others in a family see you with an honest perception of how you are? John does this in the church community to whom he is writing.

Whatever is your assessment of spiritual growth, the words in verses 15–17 need to be taken to heart. Reflect upon what is passing in your life and what lasts forever. Take the three-fold assessment that John makes of the world and meditate on them until their truth comes home to you. Take this with you today and always: **"He who does the will of God abides forever."**

Friday   *Son-Light Each Day*   **Luke 1:57–80**

And you, my child, will be called a prophet of the Most High;
for you will go on before the Lord to prepare the way for him. v. 76

There are three songs in two chapters: what a way to begin a Gospel! The first is the song of Zechariah in today's reading; the second is the song of Mary we considered last Friday; the final one is the song of Simeon in 2:29–32. Religious communities have been singing these songs for centuries as part of morning, evening, and night prayer.

The song of Zechariah is the first sound of praise that flows from his lips after he was struck dumb. After the silence of the night, a faith-filled praying of this song will have you begin your day aware of God's power. God is faithful to you now, just as in past ages. You will be "the child" to go before him to prepare the way for Jesus—the bright "Son-Light" for others in your day.

Saturday   **The Sabbath Torah Reading**

Dec 17, 2005 #8B	Dec 20, 2014 #10B	Dec 23, 2023 #11B	Dec 18, 2032 #12B
Dec 20, 2008 #9B	Dec 23, 2017 #11B	Dec 19, 2026 #11B	Dec 22, 2035 #9B
Dec 17, 2011 #9B	Dec 19, 2020 #10B	Dec 22, 2029 #12B	Dec 18, 2038 #9B

The Fourth Week in Advent

Begins on the Sunday nearest December 21. Alphabyte: Darkroom, p. 5

Sunday   *Conceiving the Word*   **Luke 1:26–38**
"I am the Lord's servant," Mary answered.
"May it be to me as you have said." v. 38

The angel Gabriel's exalted words to Mary would not have happened without her permission. God does not impose God's will on anyone. "Let it be to me according to your word," says Mary. She gives permission for God to act in her in the most extraordinary manner possible. In the quiet of Mary's soul, God shapes the deepest designs for redemption. She says **"Yes."** The Son of God takes flesh in her womb.

The same gift of conceiving the Word can happen to you; you will need to give God the same permission as Mary did.

Ponder this passage carefully and let the Holy Spirit prompt you to say with your whole being, "Let it be to me according to Your Word."

Monday   *God's Preferential Love*   **Isaiah 43**
This is what the LORD says-he who created you, O Jacob, he who formed you,
O Israel: "Fear not, for I have redeemed you;
I have summoned you by name; you are mine." v. 1

The Lord of all creation speaks tenderly and lovingly to the Chosen People. God longs that there be a loving union with God and the people. There never need be fear of anything, for the Lord will protect. God's only interest is that the people respond to the preferential love that God has for them. Why this preference? This would be to know the mind of God—something that escapes us, and needs to escape us.

Jesus came to save all. God loves everyone, yet with a love that makes it seem as though each person is the only one. The Lord of the universe longs that you love God in return. Accept this with faith. Let yourself be loved by God and with this grace, to love God in return through loving the poor; God has a preferential love for them.

Tuesday   *Into the Camp of the Enemy*   **Judges 7—8**
The LORD said to Gideon, "With the three hundred men that lapped
I will save you and give the Midianites into your hands.
Let all the other men go, each to his own place." 7:7

We encounter the man of valor who named the Gideons. Just as Gideon went into the camp of the enemy, so do the Gideons go into "camps" where the Enemy might be at work, with the prayerful hope that the Word of God would move mightily upon the lives of people away from their home.

Note the contrasts in the Book of Judges. There are mighty "Lone Ranger" types with a mission from the Lord; then there are the people who lapse right back into idolatry. The theme is constant in the Old Testament—God's chosen love and the unfaithful response of the people.

Are you being faithful to the Lord and all that God calls you to be?

Wednesday   *Redeeming Grace*   **Psalm 51**

Create in me a pure heart, O God,
and renew a steadfast spirit within me. v. 10

What a comfort this psalm is to anyone who has committed great sin! David shows us the way to abandonment to sorrow and grief over sin. His sins of adultery and murder found in 2 Samuel 11 and 12, result in an even greater repentance. His prayer has come down to us, the most well known of seven "Penitential Psalms." Feel the soul's upward movement, first humbled and purified by sorrow, then a gentle, peaceful lifting as the soul becomes open to the sweetness of being forgiven.

Notice that David does not wallow in guilt; this is self-serving and gridlocks the movement of the self toward true reconciliation with God. Only a gifted consciousness of God's great mercy can lead one out of the depths of remorse into the light of God's redeeming grace.

Thursday   *The Anointing Abides in You*   **John 2:18–29**

As for you, the anointing you received from him remains in you, and you do not need anyone to teach you. But as his anointing teaches you about all things and as that anointing is real, not counterfeit-just as it has taught you, remain in him. v. 27

We are in the final times. Whatever hour you are in right now, there is a spiritual sense that it is part of the last hour as expressed by John in verse 18. While we cannot predict just when the actual end will come, it has begun already with what took place on the last day of the old creation, Good Friday.

The anointing of the Holy Spirit gives you all you need to know about what to do. What an assertion in verse 20: "You know all things!" This is due to the anointing, gift of the Holy Spirit.

In order to access this knowledge, you need a life of prayer, union with other wise persons who are also under the anointing, and a total desire to dedicate yourself to the Lord. Trust that the Lord will indeed speak to you heart. Be willing to filter out everything else, so that you can hear.

Friday   *Jesus Comes to Stay*   **Luke 2:1–20**

She gave birth to her firstborn, a son. She wrapped him in cloths and placed him in a manger, because there was no room for them in the inn. v. 7

"No room for them in the inn." Francis of Assisi in the fourteenth century contemplated this fact, beginning the tradition of meditations on the manger with stable and animals as an expression of the poverty of Jesus' birth. While Luke would agree, there are two further points he wants to bring to our silent, prayerful attention.

First, there was no room for Mary and Joseph in the inn, because Jesus did not just come for a visit to stay awhile, as we do when we stop at a motel. Jesus came to stay!

Second, Mary and Joseph laid Jesus in a manger, the place where animals eat. Jesus rests for the first time in a place reminding us that he would become our food one day, the day before he rested on another wooden framed structure—the cross.

Saturday   **The Sabbath Torah Reading**

Dec 24, 2005 #9B	Dec 27, 2014 #11B	Dec 30, 2023 #12B	Dec 25, 2032 #13B
Dec 27, 2008 #10B	Dec 30, 2017 #12B	Dec 26, 2026 #12B	Dec 29, 2035 #10B
Dec 24, 2011 #10B	Dec 26, 2020 #11B	Dec 29, 2029 #13B	Dec 25, 2038 #10B

Christmas Week
Begins on the Sunday nearest December 28. Alphabyte: Evergreens, p. 5

Sunday   *Resting with Assurance*   **Luke 2:22–40**
**"Sovereign Lord, as you have promised, you now dismiss your servant in peace.
For my eyes have seen your salvation, which you have prepared in the sight of all people, a light for revelation to the Gentiles and for glory to your people Israel." vv. 29–32**

Themes of old and new weave themselves through the infancy stories of Jesus in Luke. The aged Zechariah and Elizabeth are types of the ancient longing, seen next to the young Mary and Joseph. Now it is Simeon and Anna contrasted with Mary and Joseph who arrive to present Jesus in the Temple. Faithful Simeon is there and Anna, who spent eighty-four years of her widowhood praying constantly in the Temple for the coming of the Messiah. The Holy Spirit tells them that the quiet, gentle couple arriving this day is the answer to their deepest prayer.

Old and new meet; patience and joy embrace. The song of Simeon sweetly lifts itself every night as those in monasteries bid farewell to a day of grace and fall asleep. May you rest assured that the Lord has indeed come, a fact that the Holy Spirit gives to you right now. Receive the child in the temple of your heart and rest.

Monday   *The Fullness of Life and Joy*   **Isaiah 44**
I will pour water on the thirsty land, and streams on the dry ground; I will pour out my Spirit on your offspring, and my blessing on your descendants. They will spring up like grass in a meadow, like poplar trees by flowing streams. vv. 3–4

The theme of blessing continues strongly in this chapter filled with God's loving move upon God's people. The blessing is the stronger as we celebrate Christmas. Look at the extent to which the Lord goes to redeem us and to have divine life present in us.

The cry of the Lord rises in verses 21 ff. after God has described the emptiness of idolatry in detail. Your Creator is also your most loving parent who wants to share everything with you, the beloved. God will forget all your sins; just return to the Lord with all your heart. Nothing less than the whole heart of God is focused upon you; God wants nothing less in return.

We have anything but a boring, distant God! Let the fresh loving joy of the Lord in this chapter quicken the fullness of life and joy in your own heart.

Tuesday   *The Evil of Self As Center*   **Judges 9—10**
**Then they got rid of the foreign gods among them and served the LORD.
And he could bear Israel's misery no longer. 10:16**

Abimelech was a son of Gideon by a concubine. He had seventy half brothers. Today you will read what Abimelech did to them. Yes, there are persons and situations in the Old Testament who perform evils so great, that it would challenge the movie industry to portray them. Abimilech is one of these persons; he had an atrocious lust for power.

While you may read his story in amazement, just know that there is a potential Abimelech inside of each one of us. The same temptation to power, control, self-centeredness, unconcern for the things of the Lord, can be at work in our own hearts. But for the grace of the Lord Jesus, there go you and I!

The Lord sends persons to liberate God's people who, in turn, lapse immediately into idolatry. God feels. Pray with a desire to experience God's hurt.

Is there anything you are doing to avoid placing God as the center of your life?

Wednesday   *Hostility and Tenderness*   **Psalm 52**

But I am like an olive tree flourishing in the house of God;
I trust in God's unfailing love for ever and ever. v. 8

This brief psalm sharp creates a distinction between the feverish, hostile plots of the wicked, and the quiet restfulness of the green olive tree planted in the house of God. Evil consumes itself, spent by Godless, self-propelled energy.

The green olive tree does nothing but enjoy its presence in the Temple of the Lord. There it is content to stay and play, trusting in the greenness of its life from being in God's presence.

Feel the contrast between this psalm and the scheming world sated and spent by the shopping season just past. Inventory and hoarding profit are its post-Christmas agenda. However, you … Go to the stable. Adore with the shepherds, Mary and Joseph. Rejoice in the tender infant Jesus, the "green olive tree." Will you allow Jesus to be engrafted onto your heart?

Thursday   *You are a Child of God*   **1 John 3:1–9**

How great is the love the Father has lavished on us,
that we should be called children of God! And that is what we are!
The reason the world does not know us is that it did not know him. v. 1

Just as Jesus was presented in the Temple as an infant, so you have been presented to the Temple of Christ's risen body. Because you live in Christ and he lives in you, you are a child of God. John is wondrously in touch with this fact as he cries out the first verse of the reading, **"We are children of God!"**

Throughout this letter, themes of darkness and light, of sin and abiding in Christ, are set in stark contrast. For John there are no "gray" areas. There is either a life of sin or a life of grace going on inside of you and me. Yes, there may be occasional acts of sin, but the torque, the momentum, the full surrender of life is to be totally within God. If you are there, then a life of habitual sin is not possible. Experience what it is like to be a child—a very own child of God.

Friday   *Your Three Gifts*   **Matthew 2**

On coming to the house, they saw the child with his mother Mary, and they bowed down
and worshiped him. Then they opened their treasures and presented him
with gifts of gold and of incense and of myrrh. v. 11

The three gifts of the King—let them be yours. **Gold**, symbol of the ultimate possession: **you** are the ultimate gift for the Christ Child. All of who you are is pure Gold to God.

Frankincense is a hard resin from Arabian trees. It looks like stone, until it falls on hot coals, becoming a sweet smelling smoke. Fall upon the fire of the Spirit and the same will become of you. **Myrrh**, from the Arabic word for bitter, is an ointment offered to Jesus on the cross to soothe his pain. He refused it.

Take your cue from Jesus. Do not anesthetize pain by habits that blunt the spirit. Give the bitterness of suffering to Jesus. Through prayer, pain is transformed and redeemed.

Saturday   **The Sabbath Torah Reading**

Dec 31, 2005 #10B	Jan 03, 2015 #12B	Jan 06, 2024 #13B	Jan 01, 2033 #14B
Jan 03, 2009 #11B	Jan 06, 2018 #13B	Jan 02, 2027 #13B	Jan 05, 2036 #11B
Dec 31, 2011 #11B	Jan 02, 2021 #12B	Jan 05, 2030 #14B	Jan 01, 2039 #11B

The First Week in Epiphany
*Begins on the first Sunday in January. Alphabyte: **Frankincense**, p. 6*

Sunday   *Jesus Embraces Our History*   **Matthew 2:13–23**

So he got up, took the child and his mother during the night and left for Egypt,
where he stayed until the death of Herod. And so was fulfilled what the Lord had said
through the prophet: "Out of Egypt I called my son." vv. 14–15

About this time of the year, Jewish people read the book of Exodus on Saturdays in synagogues throughout the world. Today's section of the Epiphany story links the ancient account of the Exodus with the history of Jesus. Just as the Chosen People's liberation began in Egypt, so does Jesus embrace the history of his people and go to Egypt. Herod is as the wicked Pharaoh who sought the life of Jesus. For Matthew, Jesus is a New Moses who is going to free his people. The weeping mothers of Bethlehem link with the weeping mothers during that other period in our history of suffering, the Exile in Babylon.

Nothing can stop what God wants to do. God is going to liberate God's people. This will happen for you, when you listen and respond to the Lord's call upon your life. God will protect you from the Evil One so that the full measure of God's anointing can flow into your soul.

Monday   *The Heavens Rain Salvation*   **Isaiah 45**

"You heavens above, rain down righteousness; let the clouds shower it down.
Let the earth open wide, let salvation spring up, let righteousness grow with it;
I, the LORD, have created it." v. 8

It is Epiphany, time of God's manifestation—the meaning of the word. Today we read about God revealing himself to a pagan King, Cyrus, who would allow Israel to go back to their homeland from Exile in 538 B.C. The ancient historian Josephus relates that King Cyrus decided to let Israel go when he read this passage about himself.

Verse 8 deserves a special focus: "Rain down, you heavens, from above …" It has happened. The Lord has come down. He desires to enter your soul as the sweetest of rains that soak the earth.

Isaiah is a poet whose images will carry your prayer along. He unfolds God as a powerful, all-encompassing presence in every aspect of creation. Exult in the Lord as you by faith, experience God's power and presence in the world.

Tuesday   *Going It Alone*   **Judges 11—12**

After the two months, she returned to her father and he did to her as he had vowed.
And she was a virgin. From this comes the Israelite custom that each year
the young women of Israel go out for four days
to commemorate the daughter of Jephthah the Gileadite. 11:39–40

The story of Jephtha's daughter is a sad one. While a tragedy in itself, the deeper sadness in this period is that for the most part, only the judges themselves were faithful. They were much like "Lone Rangers," lacking consistent support from the people to make the victories in war usher in times of spiritual peace. The people refused to follow the Lord's ways. Jephtha felt that he must keep the vow he made to God, which involved such a sad outcome for his only child.

Are you finding all the support you need to grow spiritually? One of the aspects of these daily readings is the hope that you will find others who are contemplating these passages everyday with you. Together you can reflect upon what the Lord is saying to your lives. The Lord does not want you to go it alone.

Wednesday   *Withering Fools*   Psalm 53

Note: This psalm and psalm 14 are the same, except for the latter's use of the name *Yahweh* for God.
Oh, that salvation for Israel would come out of Zion!
When God restores the fortunes of his people, let Jacob rejoice and Israel be glad! v. 6

Read this psalm with Herod in mind, along with the scheming retinue that surrounds and chokes him of life. They are fools that do not know God. The root in Hebrew for "fool," *nabal,* means to "fall away," or "to wither." Just as in Jesus' "Parable of the Sower," when seed falls on rocky ground, the plant withers and falls away, because the roots do not go deep.

Feel again the contrast between corrupt, worldly power typified by Herod, and the salvation expressed in the final verse that has come in Jesus. Do not play the fool by failing to engraft your spiritual roots onto the vine, which is Christ.

You followed Jesus to Bethlehem and adored him there; now go with him to safety in Egypt and feel an inward serenity until all that is "Herod" in your life withers away and dies.

Thursday   *Toward Life or Death*   1 John 3:10–24

This is how we know what love is: Jesus Christ laid down his life for us.
And we ought to lay down our lives for our brothers. v.16

Pray this passage, open to its simple, clear truth. As with darkness and light, here contrasts of death and life, love and hate are starkly set against each other so that John's teaching will affect his listeners.

John does the same as Moses in Deuteronomy 30 when he placed life or death before the people. As Moses invited them to choose life so that they could live, John does the same. Choose light, love, and life instead of darkness, hatred, and death.

Which way will you go today—toward life, or toward death? Pause at various moments of transition in the day to monitor your choices. As an astronaut, perhaps you need "mid-course" correction!

Friday   *Waters of Freedom*   Mark 1:1–8

The whole Judean countryside and all the people of Jerusalem went out to him.
Confessing their sins, they were baptized by him in the Jordan River. v. 5

Mark tells how people "went out" to be baptized by John in the Jordan. This is the same word in Greek for the Exodus. Jesus is the one who is going to lead you up and out of waters drowning you. Spend time with John and Jesus by the banks of these waters of freedom.

The Gospel of Mark will be our companion for the Fridays of most of this year. I suggest you spend time with a Bible Dictionary and a commentary on this Gospel so that you will appreciate the power of Jesus portrayed by Mark. The more you learn, the more the Holy Spirit will find a mind and heart receptive to the presence of God.

Just as in the Exodus, this presence will go before you as a cloud by day and a pillar of fire by night, splitting open the chaotic waters of your life!

Saturday   The Sabbath Torah Reading

Jan 07, 2006 #11B	Jan 10, 2015 #13B	Jan 13, 2024 #14B	Jan 08, 2033 #15B
Jan 10, 2009 #12B	Jan 13, 2018 #14B	Jan 09, 2027 #14B	Jan 12, 2036 #12B
Jan 07, 2012 #12	Jan 09, 2021 #13	Jan12, 2030 #15	Jan 08, 2039 #12

155

The Second Week in Epiphany
Begins on the second Sunday in January. Alphabyte: Gold, p. 6

Sunday,   **The Baptism of the Lord** *More Than a Survivor*   **Mark 1:4–11**
As Jesus was coming up out of the water, he saw heaven being torn open
and the Spirit descending on him like a dove. v. 10

Creation, old and new … Genesis and Mark—feel the blending of these two beginnings as the new year begins. The Holy Spirit hovered over the waters of chaos and gave them a limit they could not trespass so that dry land could come for us to walk upon. It happens again for Jesus by the Jordan. He plunges into the waters of your chaos and mine and emerges onto solid ground. Jesus takes all that would drown you and comes out more than a survivor, a victor! The highway between heaven and earth, blocked by Adam's sin, is wonderfully open again. Now the voice of God can be heard for you and everyone.

How are you? You can respond much more than the typical, "Hanging in there!" You are more than a survivor; you are victorious in Jesus if you will cling to the Lord as the waters rush around you.

Monday   *Carrying You in Total Care*   **Isaiah 46**
Even to your old age and gray hairs, I am he, I am he who will sustain you.
I have made you and I will carry you; I will sustain you and I will rescue you. v. 4

The image or the statue of a false god has to be carried about. Not so with our God, says Isaiah. Our God carries us, sustaining us throughout our lifetime.

The arc of a rainbow is as the span of life, as might say, "From the womb to the tomb." God has total care of you. Today's passage invites you to be in touch by faith with this protective, assertive, energetic and total care of the Lord, carrying you from one end of your life to the other.

When Jesus descended into the waters of the Jordan, he took all your sins upon his shoulders. He carries you through those waters to dry land, just as God covenanted with Noah with the rainbow after the flood and as God opened the Red Sea in the Exodus. He carried the cross, which is your cross and mine, so that the weight of our sins would not have to be borne by us. Praise Him!

Tuesday   **Totally Dedicated to the Lord**   **Judges 13—14**
You will conceive and give birth to a son. No razor may be used on his head,
because the boy is to be a Nazirite, set apart to God from birth,
and he will begin the deliverance of Israel from the hands of the Philistines. 13:5

When God is about to intervene in a unique way in history, an angel announces the coming birth of a specially anointed deliverer. Such was the case with the birth of Isaac, Samuel, and now, Samson. The season of Advent, just past, had us celebrating the angelic announcement of the two greatest persons whom God was going to use—John the Baptist and of course, Jesus.

In the case of the Baptist and Samson, there was a life style that expressed total consecration to the Lord— no wine or strong drink—and, in Samson's case, the full Nazirite vow of never cutting the hair. All these outward signs remind the individual and others of loyalty to the Lord; they were set apart and constantly reminded that their life was given to God.

What is there about your life that reminds you that you are to be totally dedicated to the Lord? In Christ you are very special, called to be a sacrament of his presence.

Wednesday   *Alive in God*   **Psalm 54**
Surely God is my help; the Lord is the one who sustains me. v. 4

The psalms are intimate prayers that join Jews, Moslems, Christians—everyone in the human family. Often, as here, the psalmist has big problems. He is aware of his enemies and begins to describe just how they are getting to him. Yet greater than the power of his enemies, the sacred writer rejoices in the power found in the name of the Lord. So awesome is this power, that Jews refrain from uttering the sacred name of God.

In Christ, we need not be so cautious. Jesus urges us to use his holy name. When prayed with faith and confidence, the same power that raised Jesus from the dead keeps you alive in God, and buoys up those people for whom you are to intercede.

When you are up against it and difficulties simply seem too much, stop, let go and place your faith in the power of the name of the Lord coming against all that comes against you.

Thursday   *The Only Teacher of the Soul*   **1 John 4:1–12**
**You, dear children, are from God and have overcome them, because
the one who is in you is greater than the one who is in the world. v. 4**

It was the first day of class in the twelve-year long course of studies to my ordination. The late Edwin Cuffe, S.J. entered the room. His gentle, kind voice flowed into the room: "Remember: the only teacher of your soul is the Holy Spirit." Then he simply walked out!

John today speaks about "discerning the spirits." Take time to give room for the Spirit to tell you about all other spirits, so that with serenity you can sift the soil of your soul and know how the Lord is at work. When you discern, it is not you who are doing this, but the Spirit of Christ.

While we need to think, consider, wait, weigh and then make decisions, let us yield from start to finish to the Holy Spirit at work throughout.

Friday   *With Jesus on Dry Ground*   **Mark 1:9–20**
**And a voice came from heaven:
"You are my Son, whom I love; with you I am well pleased." v. 11**

Water has various symbolic meanings in the Bible. In the Book of Genesis, it is a sign of chaos. As the Spirit brooded over the waters, limits to water's movements were set beyond which they could not go, as the dry land appeared.

Over the waters of the Jordan, the Spirit broods once again, appearing over Jesus as he is baptized. The chaos of sin is limited as Jesus rises up on dry land. The space between earth and heaven opens and the voice of God is heard. Just as the dove came to rest when the waters of the flood receded, so does the Spirit rest on Jesus.

A new time of salvation came with Jesus' baptism. He rose from the death that is the waters of sin, and brought you to new life in God's Spirit. Rest on the dry land with Jesus on the other side of the Jordan. Follow him in the desert of temptations. Be with him as ministry begins.

Saturday   **The Sabbath Torah Reading**

Jan 14, 2006 #12B	Jan 17, 2015 #14B	Jan 20, 2024 #15B	Jan 15, 2033 #16B
Jan 17, 2009 #13B	Jan 20, 2018 #15B	Jan 16, 2027 #15B	Jan 19, 2036 #13B
Jan 14, 2012 #13B	Jan 16, 2021 #14B	Jan 19, 2030 #16B	Jan 15, 2039 #13B

The Third Week in Epiphany

Begins on the third Sunday in January. Alphabyte: Homing Pigeon, p. 7

Sunday   *Intimacy with God*   **John 1:43–51**
Philip found Nathanael and told him, "We have found the one Moses wrote about in the Law,
and about whom the prophets also wrote—
Jesus of Nazareth, the son of Joseph." v. 45

Disciples of John the Baptist become disciples of Jesus, one by one. With each added disciple, there is a gradual revelation about who Jesus is, culminating in, **"You are the Son of God! You are the King of Israel!"**

In your heart, paint the picture of the exchange of the disciples from John to Jesus. Follow the direction of the finger of John pointing him out as the Lamb of God. Imagine you are drifting to Jesus as a new disciple. The Holy Spirit graces you with the gift of *adherence* to him; this is John's understanding of "belief." Spend the day with Jesus and the others. In your journal, write a dialogue between you and him, as though you had just met. What words of intimacy flow between you and Jesus?

Monday   *The Violation of Virgin Babylon*   **Isaiah 47**
Surely they are like stubble; the fire will burn them up.
They cannot even save themselves from the power of the flame.
Here are no coals to warm anyone; here is no fire to sit by. v. 14

As a deposed queen, the Lord confronts Babylon. She will be a virgin no longer; King Cyrus will violate her. In 539 B.C., he would come and almost destroy the entire city. The Lord gives words of justice to Isaiah about what will happen to Babylon for all her arrogance and abuse of God's people. Pray with Isaiah; feel the power of the poetry in the vivid description of victory.

The victory of the Lord in your life also needs to be real, invading areas where evil may have a stronghold. This chapter will give you confidence and trust in the Lord's entry into areas of your life where you need to yield to the Lord. Allow the Lord to crush those strongholds and throw them out of your life. Pray to know what they are and how you need deliverance—lest you get used to slavery.

Tuesday   *Grief or Joy of the Lord*   **Judges 15—16**
Then she called, "Samson, the Philistines are upon you!"
He awoke from his sleep and thought, "I'll go out as before and shake myself free."
But he did not know that the LORD had left him. 16:20

With all his strength, Samson was weak when it came to lust for women. He had no business letting his attraction for foreign women compel him into marrying one—and much less, the treacherous Delilah. Samson gave her the secret of his strength and he lost it. The tragedy became even more pathetic when Samson thought he still had the anointing of the Lord, but did not.

Feel the power of these words: "The joy of the Lord is your strength" (Nehemiah 8:10); "I can do all things in Christ who strengthens me" (Philippians 4:13). With God at work in you, you need no other power.

May you never grieve the Holy Spirit by being unfaithful to the anointing of the Lord on your life.

Wednesday   *Absolute Confidence in God*   **Psalm 55**

I cry out in distress, and he hears my voice. v. 17

Do you ever feel like wanting to run away from it all? You are in good company; so does David in today's psalm. He wishes he could just fly away like a dove to a wilderness somewhere. What makes things even worse for him is that his own friends are betraying him.

David expresses his anger fully, even imagining the destruction of his enemies. However, as though moved by how dangerous his thoughts are, David reaches out even more "dangerously" into pure trust and confidence in the Lord. As a seesaw tilting from one person shifting and the other suddenly bouncing high, so awareness of the power of God lifts David to the heights. The goodness and faithfulness of the Lord is greater than any wickedness.

Pause at morning, noon and night and at other times of transition in the day. Immediately, cast your burdens before the Lord, lest they overwhelm you.

Thursday   *Love—Beyond, Yet Within*   **1 John 4:13–21**

There is no fear in love. But perfect love drives out fear,
because fear has to do with punishment. The one who fears is not made perfect in love. v. 18

If you have any love in you at all, it is because God, who is Love, is present to you through the Holy Spirit. God does not indwell in us as a reward for our loving; rather God's presence makes it possible to love.

Love is *super-natural*; it is beyond our nature and us. Yes, it's easy to love those who love you, as Matthew 5:46 declares; but love goes beyond egoism and personal attraction and preference, giving a divine quality to our lives, not coming from ourselves, but from God.

The theme of "abiding" or "indwelling" is a central one for John, both in the letters and in his Gospel. Take each verse and let their truths sink deep. Brood over this teaching: "Perfect love casts out fear." The Lord of love dwells in you, burning away all fear until you are aglow with love.

Friday   *Fresh Divine Power*   **Mark 1:21–31**

The people were amazed at his teaching, because he taught them as one
who had authority, not as the teachers of the law. v. 22

The first action of deliverance in Mark's Gospel is the casting out of an unclean spirit. Jesus heals the person at a Sabbath service in the synagogue of Capernaum. Synagogues at that time shared the same, basic sequence of *Torah* readings that we follow on Saturdays.

Jesus' presence in the synagogue is transforming. Persons who need healing, physically or emotionally, are present. Jesus brings fresh, divine power into the covenant of healing which we read around this time in Exodus 15:26. It is basic in Mark: Jesus wins victory over the power of Satan in the movement of his ministry, just as he overcame the devil in the desert. Where the Israelites were faithless, Jesus is faithful.

Be in the synagogue with Jesus and watch him make new what is old, with his love and power.

Saturday   **The Sabbath Torah Reading**

Jan 21, 2006 #13B	Jan 24, 2015 #15B	Jan 27, 2024 #16B	Jan 22, 2033 #17B
Jan 24, 2009 #14B	Jan 27, 2018 #16B	Jan 23, 2027 #16B	Jan 26, 2036 #14B
Jan 21, 2012 #14B	Jan 23, 2021 #15B	Jan 26, 2030 #17B	Jan 22, 2039 #14B

The Fourth Week in Epiphany

Begins on the fourth Sunday in January. Alphabyte: Ice Dancing, p. 7

Sunday   *When You Grow Up*   **Mark 1:14–20**
"Come, follow me," Jesus said, "and I will make you fishers of men." v. 17

Not only being *with* Jesus, but *being* Jesus to the world—this is the meaning of the call of the first disciples. As they clean up their nets and receive the invitation to cast them over a broken, hurting world, they are to become an extension of Jesus himself.

As you "clean up" after your day of work and prepare for rest, ask the Spirit to deal with you about your life-work. Is there something that needs to change for you? Are you willing to get in touch with the pain of the discomfort that may well up with the words: "I'm just not doing what I really want to do!" Respect those feelings of disquiet; they are the beginning of being open to what the Lord is inviting you to do with your life.

What do you want to be when you grow up … in the Lord?

Monday   *Learning from Pain*   **Isaiah 48**
This is what the LORD says-your Redeemer, the Holy One of Israel:
"I am the LORD your God, who teaches you what is best for you,
who directs you in the way you should go. v. 17

Fire can either destroy or purify. "I have tested you in the furnace of affliction," says the Lord. God does not send pain our way; the sin of the world and the consequences of our personal sins result in our being afflicted. However, the Lord promises to be there to purify and transform suffering, with outcomes better than ever.

The action of the Lord teaches us how to grow from pain. The Hebrew word for teaching used in verse 17 is *lamad*. The root of the word is "to goad." Likely, it comes from the way an animal learns by being prodded. Our sufferings *goad* us to learn from them, to be transformed by them. One way is to offer your suffering for others who are not doing so well in theirs. Teach others by the example of your enduring faith in the Lord's fidelity and mercy to God's people as Isaiah declares today.

Tuesday   *The Gods of This World*   **Judges 17—18**
In those days Israel had no king; everyone did as he saw fit. 17:6

The call of the first disciples celebrated this past Sunday contrasts today with the whole tribe of Dan falling into idolatry. There is no leadership, leaving the people infected by the local pagan worship surrounding them. We find this expression here: "Doing your own thing." Life deteriorates when the value of individualism presses against the values of a whole society, which the Lord intends to lead. When God is not at the center, God either becomes unimportant, or at best, a mascot on the sidelines of life. Competition, consumerism, intrigue, vanity— all the gods of this world will move into the sacred turf of your center, if you let them. Look at the dangers when you are not bound and accountable to the integrating, renewing, recreating Body of Christ. The Dans had no accountability to the rest of the Chosen People. There was no Moses to burn their idols … no Christ to overturn their tables. However, you have the Lord.

Wednesday	*Tears Remembered*	Psalm 56

Wednesday — *Tears Remembered* — **Psalm 56**

**Record my lament; list my tears on your scroll—
are they not in your record? v. 8**

Though David overcame Goliath with one shot from his sling, it was not the same for all the enemies that came against David. However, fortunately for him, the first casting that he usually made was not with his sling, but with his prayer. However much he felt his enemies press against him in so many kinds of ways, so much the more did David's prayer press against God until the blessings of God's power were in David's heart, and only then in his hand.

Are there circumstances that bring you to tears? If God does not let a sparrow fall without God's knowledge, then neither does one tear run down your cheek without God's awareness. Consider the image that David uses in the verse for the day for this kind of remembrance of God. As the fragments of bread collected after the multiplication of loaves in the Gospel, your tears are gathered together, lest they be lost.

Today be aware that God is completely aware of your sorrow or your joy.

Thursday — *Faith Is the Victory* — **1 John 5:1–12**

**For everyone born of God overcomes the world.
This is the victory that has overcome the world, even our faith. v. 4**

John Wesley, eighteenth century founder of the Methodist movement, said that we have a sixth sense. While today we often hear a sixth sense referred to as "intuition," John affirmed that this is faith—the capacity to claim as true, realities that escape our five physical senses. Faith is at the heart of the reading for today: "This is the victory that has overcome the world—our faith."

I once had a spiritual director who was a priest and a concert violinist; his name was Cyril Schommer, S.J. Later in life, he became blind. He claimed that he could play the violin better than ever, as hearing became more sensitive to compensate for his loss of sight.

So it is with faith. When outer senses recede, the sense of faith has a chance to grow.

Though it be only the size of a mustard seed, Jesus said that faith can move mountains (Matthew 17:20).

Friday — *Pressing About Jesus* — **Mark 1:32–45**

**Jesus replied, "Let us go somewhere else—to the nearby villages—
so I can preach there also. That is why I have come." v. 38**

This is Mark's version of a typical day in the life of Jesus, beginning in the evening. People from all over crowd about him, longing to be healed. His fame spreads.

Let there arise a longing in your heart to press about Jesus. Remember, the victory over the world is faith. The world wants to control, bind, and have power over others. However, greater than what is pressing against you is Christ who presses about you. Think of this at evening time when you and other families come home. Come close to Jesus at that hour, bringing with you the crowds that are bound in traffic on their way home. Bring them to the Lord for healing, restoration, comfort, and rest.

Jesus finds the night for prayer. Let part of your nights be for that as well; rest itself can become prayer. If you rise in the morning to commute, remember that Jesus too, went on to other towns!

Saturday   **The Sabbath Torah Reading**

Jan 28, 2006 #14B	Jan 31, 2015 #16B	Feb 03, 2024 #17B	Jan 29, 2033 #18B
Jan 31, 2009 #15B	Feb 03, 2018 #17B	Jan 30, 2027 #17B	Feb 02, 2036 #15B
Jan 28, 2012 #15B	Jan 30, 2021 #16B	Feb 02, 2030 #18B	Jan 29, 2039 #15B

The Fifth Week in Epiphany
Begins on the Sunday nearest February 1. Alphabyte: Journal, p. 8

Sunday   *Spiritual Power*   **Mark 1:21–28**
Jesus rebuked him, saying, "Be silent, and come out of him!" v. 25

The triumph of the Holy Spirit over Satan is a central theme for Mark that courses through his Gospel. The Spirit at work in Jesus defeats all the dark and evil spirits keeping the human family in bondage. Whether it is an unclean spirit as here, the spirit of antagonism against Jesus in the religious authorities, or the resistance of the very disciples to the power of Jesus, it is the same: Jesus triumphs over Satan.

As you ponder this passage, get in touch with the wonder of the crowd as the fame of Jesus spreads all about. Your spirit breathes as the power of Jesus expands to cover all the areas of spiritual bondage in your life. This is true spiritual power—not the power plays of guilt and shame. Jesus is present with all the power of his love for you.

Monday   *God's Favorite Instrument*   **Isaiah 49**
See, I have inscribed you on the palms of my hands;
your walls are continually before me. v. 16

Every artisan has a favorite tool. The instrument fits snugly into his or her hand and perfectly responds to what the artist wants to do with it. This is the image behind a teaching of Ignatius of Loyola offered to me in the early years of spiritual formation: "Be an instrument closely fitted to God's hand."

There is delight and intimacy as Isaiah describes the Servant of the Lord in this second of four "Servant Songs." The Lord has a preferential love for his Servant who would lead God's people out of exile. The Servant is a type of Christ.

Make the Servant Song personal to you. God has formed you in your mother's womb to be an instrument God can use for the salvation of others. God has inscribed you in the palm of God's hand. The Lord delights in you. Is your delight in the Lord alone?

Tuesday   *From Perversity to Perversity*   **Judges 19—21**
The Israelites had compassion for Benjamin their kin, and said,
"One tribe is cut off from Israel this day." 21:6

What a harrowing series of events about the sin of idolatry and sexual perversity! In the Bible, the two relate to each other. One evil consequence is set into motion by another, as a row of dominoes falling together. The tribe of Benjamin now falls away, as the tribe of Dan did in last week's reading.

Note the setting in which the homosexual behavior is described—wanton lawlessness, anarchy, with total disregard for the rights and sensitivities of others. You will read about the atrocious symbol that the concubine's husband makes of her.

Your weakness and area of sin: ask the Lord to put an end to it. Be sensitive to the presence of God and let this grow. Look what can happen to those with a total disregard for God's ways.

Wednesday   *Awakened to Joy*   Psalm 57
Awake, my soul! Awake, O harp and lyre!
I will awake the dawn. v. 8

This psalm is attributed to David while in the back corner of a cave, escaping the wrath of jealous King Saul out to kill him. Instead of focusing on the fear in his circumstances, David does what he does best: he prays. His awareness is not limited to the dark walls of the cold cave. His spirit flies to heaven where the darkness becomes the shadow of the Lord's wings. Prayer changes the meaning of David's circumstances. He finds joy in the Lord, exalted above the heavens—certainly beyond the walls of that cave!

Your life will be totally different when you pray with the same spontaneity, intensity and intimacy as David. Each new day he makes, as it were, the dawn more joyous with his song.

Find the song in your heart, which comes to you along with the sun that gives light to the day, though the sun is hiding behind those wings of God we call clouds.

Thursday   *Flowing Pathway of Prayer*   1 John 5:13–21
This is the boldness we have in him,
that if we ask anything according to his will, he hears us. v. 14

Do you remember the famous poster used in World War I of Uncle Sam? An elderly, bearded, stern man looks out, his finger pointing right at you, saying, **"Uncle Sam wants YOU."** We can be tempted to see God's will that way—stern, unrelenting, lacking the warmth and loving feelings that we associate with the Lord in other contexts.

I remember a dear friend saying to me many years ago: *"You* are the will of God for yourself!" Now this "you" is the deepest aspect of your self. It is what you really *do* want in the depths of your soul, but which perhaps you do not fully acknowledge.

The will of God is the key to today's reading. "If we ask anything according to God's will, God hears us." When you agree with the Lord in wanting what God wants, then a pathway of prayer opens between your heart and God's. You both listen to each other, as it were, and the prayer simply flows.

Friday   *Total Healing*   Mark 2:1–12
When Jesus saw their faith, he said to the paralytic,
"Son, your sins are forgiven." v. 5

Very soon into the Gospel, the question arises about who Jesus is. In the incident of the healing of the paralytic, there is opposition on the part of the Jewish leaders. They refuse to accept Jesus walking about and healing. Now Jesus tells the man that his sins are forgiven. This presses the opposition to the ultimate; they accuse Jesus of blasphemy. They cannot wait to get their hands on Jesus, instead of begging Jesus to get his hands on them so that they too can be healed.

Jesus does not evade the issue. He confronts it even before they do, because he reads their minds and hearts. The physical healing is the sign that Jesus' power extends to the depths of the soul where there is a longing to be freed from sin and forgiven. God has power over every dimension of life.

Are you willing to let Jesus pass through the barrier, the "roof" of your heart?

Saturday   **The Sabbath Torah Reading**

Feb 04, 2006 #15B	Feb 07, 2015 #17B	Feb 10, 2024 #18B	Feb 05, 2033 #19B
Feb 07, 2009 #16B	Feb 10, 2018 #18B	Feb 06, 2027 #18B	Feb 09, 2036 #16B
Feb 04, 2012 #16B	Feb 06, 2021 #17B	Feb 09, 2030 #19B	Feb 05, 2039 #16B

The Sixth Week in Epiphany
Begins on the Sunday nearest February 8. Alphabyte: Kiln, p. 8
For 2018, 2024, 2027: This is the last week in Epiphany, beginning with Transfiguration Sunday. See p. 170 for the Sunday reading, continuing below for the Monday-to-Saturday passages. Ash Wednesday occurs this week. Next week turn to The First Week in Lent, Year B, p. 172.

Sunday   *A Day in the Life of Jesus*   **Mark 1:29–39**
**In the morning, while it was still very dark, he got up
and went out to a deserted place, and there he prayed. v.35**

While the Gospels are very different from what we know as biography, we catch a glimpse of a typical day in the life of Jesus in Galilee. The Jewish day begins at sunset. An entire city with its sick of soul and body presses at the door where Jesus is. As the sand of an hourglass waiting its turn to pass through the tiny opening of the now in the course of an hour, so does each person wait until Jesus lays his hands upon them to receive the healing and joy that only Jesus can give.

Among the precious hours in the days of Jesus are those alone with his Father. While the city sleeps in peace after the healings, Jesus quietly makes his way to a dark and quiet place for prayer. Soaked in this darkness, Jesus who is the light refreshes himself, gathering the energy for the travels to the next towns where the cycle of healing begins again.

As a disciple of Jesus, are not these cycles of prayer and healing meant to be relived in our own flesh?

Monday   *The Spiraling Light of the Lord*   **Isaiah 50—51**
**But all of you are kindlers of fire, lighters of firebrands.
Walk in the flame of your fire, and among the brands that you have kindled! 50:11**

You will think of Jesus in some of the verses in this reading, just as do Matthew and Luke in their Gospels. Again, make this Servant Song personal.

There is an image that Isaiah uses related to the basic image of these reflections—*Firestarters.* In verses 10 and 11, he describes what happens when people walk with their own fire and sparks, instead of being led by the light of the Lord. When one relies upon one's light alone, the walking will be around in circles with a frustration resulting in one "lying down in torment."

The fire that I want started for you in these introductions is the Lord's own light and fire. While there is a cycle at work in these readings, when the Lord leads the way, it is a spiral. The movement of these readings in their special weekly cycle is designed to move your life forward with the light of the Lord leading the way and God's fire igniting your heart.

Tuesday   *Embrace Wisdom*   **Proverbs 4**
**He taught me, and said to me, "Let your heart hold fast my words;
keep my commandments, and live. v. 4**

The key to this chapter is the Hebrew *musar:* "instruction." The word means "correction, chastisement, rebuke, and warning," not the kind of physical punishment that parents wrongly inflict on their children. We would say it is what happens when we "learn the hard way"; the pain of our mistakes becomes instruction for change.

Anything less than total surrender to God will bring spiritual distress to you. Take responsibility for your situation, without blaming others or punishing yourself for your sin and mistakes.

Actually, the image of a parent is not the one that Proverbs uses here, but rather of a woman who longs to be loved by a man. A feminine dimension of God's love is beautifully expressed here. Embrace wisdom.

Wednesday — *Outrage at Injustice* — Psalm 58

People will say, "Surely there is a reward for the righteous;
surely there is a God who judges on earth." v. 11

One thing about David: he feels all the emotions. The personal vengeance that David wants to bring against his enemies is at the level of his feelings; he knows that vengeance is the Lord's and that God will bring justice to bear.

Actually, that is the point of David's anger. His deepest emotions have to do with the Lord's honor and justice violated. In this respect, he is like Jesus. Christ's anger comes out, not when something personal is done to him, but when his Father's glory is at stake. Such was Jesus' anger when he overturned the moneychangers in the Temple. The business of the world was profaning the Temple.

These days, may your anger be full and free when you see God's glory diminished when one of God's little ones is being abused. Then we need the energy of anger to address the sin.

Thursday — *As a Candle Dipped in Spirit-Oil* — 2 John

Grace, mercy, and peace will be with us from God the Father
and from Jesus Christ, the Father's Son, in truth and love. v. 3

There is a little hand-painted sign in a candle store, which reads: "A candle begins as a piece of string that is dipped again and again into wax. With each dipping, more and more wax forms about the string, so that in the end, a light may be lit that burns softly and brightly."

If each day you dip yourself into the Word of the Lord, this soaking in the anointing oil of the Holy Spirit will mean that that the spark I offer here will ignite within you and keep burning.

In this little letter, John is talking in an urgent way to "abide in the doctrine of Christ." Our lives are plunged into all kinds of energies, subject to being "dipped" and surrounded by what is Antichrist. All the more do you and I need everyday to be soaked in the Word of the Lord—totally surrounded with nothing but Christ, so that nothing but Christ burns in us.

Friday — *I Need This* — Mark 2:13–28

"Those who are well have no need of a physician, but those who are sick;
I have come to call not the righteous but sinners." v. 17

One of the signs that a person is in a critical, negative, "victim" type space is the expression: "I don't need this!" When the scribes and Pharisees encountered Jesus, they saw themselves as victims of someone who was potentially going to take away their power. They in effect remarked as they observed Jesus: "We don't need this!"

It is only with those who were sick and needed the divine physician that Jesus loved to stay. It is only when you look at Jesus and say to Him: "I need this!" that you are ready to receive all the healing that Jesus desires to give you—much more than you want to ask.

Mingle with the needy crowd about Jesus. Sense in your spirit your need of him. Believe in faith that your imagination in this prayer is the connecting point to the reality that Jesus is within you. Ask for your healing and claim it in faith.

Saturday — The Sabbath Torah Reading

Feb 11, 2006 #16B	Feb 14, 2015 #18B	Feb 17, 2024 #19B	Feb 12, 2033 #20B
Feb 14, 2009 #17B	Feb 17, 2018 #19B	Feb 13, 2027 #19B	Feb 16, 2036 #17B
Feb 11, 2012 #17B	Feb 13, 2021 #18B	Feb 16, 2030 #20B	Feb 12, 2039 #17B

The Seventh Week in Epiphany

Begins on the Sunday nearest February 15. Alphabyte: Laser, p. 9

For 2015 and 2021, *this is the last week in Epiphany, beginning with Transfiguration Sunday. See p. 170 for the Sunday reading, continuing below for the Monday-to-Saturday passages. Ash Wednesday occurs this week. Next week turn to The First Week in Lent, Year B, p. 172.*

Sunday	*Bold Approach*	Mark 1:40–45

"If you choose, you can make me clean." v. 40

For a Jew, to be a leper was not only to have one's flesh whither away, but also one's spirit eaten up by loneliness. Lepers were totally isolated from the rest of the community. Surely, their sadness must have been overwhelming.

Yet greater than this consuming sickness, for the person of today's Gospel, hope stirred when he came into Jesus' presence. Likely, this hope began with a sense that Jesus was not going to keep his distance, as all the others did. The bold approach brought forth an even bolder statement of faith in the verse for the day.

Whatever is eating away at you, grab yourself, and come into Jesus' presence. He is already approaching you right now. Meet Jesus with your focus upon him and not your condition, with your faith that Jesus can do all things in you and for you. There are no "ifs" about whether Jesus wants to or not; he does. So come near; let him touch you. Be sure to obey him.

Monday	*Mountains and Valleys*	Isaiah 52—53

**How beautiful upon the mountains are the feet of the messenger who announces peace,
who brings good news, who announces salvation,
who says to Zion, "Your God reigns." 52:7**

Two mountains stand as great borders to the valley of the shadow of death and resurrection, which is the season of *Lent and Easter*. The first is Mount Tabor, where the Transfiguration of Jesus took place, celebrated at the end of the Epiphany Season. The other is the Mount of the Ascension, at the end of the season of Easter. Today's reading bears both the heights of the glory of the good news, and the depths of the suffering of Jesus. The *Lectionary* reading for Good Friday sounds the somber yet poignantly beautiful images of the fourth and final Servant Song from 52:13.

Mountains and valleys: can there be one without the other? Though you are up in the heights one day, or down in the depths the next, Jesus is the one with the good news on the heights and with you as your Suffering Servant in the depths of your Good Fridays. Even if your life seems like one big roller coaster of ups and downs, remember that the Lord Jesus is always sitting next to you.

Tuesday	*Lust Losing Its Power*	Proverbs 5

Let your fountain be blessed, and rejoice in the wife of your youth. v. 18

A special family clock rests on a table in my office. As I counsel people and see the movement of the hour, that familiar, lovely face from the past looks back at me, along with the face of the one with whom I am talking. I make sure that the clock is never near the edge; I like to see a border of table-top around it!

Is there a border, a boundary, a hedge about you and that special other person whom God may have given you to share life together? If not, then be open to the images of seduction in today's passage. Be aware of the danger of even the slightest out-of-boundary flirtation.

There is one face you surely want to have before you at all times—the Lord's face. The Holy Spirit will breathe honesty into your heart and wrench away the power of lust with the pure power of love.

Wednesday *Music in Your Being* Psalm 59

I will sing of your might; I will sing aloud of your steadfast love in the morning.
For you have been a fortress for me and a refuge in the day of my distress. v. 16

Do you like to sing in the shower? The sound of the water and the privacy invites us to add singing, good or bad, to the setting, providing a safe place to express joy, even when fears challenge us.

David does something like this in today's psalm. He sings about the wonders and the praises of God, though he is also aware of the presence of frightening enemies.

Decide to sing in your spirit to the Lord, even when you do not feel like it. A song will help to move your spirit into the presence of the Lord, showered by the waters of the Spirit. As metal to a magnet, your soul will cling more closely to the Lord as the Holy Spirit makes music in your being.

Move beyond your comfort zone and sing aloud to the Lord!

Feb. 20?22, 2003

Thursday *Prosperity and Hospitality* 3 John

Beloved, I pray that all may go well with you
and that you may be in good health, just as it is well with your soul. v. 2

Just as Jesus joins physical healing and forgiveness of sins to spiritual healing, so does John begin this brief letter. Matter and spirit link together. Signs of prosperity happen because of surrender to the Lord. God who is so maximal is not going to be minimal with those God loves.

If 2 John warns you about those you allow to surround you, 3 John reminds of the need to be hospitable to missionaries. Surround yourselves with those who believe and are on fire with the Lord. This will prevent the alternative from taking place—vulnerability to gossip, idle talkers, spending time with those who do not have a life.

You have been given the very life of God. Cherish this gift and water it by sharing your gifts from the Lord freely with others that both you and they may glorify God.

Friday *Healed for Sabbath Rest* Mark 3:1–19

Is it lawful to do good or to do harm on the Sabbath,
to save life or to kill? v. 4

Control: this is the obsession of the scribes and Pharisees. The blessing of the Sabbath to both God and the human family becomes a means of manipulating others by those in authority.

However, this authority has lost its power. When Jesus comes, the people find that he alone has true authority, a power that comes from Jesus' inner conviction that results in great wonders.

Jesus returns full power to the Sabbath by teaching that the Sabbath is made for humans and not vice versa. What greater Sabbath gift is there than to be loosed from the strongholds in life that prevent real resting on the Sabbath from taking place!

May the Lord heal you of all fears, anxieties, and pressures that keep you restless and disturbed. The Lord knows that you need Sabbath rest. Let God give it to you and see about giving this to others.

Saturday **The Sabbath Torah Reading**

Feb 18, 2006 #17B	Feb 21, 2015 #19B	May 25, 2024 #32B	Feb 19, 2033 #21B
Feb 21, 2009 #18B	May 26, 2018 #35B	May 29, 2027 #33B	Feb 23, 2036 #18B
Feb 18, 2012 #18B	Feb 20, 2021 #19B	Feb 23, 2030 #21B	Feb 19, 2039 #18B

The Eighth Week in Epiphany

Begins on the Sunday nearest February 22, unless Lent has begun. Alphabyte: Myrrh, p. 9
***For 2009, 2012, 2036 and 2039:** This is the last week in Epiphany, beginning with Transfiguration Sunday. See p. 170 for the Sunday reading, continuing below for the Monday-to-Saturday passages. Ash Wednesday occurs this week. Next week turn to The First Week in Lent, Year B, p. 172.*

Sunday	*Frontiers of Faith*	**Mark 2:1–12**

**When Jesus saw their faith, he said to the paralytic,
"Son, your sins are forgiven." v. 5**

Jesus invades the physical and spiritual frontiers of sickness, bringing complete wholeness. The teachers of religious law vigorously object. They accuse Jesus of blasphemy in his claim to forgive the sickness of sin, freeing both soul and body bound in paralysis.

For the man to be healed, however, the only frontier to be broken is that of the roof! He has already gone beyond the boundaries of unbelief, and is already by faith in the presence of Jesus. The few tiles to be removed are nothing in comparison, just as his healing from paralysis is nothing when it comes to the inner joy of being totally set free by the forgiving love of Jesus.

What physical and spiritual barriers do you need to transcend so that you find yourself dropped right into Jesus' presence? If there is a wall between you and Jesus, guess who erected it?

Monday	*Counting on the Promises*	**Isaiah 54—55**

**For as the heavens are higher than the earth,
so are my ways higher than your ways and my thoughts than your thoughts. 55:9**

Waves upon waves of compassion and love sweep across the pages of this passage. You will need to drink from each verse as from precious nectars of various flavors. Pause often. Keep your Bible close to you throughout the day so that you can take regular refreshment from the promises that lie before you.

How many such promises can you count in these chapters? All the ones you count you can count on! Take note of the various images used to convey the power of the promises. Place each one before all that may be coming against you, believing that according to 54:17, that there is no weapon turned against you that will succeed.

Tuesday	*Warm Wax*	**Proverbs 6**

**The commandment is a lamp and the teaching a light,
and the reproofs of discipline are the way of life. v. 23**

Begin your time of Bible reading with a period of pure quiet, silent presence before the Lord. Even a few minutes of simply stopping everything will prepare you as warm wax, to receive the seal of the Holy Spirit.

This kind of preparation reduces defensiveness before the Word. The book of Proverbs seeks to have you moved by the power of the truths expressed. The images and comparisons will make concrete and personal what might otherwise be abstract and distant. You will learn about the danger of indolence and the wiles of seduction. With pen poised to write, let the phrases of Proverbs loosen personal truths for you to note down. The Holy Spirit will use your own creativity and inner freedom to share God's wisdom with you.

Wednesday   *Lifting the Human Family*   **Psalm 60**

You have set up a banner for those who fear you,
to rally to it out of bowshot. v. 4

Banners are signs of encouragement to all the people of the victory, which the Lord will bring. They are symbols of hope when other evidence of defeat might be present. David prays in urgency on behalf of the people, interceding for them that the favor of the Lord return.

The Psalms have been at the heart of Christian prayer, because intercession is central to our prayer life. We read the whole book of Psalms (the Psalter), in three years; however for centuries, monastic communities would pray the entire Psalter once a week as a way of pleading before the Lord on behalf of all the people. Wednesday is a special time to lift the human family in the midst of the workweek, compassionately pleading to the Lord on behalf of those countless settings where abuse and injustice are prevailing.

Thursday   *The Vitality of Faith*   **Jude**

Beloved, build yourselves up on your most holy faith;
pray in the Holy Spirit. v. 20

This is a brief letter of Jude, said to be the brother of Jesus and James, the first leader of the Jerusalem church. Jude's words encourage his listeners to press on in the faith, contending with those settings and circumstances that would lessen the fervor of the faith. Such would be those whose doctrines amount to denying the faith itself. He refers to the book of Enoch, a respected, but non-canonical work of the first century, B.C.

Once again, notice the power of the earthy images in verses 12 and 13 used to describe faithfulness. Admonition and encouragement go hand in hand in this letter. Be strengthened by both in your walk with the Lord. Pray in the Holy Spirit. Yield to the spontaneous ways that the Spirit pours out prayer from deep within you.

Friday   *The Sin Against the Holy Spirit*   **Mark 3:20–35**

Whoever does the will of God is my brother and sister and mother. v. 35

As the Good News spreads, so does the opposition. Jesus' family thinks he has gone out of his mind. Opposition of the scribes and Pharisees increases to the point of blasphemy against the Holy Spirit, to conclude that Jesus' miracles are the work of the devil. Jesus teaches that such a sin cannot be forgiven.

Do not be afraid of this. If you are reading God's Word and want to grow in Christ, you are far from this devastating, pernicious, premeditated sin. However, we do live in a world that quietly mocks and disdains the gifts of the Lord. If there is not outright blasphemy, there is that indifference and lukewarmness that John said is worse than being cold to the Lord (Revelation 3:16).

Put on the mind of Christ and do not be afraid of those who think you are out of yours!

Saturday   **The Sabbath Torah Reading**

Feb 25, 2006 #18B	May 30, 2015 #35B	May 25, 2024 #32B	Feb 26, 2033 #22B
Feb 28, 2009 #19B	May 26, 2018 #35B	May 22, 2027 #32B	Mar 01, 2036 #19B
Feb 25, 2012 #19B	May 29, 2021 #36B	Mar 02, 2030 #22B	Feb 26, 2039 #19B

The Ninth Week in Epiphany

Begins on the Sunday nearest March 1 (Leap Year, Feb. 29), unless Lent has begun.
__For 2030, 2033:__ This is the last week in Epiphany, beginning with Transfiguration Sunday below. For the Monday-to-Saturday readings, turn to the First Week in Pentecost, Year B, p. 202. Ash Wednesday occurs this week. For next week turn to the First Week in Lent, Year B, p. 172.

Transfiguration Sundays, Year B

(The Last Sunday in Epiphany)

Feb 22, 2009	Feb 11, 2018	Feb 07, 2027	Feb 24, 2036
Feb 19, 2012	Feb 14, 2021	Mar 03, 2030	Feb 20, 2029
Feb 15, 2015	Feb 11, 2024	Feb 27, 2033	Feb 16, 2042

Transfiguration Sunday   **Mark 9:2–9**

The Mountain and the Valley
**As they were coming down the mountain,
he ordered them to tell no one about what they had seen,
until after the Son of Man had risen from the dead. v. 9**

The pitched roof of a house offers an image for this incident in the physical center of Mark's Gospel. What came before was the upward movement of healing exorcisms and liberating teaching bringing victory over evil. What follows is the "downside" 'in Jesus' approaching suffering and death. Here for a moment we are on top of the mountain with Jesus' closest friends. Jesus stands between Moses and the Elijah, just as Sunday stands between Saturday, the reading of the Torah, and Monday, our readings from the Prophets. Peter, wanting to stay forever in this heavenly bliss, suggests that they build booths there for the three heavenly guests.

Remember this moment of glory as the coming season of *Lent and Easter* begins this week with Ash Wednesday. The same Lord of glory is present in the valley of the shadow of death, just as he is on the mountain.

The monogram of Jesus on the facing page comprises the first three letters of the holy name in Greek-Iota-Eta-Sigma (ΙΗΣΟΥΣ). "Η" in the Roman Alphabet is the long "e" in Greek, Eta. The monogram became popular through Bernardine of Siena from the early fifteenth century. It was adopted as the emblem for the Society of Jesus with the addition of the cross over the central letter.

LENT
AND
EASTER

SPRING

Northern Hemisphere

Year B
2009, 2012, 2015 …

Lent begins six weeks before Easter Sunday.
See the entire cycle of readings at a glance on page xx.

The First Sundays in Lent, Year B

Mar 01, 2009	Feb 18, 2018	Feb 14, 2027	Mar 02, 2036
Feb 26, 2012	Feb 21, 2021	Mar 10, 2030	Feb 27, 2039
Feb 22, 2015	Feb 18, 2024	Mar 06, 2033	Feb 23, 2042

The First Week in Lent

Six weeks before Easter—Alphabyte: Nadir, p. 39

Sunday 　　　　　　　　*Nothing But Ashes* 　　　　　　　　**Mark 1:9–15**

"At last the time has come!" he announced. "The Kingdom of God is near!
Turn from your sins and believe this Good News!" v. 15

A forty-day journey to Easter began this past week with Ash Wednesday. We started our life's journey from dust; we will return to dust. The Holy Spirit has breathed over our dust so that we can live now as we will live forever.

Let us begin this journey with nothing but the ashes of our "stuff." Allow the things of *our* creation alone—what is outside God's will—to be brought to naught. Ashes are the leftovers when everything is gone. Burn all your "bridges over troubled waters," your escape from pain, and decide to go down into those turbulent waters with Jesus who carries you. He is with you on this journey. He goes into the desert of nothingness and temptation.

The journey is vertical as well as horizontal. The heavens are your goal and mine. The path is open now, for you are with Jesus in whom the Father is well pleased.

Monday 　　　　　　　　*The Pot and the Flask* 　　　　　　　　**Jeremiah 18—20**

But the LORD stands beside me like a great warrior. Before him they will stumble.
They cannot defeat me. They will be shamed and thoroughly humiliated.
Their dishonor will never be forgotten. 20:11

Two objects are set before you today, a pot and a flask. As you reflect upon these broken articles, become them. In what way are you broken? What would God have to do to you to remake you more fully into God's image? Is there a spirit of rebellion in you as there was for the people in Jeremiah's time?

This is a sad and tragic period for God's people. The energies of their lives burn before the altars of false gods. Jeremiah's anger and outrage find full expression in the lament that begins with 18:19. Gratefully, God does not take vengeance as fully as Jeremiah would have liked.

What does the Lord tell you about yourself as you read these vibrant images? Feel the Lord's own hurt indignation and grief over God's people. Become one, not only with the pot, but also with the potter. Let God break you and remake you.

Tuesday 　　　　　　　　*Accusations Against Job* 　　　　　　　　**Job 15**

For the godless are barren. Their homes, enriched through bribery,
will be consumed by fire. 5:34

Tuesdays and the Book of Job: open yourself to this intriguing, often tedious study of how it is that the righteous suffer. Job confronts us with the challenge to meet suffering with hope and trust in the Lord, despite our incapacity to understand.

Job has three friends who claim there must be some sin that Job committed to account for his sufferings. They go back and forth in dialogue three different times. This being *Year B*, we begin with the second series of dialogues. You might want to review the first three chapters of the book that give the entire work its setting.

Job is an especially fitting book with which to journal. When your spirit echoes his, there is a dialogue beginning in your heart—one that the Spirit wants to direct. What is this back and forth movement within you? You and who else are the participants in the dialogue? Write and see.

Wednesday   *Journey to Jerusalem*   **Psalm 125**

Just as the mountains surround and protect Jerusalem,
so the LORD surrounds and protects his people,
both now and forever. v. 2

Three make their way to Jerusalem: 1) *The psalmist* who puts this song into the mouths of the Passover pilgrims; 2) *Jesus* who moves to the sacred city as the Paschal Lamb, entering it on Palm Sunday, sacrificed on Good Friday, risen on Easter Sunday; 3) *You.* Join the throngs of rejoicing pilgrims as they pray and sing these fifteen "Songs of Ascent" (Psalms 120 to 134) that weave together our Lenten Wednesdays over the three years. We are journeying through the weeks of Lent to the spiritual Jerusalem at the center of life.

See how the psalmist is reminded of God's presence and power as the sacred writer enjoys the mountains that horizon his march. Today, take a walk and feel embraced by your surroundings, whatever they are. God surrounds you on all sides and embraces your soul from within. Walk with God!

Thursday   *Fire from the Ashes*   **Colossians 1:1–18**

For he has rescued us from the one who rules in the kingdom of darkness,
and he has brought us into the Kingdom of his dear Son. v. 13

As firelight from the darkness of ashes, comes today's reading. Paul's letter to the Colossians speaks about the exalted supremacy of Christ. Be lifted in faith to the heavenly places where you are to dwell in Christ. Each verse will do this for you, as so many wings that raise you up with resurrection power from "down" places in your life. Pray this passage, allowing the Holy Spirit to have full access to your heart.

Paul presents the theme of reconciling all things in Christ. As you begin to enter into these days of Lent, with whom do you find that you need reconciliation? Know that the Lord wants union for you with those God calls you to love. On your part, open your prayer to reconciliation. Especially pray that you and these persons together be totally reconciled to God. The Blood of Jesus has won this for you already. The red side of the spectrum fills you with joy—the blood of Jesus and the fire of the Spirit.

Friday   *Rivers from the Rock*   **John 7**

"If you believe in me, come and drink! For the Scriptures declare
that rivers of living water will flow out from within." v. 38

In John's Gospel, Jesus makes appearances at the three major Jewish feasts—Passover, Pentecost and Tabernacles. For John, Jesus completes the deepest meaning of these feasts. In this chapter, Jesus secretly goes up for the Feast of Tabernacles, called *Sukkot* in Hebrew—the harvest festival, around mid-October, recalling the times when the people would set up tents in the fields as they gathered in the crops. It also bring to mind the temporary dwellings of God's people as they journeyed through the wilderness.

The last day of *Sukkot*, is a feast called *Simchat Torah*, "The Joy of the Torah." The Torah readings are completed and the cycle begins again. At this service, prayers for rain are said. In Jesus' time, each day of The Feast of Tabernacles, water was brought, recalling the water from the rock in Exodus 17. "He who believes in me … out of his heart will flow rivers of living water." Come to your Rock and drink.

Saturday   **The Sabbath Torah Reading**

Mar 11, 2006 #20B	Feb 28, 2015 #20 B	Feb 24, 2024 #20 B	Mar 12, 2033 #24 B
Mar 07, 2009 #20 B	Feb 24, 2018 #20 B	Feb 20, 2027 #20 B	Mar 08, 2036 #20 B
Mar 03, 2012 #20 B	Feb 27, 2021 #20 B	Mar 16, 2030 #24 B	Mar 05, 2039 #20 B

The Second Week in Lent, Year B
Five weeks before Easter—Alphabyte: Olive Tree, p. 40

Sunday   *Minding the Things of God*   **Mark 8:31–38**
And how do you benefit if you gain the whole world
but lose your own soul in the process? v. 36

This is the first time that Jesus predicts his Passion. He hears the anointed confession of Peter given the gift of knowing that Jesus is the Christ. Yet Peter is not ready to hear about the suffering of his Christ. Having just received a new name, he gets another: "Get away from me, Satan! You are seeing things merely from a human point of view, not from God's."

Peter is shaken up—and needs to be. And you: do you shrink from following Jesus when you see him carrying a cross ahead of you and when he asks you to take up yours? Take it up. Do not stand with it. Carry it forward.

Think of the ashes again. What you make alone does not go with you into eternal life, but only what God makes through you. "How do you benefit if you gain the whole world but lose your own soul in the process?"

Monday   *The Fiery Hammer*   **Jeremiah 21—23**
Does not my word burn like fire?" asks the LORD.
"Is it not like a mighty hammer that smashes rock to pieces? 23:29

Open rebellion and refusal to follow the Lord: this is what has become of God's people in the 6th century B.C. God raises up Jeremiah whose hammer-like and fiery words are meant to shake the hearts of the people into repentance and recovery of God.

We know more from Jeremiah than from any other prophet about what it is like to speak on behalf of God. He finds his call repugnant and frustrating. Yet the fire still burns within. The alternative? Give up and refuse to prophesy—infinitely more difficult.

Only by doing what God calls you to do will you find inner peace and ultimate meaning to your life. The fire of God's call upon your life transforms personal preferences. Yield to God.

Tuesday   *Poetry in Pain*   **Job 16—17**
Even now my witness is in heaven. My advocate is there on high. 16:19

Imagine the terrible, sudden death of your child. A friend comes to the funeral. Instead of comforting you, the person blames you, saying that it was your entire fault! Make this personal; imagine a specific loss, with some "friend" you know coming to you in this heartless way.

This is what Job experienced, making his suffering even more dreadful. His so-called friends accuse and taunt him. They are more interested in debating their side of a theological position, than in giving love.

Job's response in today's reading has the heart-rending cry of many a psalm. There is beauty here, poetry in pain. Job teaches that it is okay to pour out one's feelings to the Lord in prayer. Can you feel the anger driving his expression? Any pockets of pain, fear, or anger inside of you that need to become chapters in your book of life?

Wednesday *Feelings as Prayer-Seeds* **Psalm 126**
Those who plant in tears will harvest with shouts of joy. v. 5

Listen to the weeping of God's people exiled in Babylonia in the 6th century B.C. Tears of anguish, torment, and grief fall into the foreign Kebar River. Now walk with them as tears become shouts of joy as these freed pilgrims make their way once again to the Holy City. As a burst dam, joy explodes.

Exile—is there a sense in which you have been "deported to some foreign land" and yearn to return to the joy of being free and of being who you are in God's sight? Lent is the season to learn the disciplines that will bring you freedom. For example, learn how to deal with your anger when you allow yourself to be manipulated by those whose will you do instead of God's.

Let your true feelings fall into the ground as prayer-seeds. The harvest of God's comforting presence will flower.

Thursday *Wider Space for the Fire* **Colossians 1:19–29**
For God in all his fullness was pleased to live in Christ. v. 19

As we read on Saturdays from the book of Leviticus, it is forbidden to eat the blood of the animals offered. Blood belongs to God. As in the case of Leviticus, there is a call to holiness that Paul places upon the Colossians. Joy increases as you read the conclusion to this first chapter. There is such spiritual energy in Paul and an unrelenting enthusiasm to share his Christ with everyone. Pray for this same desire. Open yourself to the beauty of the truths expressed here and be set on fire with need for a wider space for burning.

Someone today needs your fervor, so that his or her spirit can catch fire with yours. Be watchful in prayer for this person and others.

Friday *Enemies Brought to a Halt* **John 8:1–30**
Jesus said to the people, "I am the light of the world.
If you follow me, you won't be stumbling through the darkness,
because you will have the light that leads to life." v. 12

Rejoice in the wisdom of Jesus in his response to the tricks and dilemmas the scribes and Pharisees put before him. Today's account of the woman caught in adultery has the famous response of Jesus: "Let those who have never sinned throw the first stones!" Jesus takes the very energy of the accusers and hurls it back upon them. He knows that their own sin will convict them.

Jesus' intimate relation with the Father is revealed in the remainder of the reading. He experiences that union with the Father, which brings the power that comes against all his adversaries.

Remember that you have the Holy Spirit who helps you bring to a halt the attempts of your own enemies to harm you. In Christ, no one can really get at you. The same gift of intimacy that Jesus has with the Father is offered to you. That is all that really matters.

Saturday **The Sabbath Torah Reading**

Mar 16, 2006 #21 B	Mar 07, 2015 #21 B	Mar 02, 2024 #21 B	Mar 19, 2033 #25 B
Mar 14, 2009 #21 B	Mar 03, 2018 #21 B	Feb 27, 2027 #21 B	Mar 15, 2036 #21 B
Mar 10, 2012 #21 B	Mar 06, 2021 #21 B	Mar 23, 2030 #25 B	Mar 12, 2039 #21 B

2
Le
B

The Third Week in Lent, Year B

Four weeks before Easter—Alphabyte: ***Plumb Line****, p. 40*

Sunday   ***Cleansing the Temple***   **John 2:13–22**

**Then, going over to the people who sold doves, he told them,
"Get these things out of here.
Don't turn my Father's house into a marketplace!" v. 16**

Last week was a blow to Peter's pride. This week, Jesus literally blows away all the religious authorities as he overturns the moneychangers in the Temple. As a karate chop, Jesus powerfully breaks into "the system," so that something new, something exciting and life-giving can come in its place—his very own life.

The Temple of the Father had become a slaughterhouse. The profanity of business was set up in the most sacred place for a Jew, the Temple. Fearlessly, Jesus abandons himself to the Father's will.

Perhaps Jesus flashes back to the age of twelve when he remained in the Temple, stunning the leaders amazed by his wisdom. He remembers telling Mary and Joseph that he must be about his Father's business.

Does the temple of your life need cleansing? How about the temple of Christ's body, the church?

Monday   ***A Heart to Know the Lord***   **Jeremiah 24—26**

**I will give them hearts that will recognize me as the LORD.
They will be my people, and I will be their God,
for they will return to me wholeheartedly. 24:7**

Jeremiah, prophet of intense feelings, speaks for a God who has intense feelings. Not only is God's hurt and anger revealed in Jeremiah, but there are bursts of tender love to move your heart in sweet surrender, as well as to be broken by the hammer and the fire. Sense in your spirit the tenderness of God in the image of the two baskets of flax. Repeat 24:7 often until you know it by heart.

The Lord reveals to the people, that though they are going into exile, there will be deliverance in seventy years. This is sad news.

Jeremiah is condemned to die for what he is prophesying; Jesus and other prophets died as well for their teachings. The mobs around Jeremiah are led by their own mind, instead of the mind of God. Who has influence upon what you think and do?

Tuesday   ***A Leaping Flame of Faith***   **Job 18—19**

**"But as for me, I know that my Redeemer lives,
and that he will stand upon the earth at last. 19:25**

Enter friend Number 2. He counts Job among the wicked, furthering Job's pain. Job's response continues the conviction that he is innocent. If what Bildad says is true, then God is unjust and wrongfully afflicting Job with the worst kinds of physical and emotional pain imaginable. The insinuation that friends and family are rejecting the person in great pain is precisely one of the tortures that some countries use against political prisoners.

Watch what happens in chapter 19. A flame of faith leaps out of the ashes of the pain, an amazing gift of life in the midst of so much suffering. For Christians, this becomes a prophetic cry about the coming Redeemer.

In your flesh, you shall see God!

Wednesday   *Architect and General Contractor*   **Psalm 127**

Unless the LORD builds a house, the work of the builders is useless.
Unless the LORD protects a city, guarding it with sentries
will do no good. v. 1

"He pulled himself up by the bootstraps"—a familiar phrase, expressing the worldly value of making it on your own. However, picture it. As you pull upward on the straps of your boots, the upper body bends forward under the pressure. There is no pulling up at all, only an inner gridlock of energies pressing against themselves in frustration.

Reflect today on all your accomplishments. Who did the building: you, or God? God is meant not only to be the architect, but also the general contractor of your life's work; otherwise, your efforts will be in vain. The psalmist explores thoughts similar to these as he sees Jerusalem and its Temple coming closer and closer.

A question for you if you have children: are *you* building the "houses" which are their lives, or are you teaching them that God's will is their peace?

Thursday   *Disarmed By the Cross*   **Colossians 2**

Don't let anyone lead you astray with empty philosophy and
high-sounding nonsense that come from human thinking
and from the evil powers of this world, and not from Christ. v. 8

Human disputes, arguments, and debates pale in the face of what the cross has won for you and me. It is simply impossible to fathom the mystery of God redeeming us at the very moment when we were murdering God's Son. The shadow of the cross lifted high on that Good Friday is meant to silence our attempts to understand. Silence before the cross is what we must keep, until we adore, wonder, weep, and witness to Christ's love.

All legalism is meaningless. No keeping of rules and regulations, however holy they may be, can win us salvation. We are totally at the mercy of Christ's enduring love. Nothing else need be said!

Read the words of Paul in this chapter as you let go of your ways of thinking. Put on the mind of Christ Jesus. May this mind sweep a deep peace within your heart.

Friday   *Bookends*   **John 8:31–59**

Jesus answered, "The truth is, I existed
before Abraham was even born!" v. 58

As bookends that hold what is between, so do vv. 32 and 58 of our reading hold the center together. The left "bookend" reads, "You shall know the truth, and the truth shall make you free." The right one is: "Before Abraham was, I AM." The center area describes the mounting conflict between the Pharisees and Jesus. As typical in John, the responses of Jesus are on another level, exalted words about what happens to those who adhere to Jesus. They shall "never taste death."

In John's Gospel, when Jesus uses the words "I AM," John wants us to arc back to the very beginning of God's liberation of God's people in the Exodus when God revealed the covenantal name to Moses at the burning bush. The name of God given to Moses means, "I AM." Jesus completes the ancient covenant in himself. All that God wants of us is obedience and adherence to the Lord by faith. Bonded to the truth, we shall then become free.

Saturday   **The Sabbath Torah Reading**

Mar 25, 2006 #22–23 B	Mar 14, 2015 #22–23 B	Mar 09, 2024 #22 B	Mar 26, 2033 #26 B
Mar 21, 2009 #22–23 B	Mar 10, 2018 #22–23 B	Mar 06, 2027 #22 B	Mar 22, 2036 #22–23 B
Mar 17, 2012 #22–23 B	Mar 13, 2021 #22–23 B	Mar 30, 2030 #26 B	Mar 19, 2039 #22–23 B

The Fourth Week in Lent, Year B

Three weeks before Easter—Alphabyte: Quarters, p. 41

Sunday   *Joy in the Gold*   **John 3:14–21**

**"For God so loved the world that he gave his only Son,
so that everyone who believes in him will not perish but have eternal life." v. 16**

4
Le
B

The cross is before us again, but this time, it is still and standing tall. Ground movement is over. The cross is at rest, lifted high to connect earth with heaven. John recalls Moses and the bronze serpent in the desert in Numbers 21: 9. This was the other pole up so that when the people would look upon it, the serpent would not bite them.

Go for the gold! Keep your eyes on the prize of the cross and you will find the strength to finish the journey and come to rest. Embrace verse 16 which has been called "The Gospel in Miniature." This "Gospel Gold" needs to be committed to the memory of your heart.

Centuries ago, this Sunday was called "Laetare Sunday," a mid-Lent "Sunday of Joy." Let this mid-journey rest be filled with the joy of Jesus loving you so much, "… for the Bible tells you so!"

Monday   *A Shining Jewel*   **Jeremiah 27—29**

**For I know the plans I have for you," says the LORD.
"They are plans for good and not for disaster, to give you a future and a hope. 29:11**

Today's reading provides clues for discerning the difference between true and false prophecy. False prophets speak of promises they cannot be deliver; true ones speak of the consequences to unfaithfulness to God.

Listen to the letter of chapter 29 as though personally directed to you. Be compassionate with the lost. Pray in heartfelt intercession, moved by the tenderness of God. Does the Lord place anyone in particular upon your heart for prayer?

In the middle of the letter, a verse expresses profound love and tenderness on the part of God. May your heart, loosened, shaken, and sobered by this letter, receive this verse of comfort as a shining jewel in the midst of a rough, hard earth.

Tuesday   *The Results of Wickedness*   **Job 20—21**

**The triumph of the wicked has been short-lived
and the joy of the godless has been only temporary. 20:5**

Zophar is a good example of those so proud and opinionated, that their hearts are closed and rigid in the face of human suffering. Rather than be challenged by his thoughts and the suffering of his friend Job, Zophar is not sure that Job is good at all!

What is deceptive about Zophar's speech about the outcome of the wicked is that it is true in so many respects. Again, the power of poetry abounds in the images of this great book.

Job's energies are strong in his dispute with Zophar. Job questions Zophar's position about the wicked coming to disaster. Job does not see it that way; look how often the wicked prosper!

Get beneath the arguments, to feelings and attitudes. Does today's passage change your understandings about goodness and evil?

Wednesday	*Joy in the Walk*	Psalm 128

May you live to enjoy your grandchildren.
And may Israel have quietness and peace. v. 6

An image is forever imprinted within me. It was spring, 1968 during the days after the assassination of Martin Luther King. I was part of a great march in Newark, New Jersey. At one point, we were walking up a hill, which soon turned downward. Suddenly, as I began the walk down, an immense silent sea of people stretched before me. I felt as though I was indeed part of a people, bound together in grief over Dr. King's death, and bonded in joy, as we found meaning in witnessing to Dr. King's convictions in life and in death.

A similar feeling must have gripped our ancestor pilgrims as they walked toward Jerusalem. The joy from this psalm came from beholding families walking along with babes in the arms of their parents.

May Jews, Christians and Moslems, find unity of minds and hearts in all our festivals that celebrate in one form or another, the one God who has intervened in our lives.

Thursday	*Death—Over and Done With*	Colossians 3

Since God chose you to be the holy people whom he loves,
you must clothe yourselves with tenderhearted mercy,
kindness, humility, gentleness, and patience. v. 12

At the risk of outraging a congregation, when we celebrate Baptism, I announce, "Today we are celebrating this person's funeral!" The baptized says in effect, "I want to get death over and done with, so that I can go on living in Christ now." Death to self—death to a life without God: this is what baptism means.

Jesus did not get sick and get well on the cross; he died and rose. Paul teaches that the very same reality must happen to us. We must die in order to receive the gift of the resurrection. He assumes that since we are already dead, we will "seek those things that are above." He calls us to live in heaven now.

Using the image of clothing being put on and off, Paul makes a list of what we are to wear. As you read his list, note the clothing you need to take off and the clothing you need to put on.

Friday	*Received By Jesus*	John 9

Then Jesus told him, "I have come to judge the world.
I have come to give sight to the blind and to show those who think they see that they are blind." v. 39

The Temple in Jerusalem was destroyed in 70 A.D., and with it, the entire system of sacrifice prescribed by Moses. The local synagogue became more and more vital in the life of a Jew. Early Christians continued to share in the life of the synagogue community, until something drastic happened. If the Christians did not stop believing in Jesus, they would be expelled from the synagogue.

It appears that this situation was one of the very motives for writing the Gospel of John. It was a support and comfort to Christians who could no longer worship with Jewish communities.

This understanding will help you to appreciate the story of "The Man Born Blind." May this account bring comfort to you in any areas of life where you may be cut off, ostracized, excluded, and rejected. Fall on your knees as the man born blind and worship Jesus who receives you completely.

Saturday
The Sabbath Torah Reading

Apr 01, 2006 #24 B	Mar 21, 2015 #24 B	Mar 16, 2024 #23 B	Apr 02, 2033 #27 B
Mar 28, 2009 #24 B	Mar 17, 2018 #24 B	Mar 13, 2027 #23 B	Mar 29, 2036 #24 B
Mar 24, 2012 #24 B	Mar 20, 2021 #24 B	Apr 06, 2030 #27 B	Mar 26, 2039 #24 B

The Fifth Week in Lent, Year B
Two weeks before Easter—Alphabyte: **R***ooster, p. 41*

Sunday   *Your Hour Has Come.*   **John 12:20–33**

**The truth is, a kernel of wheat must be planted in the soil. Unless it dies it will be alone—
a single seed. But its death will produce many new kernels—
a plentiful harvest of new lives. v. 24**

Jesus celebrates the arrival of his hour. He has spoken about it often in the Gospel of John, usually noting that it is yet to come. Now the time of glory for Jesus is here.

There is no shame in the cross for Jesus. He is not a victim upon it, but a victor. In John's Gospel, Jesus is always in charge of the movement of what happens. Though it is a "passion," it is "action" as well, as Jesus allows what is going to happen to take place out of love for you.

Think about "hour" this week. Whether the electronic beep of your watch tickles your ears or you enjoy the tolling of a grandfather clock, receive each hour as your hour that has come. Reflect upon the hour just past. Let go of sin. Celebrate its ashes in the fire of Jesus' love. Continue that part of the journey, which is the hour before you.

Monday   *My Law on Their Hearts*   **Jeremiah 30—32**

**"But this is the new covenant I will make with the people of Israel on that day," says the LORD.
"I will put my laws in their minds, and I will write them on their hearts. I will be their God,
and they will be my people. 31:33**

Today's passage will be a source of comfort for you. These chapters are part of "The Book of Consolation" in Jeremiah. The exile will be over. What God says, God will do. The promises of God accelerate as the energy and the power of Jeremiah's prophesy increase with each passing verse.

Matthew quotes 31:15 when he tells the story of Herod's slaughter of the infants in his frantic effort to kill Jesus. (Cf. Matthew 2:16 ff.)

Read with a highlighter, stopping and pausing at those places that move you. Jeremiah 31:31 and following are so special! What memories and awareness come to your heart? God speaks to you very personally.

Tuesday   *From Woes to Wonder*   **Job 39**

**"Are you the one who makes the hawk soar
and spread its wings to the south?" v. 26**

For thirty-seven chapters, Job and his friends have been going back and forth. Now it is time for God to have the final word. Yet the response of God in chapter 39 consists of questions—seventeen of them. However, they are very different from the heady, judgmental, and moralistic ones that Job's friends have been posing in their tedious game of tug 'o war. God simply asks questions about creatures and nature intended to shake Job out of his woes and thrust him back into wonder. These questions come as so many karate chops to Job's spirit. There is a sense of "loving cynicism" from God, which you will catch if you read **"you"** with emphasis, referring to Job.

More importantly, let the "you" be **you!**

Wednesday   *Broken Cords*   **Psalm 129**

The LORD is good; he has cut the cords used by the ungodly to bind me. v. 4

We are just days away from Palm Sunday and the entry of Jesus into Jerusalem. The first singers of this Psalm know that the one who would lead them in triumph over all enemies would be the Suffering Servant. Jesus fulfills verses 3 and 4. These lines perfectly image death and resurrection. The resurrection has broken the cords of the scourging and the dragging of Jesus along the road leading to Calvary.

What do you experience as binding you, perhaps whipping you, and dragging you along in life? Believe that Jesus has taken your cords to himself and broken them for risen life. Be ready to know those precise, highly personal ways that Jesus is setting you free. Total, complete inner freedom is God's offer to you. Accept no substitutes!

Thursday   *Precious Moments*   **Colossians 4**

Live wisely among those who are not Christians,
and make the most of every opportunity. V. 5

There are two concepts for time in Greek. *Chronos* (our word "chronology") means "duration of time." It is the amount of time, a time-line. The other concept is *kairos*. This means "opportunity," a special moment in time, an appointed time. When Paul urges us to "redeem the time," he uses the word *kairos*. Within a movement of time, there are many "precious moments," not unlike the famous Christian figurines of the same name. Just as moments in time are precious when spent with a loved one, so in Christ every moment of life can become precious.

Time is redeemed, made worthwhile, when you live in the love that Christ Jesus has for you. Verse 6 is worth committing to memory so that all your moments of speaking will be precious. "Let your speech always be with grace, seasoned with salt, that you may know how you ought to answer each one."

Friday   *Raised Up On the Last Day*   **John 11**

Jesus told her, "I am the resurrection and the life.
Those who believe in me, even though they die like everyone else,
will live again. V. 25

Raising Lazarus from the dead is the incident that provokes the religious leaders to plot actively for the death of Jesus. See the irony. If Jesus has the power to bring another person back to life, would he not also have the power over his own life? Jesus gives another "I AM" name to Martha and Mary: "I AM the resurrection and the life."

Next Sunday is Palm Sunday and the beginning of Holy Week. Prepare now by rededicating your whole life to the Lord, being one with him in the movements of the coming holiest week of the year.

"I will raise him up on the last day." One interpretation of this phrase is to see the "last day" as Good Friday. If you are clinging to the cross when Jesus dies, you will rise with him. For John, all this happens at once on that great Friday of our salvation.

Saturday   **The Sabbath Torah Reading**

Apr 08, 2006 #25 B	Mar 28, 2015 #25 B	Mar 23, 2024 #24 B	Apr 09, 2033 #28 B
Apr 04, 2009 #24 B	Mar 24, 2018 #25 B	Mar 20, 2027 #24 B	Apr 05, 2036 #25 B
Mar 31, 2012 #25 B	Mar 27, 2021 #25 B	Apr 13, 2030 #28 B	Apr 02, 2039 #25 B

Holy Week

The week before Easter—Alphabyte: Supper, p. 42

Palm Sunday   *The Passion Hour By Hour*   **Mark 14:1—15:47**
When the Roman officer who stood facing him saw how he had died,
he exclaimed, "Truly, this was the Son of God!" v. 39

The greatest week of the year has come, Holy Week. Hour by hour, follow the movement of Jesus as your salvation and mine is won. You might read the Passion according to Mark throughout the day, taking portions of it as each hour strikes.

Go near the cross. Do not shy away and be distant. Look what happened when Peter did that! When that nightly hour struck with the cockcrow, he remembered his denial; Peter's heart was pierced along with Jesus'.

Remember the obvious: Christians throughout the world are entering into Holy Week; pray for them. May the palm you bring home be a sign of loyalty to Christ.

Monday   *Faithful As the Sun and Moon*   **Jeremiah 33—35**
Ask me and I will tell you some remarkable secrets
about what is going to happen here. 33:3

Can you imagine the sun no longer rising, or the moon changing its faithful rotation about the earth each month? So unchanging is God's Covenant with us. However, there is one condition—obedience. Slaves must be set free. How can anyone be free while controlling the lives of others through slavery?

There is a marked change in the atmosphere of this section of Jeremiah. Greater than the punishment of exile is God's desire to restore the people to their land. There is a sense of "hoping against hope" that Jeremiah is holding out to you. God is faithful, unchanging as the sun and the moon.

Are you unchanging toward God in your response? Are you letting go of the need to control others, which in our day, is a brand of slavery? As you read about the Rechabites, ask yourself, "Is there something specific that the Lord is asking of me?"

Read quietly, with joy. God will do wonderful things with your life, if you will let God do it.

Tuesday   *A Window on God's World*   **Job 40**
Are you going to discredit my justice
and condemn me so you can say you are right? v. 8

God responds to Job in a manner very different from the "friends" of Job. They are into debate, to set the mind and mouth going in the search to solve the mystery of evil. God's tactic is to silence Job's tongue so that he can peer through the lens of God's eyes and see God's world.

The Lord presents Job with some large animals of the wild. God invites him to enter their world and to exit Job's limited one. The secret is to be released from the obsession of his own thoughts, to place himself again into the mystery of the universe.

When you find that you are being obsessed with problems, look out the "window" of your world and look at of the Lord's. Get involved in something that is fun for you, so that in the joy of pure living, you give God glory.

God's wisdom and power are beyond our capacity to understand. In God's own time, the scales of justice will be balanced.

Wednesday   *Spy's Eyes and God's Eyes*   **Psalm 61**

May he reign under God's protection forever.
Appoint your unfailing love and faithfulness to watch over him. v. 7

Some traditions call today "Spy Wednesday," after the plot of Judas to betray Jesus. See in your minds eye the Lord praying this psalm, finding comfort in the prayer of King David. Today we are suspended between Jesus the King and his triumphal entry into Jerusalem on Palm Sunday, and the King on the cross, two days from now.

Imagining the trials of David, the psalm sings of the Lord's protection when David is overwhelmed. Can you find the four metaphors that weave through this psalm? As you jot them down, begin to relate to them in your spirit. What do you find in your life that links these images with David and Jesus?

The Spirit of Jesus prays this psalm. Greater than the impact of a spy's eyes upon you, is the loving, knowing, and protective gaze of the Lord upon your life. God is all-powerful in your circumstances. All that is apparently death-bound in you can move toward life, if you yield to the Lord.

Holy Thursday   *Beyond the Mind—Into the Spirt*   **1 Cor. 13—14**

Love is patient and kind.
Love is not jealous or boastful or proud. 13:4
(The *Firestarter* and the reading are repeated on Thursday, 10KiA.)

HW B

Chapter 13 is very familiar; read it as though hearing it for the first time. Sense the divine logic beyond your mind, into your spirit.

Reflect upon the spiritual gifts outlined in chapter 14. The gift of tongues is described, a spiritual language that many find the Holy Spirit continuing to give. Ordinary language tends to keep one in the mind alone. A language of the Spirit allows the Corinthians to yield their hearts to those communications from the Lord beyond the understanding. The limitations of mind are surpassed, as pure worship and praise rise forth.

Many people experience that the gifts of chapter 14 not confined to Paul's Corinthian community. Pray that the Lord give you discernment about this in your own spiritual life.

Good Friday   *Jesus in the Judgment Seat*   **John 18:1—9:42**

Pilate replied, "You are a king then?" "You say that I am a king, and you are right," Jesus said.
"I was born for that purpose. And I came to bring truth to the world.
All who love the truth recognize that what I say is true." 18:37

I am indebted to my theology professor, Edward Mally, for showing us a point in the Passion Narrative of John that I have never seen explained elsewhere. It has to do with a point of grammar, but it will illumine for you the entire approach that John has to the death of Jesus.

We are in the court called the *Praetorium* with Jesus and Pilate. Jesus is clothed with the purple cloak, bearing the crown of thorns. In chapter 19, verse 13, translations have Pilate coming out with Jesus and sitting down in the judgment seat. Do you remember transitive and intransitive verbs? The transitive ones take an object; the intransitive ones do not. The verb used by John about "sitting down" is transitive. It means that Pilate came out "and sat <u>Jesus</u> down in the judgment seat." When Pilate is apparently judging Jesus, Jesus is passing judgment on him and on the Jewish leaders! Jesus is completely in charge of the movement of his death, because it moves to LIFE!

Saturday   **The Sabbath Torah Reading**

Apr 15, 2006 Passover	Apr 04, 2015 Passover	Mar 30, 2024 #25 B	Apr 16, 2033 Passover
Apr 11, 2009 Passover	Mar 31, 2018 Passover	Mar 27, 2027 #25 B	Apr 12, 2036 Passover
Apr 07, 2012 Passover	Apr 03, 2021 Passover	Apr 20, 2030 Passover	Apr 09, 2039 Passover

Easter Week

Alphabyte: Temple, p. 42

Alphabyte: Temple, p. 42

Easter Sunday   *With Jesus in Galilee*   **Mark 16:1–8**

**The angel said, "Do not be so surprised. You are looking for Jesus, the Nazarene,
who was crucified. He isn't here! He has been raised from the dead!
Look, this is where they laid his body. v. 6**

Women were closest to the cross and therefore, closest to the resurrection. They did not come to the "front row" to see Jesus rise, but rather as the least and the last to linger near the One they loved whom they lost. They come to anoint the body with oil, which they could not do on Friday. Instead, they become the ones anointed as the glory of the resurrection is visited upon them.

Walk along with them to the tomb. Feel their overwhelming sadness, so that you can get in touch with their overwhelming joy.

Jesus goes to Galilee to meet with his disciples. Galilee was a region of many ethnic groups, "rough and ready" types, if you will, people on the margin of life. This is where ministry began for Jesus and where it is to begin for the disciples. Join Jesus there.

Easter Monday   *God Remembers Not Our Sins.*   **Ezekiel 17—19**

**"All the trees will know that it is I, the LORD, who cuts down the tall tree and helps the short tree
to grow tall. It is I who makes the green tree wither and gives new life to the dead tree. I,
the LORD, have spoken! I will do what I have said." 17:24**

Eagles soaring and ready to pounce: such are the rulers of Babylon and Egypt. Israel is exposed as the topmost branch, vulnerable to attack because King Zedekiah not only violated the covenant with God, but also failed to keep his agreement with King Nebuchadnezzar of Babylon.

The Lord has made the dry tree flourish. Indeed! The dry tree of Calvary last Friday has flourished into the eternal life we celebrate this Easter Week.

Chapter 18 puts to rest the long debated problem of whether sons pay for the sins of their father. They do not. Here Ezekiel develops one of his key themes—individual responsibility for one's own sins.

God no longer remembers our sins! What comfort in this! The only condition is a return to right living. If God does not remember your sins, why should you?

Easter Tuesday   *Wisdom in the Word and Heart*   **Proverbs 17**

If you repay evil for good, evil will never leave your house. v. 13

We have here twenty-eight "firestarters" in one chapter of Proverbs. As the positive and negative poles of a battery that allow electric energy to flow, so is there a flow of wisdom as the negative fool contrasts with the positive, wise person. Read slowly. You might take two proverbs each hour of the waking part of your day. Sift, savor, and simmer these truths until they softly sink into your soul, calling you to right living and holy thinking. Clear a few minutes of time to read and reflect as each hour comes round. The wisdom in the Word will become wisdom in the heart.

A suggestion ... Allow God's graces to well up in your heart by writing the wisdom the Lord gives to you, as God did to Solomon. Jot them on post-it notes so that they will be right in front you.

Easter Wednesday   *My Wait and My Weight*   **Psalm 62**

I wait quietly before God, for my salvation comes from him. v. 1

We are not very good at waiting in modern society. We want immediate results. Waiting implies impatience, irritation and perhaps even the doubt that what one is waiting for is going to happen.

Not so in the Hebrew mind. "Waiting for the Lord" in the Hebrew Scriptures is a serene, confident hope that the Lord is going to intervene, even if not immediately. However relentless be the attacks of evil that come upon a person, evil will have much less patience than the patience given as a grace to wait for the Lord. That is why David can say with such assurance that the weight in the scale of proud, arrogant, and wealthy people is very light in comparison to the weight of the presence of the Lord.

Augustine called God *Pondus Meum,* "My Weight." As you pray this psalm, let the weight of your centered, relaxed body by a sign of God's risen presence in Christ who now lives within you after your days of Lenten waiting.

Easter Thursday   *The Spirit Poured Out Upon All*   **Acts 10**

The voice spoke again,
"If God says something is acceptable, don't say it isn't." v. 15

Angels often appear at moments in the life of God's people when God is about to act in a special way. This chapter relates the beginning of the power of God poured out, not only on the Chosen People, but also upon all people.

The angel comes to Cornelius and Peter while they are praying at the appointed times, the quarter parts of the day. Two persons come together to realize more fully that God was about to have the Holy Spirit poured out on the Gentiles. Recall the visit of Mary and Elizabeth. They meet; Jesus and John meet; John leaps for joy.

A new era begins in the Church with the meeting of Cornelius and Peter. The Holy Spirit comes down on the people who "leap for joy" with the gift of tongues. Dwell on the significance of this incident as the Spirit is poured out upon you.

Easter Friday   *The New Community*   **John 14:1–17**

"The truth is, anyone who believes in me will do the same works I have done,
and even greater works, because I am going to be with the Father." v. 12

Jesus portrays the New Community about to come into existence. He is going to move from this world to the Father; he invites us to come with him. It is a New Exodus. Here at the foot of a new Mount Sinai, Jesus has given us a New Commandment that we love one another. He gives us the Holy Spirit as each one's personal lawyer to guide us on the way that is to come. Jesus is going to show us the way to where the Father lives. At the same time, he reveals the place where the Father and he are going to dwell; it is within the human hearts of those who believe in his name.

What are you doing to be sure that you are living in this new community with the new commandment of love? Be aware of the need to find friends in the Lord with whom you can confide, love and be loved.

Saturday   **The Sabbath Torah Reading**

Apr 22, 2006 #26 B	Apr 01, 2015 Passover	Apr 06, 2024 #26 B	Apr 23, 2033 #29 B
Apr 18, 2009 #26 B	Apr 07, 2018 Passover	Apr 03, 2027 #26 B	Apr 19, 2036 Passover
Apr 14, 2012 Passover	Apr 10, 2021 #26 B	Apr 27, 2030 #29 B	Apr 16, 2039 Passover

EW
B

The Second Week in Easter
Alphabyte: Universe, p. 43

Sunday   *The Faith Connection*   **John 20:19–31**

Jesus told him, "You believe because you have seen me.
Blessed are those who haven't seen me and believe anyway." v. 29

The name Thomas has been linked with "doubting." We might also add another—"bold"! For that's what Thomas was as he stepped outside into the streets that so recently saw the violence of Jesus' crucifixion. All his brothers were inside that room with doors and windows tightly closed for fear of their being arrested, just as Jesus was. However, Thomas needed to be where the action really was; but he was not. By cutting himself off from the community, he cut himself off from faith. Remember that!

However, it is not too late for him; he has a second chance. He comes back after his errand—and so does Jesus. While it is not a good idea to place terms on faith, Jesus lovingly meets Thomas where he is, inviting him to feel the evidences of the pain that are now signs of glory. But I wonder: did he really put his hands in there? I doubt it. The presence of Jesus was enough for him and it is more than enough for you. "Blessed are those who have not seen, yet have believed."

Monday   *Standing in the Gap*   **Ezekiel 20—22**

"I looked for someone who might rebuild the wall of righteousness that guards the land.
I searched for someone to stand in the gap in the wall
so I wouldn't have to destroy the land, but I found no one." 22:30

Keansburg, N.J. has a creek bordering it that flows into the tidal waters opposite New York City. When strong storms occurred, it often happened that the waters would rush into the mouth of the creek, flooding the town. To prevent this from happening, a great steel gate was constructed that would completely close the mouth of the creek, preventing the seawater from elbowing its way into town. The gap was covered.

Ezekiel presents this same image of the gap in 22:30. No other verse in Scripture more clearly expresses the meaning of intercessory prayer. When the protective hedge of God's grace is broken, opening the way for the onslaught of the Enemy, an intercessor needs to stand in the gap, giving protection from the forces without. The intercessor restores the broken connection to God.

The cross of Jesus bridged the gap between heaven and earth. Resurrection-life is yours.

Tuesday   *The Anesthetized Fool*   **Proverbs 18**

What dainty morsels rumors are—but they sink deep into one's heart. v. 8

You will frequently see the word "fool" used in Proverbs, as opposed to the wise person. The fool is the one whose sensibilities to wisdom, right thinking, and right living are so dull, that the fool's choices bring darkness and ultimate destruction.

Do you do anything that dulls your senses to the peace that wise living brings? Take time to reflect. Do you anesthetize your feelings of pain with overwork, alcohol, escaping what you feel inside through excessive T.V.? Take a walk with your Lord and let yourself feel the movement of your life. Know that the Lord is with you and wants to quicken you, till deep within, you know how to live with divine inspiration. This is wisdom.

Become quiet. Write. Connect with God. Share with your spouse or friend.

Wednesday — *Seeking God Early and Often* — Psalm 63

Your unfailing love is better to me than life itself; how I praise you! v. 3

David is hiding in the wilderness from his son, Absalom. Just as his ancestors in the wilderness and Jesus in the desert, it is a place of spiritual retreat for him. The starkness of the setting prevents distractions that would keep him from seeking God. He is thirsty there, in the desert, but even more does his soul thirst for the Lord. "My soul thirsts for you; my flesh longs for you."

David is completely caught up in the Lord. Notice the parts of the body and aspects of his spirit that are engaged in this prayer of praise. He reminds us of the importance of having body and soul involved in the life of prayer.

If there was any fear of his enemies, by the end of this psalm it is gone. He is left with the Lord whom he sought. He sought, and hence he found.

Seek the Lord early and often each of these days of Easter.

Thursday — *Faithful Peter* — Acts 11—12

Peter finally realized what had happened. "It's really true!" he said to himself. "The Lord has sent his angel and saved me from Herod and from what the Jews were hoping to do to me!" 12:11

Fears often beset Peter. From the time when he walked on water to Jesus, to the courtyard of the high priest and his fears of a servant girl, Peter reacted when he was afraid. The distance between Jesus and him in the courtyard opened the way for his denial. The gap then between Peter and Jesus was too much for him.

Now, however, Peter is close to his Lord in his heart, afraid of nothing, trusting in him. He moves beyond fear to faith and trust in the Lord. If God tells him to eat what is set before him, who is Peter to hold back from doing this? Read what happens when Peter is arrested in chapter 12. Nothing is impossible with God!

In a very brief reference, the news comes of James' martyrdom. He is the brother of John. Together with Peter, they were the closest friends of Jesus.

Take courage from these apostles. God is with you as God was with them.

Friday — *The New Exodus to Begin* — John 14:18–31

But when the Father sends the Counselor as my representative— and by the Counselor I mean the Holy Spirit—he will teach you everything and will remind you of everything I myself have told you. v. 26

"Arise: let us go from here." Jesus concludes his message to the apostles at the Last Supper. As so often in John's Gospel, Jesus' words have meanings on ever deepening levels.

The New Community has been founded. Now it is about to move out into the world. It will always be with Jesus who takes the lead, as the New Exodus is about to begin.

This chapter encourages the disciples, as well as you and me. As you read, do so meditatively. Take your place with the others in that room. Listen to Jesus tell you about what is going to happen.

Though the path to come is going to include great pain, Jesus is *The Way* for us to follow. Nothing that is ever going to come upon you in your Exodus to life will be without Jesus having gone there first, showing you the way. You will always have within you the Comforter, the Holy Spirit to sustain you.

Saturday — The Sabbath Torah Reading

Apr 29, 2006 #27–28 B	Apr 18, 2015 #26 B	Apr 13, 2024 #27 B	Apr 30, 2033 #30 B
Apr 25, 2009 #27–28 B	Apr 14, 2018 #26 B	Apr 10, 2027 #27 B	Apr 26, 2036 #26 B
Apr 21, 2012 #26 B	Apr 17, 2021 #27–28 B	May 04, 2030 #30 B	Apr 23, 2039 #26 B

The Third Week in Easter
Alphabyte: Vine, p. 43

3
Ea
B

Sunday   *The Sweet Presence of Jesus*   **Luke 24:36b–48**
They said to each other, "Didn't our hearts feel strangely warm
as he talked with us on the road and explained the Scriptures to us?" v. 32

Jesus appears to the frightened disciples. There is a tone of delight as Jesus gently releases them from their fears. The first signs of Jesus' presence are not enough to shake them loose from their imbedded fears. They think he is a ghost.

However, ghosts do not eat. The disciples recognize Jesus when he eats some fish and honeycomb. Then they recognize the Lord, just as did the Emmaus disciples when Jesus broke bread and gave them to eat. There is honeycomb; Jesus' presence is sweet.

Jesus opens the Scriptures for them just as he had done for the two at Emmaus. I pray that the Spirit of Jesus will open the Scriptures everyday for you. May you find the presence of Jesus soaking Genesis to Revelation, transforming your fears by the overwhelming presence of your Lord who is ever with you.

Monday   *Three Symbols*   **Ezekiel 23—24**
Ezekiel is an example for you to follow; you will do as he has done.
And when that time comes, you will know that I am the LORD. 24:24

Ezekiel confronts the people with three powerful symbols, convicting them with their chronic unfaithfulness to God. First, Samaria and Jerusalem are harlots. They prostitute themselves in alliances with foreign nations, placing trust in them, instead of in the Lord. Second, there is a filthy pot. Just as we clean a modern oven by emptying it and turning up the heat, so the pot, which is Jerusalem, is to be emptied and burned in exile, so that the city becomes clean again for the Lord. Third, Ezekiel's wife dies and God forbids him to mourn her. So too are the people forbidden to mourn for the Temple which will be destroyed in the near future.

How do you relate to these symbols? Let the fire of the Holy Spirit cleanse the "pot" which is your life so that you can be whole and pure in the Lord's sight.

Tuesday   *Proverbs Breathe*   **Proverbs 19**
Zeal without knowledge is not good;
a person who moves too quickly may go the wrong way. v. 2

Give yourself time to become quiet. Be aware of your breathing slowing down. Watch the movement of your breaths. Proverbs are the flow of the breath, with exhales and inhales. Meditate on the first line of each proverb as you breathe in, the second part as you breathe out. The satisfaction one feels when breathing deeply and completely finds its counterpart in the completeness of each proverb.

Verse 2 catches the essence of this, noting the danger of hastiness with one's feet, before one has knowledge. Wisdom is an inner spiritual knowledge that takes time to receive. Do not be rushed when you read Proverbs. Go slowly. You will be richly rewarded.

Wednesday   *Serenity Seeps into the Soul*   **Psalm 64**

The godly will rejoice in the LORD and find shelter in him.
And those who do what is right will praise him. v. 10

It is tempting to dwell on the intrigues of those opposed to us, to wonder what they might be up to next. Many become very sick with these obsessive thoughts, leading to a state of fear and paranoia. The antidote to these obsessions is prayer, focusing upon the Lord.

Of the ten verses of this psalm, over half deal with David's awareness of evil in others, the rest with awareness of what God is going to do. Yet all is prayer. You need not be concerned that it may take some "verses" of your prayer to give God all your concerns and worries. Gradually these will diminish as your soul tilts in praise of God. When your prayer is over, a peace and serenity will seep into your soul as the prayer silently flows into the hours of your day.

Thursday   *Paul's First Missionary Journey*   **Acts 13—14**

As Paul and Barnabas left the synagogue that day, the people asked them
to return again and speak about these things the next week. 13:42

Fasting, prayer, and laying on of hands are three spirit-filled actions which begin the ministry of St. Paul. This great Apostle to the Gentiles begins to realize the implications of the visions of Cornelius and peter.

Today's chapters describe Paul's first missionary journey. It will be very helpful to have a map of this area next to you as you read. Paul and Barnabas begin by setting sail from Seleucia, a seaport on the northeast shore of the Mediterranean. From there they sail to the Island of Cyprus, then going north to the southern shore of modern Turkey and the cities in that area. Paul preaches in synagogues. The order of Sabbath readings is very much the same then as now!

As you walk about today, sense yourself on a missionary journey.

Friday   *Abide in Him.*   **John 15:1–17**

"Yes, I am the vine; you are the branches. Those who remain in me, and I in them,
will produce much fruit. For apart from me you can do nothing." v. 5

Jesus uses the word "abide" eleven times in this reading. The Greek word for this, *menein*, means to "abide," "dwell in," and "remain with." The word is alive. It means to take the branch of whom you are and engraft it onto the vine, which is Jesus. A wholly new spontaneity begins to flow from you.

We find the source of this abiding in the way in which the Father and the Son abide in each other. How intimate and selfless God is! We are not God, but God shares the divine life-source with us.

Meditate and literally abide with these words today and always. You need no longer live alone. Open yourself to the power of God's life which flows within you and then outside of you in loving service.

Saturday   **The Sabbath Torah Reading**

May 06, 200 #29–30 B	Apr 25, 2015 #27–28 B	Apr 20, 2024 #28 B	May 07, 2033 #31 B
May 02, 2009 #29–30 B	Apr 21, 2018 #27–28 B	Apr 17, 2027 #28 B	May 03, 2036 #27–28 B
Apr 28, 2012 #27–28 B	Apr 24, 2021 #29–30 B	May 11, 2030 #31 B	Apr 30, 2039 #27–28 B

The Fourth Week in Easter
Alphabyte: Wax, p. 44

Sunday   *Held by the Good Shepherd*   **John 10:11–18**
"I am the good shepherd. The good shepherd
lays down his life for the sheep." v. 11

The most beloved image of Jesus is the Good Shepherd. As though recalling Psalm 23, Christians etched these pictures of Jesus in the "dark valleys" of the catacombs of Rome where they hid from persecutions. From a very early tradition as well, comes the center-piece of the Easter Season, "Good Shepherd Sunday."

Your Good Shepherd laid down his life for you and took it up again, to share it with you. He knows you by name; you are one of his beloved sheep. Do you believe this? Do you know the sweet sound of your name said with love and forgiveness? You and I know the abrasive noises of the present and the echoes of the past that poke at the heart with guilt and shame. I am sure you have many "Romans" who want to persecute you! Look at the Good Shepherd etched into your heart of flesh and rejoice.

Monday   *Against Those Around God's People*   **Ezekiel 25—26**
I will stop the music of your songs.
No more will the sound of harps be heard among your people. 26:13

As though encircling a trapped animal, six countries surround and menace God's people. They are the objects of the Lord's indignation in Ezekiel chapters 25 to 32, the readings for the rest of these weeks of the Easter Season. Phoenicia, with its capital of Tyre, borders God's people on the northwest on the coast of the Mediterranean; Ammon, Moab and Edom lie on the east and south, Philistia on the west, and Egypt on the southwest.

The previous chapters were confrontations with God's people. They were unfaithful to God through contamination with others' gods. Now Ezekiel confronts these nations directly for their arrogance not only against God's people, but also against God.

Those who despise the Lord or who simply patronize God, will be at the mercy of all the powers of darkness for destruction. Do not lose the cover of God's protection on your life. Be faithful to God alone.

Tuesday   *We're Going Back!*   **Ezra 1—2**
All of you who are his people may return to Jerusalem in Judah
to rebuild this Temple of the LORD, the God of Israel, who lives in Jerusalem.
And may your God be with you! 1:3

For the next four Tuesdays, we will consider a book of the Bible about another "Good Shepherd" who led God's people from exile in Babylon, back to the Promised Land. His name is Ezra.

Well before he led them back, he was responsible for creating a longing in the exiled people for God's Word. With the destruction of The First Temple in 587 B.C., the synagogue in local communities becomes more and more vital in bonding the exiled people of God to their God. In place of sacrifice, study of the Word becomes essential, with the example and wisdom of Ezra, upon whom was "The hand of the Lord."

In these chapters is the text of the decree of King Cyrus of Persia. He had defeated the treacherous Babylonian King Nebuchadnezzar. Think of the list of names as though you are looking in awe at the names of the immigrants who came to the United States, arriving at Ellis Island off New York City.

Wednesday   *Carpeted with the Resurrection*   **Psalm 65**

The meadows are clothed with flocks of sheep, and the valleys are carpeted with grain.
They all shout and sing for joy! v. 13

As you pray this psalm, list the number of God's actions of which David is aware. On land and sea, the Lord is at work. David describes the actions of God's bounty in the abundant fields and herds.

Your God is a God at work in your own life. If you were to make a list of the favors that the Lord has granted to you, the list would be very long. Even the things that at first glance hardly seem as blessings can become so. Nothing negative can happen to you, but that the Lord is seeking to bring about an even greater blessing for you. Will you let God do this?

Prayer is powerful. It unleashes the loving blessings of God into our lives. You need not complain. You are not a victim, but a victor in Jesus' resurrection. The resurrection has carpeted your life! Praise the Lord for who God is and for what God does.

Thursday   *The Holy Spirit at Every Turn*   **Acts 15**

There was no further discussion, and everyone listened as Barnabas and
Paul told about the miraculous signs and wonders
God had done through them among the Gentiles. v. 12

The first council of the Church takes place in Jerusalem. With joy, Paul and Barnabas announce the miracles and wonders that took place while on their recent missionary journey. It is time now for the church to establish guidelines for the expansion to come. They decide that Gentiles are to be welcomed into the life of God in Christ without having to be circumcised. However, the new Christians must adhere to some basic habits of Jews, such as not eating the blood of animals.

The Holy Spirit inspires these decisions. In every verse of Acts, the Holy Spirit is present and active. At every turn of life, the early Christians seek and find this divine presence and power. May it ever be the same for you.

Friday   *The World Hates Jesus and His Own*   **John 15:18–27**

The world would love you if you belonged to it, but you don't.
I chose you to come out of the world, and so it hates you. v. 19

Jesus leads out the New Community from the place of the Last Supper to a future fraught with suffering, yet glory. Think of Exodus. Enemies are all about. Jesus prepares his disciples for the world's hatred of them, just as it hates Jesus, a hatred which is about to move to fever pitch.

Why the hatred? Jesus refuses to let his power be used against those from Rome who were occupying the sacred lands. Instead, Jesus unleashes his spiritual power against the religious system from within, announcing a new and deeper spiritual freedom from it. The hatred against Jesus was not from Rome, but from Jerusalem.

Fear not. The Holy Spirit is promised to be with us during any persecution, for strength, for comfort, for wisdom. "When the going gets rough, the rough gets smooth"—by the Holy Spirit!

Saturday   **The Sabbath Torah Reading**

May 13, 2006 #31B	May 02, 2015 #29–30B	Apr 27, 2024 Passover	May 14, 2033 #32B
May 09, 2009 #31B	Apr 28, 2018 #29–30B	Apr 24, 2027 Passover	May 10, 2036 #29–30B
May 05, 2012 #29–39B	May 01, 2021 #31B	May 18, 2030 #32B	May 07, 2039 #29–30B

The Fifth Week in Easter
Alpbabyte: Xylophone, p. 44

Sunday   *The Last "I Am" Name*   John 15:1–8

**"Yes, I am the vine; you are the branches. Those who remain in me, and I in them,
will produce much fruit. For apart from me you can do nothing." v. 5**

Jesus gives his seventh and last "I AM" name: "I am the True Vine." There echoes in the hearts of the disciples this ancient symbol used by Isaiah (5:1–7), Jeremiah (2:21) and Ezekiel (19:10–12), among others. "Let me sing for my beloved my love-song concerning his vineyard" (Isaiah 5:1). Jesus is the one who embraces the New Vine. The only Son of God is the place to find the New Community. We are to be branches of the vine, which is Jesus. The life force is the Holy Spirit.

Pruning increases our fruit-producing power. Suffering is the passage, unique to each person that can move us from death to self, to life in Jesus.

Abide in Jesus. Rest in him. As you sit, stand or kneel in prayer, let your imagination, illumined and made real by faith, engraft you onto this wondrous vine.

**5
Ea
B**

Monday   *The Fall of an Ancient City*   Ezekiel 27—28

**"Therefore, this is what the Sovereign LORD says: Because you think you are as wise as a god,
I will bring against you an enemy army, the terror of the nations. They will suddenly
draw their swords against your marvelous wisdom and defile your splendor!" 28:6–7**

The ancient seaport city of Tyre in Phoenicia is targeted for destruction due to its wanton pride and arrogance. It was located on an island just off the northeastern coast of the Mediterranean Sea. Its power had stretched as far as Spain in the west, to Mesopotamia, the region between the Tigris and Euphrates rivers, in the east. A long list of cities is included, such as Tarshish in Spain, cities under the sway of this ancient kingdom. Though many of these cities cannot be identified any longer, the cumulative effect of the list is designed to have us feel the extent of this ancient maritime power.

Nebuchadnezzar laid a thirteen-year siege of Tyre from about 587–574 B.C. Ezekiel sees this as a consequence of the power that this country wielded from its arrogant king whom Ezekiel denounces. This phrase appears twice: "You set your heart as the heart of a god." Thus passes the glory of the world. Only those connected to the Word of God will live forever.

Tuesday   *The Joy of Worship ... and More Waiting*   Ezra 3—4

**With praise and thanks, they sang this song to the LORD: "He is so good! His faithful love
for Israel endures forever!" Then all the people gave a great shout,praising
the LORD because the foundation of the LORD's Temple had been laid. 3:11**

After seventy years, the sweet, sacred smell of sacrifice returns to the Promised Land. Ground breaking ceremonies take place for the new Temple destroyed when wicked Nebuchadnezzar razed Jerusalem and held God's people captive in Babylon. A great shout breaks out. The word used in Hebrew, *teru'ah*, is the loudest of noises that humans can make; it is a combination of shouts, weeping for joy and blasts of trumpets.

However, the neighbors complain. They write letters of protest to the then Persian King Artaxerxes who decrees that the rebuilding cease.

The Lord's will may be slowed up, but it cannot be stopped. There are two things that the Chosen People need to learn—fidelity to the Lord's will and patience. Do you have any personal reflections about these? They are gifts of the Spirit.

Wednesday   *The Self On Fire*   **Psalm 66**

You have tested us, O God; you have purified
us like silver melted in a crucible. v. 10

This Psalm joins two kinds of prayer—corporate prayer for the nation and private prayer for the self. As you pray the first twelve verses, see yourself as the intercessor for your country that needs to call upon the Lord to be present and active in the land. In verse 13 where burnt offerings and vows are promised, join your personal outpourings. While you will not be bringing burnt offerings to the altar, bring your whole self on fire with the Lord, with your egoism burnt away as in a refiner's fire. This is the kind of offering which the Lord wants—death to self and life in Christ Jesus.

At the end of the psalm, you too, have the faith of the psalmist who believes that God has indeed listened to his prayer.

Thursday   *The Gospel Comes to Europe*   **Acts 16**

Around midnight, Paul and Silas were praying and singing hymns to God,
and the other prisoners were listening. v. 25

Paul's disciple is the young Timothy. This is the second missionary journey of Paul. Models of leadership abound. People learn about leadership by becoming spiritual apprentices.

Remember that all of the Holy Lands at this time are part of the Roman Empire, which is divided into provinces. In addition to the names of cities, there are provinces such as Galatia, Asia (not the continent), Bithynia, Mysia, Phrygia, Macedonia, and Achaea (modern Greece). Soon into this journey, Paul receives a vision during the night to cross over into Macedonia. This would be the first time that the Gospel is preached in Europe.

One of the loveliest stories in Acts is the account of what happens when Paul and Silas are in prison. May your heart sing along with theirs as you too become open to the power of God in your life.

Friday   *Better That Jesus Go*   **John 16:1–15**

When the Spirit of truth comes, he will guide you into all truth.
He will not be presenting his own ideas;
he will be telling you what he has heard. He will tell you about the future. v. 13

Jesus prepares his disciples and us for the persecutions that are to come. Again, the situation for the very writing of this Gospel is disclosed: "They will put you out of synagogues." Jesus promises the Holy Spirit as the Comforter in the dislocation of Jesus' disciples from being able to worship as Jews.

Jesus announces that he is going away. He softens the sadness by stating that it is better that this be so; otherwise, "The Helper will not come to you." Jesus of Nazareth releases himself from being a limited presence on the earth. Because of the resurrection, Christ's body is beyond being bound by time and space. The Lord Christ lives in limitless space and eternity itself. Yet all the intimacy of his presence is preserved for you, because of the coming of the Holy Spirit into your heart.

Saturday   **The Sabbath Torah Reading**

May 20, 2006 #32–33 B	May 09, 2015 #31 B	May 04, 2024 #29 B	May 21, 2033 #32 B
May 16, 2009 #32–33 B	May 05, 2018 #31 B	May 01, 2027 #29 B	May 17, 2036 #31 B
May 12, 2012 #31 B	May 08, 2021 #32–33 B	May 25, 2030 #33 B	May 14, 2039 #31 B

The Sixth Week in Easter
Alphabyte: Yoke, p. 45

Sunday   *The Logic of Love*   **John 15:9–17**
I have loved you even as the Father has loved me.
Remain in my love. v. 9

The power of God's love for us is complete. Just as is the love between the Father and the Son, so is the love between Jesus and us. We can only get a glimpse at understanding this divine reality. However, beyond their human grasp is the embracing of these truths by faith.

Just accept Jesus' acceptance of you. "Greater love has no one than this, than to lay down one's live for his friends." Jesus died for you. This divine love is to flow toward one another. Remember the words of Jesus in John 13:34: "Love one another, as I have loved you." Will you die in self-sacrifice for your brothers and sisters?

Monday   *The Fall of Egypt Coming*   **Ezekiel 29—30**
The land of Egypt will become a desolate wasteland, and the Egyptians will know
that I am the LORD, because you said, "The Nile River is mine; I made it." 29:9

Ezekiel directs his prophetic power toward Egypt. The theme for all these proclamations against the nations is the growth of their power without giving glory to God.

The most vital aspect of the power of Egypt was the Nile River. The Pharaoh called the River "Mine," failing to give God the glory for its existence. Again, the power of Babylonia and its wicked king is going to come against this nation. The text of the proclamation gives us a sense of the outrage of the Lord at those nations that do not truly acknowledge God as the ultimate power and Lord of the world.

Pray for all nations that they too will trust in the Lord, and not in the power of violence to redress the wrongs that they find against each other. We live in a "Global Village." Lift it to God for God's blessing and care.

Tuesday   *The Second Temple Is Completed*   **Ezra 5—7**
This was because Ezra had determined to study and obey the law of the LORD
and to teach those laws and regulations to the people of Israel. 7:10

Haggai and Zechariah, two prophets of the Bible, appear on the scene to "jump start" the rebuilding of the Temple. Another letter of complaint is sent to Darius, King of Persia. He digs through the archives for the original decree of the former King, Cyrus. Yes, Cyrus had decreed the rebuilding of the Temple. Darius now forbids altering the decree. You will read what would happen if anyone did!

The second Temple was completed in 515 B.C. This Temple was standing in Jesus' time, with further magnificent additions done by Herod the Great.

Ezra, the holy teacher, and lover of the Word, himself leads a group of persons on the return. The phrase "The hand of our God," occurs six times in chapter 7 and the next. Greater than the hands of those who oppose, is the hand of the Lord upon this holy man.

Wednesday   *The King of All the Earth*   **Psalm 67**

How glad the nations will be, singing for joy, because you govern them with justice
and direct the actions of the whole world. v. 4

The psalms are such a central part of the life of the Church because they gather up everyone in the human family and pray in an intercessory way. This is especially the case in today's psalm. The prayer is a global one for all the nations. We intercede for the rest of the nations, which are so often about everything else, but prayer.

It is a fitting psalm for the day before the Ascension of Jesus, King of all the earth. The symmetry of this seven-verse psalm with v. 4 at the center is perfectly applied to Christ the Lord, center of the universe.

Take a map of the world or a globe. Pray over it. Are there any special countries where the Lord wants the Holy Spirit in you to brood upon, with inner groans of prayer?

Thursday   *Stirring the People*   **Acts 17**

As I was walking along I saw your many altars.
And one of them had this inscription on it—'To an Unknown God.'
You have been worshiping him without knowing who he is,
and now I wish to tell you about him. v. 23

I draw your attention to a Greek word that occurs only two times in the New Testament. In verse 6, the word *anastenazo* is used for the accusation that Paul and Silas are "stirring up" the people. The only other time this word is used is in Mark 8:12 where Jesus "sighs deeply" at the demand of the Pharisees for a sign from Jesus. The word connotes a welling up of intense emotion. May the Spirit do the same to you, loosening, and freeing you to be wholly dedicated to God.

The journeys of Paul and Silas continue. They reach Athens, center of pagan religion in the Roman Empire. You will read the sermon that Paul delivered on the Areopagus located on the famous Parthenon. However, no faith comes from Athens. Its pride in being the center of philosophical thought in the ancient world prevents it from being stirred up to faith. There would be no subsequent "Letter of Paul to the Athenians!"

Friday   *In a Little While—Joy*   **John 16:16–33**

At that time you won't need to ask me for anything.
The truth is, you can go directly to the Father and ask him,
and he will grant your request because you use my name. v. 23

Verses of great promise are here that we need to commit to memory. "Whatever you ask the Father in my name He will give you."

This will happen because ironically, Jesus is going away. He plays on the notion of a "little while." He is going to be taken away in the coming crucifixion, but soon after, he is coming again in the Holy Spirit, bringing a joy that no one can take away.

Think of it: no one can take away the joy that Jesus longs to give you in the Holy Spirit! You and I will go through various mood swings from those sinful tendencies of selfishness and fear that still lurk about, but they need not last very long. "In a little while" joy can return. Joy is to be the continual state of our lives as Christians.

Saturday   **The Sabbath Torah Reading**

May 27, 2006 #34 B	May 16, 2015 #32–33 B	May 11, 2024 #30 B	May 28, 2033 #34 B
May 23, 2009 #34 B	May 12, 2018 #32–33 B	May 08, 2027 #30 B	May 24, 2036 #32–33 B
May 19, 2012 #32–33 B	May 15, 2021 #34 B	June 01, 2030 #34 B	May 21, 2039 #32–33 B

The Seventh Week in Easter

Alphabyte: Zenith, p. 45

Next week is Pentecost Sunday, the beginning of the season of Pentecost. The readings for Pentecost and Trinity Sunday are found at the very beginning of the next season, *Pentecost*. You will also find further directions for finding the Monday-to-Saturday readings for the beginning weeks of the season of Pentecost which has slight yearly variations due to the changing date of Easter.

Ascension Sunday   *The Temple—Beginning and End*   Luke 24:44–53

They worshiped him and then returned to Jerusalem filled with great joy.
And they spent all of their time in the Temple, praising God. vv. 52–53

The traditional day for the Ascension is last Thursday. The Lord has returned to heaven, completing the Father's will in dying and rising for us, sitting at the right hand of God. Now the Spirit can come in complete measure.

The Gospel gathers the mystery of the Lord together in the moment of Ascension, also described in the opening chapter of the Book of Acts. There is one final instruction: "Wait in the city till you are clothed with power from on high."

Luke's Gospel ends as it began—in the Temple. From the lonely, aged Zechariah in the Holy of Holies, to the New Community raised by Jesus, the Temple is the place of God's praise and glory. However, what is about to happen in the Holy Spirit is that the community itself becomes the temple, the place of God's presence. You are the temple of the Holy Spirit.

Monday   *God As Lord of the Nations*   Ezekiel 31—32

Yes, this is the funeral song they will sing for Egypt. Let all the nations mourn for Egypt
and its hordes. I, the Sovereign LORD, have spoken! 32:16

Using the image of a ship, as Ezekiel did in the case of Tyre, he prophesies the destruction of ancient Egypt. Another ancient power will come against Egypt, Assyria, likened to a great cedar tree. Chapter 32 is a lamentation for Pharaoh and Egypt as poetically powerful pictures describe the downfall of this formerly strong nation.

God is in charge of all the nations. They will rise and fall in their own manipulative power. Only those nations truly dedicated to the Lord will have a power that cannot be taken away from them. It means living in the Kingdom of God and not in the kingdom of the world. We are citizens of a heavenly kingdom with roots sunk deep in the earth right now.

As you pray, feel the divine Kingdom of which you are a special citizen. Pray for this hurting world.

Tuesday   *A Model for Intercessory Prayer*   Ezra 8—10

And there by the Ahava Canal, I gave orders for all of us to fast and
humble ourselves before our God. We prayed that he would give us a safe journey and protect us,
our children, and our goods as we traveled. 8:21

One would think that after the return to the way of life of their ancestors, God's people would settle down and finally obey the Lord. Wrong! Just as happened soon after the Temple of Solomon was constructed, God's people wander from the ways of the Lord.

Ezra is a model for intercessors. Without finger pointing, as a true priest, he represents the people before the Lord and expresses the sins of intermarrying as though they were his own personal sins. Jesus did the same. For our sake, "He who knew no sin, [became] sin for us" (2 Corinthians 5:21).

Ezra desires to lift the people to God. This kind of prayer moves God. In Jesus' name, pray the same way.

Wednesday   *God Arises*   **Psalm 68**
When you ascended to the heights, you led a crowd of captives.
You received gifts from the people, even from those who rebelled against you.
Now the LORD God will live among us here. v. 18

The psalm begins with the marching cry of Moses from Numbers 10:35. Military images abound, reminding us of the adage: "Is God on our side?" I prefer this alternative: "Am I on God's side?"

For God *sides* with the rejected and forgotten expressed in the psalm by the fatherless and the widow. If you have compassion for these and others in our society, then the grace of the Lord will flow through you in a powerful way.

Paul quotes today's verse in Ephesians 4:8 in the description of the Ascension of Jesus into heaven; you might turn to that chapter of Ephesians as a counterpoint to the psalm for today.

God is beyond us, yet within us, through the Holy Spirit whom we celebrate Sunday in Pentecost.

7
Ea
B

Thursday   *A Great City Accepts Christ*   **Acts 18:1–22**
One night the Lord spoke to Paul in a vision and told him, "Don't be afraid!
Speak out! Don't be silent! For I am with you, and no one will harm you
because many people here in this city belong to me." vv. 9–10

Embedded in the midst of the most pagan of cities, there are those hungry and waiting for the Gospel. After a failure in Athens, Paul is lead to turn to another Greek city—Corinth.

It would be different for Corinth. Located on a small isthmus, it was the center of trade in the ancient world, shipments briefly passing over land in the traffic from east to west across the Mediterranean and Aegean Seas. Similar to New York City, it was a cosmopolitan city with a great diversity of peoples. It became open to the Gospel. Paul wrote two great letters to this Church.

The verses for today deserve special meditation. What might they mean for you? Are there tasks that God has placed on your heart that in the natural realm, do not seem possible?

We return to the Book of Acts next year at Easter time, with Paul's third missionary journey.

Friday   *Another Lord's Prayer*   **John 17**
My prayer for all of them is that they will be one, just as you and I are one, Father—that just
you are in me and I am in you, so they will be in us, and the world will believe you sent me. v. 21

The final passage from John this Easter Season is "The High Priestly Prayer, sometimes called another "Lord's Prayer," since we are taken right into the very heart of Jesus where he is one with the Father.

The prayer is in three parts: Glory for Jesus (vv. 1–5); that the apostles be sanctified (vv.6–19); that the Church be one (vv. 20–26).

It is the prayer of Jesus' hour. John does not describe what the other three evangelists treat—the agony in the garden. The prayer of Jesus here takes place on the way, perhaps in a space just before he crosses the Brook Kidron and enters the garden. John's entire Gospel is a Gospel of glory.

Pray this prayer slowly, letting the Spirit pray it within you, as you become one with the Lord.

Saturday   **The Sabbath Torah Reading**

June 03, 2006 Pentecost	May 23, 2015 #34 B	May 18, 2024 #31 B	Jun 04, 2033 Pentecost
May 30, 2009 Pentecost	May 15, 2018 #34 B	May 14, 2027 #31 B	May 31, 2036 #34 B
May 26, 2012 #34 B	May 22, 2021 #35 B	June 08, 2030 Pentecost	May 28, 2039 #34 B

PENTECOST

SUMMER

Northern Hemisphere

Year B
2009, 2012, 2015 …

Pentecost begins the Sunday after the Seventh Sunday in Easter.
See the entire cycle of readings at a glance on page xxi.

The Beginning of the Season of Pentecost

season of Pentecost varies a few weeks from year to year. The First two Sundays of the season are always Pentecost and Trinity Sundays. When Easter is early, up to two weeks (rarely three) at the end of the season of Epiphany "leap ahead" Lent and Easter and become the Monday-to-Saturday readings for the season of Pentecost. When Easter is late, one week (rarely two) "leaps back" before Lent and Easter begins and becomes the Monday-to-Saturday readings for the end of the season of Epiphany. For the changes this year, simply follow the table below. After these initial weeks, continue in the usual method of determining the week by finding the date nearest the previous Sunday.

For more detailed information on suggested revisions of the Christian year, see the article "Solar and Sacred Seasons" in the Appendix.

Year B	Pentecost Sunday *See facing page*	Monday-to-Saturday Readings	Trinity Sunday *See facing page*	Monday-to-Saturday Readings
2009	May 31	First Week in Pentecost	June 7	Second Week in Pentecost
2012*	May 27	1 Extra Week No Mon-Fri Readings Torah Reading for Jun 02: #35B	June 3	First Week in Pentecost
2015	May 24	1 Extra Week See Eighth Wk in Epiphany	May 31	First Week in Pentecost
2018	May 20	1st of 2 Extra Weeks See Seventh Wk in Epiphany	May 27	2nd of 2 Extra Weeks See Eighth Wk in Epiphany
2021	May 23	1 Extra Week See Eighth Wk in Epiphany	May 30	First Week in Pentecost
2024	May 19	1st of 2 Extra Weeks (7th Wk in Epiph) p. 129	May 26	2nd of 2 Extra Weeks (8th Wk in Epiph) p. 133
2027	May 16	1st of 2 Extra Weeks See Seventh Wk in Epiphany	May 23	2nd of 2 Extra Weeks See Eighth Wk in Epiphany
2030	June 9	Second Week in Pentecost	June 16	Third Week in Pentecost
2033	June 5	Second Week in Pentecost	June 12	Third Week in Pentecost
2036	June 1	First Week in Pentecost,	June 8	Second Week in Pentecost
2039	May 29	First Week in Pentecost	June 5	Second Week in Pentecost

As always, the Sabbath readings will be indicated right after Friday of each week.
*Years that have fifty-three weeks in the Christian Year. No Monday-to-Friday readings. This is a "sabbatical week." Reflect on how this whole journey is going for you.

Pentecost and Trinity Sunday
at the Beginning of
the Season of Pentecost

Pentecost Sunday   *Tongues of Fire*   **John 15:26–27; 16:4b–15**
(See also: Acts 2:1–21)

I tell you the truth: It is for your good that I am going away.
Unless I go away, the Counselor will not come to you. Jn 16:7

The Gospel promises that with the coming of the Holy Spirit, the disciples will become strong, empowered by the very glory of Christ visited upon them in the Spirit. The tongues of fire upon their heads, become "tongues of fire" in their hearts and mouths. All fear is gone. Peter is bold, giving the first sermon that gathers so many into the Body of Christ that very first day. Babel is reversed. That cursed attempt to build a tower of gathered people that scatters them more than ever, now yields to a new communication that has each one understand in their own language (Genesis 11).

Get ready for the gift of Pentecost to flow into your soul. Claim it. The promises made by Jesus in the Gospel are for you. You have a permanent advocate, helper, comforter, and counselor in the Holy Spirit.

Trinity Sunday   *Lingering on the Heights*   **John 3:1–17**
I tell you the truth, no one can enter the kingdom of God
unless he is born of water and the Spirit. v. 5

Lingering on the heights of Pentecost, Trinity Sunday prompts us to look once again at this deepest mystery of God, and adore. A searching Pharisee in the middle of the night is lead to the heart of Jesus.

The Trinity, not bound by our brains, is adored in our spirits. What the mind cannot grasp, the heart receives. God is community—Father, Son and Holy Spirit. God wants nothing less than the intimacy of community with the human family.

We have come to the middle of the church year. In *Advent and Epiphany*, we looked to the Father in preparing for the coming and manifestation of the Son. In *Lent and Easter*, we contemplated Jesus and his passage from death to life, which became our passage as well. Now the time of the Holy Spirit is here—*Pentecost*. Be ready for what the Spirit is going to do in your life!

The First Week in Pentecost

Begins on the Sunday nearest June 1, unless the Easter Season is still in effect. Alphabyte: Arc, p. 77

Sunday   *Jesus Is Your Sabbath*   Mark 2:23—3:6

The Sabbath was made for man, not man for the Sabbath.
So the Son of Man is Lord even of the Sabbath. 2:28

Bound by legalism, the Pharisees could not rest; they were always "working" at accusing Jesus, refusing to rest in him. There was always some other ordinance that must be kept. They were never satisfied, projecting that God also was never satisfied.

Jesus came to release us from bondage, setting us free to enjoy a continual Sabbath by exulting in life. Every day with Jesus is Sabbath rest, for he shares the yoke of our lives. "Come to Me all you who labor and are heavy laden, and I will give you rest" (Matt. 11:28).

Jesus is your Sabbath. Let him give you rest as he does his work in you. He came to relieve you of all other negative movements that work against the rest he longs to give you.

Monday   *The Anguish of Infidelity*   Hosea 1

I will have pity on the house of Judah, and I will save them by the Lord their God;
I will not save them by bow, or by sword,
or by war, or by horses, or by horsemen. v. 7

Marriage is the most intimate of relationships; that is how the Lord wants to embrace the people. Our Israelite ancestors were continually unfaithful. As a jolt to the people, God commands faithful Hosea, the prophet, to take a prostitute as a wife. His unfaithful wife is God's way of confronting our ancestors with their infidelity.

The Lord longs to marry you in fidelity and love. Nothing less than total intimacy is God's desire. At this very moment, God wants to refashion your soul-pain. What symbol does God use for you as energy to draw you closer to the Lord?

To love is to be poured out. The Holy Spirit was poured out, as Jesus' blood was shed for you. "Till death do us part?" Not for Jesus … His death means life and union for you!

Tuesday   *The Examined Life*   Proverbs 20

Differing weights are an abomination to the Lord,
and false scales are not good. v. 23

We often consider an examination of conscience as a judgmental, knitted eyebrow, pointing the finger at our own soul, bringing up feelings of guilt and shame. The word comes from the Latin *examen*, which literally means the "marker on a scale." Think of the careful, gentle look you give a postal scale to see if you need to add extra postage to that special piece of mail.

The scale, or a see saw, is how Proverbs are. Each side is balanced with its opposite. Read today's proverbs slowly, placing your soul in the balance of each one, literally **weighing** your life according to the measure of each proverb. Notice how your soul tilts as you pray them. Speaking of scales, beware of any double standards in your life.

The ancient Greek philosopher, Socrates said: "The unexamined life is not worth living."

Wednesday *From Pain to Praise* **Psalm 69**

**Do not let those who hope in you be put to shame because of me,
O Lord God of hosts; do not let those who seek you be dishonored
because of me, O God of Israel. v. 6**

"Dear Diary": perhaps these are the most familiar words we associate with keeping a journal. It is always there for you, always ready to listen and receive without judgment, criticism, blame, or condemnation.

This is the way David approaches his Lord in the many psalms attributed to him. They are personal. He hardly imagined that you and I would be praying them thousands of years later!

This psalm is typical of many that move from pain to praise. Do what David does. Share your pain with the Lord in writing. You will find images emerging as vehicles for the pain to move out from you. Image gives birth to image as deliverance takes place. Your soul will then be free and empty to be filled with the praises of the Lord. The more you pray, the less likely your struggles with evil will be a cause for you neighbor to stumble.

Thursday *The Comfort of God* **2 Corinthians 1**

**Blessed be the God and Father of our Lord Jesus Christ,
the Father of mercies and the God of all consolation. v. 3**

Five times in verses 3 and 4 the word "comfort" appears. Paul begins his letter with the assurance of the comfort of God in all sufferings, this comfort being the source of the same for others. Read slowly; savor these verses.

The word for "comfort" is the same word used in John's Gospel for the Holy Spirit, "the Comforter," from the Greek, *Paracletos,* "to be called to one's side." The Holy Spirit is the one at your side, poured forth to heal, restore, and deeply comfort your entire being.

Belief in the Holy Spirit is also the guarantee of all the promises of God in this world and the next. When the Holy Spirit is in evidence in you, you have a passport to the heavenly places you are entering right now.

**1
Pe
B**

Friday *Seed, Soil and Soul* **Mark 4:1–25**

**These are the ones sown on the good soil: they hear the word and accept it
and bear fruit, thirty and sixty and a hundredfold. v. 20**

Picture you soul as soil. What kind is it? Is it hard and stony with no place for roots to go deep? If the Lord promised in the prophets that God would turn stony hearts to hearts of flesh, how much more will he soften yours through his Spirit! The hardness and harshness of your soul becomes as soft as sifted soil. The finger of God pushes the seed of the Word into your heart.

Firestarters are as "Fire Seeds." Open yourself to receive God's Word be planted in you. Be alert throughout the course of your day to what God is speaking to you. Keep a journal of fresh notes that reveal how the Word meets you. Just as soil embraces seed, your soul embraces the Word.

Saturday **The Sabbath Torah Reading**

June 10, 2006 #35B	June 06, 2015 #36B	June 08, 2024 #34B	Mar 05, 2033 #23B
June 06, 2009 #35B	June 09, 2018 #37B	June 05, 2027 #34B	June 07, 2036 #35B
June 09, 2012 #36B	June 05, 2021 #37B	Mar 09, 2030 #23B	June 04, 2039 #35B

The Second Week in Pentecost

Begins on the Sunday nearest June 8. Alphabyte: Beach Ball, p. 77

Sunday   *Who's In Charge?*   **Mark 3:20–35**

If a house is divided against itself, that house cannot stand. v. 25

The Pharisees commit the sin of blasphemy against the Holy Spirit, accusing Jesus of healing by the power of Satan. In their spiritually stubborn position, they paint themselves into a corner with no escape.

It is very hard to commit this great sin, but there are smaller versions of it that can undermine your spirit, such as living as though you are Number One instead of God.

You will notice many kinds of demons that Jesus had to cast out. Not only were there ones of disease and infirmity, but there were those who dominated the spiritual real in envy, pride, and blasphemy. Even Jesus' own family, who know him from the beginning, thought he was out of his mind. They "over-knew" Jesus on one level and refused to see him as the Anointed One of God.

For you: who is Jesus?

Monday   *Comfort in the Wilderness*   **Hosea 2**

**I will now allure her, and bring her into the wilderness,
and speak tenderly to her. v. 14**

A spiritual wilderness of emptiness and loneliness is the perfect place for the Lord to comfort you with the Word. Note the shift that takes place half way through this chapter, moving from the pain and grief of God as of a husband of an outrageously unfaithful wife, to the luring, seductive words of the husband calling the wife to true love and fidelity.

If you have been seeking other "spouses" for your soul, there will come a time when nothing will satisfy you and you will know it. This is wilderness. Only here can you come to know the joy of the oasis of God's presence. You will experience for yourself the words of Augustine: "You have made us for Yourself, O God: and our hearts are restless until they rest in Thee."

Tuesday   *A River in God's Hands*   **Proverbs 21**

**The king's heart is a stream of water in the hand of the Lord;
he turns it wherever he will. v. 1**

Rafts roll over rocks in mild white water rafting as though one were riding gently on horseback. This is the image of the first proverb. As your read, gently let your spirit dip and rise as you flow over the waters of life in God's Word.

How are you with the Lord? Do you resist and push the gentle holding of the Lord, or are you as waters that take their shape and movement from the contours of God's hand? Sense in your spirit this image in the rest of the Proverbs for today. The positive halves flow with abandon; the negative sides are resistive, self-willed, and unresponsive to the call to justice intended to flow into the seas of God's peace. Pray until you are one with the wisdom of the proverbs.

Wednesday   *Deliver Me, O God!*   **Psalm 70**

Be pleased, O God, to deliver me. O Lord, make haste to help me! v. 1

This small psalm of five verses has strong similarity with the first Beatitude in Matthew 5:1. **"Blessed are the poor in Spirit, for theirs is the Kingdom of heaven."** The New English Bible translates it this way: **"Blessed are those who know their need of God."** To be poor in spirit means awareness of a total need for God. Absolute need becomes absolute blessing. The only other alternative to choosing God is despair.

The Hebrew word *'ebyon* in verse 5 carries this same concept of "poor in spirit." A group of Jewish disciples of Jesus gave themselves the name "Ebionites." They found joy in their needy state, for then they knew that the riches of the resurrected life would be theirs.

When you have given up on everything and everyone as being the source of your happiness, then you are in the place where only the Lord alone can meet your deepest need of soul.

Thursday   *The Victory Parade*   **2 Corinthians 2**

Thanks be to God, who in Christ always leads us in triumphal procession,
and through us spreads in every place
the fragrance that comes from knowing him. v. 14

Paul refers to someone who has offended him grievously. Feel his pain. Yet even more, sense his desire that there be healing and reconciliation. Unforgiveness gives Satan a foothold leading toward death instead of life.

Victory parades in ancient times had captives as well as conquerors march. There was no ticker tape. Instead, burnt fragrant spices filled the air as the way to expand the pervading sense of joy.

The victory parade of Jesus is on. The fragrance of the Holy Spirit is all about. Do not be in the parade as a captive of darkness through unforgiveness. The aroma will mean spiritual death for you. Let go. Forgive. When you do, you immediately march as a victor with all the joy of Christ who has won this victory for you.

Friday   *The Sleeping Seed*   **Mark 4:26–41**

He woke up and rebuked the wind, and said to the sea, "Peace! Be still!"
Then the wind ceased, and there was a dead calm. v. 39

Farmers have completed their work of planting the seeds. Only the power of God in life itself is going to take over now. God's Kingdom life is like that. It *will* prevail, despite its being hidden and small at first.

Jesus sleeps as a seed in the bottom of the boat. He awakens and rebukes not only the wind and the waves, but the unbelief of the disciples as well.

Believe that the Spirit deep within you, apparently asleep, is really at work bringing Pentecost life to flourish in you. It will happen, if you let it. Spend time in the silence, just being with the Lord as the seed of God's love grows within you. Others will then find rest in the shadow of your arms as branches of God's own love for them.

Saturday   **The Sabbath Torah Reading**

June 17, 2006 #36	June 13, 2015 #37	June 15, 2024 #35	June 11, 2035 #35
June 13, 2009 #36	June 16, 2018 #38	June 12, 2027 Pentec	June 14, 2036 #36
June 16, 2012 #37	June 12, 2021 #38	June 15, 2030 #35	June 11, 2039 #36

2
Pe
B

The Third Week in Pentecost
Begins on the Sunday nearest June 15. Alphabyte: Clock, p. 78

Sunday   *Small Is Big*   Mark 4:26–34
**The earth produces of itself, first the stalk,
then the head, then the full grain in the head. v. 28**

Jesus, the grain of wheat, has fallen into the ground and died. Nothing or anyone can stop the resurrection-kingdom that is coming.

Assurance of growth: that is what Jesus promises. However, you must let yourself fall into the ground as Jesus and die, just as the seed in the parable. Then you will bear Kingdom fruit that glorifies the Lord.

A mustard seed is this size of a dot on this page. Yet it becomes a strong tree, offering itself as a home and shade for many birds. That is the way the Kingdom is. Small is big! Even if you see yourself as tiny as a mustard seed, once you are into the ground of your being, which is Christ, no one can stop you!

Monday   *Startled By Love*   Hosea 3—4
**My people are destroyed for lack of knowledge;
because you have rejected knowledge. 4. 6**

Feel the tension in these two chapters. On the one hand, there is the everlasting love of God who decides to be faithful to God's faithless people; on the other hand, there is divine justice, which requires consequences to continued indifference and rebellion against God. The strategy of God in chapter 3 is to shock the people into fidelity by holding up the image of Gomer, the adulteress wife of Hosea. Just as Hosea takes her back, so does God decide to be faithful. However, if this shock treatment does not work, there are the consequences in chapter 4.

These strong words are to shake us into intimate knowledge of the Lord who alone gives direction to our lives. Otherwise, there will be visited in our own day, verse 6 of chapter 4. It is not about a heady, theological knowledge of which the prophet speaks; it is the intimate knowledge of spouse-to-spouse.

Tuesday   *After David*   1 Kings 1—2
**I am about to go the way of all the earth. Be strong, be courageous, and keep the charge of the Lord
your God, walking in his ways and keeping his statutes, his commandments, his ordinances, and his
testimonies, as it is written in the law of Moses, so that you may prosper in all that you do and wherever
you turn. 2:2–3**

In the first book of Kings, we trace the early history of the Jewish people after the death of David, the shepherd king, through the greatness of wise Solomon. Tragedies occur when the First Commandment is constantly broken. Despite the magnificence of the Temple that we will hear described, the "house" of God's people is built on the sands of idolatry, arrogance, power, and pride; it eventually divides into two. Remember what Jesus said about houses divided: they "cannot stand" (Matt. 12—25).

The sacred writer's purpose is to make this history personal to you. May this book awaken longings in you to be faithful as a member of the New Temple—the very Body of Christ alive in the Holy Spirit.

Wednesday   *In You, O Lord, I Put My Trust.*   **Psalm 71**

Even to old age and gray hairs, O God, do not forsake me,
until I proclaim your might to all the generations to come. v. 18

We live in a society that fears death. There is a desperate attempt in the cosmetic industry to make death seem far away by keeping us looking young. Children often reject their aged parents, placing them in nursing homes, even when it is possible and a blessing for them to live with their families.

An anonymous old man appears to be the author of this psalm. A whole life of dedication to the Lord and trust in God shines through these verses. He has had his times of rejection, yet there is serenity shining through this psalm, for the Lord has constantly upheld him from birth.

In verse 14, he will praise the Lord "yet more and more." The idea in Hebrew is to find new ways to praise God. Old age has not taken away inventive, creative, and alive ways to praise His God. May we all be the same as we learn how to praise God more fully, even into our old age.

Thursday   *From Glory to Glory*   **2 Corinthians 3**

And all of us, with unveiled faces, seeing the glory of the Lord
as though reflected in a mirror,
are being transformed into the same image from one degree of glory to another;
for this comes from the Lord, the Spirit. v. 18

From the deepest essence of God comes the glory of Christ radiant in your heart. Move from what is limited and hidden, to what becomes manifest. Let this chapter be a sacred vehicle that transports you into fullness.

Inwardly taste the terms of the comparison so that you can feel the shift to the new and glorious covenant right now being freshly engraved on your warm heart of flesh. In Christ, the veil has been removed. Look into his heavenly face that shines transparently at you. Do this when you pray the Scriptures each day. Jesus abiding inside of you in his Spirit will teach you all things and will take away the veil of ignorance, giving you all wisdom. As you read the Scriptures, you yourself will be moving from glory to glory.

Friday   *Delivering the Possessed*   **Mark 5:1–20**

Go home to your friends, and tell them how much the Lord has done for you,
and what mercy he has shown you. v. 19

Join the crowd in Gadara. You are accustomed to see this demon-possessed man, violent and uncontrollable. Jesus delivers him. He has peace for the first time in his life.

Observe the townspeople and their fear of the divine power that brings this about. It is ironic: they take for granted the demonic possession in that man; fear comes when a new power over demons arrives on the scene.

Are you getting used to violence in word and deed, even your inner thoughts? Are there dark spirits that harass you at times? Are you afraid of the alternative—complete freedom and peace in the power of Jesus in your life? Pray: "Spirit of fear, in the name and power of Jesus, be gone forever in my life and never return."

Saturday   **The Sabbath Torah Reading**

June 24, 2006 #37	June 20, 2015 #38	June 22, 2024 #36	June 18, 2035 #36
June 20, 2009 #37	June 23, 2018 #39	June 19, 2027 #35	June 21, 2036 #37
June 23, 2012 #38	June 19, 2021 #39	June 22, 2030 #36	June 18, 2039 #37

The Fourth Week in Pentecost

Begins on the Sunday nearest June 22. Alphabyte: Drink, p. 78

Sunday   ***The Calm Within***   **Mark 4:35–41**

They were filled with great awe and said to one another,
"Who then is this, that even the wind and the sea obey him?" v. 41

When there is a storm at sea, the surface is where it is felt. Far below, the water currents move silently, slowly, untouched by outer weather.

The disciples become frightened at the storm on the lake. They focus more on the waves outside of the boat, than on the One who is *in* the boat with them. The surface of their souls is tossed back and forth; they forget that deep inside their beings there already is a great calm,

Renew the gift of your life to Jesus. The Lord lives inside you. While he may be "asleep" to your situation that is tossing and turning you about, he is there. Go to that place of calm and cling to Jesus.

Monday   ***Tampering with the Sacred***   **Hosea 5**

The princes of Judah have become like those who remove the landmark;
on them I will pour out my wrath like water. v. 10

One's property for an Israelite was one's inheritance. To tamper with this was to touch something sacred. Deuteronomy 27:17 proclaims, **"Cursed is the one who moves his neighbor's landmark."**

The wickedness of idolatry described in today's passage tampers with the sacred boundaries of worshiping the Lord alone. Other interests, passions, and gods have come on the scene displacing the only spouse of the soul there is.

Reflect on forms of idolatry in your life. Repent. Cast them out in the name of the One who longs to share the divine inheritance with you. It is an affront to the living God to be indifferent to God's love.

Tuesday   ***Solomon's Prayer***   **1 Kings 3—4**

Give your servant therefore an understanding mind to govern your people,
able to discern between good and evil;
for who can govern this your great people? 3:9

Solomon's greatness lies in his prayer. Here, as in later chapters, he can be a model for your prayer. He had his priorities in order as he presents himself as the new king. As you read the vivid story beginning in 3:16, marvel how a shift in the ways of looking at a situation can give wisdom.

Is there something or someone that you need to look at from a fresh point of view? Pray as did Solomon and wait for the Lord to show you. God will respond because in Christ Jesus, you are a priest, a prophet, and a king. You may find it helpful to write out your prayer, waiting for the Lord to share responses through your hands.

Wednesday   *God's Judgments*   **Psalm 72**
In his days may righteousness flourish and peace abound,
until the moon is no more. v. 7

It is said in 1 Kings 4:32 that Solomon wrote 1,005 songs. Just two of them are attributed to him in the psalms: 72 and 127. Today's is a song of glory in the Lord whom we celebrate in God's Spirit released for us. Verse 10 of the psalm connects with the visit of the Magi to the Christ Child. Adoration, praise, and glory, so fitting for Epiphany, now find their fulfillment in the complete power of Jesus risen and the presence of the Holy Spirit.

Verses 18 and 19 celebrate the victory of the Lord and his domain over the earth. The last verse is a conclusion to "Book Two" of the psalms.

God's tender mercies are here for you right now. Open your heart to the Lord who wants to show you his face and let you into his heart. The condition? … total surrender. Let go of any person, place, or thing that does not lead you to God.

Thursday   *The Light of Jesus Within*   **2 Corinthians 4**
So we do not lose heart. Even though our outer nature is wasting away,
our inner nature is being renewed day by day. v. 16

I once had a dear friend who needed healing in his foot. As a way of reminding himself of the Lord's power to heal, he slept each night embracing the Bible. He wanted to touch the close, healing power of God.

For Paul too, Jesus was closer to him than all the persecutions pressing and seeking to crush him. He writes of the glory of all this to uplift the Corinthians.

Paul's body-vessel was weak; so are yours and everyone's. Thus we are reminded that the power of freedom is not our own, but given to us from God. God is the "furthest without" as well as the "closest within." The light of Jesus shines within you.

Friday   *Faith Connection*   **Mark 5:21–43**
He said to her, "Daughter, your faith has made you well;
go in peace, and be healed of your disease." v.34

Crowds press about while Jesus is on his way to heal a young girl. A woman with a hemorrhage has one focus: "I've just got to come near him. Even if I touch the hem of his cloak, I'll be healed." She insists, refusing to allow the crowd to put her off. She keeps the focus, moving nearer and nearer to Jesus, as she crawls on the ground among the people.

Then the moment of contact … Power flows forth from Jesus to heal her. It is like being jump-started. The good battery of Jesus' power is "ever-ready". However, there needs to be faith-cables of good conduction. The woman's faith connected with Jesus' healing power. Her faith saved her.

How are your cables? Are they broken or connected to Jesus?

4
Pe
B

Saturday   **The Sabbath Torah Reading**

July 01, 2006 #38	June 27, 2015 #39	June 29, 2024 #37	June 25, 2033 #37
June 27, 2009 #38	June 30, 2018 #40	June 26, 2027 #36	June 28, 2036 #38
June 30, 2012 #39	June 26, 2021 #40	June 29, 2030 #37	June 25, 2039 #38

The Fifth Week in Pentecost

Begins on the Sunday nearest June 29. Alphabyte: Eyes, p. 78

Sunday   *In the Name of Jesus*   **Mark 5:21–43**

He took her by the hand and said to her,
"Talitha cum," which means, "Little girl, get up!" v. 41

Jesus heals two women, one well into her life with serious feminine problems, the other, a little girl just at the beginning of her maturity. In the *Firestarter* for the previous Friday, we focused on the woman; today, consider the girl. Mark gives us Jesus' exact words in Aramaic, *"Talitha, cum"*: **"Little girl, I say to you, get up."**

You have been given the Holy Spirit in full measure; may *full* be the measure of your acceptance of this Spirit. Today consider the women in your life, from young to old, for whom the Lord would have you intercede. Use the words of Jesus given to you here to have them arise in fullness of resurrected life through the power given to you in Jesus' name.

Monday   *The Longing of God*   **Hosea 6**

For I desire steadfast love and not sacrifice,
the knowledge of God rather than burnt offerings. v. 6

As you slowly move through this passage, note two currents that flow—the fickle, vain intents of the people to repent, lasting as long as morning fog and the longing love of God for the people to return. What promise to you see in verse 2? There is anguish in this yearning, as when Jesus lamented over Jerusalem just before his passion, in Matthew 23:37. Verse 2 lifts itself from this chapter with a stunning reminder of the resurrection.

Meditate deeply on today's verse. "Mercy" here is the Hebrew *hesed*, the covenantal love of God for God's own. Nothing outer will do—only inner-driven love and intimacy with the Lord. Open yourself to this. With the Lord's grace, become one of God's truly faithful ones.

Tuesday   *Building the Temple*   **1 Kings 5—6**

When Hiram heard the words of Solomon, he rejoiced greatly, and said,
"Blessed be the Lord today, who has given to David a wise son
to be over this great people." 5:7

As you read about the magnificence of the Temple plans and its construction, picture its size: 90 feet long by 30 feet wide by 45 feet high. Imagine 30 yards on a football field for its length.

One of the wise moves Solomon makes is to get help from others who would "own" the project. This is a sign of true leadership: when *following* feels part of the *leading*! Solomon invites an unbelieving neighboring King, Hiram of Tyre, to be a subcontractor; his is the prayer in the verse for today.

Ask the Lord to let you see the spiritual gifts of those around you so that together you can "build" the spiritual temple, a community of love and peace that praises the Lord.

Wednesday   *God is Good*   **Psalm 73**
My flesh and my heart may fail,
but God is the strength of my heart and my portion forever. v. 26

While the psalmist asks God to remember, this is really a projection due to the psalmist's tendency to forget. We are the ones that need to remember the fidelity of God and God's power to intervene on our behalf. Once again, you will notice what frequently happens in the psalms; the writer pours out his grief, distress, anger, etc. until it is spent. Then there is room for the rush of God's presence to fill him.

Such is the case here. It was not until the psalmist has gone into the sanctuary of the Lord in verse 17 that he understands the ultimate justice of God. Just as in the case of Job, only the presence of God gives him peace. So also for "Doubting Thomas," the night of the Resurrection; only in the sanctuary of the open side of Jesus' wound could Thomas find an end to doubt and the beginning of faith: **My Lord and my God!**

How lovely are verses 21 to 26!

Thursday   *A Heavenly Tent*   **2 Corinthians 5**
We live by faith, not by sight. v. 7

Ponder each verse, each word; transforming power fills them. As a building is to a tent, so is our future body compared with our present one. Feel the intensity of Paul's longing for salvation for his beloved Corinthians. Sense the joy he has in Christ who has won the gift of reconciliation with the Living God. What no one, however good, could bring about, Jesus has done and has given the Holy Spirit as the guarantee that we are now right with God. All that needs to happen is to allow Jesus to live inside you making your body—your tent—the dwelling place of God. You become the space of heaven now, and a body in glory is promised.

You will not hear today's verse from the bombarding media! Etch it upon your heart. Walk by faith today.

5
Pe
B

Friday   *Contempt for the Familiar*   **Mark 6:1–29**
If any place will not welcome you and they refuse to hear you,
as you leave, shake off the dust that is on your feet
as a testimony against them. v. 11

High school yearbooks throughout the land have predictions of those "Most likely to succeed." Reunions years later often belie these predictions.

Jesus' classmates in Nazareth missed it too when it came to Jesus' future. Their familiarity with him bred a kind of contempt—at least blindness to what he could become. In a Gospel filled with wonders, miracles and amazement on the part of the people about Jesus, it was in Nazareth that Jesus was amazed at the lack of faith of the people. Hardly any healings took place there.

Accompany the Twelve on their first missionary journey. Grieve with them and with Jesus over the beheading of John the Baptist.

Saturday   **The Sabbath Torah Reading**

July 08, 2006 #39–40	July 04, 2015 #40	July 06, 2024 #38	July 02, 2033 #38
July 04, 2009 #39–40	July 07, 2018 #41	July 03 2027 #37	July 05, 2036 #39
July 07, 2012 #40	July 03, 2021 #41	July 06, 2030 #38	July 02, 2039 #39

The Sixth Week in Pentecost
Begins on the Sunday nearest July 6. Alphabyte: Firestarter, p. 79

Sunday   *Faith that Makes Whole*   **Mark 6:1–13**
They cast out many demons,
and anointed with oil many who were sick and cured them. v. 13

Jesus was human; his rejection by his own family must have been painful for him. With the special love he felt for them, Jesus would have wanted them to be healed among the first. However, he could not do it! Think of it: Jesus is powerless where there is no faith. Where there is faith, Jesus' presence celebrates the healing that takes place. "Your faith has made you whole."

Right after the rejection of his family of blood, Jesus becomes one with his family in the Spirit—the first disciples. They are commissioned to go out just as he has done, bringing the healing presence of God.

The power that Jesus has, he gives away. He wants to give it to you, for your own healing, and to have you become an agent for the healing of others. May the Holy Spirit move you to profound faith in the healing power of God.

Monday   *God: Now and Then or Always*   **Hosea 7**
They do not cry to me from the heart, but they wail upon their beds;
they gash themselves for grain and wine; they rebel against me. v. 14

Images abound expressing the constant infidelity of the people to their God. They are as faithless as their idolatrous neighbors after whom their lust burns with a heat as constant as a baker's oven. Recall Samson, who lost his power and anointing from the Lord and did not know it. Likewise does Ephraim, as an example of all the people, think that it still has power as deceptive alliances are made with powerful Egypt and Assyria.

Make these chapters in Hosea personal to you. Are there inner echoes in these verses? Where do you place your confidence in life? Is it in banks, works, contracts, plans, relationships—the Lord on the sideline of your life? Repent from being only with God now and then, instead of always.

Tuesday   *Prayer of Dedication*   **1 Kings 7—8**
But will God indeed dwell on the earth?
Even heaven and the highest heaven cannot contain you,
much less this house that I have built! 8:27

Until the Temple was constructed, the Ark of the Covenant, which contained the Ten Commandments, was portable, resting inside a tent moved from place to place during the Exodus. That there would be a temple means that the People of God had not only come to rest in the land that was promised them, but that they would have a magnificent center of worship in the heart of Jerusalem, their sacred city.

Follow closely Solomon's prayer of dedication. Tragically, we will soon read how the people did not honor God as Solomon did. People would direct their adoration to what is not God, abandoning the deepest meaning of the Temple. Are you tempted in the same way?

Wednesday	*O God, Why?*	Psalm 74

Yours is the day, yours also the night; you established the luminaries and the sun.
You have fixed all the bounds of the earth; you made summer and winter. vv. 16–17

The Lord is greater than the power of any enemy. However, this only occurs to the psalmist after he confronts himself with his tendency to doubt. What helped Job helps the psalmist—placing his own enemies against the backdrop of creation, remembering the obvious: God made the summer and winter, and is the one who breaks the heads of Leviathan, the great sea beast. Note the repetition of *you* as the psalmist makes a list of all the wonderful things God can do.

When your brand of Leviathan raises it head against you, get in touch with the way this and other psalms move—expression free and unhampered before God, followed by savoring the renewed trust found in the power of God to liberate.

Join the sacred writer responsible for this psalm and *write!*

Thursday	*The Acceptable Time*	2 Corinthians 6

For he says, "At an acceptable time I have listened to you,
and on a day of salvation I have helped you."
See, now is the acceptable time; see, now is the day of salvation! v. 2

Imagine a pencil held in a vertical position by gently pressing down upon the eraser end with the point on the paper. The pencil will almost hold the weight of your hand and arm as long as it is perpendicular to the table. The entire pencil hovers over the point beneath. If you move the hand away from the vertical, it will fall.

When you move away from the present moment, guilt and shame over the past, or anxiety about the future, will have you fall. **"Now is the acceptable time,"** says Paul. Another expression goes: **"The point of power is the present."**

Relax into the chair or floor that supports you. Be in the Lord's presence that fills this present moment with power and grace.

Friday	*Explosion of Bread*	Mark 6:30–56

He said to them,
"Come away to a deserted place all by yourselves and rest a while."
For many were coming and going, and they had no leisure even to eat. v. 31

The Baptist is beheaded—time out for Jesus and the disciples. The seeking crowds find and press about Him. Forgetful of food, they hang on every word from his mouth, rejoicing in his healing presence. The multiplying loaves and fish only increase the crowd's intensity; but it is the wrong kind. Jesus abruptly dismisses them, sends the disciples onto the storm-tossed sea, and seeks the solitude that soaks his soul in the presence of the Father. Back to the disciples in the middle of the night, walking on water … No barriers of time or place keep Jesus long away from those he has chosen.

Feel all the shifts and movements of the latter half of this chapter. Roll with the waves on the sea as you walk on the waters of your life toward Jesus.

Saturday			The Sabbath Torah Reading
July 15, 2006 #41	July 11, 2015 #41	July 13, 2024 #39	July 09, 2033 #39–40
July 11, 2009 #41	July 14, 2018 #42–43	July 10 2027 #38	July 12, 2036 #40
July 14, 2012 #41	July 10, 2021 #42–43	July 13, 2030 #39–40	July 09, 2039 #40

6
Pe
B

The Seventh Week in Pentecost
Begins on the Sunday nearest July 13. Alphabyte: Gears, p. 79

Sunday   *John the Baptist Beheaded*   **Mark 6:14–29**
And Herodias had a grudge against him,
and wanted to kill him. But she could not. v. 19

After Jesus' family rejects him, further family pain comes in the murder of his cousin, John the Baptist. Herod Antipas beheads this last and greatest of the prophets.

This Herod is the son of Herod the Great, the one that made magnificent expansions on the Second Temple; he murdered the innocent babies of Bethlehem when the Magi went back to their countries.

Notice the vices present, all of the seven traditional ones: **pride, covetousness, lust, anger, gluttony, envy, and sloth.** One vice breeds another, especially when pride is embedded in a person.

Be sobered by this evil, and the atrocious murders that take place in our day because the same evils are present. Be with John's disciples as they quietly come and bury him; stay close to Jesus and feel his pain.

Monday   *Indifference*   **Hosea 8**
They made kings, but not through me;
they set up princes, but without my knowledge.
With their silver and gold they made idols for their own destruction. v. 4

The message keeps pounding away when the people ignore God. Infidelity in marriage means more than actual adultery; indifference to the other is unfaithfulness as well.

In verse 4, the Lord speaks through Hosea about decisions made without consulting the Lord. This can happen at a church meeting or a family gathering. The group prays first, but the discussion following is often barren of Godly awareness—no ongoing seeking the Lord's guidance, direction and will.

Do not grieve the Holy Spirit by indifference. Treasure the love of Jesus for you. The grace of God won for you on the cross is free, but it is not cheap.

Tuesday   *Hinges*   **1 Kings 9—10**
The Lord said to him, "I have heard your prayer and your plea, which you made before me;
I have consecrated this house that you have built,
and put my name there forever; my eyes and my heart will be there for all time. 9:3

A hinge is a small piece of hardware, securing the movement of a great door. When two are carefully in place, the heaviest of doors floats on air. A slight touch of the hand opens it easily.

There are hinges in the interaction between God and Solomon in chapter 9. The first is the tiny word "IF." "If you walk before me as your father David walked, in integrity of heart and in uprightness …" The second hinge is the little word "THEN." "Then I will establish the throne of your kingdom over Israel forever."

While God loves us without any "IFS, ANDS, or BUTS," there are conditions when it comes to having a relationship with the Lord. Just as in marriage, as we see in Hosea, God demands us to be faithful to God alone. Are you?

Wednesday   *We Give Thanks to You*   **Psalm 75**

But I will rejoice forever; I will sing praises to the God of Jacob.
All the horns of the wicked I will cut off,
but the horns of the righteous shall be exalted. vv. 9–10

From the songs of the mothers of Samuel and Jesus, to Jesus himself, the Bible often speaks about the humble being lifted up and the proud being brought low. Praying this psalm brings serenity, in case your heart has the thoughts here reversed, perhaps entertaining jealousy toward those who boast about all they have.

The big "horn" of power of those who are boastful will be brought low. Similar to the wisdom of Proverbs, the wisdom present in these and many psalms can reorient you to the way God sees and orders all things by the might of God's hand.

Verses 9 and 10 place the proper order of exaltation. Singing "praises to the God of Jacob" will free your mind and heart from obsessing about anyone or anything. The Lord will lift you up on high into the presence of the One whom you are praising.

Thursday   *From Guilt to Sorrow*   **2 Corinthians 7**

For godly grief produces a repentance that leads to salvation
and brings no regret, but worldly grief produces death. v. 10

The details of the pain of the Corinthian Church escape us; however, Paul's love for this church flows out so clearly. He longs that all sin and pain turn to good. He seeks to steer his people into a positive and "better than ever" outcome.

The heart of his teaching is in verses 9 and 10. Think of "Godly sorrow" and "the sorrow of the world" as on a time line. *Guilt* and *shame* is worldly sorrow: its time-line is constant, unrelenting, because the world is unforgiving. Godly sorrow, on the other hand, is *contrition*. This is an experience in a single point of time. It is sorrow and repentance for sin that leaves the soul clean, clear, and energized by the Lord's total forgiveness.

Reflect on how you deal with guilt and shame. Ask the Lord to help you gather their energies into one great expression of contrition, and be done with it!

Friday   *Inner and Outer Responses*   **Mark 7:1–23**

Then he called the crowd again and said to them, "Listen to me, all of you,
and understand: there is nothing outside a person that by going in can defile,
but the things that come out are what defile." vv. 14–15

Religion can become dangerously "outer." Customs, traditions and "the way *we* do things" can substitute for that powerful, inner presence of the Lord, which alone makes religion breathe with true spirituality.

Works can be merely external. While there must be action in our lived response to Christ, works unenergized by a loving, surrendered heart to the Lord, will not produce the kind of fruit about which Jesus teaches.

What is within defines what comes out. If your heart is right, then what you say and do will be expressive of the goodness of your inner state of soul. However, if your heart is insincere, then the outer feigning of religious activity will be a sacrilege that defiles you.

Saturday   **The Sabbath Torah Reading**

July 22, 2006 #42–43	July 18, 2015 #42–43	July 20, 2024 #40	July 16, 2033 #41
July 18, 2009 #42–43	July 21, 2018 #44	July 17, 2027 #39–40	July 19, 2036 #41
July 21, 2012 #42–43	July 17, 2021 #44	July 20, 2030 #41	July 16, 2039 #41

215

The Eighth Week in Pentecost
Begins on the Sunday nearest July 20. Alphabyte: Hurricane, p. 79

Sunday   *Your Healing Shepherd*   Mark 6:30–44; 53–56

**As he went ashore, he saw a great crowd; and he had compassion for them,
because they were like sheep without a shepherd;
and he began to teach them many things. v. 34**

We need space for rest and quiet after strong experiences, especially after the death of a loved one. It is the same for Jesus after the death of his cousin John the Baptist. However, the crowds do not give him a chance; they find where he is.

You and I become annoyed when rest is interrupted. Jesus entrusts all his needs to the Father. Immense compassion wells up within him. The people have no shepherd.

Keep searching and finding Jesus today and everyday. The Lord has immense compassion for you and wants to gather you into the sheepfold of his healing. Do not give up. Only the hem of his garment is all you need; Jesus gives you much more than that!

Monday   *God Hurts*   Hosea 9

**Because your sins are so many and your hostility so great,
the prophet is considered a fool ... v. 7**

Put yourself in God's place as a scorned spouse. Experience the indignation and hurt of the Lord. You know that the Lord is forgiving, put what affronts are made to God! God feels; the Holy Spirit grieves.

Never presume on the Lord's mercy. Decide now to be a faithful spiritual spouse of the Lord who wants nothing but the closest intimacy with you. God is ready to forgive, but you must repent of any brand of unfaithfulness in your life toward the Lord.

May God's fidelity be an incentive for you to go deeper into your own soul, rooting out indifference and infidelity to the Lord, until your surrender to the Lord is total.

Tuesday   *The Center Collapses*   1 Kings 11—12

**For when Solomon was old, his wives turned away his heart
after other gods; and his heart was not true to the Lord his God,
as was the heart of his father David. 11:4**

Solomon's shame—he no longer practices what he is said to have preached in Proverbs. His attraction for foreign women results in adding to his harem, along with their idolatrous practices. God removes the sacred canopy of divine protection. It is the beginning of the split of God's people into two nations. The story is in the center of 1 Kings—a center that collapses. Only one tribe, Judah, remains faithful to the one Temple where all the tribes were to converge.

Place all your trust in the Lord alone; everyone else has feet of clay. Pray for those in spiritual leadership that they be faithful to the Lord. When tempted to criticize, "Let the one without sin cast the first stone!"

Wednesday   *Glory in the Power*   **Psalm 76**

Glorious are you, more majestic than the everlasting mountains. v. 4

The psalmist glories in the power of God over his enemies; we need to do this as well. There are many temptations of the Evil One to discourage us and have us think that God does not have power after all.

God power invites us to respond in faith and not to leave ourselves to our own devices when it comes to discerning where power is. We can be deceived. That is why the Lord told Adam and Eve not to eat of "The Tree of the Knowledge of Good and Evil." We cannot handle that: only God can. When your natural instincts say that everything is going downhill in your life, take out this psalm—pull it out, if necessary. Take a leap of faith and proclaim the greatness of the Lord. Copy key words and phrases to fully to pray this psalm in your spirit.

Thursday   *Offerings to the Lord*   **2 Corinthians 8**

**For you know the generous act of our Lord Jesus Christ,
that though he was rich, yet for your sakes he became poor,
so that by his poverty you might become rich. v. 9**

This passage will help you understand the spirit behind all giving to the Lord. Philippians 2: 5–11 gives further understanding of the abandon of God into our humble estate, in order that we might be lifted to the heights of divine life.

When you give to the Lord, God does not actually take. The Lord is pure giving. In the mystery of this, your giving frees the Lord to become even more abundant for you in God's riches and grace. This is the point behind the specific details of this passage.

Apply the reading to your own life. How are you when it comes to trusting in the Lord as you make your tithes and offerings? Will you surrender all your cares to God who loves you and gives you the provisions for each day?

Friday   *Faith of a Foreigner*   **Mark 7:24–37**

**But she answered him,
"Sir, even the dogs under the table eat the children's crumbs." v. 28**

Words of Jesus abrupt and even rude … Such seems to be the case today. Recall the Marriage Feast of Cana when Jesus said to Mary about the wine running dry: "What is that to you and to me?" Here too, it appears to be unkind of Jesus to refer to the Syro-Phoenician woman as a dog!

However, the intent of Jesus is to place the faith of the foreign woman into strong relief. Jesus healed the woman with the hemorrhage! she knew that only a touch of the tassel on Jesus' garment would be enough to be healed. This woman as well believes that only crumbs from the table of Jesus are all her daughter needs for healing.

The whole body of Christ is given to you in a crumb from the Communion table. One touch, one taste of the Master is enough.

Saturday   **The Sabbath Torah Reading**

July 29, 2006 #44	July 25, 2015 #44	July 27, 2024 #41	July 23, 2033 #42–43
July 25, 2009 #44	July 29, 2018 #45	July 24, 2027 #41	July 26, 2036 #42–43
July 28, 2012 #44	July 24, 2021 #45	July 27, 2030 #42–43	July 23, 2039 #42–43

8
Pe
B

The Ninth Week in Pentecost
Begins on the Sunday nearest July 27. Alphabyte: Ink, p. 80

Sunday   *A Boy's Lunch Multiplied*   **John 6:1–21**
There is a boy here who has five barley loaves and two fish.
But what are they among so many people? v. 9

Here we go is again—wilderness and hunger. Does Jesus flash back to the desert and the forty-day fast, tempted by the devil to turn rocks into bread for himself? No, today will be different—no food for himself, but for others; no rocks will be magically turned to bread, but a boy's small lunch explodes to feed a crowd.

Bring what you have to the Lord. God has made you good; the Lord will multiply your goodness so you too can feed a multitude. However, first nourish your spirit with the Word of the Lord, handing you miracle bread of his life right now. Walk with Jesus on top of the turbulent waters of your life. He will bring you through a new Exodus to life on the other side of anguish and pain.

Monday   *Great Is Thy Faithfulness*   **Lamentations 3**
The steadfast love of the Lord never ceases,
his mercies never come to an end;
they are new every morning; great is your faithfulness. v. 22–23

On or about these days, Jewish people celebrate the Ninth of Av, the date in the Jewish calendar, which recalls the destruction of the two Temples in Jerusalem. It is a day of mourning and sadness for all of us, for the way in which the forces of darkness seek to reduce God's presence to rubble in the world.

For Christians, the various attempts to eradicate the temple of the living God in the members of Christ's body, the New Temple, is our way of sharing in the losses of our ancestors. Yet what martyr is celebrated with sadness! They live on in the temple in the heavenly Jerusalem.

The flow of mourning in this chapter is suddenly interrupted by verses 22–23. The late Thomas Chisholm, a former member of The First United Methodist Church in Vineland, N.J. (where I serve as pastor at this writing), composed the famous hymn "Great Is Thy Faithfulness." He beautifully expresses the profound feelings of the writer of Lamentations.

Tuesday   *People-Pleasing*   **1 Kings 13—14**
He gave a sign the same day, saying,
"This is the sign that the Lord has spoken: 'The altar shall be torn down,
and the ashes that are on it shall be poured out.'" 13:3

God-fearing to people pleasing—this is what happens when God's people split in two. It is the story of mostly evil kings. Even the account of the "man of God" in chapter 13 reminds us of what can happen when we are not careful about the company we keep.

Evil at the top as well as at the grass roots have the two nations turn away from the Lord. Look at how God's people treat the Lord after all that God has done! God brought them from slavery to freedom. How tragic—just after the Temple is built, it is emptied as the people leave and worship idols elsewhere.

How strong are your resolves to live in the Temple of the Lord's risen body?

Wednesday *From Anguish to Hope* **Psalm 77**

I will call to mind the deeds of the Lord;
I will remember your wonders of old. v. 11

This Psalm has ten verses of anguish, ten of hope. The psalmist will teach you about how to deal with your own pains of the heart. No matter how strong the suffering, he is praying.

Share your heartaches with the Lord. When you have poured yourself out, a fresh, new space expands in your heart to listen to the Lord who brings you remembrance of God's gracious presence to you throughout your life. Jesus was there for you on the cross. He unleashed the power of healing love there; it is all that you have ever needed or will ever need. The Lord is with you. Pour out your heart and listen to Jesus. He loves you. He will comfort you in his out-poured Spirit, filling your pain and emptiness with his sweet presence.

Thursday *Giving As God Gives* **2 Corinthians 9**

The one who sows sparingly will also reap sparingly,
and the one who sows bountifully will also reap bountifully. v. 6

Giving the Lord's way makes everything you give a seed. Just as a seed becomes greater when sown, so is your giving of yourself. Talents, resources, time, etc. are seeds that become fruit for others and increased spiritual abundance for you. Nothing is lost when you give with love.

Taste the energy, the joy, the cheerfulness of Paul. Reflect on those ways that you, perhaps still bound in fear, hold back from being self-giving. Pray in a surrendered way, then rise to live in a surrendered way. Recall the words of Jesus in Luke 6:38: **"With the same measure that you use, it will be measured back to you."**

Friday *Signs to Strengthen Faith* **Mark 8:1–21**

Do you have eyes, and fail to see? Do you have ears, and fail to hear?
And do you not remember? v. 18

Miracles happen to strengthen faith, not substitute for it. The Pharisees do not *want* to have faith in Jesus. Without a yearning for faith, nothing will convince.

The deep sighing from Jesus at their lack of faith translates *anastatoo,* a Greek word used only twice in the New Testament, here and in Acts 17:6. The latter is in the context of unbelievers' charges that Christians are "turning the world upside down."

Jesus' stomach was "turned upside down" by the faithlessness of the Pharisees. How much it must have upset Jesus to see the lack of understanding of those closest to him!

How is your faith? Do you bargain with the Lord instead of believe and trust God's providence over you?

9
Pe
B

Saturday **The Sabbath Torah Reading**

Aug 05, 2006 #45	Aug 01, 2015 #45	Aug 03, 2024 #42–43	July 30, 2033 #44
Aug 01, 2009 #45	Aug 04, 2018 #46	July 31, 2027 #42–43	Aug 02, 2036 #44
Aug 04, 2012 #45	July 31, 2021 #46	Aug 03, 2030 #44	July 30, 2039 #44

The Tenth Week in Pentecost
Begins on the Sunday nearest August 3. Alphabyte: Juggling, p. 80

Sunday   *Never Hungry Again*   **John 6:24–35**

Do not work for the food that perishes, but for the food that endures for eternal life,
which the Son of Man will give you.
For it is on him that God the Father has set his seal. v. 27

Bread of the earth brings hunger again—but not Jesus, the Bread of Heaven. Receive in faith. For St. John, "to believe," means, "to adhere to Jesus." If you cling to Jesus on the cross, he will draw you up in resurrection.

For the Fourth Evangelist, "the last day" is Good Friday, the sixth day of the old creation. Then there is the Sabbath, followed by the first day of the week of the new creation, Resurrection Sunday.

Dwell on this immense fact: Christ calls you to live in a New Creation. All the "old stuff" that tends to stick like glue to your spirit, has really died and lost its power. Do not give any more power to what is already dead!

Monday   *Soil for Saving Grace*   **Hosea 10**

Sow for yourselves righteousness; reap steadfast love;
break up your fallow ground; for it is time to seek the Lord,
that he may come and rain righteousness upon you. v. 12

Just as the world of farming shapes Jesus' parables, so it is with Hosea's words here. The soul is as hard ground in verse 12. It needs to be loosened so that proper seed can yield nourishing produce, in place of the poison hemlock of verse 4.

Seeds of God's justice result in the nourishing food of compassion. It is the same message as Paul, last Thursday: what you sow you will reap. Sowing without faith in the Lord yields plants poisonous to self and others.

Assume a physical posture that expresses total surrender to the Lord. With your soul now loosened in abandoned prayer, receive the Word today as seed of saving grace for each hour.

Tuesday   *The Lord Exasperated*   **1 Kings 15—16**

Since I exalted you out of the dust and made you leader over my people Israel,
and you have walked in the way of Jeroboam, and have caused my people Israel
to sin, provoking me to anger with their sins. 16: 2

Anger and sadness often go together. When we lose a dear one in death, the loss produces grief. However, first there is anger, especially when we view the loss as a violation of justice.

In this passage, the anger of the Lord comes after years of unfaithful kings, one after another. The grieving of the Holy Spirit becomes complete exasperation. In the verse for today, the Hebrew word for anger is *cha'as*: the kind of anger that wells up after being constantly provoked. It is not the reactive anger of which we are so familiar in our sinfulness.

Reflect upon anger in your life.

Wednesday *Holy Remembrance* **Psalm 78**

We will not hide them from their children;
we will tell to the coming generation the glorious deeds of the Lord,
and his might, and the wonders that he has done. v. 4

A baby in the arms of his/her parents not only senses the love that the parents have for the child, but the faith that is in them as well. How you believe and what you believe exude from your person, generating and defining the space within and without you.

This psalm begins with the joy of sharing faith with one's children. This faith is alive; it is central to the psalmist. It is not enough simply to place children into the hands of spiritual caretakers such as Sunday school teachers.

Most of the psalm is a lengthy recollection of the disobedience and infidelity of God's people, God's response, and ultimate compassion upon those faithful to God.

May your heart be inflamed with a desire to grow in your life with the Lord.

Thursday *Spiritual Warfare* **2 Corinthians 10**

We destroy arguments and every proud obstacle raised up against the knowledge of God,
and we take every thought captive to obey Christ. v. 5

I have good news and bad news. The bad news: whatever you are struggling against is bigger than you are. The good news: God gives you all the power of heaven to come against all adversity. Take command of this power as you fight the spiritual wars in your life. Jesus won the victory for you. Apply the blood of the cross— the sign of triumph for every circumstance. Bind every thought or idea as a hostage, unless it is in keeping with the Word of Christ.

The root of our word "obedience" comes from the Latin, *audire*, whence the English, "audio." It means first *to listen*, then to *act accordingly*. May it be so in your life.

10
Pe
B

Friday *Confessing Jesus, the Christ* **Mark 8:22–38**

He asked them, "But who do you say that I am?"
Peter answered him, "You are the Messiah." v. 29

Pray in total faith for your healing. If this does not happen according to your expectations, claim it still, accepting what is happening as a stage in the process. There is a powerful precedent for this in the healing of the blind man.

Peter receives the gift of extraordinary faith, and then soon lapses into his old self. He presumes to rebuke Jesus about the issue of his coming suffering. Jesus names the adversary, Satan—the one who comes to disrupt and block the powerful movement of God's redemptive love in Christ.

Pray to keep the confession of Jesus as the Christ, fresh and free in your own heart. The Anointed One lives inside you and longs to share this anointing for ministry with you.

Saturday **The Sabbath Torah Reading**

Aug 12, 2006 #46	Aug 08, 2015 #46	Aug 10, 2024 #44	Aug 06, 2033 #45
Aug 08, 2009 #46	Aug 11, 2018 #47	Aug 07, 2027 #44	Aug 09, 2036 #45
Aug 11, 2012 #46	Aug 07, 2021 #47	Aug 10, 2030 #45	Aug 06, 2039 #45

The Eleventh Week in Pentecost

Begins on the Sunday nearest August 10. Alphabyte: Knots, p. 80

Sunday *Fruit from Calvary's Tree* **John 6:35, 41–51**
I am the living bread that came down from heaven.
Whoever eats of this bread will live forever;
and the bread that I will give for the life of the world is my flesh. v. 51

Jesus offers the Bread of Life. In place of joyous acceptance, argument and complaint ensue, just as the ancient Israelites murmured about the Manna. A physical interpretation of Jesus' teaching binds the religious leaders encircling Jesus. Only those in the Spirit see into the sacramental power.

When we eat ordinary bread, the bread becomes part of the person who eats it. In the Eucharist, it is the reverse; the person becomes the Bread.

Adam and Eve ate the "bread" of the Tree of the Knowledge of Good and Evil and they died. Jesus says about the Bread from the Tree of Life: "The one who eats this bread will live forever!" The Calvary Tree has given the fruit of everlasting life. Eat of it often and live!

Monday *The Power of Tenderness* **Hosea 11**
I led them with cords of human kindness, with bands of love.
I was to them like those who lift infants to their cheeks.
I bent down to them and fed them. v. 4

Pouring out one's deepest feelings to a loved one who will receive and accept them—truly this is one of life's richest blessings. This happens in today's reading. In the previous ten chapters of Hosea, you have heard the heart of God poured out in anguish at the infidelity of God's spouse, the Chosen People. Now waves of tenderness well up from God's heart. Be sure to enter the power of the tenderness of the example of a father teaching his son to walk.

Verse 7 deserves special attention—the difference between calling on the Lord and failing to exalt God in praise. Above all, receive the Lord in your heart through praise for who God is and not only for what God does.

Tuesday *Tales of Elijah* **1 Kings 17—18**
The jar of meal was not emptied, neither did the jug of oil fail,
according to the word of the Lord that he spoke by Elijah. 17:16

As a ride on a roller coaster, 1 Kings shifts from heights of glory to depths of depravity. The splendor of Solomon tarnishes. No sooner is the Temple completed than it is abandoned for pagan shrines. The Kingdom splits into two.

Enter Elijah. The energy shifts as we feel the presence of God in this wondrous prophet. You will read a Bible story favorite of many—Elijah and the Widow of Zarephath. When you give your all to the Lord, each day will dawn with all you need. As the woman touching Jesus' tassel, as the widow giving her last coin, give your "last meal" to the Lord and Jesus will give you the Bread of Life.

Wednesday   *Intercession and Justice*   **Psalm 79**

Help us, O God of our salvation, for the glory of your name;
deliver us, and forgive our sins, for your name's sake. v. 9

This psalm is a powerful prayer of intercession for others. There is longing for God's justice, not merely for personal self-satisfaction. So too in your own life … Instead of wanting personal wrongs done to you to be made right, pray that wrongs done to the Lord would be avenged. Remember that the Lord said, "Vengeance is mine" (Deuteronomy 32:35).

The cross made the greatest wrong, right. Jesus' love on the cross wrenches from the hand of the Enemy, any more power to do harm. God will not allow the glory of the holy Name to be shamed in any way. However, allow the Lord to bring this about in God's own time and manner—not yours. Hold the final verse of the Psalm close to your heart.

Thursday   *Zeal Penetrating Strife*   **2 Corinthians 11**

If I must boast, I will boast of the things that show my weakness. v. 30

Arguments threaten to discredit Paul's ministry. He seeks to penetrate the resistance so that the church in Corinth can receive him, but more importantly, can receive Christ.

The passion of Paul for the Lord Jesus leaps like flames in his writings. The key is zeal—an inner fire for the things of the Lord. It is as the burning bush before Moses. Zeal burns without consuming.

It is not the same with jealousy—the wicked sibling of zeal. The word comes from the same parent word in Greek. Jealousy is a fire that consumes. It destroys love and foments strife. Zeal is stronger—a blowtorch that penetrates strife. Pray that you move from the dark side of this energy into the light.

Friday   *Transfiguration and the Center*   **Mark 9:1–13**

Suddenly when they looked around,
they saw no one with them any more, but only Jesus. v. 8

If you were to take the Gospel of Mark and fold it in half like a roof, this would be the top. The Transfiguration of the Lord is the centerpiece for this Gospel. The first part is going up to the top—miracles, teachings, the expansive movement of Jesus. The downside of the roof sees the prediction of the Passion and death of Jesus and the outcome of the opposition to Jesus in the Jewish authorities. This means a climb to another mountaintop. The Mount of the Transfiguration and Mount Calvary are both expressions of the glory of Jesus.

Adore your Lord. God will be with you on the downside and then on the upside—the resurrection.

Saturday   **The Sabbath Torah Reading**

Aug 19, 2006 #47	Aug 15, 2015 #47	Aug 17, 2024 #45	Aug 13, 2033 #46
Aug 15, 2009 #47	Aug 18, 2018 #48	Aug 14, 2027 #45	Aug 16, 2036 #46
Aug 18, 2012 #47	Aug 14, 2021 #48	Aug 17, 2030 #46	Aug 13, 2039 #46

The Twelfth Week in Pentecost
Begins on the Sunday nearest August 17. Alphabyte: Loops, p. 81

Sunday   *The Bond with Jesus*   **John 6:51–58**
Those who eat my flesh and drink my blood abide in me, and I in them. v. 56

Flesh and blood together mean life; their separation brings death. When Jesus speaks about eating his flesh and drinking his blood, he refers to his death. In sharing the fruits of this death, disciples receive what happened for Jesus—resurrection.

To receive the body and blood of Jesus in Communion is to share in the innermost reality of who Jesus is. Who Jesus is, is in relation to the Father. The bond that Jesus has with the Father is the union that Jesus offers with those who partake of Communion.

What stands between you and receiving Communion more frequently?

Monday   *Vanity and Idolatry*   **Hosea 12**
As for you, return to your God, hold fast to love and justice,
and wait continually for your God. v. 6

What do you do that is vain and unfulfilling? Are there activities in your life that do not satisfy you, leaving the depth areas of your spirit without nourishment? Vanity is a form of idolatry. God will not remove its consequences. We often need pain to seek and find the Lord.

Ephraim was the last son of Joseph, the "youngest" tribe of Israel. The name stands for the whole of the Chosen People who have gone astray. By referring to the youngest son, Hosea wants us to feel the tenderness that God has for all the people. For God's people and for you personally, the Lord does not want us to feed on the futility of the wind (v.1).

Tuesday   *The Still, Small Voice*   **1 Kings 19—20**
After the earthquake a fire, but the Lord was not in the fire;
and after the fire a sound of sheer silence. 19:12

Action ceases; the roller coaster stops. For Elijah, a time of quiet has come, setting for the strong experience of the presence of the Lord in the "still, small voice." Sweetly and intimately, God communicates with the prophet. Then Elijah has a close companion who is anointed with prophecy as he—Elisha.

Action picks up again in the arrogance of a pagan king, Ben-Hadad, and the punishment of Ahab for letting Ben-Hadad get away. May you feel the disgust in your heart as you read about Ahab and Jezebel's contempt for God's ways. Let the Spirit stir you strongly to follow the Lord. Separate yourself from those people, places, and things that tempt you to put yourself in the center again.

Wednesday   *God's Smile*   **Psalm 80**

Restore us, O God; let your face shine, that we may be saved. vv. 3, 17, 19

Picture what would happen if a dearly loved person from your past were suddenly to stand before you right now, face lit in a broad, open smile. Taste the joy and the jolting change of your mood. The Lord at this very moment is smiling at you with the greatest love there is. When God smiles, nothing remains the same. The Holy Spirit engrafts you onto the vine, which is Jesus.

As corks holding up a net, so does the threefold repetition of this verse lift God's people. "Restore" (in Hebrew: *shuwb*), means a plea for God to make things go back to the way they were when God's presence and power were freshly felt by the people. May this psalm clear the space between you and the Lord, so you can see God's smile.

Thursday   *Boasting in Weakness*   **2 Corinthians 12**

He said to me, "My grace is sufficient for you, for power is made perfect in weakness.
"So, I will boast all the more gladly of my weaknesses,
so that the power of Christ may dwell in me. v. 9

Grace and joy in Greek are the same word, *charis*. When Paul says that the grace of the Lord is sufficient, he is proclaiming as Nehemiah in 8:10: **"The joy of the Lord is your strength."**

Paul was in situations that could be described by the images of many a psalm. His experience of being with the Lord during all the persecutions had him even boast in his weakness, for the contrast made the power and strength of the Lord more evident. This is positive thinking. When things are the *worst*, they are about to be the *best*, if you let the Lord be with you, with power ready for release into your circumstances.

Turn to the Lord. God loves you and **en-joys** you!

Friday   *Prayer and Fasting*   **Mark 9:14–32**

Jesus said to him, "If you are able!—
All things can be done for the one who believes." v. 23

The question is not: "Does God wish to heal?" but rather, "Is discouragement, anger, or lack of faith getting in the way of the healing and salvation God wants for others and for me?" May any stoniness of heart in us become flesh alive with God's desire for healing and wholeness for every person.

Seek settings of faith. The gathering of a small community of those who believe and intercede becomes the vehicle for the Lord's saving acts to flow. Fasting means that the only *input* is the Word of the Lord, God's grace, and the power of divine healing; the only *output* is prayer. Prayer and fasting prepare the heart to receive God's grace coming as a laser with God's healing response.

Saturday   **The Sabbath Torah Reading**

Aug 26, 2006 #48	Aug 22, 2015 #48	Aug 24, 2024 #46	Aug 20, 2033 #47
Aug 22, 2009 #48	Aug 25, 2018 #49	Aug 21, 2027 #46	Aug 23, 2036 #47
Aug 25, 2012 #48	Aug 21, 2021 #49	Aug 24, 2030 #47	Aug 20, 2039 #47

12
Pe
B

The Thirteenth Week in Pentecost
Begins on the Sunday nearest August 24. Alphabyte: Metal Detector, p. 81

Sunday   *Flesh and Spirit*   John 6:56–69
**"Lord, to whom can we go? You have the words of eternal life.
We have come to believe and know that you are the Holy One of God." v v. 68–69**

Sense the struggle between *flesh* and *spirit*. *Flesh* is power, dominance, control; *spirit* is surrender, love, service, and strength in weakness. *Flesh* is bound to law; the *spirit* is freed by love. Surpassing doctrines and systems, law and love is now a person. It is only by assimilation into that person of Christ that keeping the law has any validity and energy.

Jesus said at the Last Supper, "Do this in memory of me." The "this" to which he is referring is Communion, the sacramental gesture of sharing in the death of Christ and a sign of our own willingness to die for one another. This fulfills the new commandment to love one another as Jesus loved us.

What do you think became of those who once were disciples of Jesus, and then no longer?

Monday   *Faithful At Last*   Hosea 13—14
**I will heal their disloyalty; I will love them freely,
for my anger has turned from them. 14:4**

As two pictures that face each other, so are the final two chapters of Hosea. Infidelity to God is on one side, God's mercy is on the other. The Lord's loving kindness wins out over God's anger. Though in justice God could banish God's unfaithful people, God chooses faithful love, which eventually draws the people back to the Lord.

Persistent faith needed for healing is similar to faithful, long lasting love. Failing to place faith in the Lord to answer all our needs is to be unfaithful to God in a spousal sense.

Take the last verse of Hosea as the theme for the whole. May you know the ways of the Lord and walk in them down the aisle in union with your Spouse.

Tuesday   *Ending on the Downside*   1 Kings 21—22
**Also concerning Jezebel the Lord said,
"The dogs shall eat Jezebel within the bounds of Jezreel." 21:23**

Conspiracy to steal and murder—all evils break out when there is the kind of contempt for the Lord that Jezebel has. How terrible are the descriptions of these evils! Jezebel has violated the first commandment; how easy it becomes to violate all the others. Beauty found in the beginning of the book in the death of King David, the glory of his son Solomon and the building of the Temple, all fade into the ugliness of two kingdoms with mostly evil kings reigning on both sides.

How the Lord must have been grieved! Now you know God's sadness in Hosea's time as well as in our day. Grieve with the Lord until your groaning is one with the groans of the Spirit. These are the birth pangs of new life.

13
Pe
B

226

Wednesday	*A Festival Song*	Psalm 81

I would feed you with the finest of the wheat,
and with honey from the rock I would satisfy you. v. 16

Are you sometimes your own worst enemy? This is likely due to stubbornness—ears and heart blunt to the Word of the Lord. Join with the many praying this psalm with you today, along with generations down countless ages who likely sang this song at the time of the Jewish New Year and at other festivals. Listen carefully to the promises at the end of the psalm. The finest of wheat is offered—the Body of the Lord Jesus in Holy Communion. Receive the Lord often. Become as the Food you eat—open, receptive, abandoned to the Father, as is the Son in the joy and love of the Holy Spirit.

Let every day, every hour, be a new beginning.

Thursday	*The Self Made Whole*	2 Corinthians 13

Examine yourselves to see whether you are living in the faith. Test yourselves.
Do you not realize that Jesus Christ is in you?—
unless, indeed, you fail to meet the test! v. 5

Take a step back and look at your life, not with eyes of judgment, but with kindness, even though the Spirit may sweetly convict you of sinfulness. This will incline you less to feel guilt along with the accompanying blame of others or defensiveness in yourself. Release the flow of your life, whether its present movement is joyful or painful. Get out of your own way and let the reconciling, healing powers of the Lord bubble up from deep within. Then you will be more disposed for Paul's encouragement in v. 11 that we "aim for perfection." The Greek word for this is *katartizo*, the same word for the disciples "mending" their nets just before Jesus asked them to cast their nets out into the sea again.

May you be mended, healed, made whole and blameless in the sight of the Lord.

13
Pe
B

Friday	*As a Child*	Mark 9:33–50

He sat down, called the twelve, and said to them,
"Whoever wants to be first must be last of all and servant of all." v. 35

What makes for true greatness?—a question pondered long and hard by sages from all cultures. Jesus' disciples enter the dispute, arguing among themselves, forgetting that incarnate Wisdom walks with them. Jesus stops, takes a child, sets him in their midst, and shares the essence of greatness that is wrapped in a child's heart. Listen as Jesus speaks to your heart.

There is a child inside of you. Would that the evil kings of Judah and Israel would have listened as this child to God's voice! One wonders just where they "rested", when they "rested with their fathers." You will rest in the bosom of the Father forever in heaven, if you live as God's beloved child now upon earth.

Saturday   The Sabbath Torah Reading

Sep 02, 2006 #49	Aug 29, 2015 #49	Aug 31, 2024 #47	Aug 27, 2033 #48
Aug 29, 2009 #49	Sep 01, 2018 #50	Aug 28, 2027 #47	Aug 30, 2036 #48
Sep 01, 2012 #49	Aug 28, 2021 #50	Aug31, 2030 #48	Aug 27, 2039 #48

The image of a fish was used by early Christians as a secret symbol for Jesus. Ichthus (ΙΧΘΥΣ, Greek for fish) is an acronym of "Jesus Christ, Son Of God, Saviour ('Ιησοῦς Χριστός, Θεοῦ Υἱός, Σωτηρ). The image of three interlacing fish on the facing page is found in the catacombs, combining the symbol for Jesus with the triquetra, symbol of the Trinity. It is used here as an image for Kingdomtide as the fourth season of the year, celebrating the fullness of God in the Trinity, after the three previous seasons with their respective associations of the Father (Advent to Epiphany), the Son (Lent and Easter) and the Holy Spirit (Pentecost.).

KINGDOMTIDE

AUTUMN

Northern Hemisphere

Year B
2009, 2012, 2015 …

Kingdomtide begins on the Sunday nearest August 31.
See the entire cycle of readings at a glance on page xxi.

The First Week in Kingdomtide

Begins in the Sunday nearest August 31. Alphabyte: Nose, p. 110

Sunday *The Lord's Mirror* Mark 7:1–8,14–15,21–3

**There is nothing that enters a man from outside which can defile him;
but the things which come out of him, those are the things that defile a man.** *v.15*

With eyes of hawks, the Pharisees confront Jesus. They find him not washing their hands before eating. Jesus confronts them with Isaiah 29:13. If there is anything that God abhorred in the Old Testament, it was making a display of fervor from the outside, with nothing but frigidity within.

An instruction of Jesus follows, lest the Pharisees tempt the crowd to be impressed by their outer show. What defiles, is what comes out of a person, not what goes in. The outer is the reflection of the inner. If your heart is right with the Lord, it will mirror the divine presence; if it is not, your face will reflect only the sordid world. Do you mirror the Lord?

Monday *The Protection of Fidelity* Daniel 1

**Daniel purposed in his heart that he would not defile himself
with the portion of the king's delicacies, nor with the wine which he drank. v. 1**

The year is 605 B.C. The Hebrews are being taken into exile into Babylon, modern day southeast Iraq. The Lord raises up the prophet Daniel in the crisis. This is the account of this one faithful young Hebrew lad, probably a teenager.

Sense the purity of heart in this radiant man, confident in his God, faithful to the details of following the Lord. In a foreign land, these reminders will form sacred boundaries in his heart for adhering to the Lord alone. Recall the fidelity to God of the patriarch Joseph in Egypt. Fidelity and total trust in the Lord brought the Lord's protection in the favor of the Pharaoh. The same happens for Daniel and the King of Babylon.

What can you do each day to remind you of the divine presence as you live in a world that ignores God?

Tuesday *Released by Wisdom* Proverbs 22

**Train up a child in the way he should go,
And when he is old he will not depart from it. v. 6**

Memorize this verse if you are a parent—or will be one day. Meditate carefully on it and let the Holy Spirit teach your soul and sober you with the awesome responsibility that is yours.

Pause often as you prayerfully read these proverbs. Repeat them until they touch that place in your soul where they will rest secure. Look for that gentle shock to your spirit that is the sign from the Lord that the Word is hitting home.

What happens when you finally remember someone's name that you were forgetting, or you recall something that you need to do and finally remember it? There is a release in your whole body that takes place. This is the way Proverbs can touch and release your spirit.

| Wednesday | *The Court of Heaven* | Psalm 82 |

**"Defend the cause of the weak and fatherless;
maintain the rights of the poor and oppressed." v. 3**

The priorities of the Lord are urged to become our own. True worship increases our love for those who do not worship. These are ones "turned off," who do not experience justice, perhaps because they have not received *hesed,* the love, and mercy of the Lord through you.

Keep open. You cannot do it all, but the Lord through you can do all things. Pray this psalm in a personal way, asking the Lord to show you how you are to complete the works of mercy in your own life. Wait. Listen. Believe that the Lord will speak to your heart about the poor ones who are closest to God's own heart. Jot down notes in your journal; the Lord may become very explicit with you and you will want to remember.

| Thursday | *Faith, Hope and* | Love 1 Thessalonians 1 |

**… Remembering without ceasing your work of faith, labor of love,
and patience of hope in our Lord Jesus Christ … v. 3**

Faith, hope and love—familiar virtues that receive a fresh touch from St. Paul as he celebrates and praises a local church in Thessalonica. This was the second major church established in Europe. As Corinth, it was a busy commercial seaport on the Aegean Sea, in the northeast corner of the Grecian peninsula.

Place yourself among those gathered, perhaps in someone's house by the sea as you listen to this letter for the first time. Are you grounded in faith, hope, and love? Hope is faith's extension, confident that something of God is going to be accomplished from the faith planted in your heart. Love is the power of God at work radiating from the center of your soul.

| Friday | *Openness of a Child* | Mark 10:1–22 |

**"Whoever does not receive the kingdom of God
as a little child will by no means enter it." v. 15**

The sacredness of marriage is uplifted, its rupture denounced as sin. If this applies to you, repent of wherever there was sinfulness in your divorce. In the Lord's forgiveness, you will find the grace to follow God's will, most likely living with the blessing with the one to whom you are now married.

Become as a child. Do not be afraid of intimacy with the Lord, however great is the sinfulness in your life. God receives you and loves you. The Lord wants you to be wonderfully happy. Feel the sadness of the rich young man who walks away from joy, due to his attachment to wealth, instead of to the Lord.

Be very alert as the Word of the Lord comes to bring you life.

Saturday

The Sabbath Torah Reading

Sep 09, 2006 #50	Sep 05, 2015 #50,	Sep 07, 2024 #48	Sep 03, 2033 #49
Sep 05, 2009 #50	Sep 08, 2018 #51	Sep 04, 2027 #48	Sep 06, 2036 #49
Sep 08, 2012 #50	Sep 04, 2021 #51	Sep 07, 2030 #49	Sep 03, 2039 #49

**1
Ki
B**

The Second Week in Kingdomtide

Begins in the Sunday nearest September 7. Alphabyte: Oak, p. 110

Sunday   *Healing the Tongue*   **Mark 7:24–37**
Immediately his ears were opened,
and the impediment of his tongue was loosed, and he spoke plainly. v. 35

A gentile woman's strong faith and the healing of a deaf mute are today's examples of so many miracles. Despite the command of Jesus, the man who could now hear and talk could not be kept silent. The purpose of the silence is to downplay the "wonder-worker" name given to Jesus. People might be drawn only for the miracle and not for the relationship with the One who performed it.

Invite Jesus to come and touch your ears and your tongue. May what you hear lead you to the Word of the Lord; may what you say lead others to the same. The Letter of James, chapter 3 teaches about the wiles of the tongue. Today be aware of your tongue, and especially of the grace of God to heal it.

Monday   *Knowledge from God*   **Daniel 2**
"I thank You and praise You, O God of my fathers;
You have given me wisdom and might,
And have now made known to me what we asked of You." v. 23

Daniel lives in such intimacy with the Lord that he *knows* he will receive all he needs in the crisis in which he finds himself. He already has the prayer of thanksgiving and praise in his heart that he expresses after he receives the answer from the Lord about the King's dream. Daniel's commitment to the Lord alone results in receiving God's protection, comfort, and power against all adversities. Daniel is a model of intimacy maintained with the Lord. God alone is sovereign.

All you need to know spiritually will be given to you as you pour out your heart in prayer before the Lord. As Daniel, stand out against the crowd in your trust in the Lord. It will give you a serenity that no one can take from you.

Tuesday   *Jolts to the Spirit*   **Proverbs 23**
Do not withhold correction from a child,
For if you beat him with a rod, he will not die. v. 13

In an age of frequent child abuse, teachings about "beating with a rod" are hard to take. Though there is controversy today over the appropriateness of spanking, the selected verse intends nothing more than this. Spanking a child as a release of a parent's anger is in no way condoned. This comes from revenge, and is totally outside of the intent of the proverb.

However, here is another interpretation. In addition to being a stick with which to strike, a rod is also a *measure*, a standard to gage anyone's behavior. For example, when a child is consequenced by removing his or her stereo, the child is "hit" by the absence of music in the room. This reminds the child that he or she did not follow a proper standard of behavior.

Be jolted by the "rod"—the standard of God's Word.

Wednesday   *A Prayer for Victory*   **Psalm 83**

**Let them know that you, whose name is the LORD—
that you alone are the Most High over all the earth. v. 18**

We long for God to intervene in the presence of enemies; so does the psalmist. He uses images of victory and conquest to stir belief that the Lord indeed has power over all enemies.

Those who call themselves your enemy need not be named so by you. Jesus commanded us to love our enemies. Intercede for them with love—much more powerful than all the hatred that might rise before your face. Pray with love so that the kind of shame and confusion described in verse 17 will move your enemies beyond all intrigues, to surrender their lives into God's great love.

Remember what happened when God's people ignored divine power when it was needed.

Thursday   *Fresh Power and Intimacy*   **1 Thessalonians 2**

**When you received the word of God which you heard from us, you welcomed it
not as the word of men, but as it is in truth, the word of God,
which also effectively works in you who believe. v. 13**

The Bible we read every day is not a human word, but the very Word of God. The Lord speaks to your heart with the same tenderness and family affection with which Paul addresses the new Christians whom he loves so much.

Read slowly and prayerfully, entering into the sacred space that the inspired Paul creates for you. The freshness of the message speaks to your heart, awakening you by its power to a new way of seeing your own world. The Word of God is a sacred canopy over your life. Believe in the active presence of the Lord, bringing that power to you of which Paul speaks. What plans God has for you today!

Friday   *Clothed Only with Jesus*   **Mark 10:23–52**

And throwing aside his garment, he rose and came to Jesus. v. 50

That Jesus could predict his passion and not protect himself from it, means he is in charge of what is coming. He goes to Jerusalem to be offered as the Paschal Lamb. He came to earth for this. The forces are mounting against the Lord.

Just before the entry in triumph into Jerusalem, there is one last miracle. The man's name is Bartimaeus. He is blind. In those days, the blind wore a special garment as an indicator to passersby that the person could not see, thus needing alms. As a sign of his total surrender to the Lord, Bartimaeus throws away the protective cloak. Jesus is everything to him.

Throw off what you often use for your own self-defense and put on Jesus alone.

Saturday   **The Sabbath Torah Reading**

Sep 16, 2006 #51–52	Sep 12, 2015 #51	Sep 14, 2024 #49	Sep 10, 2033 #50
Sep 12, 2009 #51–52	Sep 15, 2018 #52	Sep 11, 2027 #49	Sep 13, 2036 #50
Sep 15, 2012 #51	Sep 11, 2021 #52	Sep 14, 2030 #50	Sep 10, 2039 #50

**2
Ki
B**

The Third Week in Kingdomtide

*Begins in the Sunday nearest September14. Alphabyte: **Pencil**, p. 111*

Sunday   *If You Lose Your Soul*   **Mark 8:27–38**

**"What will it profit a man if he gains the whole world,
and loses his own soul?" v. 37**

Peter's typical reactive behavior snatches away a moment of grace and glory. He has just confessed Jesus as the Christ, but then succumbs to arrogance when he rebukes Jesus for predicting his passion. Christ pounds Peter's spirit into coming to an awareness of his foolishness by calling him "Satan." That must have gotten Peter's deep attention!

The suffering of Jesus implicates all those who follow him. Yet Jesus leads the way. Keep the focus upon the Lord; Jesus will meet the deepest needs of those who have given their lives to him.

If you are one with Jesus, your eternal salvation is secure, a salvation that is beginning *right now*. Let the question of Jesus in the verse for the day mull around your heart every hour. It will sober your spirit.

Monday   *Absolute Protection*   **Daniel 3**

**"Our God whom we serve is able to deliver us
from the burning fiery furnace." v. 17**

The faith of the three in the furnace has been **"tested as fire and come off safe"** (1 Peter 1:7). They have an absolute sense of the power of God in the fire. Their adherence to God alone is as gold; the fire can do them no harm.

May your heart be totally on fire with love for the Lord. Nothing need ever harm you. Perhaps the anger of another is turning up the "heat" in your life.

Likely, this includes efforts to manipulate through guilt. It matters not how the adversity comes. Only be true to yourself and faithful to the Lord in the absolute protection God offers you.

Christ has been interpreted as the fourth person among the three; so is the Lord with you as your refuge, your *heat shield* against **"all the fiery darts of the wicked one"** (Eph. 6:16).

Tuesday   *The Power Goes On*   **2 Kings 1—3**

**"Ask! What may I do for you, before I am taken away from you?" Elisha said,
"Please let a double portion of your spirit be upon me." 2:9**

God's faithless people: this is theme threading its way through the Second Book of Kings. See what happens when the King consults an idol instead of turning to the Lord.

Reflect on your own life. What place do you give the Lord when you look for wisdom about important decisions in your life? In seeking the well-intended advice of others, we can be vulnerable to their bias, their prejudice—reactions from what is unhealed in their lives ... hardly the wisdom we need!

Elijah "passes the torch" to Elisha. The Spirit came at Pentecost as tongues or torches of fire on each one. The same can happen to you right now. In Jesus, you are greater than the Old Testament prophets are. Do not resist, or much less rebel, as those in chapter 3. The power of God is with you.

**3
Ki
B**

Wednesday　　　　　*The Court of the Heart*　　　　　**Psalm 84**
Better is one day in your courts
than a thousand elsewhere. v. 10

Would that we loved the house of the Lord as much as the psalmist does! Though the church means much more than a physical building, still it does include those places in life where we especially find ourselves in the presence of God.

Are there such places in your life now? Do you long for time with the Lord in special settings? If not, pray that you desire this with the same passion as today's prayer.

Can you feel the love of the Lord that the psalmist has in today's verse? Memorize it and repeat it often throughout the day. Be drawn to the inner court of the heart—God's favorite place to dwell. With God inside you, wherever you are can become a cathedral.

Thursday　　　　　*Friends in the Lord*　　　　　**1 Thessalonians 3**
May the Lord make you increase and abound in love
to one another and to all, just as we do to you. v. 12

St. Paul's greatness may have us envision him as a wondrous "Lone Ranger." Today's reading will change that. "Now we live, if you stand fast in the Lord," says Paul. Is he co-dependent to others' faith? No, but he is intimately inter-dependent to them, with bonds of faith and love that are the sinews of the Body of Christ. We belong to each other in Christ.

Do not go it alone, gritting your teeth, faking a smile that everything is just fine when it is not. The Lord wants you to trust in him with bonds extending into a community of faith, hope, and love that is immensely *real* to you.

What are you doing to be sure that you have friends in the Lord?

Friday　　　　　*Autumn for Jesus*　　　　　**Mark 11:1–14**
Others cut down leafy branches from the trees
and spread them on the road. v. 8

Autumn has always been a nostalgic time for me—smells, sounds of crunching leaves, fresh pencils and books for a new year of school. This sober, inward season is the setting when our Jewish brothers and sisters celebrate **Rosh Hashana**. It is a solemn beginning of a new year. Autumn is a season to meditate upon life and to discover the sacredness of time.

We have come to that place in Mark's Gospel, which is the "autumn," of Jesus' earthly life. Jesus will be speaking about the End Times. It is the beginning of the end, which turns out to be a new beginning.

Today we flash back to Palm Sunday as Jesus, your King, rides into the heart of Jerusalem to take possession of God's Kingdom. Walk beside the donkey.

3
Ki
B

Saturday　　　　　　　　　　　　**The Sabbath Torah Reading**

Sep 23, 06 Rosh Hash	Sep 19, 2015 #52	Sep 21, 2024 #50	Sep 17, 2033 #51–52
Sep 19,09 Rosh Hash	Sep 22, 2018 #53	Sep 18, 2027 #50	Sep 20, 2036 #51
Sep 22, 2012 #52	Sep 18, 2021 #53	Sep 21, 2030 #51–52	Sep 17, 2039 #51

The Fourth Week in Kingdomtide

Begins in the Sunday nearest September21. Alphabyte: Quilt, p. 111

Sunday　　　　　　　　　*Complete Reversals*　　　　　　　**Mark 9:30–37**

**"Whoever receives one of these little children
in My name receives Me." v. 37**

How often the disciples are "missing the boat" that Jesus is on! For the second time, Jesus tells about his coming suffering and death. So strong is their denial, they distract themselves arguing about who is the greatest and most important among them.

Jesus confronts them with their foolishness. Values are reversed when it comes to being with Jesus; the humble are exalted, the littlest become the biggest, the greatest is the one who serves; the one that dies is the one that lives. Serving the poor, the forgotten, the cast aside—they will reveal the face of the Anointed One. Pray fervently that you understand this teaching of Jesus to the full.

Monday　　　　　　　*To God Alone Be the Glory*　　　　　　**Daniel 4**

**Now I, Nebuchadnezzar, praise and extol and honor the King of heaven,
all of whose works are truth, and His ways justice. v. 37**

Though we can be inspired by another's faith, there comes a point when faith needs to become one's own. Nebuchadnezzar is moved by the faith of Daniel and his friends in the power of the God of Israel, but the King has not come to personal faith and abandon. His is self-centered. The Lord confronts him about this in the dream that comes to him in the night, brought to the light of day by Daniel.

Notice familiar themes about exalting self and being humbled. Recall the Tower of Babel in Genesis 11, the Parable of the Rich Fool in Luke 12:13, ff., as well as themes being read in Proverbs. The Lord accepts no substitutes; God wants the "real thing." Place God at the center of your world and give God alone the glory. If you find that you are being humbled by some event or by some person, then give God even more praise.

Tuesday　　　　　　　*Five Wonders of Old*　　　　　　**2 Kings 4—5**

**"Please, let us make a small upper room on the wall … so it will be,
whenever he comes to us, he can turn in there." 4:10**

Whom do you trust to get you out of debt? Is it only your own pondering, planning and plotting? Turn everything over as does today's widow. God's oil pays her debt and Gods anointing will pay yours.

Get inside the joy of the woman who makes a room in her house for Elisha. Is there a room in your inner house for the Holy Spirit to live? Keeping your home neat and having a place for prayer can reflect an inner house in order. The Lord abides in you so that you can abide in God.

Be careful what you throw in the pot of your life; it might poison the whole. Pray through God's wonders of old until they become wonders of *new* within you.

Wednesday   *The Kiss*   **Psalm 85**
Love and faithfulness meet together;
righteousness and peace kiss each other. v. 10

Only God has the power to restore. The exiled Israelites now receive the promise of restoration. For those exiled from life with the Lord, the power of the Lord is there to bring back total union. Find comfort in this.

The Lord speaks peace as he does in John's Gospel, chapter 14, v. 27. Know how absolute is the Lord's forgiveness and God's desire that intimacy be restored for you. There are verses in this psalm that you will surely want to lift up, write down and place where you can see them often. Taste and eat these words of life that God has offered for you.

Thursday   *Swept Up By Holiness*   **1 Thessalonians 4**
If we believe that Jesus died and rose again,
even so God will bring with Him those who sleep in Jesus. v. 14

Sexual impurity and idolatry—the two go together in the Bible. Paul understood purity as that holiness needed to worship and serve the Lord alone. Impurity places self at the center. This violates the First Commandment, as well as the commandment against adultery.

"Mind your own business"; the saying is from the Bible. We need purity of heart and simplicity in order to see God, as Matthew 5:8 expresses in the Sixth Beatitude. Verse 17 is the central text in the Bible about the Rapture. Here is the essence of pure love: being swept away by the love of the other. Lust pushes; love lets go. Let your spirit be caught up *now* in the Lord who longs to take you into the Holy of Holies in the heart of the risen life.

Friday   *The Cleansing of the Temple*   **Mark 11:15–33**
"My house shall be called a house of prayer for all nations." v. 17

It is time to clean house. All the previous efforts of Jesus to avoid his enemies are no longer. The hour of our deliverance is at hand. Jesus turns the Temple upside down. He breaks centuries of abuse and bondage. The Lord wants the people free. God does not tolerate religion that controls and manipulates people.

The boldness of the Lord is held up as a model for faith, as he challenges us to have belief that moves mountains. Believe when you pray. Claim what it is that you are praying for in the Name of Jesus, even when you don't see the answer in the natural realm. If Jesus turns your heart upside down, it is so that you will fully believe in God's power.

Saturday   **The Sabbath Torah Reading**

Sep 30, 2006 #53	Sep 26, 2015 #53	Sep 28, 2024 #51–52	Sep 24, 2033 Rosh Hash
Sep 26, 2009 #53	Sep 29, 2018 Tabern.	Sep 25, 2027 #51–52	Sep 27, 2036 #52
Sep 29, 2012 #53	Sep 25, 2021 Tabern.	Sep 28, 2030 Rosh Hash	Sep 24, 2039 #52

The Fifth Week in Kingdomtide

*Begins in the Sunday nearest September 28. Alphabyte: **R**ainbow, p. 112*

Sunday   *Serious Warnings*   **Mark 9:38–50**

**It is better for you to enter into life maimed,
rather than having two hands to go to hell … v. 42**

Jesus does not mince words when it comes to eternal life; the stakes are too high. Read these warnings as though for the first time.

Do you readily share your deepest conviction about absolute values? We are called to witness to others about eternal life. This means confronting others, not with *judgments* but with *convictions*. It includes sharing your faith in eternal life and the concern that others might be placing their eternal life in danger by the way in which they live.

Co-dependency means that we allow others to determine our actions, instead of God. Are you bold enough not to allow your actions to be a function of what others think of you?

Monday   *The Handwriting on the Wall*   **Daniel 5**

[Daniel to Belshazzar:] **"The God who holds your breath in His hand
and owns all your ways, you have not glorified." v. 23**

Belshazzar, son of Nebuchadnezzar becomes king. Arrogance engulfs him, as he commits sacrileges against the sacred vessels captured from the Hebrew Temple. The handwriting is literally on the wall for him! The description of this intervention of the Lord makes his whole being quake with fear.

Fear alone is not enough to make those lasting spiritual changes needed in life. Ponder deeply. *You* are the sacred vessel of the Lord. *You* are a unique part of the holy temple of the Spirit who dwells in you.

Is there any "handwriting on the walls" of your heart? Where do you need to change? Take a pencil, your journal, and ask the Spirit to reveal to you what you need to know about this. The Holy Spirit will inspire you as you dialogue with God.

Tuesday   *Syrian Siege*   **2 Kings 6—7**

**"Do not fear, for those who are with us are more
than those who are with them." 6:16**

Intrigue, unbelief, fear, famine, cannibalism—witness the extent of the sufferings of the people at the hands of the enemy Syrians. Yet the Lord is with the people. Marvel at God's intervention in causing the Syrians to hear the sounds of approaching horses and chariots coming after them when this does not actually happen.

God will intervene on your behalf. When you have enemies coming against you in sieges of disease, strife, quarrels, call upon the Lord. God's power is more within you then whatever is coming against you from without.

Recall the disciples besieged by fear in that upper room after Jesus was crucified. He comes right through the wall and shares the power of his peace. Even when your senses tell you he is not coming to you, believe that Jesus is already here.

Wednesday	*Confident Prayer*	Psalm 86

Hear, O LORD, and answer me,
for I am poor and needy. v. 1

My first encounter with this Psalm was a young person in a religious community. Martin Neylon, Master of Novices, shared this prayer with me, calling it his favorite psalm. I can still hear the tender regard he had for it, even as the psalm itself breathes a sweet relation between the pray-er and the Lord.

The psalm implies a deep level of communion with the psalmist and the Lord. He presumes much, because he knows in faith upon whom he can rely. This same God of tender compassion is available for you right now. Do not let anything stand between you and the Lord.

The Bible is God's intimate Word for you. Take each word personally. May these daily *"Firestarters"* be my way of making the Bible personal to you, just as others did for me.

Thursday	*Watch and Be Sober.*	1 Thessalonians 5

Let us not sleep, as others do, but let us watch and be sober. v. 6

Watch and be sober—two imperatives in Paul's admonition today. The Greek root of the word for "watch" is *egeiro*, whence comes the name, Gregory. The image recalls the security guards of old who stayed up for three hours at a time during a night watch, making sure that no enemies would sneak across the boundary. The root means "to gather together" the senses into a wakeful whole. The notion is linked with being sober, the absence of which shatters and scatters the focus and attention needed to live the realities of the final words of Paul in this letter.

Listen carefully. Is the Spirit sweetly convicting you of anything? The Lord gives you the gift of discernment. Treasure it. Watch and be sober.

Friday	*Protecting the Vineyard*	Mark 12:1–27

They sought to lay hands on Him, but feared the multitude,
for they knew He had spoken the parable against them. v. 12

A hedge protects; be aware of this as you read today's parable. Evil powers break into the Lord's sacred vineyard. This is what happened on Calvary, yet not without the Lord's permission.

Love is vulnerable. Jesus does not protect himself from the onslaught of destructive forces. Yet his love is stronger than evil, stronger than death, and thus the resurrection has created a hedge around a new garden, a new vineyard, a new temple, protecting us by the power of the Spirit from any evil that would further break through.

As you read the arguments and "set-ups" of the religious authorities, be sobered by this. Do not argue with the Lord; just listen and be saved. Rest in the Lord within the "hedges" of God's protective arms.

Saturday

The Sabbath Torah Reading

Oct 07, 2006 Tabern.	Oct 03, 2015 Tabern.	Oct 05, 2024 #53	Oct 01, 2033 #53
Oct 03, 2009 Tabern.	Oct 06, 2018 #54–1C	Oct 02, 2027 Rosh Hash	Oct 04, 2036 #53
Oct 06, 2012 Tabern.	Oct 02, 2021 #54–1C	Oct 05, 2030 #53	Oct 01, 2039 #53

5
Ki
B

The Sixth Week in Kingdomtide

Begins in the Sunday nearest October 5. Alphabyte: Streams, p. 112

Sunday   *Grateful for Saving Grace*   **Mark 10:2–16**

What God has joined together, let no man separate. v. 9

Jesus has strong words about divorce and remarriage. Does this situation apply to you? Rather than rationalize what Jesus teaches, let the Lord convict you where there was sin in your life in this regard. It does not mean that God wants you to return to a shattered or abusive relationship.

The Eastern Church sees marriage and divorce in the following way. There is a difference between a precious, ceramic vase that is cracked and can be fixed and one that is shattered into smithereens on the floor. In keeping with the analogy with marriage, both circumstances involve sin. In the one, effort needs to be made for repair. In the other, grief over the loss and moving on, humbled by sin and grateful for saving grace.

Monday   *The Window Facing God*   **Daniel 6**

My God sent His angel and shut the lions' mouths,
so that they have not hurt me, because I was found innocent before Him. v. 22

What does Daniel do in response to an insidious plot against him? He keeps daily contact with the Lord, praying three times everyday. He pours out his need to the Lord through the open window that faces Jerusalem. Not only is his prayer one of petition to God for his crisis, but prayer strengthens his faith as he recalls that his God, always faithful in the past, will be with him in the den to shut the mouths of the lions. And so it happens.

When anything or anyone comes against you, face God, not the evil. Remain faithful to fervent prayer. The Evil One wants to stop your prayer. Increase it! When greater love for your enemies comes about, then the Lord is ever more glorified. What is more: your enemy is more likely to turn to the Lord through your prayer.

Find your "window" that faces God.

Tuesday   *On God's Side*   **2 Kings 8—9**

Who is on my side? 9:32

It finally comes—the end of a line of wicked kings and a super-wicked woman. Over at last are years of organized idolatry and murder of prophets at the hands of Jezebel. For not having a window in her life that faces God, she is thrown out of one! Be careful not to open a window to wrongdoing. A foothold becomes a stronghold and you can become tossed about by every wind of evil.

A verse repeats in this part of the history of God's People: **"They did evil in the sight of the Lord"**—bold, brazen, defiant evil. Look for all the adjectives that describe evil. Can you come up with some more?

Poisonous fruit begins as a seed the Evil One seeks to plant in human hearts, yours and mine. The seed? **Pride**—placing anything or anyone as Number One in your life, except the Lord.

Sometimes people ask, "Is God on our side?" The question is rather, "Am I on the side of God?"

Wednesday   *Name is Written in Heaven*   **Psalm 87**
The LORD will write in the register of the peoples:
"This one was born in Zion." v. 7

If you want a copy of your birth certificate, you write to the place where you were born. This city or town is special in your life. The same sense is felt in this psalm. How proud is the one who finds his birth certificate in the registry of Zion!

Hebrews chapter 12 from verse 18 is a New Testament parallel to this passage. To be born into Christ means that you are born into Zion, the heavenly city. It is in Christ that your life really begins.

When the disciples return from their first missionary journey, they rejoice that the power of Jesus is with them. In Luke 10:20, Jesus says that even more important—their "names are written in heaven" … Where to go for your true birth certificate!

Thursday   *Faithful to the End*   **2 Thessalonians 1**
… that the name of our Lord Jesus Christ
may be glorified in you, and you in Him. v. 12

Common themes flow through the readings of the week: faithfulness to prayer, good works, having a spirit of trust, not complaining when difficulties take place. We are encouraged in ways similar to those John Wesley uplifted for the early Methodists in "The Ordinances of God:" the public worship of God, the ministry of the Word, either read or expounded, the Supper of the Lord, family and private prayer, searching the Scriptures, fasting or abstinence.

May these spiritual disciplines work their way deeper and deeper into your life, healing you wherever there may be fear, anger, or grief over your past. Read slowly the last two verses of this chapter; they will be a soothing balm to your spirit and make it possible for an unshakable joy to well up in your soul.

Friday   *Living for God Alone*   **Mark 12:28–44**
Hear, O Israel, the LORD our God, the LORD is one. And you shall love the LORD
your God with all your heart, with all your soul,
with all your mind, and with all your strength. vv. 29, 30

The 1990s saw an increase of Christians converting to the religion of Islam in the United States; some even saw it then as the fastest growing religion. Film clips show large groups bowing in the direction of Mecca as they paused for prayer various times in the day.

Christians often fail to present a truly distinct way of life, an orderly and timely way to pray, and an authentic, public witness to Christ. What we believe and what we do is often much too private.

An observant Jew prays this verse every morning and evening: **"Hear, O Israel, the Lord our God, the Lord is one"** (Deut. 6:4–5). May you and your loved ones embrace the spiritual disciplines suggested yesterday.

6
Ki
B

Saturday   **The Sabbath Torah Reading**

Oct 14, 2006 #54	Oct 10, 2015 #54–1C	Oct 12, 2024 Yom Kipp.	Oct 08, 2033 Tabern.
Oct 10, 2009 #54	Oct 13, 2018 #2C	Oct 09, 2027 #53	Oct 11, 2036 Tabern.
Oct 13, 2012 #54–1C	Oct 09, 2021 #2C	Oct 12, 2030 Tabern.	Oct 08, 2039 Tabern.

The Seventh Week in Kingdomtide
Begins in the Sunday nearest October 12. Alphabyte: Trapeze, p. 112

Sunday   *Walking To or From Jesus*   **Mark 10:17–31**
With God all things are possible. v. 27

Sense the shifts in the emotions of the rich young man who comes to Jesus. There is sincerity in his search for eternal life. Jesus reviews the basics with him. Yet the young man wants more. "Oh," says Jesus, in effect: "You want something more? You want to enter into the *Kingdom*?" Hear the strong, but liberating words of Jesus about letting go of everything but the cross.

The rich young man did not have riches; riches had him. Reflect on your own situation. Is there some person, place, or thing that has a hold on you? Do not be too quick to dismiss this question; there could be denial here. Find out who or what it is, otherwise there will be great sadness in the depths of your heart as you walk away from Jesus.

It is not too late. Throughout your day, walk toward the Lord in all you do. Remember: With God, all things are possible.

Monday   *Victory in Spiritual Warfare*   **Daniel 7**
To Him was given dominion and glory and a kingdom,
That all peoples, nations, and languages should serve Him. v. 14

While there are various interpretations of the visions of Daniel, do not forget the obvious: it is about spiritual warfare. Let the grandeur of the images do their work within as you identify with this young, faithful hero, our model for Mondays this season. A commentary will help you find various lenses through which to see these visions.

Someone once said that the battleground for spiritual warfare is the space between your two ears. We have victory in the sign of the cross. Place your present struggles against the assured victory in the end. No matter how things look to you, remember, we "walk by faith and not by sight" (2 Cor. 5:7). The victory has already taken place in the heavenlies, as well as in the bottom of your own soul.

Tuesday   *Hands Together, If Hearts Are One*   **2 Kings 10—11**
Is your heart right, as my heart is toward your heart?
… If it is, give me your hand. 10:15

Amid the stench of death, God is constantly at work to put an end to the evil that leads the Chosen People to ruin and apostasy. The Lord is *cleaning house*!

Shining as a gentle light of life comes today's verse, so dear to John Wesley. We need others in our lives with whom hearts and hands can be joined, freed from the fears of sharing life closely, discovering the comfort and the joy of the body of Christ in whom we live, move and have our being.

Do not accept an external type of church-life as a substitute for the vibrant, spiritual intimacy of being one with a community of "Friends in the Lord."

Wednesday *Prayer in Desperation* **Psalm 88**

I cry to you for help, O LORD;
in the morning my prayer comes before you. v. 13

Pure desperation fuels the prayer of the psalmist's plea and gives him power. He knows where to go with all his pain. Inflating self with positive feelings when one is afraid or angry is not being honest with God. The soul poured out in intimacy with the Lord will eventually bring a peace that is greater than the negative emotions that might be present as prayer begins.

Take this psalm as a pattern for your own prayer, especially if you are experiencing trouble in your life. Say this psalm for others who may not know where to go with their pain. Today's verse comes as a candle in the middle of the darkness. The morning brings a new day, a new perspective, and the confidence that prayer is reaching the heart of God.

Thursday *Stand Fast.* **2 Thessalonians 2**

Now may our Lord Jesus Christ Himself, and our God and Father,
who has loved us and given us everlasting consolation and good hope by grace,
comfort your hearts and establish you in every good word and work. vv. 16–17

Buffalo, New York and Chicago, Illinois become so windy at times that the downtown areas are fitted out with ropes for people to hold onto as they walk, lest they be blown away.

This passage urges us to "stand fast." We would say in current jargon, "Hang in there," lest you be "tossed to and fro and be carried about with every wind of doctrine" (Eph. 4:14). Paul describes what happens when the role of Creator to creature is reversed—absolute arrogance and lawlessness, the creature despising the order set by the Creator. All evil results from this.

Stand fast against this usurped power. Cling to the cross as your rope when the lawless, evil winds of pride and power blow strongly against you.

Friday *Pain and Joy As Never Before* **Mark 13:1–13**

It is not you who speak, but the Holy Spirit. v. 11

Good news and bad news are mixed in this passage. The bad news: things are going to get worse as peoples rise up in rage against each other; the good news: the power of the Holy Spirit will be present as an inner strength of word and action against the power of darkness. Though the Temple would be destroyed in 70 A.D., and there would not be left a stone upon a stone, yet the New Temple of the presence of God, the risen body of Jesus, will be the sacred house where you can live now and forever.

Jesus likens this to a woman at the time of birth—pain as never before yet joy as never before. Each hour of this day is a time for you to deliver. What is the pain you need to experience so that new birth can happen?

Saturday **The Sabbath Torah Reading**

Oct 21, 2006 #1C	Oct 17, 2015 #2C	Oct 19, 2024 Tabern.	Oct 15, 2033 #54
Oct 17, 2009 #1C	Oct 20, 2018 #3C	Oct 16, 2027 Tabern.	Oct 18, 2036 #54–1C
Oct 20, 2012 #2C	Oct 16, 2021 #3C	Oct 19, 2030 #54	Oct 15, 2039 #54–1C

7
Ki
B

The Eighth Week in Kingdomtide

Begins in the Sunday nearest October 19. Alphabyte: Usher, p. 113

Sunday   *The Fire of Service*   **Mark 10:35–45**

Whoever desires to become great among you shall be your servant.
And whoever of you desires to be first shall be slave of all. vv. 43–44

Pride versus humility—the age-old them is here again. The disciples of Jesus do not understand the answer; they will not until the resurrection comes and the Holy Spirit empowers them.

These sayings about service and surrender are soaked in the power of the Spirit, not only in their writing, but also in your reading. You further the power when you share the daily passage with others. You are encountering the very Word of God tailored to fit your life and your circumstances. May these *Firestarters* do their work— start the fire in the hearth of your heart. Reflect. Allow *embers* to remain as gentle, inward writings. Read, meditate, pray, and do what the Lord tells you to do about your life.

Monday   *Diving Deeper*   **Daniel 8**

[Gabriel:] Look, I am making known to you what shall happen
in the latter time of the indignation. v. 19

Daniel dives so deep into the presence of the Lord that he is receives visions about the end times. A description of the Antichrist is presented. A commentary will help. Ever increase your contact with the Lord in your conscious life. God will entrust you with gifts of knowledge, as outlined in Paul's first letter to the Corinthians, 12:8. Remember Jesus' words in Luke 16:10: "He who is faithful in what is least is faithful also in much."

Do not be afraid. Though nations war against one another, the power of God will ultimately prevail. When strife around you increases, do what we used to do as children playing in the strong waves in the ocean after a storm—dive even deeper into the Word and let the world's strife pass right over you.

Tuesday   *Evil Kings/Death of Elisha*   **2 Kings 12—13**

When the man was let down and touched the bones of Elisha,
he revived and stood on his feet. 13:21

As the bong of a somber, tolling bell, the convicting verse of 2 Kings rings again and again, referring to a dead king: "He did evil in the sight of the Lord." Even in chapter 12 :2, Jehoash's rightness is short lived; he is swept into the evils round about him.

The Lord's ways and thoughts are not ours. Be sensitive to Elisha's personal pain as he experiences the loneliness of being part of a people who have gone astray after other gods. Do you share this pain in some way?

Elisha needs the prayers of the people. The great worker of miracles, himself dies of an illness. The people not being there for him suggest a connection between his death and the lack of intercessors for him. Yet even in his death, a miracle happens. What life will come when you and I die to self!

Wednesday   *Problems Eclipsed by Praise*   **Psalm 89**

I will sing of the LORD'S great love forever;
with my mouth I will make your faithfulness known through all generations. v. 1

Many psalms are written in the first person pronoun. The soul of the psalmist is poured out in pleas from the heart. This one, however, has the first three-quarters of it completely focused on the wonder and power of the Lord. A self-forgetfulness is refreshing. Praise eclipses problems. The only purpose in creation is to praise and serve the Lord.

After praying the psalm, continue to pour out your soul spontaneously in praise, adoration, and worship. Be comforted by God's fidelity to the promise about the seed of David. Jesus is this promise, realized in the Holy Spirit who tenderly longs to dwell more deeply in your heart. Once you know this by faith, your problems, as you know them, are over!

Thursday   *That Beautiful Something*   **2 Thessalonians 3**

May the Lord direct your hearts
into the love of God and into the patience of Christ. v. 5

Stand before the Lord at the end of your life. Is there some contribution you wished you could have made for the world? You are not dead yet. There is time for you to discover more clearly, what you could do to make a difference for the Lord in a world so indifferent to God.

Take this suggestion as you read the warning that Paul makes against idleness. It is not about being busy for the sake of being busy; rather it means to keep at your **life-work**—that beautiful something that you and only you can make for God.

Keep company with those who have a life, because they *live life* for the Lord.

Friday   *The End Is Near.*   **Mark 13:14–37**

Heaven and earth will pass away,
but My words will by no means pass away. v. 31

You have heard the expression: "Things have to get worse before they get better." Jesus describes the end times in this way. There are many indicators that today's world resembles the picture that Jesus makes. However, speculation about the time of the end distracts from the personal work that still needs to be done right now.

The end can always be near—the end of your life uncommitted totally to the Lord; the end of resentment, pain, confusion. Once you have died to yourself and are alive in Jesus, you are in heaven. You need not worry when "the curtain comes down" on everything. Watch for the signs that come your way telling you that you need more trust in the Lord.

Saturday   **The Sabbath Torah Reading**

Oct 28, 2006 #2C	Oct 24, 2015 #3C	Oct 26, 2024 #54–1C	Oct 22, 2033 #1C
Oct 24, 2009 #2C	Oct 27, 2018 #4C	Oct 23, 2027 #54	Oct 25, 2036 #2C
Oct 27, 2012 #3C	Oct 23, 2021 #4C	Oct 26, 2030 #1C	Oct 22, 2039 #2C

8
Ki
B

The Ninth Week in Kingdomtide

Begins in the Sunday nearest October 26. Alphabyte: Violin, p. 113

Sunday　　　　　　　*Following Jesus Down the Road*　　　　　　**Mark 10:46–52**

Immediately he received his sight and followed Jesus on the road. v. 52

Here is Jesus' final miracle before his triumphal entry into Jerusalem, his passion and death. Ponder the wonder of it; a blind man receives sight.

Blind persons wore a specially marked cloak that told people that they needed alms. Bartimaeus takes a leap of faith that he is going to be healed. He need no longer be treated with special privileges granted to the blind. As happens in the miracles of Jesus, by stepping out in faith, he comes closer into Jesus' presence. In seeing Jesus more clearly, he can follow him more closely

Ask to see those areas where you are blind to the presence and power of Jesus in your life. There is a deeper miracle yet to take place in your life so that you too can follow him more closely and love him more dearly.

Monday　　　　　　　*Laser Beam of Devotion*　　　　　　　　**Daniel 9**

"O Lord, hear! O Lord, forgive! O Lord, listen and act!
Do not delay for Your own sake, my God ..." v:19

Daniel offers a pattern for intercessory prayer. Agree with him in prayer as he bears the lives of those who are not praying, those still caught up in infidelity to the Lord in one form or another.

As a grace given by the Lord, intercessory prayer takes the laser beam of your own devotion and sends its ray into the circumstances and lives of those who need God's grace to implode in their lives.

Daniel begins with praise. This awakens a desire for God inside the heart. Next confession comes. Daniel takes on the sin of the people, as Jesus did on the cross. He "Who knew no sin [became] sin for us" (2 Cor. 5:21). Finally, there is supplication in the plea on behalf of all on the part of one.

Is there someone's burden the Lord is placing on your heart?

Tuesday　　　　　　　*Preparing the Epitaph*　　　　　　**2 Kings 14—16**

Fathers shall not be put to death for their children, nor shall children be put to
death for their father; but a person shall be put to death for his own sin. 14:6

If you think it is tedious to read about wicked king after wicked kind who "did evil in the sight of the Lord," how do you think God feels about all this! A brief phrase brings to an end the history of a king: "He was buried with his fathers." It is sobering to wonder just where they all wound up!

As the list of kings and a summary of their reigns flow along, remember that you too will be part of a long history of people in your own family and community in which your life will be summarized along with all the others. When you are buried in the family plot along with your ancestors, what do you want to have written on your tombstone? How will you want to be remembered? May every act of love engrave itself as an epitaph.

Wednesday   *The Lord, Our Refuge*   **Psalm 90**

For a thousand years in your sight are like a day
that has just gone by, or like a watch in the night. v. 4

At this very moment, many people are not praising the Lord. *You* do it for them. Intercede for them, as you go into the presence of the Lord—our dwelling place in all generations.

Psalms 90 to 99 form a cluster of ancient songs the Hebrews used for worship on the Sabbath. Join with this communion of saints as you pray this first one. Be part of God's sacred people linking us vertically with heaven's saints and horizontally with God's faithful ones on earth

From the inner place of refuge in God's presence, look out at the whole, wide expanse of this world. Place particular problems into the wider setting of the glorious absolutes sung in these psalms. God dwells in you and you in God.

Thursday   *Hymns of Heaven*   **Revelation 4—5**

Blessing and honor and glory and power be to Him
who sits on the throne, and to the Lamb, forever and ever! 5:13

Imagination, fueled by faith, transports us into the divine presence. Clear a space within so that a slow reading of these verses can allow you to paint the picture of the wondrous vision which John shares with us.

These are the final weeks of God's year of grace. Enjoy five Thursdays that lift us on high, far above the hassles of earth, to spiritual places that will renew your life and fill you with joy. Though there will be visions of intense struggles between good and evil in the heavenly plane, this assurance courses through every verse: God is the ultimate victor.

As flashes of light that brighten the night, come hymns of praise sung in heaven that give an audio dimension to what our eyes see by faith. Four of these refrains are present in today's' passage. Pray them aloud over and over, perhaps creating spontaneous tunes.

May all that you see and hear, fill your day with heaven.

Friday   *Surges of Love and Hatred*   **Mark 14:1–31**

"Wherever this gospel is preached in the whole world,
what this woman has done will also be told as a memorial to her." v. 9

The final month of God's year of grace is here. Leaves lie on the ground; days are getting colder and shorter. Autumn, as well as spring, is a prayerful time to ponder the death and resurrection of Jesus.

The plot to kill Jesus, woven beneath the fabric of the Gospel itself, now comes to completion with the co-operation of someone from the inside—Judas. In the Anointing at Bethany, extravagant love for Jesus is literally poured out at the same time as extravagant hatred surges ahead.

Take the alabaster flask of your life and empty it out in love and abandon, as do the very leaves pour themselves from the trees. The anointing is a symbol of resurrection. Go inward and adore your Lord.

9
Ki
B

Saturday   **The Sabbath Torah Reading**

Nov 04, 2006 #3C	Oct 31, 2015 #4C	Nov 02, 2024 #2C	Oct 29, 2033 #2C
Oct 31, 2009 #3C	Nov 03, 2018 #5C	Oct 30, 2027 #1C	Nov 01, 2036 #3C
Oct 03, 2012 #4C	Oct 30, 2021 #5C	Nov 02, 2030 #2C	Nov 29, 2039 #3C

The Tenth Week in Kingdomtide

Begins in the Sunday nearest November 2. Alphabyte: Well, p. 114

Sunday *All the Way Into the Kingdom* **Mark 12:28–34**

**To love God with all the heart, and with all the understanding,
and with all the strength, and to love one's neighbor as oneself ... v. 33**

Jesus compresses all the laws and ordinances that the Pharisees believed must be kept in order to attain God and reduces them to two—love of God and love of neighbor as oneself. These bring one to the brink of the Kingdom.

Yet what is it that has one enter all the way into the Kingdom? The final movement is from Jesus alone. Believe in the Lord's sacrificial death for love of you and me; live while being open to die out of love; this completes your entry into the Kingdom. "No one has greater love than this, to lay down one's life for one's friends" (John 15:13).

With this incident, Jesus' adversaries question him no more. A Rabbi once said: "Where there is faith, there are no questions; where there is no faith, there are no answers."

Monday *Spiritual Warfare* **Daniel 10**

**Do not fear, Daniel, for from the first day that you set your mind to gain understanding,
and to humble yourself before your God,
your words have been heard ... v. 12**

Enter yet more deeply into the vision that God offers Daniel. The prophet is shown the counterpart in the spiritual realm of the forces of nations pitted against one another. Earthly struggles reflect warfare in the heavenlies, as described also in Ephesians 6:11–12. God decides the one to receive such visions; the prophet must be a person transparent to the Lord whose life and commitment to God are unwavering.

Know that the struggles you experience in life, as well as the international conflicts that take place, have their origin in spiritual domains. Angels and demons are real. If we were to see what is happening in its totality, we would be overwhelmed, just as Daniel was.

The Lord is in charge. Give God total sway of your life. Jesus has won the victory!

Tuesday *Your Case Spread Before the Lord* **2 Kings 17—19**

**Hezekiah went up to the house of the LORD
and spread it [the letter] before the LORD. 19:14**

10
Ki
B

Finally, a good king comes on the scene, Hezekiah. Yet even he waffles from total fidelity to the Lord. Take special note of verses 5 and 6 in chapter 18 and embrace the terms of greatness in the sight of the Lord.

Adventure, excitement, and faith increase in chapter 19. Be moved by what King Hezekiah does when he gets that letter from King Sennacherib of Assyria, defying and blaspheming the God of the Hebrews. Hezekiah spreads the letter before the Lord in the Temple.

Hezekiah's gesture is a sacrament of his faith in the Lord—a physical act whose meaning and energy are found in the world of the Spirit. Lay your case before the Lord, wide open, with nothing concealed. Abandon yourself to God. Divine power is released in a heart open to it.

| **Wednesday** | *Absolute Trust* | **Psalm 91** |

I will say to the LORD: "My refuge
and my fortress, my God, in whom I trust." v. 2

Make this psalm more personal by changing the pronouns. If you are praying this on your behalf, place the first person personal pronoun in place of the second person. If you are praying with someone else, place his or her name into the psalm.

The loveliness of the psalm is found in savoring the secret place, the refuge, the dwelling place. All these words in Hebrew suggest the absolute *safety* of being in the presence of the Lord. There is protection from all outside attacks, the Lord being a place where you can run and hide, just as a little child runs to hide in the arms of a loving parent. The whole psalm breathes the air of trust, confidence, peace, and assurance. As you read the psalm, what other words come to your heart to describe what it is like to be one with the Lord?

| **Thursday** | *Colors from Deep Within* | **Revelation 6** |

Then I saw the Lamb open one of the seven seals, and I heard one of
the four living creatures call out, as with a voice of thunder, "Come!" v. 1

Sealed inside each of us are energies both dark and bright. Danger comes when the darker side of us is repressed. Better to break open the seal and let the darkness find appropriate and even creative expression, than to deny the darkness and have its energies explode in rage, irritable reactions, unkindness, and gossip.

Accept the entire range of your feelings. Feelings are neither good nor bad: they just are. Recognize and accept them and they will tend to flow outward in ways similar to the images of today's reading.

Inner energies: be aware of this as you read about the opening of six of the seven seals. Strong contrasting images explode in each one. Color vary from bright to grotesque. How do you identify with these vibrant images?

Revelation: it is the book, as well as God showing you God's face from deep within your being.

| **Friday** | *The Hour Has Come* | **Mark 14:32–72** |

I am deeply grieved, even to death; remain here, and keep awake. v. 34

Join Jesus and his intimate friends in the garden of his agony. Three times the word *hour* is used; sense the power of this hour in Jesus' life and in yours right now as you pray.

Sleepiness can be a sign of an inner resistance to facing something. Does this happen to you? Pray to the Spirit that you receive a breakthrough in this area so that you can watch and be with the Lord in the communion of intimate prayer.

The hours of the day are as sacred vessels in which the Lord's grace is present. Be encouraged to grow in awareness of each hour as a sacred space where the events of your life can become encounters with the Lord. When a new hour begins, pause for a moment and thank the Lord for the hour just passed, rededicating yourself to the hour that has just begun.

10
Ki
B

Saturday

The Sabbath Torah Reading

Nov 11, 2006 #4C	Nov 07, 2015 #5C	Nov 09, 2024 #3C	Nov 05, 2033 #3C
Nov 07, 2009 #4C	Nov 10, 2018 #6C	Nov 06, 2027 #2C	Nov 08, 2036 #4C
Nov 10, 2012 #5C	Nov 06, 2021 #6C	Nov 09, 2030 #3C	Nov 05, 2039 #4C

The Eleventh Week in Kingdomtide

Begins in the Sunday nearest November 9. Alphabyte: Xerography, p. 114

Sunday   *God's Life-Support System*   **Mark 12:38–44**

**All of them have contributed out of their abundance; but she out of her poverty
has put in everything she had, all she had to live on. v. 44**

Place two persons before you—an aloof Scribe, long-robed, tall-standing, loving to be greeted in the marketplaces or sitting in the reserved seats at celebrations; the other, an elderly lady, bent over, alone, silent, putting her last coin into the Temple treasury. Jesus and his disciples first watch the scribe, and then they spot the elderly woman. She is not even aware of Jesus' gaze and comment, but for centuries ever after, her praises will be sung for the absolute trust she places in the Lord. Picture the scene—its quiet quality, different from the frenzied activity that had Jesus overturn the moneychangers in the Temple at Passover time.

Quietly surrender all you are to the Lord. Then God's "life-support system" is activated—grace, divine power, and love especially designed to fill the empty places in your heart.

Monday   *Mad with Earthly Power*   **Daniel 11:1–28**

**The two kings, their minds bend on evil, shall sit at one table and exchange lies.
But it shall not succeed, for there remains an end at the time appointed. v. 27**

Death-like struggles of arrogance, greed, and thirst for earthly power violently tug at the nations of the world. All this crashes in upon Daniel in a vision. The nations two centuries before Jesus face off with each other. In the north is Syria, the south, Egypt; the "mighty king" of v. 3 refers to Alexander the Great and the conquest of Persia by Greece.

The Syrian king Antiochus IV gave himself the name Epiphanes, meaning "God is Manifest." Such arrogance and blasphemy! So crazy did this puffed-up state make him that he was nicknamed Epimanes: "Madman!"

Power forged for selfish ends leads to madness. Contemplate God's use of power. Instead of crushing his enemies, Jesus chooses the power of his love and dies for us. There is no greater love. There is no greater power.

Tuesday   *Familiarity with God*   **2 Kings 20—22**

**The high priest Hilkiah said to Shapan the secretary,
"I have found the book of the law in the house of the LORD." 22:8**

Connect with last Monday and King Hezekiah spreading his case before the Lord. The experience of counting on the Lord gives him the confidence in today's reading to pour out his soul at this point of facing death. The Lord hears him.

While the good thief next to Jesus turned his life around at the hour of his death, don't you do the same. A bumper sticker reads, "Those who wait for salvation until the 11th hour may find themselves dead at 10:30!" Familiarity with God throughout life will be a powerful energy sending those extra-needed prayers as arrows from the bow of your heart to the heart of God.

Finally, good King Josiah arrives. Imagine: the People of God discovering the Word of God as buried treasure. It was hidden for generations. Get in touch with the treasure of God's Word as though for the first time.

11
Ki
B

Wednesday   *Confidence in God's Power*   **Psalm 92**
It is good to give thanks to the LORD,
to sing praises to your name, O Most High. v.1

Allow praise and thank to be the beginning of your prayer, just as they are at the opening of this psalm. More basic than all the troubles that push and shove to get priority in the heart, is the loving-kindness of the Lord that is present to you. It is as the first light of everyday.

Rejoice with the psalmist in the glory and the power of God. The Lord sees you and your world from the perspective of the whole. God wants to share this perspective with you, along with the power of God's love. You will see your enemies scattered before your feet as thousands of ants flee your coming.

Who have made themselves enemy to you? Pray for them that the full power of God will come upon them through you, scattering from them, the evils that beset them.

Thursday   *White in the Blood*   **Revelation 7**
These are they who have come out of the great ordeal;
they have washed their robes and made them white in the blood of the Lamb. v. 14

The stain of blood is one of the most difficult to lift from a garment. Yet, imagine—washing cloth in blood and having it come out white! This is what happens to the faithful disciples of the Lamb. Take note of the active voice; they have not *been* washed in blood, but they *do* the washing.

What is your brand of tribulation? Rather than feel yourself a victim, know that you can be actively growing in the purity and power of the Lord through your choice to be more like Jesus. The Lamb of God chose to wash us with the blood and water that flowed from his side so that you and I could become white.

The chapter begins with an awesome stillness as the winds of strife and evil are held in check. The tribulation for God's servants comes only after they have been sealed. Nothing can harm them; nothing can harm you, if you are sealed by the blood of the Lamb.

Friday   *The Power of Silence*   **Mark 15:1–20**
But Jesus made no further reply, so that Pilate was amazed. v. 5

The silence between Pilate and Jesus is awesome. Jesus refuses to defend himself or negotiate his outcome with this spineless man. Pilate is nothing but a puppet administrator, a lackey for the Roman emperor in this distant province.

Jesus' hour has come—humiliating, painful, and overwhelmingly sad. Yet his hour moves closer to death and resurrection; Jesus surrenders himself for your salvation.

When you experience injustice, mockery, and suffering, may you discover a unique joy in Jesus and love for him, for being found more like him; so was Jesus treated out of love for you. When you come away from suffering with more union with your Lord, how can you lose?

11
Ki
B

Saturday   **The Sabbath Torah Reading**

Nov 18, 2006 #5C	Nov 14, 2015 #6C	Nov 16, 2024 #4C	Nov 12, 2033 #4C
Nov 14, 2009 #5C	Nov 17, 2018 #7C	Nov 13, 2027 #3C	Nov 15, 2036 #5C
Nov 17, 2012 #6C	Nov 13, 2021 #7C	Nov 16, 2030 #4C	Nov 12, 2039 #5C

The Twelfth Week in Kingdomtide

Begins in the Sunday nearest November 16. Alphabyte: Year, p. 115

Sunday　　　　　　　*The End Times Are Here.*　　　　　　　**Mark 13:1–8**

**Do not worry beforehand about what you are to say; but say whatever is given you at that time,
for it is not you who speak, but the Holy Spirit. v. 11**

The only remnant of the Second Temple in Jerusalem, destroyed in 70 A.D., is the Wailing Wall. Jewish people pray as their hands touch this relic; they grieve over the loss of their sacred space.

Whether the date of the end of the world is near or far, it matters not: these are the end times. Jesus risen is the New Temple. There is no other place of safety but in Jesus. There is a New Creation because of the resurrection. In this sacred temple, the Holy Spirit will prompt your responses to those coming against you from the kingdom of the world.

Pray for the redemption of those presently lost, that when the temple of their body is taken away, they will be saved and found living forever with the saints in the Heavenly Kingdom.

Monday　　　　　　　*The Abomination of Desolation*　　　　　　　**Daniel 11:29–45**

**He shall seduce and intrigue those who violate the covenant;
but the people who are loyal to their God shall stand firm and take action. 11:32**

Daniel and Jesus speak of "The Abomination of Desolation." Jesus tells the disciples about this before the Passion, announcing the end of the Temple and of Jerusalem itself. The phrase refers to the altar to Zeus placed on top of the altar of burnt offerings in the Temple. It is the ultimate sacrilege. The rest of the chapter in Daniel continues the theme of the arrogance of national rulers as their passion for power sweeps them away.

Notice what happens in your heart as you read about these godless energies described. The opposite quality to pride and arrogance is meekness. Jesus said that it was the meek who will possess the earth (Matt. 5:5)—those who let the energies of life pass through them, and move on, without seeking control over others.

Tuesday　　　　　　　*Radical Reformation and Exile*　　　　　　　**2 Kings 23—25**

**Josiah read in their hearing all the words of the book of the covenant
that had been found in the house of the LORD. 23:2**

In your imagination, transport yourself back 2,500 years when our spiritual ancestors were besieged and wrenched away from their homeland. Their homeland was also a God-land. Josiah takes radical steps to root out idolatry. The same purity of heart and Godlike focus are essential today.

Those of us in the United States have no direct experience of a foreign invader coming against us to take us captive into exile. Yet a condition of spiritual exile exists for so many. The Holy Spirit will teach you about the Godly changes needed in society and in your own life as well. The cover of God's protection has so often been broken, not by foreign invaders, but by indifference to God and preference for self. This is nothing but idolatry.

Wednesday	*The Lord Reigns*	Psalm 93

Your throne is established from of old; you are from everlasting. v. 2

Do the circumstances of your life push and shove you about? If so, then ask the Lord to let this Psalm leave its impact on you. Images of permanency, stability, constancy, and timelessness move through the psalm. Pray slowly, until you are resting before the throne of God. No outer or inner source need ever move you from there. Your God is higher and mightier than what is coming against you. Trust God's changeless love for you and God's power over your circumstances. May you come to know this with such assurance, that you are totally resting in the Lord.

Teresa of Avila expressed it this way: "This too will pass … God alone suffices."

Thursday	*The Protective Hand of God*	Revelation 8—9

When the Lamb opened the seventh seal,
there was silence in heaven for about half an hour. 8:1

Horrors are described that would be put the most advanced cinema technology to the test. Chaos irrupts in these chapters of the last book of the Bible that make us wonder if the order God created in Genesis has been totally reversed.

Yet three aspects of this reading remind us that order is still in effect. First is the half-hour of silence and tranquility just after the seventh seal is opened. Second, the prayers of the saints blend with the incense rising before the heavenly altar. Third, what happens is at the direction of God. These are not actions of a whimsical, reactive, wrathful God, but rather the consequences of arrogant, human violence that has been disrupting the order of creation. Evil will ultimately be vanquished; God will prevail.

If you and I were to have that half-hour of silence, prayer, and God's Word each day, we would be drawn by faith to know that all that happens in the course of the day must yield to the protective hand of God upon us.

Friday	*The Breath of Peace*	Mark 15:21–47

Then Jesus gave a loud cry and breathed his last. v. 37

As novices in religious life, we used to walk to the Hudson River on the grounds of our former Jesuit seminary, St. Andrew-on-Hudson, near Poughkeepsie, N.Y. Conversation would cease as we paused before a large wooden crucifix. It was a gift from a community dedicated to the Passion of Jesus, from the village of Oberammergau in southwest Germany. Inscribed above it were the words, "From the arms of the Crucified, the breath of peace moves slowly across the world."

As this year of grace draws to a close with the celebration on Sunday of Christ the King, may you be in touch with the immense peace that can flow across and into your life because your King died on the cross for you. May this be a Good Friday for you, one of gratitude and tender love for your Redeemer and Lord who loves you so much.

Saturday **The Sabbath Torah Reading**

Nov 25, 2006 #6C	Nov 21, 2015 #7C	Nov 23, 2024 #5C	Nov 19, 2033 #5C
Nov 21, 2009 #6C	Nov 24, 2018 #8C	Nov 20, 2027 #4C	Nov 22, 2036 #6C
Nov 24, 2012 #7C	Nov 20, 2021 #8C	Nov 23, 2030 #5C	Nov 19, 2039 #6C

12 Ki B

The Thirteenth Week in Kingdomtide

Begins in the Sunday nearest November 22. Alphabyte: Zoom Lens, p. 115

Christ the King Sunday   *Jesus Your King*   **John 18:33–37**

**For this I was born, and for this I came into the world,
to testify to the truth. v. 37**

With eyes of faith, gaze upon Jesus your King standing before Pilate, a puppet governor. Jesus is clothed in a purple robe, the color of kings. His blood turns the cloak yet into greater kingly crimson. Listen in on their somber conversation about truth and power. Though they speak on a level plane, face to face, Jesus' word invites us to lofty heights of understanding and belief.

Pray to the Spirit that you comprehend the exalted nature of Jesus' Kingdom. Though bloodied and beaten, Jesus is the only Lord of glory, power, and might. Through his love, surrender, and total dedication to the Father's plan, Jesus finds his kingship. No other place but in Jesus will you fulfill the plan that the Father has for you.

Monday   *The Whiteness of God's Glory*   **Daniel 12**

**Go your way and rest;
you shall rise for your reward at the end of the days. v. 13**

This chapter of Daniel is similar to the Gospel accounts of Jesus speaking about the final times. The images of Daniel's vision—own them. Recall the vision of the saints in Revelation 7:14, read a few Thursdays ago, those who "Washed their robes and made them white in the blood of the Lamb."

Made white by what is red—that is transformation of suffering into glory. The blood of Jesus flows over you; pain and suffering are turned into glory.

Your King dies on the cross for you. As you are lifted onto the cross with Jesus, you are also lifted into the glory of the resurrection.

Tuesday   *Serenity*   **Ecclesiastes 5—8**

Do not be quick to anger, for anger lodges in the bosom of fools. 7:9

An aged, somber Solomon is traditionally thought to have written the Book of Ecclesiastes. Though modern scholarship shows that this is not the case, yet we can muse that long years of wisdom—and many years of not-so-wise behaviors—could beget ponderous sayings from a pessimistic spirit that perhaps pervaded the soul of this ancient king in the evening of his life. Flowing beneath the somber, sober tones, there is detachment from worldly concerns that sends a sweet flow of serenity into your soul.

It is the end of the church year and the end of the solar year as well, for autumn is the end of what has begun in spring. Jewish people read Ecclesiastes in its entirety as part of their autumn harvest holiday, the Feast of Tabernacles, *Sukkot.*

I suggest you take each of the four chapters at different times of the day, perhaps morning, afternoon, evening and before retiring. The passages are especially suited to the end of the day, as a symbol of the end of life.

**13
Ki
B**

Wednesday   *Etchings on the Heart*   **Psalm 94**
When the cares of my heart are many, your consolations cheer my soul. v. 19

When a child is about to make a sandcastle on the beach, he or she first takes the forearm and clears a smooth space in the sand, soon to receive the creative shapings. It is the same for us when we begin to pray.

Clear a space within. When the Holy Spirit speaks, your soul will receive the words as God shaping your soul. Listen inwardly to what you read so that the finger of God will etch the Word on you soul. Recall the words of St. Paul in Romans 10:17: "Faith comes by hearing, and hearing by the Word of God."

What moves you as you listen? What does the Spirit seek to etch upon your heart, turned from a heart of stone to one of flesh by God's love?

Your journal page is as the sand, waiting to receive what the Spirit says to you. Yet unlike sandcastles, the clear Word of the Lord remains forever.

Thursday   *Eating the Scroll*   **Revelation 10—11**
So I took the little scroll from the hand of the angel and ate it;
it was sweet as honey in my mouth,
but when I had eaten it, my stomach was made bitter. 10:10

Co-dependency is a modern name for an old disease, indeed an old and original sin—doing what others want instead of what God wants. God's grace can cancel this, so that we can become prophetic witnesses.

Eat the scroll of the Word today. Digest it and be aware of the spiritual feelings that accompany it—sweetness because it is the Word of God; bitterness because authentic prophesy means suffering and even death to self.

Be encouraged by these strong chapters that conclude this year's reading of Revelation. Just as we began five Thursdays ago with the three hymns of chapters 4 and 5, linger for a long time with the two hymns that conclude chapter 11, allowing them to echo in joy and triumph within the walls of your soul.

Friday   *The Great Commission*   **Mark 16**
Go into all the world and proclaim the good news to the whole creation.
The one who believes and is baptized will be saved;
but the one who does not believe will be condemned. v. 16

This is the last day for reading the Gospel in the current church year. The mystery is before you in all its brilliance—the resurrection of Jesus and your commission as a disciple. The promises of the Lord's power and presence unfold. Signs and wonders will follow those faithful disciples sent forth into the world for the conversion of others.

There is no other meaning to life than this Great Commission. Spend time reflecting over the past year. See everything in terms of the purpose of your existence—to give praise and reverence to God and to serve the Lord with all your heart.

The Lord you see with the eyes of faith ascending into heaven is coming again; the mystery is about to cycle itself through your life once again in Advent. Jesus is coming!

13
Ki
B

Saturday   **The Sabbath Torah Reading**

Dec 02, 2006 #7C	Nov 28, 2015 #8C	Nov 30, 2024 #6C	Nov 26, 2033 #6C
Nov 28, 2009 #7C	Dec 01, 2018 #9C	Nov 27, 2027 #5C	Nov 29, 2036 #7C
Dec 01, 2012 #8C	Nov 27, 2021 #9C	Nov 30, 2030 #6C	Nov 26, 2039 #7C

ADVENT
TO
EPIPHANY

WINTER

Northern Hemisphere

Year C
2007, 2010, 2013 …

Advent begins every year
on the Sunday nearest November 30, St. Andrew's Day.
See the entire cycle of readings at a glance on page xx.

The First Sunday in Advent

Begins on the Sunday nearest St. Andrew's Day, Nov. 30. Alphabyte: Advent Wreath, p. 3

Sunday   *Piercing Dark Silence*   **Luke 21:25–36**
**Be alert at all times, praying that you may have the strength to escape
all these things that will take place, and to stand before the Son of Man. v. 36**

A shrill blast pierces the silence of the descending darkness of an autumn evening. It is the *shofar*, the ram's horn, summoning the people to a sobering awareness of the end times as the Jewish New Year begins in autumn.

Today the New Year for the Church begins. The voice of Jesus sounds the call for readiness, awareness, sobriety, watchfulness—in short, for prayer. The message shakes us to our roots, loosening those places within where we are bound to a world passing away.

What the *shofar* is to the silence, the first Advent candle is to the darkness. Enter the beauty of the darkness of this season and the way in which tiny particles of light pierce the night with an expanding joy. Jesus is coming.

Monday   *Light in Womb's Darkness*   **Isaiah 56**
**Better than sons and daughters, I will give them [eunuchs]
an everlasting name that shall not be cut off. 56.5**

W hat future is there for a eunuch? No progeny—only endless cycles of boring chores, as worker bees in a hive, unable to make the queen fertile. However, the miracle of children and a future will come even for them, if they keep Sabbath sacred space—wombs of time, fertilized by fidelity to God's Word.

The first Advent candle is lit, sowing a seed of light into the dark womb of night. Place yourself before the candle at the center of those places within where there is anything like despairing darkness. Resist the smugness of those beastly types with their vain feelings of power. Each of their tomorrows will become darker and darker.

Take hope. It is Advent. Jesus the light longs to make your heart fertile. Will you let him?

Tuesday   *The Return*   **Ruth 1**
**Where you go, I will go; where you lodge, I will lodge;
your people shall be my people, and your God my God. v. 16**

A s firelight itself, imagination leaps into the remote past over three thousand years ago. The Book of Ruth as a precious jewel is before us the Tuesdays of Advent, a chapter a week. The title of each *Firestarter* outlines a four-part division of the book. Ruth is the great-grandmother of David, ancestor of Jesus. From ages past, the Lord has been carefully preparing the cast of characters in the sacred drama of salvation. A foreign woman, faithful to her family, becomes the one the Lord uses in his plan.

About two-thirds of the book is dialogue, making it like a play. Picture the scenes. Feel the emotions of the characters. Mull over the theme of *return* present in this chapter. Enter the dialogue. Find your longing for Jesus increasing, your joy expanding.

| Wednesday | *A Song in the Night* | Psalm 95 |

O come, let us sing to the Lord;
let us make a joyful noise to the rock of our salvation! v. 1

Many religious communities begin their day of prayer in the middle of the night with a gentle explosion of firelight as they begin to chant Psalm 95. So it has been for fifteen centuries, under the inspiration of Benedict, Father of Western Monasticism. It is the first psalm of Advent this year.

Sense the joy of continuity as the fire of love within you blends with the fire of intercessors around the world, praying that the peoples of the earth be open to receive the Word of the Lord. Who knows what atrocities are averted because there are faithful brothers and sisters praying in this way! Instead of being prohibited from finally resting with the Lord, conversions take place and people hear at death "Come, you that are blessed by my Father, inherit the kingdom prepared for you from the foundation of the world." (Matthew 25:34)

| Thursday | *Stars of Hope in the Darkness* | 1 Peter 1:1–12 |

Blessed be the God and Father of our Lord Jesus Christ!
By his great mercy he has given us a new birth into a living hope
through the resurrection of Jesus Christ from the dead … v. 3

As stars scattered across an Advent night's sky, so does Peter write to Christians flung across Asia Minor. His words flow down the centuries to you to this very moment. If you are lonely, dejected, rejected, or even persecuted, then this letter is especially for you. Read and embrace words of hope intended to lift you from discouragement that comes when darkness seems more basic than light. Pause at those words and phrases that touch you, repeating them as you breathe the saving words of healing salvation.

In verse 4, the word "kept" is a military one. God is a powerful sentry to guard you from the hurt that the Evil One wants to inflict pain upon you. Be embraced by the light that is this passage.

| Friday | *The Saving Move of God* | Luke 1:1–25 |

With the spirit and power of Elijah he [John] will go before him (the Lord)
to turn the hearts of parents to their children, and the disobedient to the wisdom of the righteous,
to make ready a people prepared for the Lord. v. 17

The Gospel of Luke begins and ends in the Temple. Place yourself a short distance from Zechariah and spend time in quiet prayer with him. Open your heart by faith to what is about to happen. The longing of the ages is gathered into this high priest and his aged wife, earnestly praying, patiently waiting for God to make his saving move upon the earth.

Sense the awesome moment as Gabriel announces the first words of God's intervention on our behalf. Listen slowly to each phrase of the angel. Gabriel cites the final verses of the Old Testament found in Malachi 4:5–6. The dangling thread at the end of the Old Testament is gathered and attached to the wondrous new covenant, which begins to be woven in John the Baptist.

Sink into the scene. What movements does the Spirit make upon your heart?

Saturday — The Sabbath Torah Reading

Dec 09, 2006 #8C	Dec 05, 2015 #9C	Dec 07, 2024 #7C	Dec 03, 2033 #7C
Dec 05, 2009 #8C	Dec 08, 2018 #10C	Dec 04, 2027 #6C	Dec 06, 2036 #8C
Dec 08, 2012 #9C	Dec 04, 2021 #10C	Dec 07, 2030 #7C	Dec 03, 2039 #8C

The Second Week in Advent

Begins on the Sunday nearest December 7. Alphabyte: Bible, p. 4

Sunday   *Repentance*   **Luke 3:1–6**
Prepare the way of the Lord, make his paths straight. v. 4

Another sound fills the Advent sky—the cry of John the Baptist from the barren wilderness at the heart of life. The voice was heard centuries earlier, when Isaiah promised a time when all twisted, crooked, uneven, rough, out-of-balanced parts of the world would be made straight and smooth again.

These promises will be fulfilled within us on one condition—repentance. The word in Greek, *metanoia*, means a change of heart and attitude, a total shift in the way in which we look at things. The way of selfishness and sin, of resentment, of fear, of being a victim, is over.

Are you serious about the changes that need to take place in you? What kind of repentance needs to happen that would unlock a deep rush of Godly love within you? Ask the Spirit, who will tell you—if you are serious.

Monday   *Silence and Listening*   **Isaiah 57**
I dwell in the high and holy place,
And also with those who are contrite and humble in spirit. v.15

Six identical letters make up the words "silent" and "listen." If you would listen to the sound of the voice of the Lord through Isaiah in this passage, then your heart must become silent, so that you hear only the sounds of these verses in your depths.

Notice the stunning hardness of heart of those who have yielded to idolatry. Once the first commandment is broken, all the others follow as rows of falling dominoes. The Lord takes you to the silent heights where God dwells. Feel God's pain. Believe in God's compassion—infinitely greater than the sin of idolatry. What does the Lord say to you? Do you have sanctuaries of delight other than the Lord's home within you?

Tuesday   *Gleaning the Forgotten*   **Ruth 2**
Where did you glean today? And where have you worked?
Blessed be the man who took notice of you. v.19

The word "glean" often occurs in this chapter. This is the gathering of the leftover grain after the reapers have completed the harvest.

Notice the sensitivity and reverence that fills the charm of the love story between Boaz and Ruth as the Lord *gleans* Ruth—an otherwise forgotten foreign woman. Just as Jesus' disciples glean and gather the fragments of the multiplied loaves lest they be lost, so does God gather this woman into the sacred family that will blossom into Jesus.

Be sensitive to the spiritual feelings that the Holy Spirit will give you as you enter this story. Are you ignored and passed over at times? The Holy Spirit is gathering up the fragments of your forgotten person into the Body of Jesus … lest you be lost.

	2
	Ad
	C

Wednesday *A New Song to the Lord* **Psalm 96**

Let the field exult, and everything in it.
Then shall all the trees of the forest sing for joy. v. 12

Today's psalm invites you to become a composer and sing a new song to the Lord. The psalm will lift your heart to join the chorus of creation singing praises to the Lord for the pure fact of existence. You might begin to hum or sing in a spontaneous way, just as do the birds and the sound of the wind in the trees.

We humans are the only ones that get into bad moods. The rest of creation perfectly expresses the response of joy in being created. Yet we enhance this when we "let the field be joyful and all that is in it." In the Body of Christ, we have dominion over the earth again, as Adam once had. *You* be the songwriter for creation that looks to you to make a symphony of praise!

Thursday *Walking Freely* **1 Peter 1:13–25**

Prepare your minds for action; discipline yourselves; set all your hope
on the grace that Jesus Christ will bring you when he is revealed. v.13

When we pick up a lamp or small appliance, we need to gather up the cord so that we do not trip. In New Testament times, people wore long clothes that hung down by the feet. To move quickly, they would gather the lower part of their clothing and tie it to the waist so that they would not fall. This is the meaning in "prepare" your minds.

What are the loose and hanging ends of your thoughts and attitudes? Do they tend to trip you? Gather them. Tie them up, away from your spiritual feet that need to move freely and joyfully through the power of the Word of God today. Be specific; jot down what you discover.

Verses 18–21 gather the whole Gospel into a small space. Tie these verses about your mind as you walk in the light of these truths. When the Evil One seeks to trip you, you'll be able to see clearly where you are going.

Friday *A Day with Holy Women* **Luke 1:26–56**

My soul magnifies the Lord,
and my spirit rejoices in God my Savior. vv. 46–47

Enter the joyous story of the call to Mary to become the mother of Jesus, her visit to Elizabeth, and her song. Be with Mary in the morning, as her prayer is bathed in the light of *The Annunciation*. Travel with her during the hours of the morning, till you reach Elizabeth at midday, reading the account of *The Visitation* around noon. Stay with these holy women until evening, concluding with hearing Mary sing *The Magnificat*. For ages this has been the song for Evening Prayer in the Catholic and Anglican traditions. This first of three songs in Luke's infancy narrative has a parallel in the song of Hannah (1 Samuel 2:1–10) who rejoices at the birth of Samuel.

This is the season of miracle birthings … including your miraculous rebirth in Jesus.

Saturday **The Sabbath Torah Reading**

Dec 16, 2006 #9C	Dec 12, 2015 #10C	Dec 14, 2024 #8C	Dec 10, 2033 #8C
Dec 12, 2009 #9C	Dec 15, 2018 #11C	Dec 11, 2027 #7C	Dec 13, 2036 #9C
Dec 15, 2012 #10C	Dec 11, 2021 #11C	Dec 14, 2030 #8C	Dec 10, 2039 #9C

The Third Week in Advent

Begins on the Sunday nearest December 14. Alphabyte: Chimes, p. 4

Sunday   *Winning Friends: NOT!*   **Luke 3:7–18**
Bear fruits worthy of repentance. v. 8

St. Luke is the evangelist that lets us listen in on the largest segment of John the Baptist's preaching. John astounds whole crowds with ear-piercing calls to repentance. The opening verse of the reading hardly follows the principles of Dale Carnegie's *How to Win Friends and Influence People!* John is not on a self-centered search for friends; he is out to win hearts for the Kingdom—your heart and mine.

Luke singles out three classes of people and specific changes needed for each: 1) people in general; 2) tax collectors; 3) soldiers. The essence comes down to sharing with those in need.

Place yourself among the crowd. Now is no different than then. There is no time to mince words. The Holy Spirit gets right to the point with you. Allow the Lord to burn away what is dead in you, so that what needs to come to life has inner space to grow.

Monday   *Doing What Delights the Lord*   **Isaiah 58**
**Is not this the fast that I choose; to loose the bonds of injustice,
to undo the thongs of the yoke, to let the oppressed go free,
and to break every yoke? 58:6**

Prophecies that release new energies for worship and for lively contact with the Lord—this is the passion of Isaiah. Take a piece of paper, put a line down the middle, noting on the left those actions that delight the Lord, on the right side, those in which you alone take delight. Do you notice a difference? Pray against a spirit of religiosity; this would have acts of worship be apart from making justice and peace.

Be moved by the passionate concerns of the Lord, becoming one with the priorities of God. Catch the inner sense of the meaning of the word "delight," used four times. Each of these verses has the power to make the rough places in your life smooth for the coming of the Lord.

Tuesday   *At the Feet of Love*   **Ruth 3**
Go, uncover his feet and lie down; and he will tell you what to do. v. 4

A mother-in-law's advice is followed: Ruth places herself at the feet of Boaz. Picture her there—vulnerable, chaste, respectful, trusting. A woman on the margin of Jewish life, because she is a foreigner, waits quietly before Boaz, hoping to see what will happen when love quickens in his heart. Consider how misunderstood she might be as Boaz awakes in the middle of the night to find her there.

"At the feet of love …" Play with this phrase in your heart as you pray, recalling Mary of Bethany in John's Gospel and the unnamed woman in Luke, both of whom cast themselves before another's feet—Jesus, Boaz' descendant. You do the same before Jesus. Just as Boaz was Ruth's only hope in life, so is Jesus before whom you are right now, the only one who can take you from whatever outcast state where you might find yourself, into the spousal love of Jesus who takes you to himself.

Wednesday   *Praise to the Sovereign Lord*   **Psalm 97**
Light dawns for the righteous, and joy for the upright in heart. v. 11

Here, in the center of Advent, a joyful cry wells up from God's people. While taking a stand against Godless people, the psalmist vigorously affirms the liberating truth that the world is subject to the creative power of the Lord.

Two things happen when we enter into the spirit of these ten Sabbath songs, Psalms 90—99. First, order occurs in our own hearts with respect to the power of God's presence in us and in the world. Second, by becoming spokespersons for all of creation, our faith goes far to restore the proper order of creature to creator, releasing the power of God's Spirit upon the whole of creation. As the Lord gives you specific persons and circumstances that need your intercession, yield to the Spirit. Become aware of those for whom you need to pray.

Thursday   *A Living Stone*   **1 Peter 2:1–10**
You are a chosen race, a royal priesthood, a holy nation,
God's own people, in order that
you may proclaim the mighty acts of him
who called you out of darkness into his marvelous light. v. 9

When the robot landing on Mars took place in the spring of 1997, the first item on the agenda was to name the rocks discovered. These distant, unknown objects were now placed into clear, visible light, taking on personalities. Similarly, there is a Jewish legend that tells of the pride that each rock had as it was selected to be part of the Temple of Solomon. One uneven, misfitting rock was rejected, thrown down a cliff into a refuse heap below. When the time came to complete the Temple, there was a space that needed that rejected rock. It was searched down, discovered, and placed as the capstone that completed the Temple. Peter has this in mind in today's passage.

Receive yourself as Jesus welcomes you—a unique, special rock, named and placed into the living stone, which is Christ Jesus.

Friday   *A Song of Peace*   **Luke 1:57–80**
To give light to those who sit in darkness and in the shadow of death
to guide our feet into the way of peace. v. 79

John the Baptist is born from the silent womb of Elizabeth; a song births from the silent tongue of Zechariah. He breaks out in a poetic expression that for centuries would become the hymn to close Morning Prayer in the church. Notice how the words link Jewish longing for salvation, and fulfillment in the coming Lord.

Sense the contrast between darkness and light, between silence and word. Close your eyes in silent waiting as a preparation to allow the Holy Spirit, released from the heart of Zechariah, to well up from you, as you become one with this prayer of the ages.

The hymn closes with the first of fourteen references to *peace* in the Gospel of Luke. Let peace be in your breathing and your speaking this day. Who is going to receive the comforts of this hymn from you?

Saturday   **The Sabbath Torah Reading**

Dec 23, 2006 #10C	Dec 19, 2015 #11C	Dec 21, 2024 #9C	Dec 17, 2033 #9C
Dec 19, 2009 #10C	Dec 22, 2018 #12C	Dec 18, 2027 #8C	Dec 20, 2036 #10C
Dec 22, 2012 #11C	Dec 18, 2021 #12C	Dec 21, 2030 #8C	Dec 17, 2039 #10C

The Fourth Week in Advent

Begins on the Sunday nearest December 21. Alphabyte: Darkroom, p. 5

Sunday   *Leaping for Joy*   **Luke 1:39–45**

When Elizabeth heard Mary's greeting, the child leaped in her womb.
And Elizabeth was filled with the Holy Spirit ... v. 41

A masterpiece of the great sixteenth century artist, Michelangelo, stretches across the ceiling of the Sistine Chapel in Rome. At the center, God and Adam lovingly and longingly stretch out their hands and fingers to each other. The feeling of being freshly created is awesomely captured by the artist, as their fingers are separate, yet connected. In a similar sense is the visit with Mary and Elizabeth. John in his mother's womb leaps for joy in the presence of Jesus, the new Adam inside Mary.

Clear away the debris in your heart that clutters the space between your heart and the heart of God in Christ. Then you will leap for joy at the desperate nearness of your Savior who is re-creating you right now.

Monday   *When God Seems Far Away*   **Isaiah 59:1–15a**

See, the LORD's hand is not too short to save,
Nor his ear too dull to hear. 59:1

Are you tempted to give up on God, saying to yourself: "He just doesn't hear me?" Take the first verse to heart. Repeat it often until the power of its truth loosens comfort and joy within you.

Someone once said; "If God seems far away, guess who moved?" Verse 2 echoes this truth. Isaiah provokes and incites with his images, confronting us with the full awareness that sinful behavior places barriers that separate us from the Lord. Each of us is responsible for this separation.

Habits that break communion with the Lord tend to progress into circles that become more and more vicious. Isolation is the outcome. This Advent prophet will shake your foundations until you are resting only in the Lord Jesus who is about to come.

Tuesday   *Love at the Center*   **Ruth 4**

He shall be to you a restorer of life and a nourisher of your old age. v.15

The story of Ruth is complete. In Bethlehem, she bears Obed who becomes the grandfather of David. On or about these days, we celebrate the birth of the Lord Jesus, Son of David—also born in Bethlehem.

Consider the loving care of the Lord quietly to build the house of David over long centuries. God takes the forgotten, the left out, those on the edge, and makes them the center.

It is love that moves you to the center of life. Right now, place yourself in God's center, not far away at the brink of life without God. Wait upon the Lord, praying in this way: "Lord, where would you have me go today? Whom do you want to reach through me? Remind me, lest I be among those who ignore your preferences, because I cling to mine. Amen"

An Altar of Praise
**O sing to the LORD a new song,
for he has done marvelous things. v.1**

The psalmist is a conductor of a symphony of praise. It would seem that unless he prays, the very praise of creation is inhibited.

Yes, *you* have a spiritual voice to sing a new song of praise everyday for a creation that is billions of years old. If you do not pray and work for the Lord today, there are some things that just will not be done at all. Ministry and the Lord's work will be impaired.

You are a priest of all creation. Teilhard de Chardin, the noted twentieth century theologian and paleontologist, sees the world as an altar. Place upon it your praise, intercession, joys, and sufferings. The world will come to prayer through you.

Thursday   *Suffering Shame for His Name*   **1 Peter 2:11–25**
**To this you have been called, because Christ also suffered for you,
leaving you an example, so that you should follow in his steps. v. 21**

The Greek, *hupogrammos,* "example," literally means an "underwriter." Just as insurance companies have underwriters that support legitimate claims, so does Christ's suffering and death give us the grounding and support to withstand unjust treatment that may come our way.

Rather than focus upon yourself as a victim of mistreatment, shift the focus upon a truth that gave the early Christians profound comfort when they were falsely accused. "They departed from the presence of the council, rejoicing that they were counted worthy to suffer shame for his name." (Acts 5:41). There is no spiritual or physical suffering that you can experience that Jesus did not first endure. Find joy in being treated as Jesus, being one with him in his sufferings, so that you can be one with him in his resurrection.

Friday   *His Tent Among Us*   **John 1:1–18**
**In the Beginning was the Word
and the Word was with God and the Word was God. v.1**

The Gospel of John and the Book of Genesis both begin with, **"In the Beginning."** St. John describes the pre-existence of the Son of God in a poetic expression linking heaven and earth. The frame of bounded time is set against the expanse of eternity. Into this frame enters the eternal Word.

Four times in the prologue—nowhere else in this Gospel—the Greek, *charis* is used, usually translated into English as "grace." This is the action of God as it enters our human lives. It is the New Testament term for the loving-kindness of God as found in the Hebrew Scriptures. Keeping with the sense of God's presence among the desert-wandering Jews in the tabernacle, John asserts, "The Word was made flesh and has pitched his tent among us" (author's translation).

God moves out of time to be in time—yours, so that you can be in eternity now. Pray this awesome passage.

Saturday   **The Sabbath Torah Reading**

Dec 30, 2006 #11C	Dec 26, 2015 #12C	Dec 28, 2024 #10C	Dec 24, 2033 #10C
Dec 26, 2009 #11C	Dec 29, 2018 #13C	Dec 25, 2027 #9C	Dec 27, 2036 #11C
Dec 29, 2012 #12C	Dec 25, 2021 #13C	Dec 28, 2030 #10C	Dec 24, 2039 #11C

Christmas Week
Begins on the Sunday nearest December 28. Alphabyte: Evergreens, p. 5

Sunday   *The Gospel in Small Space*   Luke 2:41–52
**After three days they found him in the temple,
sitting among the teachers, listening to them and asking them questions. v. 46**

In Matthew, the Wise Men come to Jesus; in Luke, Jesus goes to the wise men! Luke's story of "The Finding the Child Jesus in the Temple" gathers the whole of his Gospel into small space.

Picture this twelve-year-old lad in the midst of the throng approaching Jerusalem. Hear the singing of Psalms such as 122. It is Passover. Jesus, the paschal lamb, arrives in anticipation of his death. There is a hint of the resurrection as Jesus is found in the Temple "after three days."

Invite the boy Jesus into the temple of your heart. He tells you about the plans the Father has for you. Ask him to give you a feeling of the totality of your life, even finding in things that you loved as a child, anticipations of what would later come to flower in your life. Is there something that you were called to do from your youth that you still long to have happen?

Monday   *A New Consumerism*   Isaiah 59:15b–21
**When the enemy comes in like a flood,
the Spirit of the LORD will lift up a standard against him. v. 19**

Christmas for the world, is over. The presents have been bought, wrapped, given, and now lie exhausted beneath the tree. The retail world is *spent* after its meal of consumerism. The comparisons with past years will soon be in.

Isaiah shakes us, provoking us to fix our attention on the promises of Isaiah realized in Jesus. Exult with joy and confidence in the power of the verse for the day. The final one also bears the promise of the fullness and constancy of the Spirit's presence in your family for endless generations to come. Do you believe this promise? Memorize it until it is so soaked into you that unspeakable joy radiates from within, giving assurance to many others of a new consumerism—consumed *by his Love!*

Tuesday   *Vanity and the Manger*   Esther 1
**Then Ahasuerus sent letters to all the royal provinces …
Declaring that every man should be master in his own house. 1:22**

God's act of saving grace in Jesus is prefigured in many Hebrew saints and heroes. In Advent, the humble, self-sacrificing Ruth, becomes an ancestor to Jesus. Moving soon into the Epiphany portion of this sacred season, we lift up Esther, another woman totally dedicated to the salvation of God's people, risking her life, as did Jesus.

Jesus the King is born. Contrast him with the extravagance and pride of Ahasuerus and the vanity of Queen Vashti. God is quietly working out salvation amid the decrees of emperors and kings.

Chapter 1 sets the stage for this powerful and beautiful story of salvation. What personal reflections come to you about vanity and where the center of your life rests? Is it in any place other than the humble manger of Jesus' birth?

Wednesday	*From Heaven's Space*	Psalm 99

Extol the Lord our God;
worship at his footstool. Holy is he! v. 5

Let us be lifted up to the heavens to gain a perspective on the whole world. This is where the psalmist places himself as he composes this psalm. It is a song for worshipping the Lord on the Sabbath—the day of rest, the day of the Lord, the day to place all earthly works into the light of heaven.

When we are forgetful of the mighty, yet loving place that the Lord has over us, then preoccupation with the smallness of our world begins to bind with worry and anxiety. Lift your eyes to heavenly places where Jesus sits at the right hand of the Father and worship the Lord with abandon and joy. Heaven is not a far off, distant place; it is a spiritual reality where you can be whenever you give yourself in love and worship to the Lord.

Thursday	*A Quiet Spirit*	1 Peter 3:1–12

Let your adornment be the inner self with the lasting beauty
of a gentle and quiet spirit, which is very precious in God's sight. v. 4

Hesuchia is a lovely Greek word used only eleven times in the New Testament, here translated as "quiet spirit." Literally, it means, "holding one's seat." Instead of being shaken from physical or inner space by the demands and expectations of others, remain in quietness until the Lord lets you know how and when and where to respond. *Hesuchia* suggests going beyond the reactions to which we often yield, to the place where true spontaneity is born.

In terms of family relations, *hesuchia* is the eye of the hurricane, The silence of a faithful wife has power in winning over a husband without a word.

The entire passage breathes tranquility, yet energy, as well. Submission does not mean being degraded or disrespected. Neither does it mean being defensive about oneself in a prideful way. Wait. Yield. Be quiet. Soak your soul in the passage.

Friday	*Take the Child in the Arms*	Luke 2:21–40

My eyes have seen your salvation,
which you have prepared in the presence of all peoples ... vv. 30–31

Advent began with Zechariah in the Temple when Gabriel announced to him the conception of John the Baptist. Once again we are in the Temple with another aged man and woman who have been waiting and praying for salvation for God's people—Simeon and Anna. Mary and Joseph arrive to fulfill the requirements of the law, yet the Holy Spirit does the filling; three times the Spirit is referenced in verses 25 to 27.

Even as Zechariah's hymn, the *Benedictus* has been the centuries-old conclusion to the Church's Morning Prayer, so is Simeon's *Nunc Dimittis* the Church's Night Prayer. It is a brief hymn, easy to memorize, so appropriate to pray as each day closes, especially this week after Christmas and the Epiphany season coming.

As Simeon, take the Child into your arms and ask the Spirit to tell you how the salvation of the Lord was at work for you this day.

Saturday

			The Sabbath Torah Reading
Jan 6, 2007 #12C	Jan 2, 2016 #13C	Jan 4, 2025 #11C	Dec 31, 2033 #11C
Jan 2, 2010 #12C	Jan 5, 2019 #14C	Jan 1, 2028 #10C	Jan 03, 2037 #12C
Jan 5, 2013 #13C	Jan 1, 2022 #14C	Jan 4, 2031 #11C	Dec 31, 2039 #12C

The First Week in Epiphany

*Begins on the first Sunday in January. Alphabyte: **F**rankincense, p. 6*

Sunday   ***Moving With the Magi***   **Matthew 2:1–12**
We observed his star at its rising,
and have come to pay him homage. v. 2

From the outer fringes of creation and the place where the sun rises, searching wise men, the magi, "The Three Kings" yield to the gentle tug of a star. They arrive at the center of the earth, Jerusalem. There another king sits in luxury, complacency, and arrogance, surrounded by the Scriptures and those who supposedly know how to interpret them. And there is the infant king in Bethlehem—a mere five miles to the south.

Sense the irony, the contrasts, the evil, as well as the protection God gives to those who truly seek. In place of joy at the news that Jesus is born, fear grips Herod and his sickly entourage of pseudo wise men—the chief priests and scribes. Silently, prayerfully move with the magi, loosened from being held hostage by anyone or anything that is not the wondrous God who makes all things new.

Monday   ***Converging on Christ***   **Isaiah 60**
Arise, shine; for your light has come!
And the glory of the LORD has risen upon you. v. 1

The Advent candle has yielded to the intensity of the Star in the East—shining, moving, leading, drawing the entire world to the place of the glory of the Lord visited in Christ Jesus.

The trade centers of the ancient world are listed in a kind of procession of glory, all converging with their wealth upon the feet of Jesus, center of the universe. Isaiah's poetry does its work upon you as this new calendar year explodes with so much more than the passing fancy and fanfare of a New Year's Eve party.

May the joy of the season be sustained in you, growing within you as you receive the Christ whom the world is summoned to adore.

Tuesday   ***The Star-Queen***   **Esther 2**
The king loved Esther more than all the other women,
of all the virgins she won his favor and devotion. v. 17

Though God's name is never mentioned in the Book of Esther, the consuming energy of Esther and Mordecai is to protect and save God's people in the midst of a hostile and unbelieving world.

It is fitting to read the Book of Esther in the context of the story of wicked King Herod. Her name, Esther, fits the Epiphany season, for her name means "star" in Persian. Just as the Lord made smooth the way of Jesus in the midst of wicked plans, so did God do the same with the intrigues and conspiracies in the Book of Esther.

Consider your personal history. Trace the hand of God's saving grace in your life that has brought you to this day of salvation which the Lord has made for you. You have found favor in the sight of King Jesus!

Wednesday   *A Joyful Noise*   **Psalm 100**

Make a joyful noise to the LORD, all the earth. v.1

*H*alal is the word for "praise" in Hebrew. Hallelujah means "Praise Yah," the shortened name for *Yahweh*, the Covenant name for God.

Take the incentive this psalm gives to see the entire day as being in the Lord's presence—the essence of the joy in this psalm. Each hour of the day are as so many "courts" in the house of the Lord, places in time where you can encounter God. As you enter the doorway of each hour, let praise and thanks ring out along with the countless number of clocks chiming or watches beeping all across the land.

The Lord loves you very much, longs for closeness with you, and desires that you place all your cares on God. Allow whatever activity you are doing be done as a response in service to the Lord whom you love.

Thursday   *Defending the Hope*   **1 Peter 3:13–22**

Christ suffered for sins once for all, the righteous for the unrighteous,
in order to bring you to God. v. 18

*F*rom the death of the Innocents by King Herod, to the trials that you are enduring right now, all the resources for suffering with meaning are before you. In the very center of the passage, verse 18, lies the central truth that gives meaning to all unjust suffering.

Pray to move beyond self-defensiveness to intercession for your persecutors. Christ's suffering brought us closer to God; will you not let your suffering do the same for those who need salvation? How you respond to suffering is a powerful wake-up-call in others to a desire for God. As verse 15 indicates, be ready to defend the hope that is in you and not to defend the self.

Friday   *Anticipations*   **Luke 2:41–52**

Why were you searching for me?
Did you not know that I must be in my Father's house? v. 49

*S*ince I was a child, a work of art has hung in my room by C. Bosseron Chambers entitled, "Christ at Five." It depicts the boy Jesus seated on a little stool, playing with scraps of wood from Joseph's shop. Two pieces fall together forming a cross. Jesus pauses in his play … gazes upward with a look of wonder with a touch of worry … hands quietly resting on his lap … the little cross at his feet—anticipation.

Gather your childhood into your lap. What do you recall then that was an anticipation, a glimpse, of what your future life would become? Is there something back then that was lost in the temple of your heart that you need to find again? Look heavenward to your Father who holds your future in his hands. Go to the inner temple where Christ teaches your soul, as he did in the Temple.

Saturday   **The Sabbath Torah Reading**

Jan 13, 2007 #13C	Jan 09, 2016 #14C	Jan 11, 2025 #12C	Jan 07, 2034 #12C
Jan 09, 2010 #13C	Jan 12, 2019 #15C	Jan 08, 2028 #11C	Jan 10, 2037 #13C
Jan 12, 2013 #14C	Jan 08, 2022 #15C	Jan 11, 2031 #12C	Jan 07, 2040 #13C

The Second Week in Epiphany

Begins on the second Sunday in January. Alphabyte: Gold, p. 6

Sunday   *Rising to New Life*   **Luke 3:15–17; 21–22**

He will baptize you with the Holy Spirit and fire. v. 16

The early church found three Epiphanies of the Lord, contemplated this year on the first three Sundays of the New Year: The Magi, last week; The Baptism of the Lord, today; The Marriage Feast at Cana, next week.

In his baptism, Jesus begins the public ministry, taking on our sinful condition that needs to be washed clean. He descends into water as a sign of his death, rising and looking heavenward, in an anticipation of the resurrection.

Jesus takes us beyond water into the Baptism of the Holy Spirit and fire. As you pray this passage, surrender to the power of the Spirit to have you descend into the waters of your chaos, which threaten to drown you, and watch the waters become sacrament of resurrection for you. Look how God turns death-bound attacks against you into steppingstones toward life.

Monday   *Words of Comfort and Hope*   **Isaiah 61**

The Spirit of the LORD GOD is upon me, because the LORD has anointed me;
he has sent me to bring good news to the oppressed … v. 1

Epiphany light spreads out as the light of Jesus ignited in Bethlehem now lifts high before the whole earth. With the Baptism of Jesus, active ministry begins. Soon he returns to the synagogue in Nazareth. This Sabbath reading was handed to him, coming as readings of comfort and hope toward the end of the Jewish year in late summer.

The momentum of Epiphany builds; move with it. Are there personal aspects of your life or the lives of those close to you that could be described as in ruins?

Promises abound in this chapter. The Holy Spirit takes the inspired words of millennia meant for millions and tailors them just for you. When you hear the second personal pronouns from verse 10, are they not meant as though for you alone?

Tuesday   *The Power of Fasting and Prayer*   **Esther 3—4**

Go, gather all the Jews to be found in Susa, and hold a fast on my behalf
and neither eat nor drink for three days, night or day. 4:16

Esther knows the power of fasting to produce spiritual focus and hunger for God alone. Fasting also brings solidarity with her people as they intercede for her even as she intercedes for them before the King.

Haman and Herod—evil rulers cut from the same cloth of pride, arrogance, greed and hatred of goodness. Contrast the wickedness of Haman and his intrigues, with the oneness of mind and heart of Mordecai and Esther. Agreement in prayer brings power: "Wherever two or three are gathered in my name, there I am in the midst of them" (Matt. 18:20).

With whom do you find oneness of mind and heart in your walk with the Lord? Deepen this companionship as you take the power of the Lord into the courts of the world.

Wednesday   *Don't Even THINK of It!*   **Psalm 101**

I will sing of loyalty and of justice; to you, O LORD, I will sing. v. 1

The psalmist has set out to clean his spiritual, inner house. He decides what stays and what goes, according to the faith awareness of God in his life. He does not even want to think of wickedness, for this distracts him from looking upon the Lord. He protects the boundaries of his soul.

Make a list of those things that you look at that need to change in view of this psalm. Think T.V. Even when the good one wins, it is not before all kinds of violence, lying, evil speaking, and intrigue move across the screen and across your soul.

Welcome holy thoughts of love and peace as roommates in your inner house. Return to the first verse and let your heart sing of loyalty and justice, and all the fruits of the Holy Spirit that come when you let the Spirit in.

Thursday   *A Spiritual Inventory*   **1 Peter 4: 1–11**

**Like good stewards of the manifold grace of God, serve one another
with whatever gift each of you has received. v. 10**

Open your heart to the Lord in the reading, asking God to reveal to you all the spiritual gifts and qualities that you have. Take an inventory of them, without shame or withhold. Break beyond the flesh thoughts that say: "I can't do that," into the realm of the Spirit where words of Paul well up from your Spirit: "I can do all things through Christ who strengthens me" (Phil 4:13).

Take courage from today's reading. What is in the way of accepting and loving others more fully? What are you holding onto that blocks that special feeling of peace, which is the confirmation within that you are walking in love?

May you be a vessel today through whom God is glorified.

Friday   *Into the Center of History*   **Luke 3**

**The Holy Spirit descended upon him in bodily form like a dove.
And a voice came from heaven,
"You are my Son, the Beloved; with you I am well pleased." v. 22**

Each of the first three chapters of Luke's Gospel begins with a time-reference, placing Jesus in the depths of history. The ministry of Jesus begins, with its preparation in the preaching of John the Baptist. He preaches to you, readying you along with the crowd about John. The prophecy of Simeon pierced Mary's heart with the sword of suffering; so let the ax of John fall into the center of your being, unpacking the hidden recesses of sinfulness that may lurk there.

Jesus comes into the center of history, bringing transforming grace as earth and heaven unite in his Baptism. In Genesis 1:2,"The Spirit of God was hovering over the face of the waters." So here does the Holy Spirit hover over the waters of the Jordan and brings forth a new creation in Jesus.

What needs complete transformation in your life?

Saturday   **The Sabbath Torah Reading**

Jan 20, 2007 #14C	Jan 16, 2016 #15C	Jan 18, 2025 #13C	Jan 15, 2034 #13C
Jan 16, 2010 #14C	Jan 19, 2019 #16C	Jan 15, 2028 #12C	Jan 17, 2037 #14C
Jan 19, 2013 #15C	Jan 15, 2022 #16C	Jan 18, 2031 #13C	Jan 14, 2040 #14C

The Third Week in Epiphany

Begins on the third Sunday in January. Alphabyte: Homing Pigeon, p. 7

Sunday   *New Wine*   **John 2:1–11**
Do whatever he tells you. v. 5

Epiphany number three—The Marriage Feast at Cana. John places this event on "the third day." The number three is a symbol of completion.

Jesus came to give life in this first moment of glory. Notice the signs of non-life—no wine … no wedding festivity. We do not even see the faces of the newly weds. No water is in the huge earthen pots that lie empty, lifeless; there are likely cobwebs among them. There are six—the number of incompleteness.

Jesus moves at the command of his mother. The pots are filled to the brim with water, drawn out as wine. New life flows.

From your emptiness, Jesus longs to draw forth new wine. One condition: "Do whatever he tells you."

Monday   *The Bride and the Bridge*   **Isaiah 62**
As the bridegroom rejoices over the bride,
so shall your God rejoice over you. v. 5

The Lord longs for you as a spouse in a most intimate relationship. Wrap yourself in these words of comfort as you take joy in the preferential love of the Lord for you.

Take the second person pronoun as though directed to you alone. Become deeply enthused about renewal in your life, just as a bride sees herself in a new way, due to the unconditional love that her husband has for her. The radiance of the bridegroom flows into your life and outward to others in smiles and gestures of pure love, drawing others into the same love-field in which you are rejoicing. Your soul speaks as a newly wedded bride about what it is like to be so loved by God. You become the bridge for others to God.

Tuesday   *Today's Plan Complete*   **Esther 5—6**
Esther won the king's favor
and he held out to her the golden scepter that was in his hand. 5:2

Esther receives the scepter—symbol of kingly power. The favor of the king is but a sign of the favor Esther finds before God who quietly weaves a plan of salvation for the people. Slowly but surely, God is turning the wheels of justice. Soon the elements of the conspiracy against Mordecai and God's people will be turned upon the evil Haman. Jealousy, pride, and Godlessness fill the hearts of the enemy. The quiet fidelity of those who are enacting the plan of God is in sharp contrast.

Are you content to be in the background, faithfully responding to the Lord in the little details of life? Be confident that God can do great things with you, as long as today's part of the plan is completed. Your life is a quilt—each day's grace-lived square added to all your yesterdays makes a perfect work of art for the Lord.

| Wednesday | *Images for Prayer* | Psalm 102 |

Wednesday	*Images for Prayer*	Psalm 102	3 Ep C

I lie awake;
I am like a lonely bird on the housetop. v. 7

Similes and images flow throughout this psalm. As you encounter each one, your imagination brings you close to the psalmist who pours out his grief to God. Can you sense in your spirit how these images help you feel along with him?

As you reflect upon the movement of your own life, what images come forward? Here is where journal keeping can be a help. Your hand poised to write creates an inward readiness to receive those images from the Spirit that are personal to you. With them, you can write your own psalm as you pray this one.

Whatever is causing you pain—trust that it will pass. The salvation remains.

| Thursday | *Glory Resting Upon You* | 1 Peter 4:12–19 |

If you are reviled for the name of Christ, you are blessed,
because the spirit of glory, which is the Spirit of God, is resting on you. v. 14

As shining embers amid the smoldering ashes of suffering, the word "glory" rises up four times in this brief passage. The word in Greek is *doxa*, whose root means "thought" or "opinion." It comes to mean the good opinion of another, or their reputation. Applied to God, *doxa* is the radiance of God shining forth.

The word and its variations occur over two hundred and thirty times in the New Testament. In John's Gospel, it is closely connected with the great suffering and death of Jesus as the moment of God's glory. As with John, here glory joins suffering for Christ. God's own glory shines through the shame and suffering inflicted upon those who follow Jesus.

Repeat the word often throughout your day, beneath your breath, as GLORY rests on you and shines forth from within.

| Friday | *Deliverance from Evil* | Luke 4 |

Today, this Scripture has been fulfilled in your hearing. v. 21

The darkness of pride, jealousy, and unfaithfulness in the people are pitted against the humility, compassion, and fidelity of Jesus. Whether alone in the silence of the desert, or amid the crowds that want to throw him over a cliff, Jesus faces all the wiles of Satan in the strength of the Holy Spirit.

Take comfort. Whatever be the evil that is coming against you, it cannot withstand the inner power of the Holy Spirit available to you just for the asking. The Spirit is alive, capable of completing every word of this chapter and the whole Bible in your hearing. This is especially true as you meditate upon these same words of the Lord along with the many who are living the Scriptures in these daily readings.

God wills to deliver you from evil so that you can pass through its midst and be on your way—the Lord's way.

Saturday   **The Sabbath Torah Reading**

Jan 27, 2007 #15C	Jan 23, 2016 #16C	Jan 25, 2025 #14C	Jan 21, 2034 #14C
Jan 23, 2010 #15C	Jan 26, 2019 #17C	Jan 22, 2028 #13C	Jan 24, 2037 #15C
Jan 26, 2013 #16C	Jan 22, 2022 #17C	Jan 24, 2031 #13C	Jan 21, 2040 #15C

The Fourth Week in Epiphany
Begins on the fourth Sunday in January. Alphabyte: Ice Dancing, p. 7

Sunday   *The Epiphany at Nazareth*   **Luke 4:14–21**
Today this Scripture has been fulfilled in your hearing. v. 21

For some thirty years, Jesus lives quietly among friends and relatives. Sabbath after Sabbath he is present in the synagogue as the Torah readings cycle yearly, along with the companion readings from the Prophets. Now it is time for an "Epiphany at Nazareth."

It is late summer, or early autumn, toward the end of the Jewish year. The passage from Isaiah brings hope and anticipation as the year draws to a close, stirring hope in the people for the Messiah who was to come.

This is the setting as Jesus stands before his people to proclaim the reading. Receive Jesus with joy who everyday is fulfilling the Scriptures in your hearing.

Monday   *As a Father Loves His Children*   **Isaiah 63**
In his love and in his pity he redeemed them;
he lifted them up and carried them all the days of old. v. 9

The anointing upon the prophet Isaiah and the profound devotion he has for the Lord, bring power to his poetry. Be inspired by the expressions of faith that Isaiah shares with you. He weaves the sacred history of the Exodus as a thread of images for the present tapestry that expresses the desperate need of God's people for restoration. Note the intimacy of God caring for the people as a father tenderly cares for his children.

Isaiah is overwhelmed with compassion for the people and for you. His prayer from verse 15 sets fire to yours. Place yourself before God who longs to restore you to himself much more than you could ever want this. Remember the words of Paul: "If God is for us, who can be against us?" (Rom 8:31)

Tuesday   *Remember Whom You Serve.*   **Esther 7—8**
In every province and in every city ...
there was gladness and joy among the Jews, a festival and a holiday. 8:17

The power of God in Esther turns the evil prepared by Haman for others, upon himself. He dies on the very gallows prepared for Mordecai. The time of God's victory is at hand. The people rejoice.

As we move further into the Epiphany season, the brightness of the power of God in Christ illumines our paths and strengthens our days. If the Jews in Persia can rejoice over the protective hand of their God, how much more can we rejoice in the presence of Jesus through the Spirit, continually bringing the prideful powers of the world into subjection!

Esther never forgot her heritage as she stood before the powers of the world of her day. May we never forget to whom we belong and whom we serve as we go forth into the world, bringing all things into subjection through Christ Jesus.

All in Me Is Praise   Psalm 103

**Bless the Lord, O my soul,
And all that is within me, bless his holy name! v. 1**

An explosion in the soul takes place as the grace of the Lord gushes forth in extravagant praise.

How can our soul bless God? Is not God the one who blesses, we the ones who receive? To bless the Lord is to return gratitude, praise, and adoration to the Lord for the abundant blessings of life, faith, hope, and love that God has poured out upon us. God empowers you to do this. Your blessing the Lord completes the divine energy cycle. Out from God flows life: into you it comes. This can only occur when you return all thanks and praise to the Lord. Then the life of God is totally in motion within your soul, moving outward as saving grace for others. Praise God!

Thursday   *Rest in Peace*   1 Peter 5

**Discipline yourselves, keep alert. Like a roaring lion
your adversary the devil prowls around, looking for someone to devour. v. 8**

For centuries, monastic communities have been chanting this verse at the beginning of the final sacred hour of the day called *Compline*. The word means "complete," as the final prayer takes place before retiring. It suggests that the day is now complete by the final frame of prayer that finishes the day as a sacred work of art for the Lord.

As the day ends and you drop off to sleep, there is a final reminder that the dark energies of evil are still awake and at work. The world forgets that evil is a conscious, personal, malicious, energy constantly directed at destroying goodness by blatant, blasphemous affronts to the glory of God. "Be sober, be vigilant," but never afraid. The power of God exudes in all four verbs of verse 11. However strong are the forces of evil, the power and glory of God are greater still. Rest in peace.

Friday   *Into the Depths*   Luke 5

Put out into the deep water and let down your nets for a catch. v. 4

The scholarly word for a story in the Gospels is *pericope*. The word literally means a "cutting around." Just as we take a newspaper article and clip it out, so do the evangelists stand before the immense possibilities of stories about Jesus and make their selections under the inspiration of the Spirit.

Today there are five of these pericopes—three miracle stories and two debates. I suggest that you take one for each of the quarter parts of the day and evening. Take a spiritual "coffee break" and launch out into the depths of the Spirit. Catch the openness of Peter, the joy of the leper, the inventiveness of the paralyzed man who went down the roof for Jesus. Are you as desperate as he is for your healing?

Ask the Holy Spirit to make your spiritual skin new so that you can receive the power of Jesus without breaking apart at the seams!

Saturday   **The Sabbath Torah Reading**

Feb 03, 2007 #16C	Jan 30, 2016 #17C	Feb 01, 2025 #15C	Jan 28, 2034 #15C
Jan 30, 2010 #16C	Feb 02, 2019 #18C	Jan 29, 2028 #14C	Jan 31, 2037 #16C
Feb 02, 2013 #17C	Jan 29, 2022 #18C	Feb 01, 2031 #15C	Jan 28, 2040 #16C

The Fifth Week in Epiphany
Begins on the Sunday nearest February 1. Alphabyte: Journal, p. 8

Sunday   *Familiarity Breeds Contempt*   **Luke 4:21–30**
Truly I tell you, no prophet is accepted in the prophet's hometown. v. 24

In the Epiphany to the Magi, Jesus was accepted by foreigners and rejected by his own people. The same resistance occurs when Jesus returns to Nazareth. Likely, an over-familiarity with Jesus breeds a kind of contempt for him when the ministry begins. Jealousy, pride, and indignation rob the hometown people's hearts from being able to listen. They refuse to rejoice at the Messiah coming from among them. Sense the freedom that Jesus has to "call it as it is." You might reread the Old Testament stories alluded to by Jesus in 1 Kings 17:9 and 2 Kings 5.

Reflect upon yourself. Do you live according to others' images of you, or of God's? Conversely, is there someone in your life who finds it difficult to fulfill God's plan because you lack faith in God's vision for him or her?

Monday   *Embers*   **Isaiah 64**
**From ages past no one has heard, no ear has perceived,
no eye has seen any God beside you, who works for those who wait for him. v. 4**

A desperate cry begins the reading. The outburst tears open your soul to release yet greater longing within for God with images that reveal the manifest power of God's presence. Linger at verses where the Spirit especially sets fire to your heart. Pause … ponder … pray. Become an intercessor before the Lord for your city or town, expanding to the whole world that needs your prayer to bring it before the throne of God.

Firestarters are at the beginning of entrance into the Word; *Embers* are toward the end. These could be your reflections at the close of the day after living the day's passage.

The Holy Spirit invites you to that inner place where you are still and quiet before the Lord who loves you and embraces you. See what Paul does in 1 Corinthians 2:9 with verse 4.

Tuesday   *Reliving Sacred Events*   **Esther 9—10**
**These days of Purim should never fall into disuse among the Jews,
nor should the commemoration of these days cease among their descendants. 9:28**

Birthdays and special anniversaries transform the feeling of those days by sacred remembrance. It is the same for Purim, celebrated the month before Passover. The sacred writer emphasizes repeatedly the importance of reliving this saving event by the way in which future generations re-enact it as the cycles of years return. Here is the power of true celebrations: grace once poured forth is experienced again.

What are the saving events in your life that have brought you to the spiritual place where you are right now? Enter them once again, recall, and relive them until their timeless grace is released anew into your life. Beware of empty celebrations devoid of the Spirit. They tire the soul!

Wednesday   *Bless the Lord, O My Soul.*   **Psalm 104**

When you send forth your spirit, they are created;
and you renew the face of the ground. v. 30

Ignatius of Loyola, Sixteenth Century founder of the Jesuits, closes a thirty-day retreat, *The Spiritual Exercises,* with what he calls "The Contemplation to Attain Divine Love." In it, he describes God as being at work in creation. In the same way, a profound sense of the presence of God in all creation fills the psalmist. As he contemplates his world, every aspect is seen against the background of God's presence.

God is not just "out there," in a static, detached way. Rather is the Lord dynamically present creating saving events in your life. Trace the phrases of the psalm that express how God is at work. Allow your soul to vibrate with the same faith-awareness of the psalmist.

Verse 30 is found in ancient texts of the liturgy for Pentecost.

Thursday   *An Ascending Chain*   **2 Peter 1:1–12**

Support your faith with goodness, and goodness with knowledge, and knowledge with self-control,
and self-control with endurance, and endurance with godliness,
and godliness with mutual affection, and mutual affection with love. vv. 5–7

Peter urges his first recipients and us, his latest ones, to reverse the downward spiral of earthly lust into an ascent of virtues. There is a rising chain for us to climb with the energy of eight virtues, links in the upward movement. They are found in verses 5 to 7. Meditate upon each of them, sensing in your spirit how each yields to the next. Make each of these abstractions into inner spiritual realities by applying your senses to them, especially *tasting* each virtue as you receive the next one.

All of these, along with the theme of "knowledge of the Lord," weave through this letter as gifts from God. Their source rests upon the greatest gift of all—divine life pulsing through our human, mortal flesh.

Friday   *Nourishment for the Day*   **Luke 6**

Love your enemies, do good to those who hate you,
bless those who curse you, pray for those who abuse you. vv. 27–28

No one sits down and consumes three meals of the day all at once. Similarly, you may want to take the nourishment from God's Word today and divide it into smaller portions. Sense the contrasting movements of the chapter. Be with Jesus on the mountaintop as he seeks uninterrupted union with the Father before he calls the Twelve Apostles.

Think of it: Jesus prays. If the eternal Son of God sought out times for quiet prayer, how much more do you and I need to do the same. The absence of union with God in the lives of the Pharisees had them become the plaything of the forces of Satan through pride and religiosity.

Take time to listen to Luke's counterpart to Matthew: "The Sermon on the Plain." Read slowly ... pray deeply ... ponder the questions that Jesus puts to you.

Saturday   **The Sabbath Torah Reading**

Feb 10, 2007 #17C	Feb 06, 2016 #18C	Feb 08, 2025 #16C	Feb 04, 2034 #16C
Feb 06, 2010 #17C	Feb 09, 2019 #19C	Feb 05, 2028 #15C	Feb 07, 2037 #17C
Feb 09, 2013 #18C	Feb 05, 2022 #19C	Feb 08, 2031 #16C	Feb 04, 2040 #17C

The Sixth Week in Epiphany

*Begins on the Sunday nearest February 8. Alphabyte: **Kiln**, p. 8*
For 2013 and 2016, *this is the last week in Epiphany, beginning with Transfiguration Sunday; see page 284 for the Sunday reading, continuing below for the Monday-to-Saturday passages. Ash Wednesday occurs this week. Next week turn to The First Week in Lent, Year C, p. 286.*

| **Sunday** | *Obeying the Word* | **Luke 5:1–11** |

Master, we have worked all night long but have caught nothing.
Yet if you say so, I will let down the nets. v. 5

Hours of the night—the time for a fisherman to be successful on the Sea of Galilee. Get in touch with the fatigue, the frustration, the failure, and finally that looking forward to sleep after the nets are all cleaned, folded, and readied for the next evening's return to the deep.

However, all of this changes when Jesus comes on the scene. Picture Simon Peter and his friends listening to Jesus while they finish cleaning. Something begins to shift inside them as they listen to Jesus. Hearts begin to glow. Along with the sun, gentle smiles dawn upon their faces. They are ready for the command of Jesus to "Put out into the deep." Against all odds and contrary to their professional opinion, Peter obeys; Jesus commands.

Take the net of God's Word and cast it across your day.

| **Monday** | *God Hurts* | **Isaiah 65:1–16** |

I was ready to be sought out by those who did not ask,
to be found by those who did not seek me. v.1

Feelings get hurt; we all know the experience. Anguish and anger collide, at times irrupting in strong outbursts as rejection or even betrayal occurs in our lives.

Avoid falling into fear as you read about a "punishing God" that might echo from your upbringing. God hurts; the Holy Spirit grieves. Here God expresses exasperation and profound sadness at the outright idolatry of the people. Movement beyond the Chosen People is intimated by the irony of the verse for the day. There are many who seek God in their heart without knowing it. Conversely, there are those who profess faith in the Lord, but whose hearts are devoted to everything but God.

Is God your first love?

| **Tuesday** | *From Preying to Praying* | **Proverbs 7** |

Bind them [God's Words] on your fingers;
Write them on the tablet of your heart. v.3

When we remove the Word from life, all hell breaks out. First, come the gentle tugs of seduction in all its forms. The Evil One preys upon us, seeking to put some distraction between us and God's presence to us in the Word. The poetry of this chapter is designed to shock those being seduced into an awakening to the danger.

If you do not cling to the Lord, then sin will cling to you. Spend some time today taking inventory of those persons, places or things to which you are attached—and they to you. Plunge into God's saving presence, asking for the gift of detachment from everything so that you can attach yourself to the Lord and what God offers.

PRAY when being preyed upon!

Wednesday   *Promises in Song*   **Psalm 105**

Sing to Him, sing praises to Him;
Tell of all His wonderful works. v. 2

The first fifteen verses of this psalm are found in the song of David in 1 Chronicles 16:8–22 when the Ark of the Covenant was brought to Jerusalem. The Ark was the symbol of God's redemptive presence to God's people. David gathers into song, the promises that God made to Abraham, fulfilled in the Promised Land. We are the Lord's cherished recipients of these same promises—even greater ones in Jesus.

You could compose a song about your personal history. Ask the Holy Spirit to have you feel the fingers of God's love fashioning your own story of redemption. Epiphany light shines in your darkness powered by God's grace.

As you read the promises that punctuate this psalm, how are they fulfilled personally in your own life?

Thursday   *The Word Woven into Life*   **2 Peter 1:13–25**

We have the prophetic message more fully confirmed. You will do well to be attentive to this as to
a lamp shining in a dark place, until the day dawns and the morning star rises in your hearts. v. 19

The Eternal Word has leapt from heaven and woven itself into time. It is ready to be stitched into your life's fabric, stretching you beyond the limits of time, back into eternity, completing the circle.

As you hold your Bible and inwardly hear the Word today, the Holy Spirit is active right now. Peter confesses this, finding the validity of the Word in the Transfiguration experience of Christ, which he witnessed.

What are those life experiences that are the grounding points for your own faith? These are moments of Transfiguration. Yet we are to be as Peter who could not stay on that mountain, but had to rediscover the Word transfigured in the walk down the mountain into the "valley of the shadow of death" upon the cross.

Friday   *Jesus Under Your Roof*   **Luke 7**

Lord … I am not worthy to have you come under my roof. v. 6

Down through the ages, this verse has been repeated in liturgies before receiving communion. Did the centurion ever think that his faithfulness would be so long remembered?

We are never worthy of the Lord's presence under the roof of our lives. That is not the issue. Rather it is Jesus' great love for us that has him long to dwell with us. Yet there are dispositions of the centurion that prepared him for the miracle that flowered from his faith. Consider the irony: the man was a Roman soldier just like the ones that put the nails in the hands of Jesus. However, this man spent time hammering and nailing to make the furnishings of a place of worship under which roof he was not entitled to enter, because he was a gentile!

Note the human dispositions in the four stories of this chapter. Be sensitive to what happens inside you as you perhaps pray them each in quarter parts of the day.

Saturday   **The Sabbath Torah Reading**

Feb 17, 2007 #18C	Feb 13, 2016 #19C	Feb 15, 2025 #17C	Feb 11, 2034 #17C
Feb 13, 2010 #18C	Feb 16, 2019 #20C	Feb 12, 2028 #16C	Feb 14, 2037 #18C
Feb 16, 2013 #19C	Feb 12, 2022 #20C	Feb 15, 2031 #17C	Feb 11, 2040 #18C

The Seventh Week in Epiphany
Begins on the Sunday nearest February 15. Alphabyte: Laser, p. 9
For 2007, 2010, 2037and 2040, *this is the last week in Epiphany, beginning with Transfiguration Sunday. See page 284 for the Sunday reading, continuing below for the Monday-to-Saturday passages, except in 2040 when there is an extra week with no Monday-to-Friday readings. The Torah reading for Saturday, February 18, 2040 is #19. Ash Wednesday occurs this week. Next week turn to The First Week in Lent, Year C, p. 286. (Lent has already begun in 2013 and 2016.)*

Sunday   *Nothing But the Lord*   **Luke 6:17–26**
Blessed are you poor, for yours is the kingdom of God. v. 20

St. Matthew renders the first Beatitude as "Poor in spirit," to expand the meaning of poverty beyond those socially poor. Yet there is a preferential love that the Lord has for those who find themselves at the margin of life, powerless to compete with the "haves" who have managed to create "have nots." Those that are poor, while on the edge of life, are also at the brink of the joy of relying only on the power of God alone to bless, rather than on the power of the world to curse.

"Woe" is the opposite of "blessed." In other words, it is a curse. Luke speaks plainly. Be loosened from what you have, until you have nothing but the Lord.

Monday   *The Healing Joy of the Lord*   **Isaiah 65:17–25**
The wolf and the lamb shall feed together, the lion shall eat straw like the ox ... v. 25

Glorious images fill this week and next, springing from the joy of the Lord which God has planted in the heart of Isaiah. The power of God's saving grace is expressed by the utter transformation of the physical world into complete reconciliation and exuberant life.

Soak in these images of life. The final times of which Isaiah speaks are with us now in the age of the resurrection of Jesus—the Church. Though tainted with sin, the Church is the expression of the visions that well up from these verses.

All that may be at odds with you and your past, to which you have yet to be reconciled, is happening in the realm of the Spirit. Pray until all aspects of your life—past, present and future—are before you here and now in the healing joy of the Lord.

Tuesday   *Watch Beginnings*   **Proverbs 8**
**Happy is the one who listens to me, watching daily at my gates,
waiting beside my doors. v. 34**

Contrast the call of Wisdom today with the enticements of the seductress of last week. The former leads to life, the latter, to death. The seductress dresses up as wisdom, but only for a brief moment. At times, the devil comes as an "angel of light," only later, to envelop one in darkness. With wisdom comes the gift of discernment of spirits—the spiritual power to sense at the very outset, whether a thread of thoughts and desires leads toward death or toward life.

Verses 22 and following are a poetic and profound reflection upon the Second Person of the Blessed Trinity. Recall the opening of John's Gospel where, just as the sacred writer of Genesis and the author of today's passage, John penetrates to the very beginning of creation.

Watch beginnings. See where they lead.

**Save us, O Lord our God, and gather us from among the nations,
that we may give thanks to your holy name and glory in your praise. v. 47**

The sweep of God's covenant reviewed in last week's psalm takes place again today. Here, however, the focus is upon the sinful rejection of God's promises to our ancestors. Repeated acts of infidelity on the part of God's people bring not rejection and abandonment from God, but even greater expressions of God's fidelity.

As you scan the movement of your life, where have you been unfaithful to the Lord? The purpose of this is not to call up the ravages of guilt and remorse, but rather to place the Lord's loving acts toward you into even greater relief.

Who or what is your golden calf? Make the psalm personal to you. The same evils that tempted our ancestors are focused upon us today—all variations of the golden calf.

Thursday   *Peter's Passionate Plea*   **2 Peter 2**

**The Lord knows how to rescue the godly from trial,
and to keep the unrighteous under punishment until the day of judgment. v. 9**

Passionate pleas of Peter fill this chapter. There are strong words of warning to those who have come to know the Lord, yet are subject to the arrogance and lawlessness of the proud. Pride pits itself against the Lord. It seeks to soak others with its poison, dragging its victims away from the truth. We are reminded of what happened to the fallen angels.

Watch the company you keep. While not being tempted to deny faith outright, reflect upon how media producers work us over—those whose values and motives hardly come from a devotional attachment to the Word of Life.

Is there anything or anyone undermining your faith?

Friday   *Plummeted Into Devotion*   **Luke 8:1–25**

**To those who have, more will be given; and from those who do not have,
even what they seem to have will be taken away. v. 18**

This half chapter is neatly divided into five sections. Spread them through the hours of the day. Stay with what the Scriptures say about Mary Magdalene, resisting popular traditions about her as a prostitute. She was a demon-possessed person, as were others in the Gospel. Gratitude for her deliverance plummeted her into a profound devotion to Jesus, right up to the tomb, the morning of the resurrection, as recalled in John 20.

Your life is the field of "The Parable of the Sower." What kind of soil is your soul? Learn about what it takes to become part of the family of God, and about the faith that we need when the storms of life tempt us to plummet into despair, instead of into devotion.

Saturday   **The Sabbath Torah Reading**

Feb 24, 2007 #19C	May 21, 2016 #31C	Feb 22, 2025 #18C	Feb 18, 2034 #18C
Feb 20, 2010 #18C	Feb 23, 2019 #21C	Feb 19, 2028 #17C	Feb 21, 2037 #19C
May 25, 2013 #36C	Feb 19, 2022 #21C	Feb 22, 2031 #18C	Feb 18, 2040 #19C

The Eighth Week in Epiphany

Begins on the Sunday nearest February 22, unless Lent has begun. Alphabyte: Myrrh, p. 9
For 2031 and 2034, *this is the last week in Epiphany, beginning with Transfiguration Sunday. See page 284 for the Sunday reading, continuing below for the Monday-to-Saturday passages. Ash Wednesday occurs this week. Next week, turn to the First Week in Lent, Year C, p. 286.*

Sunday   *Non-Violent Violence*   **Luke 6:27–38**
"Love your enemies, do good to those who hate you, bless those who curse you,
and pray for those who spitefully use you." vv. 27–28

Karate chops of Jesus' blessings and woes of last week continue in today's reading. The heart of Jesus' revolution is about non-violent violence. Your enemy expects you to fight back, to hate, to curse, to strike out. When he receives the unexpected, he is thrown off balance and becomes disoriented and confused. The wind is taken out of the "sails" of violence.

The underlying message of the one turning the cheek is, "Your first attempt to insult and hurt me has failed; would you like to try it again? Is there not an alternative to violence?" The turned cheek has a spiritual violence about it—a karate chop to the soul.

Notice how Jesus gives a way out of chronic anger on the part of one attempted to be made a victim by some evil persecutor. If your heart is filled with prayer, blessing, and love for your enemy, joy can never be taken away from you.

Monday   *What Is Coming Is Here?*   **Isaiah 66**
… that you may nurse and be satisfied from her (Jerusalem's) consoling breast;
that you may drink deeply with delight from her glorious bosom. v. 11

Isaiah in this final chapter joins Matthew 25 with the sheep and goats, along with Revelation 21 in proclaiming the justice of God at the end of the world. Yet the end has already begun; the New Jerusalem is the church.

Be challenged to come to true worship. Move into the fullness of joy as you rest in prayer at the bosom of the church where the Holy Spirit feeds you with the very love of God. Your imagination is the mouth that takes in all the nourishment that the mother church longs to give you as her child.

When you are troubled with the injustices that make the headlines of the morning paper, claim in your heart that the triumph of justice will come. Will you live with the faith that believes that what is coming is already here?

Tuesday   *Beckonings of the Lord*   **Proverbs 9**
The fear of the Lord is the beginning of wisdom,
and the knowledge of the Holy One is insight. v. 10

Feelings of completion, fulfillment, satisfaction, celebration, and community flow from the images of wisdom. The power of poetry takes the abstract, investing it with all the vividness of the five senses.

Engage your senses as you read about the ways of wisdom, once again contrasted with the ways of the harlot. The Lord gives us our senses so that we can find God through them, and with God, God's plan for us.

Wisdom is a practical way of living. It is not intended to fill the mind with a gluttony of ideas, but rather to bathe the heart and ready it do what the Lord wants. Read this chapter repeatedly until you fully catch the Lord's beckonings to you this day.

Wednesday	*Greater Is the One Within*	Psalm 107

Let them thank the Lord for his steadfast love,
for his wonderful works to humankind. vv. 8, 21, 31

Notice the action words of God in this prayer that begins the fifth and final book in the collection of psalms. God moves into our lives with the same saving energy as God did to our Jewish ancestors long ago. Pause at each verb and let your soul receive right now the timeless actions of God.

God's protection at sea is celebrated from verse 23. I wonder if Jesus' disciples caught in the storm on the lake in the Gospels recalled this part of the psalm. Greater is the One in your boat than all the storms from without that rage and rock to frighten you. To insure that you are in touch with Jesus within who is saving you, I suggest that you repeat the refrain of this psalm as each hour of your day strikes.

Thursday	*Urging Holiness*	2 Peter 3

Since all these things are to be dissolved in this way,
what sort of person ought you to be in leading lives of holiness and godliness … v. 11

"What will it profit them to gain the whole world and forfeit their life?" These words that Peter personally heard from Jesus are echoed here in today's reading. (Cf. Mark 8:36.) The chapter stirs a call to holiness in us, as we conclude our reflections on 1 and 2 Peter.

What do you do in your life that has value beyond physical permanency? What are the priceless spiritual features about you that are not destroyed by fire, but rather purified by it? You *can* take these qualities with you into eternal life.

I read the following on a bumper sticker: Some who put off their salvation until the 11th hour, find that they are dead at 10:30 PM!

Friday	*Beyond Comfort Zones*	Luke 8:26–56

Return to you home, and declare how much God has done for you. v. 39

Jesus' presence is bad news to demons. Those who come to torment others are themselves tormented by the presence of Jesus.

Is there anything that you are doing about which you are uneasy, or even tormented, that is a sign of the changes that the Spirit is prompting you to make? Do you define your own *comfort zones* as the limits beyond which you will not go? The discomfort of advancing in your spiritual journey is the Lord's way of preserving you from the quiet desperation, stagnancy, dull and boring feeling of torment that may be going on inside you.

Notice the varying approaches of Jesus to the kind of healing that needs to take place. How is the Spirit dealing with you about the wholeness that longs to happen for you?

Saturday

The Sabbath Torah Reading

Jun 06, 2007 #36C	May 28, 2016 #21C	Mar 01, 2025 #19C	Feb 25, 2034 #19C
May 29, 2010 #36C	Mar 02, 2019 #22C	Feb 26, 2028 #18C	May 30. 2037 #36C
Jun 01, 2013 #37C	Feb 26, 2022 #22C	Mar 01, 2031 #19C	Jun 02, 2040 #36C

The Ninth Week in Epiphany

Begins on the Sunday nearest March 1 (Leap Year, Feb. 29), unless Lent has begun.
***For 2019, 2022, 2025, 2028, this is the last week in Epiphany, beginning with Transfiguration Sunday. See below** for the Sunday reading, continuing with the Monday-to-Saturday passages from the First Week in Pentecost, Year C, p. 316. An exception to this is in 2028 when there is an extra week in the year which has no Monday-to-Friday readings. The Torah reading for Saturday, March 4, 2028 is #19. Ash Wednesday occurs this week. For next week turn to the First Week in Lent, Year C, p. 286.*

Transfiguration Sundays, Year C

(The Last Sunday in Epiphany)

Feb 18, 2007	Feb 07, 2016	Mar 02, 2025	Feb 19, 2034
Feb 14, 2010	Mar 03, 2019	Feb 27, 2028	Feb 15, 2037
Feb 10, 2013	Feb 27, 2022	Feb 23, 2031	Feb 12, 2040

Transfiguration Sunday *One More Epiphany* **Luke 9:28–36**

**Peter and his companions were weighed down with sleep;
but since they had stayed awake, they saw his glory
and the two men who stood with him. v. 32**

A Scenic Overlook on a superhighway invites a choice to both stop and refresh the soul with the beauty of a landscape, or pass the moment by, urged by the need to drive on.

We are about to enter the Lenten movement to Easter. Rather than race right into the journey, Jesus invites us to take a scenic trip to a mountaintop, there to pause in prayer, enfolded by a sense of the wholeness of the journey from death to life. Join Peter, James, and John, the disciples who will be with Jesus in Gethsemane. Curiously, sleep sweeps its covering shadow over them in both places. Can it be that the stretch from glory to suffering catches them and us asleep on either end?

Pause, pray and let the Lord give you one more Epiphany of glory before the descent into the Lenten valley of the shadow of death.

The cross on the facing page is the "Jerusalem Cross," dating from the twelfth century. The large cross represents Jerusalem, the four smaller crosses, the four corners of the earth waiting for the Gospel. The four sections further suggest the four seasons and four quadrants on the face of a clock; the cross of Jesus is present in the face of every hour.

There are many crosses embedded in the Jerusalem Cross. The large one is formed by four "Tau" crosses, after the Greek letter "Tau" drawn as our "T." Four small crosses are present in each quadrant. One interpretation suggests that the four small crosses represent the holes in the hands and feet of Jesus, the larger cross, a sign of the wound in Jesus' side. Any direction you turn the cross, will be the same.

LENT
AND
EASTER

SPRING

Northern Hemisphere

Year C
2007, 2010, 2013 …

Lent begins six weeks before Easter Sunday.
See the entire cycle of readings at a glance on page xx.

The First Sundays in Lent, Year C

Feb 25, 2007	Feb 14, 2016	Mar 09, 2025	Feb 26, 2034
Feb 21, 2010	Mar 10, 2019	Mar 05, 2028	Feb 22, 3037
Feb 16, 2013	Mar 06. 2022	Mar 02, 2031	Feb 19, 2040

The First Week in Lent

Six weeks before Easter Alphabyte: Nadir, p. 39

Sunday   *When Temptations Attack*   **Luke 4:1–13**
When the devil had finished every test,
he departed from him until an opportune time. v. 13

The beginning of the season of Epiphany saw us contemplating the Baptism of Jesus. Lent opens, with what took place immediately after—the temptation of Jesus in the desert. Jesus, who knew no sin, became sin for us. (2 Cor. 5:21)

The wilderness recalls the wanderings of our ancestors, time of temptation and sin for them. They complained about bread, fell into idolatry, and tested the Lord. Jesus confronted the same three temptations. However, Jesus did what our ancestors did not—meet the attacks with the sword of the Spirit, the living Word of God, here found in Deuteronomy 6—8.

Today and everyday, let a word or phrase from the daily passage rise forth that you can use as a weapon against the temptations you face. Come against them with God's Word, and you will not fall.

Monday   *The Mire of Disobedience*   **Jeremiah 36—38**
Just obey the voice of the LORD in what I say to you,
and it shall go well with you, and your life shall be spared. 38:20

Mondays in Lent each year are dedicated to the prophet Jeremiah. You might pray each of today's three chapters in the morning, afternoon and evening. Chapter 36 uplifts the theme of repentance. King Jehoiakim tries to destroy the Word of God by throwing Jeremiah's scrolls into the fire. Recall what King Herod did when he had the Holy Innocents killed in an attempt to do away with Jesus, the infant King. Verse 18 is the only reference to "ink" in the Old Testament.

The treatment of Jeremiah in chapter 37 will remind you of the way Jesus suffered. Just as the patriarch Joseph, Jeremiah was raised from a pit. The Lord saw to it that Jeremiah would not die in the dungeon. As the very body of the prophet rises from the pit, the verse for today (38:20) wells up from the mire of disobedience.

Tuesday   *Anguish Augmented*   **Job 22—24**
I have not departed from the commandment of his lips;
I have treasured in my bosom the words of his mouth. 23:12

A third cycle of dialogues begins between Job and his so-called friends. Eliphaz is so convinced that bad things only happen to bad people, that he accuses Job of specific, grievous offenses. Loneliness augments Job's anguish. No one understands; no one comforts. Job does not respond to Eliphaz, but simply proclaims God's righteous judgments. Job talks *about* God, instead of speaking *to* God. His words come from deep conviction; yet comfort is still far away.

Highlight the golden gems in Job's words in chapter 23 that come from his suffering. Taste the pain of Job in chapter 24. What feelings and images are stirred within you as you relate your life to Job's life? There is relief for Job through writing; find the same for yourself.

Wednesday   *Out of the Depths*   **Psalm 130**

Out of the depths I cry to You, O LORD;
Lord, hear my voice! vv. 1–2

Whether you hit bottom or quietly rest at the base of your soul, there is no other place than your depths for crying out to the Lord. From there the psalmist stretches and tunes himself to God whom he trusts will hear him. Feel peace as the psalmist becomes fully aware that no sin or iniquity on his part will block God's ears from hearing, or God's heart from responding.

This is the eleventh of fifteen *Songs of Ascent*, chanted as Jews in joyous pilgrimage would go up to Jerusalem three times a year for Passover, Pentecost and Tabernacles. Journey with Jesus from the desert to Jerusalem—from the wilderness where John the Baptist made his cries of repentance, to the heights of Calvary and death; from desert emptiness, to city strife. From there, the empty depths of the tomb will stretch to resurrection and ascended life for you and me.

Thursday   *Jesus Walks with You*   **James 1**

My brothers and sisters, whenever you face trials of any kind,
consider it nothing but joy, because you know that
the testing of your faith produces endurance. vv. 2–3

Weaving through Thursdays of Lent are the five powerful chapters in the letter of James. Almost every verse stands alone as worthy to be written and put in a prominent place for you to see. Return to these verses throughout the day as you walk through its hours. With each one, James will give you a nugget of wisdom that you will want to take with you for the journey from Lent to Easter, from struggle to freedom, from death to life.

This theme courses through the book: temptations bring strength to the inner life. Such was the case for Jesus, recalling last Sunday's Gospel. Jesus won the victory over temptation where the children of Israel failed. Now he gathers all your struggles into his own, as he walks with you through the coming journey to victory.

Friday   *The Plot to Glory*   **John 11:45–57**

You do not understand that it is better for you to have one man die for the people
than to have the whole nation destroyed. v. 50

Darkness closes in upon the highest religious officials, their vision squeezed into the tiny, dimly lit room of their own self-interest. So is the atmosphere after the raising of Lazarus from the dead as we begin the Friday Gospels of John in Lent this year. The plot to kill Jesus is fashioned. The Scribes and Pharisees are about to succumb to the temptations of power and control, just as did their ancestors in the desert—the same desert temptations that Jesus overcame.

John the Evangelist fills the account with ironic verses, such as verse 50. God is about to use the most hideous of evil plots as a *plot to glory*. From the greatest evil will rise the greatest good—the resurrection.

Saturday   **The Sabbath Torah Reading**

Mar 03, 2007 #20C	Feb 20, 2016 #20C	Mar 15, 2025 #21C	Mar 4, 2034 #20C
Feb 27, 2010 #20C	Mar 16, 2019 #24C	Mar 11, 2028 #20C	Feb 28, 2037 #20C
Feb. 23, 2013 #20C	Mar 12, 2022 #24C	Mar 08, 2031 #20C	Feb 25, 2040 #20C

The Second Week in Lent

Five weeks before Easter—Alphabyte: Olive Tree, p. 40

Sunday   *Jerusalem Focus*   **Luke 13:31–35**

Jerusalem, Jerusalem, the city that kills the prophets and stones those who are sent to it!
How often have I desired to gather your children together
as a hen gathers her brood under her wings, and you were not willing! v. 34

The face of Jesus is bold before his enemies. There is no fear in him as he confronts pride and deceit with absolute truth. Herod Antipas wants to kill Jesus, just as did his wicked father, Herod the Great, when Jesus was an infant.

Jerusalem has become the hub of all the hostility that will mount against Jesus and put him to death. Jesus longs to go there. Follow him to Jerusalem with the kind of victory songs from the Psalms that fill our Wednesdays in Lent.

Meditate with a wide, expansive heart upon verses 34 and 35. Get in touch with where there is sadness in your own life, facing what makes you sad, with the love that Jesus has for Jerusalem. Be one with your Lord. Pray that his profound inner emotions transform yours and make them as his.

Monday   *Ravaging the Remnant*   **Jeremiah 39—41**

You shall have your life as a prize of war,
because you have trusted in me, says the LORD. 39:18

The holy city, Jerusalem, has fallen into the sacrilegious hands of unbelievers. Read slowly and soberly about the fall of the city. The date is July 18, 586 B.C.

Chapter 39, verse 18 rises up in hope. Jeremiah models for us the sense of comfort and safety that comes when we place our complete trust in the Lord. Reflect upon your own life. How does it move in relation to the kind of trust that you place in God?

Evil and tragedy continue as the wicked Ishmael betrays and murders the good governor, Gedaliah, as they break bread together. Jealousy and strife ravage the remnant of God's people. What little is left becomes even smaller by the treachery of Ishmael. Read. Be sobered.

Tuesday   *Endless Arguing*   **Job 25—28**

The price of wisdom is above rubies. Nor can it be valued in pure gold. 28:18–19

Job rebukes his companions, proclaiming the power of God. Strife and dissension continue to mount and pervade this book. Arguing rarely brings resolution, for each person stubbornly holds on to his or her position. Job and his so-called friends strive to grab after the last word that will silence the others; but it never comes.

The tension causes Job to become so defensive about his innocence, that he becomes self-righteous. While innocent of the charges leveled against him, Job fails to see that he needs to learn something about his predicament. This will come when Job finally explodes with anger in God's presence, ironically disposing him to the Lord's words and the beginnings of peace.

Live the tension of these readings. You will be preparing yourself to hear God's Words in the response of God that comes in the final passage on Tuesday of Holy Week.

Wednesday   *Total Satisfaction*   **Psalm 131**

Like a child who has just been nursed at his mother's breast,
So is my soul within me. (v. 2: Author's translation)

Does it stretch the imagination to link this quiet, intimate song with throngs of noisy people on the move to Jerusalem? Surely, in the crowd there is many a mother needing to pause by the roadside to nurse her baby. At that moment, no need to think about catching up with the rest. Time stops as she gazes down upon her child—mouth slightly open, lips still dripping with milk as the baby dozes off to sleep in total satisfaction.

We typically need three meals a day to keep up our strength. Yet more than the food we eat is the nourishment we need from the Lord. Pause regularly in the journey of the day and the week to your Jerusalem. Be fed by the Lord. Rest. All that you need for total satisfaction is given to you right now.

Thursday   *Echoes in an Empty Soul*   **James 2**

Just as the body without the spirit is dead, so faith without works is also dead. v. 26

Amid the many verses that convict in this chapter, James poses ten questions to us with responses that need to echo forth from an emptied self. If the walls of your soul do not bounce with the sound of these truths, there may yet lurk hidden sinfulness that muffles their tones.

The letter challenges us with its call to integrity. The final verse overcomes the apparent opposition between *Faith Alone* of Paul and *Faith and Works* of James.

James is strong, but loving as well. So would any best friend of yours be, who saw you doing something to tarnish the goodness of God meant to shine from you. Take to heart. Repent. Be healed.

Friday   *Unbelief Is Blind*   **John 12:1–10**

Why was this perfume not sold for three hundred denarii
and the money given to the poor? v.5

Do you find situations in your life where you just cannot win? Thus, it was for Jesus as he finds himself caught more and more in the web of the plot against his life. Here is Lazarus whom Jesus had raised to life. Nothing but love consumes the heart of Mary, fed by her joy in who Jesus is. Yet there is no room for joy in Judas; greed pushes it away. Evil poisons his heart.

Do not miss the irony in verse 10. The chief priests think that they can put to death the One who has power over death. Hatred and unbelief are blind. As for those who are opposed to you: If God is for us, who can be against us? (Romans 8:31)

Saturday   **The Sabbath Torah Reading**

Mar 10, 2007 #21C	Feb 27, 2016 #21C	Mar 22, 2025 #22C	Mar 11, 2034 #21C
Mar 06, 2010 #21C	Mar 23, 2019 #25C	Mar 18, 2028 #21C	Mar 07, 2037 #21C
Mar 02, 2013 #21C	Mar 19, 2022 #25C	Mar 15, 2031 #21C	Mar 03, 2040 #21C

The Third Week in Lent

*Four weeks before Easter—Alphabyte: **Plumb Line**, p. 40*

*Four weeks before Easter—Alphabyte: **Plumb Line**, p. 40*

Sunday   *Changes from Within*   **Luke 13:1–9**

Unless you repent you will all perish as they did. v. 3

Some nibble at "The Tree of the Knowledge of Good and Evil" and approach Jesus. They bait the Lord, inviting his comment on the atrocity that Pilate committed in massacring some political protesters from Galilee. Part of the Original Sin of humankind is to presume to interpret and judge the evil that is outside of us, such as the friends of Job did.

Not only does Jesus avoid falling into this trap, but also he turns the energy of the conversation back upon those who started it. The evil that is inside oneself is the evil from which to repent. Recall the words of Jesus in Matt. 7:3–4 and Luke 6:41–42 about the speck in your brother's eye and the plank in your own.

The earth is thawing and changing from within through the power of the warmth of the springtime sun. Go within yourself. God's love thaws out places that still resist repentance.

3
Le
C

Monday   *Refuge Apart from God?*   **Jeremiah 42—45**

Whether it is good or bad, we will obey the voice of the Lord our God
to whom we are sending you ... 42:6

Fear infected God's people as they witnessed the power of the king of Babylon stretching everywhere. Jeremiah was sought out to find God's will, yet when he found it, the people rejected it. Despite their promise to do whatever God would say through Jeremiah, they did what they were told *not* to do—seek safety in Egypt.

No matter how many "kings of Babylon" are coming against you, God can turn any evil design to God's own ends. God not only is not far away from what is threatening you, but also is present within these forces, ready to turn them to your advantage and salvation. But you must obey, not seeking safety in any *Egypts* in your life.

Make this reading personal to you. What is coming against you? Are you seeking refuge apart from God?

Tuesday   *The Summation Speech*   **Job 29—31**

Oh, that I had one to hear me! 31:35

Job is totally on the defensive as he winds up his arguments with his friends. He is blind from seeing other alternatives to understanding. There are three false assumptions for Job: 1) that good things only come to good people; 2) that the dark world of evil would not attack him; 3) that God persecutes as well as prosecutes.

Just as the final movement of a symphony with the music in crescendo, the poetic power of Job courses through these chapters. What would have become of Job had he not learned how to express his feelings? Had he bottled up his emotions, an explosion much more harmful would have happened.

How are you when it comes to expressing authentic feelings? Be open to express your pent-up feelings in a positive, healthy manner. Pour yourself out in creative prayer.

Wednesday	*A Place for God*	Psalm 132

I will not give sleep to my eyes or slumber to my eyelids,
until I find a place for the LORD … vv. 4–5

A joyous restlessness comes upon the pilgrims as they recall David's sleeplessness until he finds a place for God to rest. Feel their anticipation as they come closer to Jerusalem and the Temple.

Jesus will reign not from the Temple, but from the cross in the center of Calvary's hill. From there he will come down, resting for a brief time in the tomb, then on to resurrection, ascension to the Father's right hand, and descent in the Holy Spirit. The Lord seeks to rest in your own soul—his preferred temple. God will indeed find this place if you stop using your hands to build any kingdom other than God's.

Rest in Jesus and he will rest in you. Then you will do great things for the Lord, for God will be the one doing the work in and through you.

Thursday	*Pickax to Loosen the Soil*	James 3

The wisdom from above is first pure, then peaceable, gentle, willing to yield,
full of mercy and good fruits, without a trace of partiality or hypocrisy. v. 17

This chapter blends concrete images and abstract virtues. Allow the images of the bridle, the rudder, and the small fire used to describe the tongue, bring piercing awareness to you. Reflect upon the ways your tongue sins, praying to the Lord for the quietness and restraint needed to curb its reactions.

The pickax words of James will loosen the soil of your soul. Beware of any denial or defensiveness on your part as you face James' honest confrontations with the truths about sin. Then you will be able to bear the sweet fruit of righteousness that will come as you drink in the beauty of the last two verses of this chapter. They are filled with virtues that will well up from the heart when repentance frees the way.

Friday	*The Drawing Power of the Cross*	John 12:11–50

And I, when I am lifted up from the earth, will draw all people to myself. v. 32

Greeks wish to see Jesus—the occasion for Jesus' outpoured expression that his hour has finally come. This incident has the same purpose in John's Gospel as the account of the Magi has in Matthew. There is total rejection on the part of the Chosen People. The Gentile world, on the other hand, searches and seeks to see Jesus and accept him. Victory courses through this passage, even as the forces of evil mount against Jesus. The cross becomes a great magnet, drawing all people to it, and to the victorious Savior reigning from this throne lifted on high.

Resurrection and ascension are embedded in the cross. From now on, these three are bound together for those who believe and adhere to Jesus. Surrender yourself to the drawing power of the cross and live as never before.

Saturday

The Sabbath Torah Reading

Mar 17, 2007 #22–23C	Mar 05, 2016 #22C	Mar 29, 2025 #23C	Mar 18, 2034 #22–23C
Mar 13, 2010 #22–23C	Mar 30, 2019 #26C	Mar 25, 2028 #22–23C	Mar 14, 2037 #22–23C
Mar 09, 2013 #22–23C	Mar 26, 2022 #26C	Mar 22, 2031 #22–23C	Mar 10, 2040 #22–23C

The Fourth Week in Lent

Three weeks before Easter—Alphabyte: Quarters, p. 41

Sunday   *Coming Home*   **Luke 15:1–3;11–32**

We had to celebrate and rejoice, because this brother of yours was dead
And has come to life; he was lost and has been found. v. 18

The center of Lent finds us contemplating perhaps the most beloved of Jesus' Parables: "The Prodigal Son." Reflect upon the challenge that the father has with his two sons. The brothers have likely been at odds with each other from early on. The older, a "holier-than-thou" type—the younger, "spoiled rotten." Into this setting comes a father at once delirious with joy that his beloved son has returned, yet shocked into sadness when he learns how "far away" the older son has been all along.

Stop when you find your spirit moved in positive or negative ways. These are moments of grace. Identify with the persons in the story. The parable will touch your heart as you come home to your Father who loves you. Look around and discover in faith, the welcome-home party that God is throwing for you.

Monday   *Images of Arrogance*   **Jeremiah 46—48**

Do not be dismayed, O Israel; for I am going to save you from far away,
And your offspring from the land of their captivity. 46:27

Isaiah, Ezekiel, and Jeremiah each write words of judgment against pagan nations. This year, every chapter in Jeremiah except the final one, is devoted to this. Beginning from the west with Egypt and moving east to Babylon, he singles out ten nations for judgment because of their arrogant abuse of power and their defiance of the God of Israel.

The section opens with the Battle of Carchemish by the northwestern portion of the Euphrates River. The year is 605 B.C. Egypt forever loses power in the region, overcome by Babylon.

Images of arrogance seek to shake loose any particles of pride in you. Find comfort in the Lord who is ever protecting you.

Tuesday   *Relief in the Contest*   **Job 32—34**

Truly it is the spirit in a mortal,
the breath of the Almighty, that makes for understanding. 32:8

Perhaps you've been frustrated in the back-and-forth arguing with Job and his so-called friends. So is Elihu who now enters the conversation. For him, there must be an alternative to the intolerable debate that has been going on—a testy tug 'o war wearing away at the souls of the listeners, as well as those involved in the contest.

Elihu is midway between the imperfections of human reasoning as evidenced thus far in the Book of Job, and the kind of responses that God offers in the concluding chapters. You will find humility and wisdom in Elihu, with many verses worthy of savoring as you prayerfully read the beauty of the poetry.

Go between the verses, into the silence, where the still, small voice of God will be speaking to you.

Wednesday   *The Descent of Intimacy*   **Psalm 133**
**How very good and pleasant it is
when kindred live together in unity! v. 1**

Whether it is Niagara Falls or the simple fountain in a park—flowing water makes for rest and refreshment. The psalmist discovers two images of flowing descent, similes for the pleasure of human life when people dwell as one. Catch the simple joy of noticing the crystal dew descending upon the awakening grass, replacing the white frost of winter. Feel the fresh descent of love and peace that this awareness brings.

How is it with you, your family, or the primary community in which you live? The Evil One makes frequent elbow jabs there, introducing strife. Memorize this brief psalm. Its anointing for love and intimacy descends upon you from above, passing through you, to those in your community you pray for by name.

Thursday   *Vulnerable Before Truth*   **James 4**

**You do not even know what tomorrow will bring. What is your life?
For you are a mist that appears for a little while and then vanishes. v.14**

Verse after verse stands on its own as precious truths and convictions. James uses a technique of balancing opposites in the opening verses. Just as dough is tossed back and forth from hand to hand, so do the parts of these verses move from side to side so that you, as dough, can be prepared for the oven of the Spirit.

James speaks plainly; that is one of the great benefits of his letter. Be vulnerable before truth, moving beyond guilt feelings that often come with awareness of sin, to the joy of being forgiven. A new life with the risen Lord comes in the Easter season.

A thought in keeping with the verse for the day: No one can assure you that today is not going to be the day that will appear on the memorial card for your funeral.

Friday   *A Love That Serves*   **John 13:1–17**
**If I, your Lord and Teacher, have washed your feet,
you also ought to wash one another's feet. v. 14**

Jesus stands before his destiny. The hour has come. Judas is bound; Jesus is free. Total love takes over, as when Mary of Bethany pours out the oil of her gladness and love upon the feet of Jesus. Now it is Jesus who anoints the feet of the disciples with the waters of cleansing, regeneration, and service. There is a complete reversal here: the kingly one becomes the absolute servant.

Meditate upon the persons, the words, and the actions in this passage. Join the disciples. Let Jesus wash your feet. Ask the Holy Spirit to anoint your imagination with holy faith and profound sentiments of love for your Master and Lord.

Are there reversals of attitudes such as those of Peter that need to take place in your life? There is nothing like Jesus' servant love for you to make this happen.

Saturday   **The Sabbath Torah Reading**

Mar 24, 2007 #24C	Mar 12, 2016 #23C	Apr 05, 2025 #24C	Mar 25, 2034 #24C
Mar 20, 2010 #24C	Apr 06, 2019 #27C	Apr 01, 2028 #24C	Mar 21, 2037 #24C
Mar 16, 2013 #24C	Apr 02, 2022 #27C	Mar 29, 2031 #24C	Mar 17, 2040 #24C

The Fifth Week in Lent
Two weeks before Easter—Alphabyte: Rooster, p. 41

Sunday   *The Fragrance of Goodness*   John 12:1–8
The house was filled with the fragrance of the perfume. v. 3

We often find a way of expressing the quality of a spiritual experience through the sense of smell. "I don't like the *smell* of this," refers to some negatives discerned in a situation.

Two spiritual odors rise up in the incident of the supper with Martha, Mary and their brother Lazarus whom Jesus brought back to life. There is the aroma of extravagant love in the costly oil of spikenard; there is the spiritual stench of death in Judas' greed, exploitation of the poor, and in the plot to kill Jesus. Yet the sweet smell of life and love fills the house, overpowering the stifling, musty smell of hatred and death.

Are you ready to be Mary, pouring out your life in loving service for others? Overpower the negative odors that seek to pollute the otherwise sweet fragrance of your own goodness—gift of the Holy Spirit.

Monday   *Against God*   Jeremiah 49—50
I will pardon the remnant that I have spared. 50:20

Throughout these judgments against the nations, the word *against* is used to describe the posture of these nations toward the Lord. The vivid descriptions of their downfall are all consequences of being against God.

Pride is sinful because it sets the self in opposition to God as though on an equal plane. Contests of power occur between the ego of the person, group, or nation. All of these are variations on the theme of the rebellion of the opposing angels, which has unleashed the cancer of pride into the earth and the human family.

Each verse flows over you, burning away anything in you as those arrogant nations, until you are totally limp and disposed for true spontaneity in the Holy Spirit. The Lord's plan is to preserve and pardon you.

Tuesday   *God Is the Center*   Job 35—37
**The Almighty—we cannot find him; he is great in power
and justice and abundant righteousness he will not violate. 37:23**

The sixteenth century Polish astronomer, Copernicus, demonstrated that the sun is the center, with the earth and planets circling about it. It was a revolution in his day. Elihu's intervention does the same for Job's world. Job is not the center: God is. Read today's passage very slowly, so that your spirit will sense the shift, flowing easily along with his speech. Pause after his questions, so that any egocentric ways of thinking that you have will shift to a prayerful contemplation of God as the center of your world.

Yield to Elihu's expression of faith and conviction. The images and poetry here will touch your spirit. Be open to the Lord who daily prepares you to receive God's Word more and more. The concluding passage in Job comes next week, when God finally intervenes and does the talking.

Wednesday   *Crossing the Finish Line*   **Psalm 134**

Lift up your hands to the holy place, and bless the LORD. v. 2

They've arrived! As the elation of marathon runners crossing the finish line, the hands of the pilgrims are raised high as they come into the sanctuary of the Lord. Feet come to rest; now it is hands' turn to celebrate.

For the pilgrims, it is the joy at what is coming, rather than what is finished. So also for Jesus who crosses the finish line into Jerusalem this coming Palm Sunday, "who for the sake of the joy that was set before him endured the cross, disregarding it shame" (Heb 12:2). The cross is the finish line into heaven's space. Only from there does Jesus cry out: "It is finished" (John 19:30).

Because of Jesus' completion of the Father's will, we can already be in the sanctuary of the risen life now. For you: what further journeying into that precious presence still needs to take place?

Thursday   *Confrontation with Compassion*   **James 5**

Are any among you sick? They should call for the elders of the church and have them pray over them, anointing them with oil in the name of the Lord. v. 14

Confrontation with compassion: these two words describe the tone of the final chapter of the Letter of James. God's love flows forth from the way James simply tells the truth.

Throughout the letter there have been various exhortations from James; the final chapter completes the list. Verse 14 unfolds the sacramental power of prayer for the sick and anointing with oil.

John Wesley and the first Methodists knew of the joy of confessing to one another. What would it take you to find this spiritual discipline an attractive addition to your life in community, instead of a threat?

Friday   *The New Commandment*   **John 13:18–38**

I give you a new commandment, that you love one another. Just as I have loved you, you also should love one another. v. 34

In the center of the passage is the tiny sentence: "And it was night" (v. 30). Into this darkness, Judas escapes to complete the final details of the betrayal. Within the upper room, however, Jesus announces the triumph of the glory of God. The Light of the world shines as never before, illumining us with a new commandment, bathing all former ones with the extravagant light of God's love.

The passage closes with the arrogant protestations of Peter, that he will be always faithful. The night of his sin is here, but soon will come the daybreak of repentance and forgiveness. Yet for Judas, it was into a perpetual night that he walked.

The contrasts need to move you, until all that is dark in you vanishes before the saving light of Jesus and the New Commandment.

Saturday   **The Sabbath Torah Reading**

Mar 31, 2007 #25	Mar 19, 2016 #24C	Apr 12, 2025 #25C	Apr 01, 2034 #25C
Mar 27, 2010 #25	Apr 13, 2019 #28C	Apr 08, 2028 #25C	Mar 28, 2037 #25C
Mar 23, 2013 #25	Apr 09, 2022 #28C	Apr 05, 2031 #25C	Mar 24, 2040 #25C

Holy Week
The week before Easter—Alphabyte: Supper, p. 42

The week before Easter—Alphabyte: Supper, p. 42

Palm Sunday   *Joy and Sadness*   **Luke 22:14—23:56**
Father, into your hands I commend my spirit. 23:46

J esus arrives at Jerusalem, carried upon a donkey—sign of royalty. The King is taking possession of the Holy City, soon to become the heavenly Jerusalem.

Palm Sunday is a day with mixed emotions. There is the clear joy of the triumphal entry, but soon the crowd's cry will change from **"Hosanna"** to **"Crucify Him."** How the winds of the public can change!

The contrast of feeling is present in the liturgy of Palm Sunday—the exuberant beginning, then the later sober reading of the Passion. Become present to the two apparently conflicting emotions of joy and sadness. Both are true in our lives, whenever we love greatly.

Spend time Palm Sunday afternoon and evening with the movements of the Passion of Jesus according to Luke.

**HW
C**

Monday   *Waves of God's Justice*   **Jeremiah 51—52**
Wail for her! Bring balm for her wound; perhaps she may be healed. 51:8
[Note: With the exception of verses 28 to 30 of ch. 52, all of that chapter is duplicated in 2 Kings 24:18 to 25:21 and 25:27–30, considered on Monday of the Twelfth Week in Kingdomtide, Year B.]

B abylon takes its place along with Sodom, Gomorrah, and Nineveh as wicked cities in the ancient world. With the exception of the conclusion of chapter 51 from verse 59, almost every verse details the destruction of this ancient city.

Yet there are exceptions; today's verse is one of them. Not only is human vengeance at work, but rather divine interventions against Babylon. Yet there is still hope that the city will repent and be saved.

What other verses do you find that rise up as respite from the poetic waves of God's justice? These verses are themselves as a siege against the city. They pound at your own soul, lest there be anything as Babylon in you that needs to be destroyed. As the refiner's fire, may the pure gold of who you are in Christ shine forth.

Tuesday   *Job's Restoration*   **Job 41—42**
**I know that you can do all things,
and that no purpose of yours can be thwarted. 42:2**

T he Book of Job concludes with God's invitation to Job to contemplate one of the wonders of the world. Leviathan, the great sea monster, is presented for Job's and our admiration, with the underlying awareness that God is the creator of this awesome creature.

The secret behind Job's restoration is his humility and total abandon to the majesty of God. He repents from all pride and undue anger. His three "friends" receive a rebuke from the Lord. God condemns the arrogance behind their ways of thinking; yet they still have the means to repent.

Job has come full circle. Blessings of life and children return for him. It took much pain and anguish for him to get to that place. So may you find *life* through your suffering. Jesus found risen life for you in his.

Wednesday   *Beyond Obsession*   **Psalm 108**

With God we shall do valiantly; it is he who will tread down our foes. v.13

Are there times you cannot see beyond the limits of your own world? Do obsessive thoughts about a person or situation hold you hostage in your head, tempting you to think that there is no way out? This is temptation. Let this psalm break those bonds, lifting you above, where you will touch the mercy and truth of the Lord to which the sky and the clouds cling.

The psalm has this effect for the sacred writer, who collects some of his favorite verses from Psalm 57:7–11 and 60:5–12. There will be verses that lift your spirit, stretching you into the presence of the Lord. God will be totally in charge of your situation, if you let him. Watch how each verse gradually leads you into the prayer of total victory of the final verse.

Holy Thursday   *Full Faith*   **1 Corinthians 14—15**

By the grace of God I am what I am,
And his grace toward me has not been in vain. 15:10

On this sacred day of community, ministry, and Holy Communion, ponder these chapters of Paul. Be open to the full activity of the Holy Spirit in your life. Acknowledge the manifold gifts that demonstrate the presence and power of the Spirit as expressed in chapter 14. Experience the movement of Paul's thought about the resurrection in chapter 15, preparing yourself for the gift of Easter Sunday and its impact upon the way that you live now.

Pause with Paul at those verses where you find his words touching you. Allow yourself to move into those new spiritual places of understanding and love that the Spirit will bring about in you through these powerful words. Dwell on the utter reasonableness of 15:14: "And if Christ has not been raised, your faith is futile and you are still in your sins."

Good Friday   *Jesus' Hour*   **John 18:1—19:42**

When Jesus had received the wine, he said, "It is finished." 19:30

Every hour of this day is as the sacred hour of Jesus that has come. Be moved at every moment by a holy awareness that Jesus died for you. I suggest that you take chapters 18 and 19 of the Gospel of John, dividing each one into two parts, creating four sacred quarters of the day. Be with Jesus as the movements of his passion take place. Be in the crowd, but close to Jesus in fidelity, lest distance from him draw you into the courts of temptation, as happened for Peter.

1)	**6 am** (or on rising)	*Arrest, Trial, Denial of Peter*	**18:1–27**
2)	**9 am**	*Jesus and Pilate*	**18:28–40**
3)	**12 pm**	*Scourging, Crown of Thorns, Crucifixion*	**19:1–30**
4)	**3pm**	*Piercing the Side; Burial*	**19:31–42**

Be with Jesus. Let him change you. Note the points of irony. Dwell on all the meanings of the final words of Jesus.

Saturday   **The Sabbath Torah Reading**

Apr 07, 2007 Passover	Mar 26, 2016 Passover	Apr 19, 2025 Passover	Apr 08, 2034 Passover
Apr 03, 2010 Passover	Apr 20, 2019 Passover	Apr 15, 2028 Passover	Apr 04, 2037 Passover
Mar 30, 2013 Passover	Apr 16, 2022 Passover	Apr 12, 2031 Passover	Mar 31, 2040 Passover

Easter Week
Alphabyte: Temple, p. 42

Easter Sunday   *Empty Womb—Empty Tomb*   **Luke 24:1–12**
Why do you look for the living among the dead?
He is not here, but has risen. v. 5

Sacred, silent space envelopes the world the day after Jesus' death. It is the Sabbath, fragrant as no other. The holy women are resting, grieving, and breathing the sweet smell of the spices and fragrant oils they have prepared to give closure to the death of their beloved Master.

Yet openness, not closure, is what they find early the next morning. The tomb is open. They are startled, worried, filled with wonder at the words of the angels.

Where is Mary, mother of Jesus? The tomb is empty, for surely Jesus is filling her with his presence. She, whose empty womb was blessed with the fruit of the Word made flesh, is surely the first to know the fruit of the empty tomb. Ponder all these things in your heart, as Mary so often did.

Easter Monday   *Watchman, Singer and Shepherd*   **Ezekiel 33—35**
As shepherds seek out their flocks when they are among their scattered sheep,
so I will seek out my sheep. I will rescue them from all the places to which they have been
scattered on a day of clouds and thick darkness. 34:12

Three images are used by the Lord through Ezekiel to focus on the responsibilities of spiritual leadership—watchman, singer, and shepherd. Whether you are pastor or parishioner, listen well to the accountability to the Lord required of each person. Note the power of 33:32. How easy it is for the most anointed of spiritual singers either to awaken one to action and change, or simply be a soothing sound for the ears alone!

Listen to words of judgment and challenge. Rest in the strength of your Father God who takes charge and *watches* out for you, who becomes your personal *shepherd* through Christ Jesus, and who *sings* to your soul through the Holy Spirit.

What personal changes need to take place because of your close praying of God's Word today?

Easter Tuesday   *Masterpieces in the Silence*   **Proverbs 24**
Wise warriors are mightier than strong ones,
and those who have knowledge than those who have strength. v. 5

The Holy Spirit that infused Solomon is now about to fill you with wisdom as we live more consciously in the risen body of Jesus. The first three Tuesdays in Easter time this year are devoted to three chapters of Proverbs.

When visiting a holy place filled with masterpieces of art, there needs to be a slow pace while contemplating each piece. Let the pace be as you pray these proverbs. Set every one into a surrounding silence of the heart, letting each proverb soak that area of your soul where you are most in need.

Hold verse 5 in your hand and heart. Are there spiritual friends in your life who are open to the wisdom of the Holy Spirit? When praying over verses 11–12, do not be an ostrich when it comes to wrongdoing.

Easter Wednesday   *The Well-Worn Path*   **Psalm 119:1–24**

Happy are those whose *way* is blameless,
who walk in the law of the Lord. v.1. See also vv. 3, 5, 14.

The psalmist uplifts the beauty of the ways of the Lord. The word for "way" in Hebrew is *Derek,* meaning, "to walk." After one treads the same path over and over, it becomes well-worn—a road, a way. Also implied is the meaning of habit, the pathway in our souls when we do things repeatedly. As the comfort that comes from praying a familiar prayer, receive the joy and peace that come when you are walking in the well-worn ways of the Lord.

Each week you will learn an original Hebrew word for God's will. The first stanza has seven out of ten of these words. We will take one of each of these seven synonyms for the seven Wednesdays of Easter this year. Repeat the word often in the original Hebrew. Peace will flow over you in one single psalm we pray during this year's Easter season.

Easter Thursday   *The Power of the Holy Spirit*   **Acts 18:23—19:41**

EW
C

When the handkerchiefs or aprons that had touched Paul's skin were brought to the sick,
their diseases left them, and the evil spirits came out of them. 19:12

Be alert to expressions of power of various kinds. There is the fullness of power in the presence of the Holy Spirit, imparted by the hands of Paul, and by articles of his clothing as well. There is the power of faith-filled persons who receive the Holy Spirit because of their openness to this gift.

Pride fills the noisy, arrogant mob in Ephesus. The Holy Spirit sweetly invades the ancient temple of Artemis. The power of Jesus before the demons in the Gospels is now at work in the church, the new temple of God's enduring presence in the world.

Reflect upon the areas of your life where you sense power at work. The greatest power in you is the Holy Spirit.

Easter Friday   *Emptiness and Belief*   **John 20:1–10**

The other disciple, who reached the tomb first, also went in,
and he saw and believed. v. 8

It is the first day of the new creation. As in Genesis, there is darkness in the beginning. Jesus was buried in a garden. Think Eden. The empty tomb shocks Mary Magdalene, figure of Eve, into believing that Jesus' body was robbed, not risen. The disciple whom Jesus loved, understood to be John himself, outruns Peter; was Peter slowed down by the depression of denial?

As the setting of a nuptial bed, John describes the arrangements of the handkerchief and the linen cloths. John sees the empty tomb as the waiting nuptial chamber, and he believes. The only disciple at the cross is rewarded as the first of many to be blessed for not seeing, yet believing.

Take the empty places in your heart and believe that it is from there that Jesus will rise.

Saturday   **The Sabbath Torah Reading**

Apr 14, 2007 #26C	Apr 02, 2016 #26C	Apr 26, 2025 #26C	Apr 15, 2034 #26C
Apr 10, 2010 #26C	Apr 27, 2019 Passover	Apr 22, 2028 #26C	Apr 11, 2037 #26C
Apr 06, 2013 #26C	Apr 23, 2022 Passover	Apr 19, 2031 #26C	Apr 07, 2040 #26C

The Second Week in Easter
Alphabyte: Universe, p. 43

Sunday   *Enveloped by the Resurrection*   **John 20:19–31**
He breathed on them, and said to them,
Receive the Holy Spirit. v. 22

2
Ea
C

It is the first day of the week, the first day of a new creation. In Genesis 2:7, God creates Adam by forming a clay nose out of the earth, blowing God's very own breath into it. Jesus breathes into the moist, pliable clay of the Apostles and makes them a new creation through the presence of the Holy Spirit.

The resurrection not only involves the risen body of Jesus of Nazareth, but our own bodies as well. The resurrection envelops us through the gift of the Holy Spirit. By the in-breathing of Jesus, we can cry out with St. Paul: "It is no longer I who live, but it is Christ who lives in me" (Gal 2:20).

Thomas was absent when the risen Christ first appeared. Thomas receives a second chance a week later to witness the resurrection. However, do not be like him, presuming that you will have a second chance next week to worship, if you let this Sunday go by.

Monday   *Dry Bones Live*   **Ezekiel 36—37**
I will lay sinews on you, and will cause flesh to come upon you,
and cover you with skin, and put breath in you, and you shall live. 37:6

Though you may feel as a victim, God is working right now to bring justice into your situation. Pray in consonance with God. Find strength in the victory described when God promises the restoration of the Holy Lands. Repeat over and over 36:26, which recalls the very same promise of the Lord in Jeremiah 31:31–34 about receiving a new spirit in a new heart.

Even if you feel that your life is as dry as the bones of chapter 37, the Lord can remake you into the image of Christ risen. Surrender to the same power that raised Jesus from the dead and you will find your weary bones quivering with life.

As you hear God speak this message of power, become quiet and listen to the specific words of strength and energy that the Lord is speaking to your heart.

Tuesday   *Golden-Mouthed*   **Proverbs 25**
A word fitly spoken is like apples of gold in a setting of silver. v. 11

John Chrysostom was a powerful and holy preacher in fourth century Constantinople. His given name means "Golden-Mouthed," having the reputation of being the greatest expositor of the Bible in his time. His life embodied verse 11. Would you like to be remembered in a similar way? Then let your mouth be set by the silver of silence, opening yourself to the power of the Holy Spirit so that all that you say can be as gold.

In Romans 12:20, Paul uses verses 21–22 in his teaching about overcoming evil with good.

What proverbs especially move you? Writing them will deepen their impact. Place your written copies in settings where their brilliant quality will shine all the more, transforming your thoughts—and thus your mouth—into gold.

Wednesday   *A Heart Enlarged by Love*   **Psalm 119:25–48**
I run the course of Your *commandments*,
For You shall enlarge my heart. (NKJV) v.32. Cf. vv.35, 47, 48.

The Hebrew word *mitsvah* is generally translated as "commandment." The root *tsavah* means, "to establish," "to constitute," referring to the terms of a contract between persons in a relation of intimacy, such as a father to a son, or a teacher to a pupil. Here it is the relation of God to his beloved child—you. The term *Bas/Bar Mitsvah* is used when a Jewish girl or boy has become a "Child of the Commandment" at age 13.

The psalmist does not cower before the commandments of the Lord. Quite the contrary; his heart is enlarged by completing what the Lord wants. In a relation of love and intimacy, we long to fulfill the desires, the wants, and the commandments of the beloved.

Jesus has given us a New Commandment to love one another. Returning love to Jesus is eternally linked with showing love for each other.

Thursday   *Jesus, Paul and You*   **Acts 20**
I do not count my life of any value to myself, if only I may finish my course
and the ministry that I received from the Lord Jesus,
to testify to the good news of God's grace. v. 24

As it was in Jesus, the power of the Holy Spirit is at work in the early church. Watch for similar expressions; the power that Jesus had over death in the Gospels is the same power at work in Paul. Paul responds to the opposition to him in words similar to those of Jesus. Both preached in public. This new life is not a secret teaching to an elite group, designed to overthrow the government. For Jesus, nothing but the will of the Father was important; for Paul nothing but the task that the Lord Jesus had given him had any value.

The Lord has no favorites. The same power at work in Paul is available for you. What yet remains of what you need to surrender?

Friday   *Jesus: Lover of Your Soul*   **John 20:11–18**
Woman, why are you weeping? Whom are you looking for? v.15

Mary Magdalene, figure of the New Eve, weeps at the place of sin's evidence. Robbery continues to be the only alternative, even in the face of two angels whom one would think would stir her to wonder. Place yourself in the scene so you can feel Mary's desperation and then the release of joy when recognition comes.

The power of the resurrection is in the power of love. John describes this incident in language that recalls the lover seeking the beloved in The Song of Songs, 3:2. The New Adam, the Bridegroom, is here to join in wondrous love with his Bride, the Church—the New Eve.

Remember the questions of Jesus to the first disciples (1:38): "What are you looking for?" … to his arresters (18:4) and here to Mary: "Whom are you looking for?" Let the power of the resurrection stir you to seek for Jesus, lover of your soul.

Saturday   **The Sabbath Torah Reading**

Apr 21, 2007 #27–28C	Apr 09, 2016 #27C	May 03, 2025 #27–28C	Apr 22, 2034 #27–28C
Apr 17, 2010 #27–28C	May 04, 2019 #29C	Apr 29, 2028 #27–28C	Apr 18, 2037 #27–28C
Apr 13, 2013 #27–28C	Apr 30, 2022 #29C	Apr 26, 2031 #27–28C	Apr 14, 2040 #27–28C

The Third Week in Easter
Alphabyte: Vine, p. 43

Sunday   *Denials Deleted by Love*   **John 21:1–19**
Do you love Me? vv. 15, 16,17

There is a shift in the way the risen Jesus is with the disciples. Rather than appearing to them, Jesus is already present on the shore while seven disciples fish in the middle of the lake. Fishing is a symbol of ministry. Remember the call of three of these disciples: "I will make you fish for people." (Cf. Mt. 4:19, Mk 1:17, Lk 5:10). There is abundant success in ministry and mission when we obey Jesus.

Join the disciples for breakfast with Jesus. This is the first personal encounter of Jesus with Peter since the latter's denial. Catch the poignant, tender moment. Three times did Peter deny Jesus; three times, Jesus invites him to delete the denials with expressions of humble love.

This is your day to show love and loyalty to your risen Savior.

Monday   *From Gog to God*   **Ezekiel 38—39**
They will not need to take wood out of the field or cut down any trees in the forests,
for they will make their fires of the weapons. 39:10

Gog is a symbol of all the forces of evil. However great be its power unleashed, greater still is the power of God, the Almighty, rising up to protect God's beloved. The moment of evil's apparent victory becomes the time when God releases the power to heal and restore his loved ones who are suffering.

Boldly believe beyond what the senses behold. Take courage from the central theme of this great prophet: the absolute sovereignty of God. The Enemy wants to fashion destructive weapons against you from the points of pain in your life. Note these points; allow them to be *Firestarters* for your soul.

Blockage becomes passage to new life. The stone before the tomb is rolled away, revealing its inner emptiness—faith proclaiming the resurrection. When Gog shows up, so does God—with much greater power!

Tuesday   *A Greater Than Solomon Here*   **Proverbs 26**
As charcoal is to hot embers and wood to fire,
so is a quarrelsome person for kindling strife. v. 21

Many of the sayings attributed to Solomon are similes taken from everyday life. Images evoke meanings beyond rational understanding. Feel the images. As you live today, notice how the Spirit can use all aspects of your world to instruct you in the ways of the Lord. There is no experience, good or bad, that God cannot hone into a word of truth and grace for you. Be sensitive in receiving these gratuitous gifts from the Lord.

Matthew 12:42 cites Jesus as saying about himself: "Something greater than Solomon is here!" When you let Jesus fully share his risen life with you, then you have an inner wisdom greater than Solomon's. Spend part of your prayer-time, writing sentences that the Holy Spirit inspires that can become personal proverbs for you and wisdom for others.

Wednesday   *The Presence Flowing Down*   **Psalm 119:49–72**

**The *law* of your mouth is better to me
than thousands of gold and silver pieces. v. 72. Cf vv. 51, 53, 55, 61,70**

*T*orah: the root, *yara,* means "to rain," "flow down," or "to shoot with direction," such as an arrow. While English translates *Torah* as "law," its meaning is closer to "teachings." It is God's presence *raining down* upon us according to God's will. *Torah* is revelation about God and God's ways by which we are to live according to the covenant offered to us.

The presence of the Lord flows down in a sweet anointing. Breathe each verse; every one contains some reference to God and revelation. Pray and be filled. The Lord aims the divine presence at you, flowing into you from the wells of living water springing up from within. In a few weeks, we will recall another presence of God raining down—the descent of the Holy Spirit at Pentecost. Open yourself at this moment to the flowing down of the Holy Spirit into your being.

Thursday   *Ready to Suffer All*   **Acts 21**

**What are you doing, weeping and breaking my heart?
For I am ready not only to be bound
but even to die in Jerusalem for the name of the Lord Jesus. v. 13**

*S*t. Luke himself is in the picture; notice the use of the first person plural pronoun, continuing what began in 20.7. Luke weaves the places sited as so many stitches in the tapestry of the church expanding in the Mediterranean area.

You will see similarities in the trials and suffering of Paul and those of Jesus. Paul's *hour* has not yet come. The affirmation to die for his Lord sounds similar to that of Peter's at the Last Supper; however, Paul is totally grounded in the Lord; that would come for Peter only after the terrible anguish of denying his Master.

Cling to the faith and abandon of Paul in this chapter until your surrender to Jesus is as strong as Paul's. The Holy Spirit is poised to give you this grace. Ask in faith and you will receive.

Friday   *Jolted Into Peace*   **John 20:19–23**

Peace be with you. v. 19

*T*he disciples huddle together, wrapped in choking bands of fear, doors shut and bolted from the anger outside. With no sense of moving through doors or walls, Jesus simply stands in the middle. May the first word from his mouth, designed to dissipate their fright, be the word that has all your fears vanish: "Peace be with you." As unexpected, unhoped for, and undeserved as was Jesus' appearance to them, so does he now come to you and those rejoicing with you in your meditation on this same passage.

Extraordinary shifts from grief to joy, from loss to gain, from fear to peace, from death to life, mark the resurrection appearances. For John, a pre-Pentecost fullness comes to the disciples this night of the resurrection in the giving of the Holy Spirit. Receive the Holy Spirit as you join your breath with God's.

Saturday   **The Sabbath Torah Reading**

Apr 28, 2007 #29–30C	Apr 16, 2016 #28C	May 10, 2025 #29–30C	Apr 29, 2034 #29–30C
Apr 24, 2010 #29–30C	May 11, 2019 #30C	May 06, 2028 #29–30C	Apr 25, 2037 #29–30C
Apr 20, 2013 #29–30C	May 07, 2022 #30C	May 03, 2031 #29–30C	Apr 21, 2040 #29–30C

The Fourth Week in Easter
Alphabyte: Wax, p. 44

Sunday   *Held In God's Hand*   **John 10:22–30**
I give them eternal life, and they shall never perish;
no one will snatch them out of my hand. v.28

God led the Chosen People from slavery in Egypt; however, a new kind of oppression later arose. Religious leaders became slaves to greed and power, exploiting the people as evil shepherds who rob and murder sheep—God's people. A new Exodus was needed. It came with Jesus.

The center Sunday of Easter has traditionally been "Good Shepherd Sunday." By the gentle call of each by name, Jesus leads us, his wounded and abused sheep, out of the oppressive dimension of the institution of religion, into a glorious new sheepfold. There the sheep are so one with the shepherd that the bond is the same as that between the Father and Jesus.

Let go and give yourself to the Lord, then God will hold onto you; no one will be able to snatch you out of God's hand.

Monday   *A Temple Beyond Measure*   **Ezekiel 40—42**
Mortal, look closely and listen attentively,
and set your mind upon all that I shall show you. 40:4

Visions from the Lord can be filled with many details, as in Ezekiel's vision of the restored Temple and the return of the people from Exile. You will find it helpful to refer to a translation converting ancient measurements into modern ones. Go first to the end of chapter 42, noting the dimensions of the outer court—an immense square, 840 feet on each side—almost the length of three football fields! If you want to make your own blueprint of the vision, take an 8½ x 11 inch piece of paper, folding it to make an 8½ square, each inch being 100 feet.

Yet even more expansive than the dimensions of the Temple described here, is the temple Jesus offers us—one beyond measure within which to live and move and have our being, his very risen Body.

Tuesday   *Compassion in Action*   **Nehemiah 1—4**
When I heard these words, I sat down and wept, and mourned for days
fasting and praying before the God of heaven. 1:4

Hear the prayer of this extraordinary leader who would mastermind and complete the rebuilding of the walls about Jerusalem. Compare Ezekiel and Nehemiah. Ezekiel's vision of the Temple was not intended to be completed in an earthly manner: not so for Nehemiah. Vision, planning, energy, and sweat went into the completion of a 1.5 mile, 8 foot thick wall about the city. Workers had one hand on tools of reparation, the other on weapons of defense. Chapter 3 is as a great memorial plaque.

Rejoice to be within the walls of the new temple—the risen body of Jesus. Pray in compassion for the countless others outside the boundaries of this Body who live without the full protection of Jesus against the onslaughts of all the evils of our worldly society.

Wednesday *The Comforting Witness* **Psalm 119:73–96**

In your steadfast love spare my life,
so that I may keep the decrees of your mouth. v. 88. Cf. v. 79

Join the suffering of the psalmist with yours and others. Each verse with its rhythm and variation on the single theme of God's self-communication brings comfort to the heart. God gently shares with us who God is in the gentle presence of the flow of the Word. The Holy Spirit is your beloved friend who strokes the forehead of your soul with these words. The Holy Spirit is the Comforter.

The fourth word for our Wednesday meditations is *'edah,* translated as "decrees" or "testimonies." It is a legal term, also meaning "witness." The root *'uwd* means, "to go around" or "repeat." Consistent, repetitious true witness wins the case for the defendant.

Repeat the word *'edah* throughout the day as you receive the wonders of creation as witnesses of the beauty and love of the Creator.

4
Ea
C

Thursday *A Story Retold* **Acts 22**

The God of our ancestors has chosen you to know his will,
to see the Righteous One and to hear his own voice. v.14

We read the second of three accounts of the story of Paul's conversion. Each telling is fresh, for there are a new opportunities for Paul to give praise to his Lord. Catch the joy in his spirit as Paul shares his deep conviction that no evil can ever come against him that will be able to withstand the power of his Jesus.

Cast your memory over your past life. Recall those times when God intervened in your life in clear and manifest ways. How did you respond? Spend time with the story of God's shaping of your life to be in conformity with Jesus. There is energy in the retelling of the story as you move further into your life as it continues. Writing the story as Luke does, will deepen its impact upon you and upon others when you share it.

Friday *The Community and Jesus Risen* **John 20:24–31**

Blessed are those who have not seen
and yet have come to believe. v. 29

Thomas' absence at the first appearance of Jesus becomes a handicap to knowing the presence of Jesus risen in the new community. For Thomas, an alive Jesus would be a revivified corpse. He had no idea that Jesus would live in him, rather than he in Jesus with his fingers in the open wounds.

The second encounter with Jesus eight days later begins as the first one in 20:19. There is, however, a small but very significant difference. In verse 19, the past tense is used: "Jesus came." In verse 26, it is the present tense: "Jesus comes." Even before the manifestation to Thomas, Jesus is already present in the community that loves in such a way, that his presence is manifest in them.

Are you part of a community that lives and loves in the Spirit? No personal preferences to see Jesus in any particular manner will substitute for this.

Saturday **The Sabbath Torah Reading**

May 05, 2007 #31C	Apr 23, 2016 Passover	May 17, 2025 #31C	May 06, 2034 #31C
May 01, 2010 #31C	May 18, 2019 #31C	May 13, 2028 #31C	May 02, 2037 #31C
Apr 27, 2013 #31C	May 14, 2022 #31C	May 10, 2031 #31C	Apr 28, 2040 #31C

The Fifth Week in Easter
Alpbabyte: Xylophone, p. 44

Sunday   *As I Have Loved You*   **John 13:31–35**

I give you a new commandment, that you love one another.
Just as I have loved you, you also should love one another. v. 34

Love is freed from fickle ties to affection only. Now it is living out the ongoing presence of Jesus in the world through the way that he loved—unto death. The new commandment is not a stern, military-type order, but rather a charge, a mission, a commitment.

The setting for the reading is the Last Supper before Jesus' death. It is also appropriate on this Sunday as we enter into the final three of the seven weeks in the Easter season. Jesus approaches his *last suppers* during the time of glory when he was with the disciples after the resurrection until Ascension Thursday, forty days after Easter.

Let there arise in the depths of your soul that sense of *AS* Jesus has loved you—to the death … the death of self. Let the Spirit give you the gift of giving your life for others.

Monday   *Orientation*   **Ezekiel 43—44**

The glory of the God of Israel was coming from the east;
the sound was like the sound of mighty water;
and the earth shone with his glory. 43:2

The word *orientation* comes from the Latin root meaning *to rise*—the place of the rising sun. The east is a symbol of hope, of resurrection. Ancient Christian churches were oriented with the altar facing east.

In Ezekiel's vision of the mystical temple, the doorway faces east, the glory of the Lord entering from the place of the new day. Feel the glory of the resurrection bathing you as you enter into the vision of the temple. Sense the presence of the altar in the depths of your soul as the very center of the temple-body of Jesus within whom you dwell.

All the details of these chapters have one purpose—immersion in the Holy. We become spiritually *dis-*oriented in life when we lose that deep, inner spiritual sense of God's presence and holiness. The Lord offers it to you once again. Surrender to glory in these final weeks of the Easter Season.

Tuesday   *Shaking Out the Soul*   **Nehemiah 5—7**

I shook out the fold of my garment and said, "So may God shake out everyone
from house and from property who does not perform this promise." 5:13

[The genealogy list of ch 7 is also found in Ezra 2:1–10.

Look at the list as you would the names enshrined on Ellis Island.]
Nehemiah demonstrates the power of symbolic gesture in expressing outrage at the usury Jews exacted against one another. Sense the movement of the great qualities of this leader—humility, solidarity, and shrewdness in discerning plots of evil against him. At each moment of a crisis, Nehemiah turns to the Lord in prayer, shaking out his soul in the Lord's presence, loosening any angers or fears, freeing the energies of devotion to the Lord in fulfilling the mission that "God had put in my heart to do at Jerusalem" (2:12).

What are the emotions that lurk inside of you that tend to make you spiritually paralyzed? Shake out your soul before the Lord in prayer. Face opposition from within and without that would have you give up on the work that the Lord has put into your hands.

5
Ea
C

Wednesday *Divine Prescriptions* **Psalm 119:97–120**

Hold me up, that I may be safe and have regard for your statutes continually. v. 117

Beneath the word for *statutes* (in Hebrew, *choq)*, lies the root meaning, "to engrave." It refers to written or engraved enactments, decrees, or prescriptions. It is also used for the written deed for lands, which defines official boundaries.

If it were not for the afflictions of the psalmist, he might not have learned God's statutes more deeply. Put the written words of the Lord between you and your suffering. What are the official *decrees* that God has for you— the prescription that God wants you to take so that sickness and suffering retreat from the borders of your life? Since this refers to things written, let the Lord teach you in your journal the steps to take for your total healing and happiness.

Look into *The Twelve Steps* in Alcoholics Anonymous for decrees that God uses to bring healing to millions of addicted persons.

Thursday *All in God's Time* **Acts 23—24**

**Keep up your courage! For just as you have testified for me in Jerusalem,
so you must bear witness also in Rome. 23:11**

The early Church retraces the road to Calvary. The trial of Paul bears similarities to that of Jesus—hatred, false witness, and abuse. Paul confronts his accusers just as Jesus did when the Lord was struck in the face.

Enter the joy of Jesus as he appears to Paul, telling him that his present suffering is the prelude to Rome. God uses the rejection of Paul as the means to move him to the next place where God needs him—the center of the ancient world: Rome.

Felix and Pilate: do you see the similarities? Felix's refusal to do justice has Paul further confined for two more years. The two-year wait becomes part of God's timing. All plots to deny, delay, or delete God's plan will fail. Are you becoming impatient with God's plan upon your life?

Friday *Where Are You Fishing?* **John 21:1–14**

**So they cast it, and now they were not able
to haul it in because there were so many fish. v. 6**

Fishing—this is what the disciples are about. Here, however, it is a symbol—for now they are *Fishers of People*. Though they do not recognize Jesus on the shore, they recall the impact on their hearts of the miracle that happened when Jesus gave a similar command three years ago.

The word in Greek for the great quantity of fish is *plethos,* from which the word *plethora* comes. Only one other time in the whole Gospel of John is this word used. In 5:3 John tells of the *many* invalids—blind, lame, and paralyzed at the pool of Bethesda.

What changes does Jesus command you as to where you are doing your *fishing*? Do you believe in the great catch of souls that God has planned for you to draw into the Kingdom, because of your faith, hope, and love?

Saturday **The Sabbath Torah Reading**

May 12, 2007 #32–33C	Apr 30, 2016 Passover	May 24, 2025 #32–33C May 13, 2034 #32–33C
May 08, 2010 #32	May 25, 2019 #32C	May 20, 2028 #32–33C May 09, 2037 #32–33C
May 04, 2013 #32–33C	May 21, 2022 #32C	May 17, 2031 #32–33C May 05, 2040 #32–33C

The Sixth Week in Easter
Alphabyte: Yoke, p. 45

Sunday	*Irradiating Love*	John 14:23–29

**The Advocate, the Holy Spirit, whom the Father will send in my name,
will teach you everything, and remind you of all that I have said to you. v. 26**

Taste every word and phrase in profound meditation. God promises to release divine holiness and love into the human community. Yet the coming of the Holy Spirit is not enough; there must be a **YES** from deep within, as when Mary opened herself when the Word became flesh.

The Word becomes flesh in you by the Holy Spirit, the person of God that longs to dwell inside you. The Holy Spirit will enable you to do what the world cannot do—love in an absolute and unconditional way. Then comes a peace, which the world cannot give, for it is not the world's to give.

Ready your heart to receive the Holy Spirit. It is the very love of God irradiating through you.

Monday	*Architect of Space and Time*	Ezekiel 45—46

**When you allot the land as an inheritance, you shall set aside for the Lord
a portion of the land as a holy district … 45:1**

Ezekiel's audience is an exiled people longing for their homeland. Their pain is all the more poignant, for even if they could go back, there would be nothing but a barren waste where once the glorious Temple stood. Yet visions bring hope. After lifting the aspirations of the people through the vision of the new temple and its design, Ezekiel becomes an architect of time, measuring the year once again according to sacred festivals and how the people are to observe them.

What can you do to preserve that precious sense that all space and time in which you live can be sacred? Habits and rituals for personal prayer and worship are very important. They create boundaries of time and space that give life a deepening sense that God's eternity is entering into our time.

Tuesday	*Fresh Fervor*	Nehemiah 8—10

Do not be grieved, for the joy of the Lord is your strength. 8:10

Catch the power of the preposition: Joy *of* the Lord, compared with the familiar Joy *in* the Lord. God is love and joy. God opens up the vast power of God's own joy for you to find strength in it.

Place yourself amid this vast assembly that hears God's Word for the first time. Cherish the first hours of the day, just as did our Jewish ancestors; they passed the whole morning listening to the *Torah* in the open square. You join many reading this passage with you on this very day.

Renewed festivals bring fresh joy to the people of Nehemiah's day. Routine has not yet begun its erosion of fervor. The people confess publicly as they hear the recalling of God's covenant and their ancestors' infidelity to God. Note the reordering of priorities in chapter 10—the offering of first fruits to the Lord. What changes are you called to make?

Wednesday   *The Divine Supervisor*   **Psalm 119:121–144**

Redeem me from human oppression, that I may keep your *precepts*. v.134. Cf. v.128

The Hebrew word for "precepts" is *piqud*, occurring twenty-four times in the Bible. All the references are in the Psalms, with all but three of them occurring in Psalm 119. The meaning of the root of the word is "to oversee." Precepts are the conditions of the job description that a supervisor develops for employees. They are specific. Yet much different from what often happens between bosses and workers, there is here a sense of affection and comfort the psalmist finds in his God, along with a joyful experience of protection that one rarely finds in the business world.

Are there some specific precepts that God is enjoining upon you for your spiritual growth in the Lord? Scan your life. What does your divine supervisor have to say?

Thursday   *The Inner Energy of the Story*   **Acts 25—26**

**I have appeared to you for this purpose, to appoint you to serve and testify
to the things in which you have seen me
and to those in which I will appear to you. 26:16**

For the third time, Paul rejoices to share the story of his conversion. Verses 16–18 contain promises of the Lord that Paul had not previously expressed in the first two accounts (9:1–19; 22:6–21). As Paul tells his story, his joy in the Lord expands, radiating outward, pushing back the pressing in of his persecutors. Paul verifies what John teaches in his first letter, 4:4: He who is in you is greater than he who is in the world.

May this final listening to Paul's conversion bring the same inner energy to you, as you gather the story of God's gracious dealings with you into one place. Be centered in your story. It becomes alive again in your telling and humble retelling, for the glory of the name of Jesus.

Friday   *The Place of Inner Truth*   **John 21:15–19**

Yes, Lord; you know that I love you. v. 16

When someone greets us with, "How are you," the usual response is, "Fine, thank you"—whether we are fine or not. Only with those we trust do we share how it really is with us. To reach that place, the question, "How are you" may need to asked a few times, as so many steps that descend to the place of inner truth.

So it is with Peter. Each time that Jesus asks him if he loves Jesus, Peter moves beneath the levels of his reactive nature, to the place of beauty and total love that he has for his Lord. Jesus knows that Peter loves him; yet his sadness and shame eclipse his soul. The triple question of Jesus helps Peter pass below the upper spaces of anger and violence in the garden of arrest, beneath the fear in the courtyard of denial, to the place where Peter loves, by the lakeside in the morning with Jesus.

Only in accepting and returning Jesus' love will you be able to nourish his lambs.

Saturday   **The Sabbath Torah Reading**

May 19, 2007 #34C	May 07, 2016 #29C	May 31, 2025 #34C	May 20, 2034 #34C
May 15, 2010 #33C	Jun 01, 2019 #33C	May 27, 2028 #34C	May 16, 2037 #34C
May 11, 2013 #34C	May 28, 2022 #33C	May 24, 2031 #34C	May 12, 2040 #34C

The Seventh Week in Easter
Alphabyte: Zenith, p. 45

Next week is Pentecost Sunday, the beginning of the season of Pentecost. The reading for Pentecost and Trinity Sunday are found at the beginning of the next season, *Pentecost*. You will also find further directions for finding the Monday-to-Saturday readings for the beginning weeks of the season of Pentecost which has slight yearly variations due to the changing date of Easter.

7
Ea
C

Sunday   *Advent Revisited*   Luke 24:44–53
They were continually in the temple blessing God. v. 53

Luke's Gospel ends where it began—in the Temple. Sense the contrasts between these two moments. The longing for the Messiah in the beginning with aged Zechariah in the Holy of Holies, is balanced with the new community joyfully filling the Temple with the sounds of expectant praise. A new level of God's coming is about to take place with the Holy Spirit. Spend these days in the temple of your heart, gathering in prayer with faithful believers. It is Advent revisited.

Where were you spiritually six months ago when the first Advent candle began to illumine your darkness? Cast your memory over that period, giving thanks to the Lord for the opportunities to grow that you received. Repent for time wasted. Wait again with even more expectancy, for the Holy Spirit is coming!

Monday   *Yahweh Shammah*   Ezekiel 47—48
Wherever the river goes, every living creature that swarms will live … 47:9

As the Book of Ezekiel ends, the prophet offers the vision of a river flowing and growing eastward from the temple and the mystic geographic boundaries of the Twelve Tribes. The river is an image of Jesus. Recall the water and blood that flowed from the open side of Jesus on the cross in John 19:34 and the words of Jesus in John 7:39: "Out of the believer's heart shall flow rivers of living water." (Cf. Isaiah 12:3; 43:20; 44:3; 55:1.)

Bathe yourself in these saving waters that flow through you from the new temple which is Jesus risen, now ascended. Wait in the spiritual temple of your own heart for the coming of the Holy Spirit, knowing that the presence of Jesus is ever with you in the name that comes at the end of Ezekiel: *Yahweh Shammah: THE LORD IS THERE.*

Tuesday   *Joy: God's Work Is Done*   Nehemiah 11—13
Remember me, O my God, for good! 13:31

Look upon the lists of chapter 11 and up to 12:26 as you would an Honor Roll at a city square. From 12:27, take an air balloon's view of the double choir, one processing counterclockwise, the other clockwise, merging at the Temple square. Both in Ezekiel's temple in our Monday readings, and in this passage, music and singing set fire to worship.

After you read the outrage of Nehemiah from 13:4, reflect upon any ungodly types seeking to set themselves up in the temple of your heart. Throw them out by the grace of God—memories of abuse, negative parental figures … old baggage we tend to carry with us.

After addressing the problem of Sabbath defilement and intermarriage with unbelievers, Nehemiah completes his reforms, resting with this prayer: Remember me, O My God, for good!

Wednesday   *Seven Times a Day*   **Psalm 119:145–176**
Seven times a day I praise You, for your righteous ordinances (*judgments*.)
v.164. Cf. vv. 149,156,160,175.

*M*ishpat is the Hebrew word for "judgments" or "ordinances." While it carries the forensic meaning of "verdict," the word has a richer and wider sense. It includes all the just claims of God upon us—God's righteousness. As Jesus teaches in "The Sermon on the Mount," if one hungers and thirsts for it, blessedness and satisfaction come. (Matt. 6:6).

The phrase "seven times" occurs 35 times in the Bible, 33 of them in the Old Testament. It is the number of completion and fullness. The psalmist praises God seven times. According to the ancient division of the day into quarters, we would pray at the points of transition in the day: *1*: Pre-dawn praise | *2*: 6–9am | *3*: 9am–12pm | *4*: 12–3pm | *5*: 3–6pm | *6*: 6–9pm | *7*: 9pm, retire and night prayer.

A final note: this is the *seventh* and final week of Easter.

Thursday   *To the Ends of the Earth*   **Acts 27—28**
Let it be known to you then that this salvation of God
has been sent to the Gentiles; they will listen. 28:28

*T*he designs of those who seek to kill Paul are not only thwarted, but the very arrest of Paul brings him to Rome. STOP means GO! The Book of Acts closes with the final rejection of the Gospel by the Jewish community as a whole in Rome, opening up the Gentiles for Paul who begin to receive the salvation of the Lord.

The end of the Book of Acts fulfils the promise of Jesus made in 1:8, that through the power of the Holy Spirit, the disciples would witness to Jesus in Jerusalem, and in all Judea and Samaria, and the end of the earth. For the ancient world, Rome and its empire stretching to Spain in the west was understood as the end of the earth.

Place yourself amid the new crowd of Gentiles, sensing the energy of the Kingdom that flows from Paul's little rented house. Where will you take the Good News of the Kingdom?

Friday   *Eyes Upon Jesus*   **John 21:20–24**
Follow me! v.22

*H*aving passed beyond his impulsive nature to an expression of profound and total love for Jesus, Peter reverts for a moment to yet another reactive question about the beloved disciple: "What about this man?" Jesus' final words to Peter and to us in the Gospel of John have the jolting reminder that it is none of Peter's business.

This is the week of prayerful waiting for the coming of the Holy Spirit, the nine days between Ascension Thursday and Pentecost. Spend time with the Lord about the unique call that the Lord has placed upon you to be renewed at Pentecost. Do not be distracted by the call given to others; be inspired by them. Keep your eyes upon Jesus, following him in your special call. Remember: what you are called to do is no one else's business but yours and God's.

Saturday   **The Sabbath Torah Reading**

May 26, 2007 #35C	May 14, 2016 #30C	Jun 07, 2025 #35C	May 27, 2034 #35C
May 22, 2010 #34C	Jun 08, 2019 #34C	Jun 03 2028 #35C	May 23, 2037 #35C
May 18, 2013 #35C	Jun 04, 2022 #34C	May 31, 2031 #35C	May 19, 2040 Pentecost

PENTECOST

SUMMER

Northern Hemisphere

Year C
2007, 2010, 2013 …

Pentecost begins the Sunday after the Seventh Sunday in Easter.
See the entire cycle of readings at a glance on page xxi.

Adjustments at
The Beginning of the Season of Pentecost

Due to the varying date of Easter, the beginning of this season varies a few weeks. The First two Sundays of the season are Pentecost and Trinity Sundays. With respect to the Monday-to-Saturday readings, simply follow the table below. Readings from the end of the season of Epiphany are needed when Easter is early; when Easter is late, the season of Pentecost begins with the numbered weeks as indicated, since the first week(s) of Pentecost were read at the end of the season of Epiphany.

After these initial weeks, continue in the usual way for the weeks, finding the Sunday nearest a given date. See the article "Solar and Sacred Seasons" in the Appendix.

Year C	Pentecost Sunday *See facing page*	Monday-to-Saturday Readings	Trinity Sunday *See facing page*	Monday-to-Saturday Readings
2007	May 27	1 Extra Week See Eighth Wk in Epiphany	June 3	First Week in Pentecost
2010	May 23	1 Extra Week See Eighth Wk in Epiphany	May 30	First Week in Pentecost
2013	May 19	1st of 2 Extra Weeks See Seventh Wk in Epiphany	May 26	2nd of 2 Extra Weeks See Eighth Wk in Epiphany
2016	May 15	1st of 2 Extra Weeks See Seventh Wk in Epiphany	May 22	2nd of 2 Extra Weeks See Eighth Wk in Epiphany
2019	June 9	Second Week in Pentecost	June 16	Third Week in Pentecost
2022	June 5	Second Week in Pentecost	June 12	Third Week in Pentecost
2025	June 8	Second Week in Pentecost	June 15	Third Week in Pentecost
2028*	June 4	First Week in Pentecost	June 11	Second Week in Pentecost
2031	June 1	First Week in Pentecost	June 8	Second Week in Pentecost
2034*	May 28	1 Extra Week No Mon-Fri Readings Torah Reading for Jun 03: #36C	June 4	First Week in Pentecost
2037*	May 24	1 Extra Week See Eighth Wk in Epiphany	May 31	First Week in Pentecost
2040*	May 20	1st of 2 Extra Weeks No Mon-Fri Readings Torah Reading for May 26: #35C	May 27	2nd of 2 Extra Weeks See Eighth Wk in Epiphany

As always, the Sabbath readings will be indicated right after Friday of each week.
*Years that have fifty-three weeks in the Christian Year. No Monday-to-Friday readings. This is a "sabbatical week." Reflect on how this whole journey is going for you.

Pentecost Sunday   *Released in the Spirit*   **John 14:8–17**

See also: Acts 2:1–21

**This is the Spirit of truth, whom the world cannot receive,
because it neither sees him nor knows him.
You know him, because he abides with you and he will be in you. v. 17**

With the death of Jesus, the veil separating heaven and earth is lifted. Total access to God is restored once again as God makes a new creation in and through the risen Jesus.

The *world* for John is that autonomous, self-centered, exploitive reality remaining in darkness. The world has constructed a veil once again, obscuring the vision of God. The only vision that the world has is the narcissistic gaze into its own face. No wonder the world cannot receive Jesus … it does not even see him!

On Pentecost, the full release of the Holy Spirit comes upon the disciples, freeing them from all connection with the world. No longer manipulated by fear of what the world can do, boldness and expansive joy fill their hearts. Join the crowd of those who receive Jesus in the Holy Spirit today and forever.

Trinity Sunday   *The Wholeness of God*   **John 16:12–15**

(In 2007, Luke 7:1–10)

**When the Spirit of truth comes, he will guide you into all the truth;
for he will not speak on his own, but will speak whatever he hears and
he will declare to you the things that are to come. v. 13**

The indwelling of the Holy Spirit offers the very presence of God to our own souls. With this presence, comes the action of God upon our lives. The Spirit is our advocate, counselor, lawyer, advisor, teacher and here— our guide. Many roles that we assign to others in our lives are gathered up in the Holy Spirit who leads us further and further into the mystery of all truth. Where the Spirit is, there is also the Father and the Son. The heart embraces the Trinity, unable to be grasped by the mind.

In 1334, the church named the Sunday after Pentecost as Trinity Sunday. We contemplate the whole mystery of what God has been doing as the Father in creation (*Advent-Epiphany*), the Son in salvation (*Lent-Easter*), and now as the Holy Spirit in sanctification (*Pentecost*).

The First Week in Pentecost

Begins on the Sunday nearest June 1, unless the Easter Season is still in effect. Alphabyte: Arc, p. 77

Sunday *Say But the Word* **Luke 7:1–10**

"Lord, do not trouble yourself, for I am not worthy to have you come under my roof;
therefore I did not presume to come to you.
But only speak the word, and let my servant be healed. vv. 6–7

A nameless military leader from a pagan empire has more faith than the leaders of God's people … to say the least! The religious leaders are jealous and hostile in their confrontations with Jesus. The centurion, on the other hand, has a perspective that frees him for only on purpose. "My dear servant is sick and I believe that Jesus can heal him." His love and need pierce beyond religious establishment. The centurion is simple, humble, and direct. He believes that Jesus does not have to come to his house; the Word of Jesus is sufficient to heal his servant.

Stand close to the centurion as a silent aide so that you can see and feel all that takes place. This is a key healing incident, one to which you can relate. When you take Holy Communion, especially hear the words of the centurion that have come down through the ages "… Say but the Word and my soul will be healed."

Monday *The Release of Prophecy* **Joel**

Then afterward I will pour out my spirit on all flesh;
your sons and your daughters shall prophesy,
your old men shall dream dreams, and your young men shall see visions. 2:28

From the center of the surrendered heart of Joel, there wells up a prophet's voice, which would resound hundreds of years later in Peter on Pentecost. The tension in Joel between judgment and salvation makes a trampoline-like energy that releases God's Word from the prophet.

For those whose spirits are deaf, blunt and opaque to the presence of the Spirit, the outcome is one of harsh judgment. For those with Jesus in their hearts, there is the joy of salvation.

Take time to let the bottom of your soul spring upward with an energy that comes from knowing that you are a prophet in Jesus. Joel will loosen your heart from sluggishness and self-consciousness into a new freedom and spontaneity in the Lord.

Tuesday *The Instant Claims of God* **Proverbs 27**

Do not boast about tomorrow,
for you do not know what a day may bring. v. 1

Hold each proverb in the palm of your hand, contemplating every one as you would a precious jewel. Feel the texture, admire the colors, and listen inwardly as each one speaks to your heart. Taste the wisdom offered to your spirit.

Verse 6 is a way of talking about "tough love." Verse 8 relates to being at home with God and God with you … wherever you are.

There is a prayer in the 1965 Book of Worship for the Methodist Church that incorporates verse 1: "Since we know not what a day may bring forth, but only that the hour for serving thee is always present, may we wake to the instant claims of thy holy will, not waiting for tomorrow, but yielding today. Consecrate with thy presence the way our feet may go; and the humblest work will shine and the roughest places be made plain …"

Receive God into your heart, moment by moment.

Wednesday   *From Anger to Compassion*   **Psalm 109**

For the LORD stands at the right hand of the needy
to save them from those who would condemn them to death. v. 31

Take the psalmist as your model for prayer. Trust in God gives him space to express rage at injustice in words that even include cursing his enemies and wishing them destruction.

When we are angry with someone, we may *feel like* harming him or her. Begin to pray when anger surges. Give your thoughts and feelings to the Lord. Anger is best spent in the arena of prayer. You will come to that place of resting in the Spirit where you will move beyond anger at your enemies, to compassion for them, which ignites desires for their salvation.

We come to feel about others by the way in which we think about them. However, if we go further and *pray* for them, as Jesus teaches us, then our hearts will find peace, and joy will return.

Thursday   *Trivial or Edifying Pursuits?*   **1 Timothy 1—2**

The aim of such instruction is love that comes
from a pure heart, a good conscience, and sincere faith. 1:5

Beneath the issues this letter addresses to a church of a particular time and place, an atmosphere flows into our own day. The words breathe the air of that peace which comes when a person's life is centered upon the Lord. All pursuits are trivial if they lack the energy that comes from total immersion into Jesus.

Catch the joy of Paul as he offers words of encouragement to Timothy and to us. Feel yourself released from the tense bonds of disputes that often go nowhere but into greater triviality.

Make an inventory of your pursuits, ranking them according to whether they are trivial or edifying. Place everything you do into the hands of the Lord, asking Jesus to give you back only those pursuits that build up Christ's sacred body.

Friday   *The Power and the Presence*   **Luke 9:1–17**

Jesus called the twelve together and gave them
power and authority over all demons and to cure diseases. v. 1

Up to this point in the Gospel of Luke, Jesus alone demonstrates the power of the Kingdom over demons and diseases. Now this power passes into the hearts and hands of the Twelve Apostles. They have left all to follow Jesus. They have nothing, yet possess everything. These powerless ones by the world's standards begin to share all the power of the creating and saving God present in their Master.

They move outward from the center, bringing the presence of the One whom they love. As the hands of a clock that radiate outward and fill the twelve hours of the day, so these twelve fill their world with the presence and power of Jesus.

This same presence and power is ready to move further into you. Are you ready for your gifts to multiply just as the loaves and fishes?

Saturday   **The Sabbath Torah Reading**

Jun 09, 2007 #37C	Jun 04, 2016 #33C	Mar 08, 2025 #20	Jun 10, 2034 #37C
Jun 05, 2010 #37C	Mar 09, 2019 #23C	Jun 10, 2028 #36C	Jun 06, 2037 #37C
Jun 08, 2013 #38C	Mar 05, 2022 #23	Jun 07, 2031 #36C	Jun 09, 2040 #37C

The Second Week in Pentecost

Begins on the Sunday nearest June 8. Alphabyte: Beach Ball, p. 77

Sunday | ***Raised to Serve the Lord*** | **Luke 7:11–17**
Young man, I say to you, rise! v. 14

A new day of joy and wonder comes upon a dead young man and his grieving, widowed mother. Jesus raises him to life. What would his life be like after that!

This is the point of inspiration in engraving the following words on an altar at a retreat house for adolescents. "You man, I see to thee, arise." I knelt before this altar as a senior in high school, beholding this saying. I began to realize then and afterward the full implications of that verse, as though written for me alone. I was to arise to a life of ministry that God had designed for me.

What does the verse say to you—man or woman? The new life for you and me means a death of a previous one before the Risen One can raise us. How will today be different for you because the Lord is raising you now to new life?

Monday | ***Flowing Down the Mountains*** | **Amos 1—2**
The LORD roars from Zion, and utters his voice from Jerusalem.
The pastures of the shepherds wither, and the top of Carmel dries up. 1:2

From the quiet, prayerful heights of the hills of pasture, Amos hears the word of the Lord in judgment to the nations that lie below.

Take your arm and make a grand sweep in a figure eight, beginning from your upper right to lower left, upper left to lower right. This marks the geographic relation of countries indicted by Amos, crisscrossing from the northeast to southwest, from the northwest to southeast. The cross closes in at the center, as Judah and Israel are included in the judgments.

The energy of the voice of the Lord flowing down the hills through Amos must match the energy of the evils to be requited. Rather than be threatened by a God who punishes, rejoice to know a God who sees to it that pernicious evils will come to an end.

Tuesday | ***The Pace of God's Peace*** | **Proverbs 28**
Anyone who tills the land will have plenty of bread,
but one who follows worthless pursuits will have plenty of poverty. v. 19

I passed a little plot of ground on a street in New York City. It had been spared from having a building upon it or black-top for parked cars. The space was carefully cleared, grass and flowers planted, a sign fixed to the chain link fence about it, inviting passersby to pause and enjoy the garden.

Do you feel as though your days are as busy and crowded as a street in a big city? Proverbs are as little gardens for you to pass along the way, watering your soul with the refreshing and sobering truths contained in each perfect, tiny space of earthy wisdom. Take time to rest and relish the riches that God offers you in the Word. The Spirit waits for you to stop plummeting forward in haste, but to pause often.

May your pace not be so fast that the Lord has to run to catch up with you!

2
Pe
C

318

Wednesday   *The Beauty of Holiness*   **Psalm 110**

In the beauties of holiness, from the womb of the morning,
You have the dew of Your youth. v. 3

Wednesday, the middle of the week, is at the center of a cross. Spread in threes on either side, are the other days of the week. In deep, vertical descent, the psalms take us back to the times of King David. Wednesdays are rooted in the psalms as they touch the early prayer of God's people in ways that stretch upward to the promises that would come to pass. Especially in this psalm, we claim the messianic prophecy that links David to Jesus.

Your world stretches both outwardly in wide expanse, and inwardly to the quiet depths of prayer, which the Spirit of King Jesus is pouring into your heart. From the center of this cross—as from the open side of Jesus—blood and water continue to flow forth as signs of the presence of the outpouring of the Holy Spirit, filling your week.

Thursday   *Qualities of Leadership*   **1 Timothy 3—4**

Now a bishop must be above reproach, married only once, temperate, sensible, respectable, hospitable,
an apt teacher, not a drunkard, not violent but gentle, not quarrelsome, and not a lover of money. 3:2

Every Christian is a minister of the Gospel; however, certain ones are appointed to lead or "supervise," the meaning of the Greek, *episkopos*. The qualities of leadership described here are ones for us to establish in ourselves, no matter how God call us to lead. "Married only once," means faithful to one spouse.

As you read these qualities, find a place for them in your own spirit as each one touches your strings within that need to be "tuned." When you are out of tune, allow the Spirit do the adjusting, as you surrender to the Lord who alone can make you into the person God created you to be.

Chapter 5 contains sound Biblical principles that you will want to meditate upon in the course of your day. How do you measure up to them?

Friday   *Transforming the Agenda*   **Luke 9:18–50**

Those who want to save their life will lose it,
and those who lose their life for my sake will save it. v. 24

2
Pe
C

The seven units of the reading strongly contrast with each other. On the way to the Mount of Transfiguration and coming down, Jesus predicts his suffering and death. Glory and the cross are put together, faith and unbelief struggle; a demon demonstrates a final wrestling before fleeing from a boy and leaving him in peace. Then there is competition among the disciples as to who is greater, inflating them with a worldly agenda that threatens to dissipate the power they had just received from the Master.

Five of these seven units called "pericopes" are under six verses. Read slowly. May each one find a place in the movement of your waking day. You might create seven pauses in the day to read each one, meditating for a few minutes on the key verse or verses. Allow the living Word of God to gain access to your agenda and transform it.

Saturday   **The Sabbath Torah Reading**

Jun 16, 2007 #38C	Jun 11, 2016 #34C	Jun 14, 2025 #36C	Jun 17, 2034 #38C
Jun 12, 2010 #38C	Jun 15, 2019 #35C	Jun 17, 2028 #37C	Jun 13, 2037 #38C
Jun 15, 2013 #39C	Jun 11, 2022 #35C	Jun 14, 2031 #37C	Jun 16, 2040 #38C

The Third Week in Pentecost

Begins on the Sunday nearest June 15. Alphabyte: Clock, p. 78

Sunday   *Beyond All Bounds*   Luke 7:36—8:3
Her sins, which are many, are forgiven, for she loved much.
But to whom little is forgiven, the same loves little. 7:47

Two persons focus completely upon Jesus. One is a Pharisee and host of a dinner to which Jesus is invited, the other, a noted sinful woman in town. Obsessive thoughts and criticism of Jesus cripple the Pharisee's heart. The woman is free beyond all bounds to pour out fragrant oil and love upon a man who has done something extraordinary for her.

What happened previously in each of these two person's lives to account for their behaviors? The woman's outburst of joy and love is in response Jesus' love, acceptance, and forgiveness of her. The Pharisee's heart, empty of any need to be forgiven, spawns smug and arrogant thoughts.

Place yourself in the scene; be with Jesus at the dinner; open your heart completely to the One who loves and forgives you right now.

Monday   *God's Word Exposed*   Amos 3—4
Surely the Lord God does nothing,
without revealing his secret to his servants the prophets. 3:7

Watch the power in one Hebrew word—*Galah*: "to reveal." It literally means, "to uncover," "to remove." The Hebrew Scriptures often use this word for exposing the nakedness of someone, or to strip something bare. It is also the word used to take people into captivity, making them *naked* to their enemies. The protective covering of the homeland is wrenched away. Of the ten times that Amos uses the word, all have this meaning, except the meaning of "reveal" in the verse for the day.

The strong sense of action in the word *galah* suggests the power that comes upon the prophet as he experiences the naked word of God exposed to him. The early 8th century B.C. thundering voice of Amos also becomes a written word; Amos will lead the way in making prophecy a literary form.

What unique word is the Lord uncovering for you today?

Tuesday   *The Embrace of Your Friend*   Proverbs 29
A fool gives full vent to anger,
but the wise quietly holds it back. v. 11

Imagine walking along a path when suddenly a dear friend whom you have not seen in ages comes toward you. As soon as you recognize who it is, you stop in your tracks for a moment, then rush toward the person and embrace in affection.

Proverbs are similar to these encounters. Deep in your spirit, there is already a longing for close union with God. Perhaps the concerns of your world have deprived you for a long time from being with the Lord, for whom you were created—the ultimate friend of your soul. As you walk through your day, these twenty-seven expressions from your friend, the Holy Spirit, greet you along the way. Their truths bring you to a full stop. Spend a few minutes embracing these words from the Lord. Then continue to walk with the Lord more closely, more deeply, for the rest of your day.

Wednesday	*From Beginning to End*	**Psalm 111**

I will give thanks to the LORD with my whole heart,
in the company of the upright, in the congregation. v. 1

Praise and comfort in the power and goodness of God abound in this psalm. It is an acrostic poem, as each of the twenty-two lines begins with a successive letter of the Hebrew alphabet. Every verse contains two lines, except verses 9 and 10, which have three. In the original Hebrew, each line usually consists of just three words.

Could you find English words from **A** to **V** that would summarize the sense of each of the lines for you? For example, the world **ALL** comes to my mind for the first verse—**with ALL of my heart.**

Another idea … Take each verse for ten of the waking hours of your day. You will be held aloft by the verses of this psalm from the beginning to the end of your day. From *A* to *Z* Jesus will be your *Alpha* and *Omega*.

Thursday	*Touchstones for Right Living*	**1 Timothy 5—6**

We brought nothing into the world,
so that we can take nothing out. 6:7

Unique circumstances in Paul's society are contained here; still you will find what is relevant to our own day. There are similarities with the plight of widows and single parent mothers today.

Look for the Godly principles present that are universal. These are the touchstones to use when it comes to consider what to do for others and to maintain yourself in correct thinking and acting. Idleness erodes the boundaries between our lives and those of others, tempting us to mind what is not our business.

As the weeks of summer pass before your life and you are on vacation, find activities that truly renew your spirit. Paul is on the move. Take him with you in your travels. Respond wholeheartedly to his exhortations that close the letter.

Friday	*No Turning Back*	**Luke 9:51—10:24**

No one who puts a hand to the plow and looks back
is fit for the kingdom of God. 9:62

Have you ever been on a bicycle or in your car while a dog runs along, barking frantically at the wheels? Someone once described the church as a covered wagon, making its way through the world, while dogs bark noisily though harmlessly at the turning, great spokes of the wheels.

Jesus begins his journey to Jerusalem. Nothing distracts him and no one can turn his face away from this focus—at once the place of death and triumph. There is no turning back for Jesus. No barking "*Crucify him! Crucify him!*" will turn Jesus from the cross.

From 9:57–62, three kinds of persons are presented as those fit to be disciples of Jesus. Dwell on the characteristics, sensing similarities in your own life. The Lord's call upon your life is very personal.

Saturday   The Sabbath Torah Reading

Jun 23, 2007 #39C	Jun 18, 2016 #35C	Jun 21, 2025 #37C	Jun 24, 2034 #39C
Jun 19, 2010 #39C	Jun 22, 2019 #36C	Jun 24, 2028 #38C	Jun 20, 2037 #39C
Jun 22, 2013 #40C	Jun 18, 2022 #36C	Jun 21, 2031 #38C	Jun 23, 2040 #39–40C

The Fourth Week in Pentecost
Begins on the Sunday nearest June 22. Alphabyte: Drink, p. 78

Sunday   *Infected with Joy*   **Luke 8:26–39**
He went away, proclaiming throughout the city
how much Jesus had done for him. v. 39b

Two responses are announced after Jesus delivers the man with the legion of demons. The first is from the people of v. 36 who have seen the deliverance; the second comes from the man himself. The first reporters are shocked and frightened by the miracle, infecting the people with their fears; they ask Jesus to leave. The second telling comes with the joy, the peace, the energy of the man who had received such a wondrous gift. Both Mark and Luke use the Greek word for "preaching," *kerusso,* to describe how he witnesses to the people. Know how different must have been the response of the people infected with joy!

Just as this man, do not stay at the feet of Jesus, but go and share the joy and radiance of your miracle contact with the Lord with many others in your day.

Monday   *Thirsting for Justice*   **Amos 5—6**
Let justice roll down like water,
and righteousness like an everflowing stream. 5:24

During World War II, German soldiers used to go to the theater at night with their wives after having spent the day gassing thousands of Jews. Comfortable in their seats, they would weep at the beauty of the music, unmindful of the atrocities that went on during the day, ears deaf to the screams and the sobs of those in the camps occurring at the same time as the concerts.

The Holocaust of the Twentieth Century A.D. had its precedent in the Eighth Century B.C. In today's passage, Amos mourns for the virgin of Israel as though she has already died. He shares his grief in the hopes that the comfort and complacency of those moved only by music, would be shaken to a hunger and thirst for justice.

What are the changes that need to take place in you when it comes to making justice? Without it, the most beautiful music turns worship into vanity, and even blasphemy.

Tuesday   *A Sacred Sequence*   **1 Chronicles 1—3**
Abraham became the father of Isaac.
The sons of Isaac: Esau and Israel. 1:34

Almost the entire Sixth Century, B.C. saw God's people living in exile in Babylonia. Permitted by the Persian Kings Cyrus and Darius to return, the Jewish people began to rejoice once again in the power of God's saving presence. The Temple in Jerusalem was reconstructed in 515 B.C. and the full life of worship for God's people resumed once again. As a way of reconnecting the sacred thread of God's saving grace, the compilers of 1 and 2 Chronicles gather the history of God's action among God's people. This begins with nine chapters of genealogies. Today's reading traces the thread from Adam to Jacob with a focus upon Judah; from this tribe comes the line of David.

God had you in mind when he spread out this array of families. Place yourself into this sacred history. Let this day be another in the sacred sequence of your personal history.

Wednesday   *Delight in the Lord's Ways*   **Psalm 112**
Praise the Lord! Happy are those who fear the Lord,
who greatly delight in his commandments. v. 1

Qualities of a person righteous in the Lord are uplifted along with the blessings that flow from true surrender to God's power. Examine your heart. How does your life measure up to the virtues celebrated in this psalm?

Once again, the acrostic style of this psalm suggests that we be as creative as the psalmist is. After you pray the psalm, ask the Holy Spirit to bring to your mind those qualities that you need in order to live more fully according to the Lord's ways. Take the letters of the alphabet and allow a list from A to Z to well up from within as you pray to respond more fully to the call of the Lord upon your life.

A key word in Hebrew that you could use for "c" is *chafets*. It means "to delight" in the Lord's ways. Do you find that your spirit truly enjoys growing in the command of Christ Jesus that we love one another?

Thursday   *Revelation for You*   **Hebrews 1**
Long ago God spoke to our ancestors in many and various ways by the prophets,
but in these last days he has spoken to us by a Son, whom he appointed heir of all things,
through whom he also created the worlds. v. 1

This exalted letter about Christ's pre-eminence begins by making a grand sweep of revelation from the beginning to this present moment of your prayer. The superiority that Christ has over the angels serves to remind us of the complete and total access that Christ has to our hearts. References to five Psalms and other Old Testament texts fill most of the 14 verses of the opening chapter.

Enter these references deepening your appreciation, not only of the supremacy of Christ, but of Christ's intimacy with you at your own level.

No longer is God's revelation every once in a while. Rather is it ongoing, all pervasive, flooding your soul at this very moment and for always. What will you do today to be alert to those personal communications of the living God to you, God's beloved creature?

4
Pe
C

Friday   *Two Ways to Be Near Jesus*   **Luke 10:25–42**
When the Samaritan saw him, he was moved with pity. v. 33

The Evil One often uses the mixed motives of others in an attempt to distract us from God's will. The root of the word for the "testing" by the lawyer is the same one Luke uses to describe the temptation of Jesus by the devil in the desert (Luke 4:2)—even a more intense form of the word. Yet Jesus is up to the challenge.

Heady questions that fill committee rooms can distract us, while abuse and mugging could be taking place just outside the door. The two priestly types missed the chance to be near Jesus who was within the man in great need. "I was sick and you took care of me" (Matt 25:36).

There are moments to find Jesus in another in need … and moments—as Mary found—to sit at his feet and listen to his Word. Do not miss either today.

Saturday   **The Sabbath Torah Reading**

Jun 30, 2007 #40C	Jun 25, 2016 #36C	Jun 28, 2025 #38C	Jul 01, 2034 #40C
Jun 26, 2010 #40C	Jun 29, 2019 #37C	Jul 01, 2028 #39C	Jun 27, 2037 #40C
Jun 29, 2013 #41C	Jun 25, 2022 #37C	Jun 28, 2031 #39C	Jun 30, 2040 #41C

The Fifth Week in Pentecost

Begins on the Sunday nearest June 29. Alphabyte: Eyes, p. 78

Sunday   *No Place to Go But Up*   **Luke 9:51–62**
When the days drew near for him to be taken up,
he set his face to go to Jerusalem. 9:51

A runner seeing the finish line in the distance finds a burst of energy to complete the race. So does Jesus fix his eyes upon Jerusalem straight ahead to be then taken straight up to Heaven.

The Greek word for "taken up," *analepsis*, is the word for the Ascension of Jesus. Mount Calvary is as the Mount of the Ascension; the raised cross prefigures, and is at once, the Ascension.

From the deepest of suffering and darkness, there is no place to go but up. Yet for this to happen there is no place to go but straight ahead in following Jesus. He has blazed the trail for you; all you need to do is follow. Keep your eyes upon him, and nothing from the sidelines will distract you, or prompt you to leave the race before the finish.

Monday   *Final Restoration*   **Amos 7—9**
I will plant them upon their land, and they shall never again
be plucked up out of the land that I have given them, says the Lord your God. 9:15

We know about Amos only from what he tells us in 7:14. No human credential or pedigree warrants God choosing him to be a prophet. Recall what Paul said in 1 Corinthians 1:27: "God chose what is foolish in the world to shame the wise; God chose what is weak in the world to shame the strong."

Through the dark passage of pain for not living according to the Lord's way, to the heights of contemplating God's grandeur in 9:6, Amos lures his shepherd people back into believing in the promise of ultimate salvation and security in the Lord. Read and reread the promises of a restored Israel, culminating in the final verse.

Is there pain in your path? Amos will move you to hope in the victory in Jesus.

Tuesday   *The Past in the Light of the Call*   **1 Chronicles 4—6**
These are the men whom David put in charge of the service of song
in the house of the Lord, after the ark came to rest there. 6:31

The Books of Kings were written as prophetic calls to awaken God's people to awareness that their exile was the result of profound moral and religious degradation. 1 and 2 Chronicles, while covering much of the same time period, write this history in the light of the community of God that has already returned to freedom after the exile. The emphasis is upon worship; hence, the priestly tone of this work, as contrasted with prophecy.

In the passage for today, genealogies outline the tribes of Judah, Simeon, Reuben, Gad, Manasseh and Levi, with further information about this latter line of priests.

God wants you to see your personal history in the light of God's present call to you. Pray for a deep awareness of this call, asking the Spirit to help you interpret your past in the light of the blessed future that God is unfolding for you.

Wednesday	*Saturation Praise*	Psalm 113

Who is like the LORD our God, who is seated on high,
who looks far down on the heavens and the earth? vv. 5–6

Psalms 113 to 118 form a group called the *Hallel* songs, taken from the Hebrew word for "praise." Wednesdays in the middle weeks of the Pentecost season this year find us lifting our voices in these special songs that were sung in homes at Passover time. They all contain *Alleluia*, the Hebrew word that means "Praise Yah." *Yah* is the shortened form for the covenant name *Yahweh*.

Alleluia: this unique word of joy and praise only occurs in the Psalms—twenty-six times to be exact. Today let your hours be flooded—saturated with Alleluia. When you are tempted to become a victim and self-conscious with *poor me*, take on the heavenly perspective of the Lord looking down on the whole earth, not losing the smallest detail of your need. If your heart is barren as the childless mother in the final verse, *Alleluia* prayed with faith can fill your empty heart with God.

Thursday	*Extraordinary Truths*	Hebrews 2

It was fitting that God, for whom and through whom all things exist,
in bringing many children to glory, should make the pioneer
of their salvation perfect through sufferings. v. 10

If angelic annunciations were such powerful moments of God's intervention in history, how much more are the words of Jesus to you right now! The writer uses Psalm 8 to ground the argument so that we understand and rejoice in the accessibility that we have to Jesus. Christ has completely entered our history, even taking on death that he might deliver us from this last and final enemy to life and love. The triumph of Jesus in his suffering is the source of the victory that we have over all that would diminish us.

The first listeners to this letter needed to be reminded of the truths this letter teaches. Find yourself in similar need as you drink in these words of extraordinary truth about God and about you.

Friday	*Protecting the Planted Word*	Luke 11

Blessed are those who hear the word of God and protect it.
(v. 28, Author's translation)

A newly seeded garden needs daily gentle care and watering to nurture the growth to full maturity. However, when it is time to move a plant to a garden, to change it from pot to plot, we turn the plant upside down and give it a strong whack on the bottom to loosen the clinging hold that the soil has to its first home.

The chapter opens with the disciples moved by the results of Jesus' personal time of prayer. They want to receive this gift—to learn how to pray. Jesus opens the treasures of his heart and talks to them about prayer. They are like the freshly seeded garden needing nurture and protection for the seed-word to grow.

There are those who resist being transplanted from a religion of law, manipulation, self-interest, and greed, into the fresh garden of the Kingdom. Jesus' harsh words to them are designed to jolt them into saving space. Protect the planted word in your heart.

Saturday
The Sabbath Torah Reading

Jul 07, 2007 #41C	Jul 02, 2016 #37C	Jul 05, 2025 #39C	Jul 08, 2034 #41C
Jul 03, 2010 #41C	Jul 06, 2019 #38C	Jul 08, 2028 #40C	Jul 04, 2037 #41C
Jul 06, 2013 #42–43C	Jul 02, 2022 #38C	Jul 05, 2031 #40C	Jul 07, 2040 #42–43C

5
Pe
C

The Sixth Week in Pentecost

*Begins on the Sunday nearest July 6. Alphabyte: **Firestarter**, p. 79*

Sunday   *Following the Followers*   **Luke 10:1–11; 16–20**

**The Lord appointed seventy others and sent them on ahead of him
in pairs to every town and place where he himself intended to go. v. 1**

"He set his face to go to Jerusalem:" So does St. Luke begin the account of Jesus' journey to Jerusalem in 9:51. Crowds follow Jesus as he leads the way, his eyes and heart focused relentlessly on the great city from where salvation will flow forth. Into this journey narrative, savings events of teaching and healings occur.

Between Jerusalem and Jesus' face, the disciples fan out two by two ahead of him. The people along the way are not to miss the moment of saving grace that is about to happen for them. The first faces the people see are the ones of those in love with Jesus—those who believe in him and in his power to bring to life those wallowing in the shadows of death.

The Leader follows the followers! When people see your face and sense your heart, will they know that Jesus is not far behind—but in fact is within you?

Monday   *The Vengeance of Esau*   **Obadiah**

**On Mount Zion there shall be those that escape,
and it shall be holy. v. 17**

Strife continues through the generations of Esau and Jacob. Then an event of profound sadness, as descendants of Esau, the Edomites take vengeance on Israel, their hated neighbors. The Edomites become allies of the Babylonians in the sack of Jerusalem and the destruction of the Temple in 586 B.C. Sometime around now, Jewish people begin a three-week period of mourning recalling the destruction of the two Temples: the first one, mentioned above, and the second one, in 70 A.D.

This is the shortest book in Bible–21 verses. The first part reflects human sinfulness that abounds in the Bible; the second part from verse 17 anticipates God's ultimate victory from the new Mount Zion, the Church, after the ultimate treachery of the murder of the Son of God.

Do impulses of revenge lurk inside you, bending your spirit away from forgiveness?

Tuesday   *God's Data Base*   **1 Chronicles 7—9**

**So all Israel was enrolled by genealogies;
and these are written in the Book of the Kings of Israel. 9:1**

It is possible to access the history of your family from immense data bases prepared for computers. This has spurred interest in the discovery of one's ethnic origins. With today's passage, we conclude the nine chapters of genealogies that has been God's "data base" for the narrative that follows. For people in exile for almost a century, there was need to find themselves flowing from the great list of ancestors through the tribes of Israel and to remain faithful, as later ancestors did not.

Who are the ones close to you in your past that have connected you to the faith of our fathers and mothers? A myriad number of ancestors have conspired with God that you come into existence and believe in Jesus. Nothing is by chance—all is the design of God. What difference will you make to your progeny in the light of your growing love for the Lord and God's Word?

Wednesday	*The Radiating Presence*	Psalm 114

Tremble, O earth, at the presence of the LORD,
At the presence of the God of Jacob. v. 7

Crowds make a border of cheers in support of the runners in city Marathons. In such a manner does the psalmist describe the hills and rivers skipping and dancing as rams and lambs in their joy as they witness the race of God's people to freedom in the Exodus.

As you run the race and grow in holiness and perfection in the Body of Christ, all creation cheers you along. Just as the earth is described in verse 7 as trembling at the presence of the Lord, so does the Spirit of Jesus within you command a power that radiates to the world about you. Humbly accept this power—it is not yours, but God's. Release this power in loving acts of prayer and service with a joy that cheers others along their race in its course in mid-week and mid-summer.

Thursday	*Resting in Jesus*	Hebrews 3

Exhort one another every day, as long as it is called *today*,
so that none of you may be hardened by the deceitfulness of sin. v. 13

The nature of Christ is exalted high above the greatness of Moses. Christ draws us to himself, embracing us, longing that we rest in the security and comfort of being one with his own body.

Let us not be as God's people in the desert—as children squirming and pushing away from the cuddling arms of a loving parent. Rebelliousness, restlessness, and resistance took place, coming from that hardness of heart that happens when unbelief is at the core.

Sink into this day, this moment as into the arms of Jesus who waits for you to rest with him and in him. Beware of the negative movement of the deceitfulness of sin and of disobedience to God's Word. What is it in you that tends to push you away from that quiet peace that comes when you are resting in Jesus?

Friday	*The Leaven of the Word*	Luke 12

Beware of the yeast of the Pharisees,
that is, their hypocrisy. v. 1

Four New Testament writers: Matthew, Mark, Luke, and Paul each find in the image of yeast or leaven, a way to describe spiritual realities, positive and negative. It is sometimes used as an expression of the Kingdom rising as dough; in this context, it is the wicked yeast of the hypocrisy of the Pharisees that works its way into the mass of the community and damages it.

The word hypocrisy originally meant to act a part in a play. Literally it means "to judge beneath." It came to have a negative meaning, a hidden agenda, beneath the false front that someone presents.

Just a little bit of leaven changes the whole mass. So here, only a tiny bit of hypocrisy blocks that honesty needed to reveal the Lord's presence through your own transparency. Divide this powerful chapter into sections and let the leaven of the Word transform your day.

6
Pe
C

Saturday The Sabbath Torah Reading

Jul 14, 2007 #42–43C	Jul 09, 2016 #38C	Jul 12, 2025 #40C	Jul 15, 2034 #42–43C
Jul 10, 2010 #42–43C	Jul 13, 2019 #39C	Jul 15, 2028 #41C	Jul 11, 2037 #42–43C
Jul 13, 2013 #44C	Jul 09, 2022 #39C	Jul 12, 2031 #41C	Jul 14, 2040 #44C

The Seventh Week in Pentecost

Begins on the Sunday nearest July 13. Alphabyte: Gears, p. 79

Sunday   *Coming Near*   **Luke 10:25–37**

What must I do to inherit eternal life? v. 25

Though the lawyer's question lacked the sincerity needed to show hunger for Jesus' answer, may this not be so for you. Pray over the question, until your heart throbs for the answer. Only then will you not be as the priests in the parable who lost the chance to know their God in a new way.

The word *neighbor* in English means "the boor who is neigh." The original meaning of "boor," however, was not an insult as it is today; it simply meant another peasant farmer who lived nearby.

The issue for Jesus is not the one who is near you, but rather the one to whom you come near. Who are the ones in your life from whom you pull away because you do not like them—boors in the bad sense of the word ... or maybe just bores? Underneath, there is a hurting, wounded soul needing the bandages of your love.

Monday   *From the Belly*   **Jonah 1—2**

**I called to the LORD out of my distress, and he answered me;
out of the belly of Sheol I cried, and you heard my voice. 2:2**

God's heart is warm and tender to Nineveh—Jonah's is not. God singles out for salvation, this pagan capital of the empire that wreaked havoc on the Israelites from the ninth to the seventh centuries B.C. Jonah flees to Spain—the ends of the earth—refusing to be involved with God's mercy on a city Jonah hates. However, wherever he goes, Jonah brings faith in the God of the Hebrews. The Phoenician sailors cry out to God whom they have come to know by someone avoiding doing God's will. Even the great fish obeys and throws up!

God's patience with the prophet rivals God's patience with Nineveh. Is there something that you know way down in your own belly that you are called to do and are avoiding? Even greater than flight away from God's will is God's pursuit of you until you complete what God wants.

Tuesday   *The Army of God*   **1 Chronicles 10—12**

**Indeed from day to day people kept coming to David to help him,
until there was a great army, like an army of God. 12:22**

(See 1 Samuel 9—31; 2 Samuel 5:1–7; 2 Sam 23:8–39)

God's people were unfaithful, resulting in their exile in Babylonia. The tragic end of Saul is an example of the dreadful consequences to infidelity to God. He too was unfaithful. By contrast, the faithful heart of David begins to attract the whole nation toward him. He names leaders with their followers who gather into a great unity around King David.

Picture in your mind this crescendo of support. Reflect upon your own life and those who are one with you in their Christian walk. In turn, are you a support for others to find strength and unity in the Body of Christ? In the spiritual warfare waged day by day, the Lord does not want you to be minimal in the experience of prayerful intercession and community love. You are not meant to be only a survivor, but as Paul, "more than a conqueror" (Romans 8:37).

Wednesday	*Dead Idols and the Living God*	Psalm 115

O Israel, trust in the LORD;
He is their help and their shield. v. 9

Bursting with trust, verse 9 rises forth in the center of the psalm. The cry is the exploding result of the growing awareness in the previous verses of the emptiness and the powerlessness of all idols and false gods.

Further your inventory of those persons, places, and things that sometimes elbow their way into the sacred center of your life where God alone is to dwell. However much your physical senses may delight in them, in contrast to the power of God they are as dead idols "that have mouths but do not speak, eyes, but do not see."

As you conclude your list, feel the shift in today's verse into the second part of the psalm that tilts toward intercessory prayer, especially in verses 14 and 15. Join in with the exuberant ending: **Alleluia: Praise the Lord!**

Thursday	*The One and the Many*	Hebrews 4

The word of God is living and active, sharper than any two-edged sword,
piercing until it divides soul from spirit, joints from marrow;
it is able to judge the thoughts and intentions of the heart. v. 12

Do we draw water, or does water draw us? Oceans, rivers, lakes, streams each invite us to come to the side, resting as we gaze upon the liquid body. Whether it is a mirror-like lake, or waves crashing upon soft sand, water calls to quiet and to rest.

My favorite lake is always the same, yet always different. Never does the same water fill this cup of earth. Before me is the age-long dilemma of "The One and the Many."

The Letter to the Hebrews takes the same theme. The *many* attempts that there be rest after sin's atonement are contrasted with the *one*, total sufficiency of the priest and king—Jesus.

Take verse 12. There is the one Word of God, the Greek, *logos,* and there are the particular moment-by-moment words and promises for you, the Greek, *rhema.* What is the *rhema* that God has for you today?

Friday	*Slow Up and Pass Through*	Luke 13

Strive to enter through the narrow door;
for many, I tell you, will try to enter and will not be able. v. 24

Jesus continues to make his way to Jerusalem. Along the road, opportunities for teaching, healing, and confrontation offer themselves, depending upon the kind of response that Jesus needs to give.

As an image of movement from one place to another, Jesus speaks about the narrow door—that special opening through which one enters into Kingdom life. This is not unlike the narrow barriers that we pass through on toll highways. We must slow down in order to make the entry safely.

Take this chapter and its simple divisions and let them be as moments in your day to slow up and pass through the narrow gate of God's Word. Take nourishment, take heart, and be on your way. Remember: any toll that has to be paid was already done by Jesus on the cross!

Saturday   The Sabbath Torah Reading

Jul 21, 2007 #44C	Jul 16, 2016 #39C	Jul 19, 2025 #41C	Jul 22, 2034 #44C
Jul 17, 2010 #44C	Jul 20, 2019 #40C	Jul 22, 2028 #42–43C	Jul 18, 2037 #44C
Jul 20, 2013 #45C	Jul 16, 2022 #40C	Jul 19, 2031 #42–43C	Jul 21, 2040 #45C

7
Pe
C

The Eighth Week in Pentecost

Begins on the Sunday nearest July 20. Alphabyte: Hurricane, p. 79

Sunday   *At the Feet of the Master*   **Luke 10:38–42**

Martha had a sister Mary, who sat at the Lord's feet
And listened to what he was saying. v. 39

A woman in a church I served claimed that we needed to come to the defense of Martha in this story. After all, she was offering hospitality and needed her sister's help.

Yet instead of quietly, politely asking her sister to help, Martha turns to the guest and scolds Jesus for not sending Mary her way! Beneath this charming incident that only Luke reports, there are two kinds of dispositions. Martha is the impulsive type, quick to help another right away; Mary is open, receptive, needing time with Jesus before she does anything else.

There comes a time to move from the feet of Jesus to share more widely, as the Gadarene demoniac of a few chapters before. However, beware of the Martha in you who has no time to be at the feet of Jesus—being first fed by the one whom she will later serve. If you never rest and listen at Jesus' feet, what good is it wherever else you go?

Monday   *A Sense Deeper than Feeling*   **Jonah 3—4**

Should I not be concerned about Nineveh, that great city,
in which there are more than a hundred and twenty thousand persons
who do not know their right hand from their left ...? 4:11

Shall we try this again, Jonah? This man, who spends more time sulking than prophesying, finds himself back to square one. "What might happen if I avoid God's will again? More nights in the belly of a whale? I think not!"

So it is that Jonah makes his way through Nineveh obeying the command from God, yet with no energy to do it. The people repent in grand style! Jonah's anger flares up. Then he sulks again when the little bush withers up.

The Lord's compassion is never-ending. The last verse is similar to the final words of Jesus on the cross: "Father, forgive them; for they do not know what they are doing" (Luke 23:34).

Be careful about sulking. Do God's will, even when you do not feel like doing it. In the belly of your person, there is a sense deeper than feeling—you simply *know* what God is asking of you.

8
Pe
C

Tuesday   *Symbols of God's Presence*   **1 Chronicles 13—14**

David and all Israel were dancing before God with all their might,
with song and lyres and harps and tambourines and cymbals and trumpets. 13:8
(See 2 Sam 6:1–11; 2 Sam 5:17–25)

With the death of Saul, strife within the Israelites ends. Now David can turn the people's attention to a heightened awareness of God's presence by having the Ark of the Covenant returned to Jerusalem.

The Ark was the most sacred symbol of the presence of God to the people. Enter into the joy of David and the people in the all-night dance of joy before this precious symbol.

What would it be like for you to dance for the Lord? You will want to do this the more you relish those symbols that quicken God's presence to your mind and heart. From this close awareness of God, you will want to turn often to God, just as David did. He frequently asked God for direction, for example, what to do about the Philistines. Know by faith that God has an answer for you when you truly want to know what God wants.

Wednesday   *Bounties Bursting Forth*   **Psalm 116**
Return to your rest, O my soul,
For the LORD has dealt bountifully with you. v. 7

Jesus and his disciples sang portions of these Passover *Hallel* songs as they walked from the upper room of the Last Supper to the Garden of Gethsemane. He must have felt the comfort of these verses that move between threat and divine protection as he entered into the first anguished feelings of the Passion in the agony in that garden.

This psalm that Jesus said before the Passion journey is a perfect one for you to pray before moments of challenge, suffering and anguish. You could well engrave and frame verse after verse as the psalmist lists the goodness of the Lord to him.

Take one minute by the clock and let your heart make a list of God's bounties that burst forth from your spirit.

Thursday   *Perfected By Suffering*   **Hebrews 5**
Having been made perfect, Jesus became
the source of eternal salvation for all who obey him. v. 9

The wholly Other becomes one with us. Ponder the verses that tell again of Jesus' absolute identity with us. Jesus knows the weakness in being human. Our experience is his experience—all of it—sin alone excepted.

Dwell on the comfort of the words that tell of Christ's compassion for you. The rejection of others and ourselves comes from what we do not know. If the thread from our own pain to others' suffering were not broken, we would be compassionate, not critical.

Jesus is one with you in all that you suffer. He will teach you how to surrender your suffering and become one with him. Verses 12–14 invite us to reflect upon the level of spiritual maturity we bring to the faith facts of this letter. Are you ready to live the truths held before you?

Friday   *Our World Upside Down*   **Luke 14**
All who exalt themselves will be humbled,
And those who humble themselves will be exalted. v. 11

Jesus turns our world upside down. Those who take the first place are told to go to the last; those in the last place are invited to assume the first; the exalted will be humbled and the humbled with be exalted, etc.

The root meaning of "repentance" in the Greek, *metanoioa,* is "to change the attitude"—the way we look at things. What are your habitual ways of seeing things that the Lord invites you to change 180 degrees?

Keep you eyes fixed upon Jesus—not with the narrow, squinted eyebrows of the critical Pharisees, but with eyes wide open, searching for God's presence and that meaning about your world that only God can give.

Saturday   **The Sabbath Torah Reading**

Jul 28, 2007 #45C	Jul 23, 2016 #40C	Jul 26, 2025 #42–43C	Jul 29, 2034 #45C
Jul 24, 2010 #45C	Jul 27, 2019 #41C	Jul 29, 2028 #44C	Jul 25, 2037 #45C
Jul 27, 2013 #46C	Jul 23, 2022 #41C	Jul 26, 2031 #44C	Jul 28, 2040 #46C

The Ninth Week in Pentecost
Begins on the Sunday nearest July 27. Alphabyte: Ink, p. 80

Sunday   *At One with God*   **Luke 11:1–13**

If you then, who are evil, know how to give good gifts to your children,
how much more will the heavenly Father
give the Holy Spirit to those who ask him! v. 13

The disciples long to enter those spaces of communion that Jesus demonstrates he has with the Father. Join with their longing and their cry: "Lord, teach us to pray!"

What follows is Luke's version of The Lord's Prayer. Embrace every word until the familiarity of this prayer becomes brand new.

Jesus confronts the temptations that often lurk within us to distrust prayer. Jesus offers images for confidence in prayer. Fervently believe that the Lord wants to share his saving grace with you, inviting you to ask with the same confidence of a child to a loving Father. After all, this was the experience of Jesus. He shares with you the total intimacy in the bond of trust and love that he has with the Father.

Monday   *The Third Temple*   **Lamentations 4—5**

Remember, O LORD, what has befallen us;
look, and see our disgrace! 5:1

Is there an anniversary of an event of great sadness for you? For Jewish people, it is *"The Ninth of Ab,"* the day around now when the Temple of Solomon was destroyed by the Babylonians in 586 B.C. Also mourned is the Roman destruction in 70 A.D. of the rebuilt Temple. It is a day of complete fast, just as on *Yom Kippur*. The Book of Lamentations is read.

We are one with our Jewish brothers and sisters as we all mourn the loss of these sacred sanctuaries. Pray that all people will come to rejoice in the "Third Temple" that will never be destroyed—the Body of Christ in which we live, move and have our being.

Mourn with all those who have sustained great losses in national and personal tragedies. Let the verse for today be profound intercession for them, praying in faith that joy and comfort will rise from the ash heap of their sorrow.

Tuesday   *The Ark that Carries God*   **1 Chronicles 15—17**

(See 1 Sam 6—7; Psalm 105:1–5)

When your days are fulfilled to go to be with your ancestors,
I will raise up your offspring after you, one of your own sons,
and I will establish his kingdom. 17:11

David makes all decisions after prayer, consulting the Lord about the proper order (15:13). Spend time reflecting what this verse means in terms of your daily priorities.

Notice the frequent references to music as the Ark is returned to Jerusalem. Michal, Saul's daughter, still carries old resentments and jealousies; she disdains David and his way of worshipping. Is there anything of Michal in you when you see the way others express their praise of God?

Enjoy the psalm that fills chapter 16. Verses in chapter 17 tilt to the coming of Jesus. Much more important than the house that David is going to build for God is the one that God is going to build for him. You and I are to be the ark that carries God!

Wednesday   *Alleluia!*   **Psalm 117**

Praise the LORD, all you nations! Extol him, all you peoples!
For great is his steadfast love toward us,
and the faithfulness of the LORD endures forever. Praise the LORD! vv. 1–2

Today's passage is short enough to be presented in its entirety as the verse for the day. Memorize it, repeating it often throughout the course of your day. Feel the imperative mood in the words *Praise* and *Extol.* Sense the connection that this psalm has with the reading from Lamentations on Monday, as we recall the destruction of the two Temples. God has seen to it that this disaster has been surpassed by the temple-body of Jesus, which cannot be destroyed. With God, there is always a way out, even when there does not seem to be one.

May your heart and voice sing out in praise for our God who rebuilds all that is shattered and destroyed in our lives into resurrection, Holy Spirit space—all because God's love is constant and unfailing.

Thursday   *The Bond of Faith*   **Hebrews 6**

We want each one of you to show the same diligence so as to realize the full assurance of hope to the very end, so that you may not become sluggish, but imitators of those who through faith and patience inherit the promises. vv. 11–12

Strong words are addressed to the first recipients of this letter, those on the verge of renouncing the faith they once had in Jesus. To save those about to make the suicidal plunge into apostasy was likely the motive for writing the letter.

Though you may not identify with those about to renounce Jesus, remember what happened to Peter in a moment of fear and weakness. Does your life-style and activities tell the world that you are a disciple of Jesus? Is your heart as well as your lips centered upon the Lord? Pray for a deepening of your commitment to Jesus in everything. Intercede prayerfully for the countless numbers at this very moment whose suffering and persecution would cease if they would renounce their faith in Jesus. They need the bond of your faith to uphold theirs.

9
Pe
C

Friday   *Healing Tears*   **Luke 15**

We had to celebrate and rejoice, because this brother of yours was dead
and has come to life; he was lost and has been found. v. 32

Many years ago while on a thirty-day retreat of renewal, the Lord ministered to me in a special way while meditating on the Parable of the Prodigal Son. I was sitting beside the exquisite Carrousel in Spokane, Washington, listening to old time favorites from the band organ. All of a sudden, I heard "Cruising Down the River on a Sunday Afternoon." This had been our "family song" when I was a boy. Tears began to well up in my eyes in this instant connection to my past. I experienced the love of the Lord that was always with me, even when I had sometimes grabbed at the inheritance of grace in my life and squandered it.

The merry-go-round became a symbol for the party that the Father was throwing for me, as I, his prodigal son, returned. The music distracted me from the pitfall of guilt and I wept in healing. May the Parable do something similar for you.

Saturday   **The Sabbath Torah Reading**

Aug 04, 2007 #46C	Jul 30, 2016 #41C	Aug 02, 2025 #44C	Aug 05, 2034 #46C
Jul 31, 2010 #46C	Aug 03, 2019 #42–43C	Aug 05, 2028 #45C	Aug 01, 2037 #46C
Aug 03, 2013 #47C	Jul 30, 2022 #42–43C	Aug 02, 2031 #45C	Aug 04, 2040 #47C

The Tenth Week in Pentecost
Begins on the Sunday nearest August 3. Alphabyte: Juggling, p. 80

Sunday   *The Barn*   **Luke 12:13–21**

**You fool! This very night your life is being demanded of you.
And the things you have prepared, whose will they be? v. 21**

As you turn to the Word of the Lord today, are there worries buzzing around in your head right now? Perhaps they are variations of the plea someone blurted out from the crowd in the first verse of the reading: "Teacher, tell my brother to divide the family inheritance with me." The response of the Lord is not for him only, but for you as well, as you find yourself hemmed in by the crowd of your own thoughts.

Perhaps your problem is the opposite of the foolish man in the parable—not having enough funds to pay into the large barn of debt that you may have. Whether you feel secure because you have plenty, or scared because you do not, the Lord invites you to be disposed to receive the greatest of riches, the grace of God. Are you preparing the barn of your soul for this?

Monday   *Shock Treatment*   **Micah 1—2**

**I will surely gather all of you, O Jacob, I will gather the survivors of Israel;
I will set them together like sheep in a fold, like a flock in its pasture. 2:12**

Waves of judgment and compassion clash against each other throughout Micah's prophecy. His poetry and personal gestures are as shock treatments. He walks through the streets naked to awaken people from the evil of idolatry. The English translation misses the impact of Micah's word-plays on the names of cities. For example, Achzib means "Town of Deceit."

The ultimate intent of God is that there be repentance and not punishment for the evils against the First Commandment. There is the promise intimated here and prophesied later more fully, of a Shepherd King that will come to redeem. With this image, God dismisses the charges against the people and instead, comes to their aid.

Is there anything that you are doing that you need to be shocked into undoing?

Tuesday   *Victory When God Is Center*   **1 Chronicles 18—20**

**Be strong, and let us be courageous for our people and for the cites of our God;
and may the LORD do what seems good to him. 19:13**

(See 2 Samuel 8; 11–12)

Declaring the triumph of David over God's enemies is the motive that the writer of 1 Chronicles finds to encourage God's people having just returned from exile. Continuity with sacred history brings inner strength to the people. With God at the center of life, victory comes in great measure. "The LORD preserved David wherever he went" (18:6).

Military images might not appear fitting for successes that have come your way. Still, there is spiritual warfare taking place as evil *giants* seek to come against you. Do what David does and victory will be assured—prayer, recourse to God, confidence in the Lord, worship, and that joy that comes from knowing that you are very special to the Lord. Remember Paul's words in Romans 8:31: If God is for us, who is against us?

| Wednesday | *A Favorite Psalm* | Psalm 118 |

This is the day that the Lord has made;
let us rejoice and be glad in it. v. 24

The psalm stretches to God beyond the grasp of enemies. This made it the favorite of Martin Luther. As a lover of sacred music, Luther must have found solace recalling our Israelite ancestors and the festival marches to Zion, the hill where Jerusalem rests. Jesus sung this and the other *Hallel* psalms (113–118) while going from the Last Supper to the Garden of Gethsemane. As did Jesus, Luther knew how many and great were the adversaries against him as the vision of a more pure church gripped his entire being. He writes, "This is the psalm that I love … for it has often served me well and has helped me out of great troubles, when neither emperors, kings, wise men, clever men, nor saints could have helped me" (Quoted by Kittel, *Die Psalmen*, p. 371).

Psalm 118 is the traditional psalm for Easter. The sun on that day the Lord made has never set!

| Thursday | *Always Making Intercession* | Hebrews 7 |

Jesus is able for all time to save those who approach God through him,
since he always lives to make intercession for them. v. 25

The Lone Ranger would mysteriously appear on the scene when someone needed help. The mask served to obscure his origin; the only focus was the immediate mission he was called to fulfill.

By relating the priesthood of Jesus to that of Melchizedek, the author of the letter to the Hebrews does two things similar to the sagas of "The Masked Man." First, Jesus' priesthood is linked to the king and priest of Salem whose origins are mysterious and unconnected to the house of Levi, the expected source for the Aaronic priesthood. Secondly, Jesus "suddenly meets us," the literal meaning of the Greek, *entunchan*o, which has come to mean "to make intercession."

Unlike The Lone Ranger, however, Jesus meets up with you at every moment and will never leave you. Dwell on this awesome fact of union.

| Friday | *Do You Smell Good to God?* | Luke 16 |

What is prized by human beings
is an abomination in the sight of God. v. 15

The root meaning of the Greek word, *bdelugma,* is often translated as "abomination," means "a foul thing." Thus, the verse for today could be rendered, "What society finds valuable is a *stench* to God!"

The parables of "The Unjust Steward" and "Dives and Lazarus" form bookends for this verse, along with a few other teachings of the Lord that we often disregard. The stories have to do with covetousness in two forms—greed and lust, the latter being the underlying point of the prohibition against divorce.

Where do you find yourself as you pray these stories and teachings? It is about setting the Lord's priorities in our lives. Spend time today being honest with yourself. Is there preoccupation with riches that is turning your life from being a sweet smelling fragrance into something that just doesn't smell good to God?

Saturday | The Sabbath Torah Reading

Aug 11, 2007 #47C	Aug 06, 2016 #42–43C	Aug 09, 2025 #45C	Aug 12, 2034 #47C
Aug 07, 2010 #47C	Aug 10, 2019 #44C	Aug 12, 2028 #46C	Aug 08, 2037 #47C
Aug 10, 2013 #48C	Aug 06, 2022 #44C	Aug 09, 2031 #46C	Aug 11, 2040 #48C

The Eleventh Week in Pentecost

Begins on the Sunday nearest August 10. Alphabyte: Knots, p. 80

Sunday   *The Treasure of God's Presence*   **Luke 12:32–40**
Blessed are those servants whom the master,
when he comes, will find watching. v. 37

A Maltese dog used to be part of our household. At mealtime, he would sit with eyes focused upon me, waiting for the moment when a few morsels were tossed his way—eyes glued to mine. His whole being was nothing but watching and waiting.

The Lord uses similar images to call us to watch and wait for God's nourishing word. More than scraps from the table, Jesus longs to give you his very life. This is the only absolute value, one that needs selling and letting go of everything else.

The element of surprise is imaged in the thief coming when least expected. The only alternative is to expect the Lord all the time. Now is the time when the Lord wants to touch you with the treasure of his presence.

Monday   *The Margin Becomes the Center*   **Micah 3—4**
The lame I will make the remnant, and those who were cast off, a strong nation;
and the Lord will reign over them in Mount Zion now and forevermore. 4:7

Just as in last week's passage, Micah uses shocking images followed by words of comfort to awaken God's people to conversion. Wicked rulers have exploited the people as cannibals devouring human flesh. Images of this horrific practice continue in 3:1–5.

Chapter 4 marks a strong shift. The words are virtually identical to Isaiah 2:2–4. Abused by worldly power, God's people will find themselves filled with strength from the Lord. Having been cast off to the margin, the powerless will find themselves in the center; worldly powers will be the ones on the sidelines.

The sharp contrast of poetic images call you forth to total freedom and availability for the saving work that God wants to do through you.

Tuesday   *Counting on God Alone*   **1 Chronicles 21—23**
Is not the Lord your God with you?
Has he not given you peace on every side? 22:18
(See 2 Sam. 24)

The Hebrew Scriptures have only three references to Satan by name; here is one of them. Apparently, David yielded to the temptation to rest on his laurels, numbering the men he could count on in battle. The focus for David shifted away from relying upon the Lord, to measuring strength in the number of men in his army.

The Chronicler's purpose is to set the stage for the building of the Temple and the passing of the torch of this great work into the hands of Solomon. His name means "peaceable." All those whose hands go into the building of the Temple need to be soaked in peace, and not in the blood of battle. The ultimate purpose of the people is to worship God; hence the list of those who contribute to worship and not to war.

Are you counting on God alone as the only one who can give you peace on every side?

11
Pe
C

Wednesday   *Deep and Wide*   **Psalm 135**
Your name, O LORD, endures forever,
You fame, O LORD, throughout all generations. v. 13

The psalmist worships with breadth and depth. He begins by praising God as the source for the great expanse of the universe. Next, he goes down into the nation's past, recalling the pervading power of God's saving presence. Each verse envelops the psalmist in praise.

Do the same. The psalm wants to widen and deepen your perception by faith of God's presence to your world, both outer and inner. Move beyond self-absorption, tunnel vision, and narrow mindedness, into the wide courts of the Lord, which stretch before you in the very hours that are ahead. The sky, the horizon, and the expanse of the physical day or night, remind you of the limitless, all pervading presence of God to your world, deep and wide. Drop to your knees in adoration and praise.

Thursday   *The Earthly and the Heavenly*   **Hebrews 8—9**
How much more will the blood of Christ, who through the eternal Spirit offered
Himself without blemish to God, purify our conscience from dead works
to worship the living God? 9:14

Trace with the sacred writer the comparison between the old and new covenants, the earthly, and the heavenly. What is of earth is external, bound to time and repetition, as the example given of the once-a-year entry into the Holy of Holies of the Jewish priest. The heavenly is beyond time and space. What happens in heaven happens once and for all. So it is that Jesus, clothed with humanity and divinity as well, blends both priest and victim, offering his own blood in the heavenly sanctuary. At once, he gathers all of us with him in permanent and perpetual atonement.

Live this day more conscious of the heavenly realm where God calls you to live right now—not only when you die. Moments of silence will help you be aware of the present and perpetual shower of God's healing grace upon you.

11
Pe
C

Friday   *Moving with the Kingdom*   **Luke 17**
The kingdom of God is among you. v. 21

Jesus continues the journey to Jerusalem. The passage can be divided into seven sections—six teachings and a healing. Plan the "journey" of your day to have seven pauses in it. There are teachings of only two verses long concerning: 1] **Scandal** (1–2), 2] **Forgiveness** (3–4), 3] **Faith** (5–6), 4] **Duty** (7–10); then comes 5] **The Healing of Ten Lepers** (11–19), 6] two verses about **The Kingdom** (20–21) and 7] **The Last Days** (22–37).

The kingdom of God moves through the hours of the day. In order to access this movement in ways that touch your awareness, there needs to be a blend of your outer life with the Word of God at your depths. A union of outer and inner will come when you pause to find the connection between these seven Words from the Lord, and the events of your day.

Saturday   **The Sabbath Torah Reading**

Aug 18, 2007 #48C	Aug 13, 2016 #44C	Aug 16, 2025 #46C	Aug 19, 2034 #48C
Aug 14, 2010 #48C	Aug 17, 2019 #45C	Aug 19, 2028 #47C	Aug 15, 2037 #48C
Aug 17, 2013 #49C	Aug 13, 2022 #45C	Aug 16, 2031 #47C	Aug 18, 2040 #49C

The Twelfth Week in Pentecost

Begins on the Sunday nearest August 17. Alphabyte: Loops, p. 81

Sunday	***Jesus Between Us***	**Luke 12:49–56**

Do you think that I have come to bring peace to the earth?
No, I tell you, but rather division! v. 50

Chapter 12 is an awesome message about the priorities for the Kingdom. There is no peace without cost to complacency; no serenity if there is compromise with the criteria for the Kingdom.

Recall the covenant that God made with Abraham in Genesis 15. Abraham was told to cut three animals in half—a heifer, a goat and a ram. A smoking torch passed between the halves as a sign of the sealing of the covenant of blood. In the same manner is the fire of Jesus' passion for the covenant of the Kingdom expressed. The flame of his presence is to pass between the divisions that Jesus says will exists within families, spelling out in detail the oppositions that are to come.

Reflect upon the quality of the peace that exists in your household. What is it that tends to divide you? Are there aimless arguments that stem from pride, or the issues of the eternal Kingdom?

Monday	***Assurance***	**Micah 5—7**

I will look to the LORD, I will wait for the God of my salvation;
my God will hear me. 7:7

May you feel joy as you read the remarkable prophecy about the Messiah. Matthew 2:6 quotes Micah; Luke and John concur (Luke 2:4; John 7:42). Be alert to engrave special verses in your heart by writing with your hand.

The traditional liturgy for Good Friday uses 6:3–5 as the basis for "The Reproaches." As a wounded lover, God asks the people what he has done to merit such rejection, then recalls the blessings poured out upon the Chosen People.

In 6:6, there is a contrast between the anxiety of the people when they come to conviction, and what the Lord requires: "Only this: to act justly, love tenderly, and walk humbly with your God" (6:8, Jerusalem Bible).

Find peace in the concluding image in v. 19. Unlike the Titanic, your sins will never be retrieved from the ocean floor!

Tuesday	***Sacred Tasks***	**1 Chronicles 24—26**

David and the officers of the army also set apart for the service the sons of Asaph,
and of Heman, and of Jeduthun, who should prophesy
with lyres, harps and cymbals. 25:1

This passage lists the names of those assigned sacred charges in the life of worship—priests, musicians, and gatekeepers. The roster was designed by lot—twenty-four groupings, each group taking a two-week period a year.

Chapter 24, verse 10 gives the name of Abijah. Zechariah belonged to this house. Luke 1 tells how his turn had come to intercede for God's people in the Holy of Holies during *Yom Kippur*. This was the moment when the Angel Gabriel announced the conception of John the Baptist.

Many people fulfill the tasks of the Temple—not just a few, as often happens in church life. Be filled with admiration at the respect that worship had for God's people, and the privilege that each experienced at being called to serve. Would you not want to have your name written in the book of life for having served the Lord so that true worship could take place?

Wednesday	*Chesed le'olam*	**Psalm 136**

<u>Great</u> is God's <u>Love</u>, <u>Love</u> without <u>End</u>.
(Trans: Gregorian Institute of America)

My days in early religious life were filled with this psalm. We used to sing it to the psalmody of Joseph Gelineau, a Jesuit priest from France, who set the entire Psalter to music. You will catch the sweet flow of the rhythm if you swing from side to side accenting the underlined words.

Chesed (the first syllable has a guttural sound), is the Hebrew word for God's loving kindness, God's faithful love which is constant and forever, *'olam*. This latter word expresses the immensity of God's reign, infinitely extending in time and space. The verse for the day is *Chesed le' olam*. It has the feeling of a sigh to it. What a lovely way to spend your day, often breathing out this verse as you sigh in gratitude for the long list of loving kindnesses that the Lord has bestowed upon you!

Thursday	*By Faith*	**Hebrews 10—11**

**Let us hold fast to the confession of our hope without wavering,
for he who has promised is faithful. 10:23**

Seventeen times in these two chapters the phrase "by faith" is used. The final parts of the letter offer great encouragement to the Hebrew Christians who are being tempted to deny their Christ.

Ponder the opening verse of chapter 11 about the nature of faith. Follow the sweeping review of Old Testament saints as the writer lifts them as examples of faith. They gave their lives for what they believed in their heart, without seeing it with their eyes.

You too are in the possession right now, of what you do not fully see—the perfect salvation won for you by Jesus. As you receive it, you anticipate by faith the joy you will experience completely when the veil of this life is removed and your life in heaven unfolds. What links *now* with *then*, is your faith. Exult in these chapters.

**12
Pe
C**

Friday	*Two Models for Prayer*	**Luke 18**

God, be merciful to me, a sinner! v. 13

The Lord invites you to welcome two persons to accompany you today—one, a widow, the other, a tax collector, also known as a publican. You will come to know them by how they contrast with other characters in two parables unique to St. Luke. Joining with the widow is a judge who likely basks in being called "Your Honor," but who has honor neither for God nor for humans. The person forever linked to the publican is the arrogant Pharisee who spends his time, not in praying, but in boasting in self-righteousness. The widow is a model for persistent, confident prayer; the publican is an example of total abandon, humility, and trust before God. These two are your teachers today about how you need to grow in prayer.

Saturday   The Sabbath Torah Reading

Aug 25, 2007 #49C	Aug 20, 2016 #45C	Aug 23, 2025 #47C	Aug 26, 2034 #49C
Aug 21, 2010 #49C	Aug 24, 2019 #46C	Aug 26, 2028 #48C	Aug 22, 2037 #49C
Aug 24, 2013 #50C	Aug 20, 2022 #46C	Aug 23, 2031 #48C	Aug 25, 2040 #50C

The Thirteenth Week in Pentecost

Begins on the Sunday nearest August 24. Alphabyte: Metal Detector, p. 81

Sunday   *Draw Near to Jesus*   **Luke 13:10–17**

He laid His hands on her, and immediately
She was made straight, and glorified God. v. 13 *NKJV*

Eighteen years bent over … Ponder this long time for the woman. Her eyes focus only on the ground beneath her—rarely on the sky. She is utterly "weakened" by her condition—the root meaning of "illness" in the Greek word, *astheneia*.

She comes to the synagogue to hear Jesus. At least she can receive some consolation from this now famous itinerant preacher. Jesus spots her and calls her to come near, lays healing hands on her and she stands up strong and free.

Be that woman. Draw near to Jesus and he will do the rest, calling you into his intimate presence where he rests his sacred hands upon you. Picture this in your faith-filled imagination. The woman in the Gospel stands in for you!

Monday   *The Sands of Sinfulness*   **Nahum**

The Lord is good, a stronghold in a day of trouble;
he protects those who take refuge in him, even in a rushing flood. 1:7

Vivid poetry describes the destruction of the capital city of one of the severest of the enemies of God's people—Nineveh. The ultimate triumph of God over continuously unrepented evil, balances God's compassion for the city that we encountered in the book of Jonah.

The meaning of Nahum's name is "comfort." Though the book's three chapters describe anything but comfort to the people of Nineveh, still it is consolation to know that ultimate justice will prevail, that God and God's goodness is finally going to triumph.

Nations, cities, enterprises, and even minor projects are doomed to defeat if they are built on the sands of sinfulness, pride, deceit, and exploitation, instead of upon the rock of Jesus. The reading will sober and awaken you to deeper justice and mercy in your own life.

Tuesday   *The Everlasting Temple*   **1 Chronicles 27—29**

For all things come from you,
and of your own have we given you. 29:14

We conclude the description of the tightly organized community around King David with the army's twelve divisions, one for each month of service. We catch a glimpse into the economy of the kingdom in 27:25. Finally, as the architect of the Temple, David charges Solomon with the task of actually building it.

The prayer of David from 29:10 is acclaimed as one of the finest in the Old Testament. It is David's way of saying what Jesus did from the cross: "It is finished!" The prayer flows from David's serene and joyous heart at one with God. His task is over; the rest is in the hands of Solomon.

Jesus' task on the cross is finished. But as the Temple yet to be built by Solomon, you are the one in whose hands is the task of continuing to build up the Body of Christ, the everlasting temple.

Wednesday   *Outside Jesus—Exile*   **Psalm 137**

By the rivers of Babylon—there we sat down
and there we wept when we remembered Zion. v. 1

Imagine what it is like to be in exile. You no longer feel that special connection to life that comes with the simple joy of coming and going as you wish. Exquisite was the pain of God's people in Babylon. Once in bondage in Egypt to the west, now in exile in Babylon to the east, there are evil enemies on either side of the sacred land of promise.

Pray this psalm for those persecuted right now in foreign prisons just because they want to spread the name of Jesus and for encouraging people to live in the Lord. Living outside of Jesus is to live in exile.

When you come to the shocking last verse, receive, and accept the feelings of anger on the part of those with such bitterness in their heart. Even for the psalmist, more important than these atrocities actually happening is the experience in prayer that God accepts his deepest feelings and receives his anguish

Thursday   *Living the Kingdom*   **Hebrews 12—13**

Now may the God of peace, who brought back from the dead our Lord Jesus,
the great shepherd of the sheep, by the blood of the eternal covenant,
make you complete in everything good so that you may do his will,
working among us that which is pleasing in his sight,
through Jesus Christ, to whom be the glory forever and ever. Amen. 13:20–21

Chapters of instruction now shift to exhortation in the last two chapters of Hebrews. Savor the love of the writer as he longs that the final expressions of his letter ignite readers with a holy enthusiasm for living in Jesus. There is great beauty here. Take time to let each verse soak your soul; every one could be selected as the verse for the day. Which one will most move your heart?

The reading is especially appropriate as summer ends. Children will soon return to school and familiar schedules of home life will come once again. Take the reading as encouragement for the weeks to come. The final season of the year, *Kingdomtide,* begins next week. How could you more perfectly live in Christ's heavenly kingdom now, because of what you take to heart from God's Word today?

Friday   *Out on a Limb for Jesus*   **Luke 19:1–27**

Zacchaeus, hurry and come down,
for I must stay at your house today. v. 5

Ancient Rome used to hire tax collectors called publicans to be sure that Jews in the time of Jesus paid revenue to the Empire. Often, as in the case of Zaccheus, they were themselves Jews. They were looked upon as betrayers. Zacchaeus was hated all the more, for he was subcontracted as a manager to further organize the process. One imagines him taking advantage of his short stature, as he moved among the people, literally keeping a low profile.

But not today: Jesus is passing by! The Holy Spirit shakes him into a spontaneous, intense desire to see the Lord. Jesus rejoices in Zacchaeus' vulnerability in climbing a tree to see him; the Lord becomes spontaneous and open with him as well, inviting himself to Zacchaeus' house.

Will you move beyond what people think and take risks to know and love Jesus? Will you go out on a limb for Jesus today?

Saturday   **The Sabbath Torah Reading**

Sep 01, 2007 #50C	Aug 27, 2016 #46C	Aug 30, 2025 #48C	Sep 02, 2034 #50C
Aug 28, 2010 #50C	Aug 31, 2019 #47C	Sep 02, 2028 #49C	Aug 29, 2037 #50C
Aug 31, 2013 #51–52C	Aug 27, 2022 #47C	Aug 30, 2031 #49C	Sep 01, 2040 #51–52C

The facing page depicts the interlacing of the first and last letters of the Greek alphabet, Alpha and Omega. This is one of the forms in which the cosmic Christ is represented by these letters.

Three verses in the Book of Revelation make references to Christ as Alpha and Omega: 1:8; 21:6; 22:13. The final verse, "I am the Alpha and the Omega, the first and the last, the beginning and the end," suggests that this final season in the three-year cycle be linked to the first one, *Advent to Epiphany* in Year A. The interlacing of these letters catches the sense of T.S. Eliot in the first and final verses of "East Coker" in *The Four Quartets,* "In my beginning is my end…in my end is my beginning."

KINGDOMTIDE

AUTUMN

Northern Hemisphere

Year C
2007, 2010, 2013 …

Kingdomtide begins on the Sunday nearest August 31.
See the entire cycle of readings at a glance on page xxi.

The First Week in Kingdomtide

Begins in the Sunday nearest August 31. Alphabyte: Nose, p. 110

Sunday   *Kingdom Etiquette Luke 14: 1, 7–14*   **Luke 14:1,7B14**

When you give a banquet, invite the poor,
the crippled, the lame, the blind, and you will be blessed. v.13

Seeing is much more than simply noticing that something or someone is before you. It involves *how* you receive, understand, and are moved by what is there. More than eyes, the heart is the organ of sight.

We begin this final thirteen-week season that stretches before us with Jesus at a dinner with Pharisees "watching Him closely." Imagine their squinted eyes and knitted brows as they behold Jesus' every move. These are not the wide-eyed eyes of those lost in wonder at the presence of God in Christ; rather they are the strife-filled glances of judgment, condemnation—stares that want to bind Jesus as tightly as the eyelids pressing about their eyes.

How do the eyes of your heart receive the teaching of Jesus about the etiquette of dinner invitations? Are you open to see beneath and beyond the world into the Kingdom? This week, be aware of your senses of sight and smell.

Monday   *Embracing with the Heart*   **Habakkuk**

The righteous will live by his faith 2:4

Habakkuk's name means, "embrace." To embrace with the heart what eyes do not see, this is the essence of faith and the power of the verse for today. It was the byword of the Reformation of the sixteenth century.

Habakkuk and God relate through questions and answers similar to the Book of Job. But there is more intimacy and "give and take" here, than in Job. Yet as Job, the prophet has eyes of wonder at his world. Join your eyes with his as you read. Notice the contrast between how the book begins and how it ends.

Place yourself at a vantage point such as the prophet takes at the beginning of chapter 2. With eyes of faith, watch what God is going to say to you today in this reading and in the events of your day, which will be soaked with grace.

Tuesday   *The Word-Wide Web*   **Proverbs 30**

For as churning the milk produces butter, and as twisting the nose produces blood,
so stirring up anger produces strife. v.33

Beneath the proverbs of Agur, the unknown writer of this chapter, there lies a method to open yourself to the inward rush of wisdom. The writer is a contemplative. There are five groups of sayings, each characterized by the way that simple observation of God's creatures brings the sacred writer to applications in human life.

Listen to Agur as he speaks to you while he is observing creatures, commenting to you about each one. The Holy Spirit teaches you to do the same. Look about your life, your day—the simple details you may overlook or even resist that can teach you about God's ways. That spider of which you are afraid … Look at the web. What is God telling you about patience, delicacy, method, weaving, silence, planning, the Bible: *The Word-Wide Web*!

Wednesday *Facing the Church* **Psalm 138**
I will bow down toward your holy temple
and will praise your name for your love and your faithfulness. v. 2

Muslims pause five times each day to pray. They face the great mosque in Mecca. Jewish synagogues face Jerusalem. The physical turning of the body toward these holy places elevates awareness that only God is center of life. There is a tradition of churches facing east, place of sunrise and symbol of the resurrection of Jesus.

Face the direction of your church. How does this feel? Sense the gentle tension in the sacred thread that joins you and your community to that place in your life. Let this be a symbol of your facing the Lord who is more powerful than whatever else you are "facing" in life.

David prays in the last verse similar to Paul: "He who began a good work in you will carry it on to completion until the day of Christ Jesus" (Phil 1:6).

Thursday *Fanning the Flame* **2 Timothy 1—2**
I remind you to fan into flame the gift of God,
which is in you through the laying on of my hands. 1:6

Beyond Timothy, the recipient of this warm and personal letter from Paul is the Spirit's intent that this letter reach you just as personally. It is Paul's "Last Will and Testament," just as are the words of Moses in the Sabbath readings from Deuteronomy.

Take your eyes inward to those places where the frequent imperatives from Paul stir you to action. Respond as Timothy to the urging of Paul that Timothy "fan the flame" of the gift. Do the same with your gift for ministry—a gift that perhaps yet lies smoldering in the depths of your spirit.

The letter is one of great encouragement. Is there someone who will hang on your words of love and strength just as you and Timothy hang onto Paul's words?

Friday *Gateway to the Kingdom* **Luke 19:28–48**
If you, even you, had only known on this day
what would bring you peace … v. 42

The solemn entry of Jesus into Jerusalem marks the gateway to his entry into the heavenly Jerusalem. The people of this central city of God will soon abandon their loyalty to Jesus as quickly as the branches thrown beneath Jesus will be brushed to the side and die.

We enter autumn, season of harvest and return to routines as defined by children going back to school. Soon the leaves will emit a final gasp of color before they die and lie strewn beneath your feet as you walk into this season and smell its unique fragrance.

Two episodes of action, the entry of Jesus into the sacred city and the table-turning in the Temple, frame a setting of stillness as Jesus weeps over resistant Jerusalem of earth. Soon will there be the foundations of the New Jerusalem coming down from heaven.

Walk with Jesus into the Kingdom; it is the name given to this sacred season.

1
Ki
C

Saturday **The Sabbath Torah Reading**

Sep 08, 2007 #51–52C	Sep 03, 2016 #47C	Sep 06, 2025 #49C	Sep 09, 2034 #51–52C
Sep 04, 2010 #51–52C	Sep 07, 2019 #48C	Sep 09, 2028 #50C	Sep 05, 2037 #51–52C
Sep 07, 2013 #53C	Sep 03, 2022 #48C	Sep 06, 2031 #50C	Sep 08, 2040 Rosh Ha

The Second Week in Kingdomtide
Begins in the Sunday nearest September 7. Alphabyte: Oak, p. 110

Sunday   *Disciplines for a Disciple*   **Luke 14:25–33**
**Any of you who does not give up everything he has
cannot be my disciple. v. 33**

Pinging sounds of acorns on the sidewalk awaken a soul sensitive to silence; so let the words of Jesus summon your to the response of absolute love for Jesus above all else.

Jesus turns and confronts the crowd, stinging them with his words, seeking to find out who among them will remain as disciples.

The word "discipline," the root meaning of "disciple," means, "to teach." In this season when children go back to school, what is it that the Lord is teaching you about disciplines for a disciple? What new habits for learning can you develop to ensure that the everyday the Word of God will loosen from you what you need to forsake?

Monday   *The Lord Protects*   **Zephaniah**
**Seek the Lord, all you humble of the land,
you who do what he commands. 2:3**

The meaning of the name of this prophet will bring you comfort: "The Lord Protects." The deeper sense is that of God hiding you from the attacks of The Enemy.

Zephaniah's message is a transition from the previous eight Minor Prophets and their words of judgment, to the final three prophets and their message of salvation and restoration. Still, the words are strong. Let them awaken you from complacency, just as the words of Jesus in yesterday's Gospel.

The prophetic message comes in the form of a dialogue between God and Zephaniah. There are seven units. You will hear the words of God in the first person singular, and those of Zephaniah's response in the third person; this is especially so when he describes "The Day of the Lord" when God's justice will ultimately prevail.

Tuesday   *Spindle of Peace*   **Proverbs 31**
**Charm is deceptive, and beauty is fleeting;
but a woman who fears the Lord is to be praised. v. 30**

A diligent, loving, serving wife is uplifted for us in the conclusion of the Book of Proverbs. Throughout the listing of the many activities and qualities that make her so admirable, weaving is central. The verses themselves carry joy and peace to weave themselves into your spirit. There is a pattern to the poem, an acrostic. Each of the twenty-two verses begins with the next letter of the Hebrew alphabet.

The Book of Proverbs itself has been a thread stitching the four seasons together over the three-year cycle. With this poem at the end of the cycle, may you find a special energy and peace as you seek to imitate what this woman did in her call to do God's will, with your own call to discipleship. She is highly organized, yet not compulsive. Surely, she discovers the presence of God in her activities. Pray that the same be true for you.

Wednesday   *Weavings in the Womb*   **Psalm 139**
When I was woven together in the depths of the earth,
your eyes saw my unformed body. vv. 15–16

As I write, I sit in a dimly lit hospital room with my daughter, Laura, and her boy, Richie. He rests quietly while undergoing a brain scan. I recall that other day in 1987 when I was with Laura who was about to give birth to him.

I gaze at the long, slender body of my grandson, scanning the years from birth to the present, admiring the constancy of God's gift that has continued the stitching of his body and his life, long after the initial weaving was completed in Laura's womb. It is a perfect setting to pray and write about Psalm 139, a piece that breathes the awesome wonder of the sacred writer as he contemplates his own being and praises his all-knowing and ever-present God.

There are four stanzas of six verses each in the psalm. Find a place of quiet four times today to pray each stanza. The psalmist hands you a sacred thread; pick it up and let wonder weave itself within you, as steadily and permanently as the weaving of yesterday's woman of Proverbs.

Thursday   *A Gentle, Faithful Disciple*   **2 Timothy 3—4**
The Lord's servant must not quarrel; instead,
he must be kind to everyone, able to teach, not resentful. v. 24

Comfort and encouragement intended for a first-century church leader, are here for you. Every passage from the Bible is loosened from its time-bound setting of "there and then," to become "here and now" for you.

Are there trials coming against you in your life? This was the case for Timothy. Imagine the strength he received from these words of Paul, his beloved master-teacher. Is there someone in your life who loves you, challenges you, strengthens you, and encourages you? There are persons called by God to be in fellowship with you; pray that you discover them. Meanwhile, may the Spirit breathing through Paul and all true teachers, teach your soul and encourage you to become a more disciplined, gentle and faithful disciple of Jesus.

Friday   *Pain in the Heart of Jesus*   **Luke 20:1–26**
Give to Caesar what is Caesar's, and to God what is God's. v. 25

The usual interpretation of this famous verse is Jesus' endorsement about paying taxes. Actually, it simply illustrates his masterful skill in dodging the malicious traps laid by adversaries.

There is something deeper happening for Jesus. Enter the divine heart and experience the gnawing pain, frustration, and sadness that are there. Here is the Caesar of all Caesars, the King of all kings, spending precious time dodging barbed questions from leaders of God's people, instead of being able to unfold for them the Words of life.

Do you play any games with Jesus similar to those of the Pharisees? Be silent … Let Jesus do the talking and the questioning, while you listen and surrender to being a disciple.

2
Ki
C

Saturday   **The Sabbath Torah Reading**

Sep 15, 2007 #53C	Sep 10, 2016 #48C	Sep 13, 2025 #50C	Sep 16, 2034 #53C
Sep 11, 2010 #53C	Sep 14, 2019 #49C	Sep 16, 2028 #51–52C	Sep 12, 2037 #53C
Sep 14, 2013 Yom Kip	Sep 10, 2022 #49C	Sep 13, 2031 #51–52C	Sep 15, 2040 #53C

The Third Week in Kingdomtide

*Begins in the Sunday nearest September14. Alphabyte: **Pencil**, p. 111*

Sunday   *Found at the Center*   **Luke 15:1–10**

**There is rejoicing in the presence of the angels of God
over one sinner who repents. v. 10**

As an irresistible magnet, the lost of society are drawn to Jesus. The more they converge about his acceptance and love of them, the more joy and festivity burst forth.

There is a special kind of being lost when one thinks that one is found, but is not. The Scribes and Pharisees pride themselves in thinking that they are at the center, yet are lost at the margin. They take the essence of the Gospel, "This man welcomes sinners and eats with them," as the source of their greatest complaint.

As the *alphabyte* "Pencil" suggests, the center is where the power. Stop. Rest. Be drawn toward the inward center where Christ is ready to embrace you. If you are any place other than this, you are lost.

Monday   *Kingdom Energy*   **Haggai**

**This is what I covenanted with you when you came out of Egypt.
And my Spirit remains among you. Do not fear. 2:5**

Exiles newly returned to the Promised Land continue in a mood of discouragement. "Gone are the days of the glory of Solomon and the Temple." They settle for only building houses for themselves. Though found at home once again, they are lost in the consuming pressure of their own need, bringing them to the brink of despair.

God calls Haggai to prophesy and to minister to these lost ones. His name means "Festivity." The Spirit also moves within the governor, Zerubbabel, to ignite the people into a common energy to rebuild the Temple so that the glory of God will be present with them once again as in days of old.

The prophet seeks to free you from preoccupations with your concerns alone, to a desire to "Seek first the Kingdom of God" (Matt 6:33). Worship the Lord present in the temple of your own body and the glory of the Lord will shine from you, filling you with Kingdom energy.

Tuesday   *God's Preferred Temple*   **2 Chronicles 1—3**

**Give me wisdom and knowledge, that I may lead this people,
for who is able to govern this great people of yours? 1:10**

After yesterday's explosion of divine energy to rebuild the Temple, we find ourselves in 2 Chronicles returning to the original inspiration of the Temple God gave to Solomon. The Chronicler at times repeats the history of the two books of Kings, at other times recasts and remolds it according to his purpose. He offers Solomon and the first Temple as models to imitate. The emphasis is upon worship.

Solomon's prayer will inspire yours. Come to that central point of your "here and now," drawing strength for the present and the future in the "there and then" of three millennia ago when God moved through the heart of Solomon. Dwell in faith upon this awesome fact: God prefers your own quieted, surrendered soul to all the wonders of the Temple.

| Wednesday | *Praise of God's Name* | Psalm 140 |

**Surely the righteous will praise your name
and the upright will live before you. v. 13**

Many times the sinner and tax collector of last Sunday's Gospel felt as David in this psalm. The ones persecuting David were not foreigners, but his own people. In Jesus' time, it was the highest level of God's chosen people, the Scribes and Pharisees, who made themselves the enemies of Jesus.

Here in the center of the week, hinged between the two Testaments, find the eye of the hurricane of accusers that may be spiraling about your own life. Perhaps your own family or church members are the ones hostile to you.

Descend into your feelings until you are at the quiet place beyond the noise of accusers. Trust God. Share the anguish and pain that burns within you. Your pain can become a purifying prayer, just as the one that concludes this psalm.

| Thursday | *Clinging to the Word* | 2 Timothy 3—4 |

**All Scripture is God-breathed and is useful for teaching,
rebuking, correcting and training in righteousness, so that the man of God
may be thoroughly equipped for every good work. 3:16**

Paul's words, as those of Moses in the Sabbath *Torah* readings, reveal the urgency of those nearing the end of their lives. There is passion in the words of Paul to a beloved disciple. Cling to them as you would to the deathbed words of a beloved friend; the same is true in the final words of Jesus in the Friday readings that occur just a few days before the crucifixion.

Pray with a light and steadied heart, so balanced, that you move to action only when Christ's Word prompts you to do so. Listen with the inner ears of the heart to those special movements of the Holy Spirit in your daily readings that especially bear witness to the truth contained in the verse for today. What are the special teaching points that God calls you to incarnate in the way in which you will live today?

| Friday | *The Pulse of Risen Life* | Luke 20:27–47 |

**He is not the God of the dead, but of the living,
for to him all are alive. v. 38**

The Sadducees did not believe in the resurrection of the body. Jesus resists being confounded by them. He not only turns the tables of debate on them, but further questions to Jesus serve to reduce these religious naggers to silence.

Relate the stern warning of Jesus about the scribes to the "bewares" of Paul in yesterday's reading—those "having a form of godliness but denying its power" (2 Tim. 3:5). Resist the sacrilegious behavior of those whose only purpose in speaking about spiritual matters is to exalt themselves, not God.

The Holy Spirit plants the seed of the resurrection in you, dead to sin, but alive in Christ. The pulse of Christ's love becomes one with the beating of your heart.

**3
Ki
C**

Saturday			**The Sabbath Torah Reading**
Sep 22, 2007 #54C	Sep 17, 2016 #49C	Sep 20, 2025 #51C	Sep 23, 2034 Yom Kip
Sep 18, 2010 Yom Kip	Sep 21, 2019 #50C	Sep 23, 2028 #53C	Sep 19, 2037 Yom Kip
Sep 21, 2013 Tabern	Sep 17, 2022 #50C	Sep 20, 2031 #53C	Sep 22, 2040 Tabern

The Fourth Week in Kingdomtide

Begins in the Sunday nearest September21. Alphabyte: Quilt, p. 111

Sunday   *A Heavenly Roof*   **Luke 16:1–13**

**If you have not been trustworthy in handling worldly wealth,
who will trust you with true riches? v.11**

A crisis in personal finances calls forth great inventiveness from this manager. "I've got to be sure that I have a roof over my head when I'm fired!"

A glance at the whole line of the week's readings in the quilt of this season reveals a temple theme threading its way through the days. Today Jesus contrasts the creativity of this man in caring for the temple of his earthly home with the lack of concern of so many for the spiritual, heavenly temple and the eternal "roof" intended to cover us.

Become quiet so that you will sense the contrasts of these priorities. Sift, evaluate, feel what is truly central in your life. Will you be as creative and inventive about the call upon your life, as you are with caring for yours and your family's temporal needs?

Monday   *Waves of Comfort*   **Zechariah 1—2**

**"I myself will be a wall of fire around it," declares the Lord,
"and I will be its glory within." 2:5**

The lack of concern of yesterday's unjust steward is set beside the call of God's people in today's reading to rebuild the Temple. Destruction of Solomon's Temple and exile had plummeted God's people into despair. While they have returned to their homeland, discouragement still hovers as a dark cloud over the people, de-energizing them from rebuilding the Temple. "How can we build a temple as magnificent as Solomon's?"

Zechariah, whose name means "Yahweh Remembers," receives eight visions of comfort and energy from God to empower the people to rebuild the Temple, sign of God's life among them. Today's reading has the first three of these visions. Read them as waves of comfort God is sending your way to enable to you to rebuild your own life according to the plans of the temple of Christ's body in which you live, move, and have your being.

Tuesday   *A Model for Praye*   **2 Chronicles 4—6**

**O LORD, God of Israel, there is no God like you in heaven
or on earth—you who keep your covenant of love
with your servants who continue wholeheartedly in your way. 6:14**

The purpose of the writer of Chronicles and of Zechariah is the same—to have God's people recently returned to Jerusalem, find connectives to their past and God's fidelity to them. The history of the earliest beginnings comes alive for them in these writings, sometimes copies of the history of 1 and 2 Kings.

The newly constructed Temple finds the vast, inward, empty space filled with the sacred articles used at worship. Solomon's work is done. He pauses as he looks at everything in place. He prays a model for prayer across the ages and through the seasons.

Place yourself among the throng of people hearing Solomon's prayer. May the earnest pleas for his people become yours. What specific calls for prayer does the Spirit bring to mind as you pray along with this great King?

Wednesday *Evil Coming and Going* **Psalm 141**
Set a guard over my mouth, O LORD;
keep watch over the door of my lips. v. 3

Solomon learned how to pray from his father, David. The closeness of David to God peacefully reveals itself in this prayer of protection from the forces of evil that circle about him. He asks God to protect him from the seductive quality of evil as it threatens to enter him. He prays that God guard his mouth from evil; it is a prayer of protection against the comings and goings of wickedness.

Here in the center of the week, when the human family is beset with so many attacks from evil, let this gentle, confident prayer become yours. Pray not only for personal protection against evil, but allow this psalm to be a spark of fire the Spirit fans in you for intercessory prayer.

Thursday *Cosmic Images for the Soul* **Revelation 12**
A woman was pregnant and cried out in pain
as she was about to give birth. v. 2

The persecution of God's people in the first century is described in bold images on a cosmic scale. The images stir within us a sobering awareness that the struggles of the first-century church are mirrored in our own day, with portents of what is to come. We will devote the last ten Thursdays of this year of grace to the second half of the Book of Revelation.

The woman clothed with the sun recalls the woman in Genesis 3, the twelve stars reminding us of God's people in the twelve tribes. The ancient church also saw the woman as Mary, mother of Jesus. This image, as well as all the images of Revelation, evokes varying levels of meaning. The images are vehicles of God's power at work in you bringing about victory against evil.

Friday *Two Small Coins* **Luke 21:1–19**
I will give you words and wisdom that none of your adversaries
will be able to resist or contradict. v. 15

The cosmic image of the woman of yesterday is in marked contrast with the humble woman of today's reading. We are in the Temple with Jesus and some disciples. Similar to the grand furnishings of the Temple described in Tuesday's reading, proud Pharisees stand about in long robes. They form a border to the scene. An old woman enters, bent over, slowly making her way to the box that receives her offering of two small coins. Picture her, there in the center, in the spotlight of Jesus' gaze; the Temple adornments and Pharisees are lost in the shadows.

Find comfort in the words about this remarkable, unnamed woman whom Jesus exalts. Quietly discover your brand of the two small coins and simply give them to the Lord. Empty yourself of everything, so that Jesus can fill you with everything.

4
Ki
C

Saturday **The Sabbath Torah Reading**

Sep 29, 2007 Tabern	Sep 24, 2016 #50C	Sep 27, 2025 #52C	Sep 30, 2034 Tabern
Sep 25, 2010 Tabern	Sep 28, 2019 #51C	Sep 30, 2028 Yom Kip	Sep 26, 2037 Tabern
Sep 28, 2013 #54C-#1A	Sep 24, 2022 #51C	Sep 27, 2031 Yom Kip	Sep 29, 2040 #54C

The Fifth Week in Kingdomtide

Begins in the Sunday nearest September 28. Alphabyte: Rainbow, p. 112

Sunday   *The Lines Are Drawn*   **Luke 16:19–31**

"If they do not listen to Moses and the Prophets, they
will not be convinced even if someone rises from the dead." v. 31

Rich and poor, good and evil, death and life, worship of self instead of God—there are stark contrasts in the readings for this week. The rainbow image from the *Alphabyte* suggests that we be alert to colors that would further the impact of all the readings upon your days. From the purple finery of Dives, to the garish colors of the dragon and the beasts of Revelation, your imaginations lead you through the inward senses of sight, sound and smell to the Lamb of God resting within.

Dives only saw the riches on his table. Blind to the beggar, he was blind to the Jesus present in the poor, recalling Matthew 25: "Lord, when did we see you hungry or thirsty …?" The rich man did not see Jesus on this side of the grave; neither will he see Jesus on the other side. Self-absorption and self-worship—he will only have himself for all eternity: how tormenting!

Monday   *By My Spirit*   **Zechariah 3—4**

"Not by might nor by power, but by my Spirit,"
says the LORD Almighty. v. 6

Rags of poverty on Joshua become rich robes. This is not his doing, but the Lord's. Contrast the robes and rags of Dives and Lazarus in yesterday's reading. The rich man's robes came from exploitation, manipulation, and the denial of the balance that comes when we share God's good things.

The task before Joshua the priest and Zerubbabel the governor is to work together with the Spirit providing the energy for the completion of the Temple and the reviving of God's people after the devastation of exile. The olive trees symbolize what we would come to know as "church and state." These are set before Zechariah who prophesies under the power of the Spirit.

What are the divine tasks that the Lord puts before you? You will be given the courage to face them, for it is not you who will complete them, but the Holy Spirit.

Tuesday   *Filled with the Glory*   **2 Chronicles 7—9**

If my people, who are called by my name, will humble themselves and pray and seek my face
and turn from their wicked ways, then will I hear from heaven and will forgive their sin
and will heal their land. 7:14

The glory of the Lord fills the Temple because of the abandoned prayer of Solomon. God was his first priority, and so the divine presence is full as temple life begins for God's people. The verse for today is one of the most comforting in all the Old Testament. Humility and abandonment to God open the way for God to respond in like manner with forgiveness and healing.

The achievements of Solomon, just as those promised in yesterday's reading, are the result of the Spirit of God at work in Solomon. Recall that Solomon's first request was for wisdom, not wealth; the world sees this in reverse order.

Dedicate the temple of your body to God; the glory of the Lord will fill it.

Wednesday   *All Poured Out*   **Psalm 142**

Set me free from my prison, that I may praise your name. v.7

Davide is as Lazarus of last Sunday. Pray this psalm interceding for the millions who lie in poverty outside the range of ears to hear the cry, but near to the heart of those willing to be moved by others in need.

There is power in the word "pour" as David expresses his complaints, his angers, and all his emotions. They do not come out drip by drip, hedged in by guilt and shame, as so often happens when it comes to feelings. Be as David. Take all of who you are in confident pouring into the lap of the Lord's compassion. When these energies are spent, there will be a space of pure emptiness for the glory of the Lord to fill you and the hearts of the desperate in expressions of glory as is in the final verse.

Thursday   *The Blasphemy in Evil*   **Revelation 13**

If anyone is to be killed with the sword,
with the sword he will be killed. v.10

From the sea and the land come the beasts born of the dragon. They are blasphemous counterparts of the Blessed Trinity. Five times the Greek word, *exousia,* is used, translated by the English, "authority." This is the constituting power of God alone, here usurped by evil in a sacrilegious pretence at being divine. The evil of those who bear the mark of the beast replaces God's brand of ownership.

Chapters 12 to 14 reveal the characters that will play their parts in the second half of the Book of Revelation. Evil is portrayed in these outlandish images—the same evil of Dives who despised Lazarus.

Hear the words of Jesus in his arrest in the Garden of Gethsemane: "All who draw the sword will die by the sword" (Matt. 26:52). Is there any violence in you?

Friday   *Your Redemption Is Near*   **Luke 21:20–38**

"When these things begin to take place, stand up and lift up your heads,
because your redemption is drawing near." v. 28

Jesus reveals the destruction of Jerusalem as a sign of the end of the ages. With images similar to those in Revelation, he describes the mounting power of evil. The descriptions of the explosions of evil serve to awaken in the faithful the yet greater power of God to triumph in the end.

Are there people and events in your life that are coming against you with strength similar to what Jesus outlines? The overwhelming power of these energies only serves to scream out all the more that your redemption is near.

Once again, it is a matter of things getting worse before they get better. You have models for prayer this week—Zechariah, Solomon, David and John. They heighten awareness that the Holy Spirit is praying in you and working out the victory.

Saturday   **The Sabbath Torah Reading**

Oct 06, 2007 #1A	Oct 01, 2016 #51C	Oct 04, 2025 #53C	Oct 07, 2034 #54C-#1A
Oct 02, 2010 #54C-#1A	Oct 05, 2019 #52C	Oct 07, 2028 Tabern	Oct 03, 2037 #54C-#1A
Oct 05, 2013 #2A	Oct 01, 2022 #52C	Oct 04, 2031 Tabern	Oct 06, 2040 #1A

5 Ki C

353

The Sixth Week in Kingdomtide

Begins in the Sunday nearest October 5. Alphabyte: Streams, p. 112

Sunday   *The Flow of Saving Grace*   **Luke 17:1–10**

**"Things that cause people to sin are bound to come,
but woe to that person through whom they come." v.1**

Convergences of three streams of church energies unite into a powerful river. At the mouth of the river, there is a delta of rich, fertile soil where wheat for the bread of life can grow. Nothing is to impede the sacred flow that brings the richness of God's grace to all.

The week begins with four power-principles that Christ lays before his disciples to ensure access to grace. First: the strong warning against scandal; the word in Greek, *skandalon,* refers to the stick that holds up a trap for an animal; second: freeing the other by forgiveness; third: faith, even as minute as a mustard seed; fourth: God owes us nothing; all that we receive from God is pure, gratuitous grace—unmerited, free, ever-flowing.

Pray that you receive the impact of today's reading so that the flow of saving grace can move out from you into the sea of peace.

Monday   *Total Freedom in the Spirit*   **Zechariah 5—6**

**Here is the man whose name is the Branch,
and he will branch out from his place and build the temple of the LORD. 6:12**

Three more visions awaken the spirit of prophecy in Zechariah, making eight in all. An immense scroll, fifteen by thirty feet, wafts thieves and perjurers away in something like a magic carpet. Wickedness flies away in a basket. Connecting with yesterday's Gospel, this is the removal of the scandals, the traps set for God's people. The image of the four chariots sweeping from the four directions continues images of movement and completeness, as God's power envelopes the entire earth. The divine gifts of kingship and priesthood are now united in one crown for Joshua, a messianic figure.

What do these images do for you? Is there anything yet coming between you and the Lord Christ who wants nothing less than your total freedom in the Spirit?

Tuesday   *Humble Before Grace*   **2 Chronicles 10—12**

**Because Rehoboam humbled himself,
the LORD'S anger turned from him, and he was not totally destroyed.
indeed, there was some good in Judah. 12:12**

The grace of God, so abundant and flowing in David and Solomon, ceases in the life of the next son and king, Rehoboam. Arrogance, a vice that gives a halt to grace and is a scandal to others, seethes in the heart of David's grandson, rending asunder what God had put together—one sacred people. The evil of power and control turns the one sacred river of life, into two; Judah and Israel will separate.

The united cover of grace now lost, Judah becomes vulnerable to an attack from the age-old enemy of God's designs, Egypt. The threat offers an opportunity for Rehoboam to become humble, opening himself once again to some measure of God's saving help.

Anything fresh come to mind? Become humble before the saving hand of the Lord upon your life.

Wednesday   *Yearning for God*   **Psalm 143**
Do not bring your servant into judgment,
for no one living is righteous before you. v.2

The millstone of persecution presses at David's soul, grinding it into the flour of prayer. The burdens of life loosen more and more supplications. The outpourings stretch him to God. Waves of comfort crescendo as David yearns for God's help. The very longing for God is a sign of God's presence.

Find those points of connection between you and David. Does the Lord bring anyone to mind who is similarly burdened? A fervent praying of this psalm will be the conduit for the stream of grace to reach that one's heart.

If only Rehoboam had prayed this psalm of his grandfather, David, with all his heart! Will you pray the psalm?

Thursday   *The Sounds of Heaven*   **Revelation 14—15**
I heard a sound from heaven like the roar of rushing waters
and like a loud peal of thunder. v. 2

Water flowing swiftly across rocks in a river … sounds of surf splashing upon the sand … the voice of peace within erasing harsh accusations and judgments from within and without … Let your imagination transport you to a refreshing place in your life. That setting can be the means God uses so that you experience the peace that begins this chapter of Revelation. You will find a mark difference from the abrasive, horrific images of the previous chapters.

144,000—twelve groups of twelve thousand … Picture the vast assembly, just as the tribes gathered to listen to Moses' final words in Deuteronomy. As the hours that radiate from a clock, there are four groups of three, from each direction, clustered about the Word. You are listening to the sounds of heaven; be revived.

Friday   *The Stream from Jesus' Side*   **Luke 22:24–46**
The Son of Man will go as it has been decreed,
but woe to that man who betrays him. 22:22

From the very depths of Jesus, comes the cry "Woe!" We heard it in last Sunday's Gospel referring to those who are a scandal to God's little ones. Here it refers to Judas. The word is used 106 times in the Bible—virtually the same word in Hebrew, Greek, and English, for the word itself is the sound of the soul groaning in grief. It also carries a call of warning, recalling the "Woes" in Luke's "Sermon on the Plain" which offers a counterpoint to the Beatitudes (Luke 6:24–26).

Today we begin six Fridays of reading the Passion of Jesus. Contemplate the mysteries of the Lord's suffering in the context of the rest of the week's readings as this year of grace begins to end. Be with Jesus and the disciples. Place your life into the bread and cup of communion. The sacrament of Christ's blood is the stream of grace flowing from his side.

6 Ki C

Saturday   **The Sabbath Torah Reading**

Oct 13, 2007 #2A	Oct 08, 2016 #52C	Oct 11, 2025 Tabern	Oct 14, 2034 #2A
Oct 09, 2010 #2A	Oct 12, 2019 #53C	Oct 14, 2028 #54C-#1A	Oct 10, 2037 #2A
Oct 12, 2013 #3A	Oct 08, 2022 #53C	Oct 11, 2031 #54C-#1A	Oct 13, 2040 #2A

The Seventh Week in Kingdomtide

*Begins in the Sunday nearest October 12. Alphabyte: **T**rapeze, p. 112*

Sunday   *The Healer and the Healed*   **Luke 17:11–19**

**One of them, when he saw he was healed, came back,
praising God in a loud voice … and he was a Samaritan. v.15**

The distance that God's people kept from lepers was as great as that between Jews and Samaritans. However, for a person to be both—that is to be an outcast, indeed. Ten lepers in misery, while keeping their distance, somehow know that Jesus is not going to pull away. They cry out for divine mercy.

The ten are healed, but nine soon forget, failing to return to give God glory and praise. We know nothing about them, but the silence invites us to wonder: did the healing last without the total trapeze-like abandon to the One who could do *more* than have them look good from the outside?

Surrender all outer and inner needs to Jesus. Grasp the hand of God in Jesus, as the healer and the healed become one.

Monday   *The Sleeve of a Believer*   **Zechariah 7—8**

**"In those days ten men from all languages and nations
will take firm hold on one Jew by the hem of his robe and say,
"Let us go with you, because we have heard that God is with you."' 8:23**

God's call to obedience courses through these two chapters of sermons from Zechariah. Disobedience on the part of our ancestors made them vulnerable to foreign attacks and the destruction of Jerusalem and their sacred Temple.

Just as the salvation of the one leper who returned is better than all ten healed of leprosy, so fasting and worship may be external only, never going to the heart of total obedience—that surrender which has us walk in God's ways with our hands in God's.

Notice what happens. Just as the ten lepers of yesterday, ten persons from every foreign nation will let go of their unfaithful ways and cling to the sleeve of a believer. Your obedience and fidelity to the Lord can prompt others to let go of the "trapeze" of their vain works and cling to the Lord by grasping the sleeve of your faith.

Tuesday   *Burnt Offerings*   **2 Chronicles 13—16**

**Every morning and evening they present burnt offerings
and fragrant incense to the Lord. 13:11**

King Abijah, Solomon's grandson, reigns in Judah, the southern kingdom. In general, the south remains faithful to God at this time, the northern kingdom yielding to idolatry.

In the sixth century B.C., the captives return to find their lost history, aware that "for a long time Israel has been without the true God, without teaching priest and without law" (15:3). Though similar to 1 Kings 15, the chronicler places emphasis on the life of worship in tenth century B.C., as summarized in the verse for today.

The *Firestarter* in the morning and the daily reading—your morning "burnt offering." In the evening, let there be an ember-like reflective glow over the day and its union with the day's passage—your evening burnt sacrifice. Thus from morning till evening there will be sweet incense rising from your life bringing God's presence and love to many others.

| Wednesday | *Song for Spiritual Warfare* | Psalm 144 |

**I will sing a new song to you, O God; on the ten-stringed lyre I will
make music to you, to the One who gives victory to kings ... v. 9**

A song of joy wells up in the middle of the week. David rejoices to find his God Almighty, so close and protective of him. God is the one who trains his faithful for spiritual warfare and is the source of all victory.

Meditate on the lists that David uses: 1) Images of protection; 2) A summary of God's power; 3) An inventory of the blessings that David has received. Read the lists slowly so that your creative imagination can bring the items from head to heart. Add to the list those particular ways you experience God's protection and power, and the blessings that God showers upon you.

Will you let the Spirit inspire a new song in your heart and on your lips?

| Thursday | *Seven Bowls of Judgment* | Revelation 15—16 |

**"Great and marvelous are your deeds, Lord God Almighty,
Just and true are your ways, King of the ages." 15:3**

Images from the Exodus are mixed into the seven bowls of judgment prepared for those committed to evil and blasphemy. The Song of Moses sung after the crossing of the Red Sea and the song at the end of his life recently sung on the Sabbath reading, keep the focus upon God's ultimate triumph over all evil. There is simply no way that evil is going to be victorious; God's love will triumph.

Do not be afraid of the images of the blood that flows in the plagues listed. Indeed, God's love and victory over evil began on the cross where the sea of God's own blood in Christ streamed down for the salvation of us all. The plagues of wrath will come to an end; God's love will not.

What impressions does this reading make on you? Write them down, so you will remember.

| Friday | *Commotion after Communion* | Luke 22:24–46 |

**The greatest among you should be like the youngest,
and the one who rules like the one who serves. v. 26**

Jesus faces one of the Twelve about to betray him, another who will deny even knowing Jesus at all. Added to this, all of them argue with each other about who is the greatest among them. Betrayal, denial, and pride mix themselves together, playing themselves out among the most intimate of Jesus disciples.

Listen in upon the commotion at the Last Supper—this, just minutes after the Apostles had received Holy Communion for the very first time. Contemplate the scene with all its shifts of energy and focus—from communion to commotion, from fellowship to loneliness, from pure love to agony, from friendship to betrayal, from the One who sets others free to the One is arrested. Will you be awake for at least an hour, to the full Jesus who is praying in his Spirit within you right now?

**7
Ki
C**

Saturday

The Sabbath Torah Reading

Oct 20, 2007 #3A	Oct 15, 2016 #53C	Oct 18, 2025 #54C-#1A	Oct 21, 2034 #3A
Oct 16, 2010 #3A	Oct 19, 2019 Tabern	Oct 21, 2028 #2A	Oct 17, 2037 #3A
Oct 19, 2013 #4A	Oct 15, 2022 Tabern	Oct 18, 2031 #2A	Oct 20, 2040 #3A

The Eighth Week in Kingdomtide

Begins in the Sunday nearest October 19. Alphabyte: Usher, p. 113

Sunday   *The Gush of God's Grace*   **Luke 18:1–8**

**Will not God bring about justice for his chosen ones,
who cry out to him day and night? v. 7**

Here is a parable with contrasts of energy—the lazy judge and the relentless widow, the care of God and the weak faith of God's children. The widow has the persistence of a battering ram against the hard heart of the judge. Lack of faith blocks God's people from receiving the current of God's healing grace. Jesus said previously that the faith of a tiny mustard seed would be sufficient to hurl a mountain into the sea—certainly enough to move the heart of God already filled with love and tender care for God's children.

What are the obstacles to your faith that prevent God's grace from gushing into your soul? Recall the root meaning of the word, "usher." It is about *opening* a way for God to move. Let the parable literally usher in a week of flowing communion between you and God.

Monday   *Jesus' Entry into the Heart*   **Zechariah 9—10**

**Rejoice greatly, O Daughter of Zion! Shout, Daughter of Jerusalem!
See your king comes to you, righteous and having salvation,
gentle and riding on a donkey … v. 9**

Receive the absolute assurance of God's promise of restoration for Israel and Judah as renewal and restoration for your own soul. As you read Zechariah's list of the enemies of Israel that shall be overcome, become sensitive to your own list of all that would place itself as enemy in your life—sickness, family challenges, antagonists, etc.

In the verse for the day, there is joy in the description of the Messianic King that will bring about these victories. You are familiar with this verse, used by all four evangelists as they discover its fulfillment in the triumphal entry of Jesus into Jerusalem on Palm Sunday.

The *Alphabyte* "Usher" for this week offers a personal image, as you usher Jesus into the inner recesses of your own heart, there to take dominion of it, winning victory over all your enemies.

Tuesday   *The Weapon of Praise*   **2 Chronicles 17—20**

**Do not be afraid or discouraged because of this vast army.
For the battle is not yours, but God's. 20:15**

Saint Paul would want you to remember his words: "What you sow you will reap," as you read about the consequences of good and evil kings (Gal 6:7). The reference in Zechariah yesterday (10:2) about the sheep having no shepherd is present in today's reading (18:16), an image that would become familiar in the Gospels.

Chapter 20 provides respite from the intrigues and infidelity of some of the leaders of God's people. Give yourself special meditative time to pray through this chapter. Notice the power of praise as the weapon of victory over all enemies. Shift your focus away from what is coming against you in life, to praise for the One who is working out the victory for you at this very moment. The battle is not yours, but God's!

Wednesday   *A Symphony of Synonyms*   **Psalm 145**
The eyes of all look to you,
and you give them their food at the proper time. v. 15

The subtitle for this Psalm is "A Praise of David." From this prayer until we come to the end of the Wednesday cycle in Psalm 150, praise will pervade every psalm.

This is another example of an acrostic poem—each verse beginning with the next letter of the Hebrew alphabet. This structure offers a sense of movement and completion to the prayer. Further adding to the feeling of completion, the psalmist exhausts all the possible words for "praise" in Hebrew, making a kind of symphony of synonyms. How many words in English can you find that will fill your soul with praise?

This is a fitting psalm for all the readings for this week, as well as for the ones in these final weeks God's year of grace.

Thursday   *The Blood of the Lamb*   **Revelation 17**
They will make war against the Lamb, but the Lamb
will overcome them because he is Lord of lords and King of kings—
and with him will be his called, chosen and faithful followers. v. 14

With powerful images of evil, John portrays the arrogance and idolatry of the Roman Empire, great enemy of the early Christians. Recall the words of St. Paul in 1 Cor. 1:27: "God chose the weak things of the world to shame the strong."

The Book of Revelation was intended to be a source of strength as Christians endured cruel persecution at the hands of that evil empire. Connecting with the image of the king riding in victory on a donkey in Monday's reading from Zechariah, the image of the meek and vulnerable Lamb is John's way of reminding us of the victory of the blood of Jesus over all adversaries.

Picture yourself in the Coliseum in Rome as lions are about to tear your flesh to shreds. The flesh of the Lamb of God was first torn for you, assuring you of the loving, sustaining presence of your Jesus when the flesh of your soul is about to be ripped.

Friday   *The Lamb Alone*   **Luke 22:47–71**
Peter went outside and wept bitterly. v. 62

We enter the scene of the betrayal and arrest of Jesus and the poignant denial of Peter. Jesus experiences the loneliness of being abandoned by his intimate friends. Only after the resurrection and the coming of the Spirit will Peter and the other disciples who had deserted Jesus surround the Lamb once again, as promised in the verse from yesterday's reading. The blasphemies described in that reading are present on the lips of Jesus' persecutors. What irony: after such atrocious behavior before the Lamb, Jesus' persecutors accuse him of blasphemy!

Be present as a silent, faithful witness of Jesus sufferings. Feel every word and turn of events. Slow down the movement of Jesus' suffering so that you can receive each one as so many drops of his blood filling your life-cup with the sacrament of his presence.

8
Ki
C

Saturday   **The Sabbath Torah Reading**

Oct 27, 2007 #4A	Oct 22, 2016 Tabern	Oct 25, 2025 #2A	Oct 28, 2034 #4A
Oct 23, 2010 #4A	Oct 26, 2019 #54C-#1A	Oct 28, 2028 #3A	Oct 24, 2037 #4A
Oct 26, 2013 #5A	Oct 22, 2022 #54C-#1A	Oct 25, 2031 #3A	Oct 27, 2040 #4A

The Ninth Week in Kingdomtide

Begins in the Sunday nearest October 26. Alphabyte: Violin, p. 113

Sunday   *The Song of the Dead Self*   **Luke 18:9–14**
God, have mercy on me, a sinner. v. 13

Listen this week for the sounds of the sweet song that rises from the soul of the dead self. We begin with the parable of "The Pharisee and the Publican." These two figures contrast the garish song of vanity of one with the humble chant of repentance of the other; between pride and humility, between true and false worship. The week's readings will be filled with these contrasts—simply put, between good and evil.

Luke's parable could have begun with him saying, "Two men went up to the Temple to pray; one did, the other didn't." The protestations of thanks on the part of the Pharisee are empty echoes on the walls of the temple of self-righteousness, pride and ultimately the vilest form of idolatry—self worship under the guise of prayer.

Enter the depths of your own soul and listen there to the music the Spirit makes.

Monday   *Grief in and for Jesus*   **Zechariah 11—12**
I will pour out on the house of David and the inhabitants of Jerusalem
a spirit of grace and supplication. They will look on me, the one they have pierced ... 12:10

Arrogant shepherds appear at the beginning of the reading, boasting as the Pharisee in yesterday's parable. Hear the Lord's outrage against such ones.

We are reminded of the suffering of Jesus, as we encounter verses from this prophet that Matthew and John have on their hearts in their passion narratives (Matt 27:3 ff; John 19:37).

Listen for the sounds of mourning that rise up from the people as they grieve—sounds in harmony with the expression of sorrow of the Publican of yesterday's Gospel. The verse for the day reminds us the Holy Spirit stirs such groans as birth pangs of the new creature you will become when you are dead to self.

Tuesday   *An Unholy Family*   **2 Chronicles 21—24**
Jehoiada stationed doorkeepers at the gates of the Lord's temple
so that no one who was in any way unclean might enter. 23:19

A most unholy family rules Judah—Jehoram, his son Ahaziah (also called Jehoahaz) and Jehoram's wife, Athaliah. The utmost of brutal power and idolatry infect God's people. The gushing forth of Jehoram's intestines bear witness to the maxim: "As you live, so will you die."

There are echoes in the protection of Moses and Jesus in their births as you read about the divine protection of Joash during the reign of the wicked Athaliah. He repairs the Temple and restores proper worship for God's people. How sad to hear about how he ended his life, slipping into the apostasy that had driven its way into his life from previous generations!

Inspired by the verse for the day, pray that no similar intergenerational sin have any effect upon you.

Wednesday   *Sacred Bookends*   **Psalm 146**

I will praise the LORD all my life;
I will sing praise to my God as long as I live. v. 2

ALLELUIA: the only Hebrew home for this word is in the psalms. Alleluias are sacred bookends embracing either end of each of these last psalms, conclusions to the three-year cycle of Wednesdays.

This is the resurrection song of the soul dead and risen in Christ Jesus, the ultimate song of praise that the Spirit sings from within. Its strength and power is in proportion to the ashes of the song of repentance—a song the stronger and more sober because of the readings of this week.

Keep together the "medley" songs that the Spirit inspires within as you recall the week's themes of goodness and evil, arrogance and humility that weave themselves throughout the week. While each day has its own reading, there is a stitch holding each one together.

Thursday   *No Music from Babylon*   **Revelation 18**

Rejoice over her, O heaven! Rejoice, saints and apostles and prophets!
God has judged her for the way she treated you. v. 20

CRUEL persecutions from Roman emperors cause the blood of early Christians to flow on the ground of the Coliseum. How true the saying of Tertullian is: "The blood of martyrs is the seed of Christians"! Overwhelmed by the tide of evil from this Empire, John receives visions of its ultimate downfall about Babylon, image of Rome.

Arrogance and pride find vicious voice in the expressions of Babylon. However, equally horrific is the fall of the empire of evil. Such visions gave hope to the sufferings of early Christians. May the same be true for you, when evil rises as a tide against you. Believe that the victory has already been won in the blood of the Lamb.

Do you find similarities that contemporary economic and political structures have with Babylon? All systems that stand in the temple of God's presence boasting in Pharisaic arrogance are doomed to fall. No more music from them!

Friday   *A Silent, Steady Stare*   **Luke 23:1–12**

Herod plied him with many questions,
but Jesus gave him no answer. v. 9

PILATE and Herod are as kings of "Babylon." Hear Jesus' silence in his encounters with them. While there are a few words of Jesus to Pilate expressing who Jesus is, there is not a word in the presence of Herod. As the evil kings of his ancestors from the readings from 2 Chronicles, all the pomp and noise of Herod produces nothing but Jesus' steady silent stare into his face.

Just before today's account in Luke of Jesus brought before Pilate, Matthew has inserted the account of the tragic end of Judas, using verses that occur in our reading on Tuesday from Zechariah. If only he, as Peter, had found a moment to behold Jesus' look of sadness and love upon him! Being in such a presence might have changed him. Look what it did for Pilate and Herod; they became friends!

Feel the silent, steady stare of Jesus and be changed.

9
Ki
C

Saturday   **The Sabbath Torah Reading**

Nov 03, 2007 #5A	Oct 29, 2016 #54C-#1A	Nov 01, 2025 #3A	Nov 04, 2034 #5A
Oct 30, 2010 #5A	Nov 02, 2019 #2A	Nov 04, 2028 #4A	Oct 31, 2037 #5A
Nov 02, 2013 #6A	Oct 29, 2022 #2A	Nov 01, 2031 #4A	Nov 03, 2040 #5A

The Tenth Week in Kingdomtide

Begins in the Sunday nearest November 2. Alphabyte: Well, p. 114

Sunday   *Surge of Saving Grace*   **Luke 19:1–10**

The Son of Man came to seek and to save what was lost. v. 10

One would have to know the kind of person Zacchaeus was before knowing Christ, to appreciate who he became afterward. He was a publican, a tax-collector, just as the one who prayed in the Temple with great repentance in last Sunday's Gospel. Zacchaeus benefited from his short, stocky build to move cautiously and carefully amid God's people. They hated him, because he, a Jew, exacted the taxes due to the Roman Empire.

However his soul, short and crouched as his body, expands and lifts itself to the height the tree he climbs to see Jesus. He had heard about Jesus and witnessed the power of the Kingdom near at hand from the disciples that went ahead of Jesus as Jesus made his way to Jerusalem. These faithful disciples opened up a well of deep, spontaneous love in Zacchaeus, breaking the bonds of greed and self-centeredness that bowed him to the ground.

Who will want to see Jesus because of you?

Monday   *Refined by the Fire*   **Zechariah 13—14**

On that day a fountain will be opened to the house of David and the inhabitants of Jerusalem, to cleanse them from sin and impurity. 13:1

The opening verse of the passage, along with the living waters in 14:8, further the theme of the *Well* for this week. Apocalyptic images will have you feel the connection with the Book of Revelation as the energy of the year's end mounts to conclusion. Also, see if you can find some verses that Matthew and Mark place on the lips of Jesus in the narrative of the Passion.

The nineteenth century German philosophy Nietzsche said: "That which doesn't destroy me makes me stronger." Zechariah expresses a similar conviction in using the image of the refiner's fire as suffering comes upon the people. Who or what in your life are you resisting that, if embraced and accepted, would lift you to a higher place, as Zacchaeus, so that you can see Jesus?

Tuesday   *Life at a Glance*   **2 Chronicles 25—28**

Jotham grew powerful because he walked steadfastly before the LORD his God. 27:6

Photos of the earth from a satellite reveal cities as tiny blotches of color flung across the globe. In one glance, the congestion, commotion, and conflict of whole cities are beheld in silence. In a similar way, the chronicler sweeps across the history of Judah in summaries of kings—some good, most evil.

Kings come and go. Whether good or bad, God continues to weave sacred history even with wicked thread. Life is short, especially when seen from above; remember Zaccaheus!

If you were to write a summary about your life, what would you want it to be? There is still time for you to update and upgrade your life according to the image that God had of you when you were first conceived. Keep the end and purpose of your existence in sight. The tiny details of today lived with love can make a magnificent mosaic tomorrow.

Wednesday   *The Grandeur of God*   **Psalm 147**

He grants peace to your borders
and satisfies you with the finest of wheat. v. 14

Embrace this psalm as a connective to your whole week, a song of praise for God celebrated as the center of life. The psalmist is your guide on a tour of God's universe. God has loving care for the world and for you.

The catalog of God's grandeur moves from inner to outer manifestations. There is an air of spontaneity about the order of things, as the sacred writer simply expresses what comes to his heart in whatever order the Spirit prompts. You might write a psalm that follows a similar movement. What elements of God's goodness does the Spirit give you to express?

The ultimate gift is the finest of wheat that becomes the sacrament Christ's body.

Thursday   *The Joys of Water and Fire*   **Revelation 19**

I heard what sounded like a great multitude, like the roar of
rushing waters and like loud peals of thunder, shouting:
"Hallelujah! For our Lord God Almighty reigns." v. 6

Our reading today contains the only times that the word "Alleluia" is used in the New Testament. Alleluia— only found elsewhere in the psalms—is sung four times in the first six verses of the reading. Even as the final five psalms begin and end with alleluia, concluding this year of grace, so also does the Book of Revelation mount in songs of joy and praise as God's final triumph over evil is celebrated.

Listen to the sounds of many waters in the wells of grace that God is sending upward from within you. See the points of fire in the eyes of Jesus against the white background of your day. Once again, be lifted high as Zaccaheus and let the Spirit share with you the fruit of joy as the living waters of grace, flowing as the blood of Jesus, reveal the victory over all the evils that are coming against you. Rededicate yourself to how you are living in the Church, the Bride of Jesus.

Friday   *The Way of the Cross*   **Luke 23:13–43**

"I tell you the truth, today you will be with me in paradise." v. 43

Pilate's cowardice brings Jesus to the point of crucifixion. The Way of the Cross is laid out, the final steps of Jesus' Jerusalem journey that bring him to rest upon the new tree of life. Accompany Jesus. Be there—not in memory only, but right now; today Jesus completes the cross in countless others.

Once again as Zaccaheus, high upon the tree, the "Good Thief" has the gift of seeing Jesus. Unlike the other thief, this one looks for and finds the silent spaces between shouts of hatred and groans of pain. He goes inward to where he can truly see Jesus and there makes his protestations of love for Jesus, belief in Jesus, and then his final "robbery" of paradise: "Remember me when you come into your Kingdom."

Even if your soul is a soiled as the wicked kings of Judah, there is still time!

10
Ki
C

Saturday   **The Sabbath Torah Reading**

Nov 10, 2007 #6A	Nov 05, 2016 #2A	Nov 08, 2025 #4A	Nov 11, 2034 #6A
Nov 06, 2010 #6A	Nov 09, 2019 #3A	Nov 11, 2028 #5A	Nov 07, 2037 #6A
Nov 09, 2013 #7A	Nov 05, 2022 #3A	Nov 08, 2031 #5A	Nov 10, 2040 #6A

The Eleventh Week in Kingdomtide

Begins in the Sunday nearest November 9. Alphabyte: Xerography, p. 114

Sunday   *In the Light of the Mast*   **Luke 20:27–38**
He is not the God of the dead, but of the living,
for to him all are alive. v. 38

The Sadducees waste awesome moments in Jesus' presence. Here they pose a question only designed to catch Jesus in the awkwardness of a dilemma. Puffed up in themselves, they resist the light of the Master, remaining in their darkness—smug and self-assured in denying that there is a resurrection. See the sneers on their faces as they put their question to Jesus, confident that he would be reduced to an embarrassing silence.

Jesus responds with a glimpse into the future life of the saints in heaven. The only spouse in heaven will be Jesus, the one in whom marriage finds its bond and meaning here on earth.

The arrogance of the Sadducees prevents them from dying to self so that they can rise in Jesus. The "dead" ashes-toner of a copier is stirred to resurrection only when it recognizes the light shining on the face of the "Master."

Monday   *Compassion and Worship*   **Malachi 1**
My name will be great among the nations,
from the rising to the setting of the sun. v. 11

The final weeks of the cycle of prophets are dedicated to the last sacred writer of the Old Testament, Malachi. From him the torch would be passed to Matthew.

We are in the middle of the fifth century, B.C. The Temple has been rebuilt. Just as in the case of the original Temple of Solomon, when many lost interest in faithful worship and drifted to idolatry, so does Malachi call for authentic worship along with compassion. He teaches that the union of mercy and sacrifice is the kind of worship that God wants.

The slogan for Hallmark Cards has been applied to God the Father sending Jesus to us: "He cared enough to send the very best." Will you return your very best to God in a fervent life on fire by personal and communal worship together with dedication to service?

Tuesday   *The Sanctuary Swept Clean*   **2 Chronicles 29—32**
"Listen to me, Levites! Consecrate yourselves now and
consecrate the temple of the Lord, the God of your fathers.
Remove all defilement from the sanctuary." 29:5

At last, there is relief from chapters summarizing wicked deeds of kings! The good king Hezekiah sets out to restore true worship. The first step is to take out the rubbish that has accumulated in the sanctuary.

If you compare this account with the similar one in 2 Kings 18–20, you will notice expansions on the theme of worship. The momentum of fervor in celebrating the Passover carries them into another seven days! Singing has great importance in the life of renewed worship.

Do you have any rubbish—or at least excess baggage—that is filling your inner sanctuary? Catch the fresh fervor of this reading. Together with the reading from Malachi yesterday, let the Spirit sweep your inner house clean as you pattern your life after the sacred words you are hearing these days.

Wednesday   *At the Heart of Creation*   **Psalm 148**

Let them praise the name of the LORD, for his name alone is exalted;
his splendor is above the earth and the heavens. v. 13

Preoccupation with something or someone, obsession with a thought or habit—all these constrict the wide-angle view of creation which we need to maintain. The psalmist has this perspective. At the very heart of matter—more intimate than the bustling movement of atoms and molecules—lies the creative activity of God lifting every thing, animal and person into existence. It is there, at the deepest core that each article of creation is in praise of its creator. From the heights of heaven where God dwells, every creative thing finds its master-image. The dust of the earth—as toner in a copier—arranges itself according to this image.

Enter into God's creation at the inspiration of the psalm for today. Find your life, with all its details, thoughts, and feelings, set against the background of creation ever-singing praise to God.

Thursday   *"Already" and "Not Yet"*   **Revelation 20**

Then I saw a great white throne and him who was seated on it.
Earth and sky fled from his presence, and there was no place for them. v. 11

Some people in remote parts of the world did not receive the news of the end of World War II until long after the victorious countries held parades of celebration. In somewhat the same manner, John keeps a tension between the victory in Jesus already won, and its not yet realization in all levels of creation. A new thousand-year period is upon us, heightening the awareness of the millennium of which John speaks.

There are various interpretations of the thousand-year period of Jesus' reign. However, beyond calendars and literal verifications of the events in Revelation, the images of the triumph of good and the defeat of evil are meant to work there way into our lives until the Word of God's victory touches the heart with praise.

Psalm 148 of yesterday continues its energy of praise into today's chapter.

Friday   *Scent of the Resurrection*   **Luke 23:44–56**

"Father, into your hands I commit my spirit." v. 46

Evil has apparently had its day. All creation is distracted from praise of the Creator as immense sadness overwhelms it. The cross pierces the earth, even as the lance opens the side of Jesus. The eternally begotten, uncreated Son of God drinks the dregs of death, and everything is in mourning.

With the death of Jesus, however, there is a shift in the narrative. No longer do we hear blasphemous cries. Instead, a witness of faith rises up in a Roman centurion. In addition, those about the cross move toward salvation with signs of repentance.

Ponder the details of the burial of Jesus. Dwell with expectancy on the final verse where the scent of the resurrection can already be smelled. May this evening be peaceful for you, the Sabbath tomorrow, especially restful, as you prepare for the resurrection on Sunday.

11
Ki
C

Saturday   **The Sabbath Torah Reading**

Nov 17, 2007 #7A	Nov 12, 2016 #3A	Nov 15, 2025 #5A	Nov 18, 2034 #7A
Nov 13, 2010 #7A	Nov 16, 2019 #4A	Nov 18, 2028 #6A	Nov 14, 2037 #7A
Nov 16, 2013 #8A	Nov 12, 2022 #4A	Nov 15, 2031 #6A	Nov 17, 2040 #7A

The Twelfth Week in Kingdomtide
Begins in the Sunday nearest November 16. Alphabyte: Year, p. 115

Sunday | *Yoked with Christ* | **Luke 21:5–19**
By standing firm you will gain your life. v. 19

The harsh, pointed tip of the plow would have preferred to be silently stuck, jutting from the untilled soil. If it were thus, there would be no harvest to celebrate at Thanksgiving. If you have been tilling your soul with the seed-word of God each day, there will be fruit in your life. You are yoked with your Christ who is "pulling for you."

This is the point behind Jesus' prediction of the harsh events to come. The "end" is not something in the indefinite future, as many find themselves distracted by calendar-makers about what is to come; it is rather a quality of the present moment. Jesus invites you to continue to be in movement before the forces of darkness. There is no need to hide in an underground shelter, away from it all. With Jesus, you can plow your way into the very heart of evil itself and be victorious.

Be yoked with Christ.

Monday | *Lubricant for the Way* | **Malachi 2**
The lips of a priest ought to preserve knowledge,
and from his mouth men should seek instruction—
because he is the messenger of the LORD Almighty. v. 7

Malachi decries corruption on the part of the priests and infidelity in marriage in God's people. He rejects expression of emotion as a substitute for true offering in worship. In the midst of the very refuse of false worship and other abuses that Malachi would smear in the faces of the unfaithful, there are verses that warrant profound reflection. Take vv. 5–7, reading them not as applied only to the Levitic priesthood, but to yourself; you are called to be a priest in Christ Jesus. The qualities described in those verses are for you to live.

Do not pull apart from the yoke of the Lord, but tie these words to you, as a link between you and Jesus. Let the words be as a kind of spiritual lubricant for your way—peace, reverence, trust, justice, equity, knowledge.

Tuesday | *The Final Four* | **2 Chronicles 33—36**
"The LORD, the God of heaven, has given me all the kingdoms of the earth and he has appointed me to build temple for him at Jerusalem in Judah. Anyone of his people among you—may the Lord his God be with him, and let him go up." (Words of Cyrus, King of Persia) 36:23

Goodness and evil oscillate, along with celebration and disaster, as the final four of the twenty kings of Judah are accounted. The reign of the worst of these, Manasseh, is described in a few horrific verses; yet even he repents and is restored.

The pendulum swings to Josiah, great king of reform for God's people. Feel the joy in the restoration of the Temple, the discovery of God's Word and the especially memorable celebration of the Passover. Then disaster takes place again in the fall of Jerusalem, the destruction of the Temple, and the captivity in Babylon. However, good will triumph. God uses Cyrus, the pagan King of Persia, to be the means of restoring God's people to their homeland.

Do not fail to see the many meanings contained in the final verse of this book of the Bible, as another year of grace begins to draw to a close.

Wednesday *Battering Ram of Praise* **Psalm 149**

The Lord takes delight in his people;
he crowns the humble with salvation. v. 4

Praise is the ultimate weapon of victory in spiritual warfare. Because God is to be praised, the Enemy rises up in arrogance and anger. Praise, uninterrupted by the forces of darkness, brings the victory. When there is nothing to stop us from praising the Lord at every moment, no matter what the assault or temptation, then the Enemy has already been defeated before the battle is very much underway!

Praise is especially powerful in song. May there be one in your heart, if not on your lips, as you live today. Be watchful for the tactics of the Enemy getting into your mind and heart to discourage you from praise—perhaps by temptations to discouragement that come from seeing yourself as a victim. Use the battering ram of praise against that!

Thursday *The New Jerusalem* **Revelation 21**

I saw the Holy City, the new Jerusalem, coming down out of heaven from God,
prepared as a bride beautifully dressed for her husband. v. 2

Heaven and earth are bonded together in the striking image of the verse for the day. Evil is forever defeated. Wickedness no longer impedes the sweet commerce intended to take place between heaven and earth. It is the ultimate answer to the plea in the Lord's Prayer that God's "will be done on earth as it is in heaven."

The image of the flow between heaven and earth is similar to the dream of Jacob in Genesis 28:12, reiterated in John 1:51 with the image of "angels ascending and descending."

As you receive the images of the New Jerusalem, which abound in purity and perfection, may you rest in victorious peace at the heart of the Church. This is the temple.

Friday *The Opened Scripture* **Luke 24:1–35**

"Were not our hearts burning within us while he talked with us
on the road and opened the Scriptures to us?" v. 32

Yesterday's reading about the New Jerusalem came as a marked contrast with the previous chapter in Revelation; so also for today's Gospel of the resurrection. Evil has been defeated on the cross. The glorious presence of Jesus, the Bridegroom, fills the final chapter of Luke as we conclude this year of grace next week.

Be a silent, observant partner as you walk with the two disciples on the road to Emmaus. Jesus joins them. He is the yoke between them and the power within. Watch their hearts begin to burn as Jesus reveals the inner meaning of the Scriptures to them.

You might divide the reading into two parts, one for the morning, one for the evening. Spend your whole day with the risen Lord. Jesus walks with you and talks with you.

12
Ki
C

Saturday **The Sabbath Torah Reading**

Nov 24, 2007 #8A	Nov 19, 2016 #4A	Nov 22, 2025 #6A	Nov 25, 2034 #8A
Nov 20, 2010 #8A	Nov 23, 2019 #5A	Nov 25, 2028 #7A	Nov 21, 2037 #8A
Nov 23, 2013 #9A	Nov 19, 2022 #5A	Nov 22, 2031 #7A	Nov 24, 2040 #8A

The Thirteenth Week in Kingdomtide

Begins in the Sunday nearest November 22. Alphabyte: Zoom Lens, p. 115

Sunday   *The King on the Cross*   Luke 23:33–43

"Jesus, remember me when you come into your kingdom." v. 42

The final Sunday dedicated to Christ the King has us contemplate our Lord upon the throne of the cross. Place yourself before the cross, aware of the two thieves on either side. Hear the blasphemies of the one, and the tender response of the other. The late Bishop Fulton J. Sheen remarked, "The thief on the left wanted to be taken down; the thief on the right wanted to be taken up!"

As you look upon your King and the ignominy of his throne, may your heart be filled with the same grace with which the good thief responded. Jesus has taken possession of the Kingdom; he will share the paradise of his Kingdom presence with you now, if your prayer is as simple and direct as the one of the saved thief. The cross is the throne upon which Jesus shares his kingship with you. The victory and the joy are there.

Monday   *The End and the Beginning*   Malachi 3—4

For you who revere my name, the sun of righteousness
will rise with healing in its wings. 4: 2

God's love, like circles and cycles, has no beginning or end. While we mark the conclusion of the three-year cycle of Bible readings and its beginning next week in Advent, the movement of God's Word is all of one piece. These final chapters of the Old Testament are sutured to the New. The "coming messenger" is John the Baptist. There is unity of ends and beginnings, even as Advent begins the story of God's grace, yet points to the end, in the Second Coming of Christ.

Verses 8–10 are among the principle texts in the Bible about tithing and giving the first fruits to the Lord. Make connections with economic systems of injustice that exploit the Third World. Linger on the blessed promises of the concluding verses of the Old Testament, and the curse upon those whose hearts are hardened.

Tuesday   *Life from Beginning to End*   Ecclesiastes 9—12

Remember man—before the silver cord is severed, or the golden bowl is broken;
before the pitcher is shattered at the spring,
or the wheel broken at the well … 12: 6

Solomon in the evening of his life offers a sobering sense of the theme of the end of all things. While he fell short of the revelation about eternal life, still the perspectives he offers are valuable for personal detachment, setting priorities in life and realizing that the end of earthly life will come for everyone. God's judgment will be the next event after our death as we all gaze alone with God upon the open pages of each one's Book of Life.

Read slowly as though you are sipping hot cider on a cold autumn evening. Take the verse of the day, linking it with the encounter of the Good Thief upon the cross. The Lord will remember you in his Kingdom in heaven if you remember your Redeemer in his Kingdom upon earth.

| **Wednesday** | *Praise with Every Breath* | **Psalm 150** |

Let everything that has breath praise the LORD.
Praise the LORD. v. 6

Praise completes the collection of 150 psalms that comprise the longest book of the Bible. The word "praise" occurs in every one of the six verses—in fact, in every line of the psalm. It begins by saying *where* God is to be praised, then *why* God is to be praised, followed by four verses that direct *how* the praise is to be expressed. There is no time indicated as to *when* God is to be praised; but then there is the final verse summoning every creature with breath to praise the Lord. Since breathing takes place at every moment, perhaps the psalmist suggests that God be praised with every breath.

Today, allow your breathing to be praise, along with every word you express that fills the space about with your exhales. May many "Alleluias" be sweet smells of praise that flow from your heart.

| **Thursday** | *Come, Lord Jesus* | **Revelation 22** |

I am the Alpha and the Omega, the First and the Last,
the Beginning and the End. v. 13

The Bible begins with day and night, the Tree of Life and the Tree of the Knowledge of Good and Evil. It ends with day only, and the River of Life. Darkness and evil are gone. Only grace flows from the river.

Images of permanent abundance characterize this final chapter of the Bible. While there is no physical temple in space, there is a reference to time in the twelve crops of fruit harvested in each of the twelve months. Time, not space, survives as the link that makes eternity descend into the months and days of our lives.

The final words of the Bible echo deeply in the emptied stillness of the heart. As the clarion cry, **"Come Lord Jesus"** sounds and fades away, the stillness of Advent is days away. Prepare for an ever more complete coming of the Lord Jesus into your life.

| **Friday** | *The Whole Bible* | **Luke 24:36–53** |

Then he opened their minds
so they could understand the Scriptures. v. 45

St. Luke's Gospel ends as it begins, in the Temple. From the glowing lights of the Holy of Holies and the annunciation of the birth of John the Baptist to Zechariah, to the inner glow in the hearts of the disciples waiting for the coming of the Holy Spirit, the glory and presence of God has moved through this year of grace.

Apart from the cycle of Torah readings, today concludes the three-year cycle of readings from the Bible. Each day the Holy Spirit has been doing in your heart what the Spirit did with the first disciples—opening your understanding to receive the Scriptures. As the cycle begins again next week with the flickering of the first Advent Candle, pause today with gratitude as the whole Bible lies open before you. Look through the "zoom lens" of the present moment, which embraces all of God's Word.

13
Ki
C

Saturday

The Sabbath Torah Reading

Dec 01, 2007 #9A	Nov 26, 2016 #5A	Nov 29, 2025 #7A	Dec 02, 2034 #9A
Nov 27, 2010 #9A	Nov 30, 2019 #6A	Dec 02, 2028 #8A	Nov 28, 2037 #9A
Nov 30, 2013 #10A	Nov 26, 2022 #6A	Nov 29, 2031 #8A	Dec 01, 2040 #9A

THE SABBATH
TORAH PORTIONS

When the exiles returned to Jerusalem and rebuilt the Temple in 515 B.C., a tradition began of reading the *Torah* every year on the Sabbath services of worship. The first five books of the Bible were divided into fifty-four portions called *Parashahs*. In order to complete the entire Torah, a great amount of time was needed at worship; in addition, the passages were sung according to Jewish cantilation. Thus, sometime around the time of Jesus, a lectionary was designed that extended the *Torah* over a three-year period. Around 1200 A.D., reading the entire Torah each year was again honored by returning to a one-year cycle.

In the course of time, the Conservative tradition devised a way of retaining the advantages of both a one-year and a three-year cycle. Each portion is divided into three parts—a third of each portion per year. This is the method in *The Bible through the Seasons*. The yearly cycle ends and begins again in October at the end of *The Feast of Tabernacles (Succoth)* at a special celebration called *The Joy of the Torah (Simhath Torah)*.

The three parts of the *Torah* passages roughly coincide with years A, B, and C, according to *The Revised Common Lectionary*. However, since the Jewish Year begins in autumn and the Christian Year in winter, reference to the Torah portions is done as "Part A, B or C," to avoid confusion.[1]

Similar to Christian naming of Sundays, each Sabbath is named after a word(s) which comes at the beginning of the portion. Uniting a spirituality of both Sabbath and Sunday observance, we discover two distinct moments of force at work in a week. The Sabbath is that to which the week builds. Together with Jewish people, we are invited to allow the Sabbath to lure us and draw us to it, as we look forward to this precious holiday. Synagogues conduct weekday morning services when sections of the coming Sabbath Torah portion are read. Preparations are made for the Sabbath as for an esteemed guest—the "Sabbath Queen" that is coming to visit the home. It is on the Sabbath that God rested and enjoyed the work of creation; we are to do the same.

Faith in the resurrection of Jesus on the first day of the week launches Christians into the week ahead. There are thus two moments of force from these traditions. On the one hand there is a drawing of life toward the Sabbath; on the other hand, a release of life as the Sunday begins the new week. The two energies come together as ebb tides on the waters of the week. Whether you are being launched and lifted into God's presence, or drawn and lured into it, the effect is the same: God wants to share life with us and longs that we enjoy the sacred intimacy that God offers.

---

1   For a complete understanding of the Jewish Calendar and the cycle of readings from 1900 to 2100, see *The Comprehensive Hebrew Calendar* by Arthur Spier. (Feldheim Publishers, New York, 1986).

The Sabbath Torah Portions (*Parashas*)

	Portion (*Parasha*)	Part A	Part B	Part C
	THE BOOK OF GENESIS—*Bereshith*			
1	*Bereshith* (Beginning)	1:1—2:3	2:4—4:26	5:1—6:8
2	*Noah* (Noah)	6:9—8:14	8:15—10::32	11
3	*Lech L'cha* (Go yourself)	12—13	14—15	16—17
4	*Vayera* (And He appeared)	18	19—20	21—22
5	*Haye Sarah* (The Lives of Sarah)	23:1—24:9	24:10-52	24:53—25:18
6	*Tol'doth* (Progeny)	25:19—26:22	26:23—27:29	27:30—28:9
7	*Vayetze* (And he departed)	28:10—30:13	30:14—31:16	31:17—32:2
8	*Vayishlah* (And he sent)	32:3—33:20	34:1—35:15	35:16—36:43
9	*Vayeshev* (And he settled)	37	38	39—40
10	*Mikketz* (At the end)	41:1-52	41:53—43:15	43:16—44:17
11	*Vayiggash* (And he approached)	44:18—45:27	45:28—46:27	46:28—47:27
12	*Vayhi* (And he lived)	47:28—48:22	49	50
	THE BOOK OF EXODUS—*Shemoth*			
13	*Shemoth* (Names)	1—2	3:1—4:17	4:18—6:1
14	*Vaera* (And I appeared)	6:2—7:7	7:8—8:15	8:16—9:35
15	*Bo* (Come)	10:1—11:3	11:4—12:28	12:29—13:16
16	*Beshallah* (Sent Out)	13:17—14:14	14:15—16:10	16:11—17:16
17	*Yithro* (Jethro)	18	19	20
18	*Mishpatim* (Laws)	21:1—22:24	22:25—23:19	23:20—24:18
19	*Terumah* (Portion)	25	26:1-30	26:31—27:19
20	*Tetzaveh* (And you shall command)	27:20—28:30	28:31—29:18	29:19—30:10
21	*Ki Tissa* (Take a census)	30:11—31:17	31:18—33:11	33:12—34:35
22	*Vayakhel* (And he assembled)	35:1—36:19	36:20—38:20	
23	*Pekude* (Reckoning)	38:21—39:21	39:22—40:38	

Portion (Parasha)	Part A	Part B	Part C
THE BOOK OF LEVITICUS—Vayikra			
24 *Vayikra* (And he called)	1—2	3:1—4:26	4:27—5:19
25 *Tzav* (Command)	6:1—7:10	7:11-38	8
26 *Shemini* (Eighth)	9:1—10:11	10:12—11:32	11:33-47
27 *Tazria* (Conceives)	12:1—13:28	13:29-59	
28 *Metzora* (Afflicted)	14:1-32	14:33-57	15
29 *Ahare Moth* (After the death)	16	17—18	
30 *Kedoshim* (Holy)	19		20
31 *Emor* (Say)	21—22	23—24	
32 *Behar* (On the mount)	25:1-28	25:29—26:2	
33 *Behukkotai* (My commandment)	26:3—27:15		27:15-34
THE BOOK OF NUMBERS—Bemidbar			
34 *Bemidbar* (In the wilderness)	1	2:1—3:13	3:14—4:20
35 *Naso* (Census)	4:21—5:10	5:11—6:27	7
36 *Behaalot'cha* (When you kindle)	8:1—9:14	9:15—10:34	10:35—12:16
37 *Shelah L'cha* (Send)	13:1—14:7	14:8—15:7	15:8-41
38 *Korah* (Korah)	16:1-40	16:41—17	18
39 *Hukkath* (Ordinance)	19:1—20:21	20:22-29	21:1—22:1
40 *Balak* (Balak)	22:2-38	22:39—23:30	24:1—25:9
41 *Pinhas* (Phineas)	25:10—26:51	26:52—28:15	28:16—30:1
42 *Matoth* (The chiefs)	30:2—31:54	32	
43 *Maseh* (Journeys)	33	34—35:7	35:8—36:13
THE BOOK OF DEUTERONOMY—Devarim			
44 *Devarim* (The words)	1:1—2:1	2:2-30	2:31—3:22
45 *Vaethanan* (I implored)	3:23—4:49	5—6	7:1-11
46 *Ekeb* (Reward)	7:12—9:3	9:4—10:11	10:12—11:25
47 *Reeh* (Behold)	11:26—12:28	12:29—14:29	15:1—16:17
48 *Shof'tim* (Judges)	16:18—18:5	18:6—19:13	19:14—21:9
49 *Ki Tetze* (When you go out)	21:10—23:8	23:9—24:13	24:14—25:19

50	*Ki Tavo* (When you will come)	26:1-11	26:12—28:6	28:7—29:8
51	*Nitsabim* (Stand)	29:9—30:20		
52	*Vayelech* (And he went)	31		
53	*Haazinu* (Give)	32		
54	*V'zot Habracha* (And this is the blessing)	33—34		

Major Jewish Holidays

When *Rosh Hashana* (The New Year), *Yom Kippur* (The Day of Atonement), and *Shavuoth* (Pentecost) occur on the Sabbath, the readings below are read, instead of the expected Torah Portion, which is postponed to the following week. *Succoth* (Tabernacles) and *Pesach* (Passover) are celebrations eight days long; hence, there is always a special Sabbath Torah reading during those festivals.

Rosh Hashana   *The New Year*   **Genesis 21**

She said, "Who would ever have said to Abraham that Sarah would nurse children?
Yet I have borne him a son in his old age." v. 7

*R*osh Hashana means "The Head of the Year." The spiritual feeling of the Jewish New Year is sober, quiet, and reflective, contrary to the energies in the secular New Year on January 1. The Jewish New Year occurs in autumn, a season that is "seasoned" with nostalgia and inwardness. There is a tradition that God made the world in the fall, for everything was made in its fullness. Seeds are for the next generation; God created Adam and Eve in their maturity. The patriarchs, Abraham, Isaac and Jacob, were believed to have been born on *Rosh Hashana*. Hence, the reading for this festival is Genesis 21: Isaac's birthday. You will find this passage in Portion 4B.

Let us greet each other with the Jewish way of saying "Happy New Year": *L'shanah tovah tikateivu:* "May you be inscribed in the Book of Life for a good year."

Yom Kippur   *The Day of Atonement*   **The Book of Jonah**

Should I not be concerned about Nineveh, that great city,
in which there are more than a hundred and twenty thousand persons
who do not know their right hand from their left …? 4:11

*I*n the course of the years of seminary, God blessed me with the friendship of a cantor in the Reformed tradition, the late Sidney Venetianer. Along with his family, Sid became my life-long, devoted friend until his death in 1993. One *Yom Kippur*, I joined him in a complete fast of twenty-four hours, prescribed by the *Torah* for this day. That day sealed for me what has become a love for Judaism and a desire that we rediscover its profound rhythms for prayer, devotion to the Lord and openness to the ongoing flow of God into our lives.

The essence of the day is prayer and repentance, with the assurance that God is listening and merciful. It is a day of closeness in the Jewish Community, both those on earth and those beyond the grave, as remembrances of names of the community rise forth at the service on this day. It is a fitting day to visit a synagogue. As Christians, we bring the assurance of God's forgiveness and atonement in Jesus Christ.

The Book of Jonah is read in its entirety on this day. (You will find *Firestarters* for this book in the Eighth and Ninth Weeks of Pentecost, Year C.)

Sukkot (Tabernacles) *God's Tent Among Us* Leviticus 22:26—23:44
I am the LORD who sanctifies you. 23:41

The Jewish calendar is grounded on three sacred feasts—Passover in the spring, Pentecost in summer and Tabernacles in autumn. Before the Temple was destroyed in the year 70 A.D., Jewish people used to make pilgrimages to Jerusalem for these festivals.

The festival of Tabernacles lasts nine days. Many believe that the pilgrims modeled their celebration of Thanksgiving after this festival. (The reading is part of Portion 31.) The tabernacles recall the tents of dwellers at harvest time as well as the Exodus in the desert.

We Christians can relate these feasts to the Triune God. The death and resurrection of Jesus is the Passover, as the descent of the Holy Spirit is Pentecost. Is there a counterpart for God the Father in Tabernacles? Curiously, we might have found it in the Transfiguration incident when Peter asked Jesus if he would allow three tabernacles to be built for Jesus, Moses, and Elijah. This never takes place. Instead, Jesus resumes his normal appearance and they walk down the mountain, learning about the coming suffering and death of Jesus.

The complete fulfillment of Tabernacles is yet to occur. We are all walking the path of God that leads us more and more into the Promised Land of God's dominion over our hearts.

Passover *(Pesach)* *The Beauty and Power of God* Exodus 33:12—34:26
Now if I have found favor in your sight, show me your ways, so that I may know you and find favor in your sight. Consider too that this nation is your people. 33:13

The center of the year for the Jewish people is Passover, as Easter is for Christians. The *Torah* reading unfolds the beauty, the power, and the presence of God. The Lord's goodness and mercy are described. Be with Moses as the glory of the Lord is revealed to him and to you, through the Holy Spirit.

Learn about the Seder, the supper that recalls the Exodus. There are foods symbolic of the suffering endured such as salt water for the tears shed, and horseradish for the bitterness experienced in suffering so much.

This is a day of solidarity with all those in bondage in one form or another. We intercede for them that the pathways to liberation would become open—that all the "Red Seas" in their lives would split apart so that they can walk on to freedom.

Pentecost *(Shavuot)* *A Night of Expectation* Exodus 19:1—20:26
I am the Lord your God, who brought you out of the land of Egypt, out of the house of slavery; *3* you shall have no other gods before me. 20:2–3

Shavuot was originally a spring harvest in Israel. The first wheat was ripe about fifty days after the first barley harvest. The crop of barley was brought to the Temple the day after Passover began. The people were then instructed to count fifty days or seven weeks from one harvest to the other.

As time passed, the festival became one to celebrate the revelation of God on Sinai, the true harvest of God's life that to the human family. The very meaning of the word *Torah* is to rain or flow down. The *Torah* Reading is the giving of the Ten Commandments found in Portion 17 B and C, God's revelation and teaching flowing down the mountain.

There is a tradition of taking a long nap the afternoon before the beginning of *Shavuot*, which begins at sundown. This is to be ready to participate in an all night vigil that many Jewish communities observe. One mystical work praises those who stay up all night in expectation of receiving the *Torah*.

The Christian expression of this revelation is the descent of the Holy Spirit upon the first disciples—the flowing down of God's Spirit upon us.

Portion 1   *Bereshith* (Beginning)   Genesis 1:1—6:8

Bereshith is the Hebrew name for the book of Genesis.

Part A   *In the Beginning*   Genesis 1:1—2:3

In the beginning God created the heavens and the earth. 1:1

We listen to the awesome words that recount the beginning of the universe. On fire with faith, our imaginations behold the work of God. God's word is God's work. This pattern recurs as a rhythm: "God said" … and then "God saw that it was good."

The word "universe" literally means "The one thing that turns." Make it personal—"The One who turns." The description of creation takes place in thirty-four "turnings" we call "verses" in the Bible.

It took over three years for Michelangelo to recreate the creation of God onto the ceiling of the Sistine Chapel in Rome. As you come to the place of the beginning of the Jewish Torah cycle, may the Bible's 30,442 verses, turn your whole being each day into a sacred chapel/temple that reflects the beauty and handiwork of God.

Part B   *Sin and the Seed of Promise*   Genesis 2:4—4:26

**The Lord God formed man from the dust of the ground,
and breathed into his nostrils the breath of life; and the man became a living being. 2:7**

A second story of creation is told, this time from the tradition that clusters around the covenantal name of God: *Yahweh.* The focus of creation is that of man and woman. With tender love, God gathers the moist clay of the earth, forming a nose as a sculptor, and breathing God's life into it. Inspirited earth: that is what you and I are. We live because the breath of God lives in us. Woman is made from the side of man, suggesting the intimate and equal relation that she has with him.

Read the familiar story of the Fall by placing yourself there at that moment of grave temptation and tragic yielding. Sin is original—yet it bears the seed of redeeming promise as the lines of Jesus' coming are traced here in the very beginning of the Bible.

Linger in prayer with your thoughts and feelings as you conclude the reading.

Part C   *Creation Goes Downhill*   Genesis 5:1—6:8

**The Lord was sorry that he had made humankind on the earth,
and it grieved him to his heart. 6:6**

Methuselah lived 969 years! He was not alone in great life spans listed for the ten Patriarchs from Adam to Noah and the flood. One of the purposes of this list is to give continuity to long periods of elapsed time and to keep the connection to our deepest roots in the human family. The shortening of the life span has been seen as a consequence to the degrading levels to which the human family had fallen. Everything went downhill. Some see the shortening as actually an act of mercy on God's part, as we might say: "Quit, while you're ahead," or "Stop before things get worse!" And worse indeed did things get with the reference that even "sons of God" (fallen angels?) took human wives. God was grieved at creating us. However, there was one good man: Noah.

How does God feel about having created you?

Part A   *The Ark of Saving Grace*   **Genesis 6:9—8:14**

**I will establish my covenant with you; and you shall come into the ark,
you, your sons, your wife, and your sons' wives with you. 6:18**

The highest form of God's creation, human life, becomes the lowest. Ask the Holy Spirit to give you a spiritual sense of the heart of God—the profound divine sadness at human corruption.

However, Noah and his family stand above the rest in perfection. Through him, the human family and all the species of the earth will be spared extinction. The ark is built, symbol of the boundaries of saving grace that would come through the body of Jesus and living in him.

Note the time references to this ancient disaster that came upon the earth. In the midst of all the chaos of water defying the boundaries of land, there are time boundaries and the absolute certainty that from the Genesis passages here, to the Revelation chapters of these Thursdays, the Lord is in charge.

Part B   *From Creation to Covenant*   **Genesis 8:15—10:32**

**As long as the earth remains, there will be springtime and harvest,
cold and heat, winter and summer, day and night. 8:22**

Noah emerges from the ark with the rest of the land animals—"birds, beasts and beetles." Just as in the first account of creation, when the dry land appeared with water taking its assigned place, here again, dry land emerges from the chaos of the Flood.

For the first time in the Bible, the word **Covenant** is used to describe a new dimension in the relation of the Creator to the creature. The term is repeated several times in chapter 9, as though to introduce the new intimacy that the Lord wants to have with the human family. It thus anticipates the great covenants to come with Abraham, Moses—and of course, with Jesus.

Is there any chaos from which you are emerging in your life? From it there arises a new relation of intimacy and joy with your Creator and Lord.

Part C   *Pushing Up to Heaven*   **Genesis 11**

**Come, let us go down, and confuse their language there,
so that they will not understand one another's speech. v. 7**

What arrogance—to think about getting to heaven by building a tower, instead of being lifted up to heaven by God! The seventeenth century Rabbi, Chaim Ibn Attar, suggested that the sin was also found in placing humans in tight, vertical space, when God had intended the population to be spread out. Naturally he made this comment before the advent of high apartments and office buildings. Though these are not evils in themselves, one wonders where the boundaries of justice are, in decisions emanating from skyscrapers around the world that result in unjust distribution of the world's resources.

The Day of Pentecost reversed Babel's confusion of tongues, as recorded in Acts 2. We need to allow our mouths to be regulated by the Spirit-tongue of fire in the head and heart.

Portion 3   *Lech L'cha (Go Yourself)*   Genesis 12—17

Part A   *A Model Human Being*   Genesis 12—13

**I will bless those who bless you, and the one who curses you I will curse;
and in you all the families of the earth shall be blessed. 12:3**

Having completed a history of the earliest ages, the sacred writer of Genesis turns his attention to the father of all patriarchs, Abraham. Not only is he a prototype of Christ, but Abraham is the model of all who would come to believe in Jesus and leave all to follow him.

God offers a unique and blessed covenant to the human family through Abraham in a people chosen and blessed by God. Previews are laid out of the coming famine and slavery in Egypt and Exodus into the Promised Land, with all the clashes and strife that this movement would entail.

Sense the sweep from the "nobody" that Abraham was, to the greatness of what he came to be—all because he left the comfort of the familiar, and followed God into the empty space of the future. What "country" do you need to forsake to follow God's plan in your life?

Part B   *The Fire of God's Covenant*   Genesis 14—15

**He blessed him and said, "Blessed be Abram by God Most High, maker of heaven and earth;
and blessed be God Most High, who has delivered your enemies into your hand!"
And Abram gave him one-tenth of everything. 14:19–20**

As though wrenching a prized object from a fire, Abraham moves in to rescue his nephew, Lot, held captive. The tradition of tithing has its beginnings as Abraham gives to Melchizedek a tenth of his spoils of war. The gift of Christ's body and blood is anticipated in this King of Salem, King of "Peace," as he brings out bread and wine to meet Abraham.

Chapter 15 is one of the great moments in Hebrew History. The Lord tells Abraham that he will be the father of a people special to the Lord above all nations of the earth.

God acts when hopelessness sets in for Abraham and Sarah, childless in their old age. The Lord acted then and is acting now in your life. May the light of God's Spirit pass between what is separated and broken in your life and make it ablaze with the fire of God's healing love.

Part C   *The Covenant with Abraham*   Genesis 16—17

**I will establish my covenant between me and you, and your offspring after
you throughout their generations, for an everlasting covenant,
to be God to you and to your offspring after you. 17:7**

Sarah's barrenness was interpreted as a curse. Rather than trust in the Lord, she took it upon herself to tell Abraham to have relations with Hagar, Sarah's maid, so that Abraham could have a son. Ishmael was born, and with it was begotten jealousy between the two women and their children, even to our own day. Modern day Arabs trace their ancestry back to Ishmael.

In chapter 17 we joyfully begin to recall the covenant that God made with Abraham. God introduces himself as *El Shaddai*, the name we translate as "The Almighty."

God offers a covenant with Abraham. The sign of this covenant is circumcision—what comes forth in generative life is to be the gift of God and not simply the productivity of the flesh alone. May your heart be circumcised in a response to God's abundant life.

Portion 4   *Vayera (And He Appeared)*   Genesis 18—22

Part A   *A Son for Sarah*   Genesis 18
**Is anything too wonderful for the Lord? At the set time I will return to you,
in due season, and Sarah shall have a son." 18:14**

Three men mysteriously come before Abraham to announce the conception of Isaac. Many scholars interpret this as a manifestation of the Trinity, coming in the early chapters of the Bible. Isaac is another type of Jesus, miracle-child of Abraham and Sarah. He comes at a moment in the evening of the lives of this couple when their "sun" would be expected to set.

There is a charming quality about the story of the back-and-forth dialogue between God and Abraham about the catastrophe soon to come upon Sodom and Gomorrah. God's desire is to save, not to destroy. Look at what a few good people in prayer could do to hold back the consequences of so much sin. However, as the disciples in the garden with Jesus, there was no one to watch one hour with him. Be among those found faithful to intercessory prayer.

Part B   *Fear in the Face of Depravity*   Genesis 19—20
**For we are about to destroy this place, because the outcry against
its people has become great before the Lord, and the Lord has sent us to destroy it. 19:13**

The depravity of the people of Sodom is expressed in this episode of brutal disregard for the sanctity of life and sexuality, as well as the sacredness of the law of hospitality to the stranger in one's house. There is a similar story in Judges 19:22ff. with striking similarities in its account.

Just as Gibeah in the story from Judges, Lot is willing to expose the women in his family to the brutality of wanton men. The completely forget God.

What do you do when it is time to take a stand when the rights of others are violated? There is a temptation to succumb to evil in the manipulative powers of people who reactively "Want what they want, when they want it." Disregard for human dignity demands a strong response with a desire to please the Lord alone—no one else.

Part C   *The Lord-Will-Provide.*   Genesis 21—22
**Abraham said, "God himself will provide the lamb for a burnt offering, my son."
So the two of them walked on together. 22:8**

Walk in Abraham's sandals with his absolute trust in the Lord. The place where Abraham sacrificed the ram in place of Isaac was called "The Lord-Will-Provide." Take a post-it note with this phrase and place it where you can see it clearly, so that you too may grow in total confidence in the Lord in all your circumstances.

Ponder the words of Isaac just before the sacrifice. "Look," he said to his father, "the fire and the wood, but where is the lamb for a burnt offering?" Hear the response of Abraham in the verse for today and know of whom he really speaks—Jesus the Lamb of God.

Isaac and Ishmael would later become symbols in Paul's letter to the Galatians representing the two covenants of law and grace (Gal. 4:28–31). Rejoice in the covenant of grace that empowers your life.

Portion 5   *Haye Sarah (The Lives of Sarah)*   Gen. 23:1—25:18

Part A   *Where do we go from here?*   **Genesis 23:1—24:9**

And Sarah died at Kiriath-arba (that is, Hebron) in the land of Canaan;
and Abraham went in to mourn for Sarah and to weep for her. 23.2

The death of Sarah has a special poignancy about it. We have come to know Abraham and Sarah in a way no other human being from Adam and Eve to the family of Noah has even been known. We see their humanness, frailty, and sinfulness—including the cynical laughter of Sarah when she heard that she would conceive Isaac in her old age.

Familiarity with Abraham and Sarah permits you to enter into the mourning of Abraham for his beloved wife. Abraham is so very human in negotiating with neighbors after the funeral about, "Where do we go from here?"

The story of God's unique intervention in history with Abraham and Sarah continues in the next couple to intrigue us, Isaac and Rebecca. Sense the shift in the story, even as the death of Jesus opens up new possibilities in resurrection.

Part B   *A Wife for Isaac*   **Genesis 24: 10–52**

The Lord, before whom I walk, will send his angel with you and make your way successful.
You shall get a wife for my son from my kindred,
from my father's house. v. 40

This is the story of how God placed the beautiful Rebecca into a setting where she would eventually become Isaac's wife. We are in Mesopotamia: "The Land between the Rivers" (the Tigris and the Euphrates) in modern Iraq.

The Lord uses the kindness of Rebecca as part of the plan to have her be a key ancestor in the life of God's people. Her name means, "to captivate," which is what her beauty did to men. Equally as captivating as her physical beauty, is the beauty of her kindness, which results in such a great change in her future life.

Never fail in being kind in all circumstances. In so doing, you make yourself more suitable for the Lord to use for increasing love in the Kingdom. Hebrews 13:2 expresses a similar truth: "Don't forget to show hospitality to strangers, for some who have done this have entertained angels without realizing it!"

Part C   *Help from Ages Past*   **Genesis 24:53—25:18**

May you, our sister, become thousands of myriads;
may your offspring gain possession of the gates of their foes. 24:60

How far back can you go with stories about your ancestors? Families that have such accounts rejoice in the sense of identity and belonging that their ancestors give them.

As you read the story of how Isaac and Rebecca married, let us remember that these are *our* ancestors too. You and I are part of God's chosen people. When Abraham was promised descendants "as the stars of the heaven and as the sand on the seashore," you were included. God's all embracing knowledge and love had you in mind. There is a song which sings about Jesus: "When he was on the cross, I was on his mind."

As the Christian year soon ends, we gratefully remember what God has done—"our help from ages past."

Part A   *Patient and Waiting Upon the Lord*   **Genesis 25:19—26:22**
The Lord said to her, "Two nations are in your womb,
and two peoples born of you shall be divided; the one shall be stronger than the other,
the elder shall serve the younger." 25:23

Within the womb of Rebecca, the twins Jacob and Esau struggle in strife—sign of the same evils that will beset future generations of the human family. Within the flow of God's gracious covenant and the responses on the part of our patriarchs, there are the shadows of selfishness and greed. Witness the tension between instant gratification, and patient waiting to fuller revelation, as described in Esau's selling his future destiny so that he could have his stomach filled in the present. Find the points of identification with these figures portrayed as so very frail and human, though at the same time touched by God with wondrous plans for the future.

Are there future possibilities you are compromising be being obsessed with some immediate desire that presses on you for satisfaction?

Part B   *Each Person Is Responsible*   **Genesis 26:23—27:29**
You shall take it to your father to eat,
so that he may bless you before he dies. 27:10

Families are like mobiles. Ideally, each of the part of the mobile hangs freely in their proper place, all of them suspended by one string. Few families are like that; most are tangled together, resulting in the term, "dysfunctional family."

The family of Isaac and Rebecca has seeds of dysfunction within it. Esau, selling his birthright for food—is he not also responsible for the loss of the blessing, which Isaac gave to the deceitful Jacob? Then there is the preferential treatment of Rebecca to Jacob, and the latter's complicity with her plan. Even Isaac needed to trust his nose more than his hands when he "smelled" something not quite right when Jacob approached him as Esau.

We are responsible for the situations in which we find ourselves. This frees us from the language of blame, reserving the discovering of our guilt when we go and pray to the Father in secret.

Part C   *Dare to Forgive*   **Genesis 27:30—28:9**
Esau said to his father, "Have you only one blessing, father? Bless me, me also, father!"
And Esau lifted up his voice and wept. 27:38

God's will is done even in the midst of deceit, as in this story of Esau, Jacob, and the blessing. The Chosen People knew the power of the tongue to bless or curse—something we need to remember today. That critical word, that unkind remark has a strong effect upon another. Yet one word of heartfelt prayer can be more powerful. When Jesus told us to pray for our enemies, he knew that the effect of prayer is greater than all the schemes of evil plotted against us.

Who are the "Esaus" in your life? May that list become one with your prayer list. If you have been deceitful toward anyone, repent. Then there is the other side: are you "Esau" to anyone? Who has done you wrong in your life? Be careful about harboring resentment as Esau did. Forgive, and the power of the Lord will flow into your life.

Portion 7   *Vayetze (And He Departed)*   Genesis 28:10—32:3

Part A   *Family Strongholds*   **Genesis 28:10—30:13**
Then Jacob woke from his sleep and said,
"Surely the Lord is in this place—and I did not know it!" 28:16

The mystic dream of Jacob is similar to the flow between heaven and earth that describes the Book of Revelation.

The ongoing deception of Laban and that of his sister Rebecca finds its beginning in the earlier deceit about Esau, Jacob and the blessing of Isaac. A stronghold of dishonesty has worked itself into that family, soon to have a strong effect upon the twelve sons born of Jacob, fathers of the Twelve Tribes of Israel.

Take a stand by faith against any family stronghold with which the Evil One seeks to stop the Spirit flow from God to you and your children. A stronghold is anything contrary to the will of God that is to be done on earth, as it is in heaven.

Part B   *What's in a Name?*   **Genesis 30:14—31:16**
She conceived and bore a son, and said, "God has taken away my reproach";
and she named him Joseph, saying,
"May the Lord add to me another son!" 30:23–24

The narrative continues with the births of more of Jacob's sons and one daughter. Names of children in Hebrew are derived from some circumstance surrounding their births.

Naming is important. If you are a parent, you will recall the careful thought you gave to the naming of your children, perhaps to remember your own parent or grandparent. Jewish people never use the name of God directly, because naming gives power over whom or what is named. Naming God, we have "power" over God, which would be blasphemous in the Hebrew mind.

If you were to give names to the members of your family associated with divine intervention and blessing in their lives, what would those names be? Such names could be the focal point for prayer for each family member.

Part C   *Praying for Those Who Wronged Us*   **Genesis 31:17—32:3**
The Lord watch between you and me,
when we are absent one from the other. 31:49

Through all the intrigue and dishonesty in this part of the Bible, the Lord is dealing with you and me. Jacob and Rachel secretly escape from Laban, Rachel's father. She has secretly stowed away the small figurines, which are the household gods of her family's religion. The couple set out with their entourage and cross the Euphrates River.

As Laban pursues Jacob, Laban is warned by God not to threaten Jacob. Within each of us, the Holy Spirit warns us not only to avoid thinking harm of anyone, but also to pray for those who have wronged us. We need to be guided by the awesome power of God.

Today's verse, the covenant between Jacob and Laban, is worthy to be engraved in wood and in your heart.

Portion 8   *Vayishlah (And He Sent)*   Genesis 32:3—36:43

T
O
R
A
H

8

Part A   *True Meeting*   Genesis 32:3—33:20

**Jacob said, "No, please; if I find favor with you, then accept my present from my hand;
for truly to see your face is like seeing the face of God—
since you have received me with such favor. 33:10**

Toward the end of the first four years of my ministry when I was a campus minister, one of the teachers at Canisius College in Buffalo, N.Y. where I was serving, criticized by efforts with the remark: "The trouble with you is that you want everybody to be friends." "No," I replied, "but I *would* like to provide opportunities for everyone to meet *at least once.*"

The enmity between Esau and Jacob, while not over for their descendants, did at least cease in the tender moment of meeting between these two brothers. How beautiful is the verse for the day! Perhaps Jacob became open to see the face of God in his former enemy Esau, because he had struggled the night before with the presence of God. Jacob wanted blessings—either by deceit, as he did with Esau, or by not letting go of God until a blessing came. Cling to the Lord in your prayer until the blessing comes.

Part B   *Holy Places in Life*   Genesis 34:1—35:15

**Jacob set up a pillar in the place where he had spoken with him, a pillar of stone;
and he poured out a drink offering on it, and poured oil on it. 35:14**

You will read about the evil act of revenge of Simeon, Levi and their men upon those who violated their sister, Dinah. Such evil will continue in them and the rest of the brothers when the story of Joseph is told.

The vengeance of his sons outrages Jacob. God comes to Jacob and tells him to go to Bethel, a place sacred in the memory of Jacob, where he met the Lord in a most special way (Gen 28:11–22). There his name is changed from Jacob to Israel. That place becomes a holy remembrance for Israel and his descendants.

Do you have a place or places in your life where you especially met the Lord? Such places bring back the sense of the original blessings the Lord has given you. Make a retreat to those places in your mind—even make plans to visit them sometime.

Memories are important. They keep us in touch with the Lord who is always with us, but which we might be forgetting in the haste and pace of life's movement.

Part C   *A People with Color*   Genesis 35:16—36:43

**As her soul was departing (for she died), she named him Ben-oni;
but his father called him Benjamin. 35:18**

Do you know any mothers who died at childbirth? There is an extraordinary sadness when this occurs. Our reading begins with the death of Rachel when Benjamin was born. There is a church between Jerusalem and Bethlehem that prides itself as being the place where Rachel is buried. As quietly as Isaac breathes his last, so are the final verses in the Bible that recount his death.

Chapter 36 gives the history of Esau and his people—only a list of names as though printed in black and white. Colors are kept for the stories of Jacob and his descendants, the Twelve Tribes of Israel, prototype of the Twelve Apostles and the New Israel, the Church. Esau's disobedience wrenches him from significant history; there are only names of those whose descendants would be bitter enemies to Israel.

Part A   *Two Josephs*   **Genesis 37**
Now Israel loved Joseph more than any other of his children, because he was the son of his old age; and he had made him a long robe with sleeves. v. 3

The story of the Patriarch, Joseph, draws our attention to Joseph, husband of Mary. Both were addressed by God through dreams; both went to Egypt as a result of attempts on life—the patriarch Joseph himself, and Jesus.

The chapter sets the stage for God to use a victim of fraternal strife to become the means of salvation for his brothers. Joseph anticipates Jesus. The leaders of God's own people complete the attempt on Jesus' life by Herod years later; the scribes and Pharisees collectively have the same power and arrogance of Herod.

The betrayal of Joseph by his brothers is not unlike that of Judas, and the denial of Peter. However, the victory will come in Joseph's fidelity to his God and Jesus' adherence to the Father.

How does this reading touch you and move you to trust what God is doing in your life no matter what may be coming against you?

Part B   *Ancestor of Jesus*   **Genesis 38**
As she was being brought out, she sent word to her father-in-law, "It was the owner of these who made me pregnant." And she said, "Take note, please, whose these are, the signet and the cord and the staff." v. 25

Around this time of the year for over 2500 years, Jewish people have been proclaiming these readings. For the first time they are integrated into a sequence of readings for Christians. Think of the power of this as we join our Jewish brothers and sisters as they lift the scroll each Sabbath and chant these stories! This is the *Torah*—God's precious communication with us.

This story fits well in Advent, for with Tamar, we have a direct descendant to Jesus. Tamar's son Perez was an ancestor to David. (Matthew gives the list 1:3.) Jesus came from the family of David.

Look what the Lord does with the sinfulness and intrigue of ancestors! The Lord can use everything and everyone. In your family tree, you probably have some with a "shady past." The Lord can use them for good.

Part C   *Spiritual Cancers*   **Genesis 39—40**
The Lord was with Joseph and showed him steadfast love; he gave him favor in the sight of the chief jailer. 39:21

The prophet Daniel and the patriarch Joseph have similar histories. Both find favor in hostile, foreign lands. Despite the intents of the enemies of Joseph—his own brothers and the wife of Joseph's master—the Lord is with him. There will always be persons of support in our lives when we surrender our cares totally to God as did Daniel and Joseph.

Jealousy and lust both grow as vicious cancers. Absolute repentance and personal responsibility will send these cancers into remission.

Listen to the story about the beauty of holiness and the single heart of Joseph. As a perfectly clear telescope that reaches into the heavens, so does the lens of his heart open to spiritual knowledge.

Does the lens of your heart need cleansing?

Portion 10   *Mikketz (At the End)*   Genesis 41:1—44:17

Part A   *Enemies*   Genesis 41:1–52

**Pharaoh said to his servants, "Can we find anyone else like this—
one in whom is the spirit of God?" v. 38**

Joseph is a supreme example of what God can do to a heart disposed to serve even one's enemies. He was free of rancor and of being a victim, either of his brothers' betrayal, or of Egyptian injustice. He slept each night in peace, and so God was able to use his dreams as a way of freeing him to find favor with Pharaoh.

Will you allow yourself to be the answer to Pharaoh's question in the verse for today? If the Patriarch Joseph has the Spirit of God, how much more do you who have received the promise, the regeneration, and renewal of the Holy Spirit! Once again, open your heart. Renounce resentment and hostility to any who have declared themselves to be your enemies. For you, there need be no enemies of *your* naming, for God is with you in Jesus.

Part B   *In God's Time*   Genesis 41:53—43:15

**May God Almighty grant you mercy before the man,
so that he may send back your other brother and Benjamin. As for me,
if I am bereaved of my children, I am bereaved. 43:14**

All the years of Joseph's trusting in the Lord come to fruition at this moment of meeting his brothers. They have come to Egypt in search of food. What restraint Joseph exhibits as he recognizes them, but does not reveal himself! Think of what he might have said to those who had sold him into slavery. He keeps silent about that. God uses him to bring ultimate joy to his family. Though we may not understand the long delay and the trips of his brothers to Canaan and back—all the territory covered in the Exodus—the suspense only serves to heighten the coming moment of total recognition.

Be patient. The Lord is working out all the details in his own time of reconciliation with those with whom you may be estranged. Seek to do God's will.

Part C   *The Way Cleared for Reconciliation*   Genesis 43:16—44:17

**Joseph hurried out, because he was overcome with affection for his brother,
and he was about to weep. So he went into a private room and wept there. 43:30**

You may feel impatient, as you anxiously wait for the recognition of Joseph by his brothers. Yet the mounting tension only serves to make the coming disclosure all the more poignant—all in the Lord's own time. Each step of the story purifies Joseph's brothers of the evil they did to him. The coming reconciliation of the brothers will be all the more complete.

Do you become impatient when some issue needs resolution in your own life? Perhaps the Lord is dealing with you as he did with Joseph's brothers, purifying your mind and heart so that you will more fully recognize your Jesus who has been with you all along, yet you did not know it. What is in the way of the deeper recognition that is delayed?

Portion 11   *Vayiggash (And He Approached)*   **Gen. 44:18—47:27**

Part A   ***Stunned By Grace***   **Genesis 44:18—45:27**
God sent me before you to preserve for you a remnant on earth,
and to keep alive for you many survivors. 45:7

Before you are one of the most tender, touching passages in the whole Bible. Absolute forgiveness and love on Joseph's part astounds his sinful brothers and plummet them into a wholly new way of living.

This reading comes on or about Christmas. Approach it as an anticipation of the total love and forgiveness of Jesus. Joseph is a figure of Jesus. As Joseph presents the meaning of his existence to his brothers, hear Jesus saying these same words to you.

Perhaps you have been unfaithful to Jesus, as Joseph's brothers were to him. The love and acceptance of Joseph is found in infinite measure in Jesus. All you can do is be stunned by this grace. Rejoice along with Jacob, after his heart stood still.

Part B   ***A Vision in the Night***   **Genesis 45:28—46:27**
I will go down to Egypt with you, and I will surely bring you back again.
And Joseph's own hand will close your eyes. 46:4

Jacob receives a comforting and wondrous vision from God during the night. This is the seventh time that God has spoken of the covenant—twice to Abraham, twice to Isaac, and now the third time to Jacob. Jacob is reassured about the promises of the Lord; he will see his son Joseph before he dies.

Respect the power of the night. When you awaken during it, turn to the Lord who wants to share with you the intimacies of the covenant God offers to you in Jesus through the Spirit. All the great revelations that God made to patriarchs and prophets are gathered in Jesus. The Lord wants to speak to your heart and tell you of the love, plans, and promises held out to you. Take time to listen to God with a pure, open heart—day or night.

Part C   ***Your Servant Dismissed***   **Genesis 46:28—47:27**
Israel said to Joseph,
"I can die now, having seen for myself that you are still alive." 46:30

Simeon in Luke 2 blesses the Lord in words similar to the verse for today. Linger with Jacob and Joseph in their meeting—so long in coming. Taste the joy of Jacob. So much of Jacob's life has been pain and sorrow; we are sad as Jacob gives a one-sentence account of himself to Pharaoh in 47:9.

Do you need to reconcile with someone in your life? The Lord is present in an experience of holy sadness as an incentive to bring this about.

The settling of Jacob and his sons in Egypt sets the stage for the coming friction between Israel and Egypt and God's liberation of the people in the next book of the Bible, Exodus. Whatever be the circumstance of your life right now, it is the one the Lord is using to bring you to freedom.

Part A   *A Fruitful Future*   **Genesis 47:28—48:22**
So he blessed them that day, saying, "By you Israel will invoke blessings, saying,
"God make you like Ephraim and like Manasseh.'" 48:20

The final portion of the Book of Genesis contains the passing of the blessing from Jacob to the two sons of Joseph, Ephraim and Manasseh. As in the case of Esau and Jacob, the younger is preferred to the older. Joseph objects with strong feelings as his father switches his hands placed on the heads of these two boys.

The names of the two sons will help to understand the verse for the day, a blessing whose importance is seen as a part of Aaron's blessing (Numbers 6:22) and the opening of the Lord's Prayer. The key lies in the meaning of the names of the sons: Ephraim, "Fruitful," and Manasseh, "One who causes forgetfulness." It is indeed a blessing from God to forget one's painful, sinful past, and that one's future be fruitful. Make this your prayer as you bless your loved ones.

Part B   *The Power of Blessing*   **Genesis 49**
By the God of your father, who will help you, by the Almighty who will bless you with blessings of
heaven above, blessings of the deep that lies beneath, blessings of the breasts and of the womb. v. 25

The nearness of Jacob's death is the moment of blessing for his sons. It is a powerful moment of transition, a kind a sacred "passing of the torch" to the next generation. Picture yourself at the deathbed of Jacob, listening carefully to the words he says to his sons. Such words have power for generations.

Perhaps you are not a parent; but you certainly had one! The beliefs and attitudes you have for your children, and the ones your parents have for you, are powerful moments of force in you and the lives of your children. So often, these beliefs are negative. They lack the spiritual awareness of *blessing* that is present in full evidence in this reading.

The words: "God bless you," said as reflexively as a sneeze, need to become conscious. Say them this way, slowly: **"God *bless* you!"**

Part C   *God Intended It For Good*   **Genesis 50**
Even though you intended to do harm to me,
God intended it for good. v. 20

The secret of Joseph's success is his unwavering faith in the Lord. From the moment his brothers threw him into the ditch until his forgiveness of them in Egypt, Joseph knew that the God of justice and mercy would eventually bring goodness out of evil.

This is the faith that made the forgiveness of his brothers possible. He anticipated Paul in Roman 8:31 who rejoiced to write: "If God is for us, who can be against us?" Such focus upon the Lord freed the heart of Joseph from nursing resentments. He was thus available to receive direct knowledge from the Lord through dream interpretations and in wisdom. He was put in charge of the affairs of the very country where he was a slave.

Repeat the verse for the day repeatedly as you pray it against the background of what may be tempting you to harbor anger.

Portion 13   *Shemoth (Names)*   Exodus 1:1—6:1

Shemoth is the Hebrew name for the Book of Exodus.

Part A   *The One Drawn from Water*   Exodus 1—2

She named him Moses, saying, "I drew him out of the water." 2:10

The Book of Exodus is called *Shemoth* In Hebrew, meaning "The Names," due to the Twelve Tribes, which link the history of the book of Genesis with the beginning of Exodus. Continuity was broken; there arose a king of Egypt who did not know Joseph.

The mounting slavery of the Hebrews is bitter. God raises up a new leader for new circumstances—Moses. He is saved at birth from an evil king, as was Jesus.

Moses' name means "The One drawn from water." He would be the one to lead God's people *through* water, prefiguring the One who came from the water of Mary's womb, the waters of the Jordan, and who let flow the saving water and blood from his open side. Spend time praising God for the wondrous intervention God makes in history.

Part B   *The Never-Ending Fire*   Exodus 3:1—4:17

**God said to Moses, "I am who I am. This is what you are to say to the Israelites:
'I AM has sent me to you.'" 3:14**

It is about 1,450 B.C. God is going deliver his people from slavery in Egypt. What God brings about becomes the symbol of all activity of God on behalf of human freedom.

It begins with Moses. He had placed himself in voluntary exile in Median, because of murder. Something makes him curious … a bush burning without being consumed. It is there that God reveals God's name. Yahweh, the Covenantal name for God, is difficult to translate. It means, "I Am the One Who will Always Be with You."

God is the One present to you in all your circumstances to liberate you through the fire of the Holy Spirit. May this *Firestarter* be a match that the Lord uses to set the never-ending fire of God's love in your heart. With the Lord present to you, no pain, hurt or abusive past need ever consume you.

Part C   *God's Saving Acts Begin Again*   Exodus 4:18—6:1

**The people believed; and when they heard that the Lord had given heed to
the Israelites and that he had seen their misery, they bowed down and worshiped. 4:31**

Joseph dragged to Egypt as a slave, becomes the means of salvation for his people. Now it is Moses who returns to Egypt as the Lord's chosen to save God's people who had all become slaves in that land. The swelling movement of God's saving acts begins again. No resistance on the part of Pharaoh is going to withstand what God is going to do. Even the periodic discouragements and angers of the Israelites against Moses do not stop the Lord from the relentless grace of salvation held out to God's beloved people.

Resistance of God's people is stronger when they fail to worship. When you find that affliction seems greater than grace, bow your head, go inward, and worship the Lord in acts of praise, trust, and surrender. Focus all the energies of faith upon the One who is delivering you right now.

Portion 14   *Vaera (And I Appeared)*   Exodus 6:2—9:35

T O R A H 14

Part A   *Bearing the Power of the Promise*   Exodus 6:2—7:7
**Say to the Israelites: "I am the Lord, and I will bring you out
from under the yoke of the Egyptians." 6:6**

A frustrated Moses comes before the Lord. Ever since Moses went before Pharaoh with the command he received from the Lord to let God's people go, life became worse for the Hebrews. However, Moses always turns his troubles over to the Lord. This will become a habit for him.

Hear the strength of the promise. Moses and God's people will need to bear the power of the promise to carry them through the continual resistance that Pharaoh will make.

Allow the promise of God do the same for you. You will encounter times of temptation, doubt, and discouragement. When that occurs, allow the power of the promise of God held out to you in Christ Jesus to fire the "internal combustion engine" of your life.

Part B   *Resistance to What God Wants*   Exodus 7:8—8:15
**Moses and Aaron did just as the LORD had commanded.
He raised his staff in the presence of Pharaoh and his officials
and struck the water of the Nile, and all the water was changed into blood. 7:20**

The first two plagues come upon the land of Egypt in response to Pharaoh's refusal to let the Hebrews go. Each of these actions of God is designed to address the various Egyptians gods and to show that they are powerless in the presence of the great **I AM**. All throughout these moves of God against Pharaoh, God is the one who is really in charge.

When you and I resist doing what the Lord wants of us, the consequences will be a kind of plague. While these may not seem as dramatic as the ones in the Book of Exodus, still many evils can come against you with more effect when you lose the protection of the Lord by resisting God's ways.

Recovering persons say, "Denial is not a river in Egypt!" You will be in denial as Pharaoh, if you expect to live a happy, free life without prayer and a deep desire to respond to who the Lord calls you to be.

Part C   *Blessing Embedded in Pain*   Exodus 8:16—9:35
**This is why I have let you live: to show you my power,
and to make my name resound through all the earth. 9:16**

God addresses Pharaoh through the mouth of Moses. However great is the hardness of Pharaoh's heart, even stronger are the consequences of his stubbornness. Plague upon plague comes against Pharaoh and the Egyptians—five of them in this year's reading.

The Bible's way of stating that God is in command at every moment is to have God be the one who sends the plagues. Actually, when we do anything outside of the Lord's will, the results will be something like the plagues. Because of Jesus, we know that God is not out to punish, but to save. The Lord is actively present in the afflictions and hardships of life, manifesting divine power to deliver us precisely through the pain that urges us to drop to our knees, not in defeat, but in worship. Pray until you find the blessing embedded in the pain.

Portion 15   *Bo (Come)*   Exodus 10:1—13:16

Part A   *The Glow of Light from Within*   **Exodus 10:1—11:3**
All the Israelites had light in the places where they lived. 10:23

The eighth plague envelopes Egypt with locusts so severe, that the land is darkened. Crops are destroyed. Then the sun itself is darkened in the ninth plague. No one can be seen, but miraculously, there is light in the dwellings of the children of Israel.

The Egyptians revered Pharaoh as an incarnation of the sun god Amon-Ra. The Lord God of the Israelites is again revealed as more powerful than the gods of Egypt. Picture in your might the total darkness and the lights glowing from the homes of the Israelites. God is with them and with his presence, comes a light that shines.

Jesus is the light of the world. "Whoever follows me will never walk in darkness, but will have the light of life" (John 8:12). Come to your center. The light of faith shines within. Trust its glow.

Part B   *The Doorposts of the Heart*   **Exodus 11:4—12:28**
Take a bunch of hyssop, dip it into the blood in the basin
and put some of the blood on the top and on both sides of the doorframe.
Not one of you shall go out the door of his house until morning. 12:22

This passage is proclaimed at the Easter Vigil, on Holy Saturday. It is the central festival for us as Christians and Jews, since it describes that primary move of God that resulted in our ancestors nor longer being slaves in Egypt. Passover is the paradigm for our freedom. It is during this festival that Jesus, the true Paschal Lamb was sacrificed. His is the blood of the covenant that truly sets us free.

In 12:22, the Lord prescribes that hyssop, a shrub-like plant, be dipped into the blood of the lamb, and be smeared on the doorpost of the house. It is hyssop that was dipped into vinegar and brought to the lips of Jesus on the cross (John 19:29–30). This detail of John is not without meaning. Then Jesus exclaims, "It is finished." Jesus won complete freedom for us by shedding his blood on the cross. Smear the doorposts of your heart with the saving blood of Jesus.

Part C   *Ready to Go*   **Exodus 12:29—13:16**
It shall serve for you as a sign on your hand and as a reminder on your forehead,
so that the teaching of the Lord may be on your lips. 13:9

The death of one's first child—is there any pain greater for a parent? This plague brought Pharaoh to let God's people go.

Rejoice in the reading, the paradigm of all freedom, the Exodus. Read about the importance of continuing its remembrance in the regulations given for the Passover. The use of unleavened bread—a tradition in Holy Communion—recalls that there was no time for the bread to rise. When the Lord says, **"GO"**, we must be ready.

God moved at night. Think of this as you drop off to sleep and end each day. "He who keeps you will not slumber" (Ps 121: 3). An observant male Jews ties leather cases on his head and left hand, which contain passages from the *Torah*. What can you do to never forget the obvious—that the blood of Jesus has set you free?

Portion 16　　　　　*Beshallah (Sent Out)*　　　　Exodus 13:17—17:36

Part A　　　　*What is in Front—Not Behind*　　　　Exodus 13:17—14:14

**By day the Lord went ahead of them in a pillar of cloud to guide them on their way
and by night in a pillar of fire to give them light. 13:21**

God led the people by wilderness—empty space where God can speak to hearts. The people do the first of what would often happen during the next forty years: they complain. Just as Peter who walked on water, but soon doubted and fell, so do the hearts of the Israelites sink as they see nothing but disaster coming behind them in the army of Pharaoh galloping toward them. See the dust clouds in the distance; hear the strident noises and rumbling of the chariots. The enemy is coming! The Hebrews are distracted from the pillar of fire and the cloud before them, mindful only of the disaster pressing from behind. They have no notion of how God is going to open the Red Sea before them.

Jesus, the New Moses, encourages you to keep your eyes in front of you where God's salvation is ever coming. Don't pay attention to the noises of the Enemy behind. Your miracle is coming!

Part B　　　　*The Covenant of Healing*　　　　Exodus 14:15—16:10

**Take a bunch of hyssop, dip it into the blood in the basin
and put some of the blood on the top and on both sides of the doorframe.
Not one of you shall go out the door of his house until morning. 12:22**

Events move rapidly in the Exodus. After the Israelites cross the Red Sea, Moses leads the people in praise of God. Then the scene shifts to one of complaint about there being no water, and later, there being no food.

How easy it is to forget the major interventions of the Lord on our behalf, and complain! After the episode of grumbling about no water, God makes a promise: if there is in the people, a heart that listens and does what the Lord wants, then God will be *Yahweh-Rapha*, "The Lord Who Heals." 15:26 has been called "The Old Testament Covenant of Diving Healing." Return to it often in those circumstances that tempt you to complain. Greater than what besets you is the Lord who promises to lead you through the Red Sea of suffering to freedom and wholeness.

Part C　　　　*The Cloud of Anger*　　　　Exodus 16:11—17:16

**Those who gathered much had nothing over, and those who gathered little had no shortage;
they gathered as much as each of them needed. 16:18**

Join today, not only with those across the globe who observe the Sabbath, but also reach down over 3,250 years ago to that Sabbath after the week of manna. Just as the Lord had ceased the work of creation and rested on the seventh day, so does God command the. The Sabbath is a sacred time to pause and celebrate God's presence and activity in life. A familiar saying is reversed: **"Don't just DO something—STAND THERE!"**

Yet instead of spending time contemplating the miracle of free bread from the skies, the Israelites complain that they are now about to die of thirst. Doubt, complaining and anger cloud their belief that the God who just did one miracle for food is about to do another for water.

After the reading, go down into your own depths and flush out any doubting or complaining going on there.

Portion 17   *Yithro (Jethro)*   Exodus 18:1—20:26

Part A   *Someone to Turn To*   Exodus 18

**Select capable men from all the people—men who fear God,
trustworthy men who hate dishonest gain—and appoint them
as officials over thousands, hundreds, fifties and tens. v. 21**

A brief, but decisive moment of intervention comes from a tender meeting with Moses' father-in-law. Likely Moses had sent his wife and children to him during the ravages of the plagues. Now that the Exodus is complete, Jethro brings Moses' family to him.

While the Midianites were descendants of Abraham through his concubine Keturah, they were considered as foreigners. However, God is at work in faith in Jethro through Moses' witness. In addition, Jethro's outside view of God's work affords him a perspective often missed by those inside. Jethro suggests that Moses delegate leadership according to the numbers indicated in the verse for the day.

Is there someone to whom you can turn who loves you, yet is not so involved in your life that he or she is still able to give you insight into areas that you are missing?

Part B   *The Three Stones*   Exodus 19

**The LORD said to Moses,
"Go to the people and consecrate them today and tomorrow.
Have them wash their clothes and be ready by the third day,
because on that day the LORD will come down on Mount Sinai
in the sight of all the people. vv. 10–11**

There is a power-pause in the journey through the desert of our Jewish ancestors. The horizon of the Promised Land is still distant, but right in front of them is wondrous Mount Sinai. God will be face to face with Moses. A cloud covers the base of the mount as the Glory of the Lord settles in.

Lose yourself at the foot of Mt. Sinai. Stone tablets of the law are coming. But another stone is coming too— the one in front of Jesus' tomb. Then the two stone tablets will become one law of flesh upon our hearts when the resurrection-stone is rolled away. The other two stones of law yield to the one commandment that we love one another as Jesus has loved us.

How God loves his people! In the wilderness, God shares the wonders of relating to him.

Part C   *An Honest Examine*   Exodus 20

**I am the Lord your God,
who brought you out of the land of Egypt, out of the house of slavery. v. 2**

The Ten Commandments are placed in the very center of the Book of Exodus. Meditate on them, especially the extended phrases that amplify the familiar summaries of the commandments. They are meant to convict you—never condemn. They are basic standards that ensure that there will be right relation between God and the human family.

As you pray over them, make your own extensions. For example, what was the particular "house of bondage" out of which the Lord brought you? Make the commandments personal; examine your conscience, gently, completely and honestly.

You need not be afraid, as the Israelites were, that God speak to you directly. Because of the freedom won for you on the cross, the Holy Spirit of Jesus can speak directly to your heart. What does the Spirit say?

Part A   *Good Order in Life*   **Exodus 21:1—22:24**
Do not mistreat an alien or oppress him,
for your were aliens in Egypt. 22:21

What must have been the previous mistreatment of others such that these various laws were designed to put some measure of justice into life! We might have come a long way from what is outlined here for a society over three thousand years ago, yet there is something we can miss so easily—the ordering of life has its initiative from the Lord.

Jesus said to his disciples at the Last Supper, "I have much more to say to you, more than you can now bear. But when he, the Spirit of truth, comes, he will guide you into all truth" (John 16:12). There has been and will continue to be a development, a refinement of how God wants us to respond to one another.

Reflect upon how you treat others. Seek the justice and mercy that God wants to express to others through your very own life.

Part B   *Principles and Sacred Celebrations*   **Exodus 22:25—23:19**
Do not blaspheme God or curse the ruler of your people. 22:28

There is a saying in recovery groups: "Principles, Not Personalities." The Lord puts forth principles for right and holy living. The first verse of today's reading has the Lord give us a sobering principle through Moses: "Do not curse a ruler of your people." Complaining about those who hold public office is a form of curse, since what is needed is prayer for the leader, not complaints. Your prayer will be a blessing upon the person; your complaining, a kind of curse. There is a sense in which we are doing one or the other—blessing or cursing; praying or complaining. Anger is to be directed to the building up of good principles, not the tearing down of personalities.

Next, there are regulations designed to keep the passions for greed and competition in check. The passage then contains the basic prescription for keeping the Sabbath and the three major pilgrim feasts. All of this comes directly from the Lord.

Part C   *Promises and Glory*   **Exodus 23:20—24:18**
You shall worship the Lord your God, and I will bless your bread and your water;
and I will take sickness away from among you.
No one shall miscarry or be barren in your land ... 23:25–26

A phone call came from our daughter one day in 1993, with fears that she had just miscarried twins. My wife and I prayed, turning to a Bible calendar for that particular day which had the verses from today's reading. We claimed these promises. The crisis passed. Beautiful twin girls were born a few months later. We rejoiced in the fidelity of the Lord.

The reading continues in verse 27 stating that terror from the Lord will go before the people, driving back the enemies coming against God's beloved. So it is with us. Those who resist the love of God coming inside them will find the power of God against them.

St. John affirms: "Perfect loves casts out fear" (1 John 4:18). Those who cast out the Lord are the ones who need to be afraid!

Portion 19   *Terumah (Portion)*   Exodus 25:1—27:19

Part A   *The Tent Among Us*   Exodus 25
**Then have them make a sanctuary for me,
and I will dwell among them. v. 8**

God turns his attention to instructing Moses to build a sanctuary for God's presence in the wilderness. Though they are a people on the move, they are to come to rest for times of worship, enjoying the presence of their God in an uninterrupted manner. The tent-like tabernacle will prefigure the Temple to come, anticipating even more, that permanent resting place of Christ Jesus in the Church: "The Word became flesh and pitched His tent among us." (John 1:14)

The design of the tabernacle begins first with the Ark of the Testimony, the place where the Ten Commandments are to be reserved. As you read these instructions, imagination saturates inner senses with colors, smells, and beauty of design.

The two angels that face each other with hovering wings … leap forward to the tomb of Jesus in John 20:21 where a similar description is given: "(Mary Magdalene) saw two angels in white sitting, one at the head and the other at the feet, where the body of Jesus had lain."

Part B   *Every Detail Sacred*   Exodus 26:1–30
You shall not revile God, or curse a leader of your people. 22:28

A cubit is the distance from the elbow of a man to the tip of his middle finger, about eighteen inches, or half a yard. This will help you to picture the dimensions of the tabernacle and the curtains described.

The Lord gave Moses precise details about the construction of the tabernacle. Every aspect had a symbolic quality. The tabernacle was *the* place that the presence of the Lord was to be especially found. While it may be difficult to picture all the details, each aspect is to be a reminder of the presence of God.

If you have any love in you at all, it is because God, who is Love, is present to you through the Holy Spirit. God does not indwell in us as a reward for our loving; rather does God's presence make it possible to love.

Love is *super-natural*—it is beyond our nature and us. It is God's way of loving granted to us.

Part C   *Sacred Space*   Exodus 26:31—27:19
**You shall make a veil woven of blue purple,
and scarlet thread, and fine woven linen. 26:31**

While the second commandment forbids the making of images adored as God, the Lord knows that our senses need to be active so that we can go beyond them to the realm of the Spirit.

In order to get a sense of the size of the court for the tabernacle in the wilderness, imagine the dimensions of a football field. Stretching across the field is the length of the tabernacle—about 50 yards. Its width is from the 25th yard line to the goal line. Within that sacred space, clear directions from the divine architect are given to Moses.

Now leave the "football field" and enter into the tabernacle as you listen to the exact dimensions, adornment, and location of every object … the color of every thread. All these are symbols, meant to act upon our senses to stimulate the awe of being in the presence of God. Sense the colors. What spiritual feelings does each one stir in you? Let all your spaces today be sacred.

Portion 20 *Tetzaveh (And You Shall Command)* Ex. 27:20—30:10

Part A *Sacramentals* Exodus 27:20—28:30

And you shall command the children of Israel that they bring
you pure oil of pressed olives for the light, to cause the lamp to burn continually. 27:20

While it is forbidden to make images of God, the Lord does command Moses that there be symbolic objects, colors and clothing in order to draw the people into a sense of prayer and the presence of God. We have come to call such articles, "sacramentals."

The Sabbath portion begins with oil for the lamp, the origin of sanctuary lamps in some church traditions. Then we move into the vestments of Aaron and the priests. Read slowly, so that you can turn the verbal instructions of the ephod and the breastplate into mental pictures.

What do you have in your house and on your person that can become constant reminders of the presence of the Lord? Just as the Twelve Tribes that were carried on Aaron's shoulders and over his heart, what can you do to be reminded of the burdens of others you are asked to carry in prayer? Hold these persons in your heart.

Part B *Holy to the Lord* Exodus 28:31—29:18

You shall make a rosette of pure gold, and engrave on it,
like the engraving of a signet, "Holy to the Lord." 28:36

There is much concern in the world with what one wears. One has to look good. While this can be only a worldly principle, there is a truth that the Lord had in mind by ordering such detail about the clothing of Aaron and the priestly family of God's people. They were a very special sign of the presence of God at work in others. That which is physically the closest to any person is the clothes worn. The sacramental quality of the clothes was thus a reminder of the closeness of the Lord.

Paul has this in mind when the clothing he encouraged Christians to wear are the inner virtues flowing outward that make God known to others—tenderhearted mercy, kindness, humility, gentleness, and patience (Col. 3:12). Engrave on your heart the phrase engraved on Aaron's gold: "Set apart as Holy to the Lord."

Part C *Anointing and the Cross* Exodus 29:19—30:10

"I will dwell among the children of Israel and will be their God." 29:45

The passage begins with the ritual of priestly ordination of Aaron and his sons. The blood of the ram is applied to the ear, thumb, and toe, organs of receptivity and action. The anointing reminded the priests *to hear* only the Word of God, *to do* only what the Lord wants, *to go* only where the Lord leads.

From the earliest times in the church, symbolic gestures came to be incorporated into the prayer of Christians, such as making the sign of the cross. There developed a variation by making three crosses with the thumb on the forehead, the lips and chest. "Christ in my mind, in my mouth and in my heart."

The origin of morning and evening prayer is outlined from 29:38. God longs to dwell with you always.

Portion 21   *Ki Tissa (Take a Census)*   Exodus 30:11—34:35

Part A   *Keeping Sabbath Time*   Exodus 30:11—31:17
With it you shall anoint the tent of meeting and the ark of the covenant. 30:25

God told Moses to have the people bring money as a response to having their lives ransomed in the Exodus. However, the priceless blood of Jesus has truly redeemed us and ransomed us from death.

The barrenness of the desert surroundings are set in marked contrast with the materials that are to become the sacred articles of the wilderness tabernacle. Three of them are the gifts of the Magi to Jesus. As sense of the sacred is heightened by having the ingredients for anointing oil and incense be used for these purposes only. The sense of smell, the most powerful sense that links us to memory, reminds the people of the sacred presence of God.

What are the articles in your life that you employ only for the service and worship of God? Do you keep Sabbath time?

Part B   *Burning Your Idols*   Exodus 31:18—33:11
Thus the Lord used to speak to Moses face to face, as one speaks to a friend.
Then he would return to the camp. 33:11

God speaks to Moses and gives him the details of the enduring relation that God longs to have with us through the Covenant. However, the people below the mountain enter into full-blown idolatry. Just as a parent who is angry with a child and refers to him or her as the child of the other parent, God does the same when talking with Moses: "*Your* people whom *you* brought out of the land of Egypt have corrupted themselves."

Just when God wants to do the most for the people, they turn away. Can you identify with this? When you get impatient, are there any idols that you construct to make up for the absence of feeling God's presence? Walk by faith, not by feelings. Repent. Throw all the idols that you have into the fire.

Part C   *The Cleft in the Rock*   Exodus 33:12—34:35
He said: I hereby make a covenant. Before all your people I will perform marvels,
such as have not been performed in all the earth or in any nation;
and all the people among whom you live shall see the work of the Lord;
for it is an awesome thing that I will do with you. 34:10

Forty days and forty nights, Moses fasts upon the mountain, filled with the presence of the Lord. Jesus, who *is* the presence of God, does the same at the beginning of his ministry. May the time of Lent find you in God's presence, your awareness of it increased by fasting and faith.

Be with Moses as you listen to his communion with the Lord, the renewal of the covenant and the promises that God makes. Moses longs to see the glory of the Lord. Moses rests in the cleft of the rock, covered by God's hand as God passes by. The rock now is Christ—the cleft, the open side of Jesus on the cross. The glory of God is Jesus' compassion and forgiveness from that cross. The people see the presence of God in the face of Moses. The glory of God will radiate from your face if you spend time in the cleft in Jesus' side.

Portion 22   *Vayahkel (And He Assembled)*   Ex. 35:1—38:20

Part A   *Time and the Holy Exodus*   35:1—36:19
**God has filled him with divine spirit, with skill, intelligence,
and knowledge in every kind of craft. 35:31**

Here, as often throughout the *Torah* readings, the law of the Sabbath is repeated. Though these readings from Exodus are about holy objects, it is well to remember that the first designation of the word holy in the Bible in Genesis 2:3 is not given to an article, or even to a person: it is given to *time*—the Sabbath.

Everyone is involved in bringing the gifts for the Tabernacle. There is frequent use of terms such as those whose "hearts were stirred" and "spirits were willing."

Moses repeats what the Lord gave to him in 31:2–6. This is among the earliest references in the Bible to the Holy Spirit filling someone. The Spirit gives Bezalel the anointing to gather all the gifts into the unity of the Tabernacle. God fills you with the Holy Spirit so that you may transform the gifts of others into a time and a place where God dwells.

Parts B and C   *Sacrament of the Lord's Presence*   Exodus 36:20—38:20
**He made the curtain of blue, purple, and crimson yarns, and fine twisted linen,
with cherubim skillfully worked into it. 36:35**

We read about the construction of the Tent of Meeting (the Tabernacle) and the Ark of the Covenant. The area where the Ark rests is called "The Holy of Holies." Here God dwells with the people. The Ark is a sacrament of the Lord's presence.

The plans may be difficult to picture. I suggest that you take a sheet of graph paper and let each box be a cubit, which is half of a yard, or eighteen inches. As you read, you can map out for yourself these dimensions. Every two squares would be a yard. The list of the precious materials and the dimensions give a sense of the presence of the Lord. There is beauty, holiness, order, value, symbol, focus, purity, joy, peace.

All that your hands will hold and touch today can become holy, because in the Lord, you are holy.

Portion 23   *Pekude (Reckoning)*   **Exodus 38:21—40:38**

Part A   *Sacred Colors and the Cloud*   **Exodus 38:21—39:21**

**The onyx stones were prepared, enclosed in settings of gold filigree and
engraved like the engravings of a signet, according to the names of the sons of Israel. 39:1**

God reveals the divine presence through the created world. In addition, this presence is manifested ever more deeply through the creations that God's children make under the anointing of the Holy Spirit.

This portion gathers all the artwork of the tabernacle into one sacred place. All are fashioned at the Lord's directions. Aside from imaging each one, sense the accumulation of holiness as each piece of sacred art finds its place in the tabernacle.

Become sensitive to those objects that surround your life; these are reminders of God's presence to you and God's gifts. Ask the Holy Spirit to anoint your senses so that all you experience and create can become avenues to the divine presence.

Parts B and C   *Fire in the Cloud*   **Exodus 39:22—40:38**

**For the cloud of the Lord was on the tabernacle by day,
and fire was in the cloud by night, before the eyes of all the house of Israel
at each stage of their journey. 40:38**

The Holy Spirit brings the presence of the Lord when the Word is read with hearts opened in faith. You are going to meet the Lord in the reading.

Aholiab was an engraver, a designer and a weaver. Be the same. God *engraves* the Word on your heart, *designs* your life, and *weaves* the very minutes and hours of your day into a sacred garment to wear as a priest of the Lord.

Four sacred colors mentioned can be symbolic of four days of the week: **GOLD** for Sundays, the Lord's Day; **BLUE** for Saturdays, the Sabbath, and the *Torah*; **PURPLE** for Mondays: the Prophets; **SCARLET** for Fridays: the words of Jesus, his blood and the Gospel.

The tabernacle is completed—the glory of the Lord comes down.

Portion 24   *Vayikra (And He Called)*   Leviticus 1:1—5:19
Vayikra is the Hebrew name for the book of Leviticus.

Part A   *From the Heights to the Sacred Center*   Leviticus 1—2
**What is left of the grain offering shall be for Aaron and his sons;
it is a most holy part of the offerings by fire to the Lord. 2:10**

Now that the tabernacle has been completed, the Lord directs Moses in the total life of worship with the seasonal and lunar celebrations that call to mind all that God has done for the people. Jewish children begin with the Book of Leviticus as the introduction to their life with God. Worshipping the Lord is the way that one comes to know God. No longer does God call to Moses from the heights of Mt. Sinai, but rather from a level plane at the sacred center of the people—the Holy of Holies.

The tabernacle and subsequent Temple no longer exist. Jesus is the living temple. His love burned for you on the cross in the sacrifice to end all sacrifices. Holy Communion brings this sacrifice into the present moment of worship. May your whole being be a burnt offering of love to God. Worship in Christ Jesus.

Part B   *Peace and Sin Offerings*   Leviticus 3:1—4:26
**It shall be a perpetual statute throughout your generations, in all your settlements:
you must not eat any fat or any blood. 3:17**

Leviticus describes the sacrificial system, which the Lord gave to Moses in the tabernacle. The priests and the Levites preserved it, hence its title from the Greek name. In Hebrew, it is called *Vayikra*, meaning "And He Called," taken from the first words of the book.

Since the destruction of the Second Temple in 70 A.D., no sacrifice has been offered; nothing is done today as described. Jesus has become the one complete sacrifice that has gathered all the varieties we read about in this book.

The call to holiness is what makes Leviticus a book of great value. The various kinds of offerings focus upon aspects of life still important to address. Today's reading has to do with the Peace Offering (expiation) and the Sin Offering (restoring purity to the sanctuary.) Move beyond the details of *what* is offered to *why*.

Part C   *Sin Burned Away by Love*   4:27—5:26
**When you realize your guilt in any of these,
you shall confess the sin that you have committed. 5:5**

We long to be reconciled to God. The sacrifice and burning of various animals correspond to various kinds of sin; this is the Bible's way of calling the people to repent from sin without further consequences. They were the acts of contrition whereby one could turn from sin and live again in communion with God and God's people. Fire made the burnt offering become a sweet smelling smoke ascending into the air, blending with the presence of God all about.

Face your sin. Confess it. In so doing, you celebrate the gratuitous fact that God has already forgiven you in Jesus. When you repent, the Lord burns your sins away with his love, for he has gathered all sin into himself. The blood of Christ shed for you, turns sorrow for sin into a sweet smelling smoke rising from the cross.

Portion 25   *Tzav (Command)*   Leviticus 6:1—8:36

Part A   *The Candle of the Heart*   Leviticus 6:1—7:10
A perpetual fire shall be kept burning on the altar;
it shall not go out. 6:13

An ever-burning candle in sanctuaries in many church traditions bears witness to the command given to Moses in today's verse. From the appearance of God in the ever—burning bush before Moses and later the faithfully burning fire by night that led God's people out of Egypt, fire has been a sign of the presence of God.

The burning of the grain offering suggests taking this basic element of life as a symbol of the substance of you. Offer yourself to the Lord. You might take a candle as a way of recalling this offering. As it burns during your prayer, your essence, your substance, your "grain," is offered to God.

St. Paul enjoins us to "Pray without ceasing" (1 Thessalonians 5:17). Light the candle of the heart to ever burn before the Lord.

Part B   *A Special Call*   Leviticus 7:11–38
Flesh that touches any unclean thing shall not be eaten; it shall be burned up.
As for other flesh, all who are clean may eat such flesh. v. 19

Details are given for making peace offerings. The sons of Aaron are the priests who may eat of this offering. While the full importance of the details may escape us, the message of Leviticus is clear: You are called to holiness.

Holiness, in Hebrew *qadosh*, means, "To be set apart." When the Lord created you, God set you apart in a special way. There is a life-call upon you, some special gift to life that you have been created to offer. This is the deepest aspect of God's will. Your peace is at stake if you do not complete it.

Original Hebrew peace offerings were celebrations. What can you do that would increase your joy in the unique call of God upon your life? Pray over this. Take a walk alone; find an object that "speaks" to you about this call.

Part C   *Senses Evoking the Sacred*   Leviticus 8:1–36
Then Moses took them from their hands and turned them into smoke on the altar
with the burnt offering. This was an ordination offering for a pleasing odor,
an offering by fire to the Lord. v. 28

The Tabernacle has been constructed, ready for worship to fill it. There is drama in the reading. Everywhere you look, all that you hear, feel, taste, touch and smell, evokes a sense of the sacred, the consecrated, the holy. These are words used to translate the Hebrew *qadosh*, that which has been cleansed, purified, and set apart for the Lord.

In Christ, you are more than the sons of Aaron. You are set apart for the things of God. The sweet aroma of the Lamb of God who died for you takes the place of all the bulls and rams of the old sacrifices that strain to make their way heavenward.

What daily rituals can you create that would increase the inner sense that your life is sacred and set apart for God?

Part A   *The Burnt Offering of the Self*   Leviticus 9:1—10:11
Fire came out from the Lord and consumed the burnt offering and the fat on the altar;
and when all the people saw it, they shouted and fell on their faces. 9:24

Here is one of the principal places in the Bible that describes ordination to ministry. Again, the presence of God is described as fire. While consuming the offering of Aaron, the fire elevates it to heaven. On the other hand, the profane offering of Nadab and Abihu is simply reduced to ashes; nothing ascends. Idol worship has contaminated their offering.

You and I are to live immersed in Jesus, one with his offering in the fire of his love on the cross. We are one with him as priest, prophet, and king. Whether or not you are an ordained deacon, priest or elder, you still have a call to ministry placed upon your life. May there be nothing frivolous or contaminated with other "gods" in what you bring—nothing less than the offering of your *self* in service to the Lord.

Part B   *The Clean and the Sacred*   Leviticus 10:12—11:32
Moses spoke to Aaron and to his remaining sons, Eleazar and Ithamar:
Take the grain offering that is left from the Lord's offerings by fire,
and eat it unleavened beside the altar, for it is most holy. 10:12

What foods to eat or not to eat might seem of minor importance to us, but what is not minor, is cleanliness. The familiar adage: "Cleanliness is next to Godliness" is the point behind all these prescriptions. The sacred is clean; the profane is unclean. When God speaks to the people about what is clean and unclean, they are to associate themselves with creatures that especially draw them into the sacred. God's presence is to pervade every aspect of life. There is a constant reminder of this when coming up against choices in creation. For something to be a sacrament of God's presence, it must be clean.

Take in inventory of what you do and with whom you associate in your life. Do the people, places, and things in your life lead you to God or not? That is the all-important question.

Part C   *Distractions Drawn into Prayer*   Leviticus 11:33–47
I am the Lord your God; sanctify yourselves
therefore, and be holy, for I am holy … v. 44

We discover what is clean and unclean from the Lord, not only from natural inclinations. Repugnance for vermin and other insects is part of God's teaching!

The routine of bathing or cleaning the house can be transformed into an activity that evokes God's presence. Think of this as you wash dishes, or clean windows. The transparent presence of God shines through.

To keep the house clean and in order means that everything in life has its proper place and assigned boundary. For example, when distractions come in prayer, think of these as intruders crossing the boundary of your sacred space of time with God. Something imposes itself to be dealt with at another time and place. Draw the distraction into your prayer, place it into your hands, and lift it to the Lord, saying, "Later about this, Lord!"

Portion 27   *Tazria (Conceives)*   Leviticus 12:1—13:59

Part A   *The Gift of Discernment*   Leviticus 12:1—13:28

**When the days of her purification are completed,
whether for a son or for a daughter, she shall bring to the priest
at the entrance of the tent of meeting a lamb in its first year for a burnt offering,
and a pigeon or a turtledove for a sin offering. 12:6**

You will be familiar with this ordinance of God from St. Luke's account of the presentation of Jesus in the Temple (Luke 2:22 ff). Jesus submits to the regulations of the Law in order to go beyond it. Jesus **IS** the Law and the Temple itself.

The priest is the one who diagnoses leprosy. This comes from the anointing for discernment outlined in the reading of last Saturday, Lev 10:9–11.

Pray to the Lord that you be given the gift of discernment. We are intended to tell the difference between what is clean and unclean in all aspects of life. We also need to discern the spiritual spaces of those with whom we associate, at the same time, never judging.

Part B and C   *Wholeness and Holiness*   Leviticus 13:29–59

**The person who has the leprous disease shall wear torn clothes and
let the hair of his head be disheveled; and he shall cover his upper lip and cry out,
"Unclean, unclean." v. 45**

Leprosy was a sign of death in a body alive. Such afflicted persons must keep apart from the rest of the people. No one was permitted to touch a leper, for fear of contagion and uncleanness coming upon the person. Such a person was obliged to call out "Unclean, unclean," so that people would stay away.

Wholeness of body and holiness of spirit were always seen together for a Jew. That is the significance of Jesus' approach to the leper, of not being afraid of becoming unclean by such contact. Jesus reverses the principle; only what Jesus *does* touch becomes whole and holy!

Invite Jesus to inspect your life and diagnose your ills. Jesus heals. Do not be afraid to touch those lacking in wholeness; they can become whole through contact with you, if you are in Jesus.

Part A   *The Power of Ritual*   Leviticus 14:1–32

Some of the oil that remains in his hand the priest shall put on the lobe of the right ear of the one to be cleansed, and on the thumb of the right hand, and on the big toe of the right foot, on top of the blood of the guilt offering. 14:17

Cleansing is a spiritual as well as a physical reality. The ritual described here has a movement and rhythm designed to deepen the healing of leprosy. Each gesture is one of caring. There is no haste, but rather a slow doing and re-doing of the movement of the Lords' command.

Be careful about being hasty in your prayer and your spiritual exercises. Clear a space for yourself to come into the presence of God, submitting your life to the cleansing and healing power of God's love. Once again, the basic theme of Leviticus: holiness before the Lord means to be dedicated, set apart, and uncontaminated from the "leprosy" of the world.

Faith makes rituals have power. Ritual becomes the vehicle for the grace of God.

Part B   *House Inspection*   Leviticus 14:33–57

Leprosy was not only diagnosed of people, but of places as well. As a modern pest or termite inspector, so the priest would come in to evaluate a house to see if leprosy was in the walls.

In the Spirit, we have been given the gift of discernment, which allows us to be as the priest in this passage. Through the Spirit, we can tell the spiritual atmosphere of a place—either the joyful spirit of holiness or the leprosy of strife.

Yet even more important than the physical house, is the house of the body in which you dwell. How is it? Do you allow feelings, resentments, fears etc. to eat away at this house which is you? Do you need an exterminator? Ask the Holy Spirit to drive far from you all the deceits and wiles of the Evil One, so that in your inner house, the Trinity may dwell with you and make you whole.

Part C   *Discharges of the Heart*   Leviticus 15:1–33

Thus you shall keep the people of Israel separate from their uncleanness,
so that they do not die in their uncleanness
by defiling my tabernacle that is in their midst. v. 31

While we no longer interpret actual bodily discharges as making us unclean in God's sight, there are truths in this reading. The key word throughout is "discharge"—what comes out of us.

Picture a fluid polluting an area as a symbol of the discharges of the heart that contaminate. Jesus said, "Those things which proceed out of the mouth come from the heart, and they defile a man" (Matt. 15:18).

Are there hurtful discharges in words that flow from your mouth? The expression on your face, the tone of your voice, the sound of your breathing, the language of your body: all these discharge either the stench of negativity or the sweet smell of holiness and love. Others can be drawn to God by the way you are.

Portion 29   *Ahare Moth (After the Death)*   **Lev. 16:1—18:32**

Part A   *The Day of Atonement*   **Leviticus 16**
**The goat shall bear on itself all their iniquities to a barren region;
and the goat shall be set free in the wilderness. v. 22**

This is the most sacred day of the year for a Jew, usually occurring in early October. This is the only time when the priest would enter into The Holy of Holies.

Every day, every moment, you can be in The Holy of Holies; it is your own heart where Jesus lives. Jesus has gathered all the elements of the Old Law into himself. Go to that place within where you are most you and where you are perhaps most hurting. The Lord longs to meet you there. Be with the Lord. It is holy there, because you have been made so by the Lord's presence.

About the scapegoat: is there someone in your life you tend to blame? Let go. The scapegoat was Jesus. It is finished. He has returned from the banishment of death to the fullness of life.

Parts B and C   *Two Aspects of Holiness*   **Leviticus 17—18**
**For the life of the flesh is in the blood; and I have given it to you for
making atonement for your lives on the altar; for, as life,
it is the blood that makes atonement. 17:11**

Blood and sexuality are spoken about as holy. Blood is life; life is to be dedicated to God, and so blood was reserved for God alone. No blood was permitted to be consumed by anyone.

The New Testament Letter to the Hebrews develops this in an exalted way, speaking about the holiness of the Blood of Christ. His blood is sacramentally consumed by us, for in Christ, we already belong to him and are one with him. Communion is the expression of the blood of Christ given back in sacrifice to God.

The world tends to degrade sexuality and eclipse its holiness. The prescriptions in chapter 18 are to remind us of the goodness and joy of human sexuality. Care must be taken to protect and maintain its sacredness, for upon this depends whether God will be present in the sexual encounter or not. May the spirit of these ordinances become even clearer to you, for the greater glory of God.

406

Parts A and B   *The Stranger and the Sacred*   **Leviticus 19**

**You shall not take vengeance or bear a grudge against any of your people,
but you shall love your neighbor as yourself: I am the Lord. v. 18**

Ceremonial and moral laws are considered again, as in Exodus and Deuteronomy. First on the list is honoring of father and mother. Four times Jesus quotes the second half of v. 18 as a summary of all the commandments with respect to our neighbor (Matthew 19:19; 22:39; Mark 12:31; Luke 10:27).

The manner of treating strangers is very sacred in the life of a Jew. Respect for them is due because the Jew was a stranger in the land of Egypt. The stranger and the sacred were very much understood together. Benedict, born about 480 A.D., the founder of western monasticism, stated in his Rule: *Hospes venit, Christus venit:* "A stranger comes, Christ comes." The spirituality of Leviticus interprets all things as either connected to God, the sacred, or disconnected from God, the profane. Doing the will of God means that all choices are in keeping with what the Lord calls the person to be. Everything is potentially sacred.

Part C   *Praying for Our Children*   **Leviticus 20**

**You shall not follow the practices of the nation that I am driving out before you.
Because they did all these things, I abhorred them. 20:23**

The sacrifice of children to gods is an abhorrent practice of the ancient pagans. Consider, however, what happens when we do not pray for our children and neglect to dedicate them to the Lord. To fail in this is to leave them exposed to the Evil One. Vulnerable to evil, are not our children in one sense handed over to Satan by our failure to pray?

The whole theme of this chapter is to warn the Israelites not to engage in the practices of their pagan neighbors. Verse 13 is a central text in the Old Testament against homosexual behavior. Rather than pound the gay community over the head with this verse in judgment and condemnation, intercede for them in love, acceptance, compassion, and kindness. Dedicate them to the Lord as your own children and pray that they live a life of total openness to the will of God for them.

Portion 31 *Emor (Say)* Leviticus 21—24

T O R A H 31

Part A *Wholeness in Jesus* Leviticus 21—22

You shall not profane my holy name, that I may be sanctified among the people of Israel: I am the Lord; I sanctify you, I who brought you out of the land of Egypt to be your God: I am the Lord. 22:32–33

Physically challenged people and persons otherwise handicapped were not permitted to serve as priests in the Old Testament. There is a valid principle at work: only that which is without defect can approach the altar. Only what is complete and the best is to be given to God.

Thank God for Jesus! He is the only perfect One who is also willing to share the perfection of grace with all those who give their lives to him. Thus, there is no need for us literally to fulfill the principle behind restricting servants of the Lord to whole persons; Jesus makes us whole.

While all this is true, still be sure that you are giving your best to the Lord. Your whole heart, your complete intention, your number-one desire is to dedicate your life to God alone.

Parts B and C *Everything Can Be Sacred* Leviticus 23—24

Six days shall work be done; but the seventh day is a sabbath of complete rest, a holy convocation; you shall do no work: it is a sabbath to the Lord throughout your settlements. 23:3

The celebrations in which Jewish people take part have their origins in the revelation of God to Moses. Here there is another listing of the feasts with details about how they are to be honored. These are the direct words of God to the people concerning how the seasons for farming and other events become sacred celebrations, ways to give God honor and glory.

I recall what Ignatius of Loyola wanted for the Jesuits: "Let them find God in all things." How can you take the things you are called to do and have them become acts of worship and honor to the Lord?

This may help; the word "profane" in Latin means: "In front of the temple." What is outside of the "temple" where the Lord dwells is profane. However, *you* are the temple of the Lord where the Blessed Trinity dwells. Actions that flow from this presence are sacred, those that do not are profane. May you grow in knowing Who lives within you.

Portion 32   *Behar (On the Mount)*   Leviticus 25:1—26:2

Part A   *Sacred Pauses for Renewal*   Leviticus 25:1–28

You shall hallow the fiftieth year and you shall proclaim liberty throughout the land to all its inhabitants. It shall be a jubilee for you: you shall return, every one of you, to your property and every one of you to your family. v. 10

Special provisions for social justice are celebrated every fifty-years—seven times seven years. It is the year of jubilee. The root of this word means, "to split the ears" with a trumpet blast that announces the beginning of this sacred period. Captives were set free. No land could be permanently sold from its original owner; in the Jubilee year, it was returned. Jesus applied the term to himself and his ministry in Luke 4:19.

Jesus ushered in a Jubilee, which will never end. With Jesus comes a never-ending Sabbath. Still, find times for Sabbath days and longer stretches of time when you can rest and find sacred renewal of energies. Make good use of all the "mini-sabbaths" in life—times of transition in your day, sacred pauses for renewal.

Parts B and C   *We Belong to the Lord.*   Leviticus 25:29—26:2

If any of your kin fall into difficulty and become dependent on you, you shall support them; they shall live with you as though resident aliens. 25:35

Principles are outlined about the transfer of land as a possession. In 25:23 God declares: "The land shall not be sold permanently, for the land is mine: for you are stranger and sojourners with me." Reflect upon this principle and its connection to private property.

Everything we have comes from the Lord and belongs to God. The Gospel parables about stewardship further develop this understanding. Keep this in mind as you read about slavery from verse 39. While our understanding of slavery has grown over the centuries to be completely excluded, still, masters in Biblical times were enjoined "not to rule over them [slaves] with rigor, but you shall fear your God." The master for right living is the Holy Spirit who will teach us all things, always prompting us to the law of universal love and equality which Jesus held up for us the night before he was crucified.

Portion 33   *Behukkotai (My Commandment)*   Lev. 26:3—27:34

Parts A and B   *Blessings and Curses*   Leviticus 26:3—27:15

If you follow my statutes and keep my commandments and observe them faithfully,
I will give you your rains in their season, and the land shall yield its produce,
and the trees of the field shall yield their fruit. 26:3–4

Here are the blessings that come from obedience and the curses that result from disobedience. When you read about the curses, focus not on the Lord who is punishing, but on the issue of not walking in God's ways.

We don't like to hear about a God who punishes. However, God will forgive where there is repentance. God will be faithful to the Covenant God established with our ancestors.

A difficulty we have with a God who punishes out of justice, is the projection of our unholy anger. Harboring resentments, dwelling on thoughts of revenge and wanting to punish those who have wronged us: this is our sin. The Lord is pure love, with justice. It is comforting to know that ultimate justice will take place. The Covenant is the Lord's. It is ultimately God's responsibility to reward or punish—not ours.

Part C   *Holy and Wholly the Lord's*   Leviticus 27:15–34

All tithes from the land, whether the seed from the ground or the fruit from the tree,
are the Lord's; they are holy to the Lord. v. 30

Specifics of these regulations no longer pertain in our lives. However, as we read this final passage from the Book of Leviticus, ponder again upon the Hebrew *qadosh*, the word for all the English expressions used for "dedication."

Something or someone is holy when set apart and dedicated for the things of God. As the Easter season ends, remember that you are to be set apart for God, to live in the new temple of the Body of Christ.

Jesus' disciples waited in the Temple after he ascended into heaven, waiting for the Holy Spirit to come upon them and to fill them completely.

Only God is holy. However, you become holy and wholly the Lord's when the "parcel of land" that you live in is the Holy Body of Christ.

Bemidbar is the Hebrew name for the Book of Numbers.

Part A   *Census and Inventory*   **Numbers 1**
Take a census of the whole congregation of Israelites, in their clans,
by ancestral houses, according to the number of names, every male individually. v. 1

The Hebrew title of the Sabbath *Torah* portions comes from a word or words in the beginning of the portion. Since this is the first third of the first portion of the book of Numbers, *Bemidbar* is the Hebrew name for this entire book of the Bible. The English name comes from the Latin translation of the title of the Book in the Greek version of the Old Testament called *The Septuagint*. Much of the book deals with census-taking and other numberings.

Names and dates give orientation to the plans that God has for the people, such as the entry into the Promised Land and the preparation of the armies to bring this about.

Take a census—an inventory—of all that you have with you that the Lord can use as you enter into the spiritual battle for God's people, bringing them into the Promised Land of the resurrection.

Part B   *When God Is at the Center*   **Numbers 2:1—3:13**
The Israelites did just as the Lord had commanded Moses:
They camped by regiments, and they set out the same way, everyone by clans,
according to ancestral houses. 2:34

Who is at the center of your life? We live in a society that has a high degree of self-centeredness. "Doing *my* thing," is a byword these days. The book of Numbers will give you a new perspective.

Place yourself as part of a family of one of the tribes of Israel. You are part of this great nation camped around the presence of the Lord. The tabernacle of God's presence is what is center, not the lives of any one person, or any group. Alas, when the people sinned, it was because they forgot the Lord as their center.

You are the tabernacle, the temple of the Lord. May God's presence radiate from your center to all those surrounding you in your life.

Part C   *God Is Helper*   **Numbers 3:14—4:20**
Eleazar son of Aaron the priest shall have charge of the oil for the light, the fragrant incense,
the regular grain offering, and the anointing oil, the oversight of all the tabernacle and all that is in it,
in the sanctuary and in its utensils. 4:16

Words such as *order, holiness*, and *sacred tasks* come to mind as we move through the lists of names and the duties assigned to each of the priestly families, the Levites and the Kohathites. Every action and object is meant to evoke a sense of God's presence. Once again the use of colors evokes spiritual feelings.

There is beauty in the sacred task appointed to Eleazar, whose name means, "God is Helper." He tends to the light and takes care that incense and anointing oil are in readiness. He is given the overall responsibility of the sanctuary.

Reflect upon your occupation in life as a call to bring the light of the Lord, the sweet aroma of God's presence, and the oil of healing to those with whom you come in contact. You are the sanctuary of the Lord. How you do what you do, either draws others to the Lord or tends to push them away.

Portion 35   *Naso (Census)*   Numbers 4:21—7:89

Part A   *Growth in the Body*   Numbers 4:21—5:10

**From thirty years old up to fifty years old you shall enroll them,
all who qualify to do work in the tent of meeting. 4:23**

Every man in the range of age indicated is assigned a task in the arrangement of the articles in the tabernacle. All the details of the adornments have spiritual meaning for worship, serving also to define the meaning of each person's part in the whole.

While the activities are restricted to men of certain ages, there is completeness with everyone having a part. Paul develops this in Ephesians 4:16 where the tabernacle is no longer an edifice with objects within, but rather the Body of the Risen Lord. Every believer is a part of the whole, each doing his/her part to have the body of Christ grow into wholeness.

Reflect upon how you can find the meaning of your life through the way you share your uniqueness with others. Anything less limits the growth in the Body of Christ.

Part B   *Married to God*   Numbers 5:11—6:27

**The Lord bless you and keep you;
the Lord make his face to shine upon you, and be gracious to you;
the Lord lift up his countenance upon you, and give you peace. 6:24–26**

Infidelity in marriage is sacrilegious because it is a reflection of the infidelity of God's people to the Lord. God's covenant is as a marriage. Think of it: the God of the universe invites his people to marry God. Keep this in mind as you read the strong ordeal that a woman suspected of infidelity must undergo. You will read about the Nazirite vow; recall that you are to be separate from all that is unholy and profane. This vow is one of the ways in which a person consciously and deliberately lived apart for God in one's daily habits.

How do your habits demonstrate that you are living for God alone, as the spouse of your soul? Memorize the blessing in verses 24 to 26. Bless your family as you do.

Part C   *In Touch with God*   Numbers 7:1–89

**When Moses went into the tent of meeting to speak with the Lord, he would hear the voice speaking to
him from above the mercy seat that was on the ark of the covenant from between the two cherubim;
thus it spoke to him. v. 89**

Go beyond the details of the offerings and the repetitions of the objects offered, to the overall feeling of the passage. These are as the memorials offered when churches are built. The names of the families give a sense that they are part of the sacred building that is now complete and ready for worship.

The first and final verses of this chapter frame the content. Moses anoints the tabernacle and its furnishings, heightening the sense of the sacred. The passage closes with a description of how God communicates with the people—to Moses first, and through him to others. The chapter is about being in touch with God.

You have access to the presence of God through those speaking who are one with Jesus through the Holy Spirit. In Christ, you are greater than Moses!

Part A   *Appointed Times*   **Numbers 8:1—9:14**
Let the Israelites keep the passover at its appointed time. 9:2

Seven lights, number of fullness, shine within the Holy Place. There is an inner light as you read God's Holy Word.

The cleansing of the Levites reminds us that those at the center of worship need to be pure. Though here limited to a single class of people, the New Covenant extends to every person found within the Body of Jesus. Your surrender to the Lord is what brings you within Jesus and makes you a priest. Every action of yours can become a gesture of worship, bearing witness to the world of the holiness of God.

The second celebration of the Passover is announced. The root of the word in Hebrew for the "appointed" time, *mo'ed,* is the same as the word in Genesis1:14 for the seasons. God has outlined cycles of time by days and nights, seasons and years, giving rhythm and serenity to the passage of time. Respond to these shifts and changes as one candle shares its light with another.

Part B   *The Lord Leads the Way*   **Numbers 9:15—10:34**
It was always so: the cloud covered it by day
and the appearance of fire by night. 9:16

The presence of the Lord in the cloud by day and the fire by night: picture this abiding presence, and the direction that this presence will give. It is time for the Chosen People to move on from Sinai. The Law has been given. The tablets become part of the sacrament of God's presence to them. Hear the sound of the trumpets as the lives of our ancestors are quickened. The Lord says, "It is time to move on." There is joy when we know that the Lord is calling us to move forward in life.

In Revelations 8 to 12, the trumpets spark the final war in the heavens. There is a spiritual war waged on the battlefield of your own soul. However, Jesus won the victory already. May the cross go before you.

Part C   *Familiarity with God*   **Numbers 10:35—12:16**
Moses said to him, "Are you jealous for my sake? Would that all the Lord's people were prophets,
and that the Lord would put his spirit on them!" 11:29

The Israelites leave the foot of Mount Sinai and renew their journey once more. Soon strife starts in again. The people keep their eyes on their need, instead of on the cloud before them by day and the pillar of fire by night—signs to them of the faithful presence of God. The fire begins to burn them, instead of leading them out of their misery, by a constant, faithful trust in the Lord.

The unique intimacy of God with Moses is described in the familiarity of their conversation. Moses places his need before God: others need to share the burden of the people that Moses otherwise has to carry alone. Watch what happens when the jealousy of Miriam and Aaron flares up.

Moses is described in 12:3 as the humblest man on earth. How are you when it comes to humility? Christ exalts the humble. If you are, God will be glorified, for he has made you part of a race of priests, prophets and kings!

Portion 37   *Shelah L'cha (Send)*   Numbers 13—15

Part A   *Fearless Before the Enemy*   **Numbers 13:1—14:7**
"The land that we went through as spies is an exceedingly good land.
If the Lord is pleased with us, he will bring us into this land and give it to us,
a land that flows with milk and honey. 14:7–8

Jewish tradition gives names to every Sabbath as Christians name Sundays in the sacred year. As you read the Torah readings, especially this year A (the first of the three-part division of each portion), see how the title relates to the subject matter of the reading. "Send" refers to the Lord's command to send out spies into the land of promise.

13:16 is the very first time that the name of Joshua appears. Moses does something to his name as God did to Abraham and as Jesus did to Simon; the name is changed or slightly altered to give it special meaning. Moses changed Hoshea to Joshua, the latter meaning **"Yahweh (the Lord) is Salvation."** It is the same name as Jesus, the Greek form of the Hebrew name.

Fear paralyses the hearts of the other spies. Notice the "Yes, but" to which they yield in 13:28. "But" cancels out all that goes before it. Pray that you face the "enemies" in your life as fearlessly as Joshua and Jesus faced theirs.

Part B   *Stop Complaining*   **Numbers 14:8—15:7**
"Forgive the iniquity of this people according to the greatness of your steadfast love,
just as you have pardoned this people, from Egypt even until now." 14:19

No one likes a complainer; neither does the Lord. If you have the Lord in charge of your life and you have surrendered to God, is it not a kind of blasphemy to complain the way things are going?

The Lord is hard on the desert complainers. This was usually the beginning of disobedience, rebellion, and idolatry. God becomes angry with the people, and talks about destroying them, making a new nation with new people. What power in the intercessory prayer of Moses! God listens to his chosen one and does not complete the plans of his rage.

Intercessory prayer is powerful. Jesus was the one who interceded for you and for me, and turned back the eternal consequence of our sins. Praise Him!

Part C   *Covered by the Blood*   **Numbers 15:8–41**
Speak to the Israelites, and tell them to make fringes on the corners
of their garments throughout their generations
and to put a blue cord on the fringe at each corner. v. 38

The details of this passage converge into one great truth: God is the absolute center of life. The Lord, who cannot be seen, establishes a visible sign as a reminder of this fact in the blue tassels at the four corners of the basic garment worn by the Israelites.

Look what happens when there is what we would consider, a minor violation of the Sabbath. The grasping energy of *having* fuels our modern society; contrast this joy of *giving* in the various offerings and contributions for the worship of God.

The word for atonement in Hebrew is *chaphar*; you are familiar with this in *Yom Kippur,* The Day of Atonement. The root of the word means *to cover.* The blood of Jesus covers your sins so that they are no longer visible. So do not keep looking at them!

Portion 38   *Korah*   Numbers 16—18

Part A   *A Destructive Power*   Numbers 16:1–40

**Then he said to Korah and all his company, "In the morning the Lord will make known who is his,
and who is holy, and who will be allowed to approach him;
the one whom he will choose he will allow to approach him. v. 5**

Jealousy and power rear their ugly heads, as they did for the fall of the evil King (or Lucifer?) in Isaiah 14. The rebels mentioned might as well have taken on God, as indeed amounts to be the case, when they challenge Moses and Aaron with such profound disrespect. What happens to them is similar to the outcome of that one that fell from heaven.

Envy is one of the Capital Sins. Its reckless, blind energy smashes headlong into the carefully woven plans that God has for each person.

If only the Korahites had minded their own sacred business—a sacred, priestly business. After you read, examine your own conscience about jealousy. The purity of God's Spirit cannot tolerate dwelling in a soul restless with jealousy. It is a very destructive power. Beware!

Part B   *The Symbol of Your Uniqueness*   Numbers 16:41—17:13

**When Moses went into the tent of the covenant on the next day,
the staff of Aaron for the house of Levi had sprouted.
It put forth buds, produced blossoms, and bore ripe almonds. 17:8**

Hear the sobering consequences for those who challenged the leadership of Moses and Aaron. Death by plague comes to those continuing to rebel and complain against the Lord. Moses stands in the gap for the people as their intercessor. (Cf. Ezekiel 22:30.)

Chapter 17 tells what the Lord does about the arrogance of the people's complaining about Aaron. His rod buds with blossoms and almonds. Together with the stone tablets of the Ten Commandments, this wondrous sign from the Lord is placed in the Ark of the Covenant in the Holy of Holies in the tabernacle.

You are called to a unique ministry that only you can fulfill. What would be a symbol of this uniqueness? Put it near the place where you pray.

Part C   *Drawn to God*   Numbers 18

**But you shall not profane the holy gifts of the Israelites,
on pain of death. v. 32**

It was a unique privilege to have been a son of Aaron, or to have been born into the tribe of Levi. The tithes of the rest of the people were dedicated to the support of these two priestly groups. The entire life of the priests was devoted to the care of the sanctuary and worship. The verse for the day describes the even greater responsibility of the Levites to honor what they do with these gifts, for they belong to the Lord.

The life of worship is central for God's people. The tabernacle is the most important place for the Israelites, for it draws the people together about their God, maintaining a consciousness of the presence of God in all life.

On our about this Thursday we will begin the Letter to the Hebrews which expresses the priesthood of Jesus in even more exalted terms. In Jesus, you are a priest. What do you do with the gifts you have been given?

Portion 39   *Hukkath (Ordinance)*   Numbers 19:1—22:1

Part A   *Waterpower*   Numbers 19:1—20:21
**Those who touch the dead body of any human being
shall be unclean seven days. 19:11**

John the Baptist and Jesus are prefigured in this portion of the Torah that treats of the spiritual power of water. John must have had this reading in mind when he chose the ritual of baptism as a preparation for Jesus. Miracle water from the rock looks to Jesus as the living water, which flowed from his open side.

Whenever death has been touched, cleansing needs to happen. So too in death-bound unreconciled negative feelings within, such as hidden resentments and unhealed pain that pull the soul toward death. Notice the period of seven days of purification; what a blessing it would be to have your whole self cleansed of inner "death" within the space of a week! The water from your own tears can be the means of cleansing.

Look what happened to Moses when he challenged God's decision to give the complaining people the water they needed! Do you complain when God is showing mercy?

Part B   *Complaining Blocks the Presence.*   Numbers 20:22–29
**"Let Aaron be gathered to his people.
For he shall not enter the land that I have given to the Israelites,
because you rebelled against my command at the waters of Meribah." 20:24**

Moses complains about having to bring water from the rock for the rebellious people (v.11). Therefore, he and Aaron are barred from entering the Promised Land. Today's reading also tells about the death of Aaron and the long period of mourning of the people—a whole month.

Even though God's people complained, it was not for Moses in turn to complain about bringing water for them from the rock.

Resist complaining about what God calls you to do. Such a complaint fails to see the Lord at work at all times. Moses lost sight of this when he said "we" (Aaron and he) were to bring water from the rock, instead of more clearly acknowledging that it was the Lord's doing. Complaining blocks the presence of God.

Part C   *Evil Becomes Source of Salvation.*   Numbers 21:1—22:1
**And the Lord said to Moses, "Make a poisonous serpent, and set it on a pole;
and everyone who is bitten shall look at it and live." 21:8**

Complaining continues. Snakes come and torment the people. The Lord tells Moses to make a serpent out of bronze, lifting it high for the people to see, that they might be healed. The consequences of sin become the means of salvation.

So too for the cross. There is no greater sin than to have crucified the son of God. However, God takes the cross, the results of the cruelest evil, and turns it into a source of salvation. St. John has this in mind in his Gospel when he relates the cross to the fiery serpent in 3:14 and 12:32.

Is there any person, place, or thing that has been sin for you? Rather than look away in guilt or shame, let the cross upon which Jesus has suffered in your sin, become a source of healing for you and others. God can turn your greatest sin into a source of grace.

Portion 40   *Balak*   Numbers 22:2—25:9

Part A   *An Animal Teacher*   Numbers 22:2–38

**Balaam said to Balak, "I have come to you now, but do I have power to say just anything?
The word God puts in my mouth, that is what I must say." v. 38**

A donkey turns out to be more responsive to God than a man gifted with spiritual powers to see. Here is a story that will warm your heart and sober your mind. As the cows of 1 Samuel 6 that brought the Ark of the Covenant back to its resting place in the center of God's people, so does this beast of the field prevent Balaam from going down the road to comply with the evil plans of Balak, king of the Moabites.

Animals seem to have a special gift of sensing fear. Be alert on this Sabbath, not to raw fear, but to a prudent sense of caution that the Holy Spirit may be sending your way when you are being manipulated. Is there a pet in your house or some other animal that you will discover as an image, a parable, that God is sending your way to teach you something very important?

Part B   *A Pagan Stands in Awe*   Numbers 22:39—23:30

**God is not a human being, that he should lie,
or a mortal, that he should change his mind. Has he promised, and will he not do it?
Has he spoken, and will he not fulfill it? 23:19**

King Balak of the neighboring country of Moab hired Balaam, a pagan prophet, to curse God's people. Balak wanted to eliminate any threat that the Israelites would have against him and his land of Moab. Today's reading is the account of what happened between God and Balaam. God declares to Balaam the unique blessing that God gives to his people.

The pagan Balaam stands in awe of the power of God. God is true to God's word. When God blesses, who can curse?

The well known hymn "Great Is Thy Faithfulness," based on Lamentations, 3:22–23, expresses this when we sing in praise of God: "Thou changest not, Thy compassions, they fail not." The Letter to the Hebrews, 13:8, expresses it this way: "Jesus Christ, the same yesterday, today, and forever."

Part C   *A Star Shall Come*   Numbers 24:1—25:9

**I see him, but not now; I behold him, but not near—
a star shall come out of Jacob, and a scepter shall rise out of Israel … 24:17**

With each successive prophecy, the pagan Balaam becomes more sweetly open to God, simpler, more childlike as he yields to the promptings of the Spirit. He is completely caught up in the prophetic word he speaks. His yielding opens his eyes to behold the beauty of God's people, as he sees the tents of the people of God.

In the center of his fourth and final prophecy, Balaam sees a star coming out of Jacob, lifting him to a vision that realized in David, and especially in Jesus. When you turn your heart totally over to the Lord, God will show you wondrous things.

Verse 1 of chapter 25 begins the shocking story of sexual immorality with foreign women. The exalted state of a pagan yielding to the gift of prophecy, is contrasted with the sin of infidelity by God's own people.

Portion 41   *Pinhas (Phineas)*   Numbers 25:10—30:1

Part A   *God Inside-ism*   Numbers 25:10—26:51

**"Phinehas son of Eleazar, son of Aaron the priest, has turned back my wrath from
the Israelites by manifesting such zeal among them on my behalf
that in my jealousy I did not consume the Israelites." 25:11**

Phineas has passion zeal almost as much as God has. There always appears at least one faithful person after the heart of God; thus God alters the chastisement planned. Phinehas reminds us of Jesus. John in his Gospel cites Psalm 69:9 in reference to Jesus: **"Zeal for Your house has consumed me"** (2:17).

Who or what in your life receives your life-energies? If any work or person outside of God consumes you, you will indeed by "eaten alive." However, spiritual zeal is like enthusiasm, the latter word literally meaning, "God inside-ism." When you consume God through prayer, Scripture and the Sacrament of the Lord's Supper, then you will be caught by the fire of God and be consumed by it.

At this point in the Book of Numbers, we are half-way through the forty years of wandering. A new generation is on the scene; a new census needs to be taken. Good news: this group does not complain!

Part B   *Women's Rights*   Numbers 26:52—28:15

**So the Lord said to Moses, "Take Joshua son of Nun,
a man in whom is the spirit, and lay your hand upon him. 27:18**

The generation of those who rebelled against the Lord in the desert has died. A new generation is prepared; they had no experience of Egypt, since they were born during the Exodus.

The Bible's first instance of women's rights is in the account of the five daughters of Zelophehad. This man had no sons; the daughters came to Moses requesting justice for them, so that they could have the inheritance of the family, which usually passed along by the sons alone. They present a delicate balance between assertiveness and yielding to the final decisions left in the hands of the Lord through his servant Moses.

Joshua is selected as the one to lead the people into the Promised Land. 27:14 recalls how the Lord denied entry to Moses, because he complained. Reflect on yourself in this regard.

Part C   *A Burnt Offering*   Numbers 28:16—30:1

You shall offer a burnt offering, a pleasing odor to the Lord ... 29:2

Spring or autumn—which one is the beginning of a new year? Obviously, there is a connection with spring as the beginning, as new life comes into existence. It was then that new life emerged from the Red Sea in the Exodus. There is also the sense that autumn is the beginning, the time when Jewish people celebrate the New Year. Jewish tradition has it that creation took place in autumn, since God created all things in their fullness.

Keep this tension in mind as God outlines all the major festivals of the Jews gathered into this passage. Burnt offerings are to be made. The phrase occurs 267 times in the Old Testament, 22 of them in this passage alone!

While *what* is burnt is no longer in effect, the *fact* of burning remains. Are you willing to let yourself be set on fire by the Holy Spirit and burn on for the Lord? God wants no other offering than *you.*

Part A   *Holy Violence*   **Numbers 30:2—31:54**

Gold, silver, bronze, iron, tin, and lead—everything that can withstand fire,
shall be passed through fire, and it shall be clean. Nevertheless it shall also be purified with
the water for purification; and whatever cannot withstand fire,
shall be passed through the water. 31:22–23

The verse for today that comes in the center of the reading is a *Firestarter* for your heart to glow with a basic truth: God wants purity for his people. This may help to interpret the warlike behavior, which seems impossible to justify by modern understanding of how God wants us to act toward our enemies. Certainly, Jesus' position is clear: we are to love our enemies and to pray for them. These "coals of fire" upon their heads are the holy violence of love designed to win people into the Kingdom. As for the Book of Numbers, there is no consistently clear position about what constitutes a Holy War. Killing defiles; hence the need for purification afterward.

There are harsh consequences for those given to idolatry. However, thank God for Jesus. The way he treats the foreign woman in Matthew 15 shows how he makes new "spoils" for the Kingdom by healing and love.

Part B and C   *Unity in the Body*   **Numbers 32**

We will cross over armed before the Lord into the land of Canaan,
but the possession of our inheritance shall remain with us on this side of the Jordan. v. 32

Two and a half tribes request Moses that they stay on the east side of the Jordan. Moses has to be sure that this is not due out of fear to enter into the Promised Land. He wants to be sure that they are not in rebellion about going into the Promised Land, as happened earlier in chapters 13 and 14. The cooperation of all of God's people is needed in order for the conquest to take place. We are "our brother's keeper," as implied in Genesis 4:9, after Cain murdered his brother Abel.

You are important for the whole body of Christ. If you do God's will in your life, then the rest of the body benefits; if you do not, then the whole is threatened. The unity in the Body of Christ is powerfully developed in 1 Corinthians 12:12 and following. May you find comfort and much joy in knowing in whom you live and move and have your being.

Portion 43   *Maseh (Journeys)*   Numbers 33:1—36:13

Part A   *Stepping-Stones*   Numbers 33

**Moses wrote down their starting points, stage by stage, by command of the Lord;
and these are their stages according to their starting places. v. 2**

The history of all the people that came to the United States through Ellis Island is available in massive data banks—where each person came from, on what boat, and to what city each migrated.

Interest in connecting to one's roots is at the heart of this chapter summarizing the history and geography of the Exodus. At this half-way point in the forty-year wandering, God wants those born after the Exodus to know the stepping-stones that enabled them come to where they are now. A map of the Exodus will help you see the journey, just as a "dot-to-dot" child's game helps to bring the latent picture into awareness.

Your life will seem as aimless as wandering dots, unless you take time to note the stepping-stones along your path. Each is a point of grace that has taken you to where you are right now. Connect the dots in your life so that the whole picture of what God is doing with you can emerge.

Part B   *Boundaries*   Numbers 34—35:8

**Command the Israelites, and say to them: When you enter the land of Canaan
(this is the land that shall fall to you for an inheritance,
the land of Canaan, defined by its boundaries), 34:2**

It is very important that there be clear boundaries for personal property, as well as for towns, counties, states, and countries. The border that defines one land from another gives a name to what is within.

From no one but the Lord come the plans for the boundaries of the Promised Land. Not only does God map out the boundaries of the land itself, but also the locations of each individual city are determined. God is the One responsible for these details. He is the "City Planner," if you will.

The Lord has given all that you have to you. Thank him for the land in which you live, the house and lot where you reside. These are gifts from the Lord, not only what you managed to acquire from your efforts. Be grateful to the Lord for all you have been given.

Part C   *Refuge in Christ's Body*   Numbers 35:8—36–13

**You shall not defile the land in which you live, in which I also dwell;
for I the Lord dwell among the Israelites. 35:34**

We make distinctions between civil and religious laws; there were no such differences for God's people. All law came from God. The Lord ordained six cities of refuge for the Israelites, places where a murderer might find protection. There is care about the various kinds of death dealing and justice.

How good it is to know that there is some place where we can be safe from the consequences of wrongdoing—a place where the anger, hatred, and revenge of enemies cannot enter! This refuge is in Jesus. Many have found the image of the open side of Jesus as the place to find this protection. This gaping wound, fashioned by our sin, becomes the place of protection against sin. Look how God turns evil into good!

Chapter 36 is a plan to insure that ones inheritance stays within the tribe of one's family. You have received all the inheritance of the very Son of God. Stay with his body.

Portion 44   *Devarim (The Words)*   Deuteronomy 1:1—3:22

Devarim is the Hebrew name for the Book of Deutronomy.

Part A   *Resume*   Deuteronomy 1:1—2:1

**... and in the wilderness, where you saw how the Lord your God carried you,
just as one carries a child, all the way that you traveled until you reached this place. 1:31**

God's people are poised for the Promised Land. It is near the end of the forty-year period. The entire book of Deuteronomy is an address of Moses to God's people. Their whole history appears before their eyes. Moses brings a generation that did not know the Exodus into vivid contact with the history of God liberating the people from slavery.

Line up with the tribes assembled together in awesome silence as they listen. How much we need to experience ourselves as part of The People of God! You are not alone. You stand in formation with saints who have gone before, and billions today who are God's children.

You might make your own resume of what God has for you as you are about to enter into a greater possession of the Promise. See your personal story as part of the great masterpiece of history as God works to bring freedom to everyone.

Part B   *The Thread of Connection*   Deuteronomy 2:2–30

Surely the Lord your God has blessed you in all your undertakings; he knows your going through this great wilderness. These forty years the Lord your God has been with you; you have lacked nothing. 2:7

With the passing of one generation, it is time to tell the story. This is sacred history brought up to the present.

History makes a people one. We step back and see the past as a whole, with connectives of grace and separations by sin. For Moses, this moment serves to bring the new generation of people up to the present by a vivid recall of where they have been. The final phase of the journey needs the energy of what God has done—and what others have undone by complaining, false worship, and strife.

The Book of Deuteronomy is the thread of connection from past to future. Moses, the great leader and instructor, gathers all that he has received into one book, leaving it as a legacy from the generation gathered then to listen, to the present generation gathered across the Jewish world. In our plan of reading, Christians join with this community to listen to the one Spirit of God speak to us today with words that have come down to us from thousands of years.

Saturday   *A New Promised Land*   Deuteronomy 2:31—3:22

Do not fear them, for it is the Lord your God who fights for you. 3:22

At the age of 120, Moses is about to die. Listen to his final words to the people on the brink of the Promised Land. From the shores of the Red Sea, to the banks of the Jordan, God has been with his people. If God has been with them thus far, will God not be present in all the challenges to come?

There is an awesome silence as the people they listen to Moses. After the reading, linger and listen in the silence of your own prayer to the support, encouragement and love that God gives you; the Spirit brings to your mind how the Lord has always been with you, no matter what. What about the struggles you are facing? The same power that raised Jesus from the dead has been given to you and will be at work for you today.

Portion 45   *Vaethanan (I Implored)*   Deut. 3:23—7:11

Part A   *Fire in the Heart*   Deuteronomy 3:23—4:49
**Then the Lord spoke to you out of the fire. You heard the sound of words
but saw no form; there was only a voice. 4:12**

There are Five references to fire in this passage. Life-giving as well as destructive aspects are given. Relate your awareness of fire here with others instances of fire in the Bible. Fire manifested God to Moses in the Burning Bush (Ex 3:2–3); it was fire that revealed the fullness of God's outpoured present to the disciples on Pentecost (Act. 2).

Though Moses speaks about the presence of God in the fire on Mount Sinai, here God's word comes to the people with Moses on a level plain, similar to the contrast of Matthew and Luke. For purposes of theology, and not only history, Matthew places the words of Jesus in a sermon "on the mount," while Luke has Jesus speak "on the level."

So let Moses speak to you—"level" with you—about God as the absolute priority in your life. You are not only reading, but also listening to the Spirit as fire in your heart is set by these words that burn within.

Part B   *Terms of the Covenant*   Deuteronomy 5—6
**Look, the Lord our God has shown us his glory and greatness,
and we have heard his voice out of the fire. Today we have seen
that God may speak to someone and the person may still live. 5:24**

The Ten Commandments are not impassioned principles of law from an impersonal ruler of the universe. The Commandments set the basic boundaries and terms of the covenant relation that the Lord is offering to us. If you want to have a life with God, then here is what *not* to do so that this can occur.

The People of God knew what would happen if God spoke directly to them; they would die. Hence, Moses was a mediator for them. We have a Mediator in Jesus who is both God and man. He makes the connection through the Holy Spirit from the heart of God to yours. Receive the Ten Commandments warmly and reflect on them deeply.

Part C   *In the Spotlight of God's Love*   Deuteronomy 7:1–11
**It was not because you were more numerous than any other people that the Lord
set his heart on you and chose you … It was because the Lord loved you and
kept the oath that he swore to your ancestors … 7:7–8**

A spotlight reveals only what is before it; everything else is cast into darkness. So is God's love for his people. It is a love of great tenderness and preference. For some reason known only to God, this saving love focused as a spotlight upon this little, insignificant people; all other nations were outside in the darkness.

The ultimate plan of God is to create a new people, born from the open side of his only Son, for whom God has a love of tenderness and preference. The Son's embrace on the cross is worldwide. No one from any nation, people, or race is excluded from this embrace. In Jesus, God has a preferential love for everyone.

God has simply decided to love you. Nothing you do can change that. Only live in the spotlight of God's love shining from the cross.

Part A   *Last Words*   Deuteronomy 7:12—9:3
Do not bring an abhorrent thing into your house,
or you will be set apart for destruction like it.
You must utterly detest and abhor it, for it is set apart for destruction. 7:26

The last words of one about to die often have a powerful urgency about them. Such is the case for Moses and the entire Book of Deuteronomy. God has told Moses that he will not be permitted to enter the Promised Land because of the complaint Moses expressed to God about God's compassion on his thirsty people in Numbers 20. Moses wants to be sure that future generations are extremely careful about their attitude to God and God's ways.

Take to heart, therefore, these words of Moses; he does not speak lightly. Reflect upon the power of suggestion. Some things can either lead us to God, or drag us away, by the connection they have either with God or what is opposed to God.

Moses speaks his last words to God's people—and to you and me. How do you know that these are not among the last words you shall ever hear?

Part B   *Rebels, But for the Grace of God*   Deuteronomy 9:4—10:11
Throughout the forty days and forty nights that I lay prostrate before the Lord
when the Lord intended to destroy you 9:25

God's people are on the verge of entering the land promised them by the Lord. Moses reminds them that this is not a reward for their good behavior, but rather is due to God's goodness and the wickedness of the original inhabitants. The Lord is faithful to the promises given to Abraham, Isaac, and Jacob, even when the people have disobeyed and rebelled.

Moses tells the story of the breaking of the tablets of the Ten Commandments to the first generation after it happened, and to us, countless generations afterward. The message is still the same: our ancestors were rebels; we must not be. We are no different from our ancestors, but for the grace of God.

Part C   *A Final Plea*   Deuteronomy 10:12—11:25
You shall put these words of mine in your heart and soul, and you shall bind them
as a sign on your hand, and fix them as an emblem on your forehead. 11:18

Have you ever been with a dear relative or friend as they say goodbye to you before they died? This is what Moses is doing in Book of Deuteronomy. Listen as this great ancestor directs his final words to you. It is the Holy Spirit that will make this message personal and tender, as Moses pleads with you and all God's people, to walk in all the ways of the Lord. Read slowly, with great care. Though you can always pick up your Bible and read these words again, listen inwardly in the heart, clinging to these final words of Moses, as though you will never hear from him again.

Try memorizing 11:18–21. What happens inside your heart as you listen? Can you catch the immensity of God's love for you and God's own longing that you live by God's ways? Be moved. Change. Fall in love with God again.

Portion 47   *Reeh (Behold)*   Deuteronomy 11:26—16:17

Part A   *Where to Find God*   Deuteronomy 11:26—12:28

You shall seek the place that the Lord your God will choose out of all your tribes
as his habitation to put his name there. You shall go there. 12:5

When I am preparing a couple requesting to be married in our church, I inquire about whether they already belong to a church community. Sometimes I hear: "You don't have to go to church in order to pray." True. But the non-verbals and lack of life in the response often make it merely a game of "one-up-manship." Very little prayer seems to be going on in some lives, and hardly any experience of the joys of being part of a community of faith.

As the objects from last week's reading, so here, places for worship are featured. The verse for today is one of three verses where Moses refers to God's instructions about where to worship. Find the other two.

Become sensitive to the places that are especially conducive to lead you into the Lord's presence—a church, a favorite spot for a meditation walk, a small table-like altar in your house where you are drawn to God just by going there. In order for you to find God everywhere, there needs to be some places where you find God's face first.

Part B   *Atheism: a False Religion*   Deuteronomy 12:29—14:29

The Lord your God you shall follow, him alone you shall fear,
his commandments you shall keep, his voice you shall obey,
him you shall serve, and to him you shall hold fast. 13:4

In Biblical times, atheism was never an option; this is a modern invention. Atheism, as we know it, is simply another false religion. The atheist is committed to something approaching an absolute—some "god" that he adheres to and "worships," as did our wandering ancestors in the desert. Then there are "theists" for whom God is nothing more than a vague reality on the margin of life.

Is there any person, place, or thing elbowing a way into your life seeking to take the place that belongs to God alone?

Part C   *Holidays … or Not So Holy?*   Deuteronomy 15:1—16:17

Three times a year all your males shall appear before the Lord your God
at the place that he will choose: at the festival of unleavened bread,
at the festival of weeks, and at the festival of booths.
They shall not appear before the Lord empty-handed. 16:16

Persons on their deathbed are often able to put their things in order and make final arrangements before they die; so too in the case of Moses. Instructions are given about how the poor are to be treated and the ordinances for the freeing slaves. Once again, the commandment is stated about celebrating the three major pilgrim festivals—Passover, Pentecost ("Weeks") and Tabernacles.

We often take for granted the yearly celebration of festivals and holidays. Of course, the word "holiday" is from "holy day." Originally, the Lord commanded such celebrations as a way to fill the year with remembrances of God's saving activity on behalf of God's people. We are responding to the instruction given by God through Moses.

How do you celebrate holidays? Are they holy … or not so holy?

Part A   *The Bible Close to You*   Deuteronomy 16:18—18:5

When he (the king) has taken the throne of his kingdom, he shall have a copy of this law written for him in the presence of the levitical priests. It shall remain with him and he shall read in it all the days of his life, so that he may learn to fear the Lord his God, diligently observing all the words of this law and these statutes. 17:18–19

Three classes of God's people are mentioned—priests, prophets and kings. Recall that Samuel, coming at the end of the period of judges, was at the same time the first of the prophets that were to follow. In Christ, you participate in all three classes, because you are engrafted onto his body. Therefore, read this passage by listening to the instructions directed to you in a special way. If the future kings need to read the law every day, how much more must we read, pray, and respond to the Holy Spirit who sets fire in our hearts from the words of Scripture! Is your Bible always close to you?

Verse 17:16 is a strong command: "You must never return to Egypt." It was tempting for the wandering Israelites to forget the slavery of Egypt when they were hungry and thirsty in the desert. So too will you be tempted at times to return to previous forms of slavery and addiction instead of following the inner call of the Spirit to an evermore complete possession of "The Promised Land."

Part B   *A Prophet to Come Like Moses*   Deuteronomy 18:6—19:13

The Lord your God will raise up for you a prophet like me
from among your own people; you shall heed such a prophet. 18:15

Turn on your television, and you will likely find a commercial for a psychic hotline. It is stated that the calls are "For entertainment only," disclaiming deception.

Chapter 18 from verse 9 explicitly prohibits these customs, calling them an "abomination to the Lord. The Lord does not speak to entertain you, but to give you life, with proper guidelines to be sure that you will grow.

In chapter 18 from 15–22, there is a remarkable prediction from Moses about a prophet like him that the Lord will raise up. Jesus fulfills this prophecy. Ask the Holy Spirit to show you God's will for your life as you read in faith and trust.

Part C   *God Longs for a People Who Will Love*   Deut. 19:14—21:9

It is the Lord your God who goes with you,
to fight for you against your enemies, to give you victory. 20:4

It will be difficult for you to read about the treatment of the inhabitants of cities that resist the entry of God's people into the Promised Land. However, thank God for Jesus! When the resistance to God's plan of salvation comes from the very center of Judaism—the chief priests, Scribes and Pharisees—then the outcome is reversed; *they* are rejected, and God's beloved ones become those of any race or nation open to God's movement in their hearts. Recall the parables of the Wedding Banquet and others that express this reversal.

The Old Testament presses against the New for fulfillment. However, one truth pervades both Testaments. God is looking for a people who will love him and follow God's ways of love. Do not resist God's plan.

Portion 49   *Ki Tetze (When You Go Out)*   Deut. 21:10—25:19

Part A   *From Curse to Blessing*   Deuteronomy 21:10—23:8
You must not defile the land
that the Lord your God is giving you for possession. 21:23

Ask the Holy Spirit to help you sift out the eternal truths that remain after some regulations are no longer in effect. The Lord has led us away from being a male-dominated society. Yet, the areas of God's concern are ever the same. For example, God cares about sexual behavior, for sexuality says a great deal about who God is and how God is related to us. Marriage imagery is often used to describe the relation of God to us. Consider too the seriousness of an incorrigible child; read what happened to such a one! Modern society is filled with examples of enabling and spoiling children by their parents. Look for the eternal sense of justice that runs through the other examples given.

Paul in Galatians 3 quotes the sentence just prior to the one in the verse for today about the curse of the cross. Not only was Jesus nailed to the cross, but also so were the curses that went with it. The curse has become the blessing. Hold the cross near you as you hear God's personal instruction to you in this passage.

Part B   *Guidelines for Right Living*   Deuteronomy 23:9—24:13
Because the Lord your God travels along with your camp, to save you and to hand over your enemies to
you, therefore your camp must be holy, so that he may not see anything indecent among you and turn
away from you. 23:14

Even in war, cleanliness is vital, for it reminds the warrior that the Lord walks in the camp that must be in good order for God to be present.

The word *Torah* in Hebrew means not only "law" but also includes the concepts of "teaching" and "guidelines." The Lord gives us the banks of the river, as it were, for the clear movement and flow of our lives.

Remember the obvious: all this comes from the Lord. God is the legislator; no congress or human being has made these laws. Receive them with faith and awe, as you come to understand what the Lord has given us that we might live.

Part C   *Compassion and Solidarity*   Deuteronomy 24:14—25:19
Remember that you were a slave in Egypt and the Lord your God
redeemed you from there; therefore I command you to do this. 24:18

Mercy and justice are blended in these laws of Israelite society. Laws of justice have changed; those of mercy and compassion have not. The essence of the motive for compassion is the word "remember" found in the verse for today and in verse 22. The energy for compassion comes from solidarity with those whose lives are being diminished. Every person in need can present him or herself before you, prompting you to utter from your heart: "I've been there; I too have been a slave in Egypt."

There we would continue to be, but for the mercy and grace of God upon our lives. Be a sacrament of love; be like Moses, who in the power of the coming Christ, led those in bondage in Egypt to freedom in the Promised Land—the Kingdom that God is ever opening to you.

Part A   *Canaan Points*   **Deuteronomy 26:1–11**
The Lord brought us out of Egypt with a mighty hand and an outstretched arm,
with a terrifying display of power, and with signs and wonders. v. 8

Canaan is the land intended by Moses when he tells the people, "When you arrive in the land … (v. 1). However, mull over "Canaan" in your heart. Where is the spiritual "place" to where the Lord is leading you? Accept where you are right now, but believe that the Lord is continuing to give you grace to move to new levels of union with God and realization of your purpose in life.

Each day is a steppingstone to move further and deeper. Whether the stone is comfortable to stand upon or not, whether you like the stone or not, it is the one that will enable you to move to the next place on your journey. Greater than any discomfort is the presence of the Lord and his love for you that give you the energy to keep on.

As you arrive at each Canaan-point of spiritual growth, be ready to offer your "first fruits" to the Lord.

Part B   *God's Prized Possessions*   **Deuteronomy 26:12—28:6**
Today the Lord has obtained your agreement: to be his treasured people,
as he promised you, and to keep his commandments. 26:18

This verse contains a word in Hebrew that describes God's people as "special" to Him: *segullah.* Used only eight times in the Old Testament, the underlying meaning of this word is "treasure." God's people are God's prized possessions. The final reference in Malachi 3:17 refers to God's people as his "jewels."

In Matthew 6:10–22 Jesus urges us not to lay up treasures on earth, but in heaven. "Where you treasure is, there your heart will be also." You are God's treasure, held in God's heart. The heart of Jesus opened on the cross for you, remains open right now to love you. Jesus has already laid you up as a treasure in heaven.

Paul expresses it this way in Colossians 3:1–4, where we are encouraged to "seek those things which are above, where Christ is, sitting at the right hand of God. For you died, and your life is hidden with Christ in God."

Part C   *Son-Block*   **Deuteronomy 28:7—29:8**
The Lord will establish you as his holy people, as he has sworn to you,
if you keep the commandments of the Lord your God and walk in his ways. 28:9

Were you sunburned badly this past summer, saying to yourself: "I should have used sun block!" "Son block"—that is what Jesus is to the kinds of curses described in this reading. Rather than be frightened at the long list of woes that seem to outweigh the blessings, remember that when you are in Jesus, the Son blocks the effects of evil upon your life. If you walk outside of the ways of Jesus, outside of the protection that his Spirit gives, then rays of evil will fall on you mercilessly.

On the cross, Jesus completely exposed himself to the evil and hatred of the world. He "took the heat," so that you would not have to. In Galatians 3:13 we read: "Christ redeemed us from the curse of the law, by becoming a curse for us, for it is written: 'Cursed is everyone who is hung on a tree.'"

After each of the curses in the reading, add this comforting refrain: "If it weren't for Jesus …"

Portion 51ABC   *Nitsabim (Stand)*   Deut. 29:9—30:20

Choose Life

The word is very near to you; it is in your mouth
and in your heart for you to observe. 30:14

As this last book of Moses begins to draw to a close, sense in your heart the tender longing of God for us to respond in love and fidelity to the covenant God is offering. These are powerful closing chapters, read in their entirety every year in Jewish synagogues on the Sabbath.

Have your highlighter ready for 29:19. What consequences for not being faithful to the covenant!

One of my favorite passages in the whole Bible is 30:11–20. May you read it as though you are truly listening to this from the Lord as you and I, along with all God's people assembled, "Choose life."

It is the time of the beginning of the school year. Read this passage with your family as you rededicate yourselves to God's ways. The Holy Spirit is the master-teacher of your soul.

52ABC   *Vayelech (And He Went)*   Deuteronomy 31:1–30

The Fidelity of the Lord

Be strong and bold; have no fear or dread of them,
because it is the Lord your God who goes with you; he will not fail you or forsake you. 31:6

Here is one of those verses that gather the entire Bible into one, as though seeing all the heavens reflected in the tiny piece of a mirror.

The tradition of the Scribes begins with verse 9, after God commanded Moses to write down the law. The Hebrew word for write is *chatab,* which means to "inscribe" or "engrave" on some material such as sheepskin. Thus, the scriptures have been preserved for 3,000 years. Remember how Jesus stopped Satan in his tracks when he responded to the temptations in the desert with quotations from Deuteronomy saying: "It is written …" (Cf. Matthew 4:1–11.)

The chapter closes with the "passing of the torch" to Joshua, and the importance of the song of Moses that comes in the next chapter.

53ABC   *Haazinu (Give)*   Deuteronomy 32

The Song of Moses

Give ear, O heavens, and I will speak; let the earth hear the words of my mouth.
May my teaching drop like the rain, my speech condense like the dew;
like gentle rain on grass, like showers on new growth. vv. 1–2

This song was intended to fill the air from generation to generation. The image of a rock appears throughout. It tells what would happen if the people go after other gods and serve them. While the song expresses the anger of God, yet deeper still, it sings of the compassion of a God who continues to lure the people into fidelity and love.

The end of Moses is near. He is reminded that he will not be permitted to enter the Promised Land because he complained about the people in Numbers 20:11–13. He failed to acknowledge the goodness of the Lord giving water from the rock to the people.

As you hear this song in your heart with countless others "listening" to it this same day, what kinds of thoughts and feelings come to you? Write them down, so that you will remember.

The Final Blessing

*This portion, along with the first one in Genesis is read
at Simchat Torah, "The Joy of the Torah" at a celebration
at the end of the eight day festival of Tabernacles.*

**There is none like God, O Jeshurun, who rides through the heavens to your help,
majestic through the skies. 33:26**

Open your hand to receive God's abundant blessings poured out upon the tribes of Israel. God is faithful. All that is asked is acceptance of the covenant and to walk in God's ways; the Lord will provide all the safety and protection needed.

The verse for the day has the name "Jeshurun" as was also used in the Song of Moses in 32:15, found also in Isaiah 44:2. It is a nickname for Israel, a term of endearment for God's people.

Moses dies on Mount Nebo. Read with awe, the death of this great man of God. Be moved with the grief of the people. Joshua is ready. Find comfort in the One who would be the prophet-like-Moses to come, whom God knew face to face as Father and Son.

With this passage, we join Jewish people as they rejoice at completing the cycle of readings from the Torah.

ARTICLES

Weaving the Word

Regular Bible reading is like knitting or embroidering; design and commitment are needed. The word "text" means, "to weave." Those who knit or embroider first began with a plan. There was that first pair of booties … There was a goal. So it is with weaving God's Word into life. Deliberate, intentional plans need to be made and daily dedication. In time God's Word will become the center design in the fabric of life.

Here are a few suggestions to build the habit of reading the Bible daily. Begin by praying for the inspiration of the Holy Spirit. Read the *Firestarter* and the passage. As you read, lightly draw a vertical line in pencil in your Bible near the verses or sections of the reading that attract your attention in a special way. This is the Holy Spirit moving in you. If you have your Bible nearby throughout the day, you can quickly refer to the reading. In this way, even brief moments of transition can become pauses that refresh and renew your day with the Word.

I find it helpful to look over the reading the evening before. In this way, a spiritual momentum will carry you into the night—perhaps through your dreams—to the waking day. If a day has several chapters, see if you can pray them in the morning, afternoon and evening. Take the passage and key verses of it as God's way of being with you that day. What rises from the page of the Bible as key issues in your life? How are you challenged to live your life as a disciple of Jesus? By being creative with your devotion to the Bible, a sacred context will be forming itself in your life, shared with many others joining you on the journey. A habit will take shape like morning coffee. If you miss a day … no bother; no need to catch up; the reading will return again in three years. This is "guiltless" Bible reading! It is not about making a project out of reading the whole Bible—feeling badly, if you fail. Rather than "covering" the Bible, the Bible will "cover" you, protecting you as the shadow of God's wings.

As you read the daily passage, be on the lookout for a small part of it that could be used as a time of devotion with members of your family or small group. The plan can enrich the spiritual lives of couples as they seek to allow God's Word to direct their lives. Sharing the three-year journey with at least one other person deepens the experience. Spiritual conversations, and what John Wesley calls "Holy Conferencing" will take place. When you are talking with another, you might describe the reading as a story in your own words and share what the reading means for you.

There is an ancient method of prayer, which takes brief phrases of seven syllables and blends them with breath—three syllables on the inhale, three on the exhale and one syllable for rest. Without necessarily being so strict, you can create what I call **Bible Breaths**, prayer-phrases or sentences that catch the main points of the daily reading. They have two parts made up of a few syllables for inhales and exhales. For example: [inhale] *You, O Lord—* [exhale] *are my shepherd.* We use the phrase, "Take a breather" when there's need to stop the pace of life for a moment. The article "Timescaping" expands on this theme.

I encourage you to keep a **Bible Journal**. God can speak to your heart by using the hand that holds your pen! It is a way to listen to God. The same Holy Spirit that was at work in the sacred writers of the books of the Bible is at work inspiring you. Various helpful formats such as a three-ring binder with pages correspond to the daily readings of the week. Smaller notebooks may be preferred—perhaps one for each of the twelve seasons across the three years. I recommend keeping a separate page for each day of the week, as well as a separate section or notebook for the *Torah* readings since these do not occur in the same weeks every year. By using the abbreviations found on the tags at the edge of each week and for the *Torah* readings, it will be easy to find your own notes on a given day of any week. For example, a separate page for *Mon. 3PeB* offers space for you to take notes on the reading for that day, Hosea 3—4. Include the current date just below the days of the sacred week or the *Torah* passage. When you return to these pages in your journal, you will be gazing at how that particular passage blended with your life three years ago. If you are faithful to this discipline, you will be creating your own, personal Bible journal that will bear the imprint of the Holy Spirit on your soul for the rest of your life.

As an added feature, object lessons called "Alphabytes" begin each week, following the alphabet two times each year. From A to Z, you will sense the movement of the year. These are found at the beginning of each of the seasons in Year A.

One more suggestion: I use seven 1-inch removable tabs or small post-it notes placed at the pages of my Bible that correspond to the readings for those days. This makes it easy to turn to all the readings of a given week. Either one of two ways is suggested:

1. Print the names of the parts of the Bible on the tabs or notes and place them descending from the top to the bottom corners of your Bible on the pages of the current reading for each book in the order in which they occur in the Bible, e.g., TORAH • WRITINGS • PSALMS • PROPHETS • GOSPEL-SUN • GOSPEL-FRI • NEW TESTAMENT or,

2. Print the days of the week and simply have them positioned from Sunday to Saturday descending from the top to the bottom corners of your Bible at the particular pages of the parts of the Bible to which the days of the week are dedicated.

The website **BibleThroughSeasons.com** will offer ongoing articles and resources along with a link to "Wesley Without Walls," an internet sharing group for those following the plan. I will be with you every step of the way, as long as God wills. One day at a time we will be bonded together in common passages from the Bible, weaving themselves year after year. The Bible text will become the Bible "texture" and context of life. Then there will come a future season when you and I will simply step into eternal communion with the Word in the Kingdom of heaven.

Timescaping

So much time, dedication and money goes into landscaping. The area about homes is shaped, manicured, studded with rocks, plants, bushes, flowers and trees so as to portray something of the feeling and the beauty of the family inside. It is a family's space; it is precious. Why not do to *time* what landscaping does to *space*? Space and time are so similar.

On New Year's Eve, we count down the minutes before 12 Midnight because a new year of life is about to begins. I invite you to let go of each quarter-part of the day and take hold of the next three-hour period with something of that New Year's Eve feeling of saying good-bye to the Old and greeting the New. You might even catch the shift of each hour. Listen to the gentle "beep" of your watch, or the chime of a clock. Step back from however the day is going—intense and stressful, or peaceful and serene. As the cock crowing for Peter, the ancient "chiming" of time, we can get in touch with the deepest call in life, give thanks for this call, and repent for failing and falling in it, as happened to Peter. Such awareness can disengage us from the compulsions that often characterize the passing of our hours. Similar to moving across the boundaries of a state or country, a new feel to life begins as we enter a new space of time.

The quarter parts of your day can be transformed by the colors, the tones, the energy of God's presence to you through the daily reading offered. Five of these waking quarter-parts of the day begin with 6, 9, 12, 3, and 6.

If you have a dear friend whom you have not seen in many years and suddenly his or her face appears with a glowing smile before you, you rush to each other and embrace. There goes any bad mood! In an instant, obsessive thoughts and worries are gone. How long did it take Peter to experience that scratch on his soul when the rooster crowed? Instantly. In a second the transmission of your car changes from one gear to the next. Were it not for that second, you would stay stuck in one gear. As suggested in the article, "Weaving the Word," *Bible Breaths* can be way of sensing a visit from God to refresh and transform the day. Read each part of your day through the lens of the Word. Take a moment at the transitions of the day and do Adoration, Contrition, Thanksgiving, Supplication.

Another method used for centuries, though rising in interest in modern times, is "Mindmapping." This is a non-linear, right brain way of clustering ideas, images and themes flowing out from a central word or image, placed in the center of a page. Page 447, "Resources," has a valuable reference; there are many sites on the internet as well

Loosen the ground … loosen the heart. Let the Word fall freely and deeply into the prepared plot of ground, which is your heart. Landscape your heart … "timescape" it. Stand where you are and enjoy the gifts of the garden. Know that the face of the Lord—as the face of time—smiles back at you and winks lovingly at every moment … when you turn and look.

Bible Study Through the Seasons

The arrangement of the sacred books in *The Bible Through the Seasons* provides many formats for group Bible Study.

Weekly Study Groups

- Short-term Bible Study of several weeks at the beginning of a new season, with option to continue further
- Thirteen-week studies of a complete season
- Focus on one of the books of a particular season.

Bands

A small group of two or more persons committed to the journey who share regularly throughout the week such as personal meetings, phone conversations, and e-mails. Such a group may agree to meet for a monthly overnight retreat, spending twenty-four hours together, after the inspiration of the *Jesus Caritas* movement.

Family Bible Time

Select a portion of the daily reading suitable for children. The author is preparing a special edition of *The Bible Through the Seasons* for families with *Firestarters* suited for young people. Go to BibleThroughSeasons.com for the latest information about this project.

Wesley Without Walls

A website managed by the author for those following the plan. Members post messages coming from personal experiences with the daily readings. Follow the link at BibleThroughSeasons.com.

The group leader guides the process; he or she is not the one to whom the members turn for answers to questions. Resources such as those listed at the end of this book can be on hand to respond to questions of participants.

The "tools" for the study are the Bible itself and the journals of the participants. The familiar greeting, "Well, how was your week?" has responses that come from the spiritual depths of a person. The journal is a constant reminder of those moments in a week when God speaks to the heart. Much of the session of an hour or an hour and half, for example, can be filled with participants witnessing to the movements of God, sharing struggles, temptations and challenges with respect to being a more faithful disciple. Such a group will be a powerful support as members encourage one another, and offer prayers of intercession for themselves and others.

This plan is complementary to the widely acclaimed *Disciple: Become Disciples Through Bible Study* (Abingdon Press, 1993). Those who have completed this thirty-four week study will find *The Bible Through the Seasons* to be an ongoing way to deepen daily contact with the Word in a covenant group.

Solar and Sacred Seasons

The weeks of the year unfold through the four seasons. While solar seasons are reversed in the northern and southern hemispheres, the origins of sacred seasons were set from Biblical times from the time of the Exodus. For example, the command to celebrate Passover in springtime assumes a northern hemisphere setting. In *The Bible Through the Seasons* the entire Bible flows through the seasons every three years with passages sensitive to the sacred seasons. References to the solar seasons are limited, so that the plan will be suitable for God's people in the southern hemisphere.

This approach incorporates the traditional sacred names for the seasons and the counting of Sundays, while suggesting some changes for ease in using the three-year cycle of daily readings. The widespread use of *The Revised Common Lectionary* for Sunday worship also urges a method of naming Sundays consistent with the structure of the *Lectionary*.

Advent to Epiphany
(Winter in the Northern Hemisphere)

Each of the four seasons is a quarter of a year with a norm of thirteen weeks. The four Sundays of Advent begin on the Sunday nearest November 30, the traditional date for St. Andrew's day. Next there is Christmas Week, occurring on or after Christmas Day. The first Sunday in January is celebrated as Epiphany Sunday, the traditional date being January 6. There are from ten to fifteen weeks in *Advent to Epiphany*, depending on the date of Easter. The week when Ash Wednesday occurs is the Last Week in Epiphany, beginning with Transfiguration Sunday.

Lent and Easter
(Spring in the Northern Hemisphere)

The Council of Nicea in 325 A.D. decreed that Easter would occur on the first Sunday after the first full moon after the vernal equinox. According to lunar variation, there is about a month's range of dates for Easter, from March 22 to April 25. *Lent* begins six weeks before Easter. Ash Wednesday was introduced in the 7th century, adding four days before the First Sunday in Lent, to make forty days of fasting for the weekdays of Lent. (Fasting was not observed on Sundays.) There are seven weeks in *Easter*. The total number of weeks in *Lent and Easter* is always thirteen.

Winter *Advent to Epiphany*		Spring *← Lent and Easter →*		Summer *Pentecost*	Autumn *Kingdomtide*

Depending upon the date of Easter, the season of *Lent and Easter* moves back and forth across the end of *Advent to Epiphany* and the beginning of the season of *Pentecost*. The mid-range of the date of Easter (April 10 to 16) results in all four seasons being thirteen weeks long. When an early Easter shortens *Epiphany* by one or two weeks (very rarely three), then *Pentecost* is lengthened by the corresponding number of weeks. In this case, the weeks at the end of *Epiphany* "leap ahead" as extra weeks needed at the beginning of *Pentecost*. When a late Easter lengthens *Epiphany* by a week (rarely two), then *Pentecost* is shortened by the corresponding week at the beginning which "leaps back" to the end of *Epiphany* and is added as an extra week.

435

Adjustments to the Seasons of Epiphany and Pentecost

Dates of Easter	Epiphany 8 Weeks + or − at the end	Pentecost 13 Weeks + or − at the beginning
From March 22 to 26 (Only occurs 6 times in the 21st Century)	−3	+3
From March 27 to Apr 2	−2	+2
From April 3 to 9	−1	1
From April 10 to 16	0	0
From April 17 to 23	+1	−1
From April 24 to 25 (Only occurs 2 times in the 21st Century)	+2	−2

Note: Every five or six years there are fifty-three weeks in the church calendar. This occurs when Christmas is on a Sunday or on a Saturday when the following year is a leap year. In those years, there is an extra week added to the Sundays after Epiphany. For the first half of the 21st century, they are as follows: '06, '12, '17, '23, '28, '34, '40, '45, and '50.

Pentecost
(Summer in the Northern Hemisphere)

Pentecost Sunday has its origins in the Jewish celebration of *Shavout*, also called "Pentecost"—fifty days after Passover. From the earliest centuries in the Christian calendar, Sundays after Pentecost were given ordinal numbers for counting—so many "Sundays after Pentecost."

The origins of the *Lectionary* date from 1969 when the Roman Catholic Church developed the *Lectionary for Mass*—the greatest revision of the Scriptures used in the Catholic Church since 1570! In order to free this half-year period of Sundays after Pentecost from being bound to a lunar, Easter reference, a new term was introduced for this time as well as for the time after Epiphany. They were called "Sundays in Ordinary Time." With the exception of the Sundays in Lent and Easter, these were based every year on a Sunday nearest a fixed date.

Many Protestant churches soon heralded this new arrangement of readings for worship. Though some changes were made in the selection of the first readings from the Hebrew Scriptures, the New Testament and Gospel selections were retained. The result was *The Revised Common Lectionary*. Many churches simply continue to name "Sundays after Pentecost" for purposes of worship. Though the term "ordinary" refers to the counting of Sundays as "ordinal" numbers, the common sense of the term "ordinary" naturally prevails. Yet time with God is anything but *ordinary*!

The Bible Through the Seasons follows the basic weekly design of the *Lectionary*; the Sunday readings are taken from that sequence. However, the following system is offered as a way to continue honoring the traditional sacred name of *Pentecost* as a season after *Lent and Easter*, without linking the numbering of the Sundays to those "after" Pentecost Sunday. Here is how it works.

With the exception of *Lent and Easter*, a fixed, solar frame of reference is provided for the remaining three seasons. The Sunday nearest June 1 is named *The First Sunday in Pentecost*. Rather than say that a Sunday is "after" Pentecost Sunday, which varies from year to year, we simply say that it is a Sunday "in" the season of Pentecost. Thus, except for some minor changes at the end of *Epiphany* and the beginning of *Pentecost* as noted above, the numbering of the Sundays in these seasons is the same for every year, since they relate to a Sunday nearest a fixed date. The last week in *Pentecost* is always the thirteenth, followed by the season of *Kingdomtide*, as explained below. By adopting this system of names, every Sunday in the year is given a liturgical name linked with the *Lectionary* readings. Rather than use the propositions "after" or "of", the common use of "in" makes for consistency. With these adjustments, an easy-to-use structure is offered for the daily lectionary, which is *The Bible Through the Seasons*.

Kingdomtide
(Autumn in the Northern Hemisphere)

The name "Kingdomtide" was introduced in 1937 by the former Federal Council of Churches as a way of dividing in half the traditionally long, six-month period of the time after Pentecost Sunday. *The Book of Worship for Church and Home* published in 1965 for The United Methodist Church indicates that the season begins on the last Sunday in August—a period of thirteen or fourteen weeks; again, variation versus constancy. *The Bible Through the Seasons* proposes that this season begin on the Sunday nearest August 31. It is always thirteen weeks long. The last Sunday is named *Christ the King Sunday*. The following Sunday begins *The First Week in Advent* in the next year in the cycle.

The Trinity in the Year

The presence of the Blessed Trinity is reflected throughout the Church year. While all the persons of the Trinity act together, it is appropriate to honor a special sense of the activity of the Father in the first season, *Advent to Epiphany*. The second season, *Lent and Easter*, expresses in a unique way the saving acts of Jesus in his death and Resurrection. The third season, *Pentecost*, celebrates the third person of the Trinity, the Holy Spirit outpoured after the Ascension of Jesus. The fourth season, Kingdomtide, is the season of fulfillment and harvest in which the nature of the Kingdom of God is celebrated in a special manner.

Living the Bible

Living the Bible through the seasons is enhanced by the following progression associated with the sacred seasons:

Advent: *Coming*   Lent: *Journey to the Cross*
Christmas: *Presence*   Easter: *The Risen Body of Christ*
Epiphany: *Manifestation*   Pentecost: *The Indwelling Holy Spirit*
                                   Kingdomtide: *The Kingdom of God Now*

New Meaning for the Days of the Week

One day of the week feeling like another—we all relate to this experience from time to time. "Today feels like a Sunday," even though it may be a Friday. We live in time frames of hours, days, weeks and seasons with affective connotations. Try singing a Christmas carol in summer!

The names of the week in English come from the seven known planets in Roman times with their Nordic equivalents on Tiw, Woden, Thor, and Frige. Beyond pagan deities, *The Bible Through the Seasons* intentionally offers a new feeling and meaning for the days of the week derived from the parts of the Bible to which each day is dedicated.

In the Transfiguration of Jesus, Moses was on one side and Elijah on the other, the Law and the Prophets, with Jesus in the middle. On either side of Sunday, the Lord's Day, are the Law (Torah) on Saturday, and the Prophets on Monday. The days of the week, as a symphony, have movements and progressions to them.

Through the Psalms, Wednesday, the day in the middle of the week, becomes the day of transition from the Hebrew Scriptures on Monday and Tuesday, to the New Testament on Thursdays and Fridays. Wednesday of Holy Week is sometimes called "Spy Wednesday," the day when Judas and the religious leaders were plotting against Jesus. It is the day in the midst of the workweek that reminds us of the plotting for gain and the often betrayal of others in one form or another. Work is sometimes at fever pitch, whether it's a Wall-Street kind of fever of increasing profits, or the actual fevers of migrant farm workers harvesting for the food industry. Such workers harvest little income for themselves! Judaism, Christianity, and Islam all look to the psalms as one of the places where we can pray together in the common covenant that God began with us through Abraham. We pray with a consciousness of the whole world community. The prayer of the church from the earliest centuries of the monastic movement had the psalms as central to the cries to God on behalf of the human family. One of these cries is that religious tensions that pull us apart, may come to a deeper and more lasting union.

Holy Thursday, sometimes called Maundy Thursday, recalls the Last Supper, Holy Communion and the Washing of the Feet. The words of Jesus narrated in all the Gospels, especially in John, unfold the reaching out of God in Christ to form an intimate relation with us. This gift of divine friendship survives the rupture of Calvary by the resurrection. Thursday's dedication to the New Testament in the Book of Acts, the Letters and the Book of Revelation, further the feeling that every Thursday can be a Holy Thursday.

Friday, the day of Jesus' offering on the cross, is dedicated to the entire texts of the four Gospels. Saturday, the Sabbath, invites us to recall the gift of God's self-revelation to our ancestors in the wilderness by honoring a day of rest and renewal with dependence upon God alone. Even though this has been transferred to Sunday for Christians because of the resurrection, still, solidarity with our Jewish sisters and brothers can transform the secular "weekend" into two days of reverent rededication to the gift of creation. On the Sabbath, we rest; on Sunday, we prepare to return to co-operating with God in the New Creation, which is Christ's risen body, the church.

Seasons, solar and sacred: may this plan which God has placed on my heart, be realized in yours and many others as well. May we grow each day in the sacred context that the Bible offers to our lives.

A Heavenly City Comes to Earth

The city of Jerusalem has been the object of conflict for three thousand years. It has been tugged at by three related, but unfortunately often viciously separated religious traditions—Hebrew, Christian and Moslem. We have behaved as three siblings at violent odds with each other, continuing the anger and jealousy of our oldest brother, Cain. At present, Jerusalem is like a square on a chessboard with two players claiming the right to occupy the same square at the same time.

Is there a way out? A resolution must transcend geography, nations and lands. Knitted eyes of anger and hands filled with violence need to change to eyes lifted upward and hands joined together. The one Creator of the heavens, the earth and each one of us, in whom we claim to believe, calls us beyond separateness to a new unity.

All religions are exiled in one form or another. We live in Diaspora, the condition of being scattered across the globe, hungry for a sacred piece of land that we can call home and it evades all of us.

The solution lies in the common sky that embraces us. A new and heavenly city is descending upon us, described in the final promise of the Bible in the Book of Revelation. May we discover this holy city, a spiritual home whose center is the heart of every human being where the Holy Spirit groans in prayer. For Jesus, this new city is the Kingdom of God. There may we live in justice, peace and great love.

Perpetual Calendar of the Church Year

Solar seasons are reversed in the Southern Hemisphere.

Winter

Except for the Sundays in January, each week begins on the Sunday nearest the date in the bottom row.

One to three shaded weeks are omitted and added to the beginning of the season of Pentecost when Easter is early.

Advent					Epiphany							
1st	2nd	3rd	4th	Christmas Week	Epiphany	2nd	3rd	4th	5th	6th	7th	8th
Nov. 30	Dec. 7	Dec. 14	Dec. 21	Dec. 28	1st Sun. Jan.	2nd Sun. Jan.	3rd Sun. Jan.	4th Sun. Jan.	Feb. 1	Feb. 8	Feb. 15	Feb. 22

Spring

The weeks take their reference from the date of Easter. Include "Easter" when reading "before" and "after."

Lent						Easter						
1st	2nd	3rd	4th	5th	Holy Week	Easter Week	2nd	3rd	4th	5th	6th	7th
6 wks before	5 wks before	4 wks before	3 wks before	2 wks before	1 wk before	Easter	1 wk after	2 wks after	3 wks after	4 wks after	5 wks after	6 wks after

Summer

Each week begins on the Sunday nearest the date in the bottom row. One or two shaded weeks are sometimes omitted, having been added to the end of the season of Epiphany when Easter is late. The counting of the Sundays is "in" the season of Pentecost, not "after" Pentecost Sunday.

Pentecost

1st	2nd	3rd	4th	5th	6th	7th	8th	9th	10th	11th	12th	13th
June 1	June 8	June 15	June 22	June 29	July 6	July 13	July 20	July 27	Aug. 3	Aug. 10	Aug. 17	Aug. 24

Autumn

Each week begins on the Sunday nearest the date in the bottom row.

Kingdomtide

1st	2nd	3rd	4th	5th	6th	7th	8th	9th	10th	11th	12th	Christ the King
Aug. 31	Sept. 7	Sept. 14	Sept. 21	Sept. 28	Oct. 5	Oct. 12	Oct. 19	Oct. 26	Nov. 2	Nov. 9	Nov. 16	Nov. 23

441

The Books of the Bible by the Seasons—ld Testament

The Books from Genesis to Deuteronomy are in sequence in the *Torah* Supplement. See also the Table of *Torah* Readings.

History and Writings: Tuesdays		Week In the Season
Joshua		1 Ad – 5 Ep A
Judges		1 Ad – 5 Ep B
Ruth		1 — 4 Ad C
1 Samuel		3 – 13 Pe A
2 Samuel		3 – 12 Ki A
1 Kings		3 – 13 Pe B
2 Kings		3 – 13 Ki B
1 Chron		4 – 13 Pe C
2 Chron		3 – 13 Ki C
Ezra		4 – 7 Ea B
Nehemiah		4 – 7 Ea C
Esther		CW – 5 Ep C
J O B	1—14	1 – 5 Le A
	15—21	1 – 4 Le B
	22—37	1 – 5 Le C
	38	HW A
	39—40	5 Le – HW B
	41-42	HW C
P R O V E R B S	1—3	6 – 8 Ep A
	4—6	6 – 8 Ep B
	7—9	6 – 8 Ep C
	10—12	1 – 3 Ea A
	13—14	1 – 2 Pe A
	15—16	1 – 2 Ki A
	17—19	1 – 3 Ea B
	20—21	1 – 2 Pe B
	22—23	1 – 2 Ki B
	24—26	1 – 3 Ea C
	27—29	1 – 3 Pe C
	30—32	1 – 2 Ki C
Eccle	1—4	13 Ki A
	5—8	13 Ki B
	9—12	13 Ki C
Song of Songs		4 – 7 Ea A

Psalms: Wednes.	Week in the Season
1—13	1 Ad – 8 Ep A
14—21	HW – 7 Ea A
22—34	1 – 13 Pe A
35—47	1 – 13 Ki A
48—60	1 Ad – 8 Ep B
61—68	HW – 7 Ea B
69—81	1 - 13 Pe B
82—94	1 – 13 Ki B
95—107	1 Ad – 8 Ep C
108	HW C
109—118	1 – 10 Pe C
119	1 – 7 Ea C
120—124	1 – 5 Le A
125—129	1 – 5 Le B
130—134	1 – 5 Le B
135—137	11 – 13 Pe C
138—150	1 – 13 Ki C

Proph-Mon		Week in the Season
I S A	1—12	1 Ad – 8 Ep A
	13—27	1 – 13 Pe A
	28—39	1 – 13 Ki A
	40—55	1 Ad – 8 Ep B
	56—66	1 Ad – 8 Ep C
J E R	1—17	1 Le – HW A
	18—35	1 Le – HW B
	36—52	1 Le – HW C
L A M	1—2	9 Pe A
	3	9 Pe B
	4—5	9 Pe C
E Z	1—16	1 – 7 Ea A
	17—32	1 – 7 Ea B
	33—48	1 – 7 Ea C
Daniel		1 – 13 Ki B
Hosea		1 – 13 Pe B
Joel		1 Pe C
Amos		2 – 5 Pe C
Obadiah		7 Pe C
Jonah		8 – 9 Pe C
Micah		10 – 12 Pe C
Nahum		13 Pe C
Habakkuk		1 Ki C
Zephaniah		2 Ki C
Haggai		3 Ki C
Zechariah		4 – 10 Ki C
Malachi		11 – 13 Ki C

The Books of the Bible by the Seasons—New Testament

Gospels (Lection.) Sundays	Week in the Season
Matthew	Ad-Ep, Pe, Ki A
Mark	Ad-Ep, Pe, Ki B
Luke	Ad-Ep, Pe, Ki C
John	Le-Ea ABC

	Gospels: Fridays	Week in the Season
M A T T	1—7	CW – 8 Ep A
	6:1—18:35	1 – 13 Pe A
	19—28	1 – 13 Ki A
M A R K	1—3	1 – 8 Ep B
	4—9	1 – 13 Pe B
	10—16	1 – 13 Ki B
L U K E	1	1 – 3 Ad ABC
	2:1-20	4 Ad AB
	2:21-40	CW C
	2:41-52	1 Ep C
	3—8	2 – 8 Ep C
	9:1—19:27	1 – 13 Pe C
	19:28—24:53	1 – 13 Ki C
J O H N	1:1-18	4 Ad C
	1—2; 4—5	1 – 5 Le A
	3, 6, 10	1 – 7 Ea A
	7—9	1 – 5 Le B
	14—17	1 – 7 Ea B
	18—19	HW ABC
	11—13	1 – 5 Le C
	20—21	1 – 7 Ea C

	New Testament: Thursdays	Week in the Season
A C T S	1—9	1 – 7 Ea A
	10:1—18:22	1 – 7 Ea B
	18:23—28:31	1 – 7 Ea C
	Romans	1 – 13 Pe A
	1 Corinthians	1 – 11 Ki A
	2 Corinthians	1 – 13 Pe C
	Galatians	CW – 5 Ep A
	Ephesians	1 – 5 Le A
	Philippians	6 – 8 Ep A
	Colossians	1 – 5 Le B
	1 Thessalonians	1 – 5 Ki B
	2 Thessalonians	6 – 8 Ki B
	1 Timothy	1 – 3 Pe C
	2 Timothy	1 – 3 Ki C
	Titus	1 – 3 Ad A
	Philemon	4 Ad A
	Hebrews	4 – 13 Pe C
	James	1 – 5 Le C
	1 Peter	1 Ad – 4 Ep C
	2 Peter	5 – 8 Ep C
	1 John	1 Ad – 5 Ep B
	2 John	6 Ep B
	3 John	7 Ep B
	Jude	8 Ep B
R E V	1—3	12 – 13 Ki A
	4:1—11:18	9 – 13 Ki B
	11:19—22:21	4 – 13 Ki C

Abbreviations for the Seasons
These correspond to the tabs occurring on each page of the *Firestarters*.
Ad-Advent; Ep-Epiphany; Le-Lent; Ea-Easter; Pe-Pentecost; Ki-Kingdomtide

Names of Sundays Corresponding to Lectionary-Based Church Years

The Bible Through the Seasons (BTS)
The Revised Common Lectionary (RCL)
The Lectionary for Mass (LFM)

Advent to Epiphany

The Sunday...	The Bible Through the Seasons	The Revised Common Lectionary Proper #	Lectionary For Mass (Roman Catholic) Numbered Sunday are those in "Ordinary Time"
Nearest Nov. 30	The First Sunday in Advent		
Nearest Dec. 7	The Second Sunday in Advent		
Nearest Dec. 14	The Third Sunday in Advent		
Nearest Dec. 21	The Fourth Sunday in Advent		
Nearest Dec. 28	Sun. on or after Christmas.	1st Sun. after Christmas [1]	1st Sun. after Christmas
1st Sun. in Jan.	Epiphany Sunday	2nd Sun. after Christmas [1]	2nd Sun. after Christmas
2nd Sun. in Jan.	2nd Sun. in Epiph Baptism of the Lord	Sun. after Epiphany Baptism of the Lord [1]	Sun. after Epiphany Baptism of the Lord
3rd Sun. in Jan.	3rd Sun. in Epiph	3rd Sun. aft. Epiph [1]	2nd Sun. in Ord. Time
4th Sun. in Jan.	4th Sun. in Epiph	2nd Sun. aft. Epiph [1]	3rd Sun. in Ord. Time
Nearest Feb. 1	5th Sun. in Epiph	4th Sun. aft. Epiph [1]	4th Sun. in Ord. Time
Nearest Feb. 8 [2]	6th Sun. in Epiph	5th Sun. aft. Epiph [1]	5th Sun. in Ord. Time
Nearest Feb. 15 [2]	7th Sun. in Epiph	6th Sun. aft. Epiph [1,2]	6th Sun. in Ord. Time [2]
Nearest Feb. 22 [2]	8th Sun. in Epiph	7th Sun. aft. Epiph [1,2]	7th Sun. in Ord. Time [2]
Nearest Mar. 1 (Leap Yr, Feb. 29) [2]	9th Sun. in Epiph	8th Sun. aft. Epiph [1,2]	8th Sun. in Ord. Time [2]
Last Sunday in Epiphany	Transfiguration of the Lord		9th Sun. in Ord. Time [2]

1   The first Sunday of the year may be celebrated as "Epiphany Sunday." However, if the first Sunday is Jan. 7, since the traditional date of Epiphany, Jan. 6, is the day before, this first Sunday becomes "The Baptism of Jesus." In *The Bible Through the Seasons* the first Sunday of the year is always "Epiphany Sunday," thus being one week behind the Gospel from *The Revised Common Lectionary* and the Roman Catholic *Lectionary for Mass* in those years.

2   Unless Lent has begun. In this case, those weeks omitted due to the beginning of Lent leap ahead to the beginning week(s) after Pentecost Sunday.

Lent and Easter

The naming of the Sundays in Lent and Easter is identical in the three systems. In order to be consistent throughout all the seasons, *The Bible Through the Seasons* prefers to use the preposition "in" rather than "of" or "after," since "in" provides a common way of naming a Sunday in any season.

Pentecost   Kingdomtime

Sunday Nearest...	BTS Sundays in Pentecost	RCL Proper #	LFM Sundays in Ordinary Time	Sunday Nearest...	BTS Sundays in Pentecost	RCL Proper #	LFM Sundays in Ordinary Time
N/A	Pentecost Sunday			Aug 31	1st	17	22nd
	Trinity Sunday			Sep. 7	2nd	18	23rd
June 1 [4]	1st	4 [4-5]	9th [4]	Sep. 14	3rd	19	24th
June 8 [4]	2nd	5 [4]	10th [4]	Sep. 21	4th	20	25th
Jun. 15	3rd	6	11th	Sep. 28	5th	21	26th
June 22	4th	7	12th	Oct. 5	6th	22	27th
June 29	5th	8	13th	Oct. 12	7th	23	28th
July 6	6th	9	14th	Oct. 19	8th	24	29th
July 13	7th	10	15th	Oct. 26	9th	25	30th
July 20	8th	11	16th	Nov. 2	10th	26	31st
July 27	9th	12	17th	Nov 9	11th	27	32nd
Aug. 3	10th	13	18th	Nov. 16	12th	28	33rd
Aug. 10	11th	14	19th	Nov. 23	13th	29	34th
Aug. 17	12th	15	20th				
Aug. 24	13th	16	21st				

4   One or two of these weeks may be omitted if the Easter season is still in effect. In this case, these weeks leapt back to the end of Epiphany which was needed to fill in for needed weeks before Lent begins. For the Proper Number, add 3 to the Sunday in Pentecost; for the Sunday in Ordinary in the Roman Catholic *Lectionary for Mass*, add 8 to the Sunday in Pentecost.

5   For worship services, the church year designation for those using *The Revised Common Lectionary* is counted "after" Pentecost Sunday. The term "Proper" with a number identifies a particular sequence of readings for a Sunday nearest a fixed date. Again, in *The Bible Through the Seasons* the term "in" is used to refer to a Sunday "in" Pentecost, named as a season, rather than a Sunday "after" Pentecost Sunday itself.

Dates of Easter and Cycle Letters
For the Twenty-first Century

Year		Easter	Year		Easter	Year		Easter	Year		Easter
2001	C	Apr. 15	2026	A	Apr. 5	2051	B	Apr. 2	2076	C	Apr. 19
2002	A	Mar. 31	2027	B	Mar. 28	2052	C	Apr. 21	2077	A	Apr. 11
2003	B	Apr. 20	2028*	C	Apr. 16	2053	A	Apr. 6	2078*	B	Apr. 3
2004	C	Apr. 11	2029	A	Apr. 1	2054	B	Mar. 29	2079	C	Apr. 23
2005	A	Mar. 27	2030	B	Apr. 21	2055	C	Apr. 18	2080	A	Apr. 7
2006*	B	Apr. 16	2031	C	Apr. 13	2056*	A	Apr. 2	2081	B	Mar. 30
2007	C	Apr. 8	2032	A	Mar. 28	2057	B	Apr. 22	2082	C	Apr. 19
2008	A	Mar. 23	2033	B	Apr. 17	2058	C	Apr. 14	2083	A	Apr. 4
2009	B	Apr. 12	2034*	C	Apr. 9	2059	A	Mar. 30	2084*	B	Mar. 26
2010	C	Apr. 4	2035	A	Mar. 25	2060	B	Apr. 18	2085	C	Apr. 15
2011	A	Apr. 24	2036	B	Apr. 13	2061	C	Apr. 10	2086	A	Mar. 31
2012*	B	Apr. 8	2037	C	Apr. 5	2062*	A	Mar. 26	2087	B	Apr. 20
2013	C	Mar. 31	2038	A	Apr. 25	2063	B	Apr. 15	2088	C	Apr. 11
2014	A	Apr. 20	2039	B	Apr. 10	2064	C	Apr. 6	2089	A	Apr. 3
2015	B	Apr. 5	2040*	C	Apr. 1	2065	A	Mar. 29	2090*	B	Apr. 16
2016	C	Mar. 27	2041	A	Apr. 21	2066	B	Apr. 11	2091	C	Apr. 8
2017*	A	Apr. 16	2042	B	Apr. 6	2067	C	Apr. 3	2092	A	Mar. 30
2018	B	Apr. 1	2043	C	Mar. 29	2068*	A	Apr. 22	2093	B	Apr. 12
2019	C	Apr. 21	2044	A	Apr. 17	2069	B	Apr. 14	2094	C	Apr. 4
2020	A	Apr. 12	2045*	B	Apr. 9	2070	C	Mar. 30	2095	A	Apr. 24
2021	B	Apr. 4	2046	C	Mar. 25	2071	A	Apr. 19	2096*	B	Apr. 15
2022	C	Apr. 17	2047	A	Apr. 14	2072	B	Apr. 10	2097	C	Mar. 31
2023*	A	Apr. 9	2048	B	Apr. 5	2073*	C	Mar. 26	2098	A	Apr. 20
2024	B	Mar. 31	2049	C	Apr. 18	2074	A	Apr. 15	2099	B	Apr. 12
2025	C	Apr. 20	2050*	A	Apr. 10	2075	B	Apr. 7	2100	C	Mar. 28

* Every five or six years there are fifty-three weeks in the church calendar. This occurs when Christmas is on a Sunday or on a Saturday when the following year is a leap year. In those years, there is an extra week added to the Sundays after Epiphany.

RESOURCES

Resources for Bible study and the history of God's people are so vast, that they cannot be adequately listed here. I offer, however, these books and websites that would be especially helpful for those following this plan for reading the Bible and aids in creative writing.

Books

Atwan, Robert and Laurance Wieder. *Chapters into Verse: Poetry in English. Volume I: Genesis to Malachi; Volume II: Gospels to Revelation.* Oxford Univ. Press. 1993.

Complete Guide to the Bible. Reader's Digest Association, 1997.

Cross, F. L. and E. A. Livingstone. *The Oxford Dictionary of the Christian Church.* Oxford University Press. 1983

Day, A. Colin. *Roget's Thesaurus of the Bible.* Harper, San Francisco, 1992

Go-Anywhere Bible. HarperSanFrancisco, 2007

Illustrated Dictionary of Bible Life and Times, Reader's Digest Association, 1997.

Kimbrough, S.T., Jr. and Oliver A. Beckerlegge, ed. *The Unpublished Poetry of Charles Wesley. Volume I: Hymns and Poems for Church and World; Volume II: Hymns and Poems on Holy Scripture.*

Metzger, Bruce M., and Michael D. Coogan, ed. *The Oxford Companion to the Bible.* Oxford Univeristy Press. 1993

Wycoff, Joyce. *Mindmapping: Your Personal Guide to Exploring Creativity and Problem-Solving. The Berkley Publishing Group, 1991.*

The Revised Common Lectionary: Consultation on Common Texts. Abingdon, 1992

The New Interpreter's Bible: A Commentary in Twelve Volumes. Abingdon, 1994.

The Bible Through the Ages. Reader's Digest Association, 1996.

The New Interpreter's Study Bible. Abingdon, 2003

Websites

biblethroughseasons.com—Website for *The Bible Through the Seasons.*

bible-history.com—Easy access to creative presentations of Bible history.

divinity.library.vanderbilt.edu/lectionary
    Complete list of Bible passages from *The Revised Common Lectionary*

chabad.org/calendar—The Jewish Calendar

crosswalk.com—Many resources for Bible study.
    Links to all the words in the Bible in the original languages

gbod.org—The General Board of Discipleship of the United Methodist Church.
    Resources for worship

groups.msn.com/wesleywithoutwalls
    Internet site for those following this plan to share insights

learn.jtsa.edu

Weekly commentaries on the Sabbath Torah Readings from the Jewish Theological Seminary.

umc.org

Main site for The United Methodist Church, history, structure and theology.

wga.hu—The Web Gallery of Art; great resource to include art with Bible study.